TEACH YOURSELF

Simply Accounting™

FOR WINDOWS™

VERSION 5

TEACH YOURSELF

Simply Accounting™

FOR WINDOWS™ VERSION 5

▲ **Addison-Wesley**

An imprint of Addison Wesley Longman Ltd.

Don Mills, Ontario • Reading, Massachusetts • Harlow, England
Melbourne, Australia • Amsterdam, The Netherlands • Bonn, Germany

M. PURBHOO • D. PURBHOO

Publisher: Ron Doleman
Managing Editor: Linda Scott
Coordinating Editor: Madhu Ranadive
Production Coordinator: Wendy Moran
Text and Cover Design: Anthony Leung
Desktopping: Mary Purbhoo
Manufacturing Coordinator: Sharon Latta Paterson
Printing and Binding: Webcom

The authors and publisher have taken care in the preparation of this book, but make no expressed or implied warranty of any kind and assume no responsibility for errors or omissions. No liability is assumed for accidental or consequential damages in connection with or arising out of the use of the information herein. The publishers will gladly receive information enabling them to rectify any errors in references or credits.

Simply Accounting is a trademark of Computer Associates Canada, Limited.
Windows is a trademark of Microsoft Corporation.

Canadian Cataloguing in Publication Data

Purbhoo, Mary, 1949–
    Teach Yourself Simply Accounting Version 5.0 for Windows
First edition published under title: Teach yourself ACCPAC Simply Accounting for Windows.
Includes 3 1/2" data disk and index.

ISBN 0-201-33223-X

1. Simply Accounting for Windows (Computer file).
2. Accounting – Computer programs. I. Purbhoo, D. (Dhirajlal). II. Title. III. Title: Teach Yourself
    ACCPAC Simply Accounting for Windows.

HF5679.P89 1998b   657'.0285'5369   C97–931726–6

ISBN 0-201-33223-X

Printed and bound in Canada.

A B C D E -WC- 01 00 99 98 97

PREFACE

Teach Yourself Simply Accounting Version 5.0 for Windows has been updated for this new Windows 95 version of the program, covering both the basics and the latest features of the popular accounting software from Computer Associates.

The fifteen accounting applications in the workbook represent a wide variety of business types and settings because our users live in all parts of Canada and work in a variety of companies. To enhance the feel of a small business, we include a company profile for each new application. By covering the Harmonized Sales Tax (HST), GST using the quick and regular methods, Employer Health Tax (EHT) for Ontario as well as examples for other provinces, we have tried to familiarize our users throughout Canada with a broad range of Canadian business requirements. For example, although HST is currently applied in only three provinces, the federal government would like the remaining provinces to adopt this tax model. Quebec's approach to sales tax is a variation of the HST model. To offer this variety, we chose to include a larger number of shorter applications rather than use a single company that we follow throughout the workbook.

As the Simply Accounting program is updated, the alternative methods of inputting data and using the program are increasing. We have tried to provide alternative ways of doing things. For example, we include different keystrokes or the choice between using menu bars or tool buttons. For the most part, however, we follow the Windows and mouse based approach rather than the DOS based keyboard commands because Simply Accounting is a Windows program. We also offer different methods of setting up new company files — starting from scratch and using two different pre-defined starter files that accompany the software program. Again, we hope that our users will thereby learn some alternative methods and will gradually learn to use the ones that are best suited to their new applications or the ones they prefer.

Input forms are provided in Appendix A to assist with the organizing and entering of the accounting data for setting up company data files. We continue to include these input forms for a number of reasons, recognizing that some of our users will choose not to use them. Many businesses use input forms as an additional method of internal control. Many users may prefer to complete these forms at a separate stage from entering the information into the computer. And finally, they provide us with a convenient method of displaying the information that users will be entering themselves. Users may choose not to use the input forms, entering data directly from the company information provided at the beginning of the setup application.

We have had lengthy discussions about the best way to organize material within each chapter, specifically the order of keystroke instructions and source documents. A certain amount of page-flipping is inevitable in a book of this nature because the description or instructions for any type of transaction will invariably occupy more than two facing pages, especially if screens are included. We believe that keeping all the source documents together and all the keystroke instructions together makes it easier to see the whole picture of what you are accomplishing. If keystrokes refer to a setup that must be completed before entering transactions, we place them before the source documents. If the keystrokes refer to the transactions, they follow the source documents. As much as possible we try to present new keystroke transactions first. However, we are cautious about sacrificing realism. Employees are not paid on their first day of work and recurring transactions are recalled only after the recurring interval has passed.

We will continue to search for ways to improve the workbook. In the meantime, we are trying to make it easier for you to find your way around the book. Beside every source document or transaction that has keystroke instructions, we have added the page number where those instructions begin. These transactions have ✔ beside them in the check box. All other transactions have a blank check box for you to check when you complete the entry. We are also providing a bookmark that we hope will serve a dual purpose. Use it to mark your place as you move back and forth between transactions and keystrokes, and use the index printed on it as a quick reference to find the beginning page for the keystrokes for all major kinds of transactions.

The accounting applications in the workbook follow the same approach as our other workbooks, introducing the six ledgers of the Simply Accounting program (General, Payables, Receivables, Payroll, Inventory and Project) in a separate application, with a detailed demonstration of keystrokes and matching screens for each new type of sample transaction. Two more applications, Bonnie Brides and HSC School Store, explain the budgeting and bank reconciliation procedures using the software, again with detailed keystrokes. These applications are set up in advance. Additional applications dealing with advanced level topics have also been set up for you.

Three applications provide a comprehensive introduction to setting up a computerized accounting system using Simply Accounting. The first, CISV, introduces an actual non-profit organization that uses only the General Ledger. The application describes the accounting for a summer village in the Toronto chapter of the international organization. The second setup, Maverick Micro Solutions, is a service organization using the General, Payables and Receivables Ledgers. The third setup application describes Hearth House, a comprehensive retail organization and covers the General, Payables, Receivables, Payroll and Inventory Ledgers, and Projects. Detailed instructions are given for each setup. The authors walk you through each step as you learn to convert, design and implement a complete accounting system.

The final application, Serene Sailing, offers another opportunity to convert a manual accounting system to a computerized one. This time you are asked to enter accounting transactions using descriptive and realistic source documents to give you the "feel" of actual company transactions.

At the end of each application, you will find one or more case problems. These are provided to supplement and extend the principles covered in the applications.

A number of appendices have been included for reference or further study. Appendix A includes a complete set of input forms for setting up a company's computerized accounting system. Appendix B describes system security — setting and removing passwords. A section for correcting errors after posting is provided in Appendix C. Appendix D provides additional case problems. The systems and control approach is further illustrated in Appendix E. This final appendix includes a discussion on how Simply Accounting reports can be integrated with other software for analysis and decision making by exporting reports, linking through Dynamic Data Exchange and creating reports using CA-RET. Examples from Excel, WordPerfect and CA-RET are included.

ACKNOWLEDGEMENTS

Many people are involved in our writing projects. We always enjoy working with Mary Watson at Computer Associates, who never fails to give us professional, friendly and timely assistance. Despite our long-distance (Vancouver to Toronto) communication, Mary seems to have developed a telepathic connection with us. Within an hour of leaving a message for her to phone, the material we were going to request arrived at the door. You can't beat that for service! Thanks, Mary.

For this edition, we benefited from several intensive reviews. Grace Credico at Lethbridge Community College, Robert Dearden at Red River Community College, Allen Dowhan at Assiniboine Community College, Imelda Engels at College of the Rockies, Alberta Fraccaro at Liaison College, Keith Johnson at DeVry Institute, and Frank Mensink and Maria Vogels at Conestoga College each examined an early draft of several chapters. We sincerely appreciate their careful examination of the material, and their timely response to our request for feedback. They offered a large number of helpful suggestions which we weighed very carefully. Where feasible, we have incorporated their suggestions in this book — to include them all in a single book would lead to some inconsistencies — and some of the ideas will be considered for future editions.

Lori Christoffer and Joanna Severino, graduates of the Business Education Program in the Faculty of Education at the University of Toronto, carried out the important task of independently checking the accuracy of all keystroke instructions and transactions. We appreciate their careful reading of the material, their professional contributions and their overall excellent work. Furthermore, by meeting the tight deadlines we provided, they helped us to keep the project on track. We also value their friendship and hope to continue working with them in the future.

Our working relationships with the staff at Addison Wesley Longman Ltd. continue to grow (as does the company and its name). We believe that our author-publisher partnership is about as good as any working relationship can be. Thank you for making it easy and fun to work with you.

The ongoing support that we receive for our professional development activities from the staff and administration of the Board of Education for the City of Toronto is still important and appreciated as much as ever.

We dedicate this book, as we have all the others, to Kevin and Adrienne.

Using This Book

The accounting applications in this workbook were prepared using **Version 5.0A** of the Simply Accounting for Windows software published by Computer Associates International, Inc. If you are using a subsequent version of the software, you may find some changes in screens and keystrokes. It is important to refer to your user's guides, readme files, update notices and bulletins when you work with a later version of the software.

We assume that you are using an IBM personal computer or compatible with a hard disk system and single or dual floppy drives, or a network system with Windows installed. You will need a copy of the licensed Simply Accounting software or access to that software through a network environment. Each user must have a formatted data disk or a pseudo data disk on a network system, with the correct attributes and permissions for each user. For network systems, the authors recommend that users work with the facilitator, site-administrator or superuser of the system under consideration.

In addition, users should have a standard accounting text for reviewing accounting principles. The workbook does provide the user with some accounting principles and procedures, but it is not intended to replace the breadth and depth of all the principles covered in most standard accounting texts. Copies of the Simply Accounting user's manuals should be available to consult with when computer and software assistance is needed.

The workbook is as simple and straightforward as we could make it, but users will still need some familiarity with computers before they work through it. Their lives will be easier still if they have acquired some of the fundamentals of troubleshooting.

In response to feedback from some of our users, the setup applications are introduced at an earlier stage in the workbook. Advanced users should have no difficulty working through the applications in the order given and may even choose to skip some applications. However, at a minimum, we recommend working through all keystroke transactions (the ones with a ✔ beside them) so that you become familiar with all the journals before starting the more comprehensive applications.

If you want more practice before starting a company setup, you may wish to deviate slightly from the order given. Completing all six ledgers before beginning the setup applications will provide this additional practice before beginning the more complex setup procedures. A recommended order for these situations would be:

1. Read and work through the two *Getting Started* chapters in Part 1.
2. Complete the six ledger applications in order: Reliable Roofing (General), Java Jean's (Payables), Grandeur Graphics (Receivables), Carnival Catering (Payroll), Meteor Mountain Bikes (Inventory) and Puretek Paving & Stoneworks (Project).
3. Complete the bank reconciliation (HSC School Store) and budgeting (Bonnie Brides) applications.
4. Complete the three setup applications in order: CISV (General), Maverick Micro Solutions (three ledgers) and Hearth House (six ledgers).
5. Complete the remaining advanced topic applications as they fit curriculum and student knowledge levels: year-end adjustments (Mighty Mack Service Centre), corporation accounting (Delhi Delights, Inc.) and depreciation (Cheshire Cheese & Butter Factory). These applications use only the General Ledger.
6. Complete the Serene Sailing setup application with realistic source documents.

This order is shown graphically in the following chart:

Notes

Another approach is to complete the source document transactions for every application (except Serene Sailing), then return to complete the three keystroke setup applications and Serene Sailing. This, of course, means setting up an application that you are already familiar with from the source documents and accounts.

AN ALTERNATIVE SEQUENCE FOR WORKING THROUGH THE APPLICATIONS

Getting Started	Ledger Applications	Supplementary Features	Setup Applications	Advanced Topics	Challenge Application

```
┌─────────────┐
│ Getting     │
│ Started (1) │
└─────────────┘
      ↓
┌─────────────┐      ┌──────────────┐
│ GST (2)     │  →   │ Reliable     │
└─────────────┘      │ Roofing      │
                     │ (3 General)  │
                     └──────────────┘
                            ↓
                     ┌──────────────┐
                     │ Java Jean's  │
                     │ (4 Payables) │
                     └──────────────┘
                            ↓
                     ┌──────────────┐
                     │ Grandeur     │
                     │ Graphics     │
                     │ (5 Receivables)│
                     └──────────────┘
                            ↓
                     ┌──────────────┐
                     │ Carnival     │
                     │ Catering     │
                     │ (7 Payroll)  │
                     └──────────────┘
                            ↓
                     ┌──────────────┐
                     │ Meteor Mtn Bike│
                     │ (8 Inventory)│
                     └──────────────┘
                            ↓
                     ┌──────────────┐
                     │ Puretek Paving│
                     │ & Stoneworks │
                     │ (11 Project) │
                     └──────────────┘
```

Bonnie Brides (12 Budgeting)

HSC School Store (14 Bank Reconciliation)

CISV Village (6 General)

Maverick Micro Solutions (10 General, Payables, Receivables)

Hearth House (13 General, Payables, Receivables, Payroll, Inventory, Project)

Mighty Mack Service Ctr (9 Year-end adjustments)

Delhi Delights (15 Corporation Accounting)

Cheshire Cheese & Butter (16 Depreciation)

Serene Sailing & Boating (17)

Notes

- Each box includes the chapter or application title, the chapter number and the topic or ledgers introduced.
- Applications within the same box may be completed in any order.

CONTENTS

Part 3: Appendices

PART 1

GETTING STARTED

Getting Started

OBJECTIVES

Upon completion of
this chapter, you
will be able to:

- *install* the Simply Accounting program under Windows
- *access* the Simply Accounting program
- *access* the data files for a business
- *understand* Simply Accounting's help features
- *save* your work
- *back up* your data files
- *finish* your session

DATA FILES AND ABBREVIATIONS

Notes

The instructions in this chapter for installing the program, starting the program and copying files refer specifically to Windows 95 procedures. If you are using an earlier version of Windows, please refer to your Windows and Simply Accounting manuals for assistance with these procedures.

The applications in this workbook were prepared using Windows 95 and version 5.0A of the Simply Accounting software package produced by Computer Associates International, Inc. Subsequent versions of the software may have changes in screens or keystrokes. Income tax tables change regularly; the most recent ones will be used in later versions of the software.

The instructions in this workbook have been written for a stand-alone IBM-PC or compatible computer, with a hard disk drive and single or dual floppy disk drives. Windows should be correctly installed on your hard disk. Your printers are installed and accessible through the Windows program. Refer to your Windows manuals for assistance with these procedures.

This workbook reflects the authors' approach to working with Simply Accounting. There are alternative approaches to setting up company accounts and to working with the software. Refer to your Simply Accounting and Windows manuals for further details.

DATA APPLICATION FILES

Company	Folder\File name	Chapter
Reliable Roofing	reliable\reliable.asc	3
Java Jean's Coffee Emporium	java\java.asc	4
Grandeur Graphics	grandeur\grandeur.asc	5
CISV Toronto Village	setup\cisv.asc	6
Carnival Catering	carnival\carnival.asc	7
Meteor Mountain Bike Shop	meteor\meteor.asc	8
Mighty Mack Service Centre	mighty\mighty.asc	9
Maverick Micro Solutions	setup\maverick.asc	10
Puretek Paving & Stoneworks	puretek\puretek.asc	11
Bonnie Brides	brides\brides.asc	12
Hearth House	setup\hh-oct.asc	13
	setup\hh-nov.asc	13
	setup\hh-dec.asc	13
HSC School Store	hsc\hsc.asc	14
Delhi Delights, Inc.	delhi\delhi.asc	15
Cheshire Cheese & Butter Factory	cheshire\ches-cca.asc	16
	cheshire\ches-sl.asc	16
Serene Sailing and Boating	user setup	17

The applications increase in complexity, with each one introducing new ledgers, setups or features as shown in the following chart.

DATA APPLICATION	LEDGER USED						OTHER
	GL	AP	AR	PAY	INV	JC	
Reliable Roofing	*						
Java Jean's	*	*					
Grandeur Graphics	*	*	*				
CISV Toronto	*						1
Carnival Catering	*	*	*	*			
Meteor Mountain Bike	*	*	*		*		
Mighty Mack	*						
Maverick Micro	*	*	*				1
Puretek Paving	*	*	*	*	*	*	2
Bonnie Brides	*	*	*	*	*		3
Hearth House	*	*	*	*	*	*	1
HSC School Store	*	*	*		*		4
Delhi Delights, Inc.	*						
Cheshire Cheese	*						
Serene Sailing	*	*	*	*			

Ledgers:
GL = General Ledger   AP = Accounts Payable
AR = Accounts Receivable   PAY = Payroll
INV = Inventory   JC = Jobcost (Project)

Other: 1 Setup application with keystrokes
2 Integrating accounting reports with word processing or spreadsheet applications (Appendix E)
3 Budgeting
4 Bank Reconciliation

SOME WINDOWS AND MOUSE BASICS

Skip this section if you are already familiar with Windows and the use of a mouse.

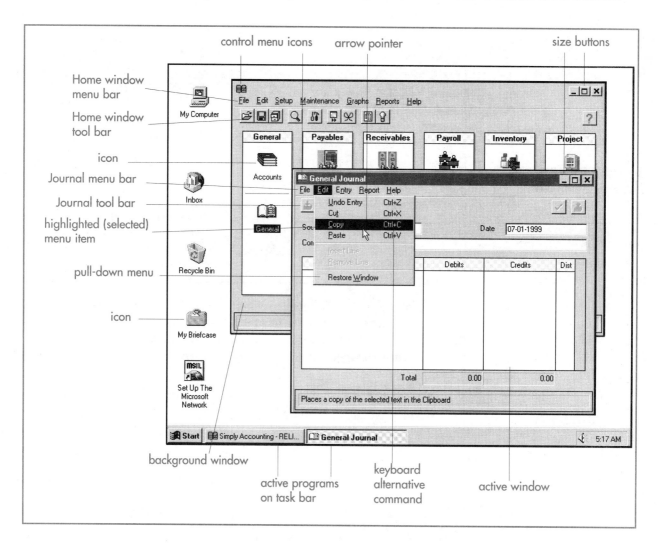

The **mouse** is used to move the cursor. When you move the mouse, an **arrow** or **pointer** moves to indicate the cursor placement. If you **click** (press) the left mouse button, the cursor will move to the location of the arrow (if this is a legitimate location for the cursor to be at the time). That is, you use the mouse to **click on** (point to and click) a screen location, item on a list, command or icon.

The arrow or pointer changes shape, depending upon what actions you may perform. When you are moving the mouse, it appears as an arrow or pointer. When you are in a field that can accept text, it appears as a long **I bar**. Clicking will change it to a flashing vertical line in a text field. When the computer is processing information and you are unable to perform any action, you will see an **hourglass**. This is your signal to wait.

Dragging refers to the method of moving the mouse while holding the left button down. As you drag through the options in a menu, each one will be successively highlighted or darkened. Dragging through text will highlight it. Point to the beginning of the text to be highlighted. Then click and hold the mouse button down while moving through the entire area that you want to highlight. Release the mouse button at the end of the area you want to highlight. You can highlight a single character or the entire contents of a field. The text will remain highlighted and can be edited by typing new text. It can be deleted by pressing the Back Space key or ⌊del⌋ . Clicking on a different location will remove the highlighting.

To **double click** means to press the left mouse button twice quickly. This action can be used as a short-cut for opening and closing windows. Double clicking on an icon or file name will open it. Double clicking on the control icon will close the window.

The **active window** is the one you are currently working in. If you click on an area outside the active window that is part of a background window, that one will become the one in the foreground. To return to your previous window, click on any part of it that is showing. If the window you need is completely hidden, covered by another window, you can reduce the active window to an icon/name on the task bar by clicking on ⌊-⌋ .

An **icon** is a picture form of your program, file name or item. **Buttons** are icons or commands surrounded by a box frame.

The **menu bar** is the line of options at the top of each window. Each menu contains one or more commands or selections (the **pull-down menu**) and can be accessed by clicking on the menu name. Each window may have different menu selections, and the options in the pull-down menu may differ. To choose an option from the menu, click on the menu name and then click on the option you want in order to **highlight** and **select** it. If an option is dimmed, you will be unable to highlight or select it.

The **control menu icon** is situated in the upper left-hand corner of each window. The icon is different for different programs and windows. It has its own pull-down menu, including the Close and size commands. To close windows, you can double click on this box, choose Close from its pull-down menu or click on the Close button ⊠ in the upper right corner of the window.

Size buttons are located in the upper right-hand corner of the window. They can be used to make the window larger ▢ (maximize) or to reduce the window to an icon at the bottom of the screen ⌊-⌋ (minimize). If the window is full screen size, it can be reduced with the ⬚ (restore) button.

The size of a window can also be changed by dragging the side you want to move with the mouse. When the pointer changes to a two-sided arrow, the window frame can be dragged to a its new size.

When a window contains more information than can be displayed on the screen at once, the window will contain a **scroll arrow** in any corner or direction next to the hidden information (bottom or right sides of the window). Click on the arrow and hold the mouse button down to scroll the screen in the direction of the arrow you are on.

WORKING IN WINDOWS WITHOUT A MOUSE

All Windows software applications are designed to be used with a mouse. However, there may be times when you prefer to use keyboard commands to work with a program because it is faster. There are also times when you need to know the alternatives to using a mouse, as when the mouse itself is inoperative. It is not necessary to memorize all of the keyboard commands. A few basic principles will help you to understand how they work and over time you will use the ones that help you to work most efficiently. Some commands are common to more than one Windows software program. For example, Ctrl (Control key) + C is commonly used as the copy command and Ctrl + V as the paste command.

The menu bar and the menu choices can be accessed by pressing ⌜alt⌟. The first menu bar item will be highlighted. Use the **arrow keys** to move back and forth to other menu items or up and down through the pull-down menu choices of a highlighted menu item. Some menu choices have direct keyboard alternatives or shortcuts. If the menu item has an underlined letter, pressing ⌜alt⌟ together with the underlined letter will access that option directly. For example, ⌜alt⌟ + F (press ⌜alt⌟, and while holding down ⌜alt⌟, press F) accesses the File pull-down menu. Then pressing O (the underlined letter for Open) will give you the dialogue box for opening a new file. Some tool buttons in Simply Accounting have a direct keyboard command and some menu choices also have a shortcut keyboard command. When available, these direct keystrokes are given with the button name or to the right of a menu choice. For example, ⌜alt⌟ + ⌜f4⌟ is the shortcut for exiting from the Simply Accounting program.

To cancel the menu display, press ⌜esc⌟.

In the Simply Accounting Home window, you can use the **arrow keys** to move among the ledger and journal icons. Press ⌜alt⌟, ⌜alt⌟ and ⊡ to highlight the Accounts icon, and then use the arrow keys to change selections. Each icon is highlighted or selected as you reach it and deselected as you move to another icon.

To choose or open a highlighted or selected item, press ⌜enter⌟.

When input fields are displayed in a Simply Accounting window, you can move to the next field by pressing ⌜tab⌟ or to a previous field by pressing ⌜shift⌟ and ⌜tab⌟ together. The ⌜tab⌟ key is used frequently in this workbook as a quick way to advance the cursor, highlight field contents to prepare for immediate editing and accept input. Using the mouse while you input information requires you to remove your hands from the keyboard while the ⌜tab⌟ key does not.

INSTALLING SIMPLY ACCOUNTING

Notes

Skip this section if your Simply Accounting program is already installed.

Notes

Your windows may look different from those shown in this chapter if you have a different computer setup or if you have selected different display options.

Start your computer and the Windows program. In the Windows 95 opening screen,

Double click on the **My Computer icon** ▣. The screen that follows will show the drives on your system. The one shown here has one floppy drive (A:), a hard drive partitioned into C:, D: and E: and a CD-ROM drive (F:):

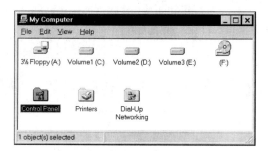

Double click on the **Control Panel icon** to see the components that are installed on your computer:

Insert the Simply Accounting program in your CD-ROM drive (or, if you have the program on diskettes, insert the first program disk in your floppy disk drive A:).

Double click on the **Add/Remove Programs icon** (and click on Install if necessary) to proceed.

The installation may begin immediately. If it does not,

Choose Start and then **choose Run**.

If you are installing from CD-ROM,

Type   d:\disk1\setup (where d:\ is your CD-ROM drive)

If you are installing from diskettes using drive A:,

Type   a:\setup

Press (enter). The following screen appears to begin the installation:

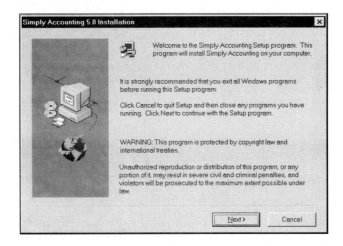

If you have any other programs running, Click on Cancel, close the other programs and start again. Otherwise,

Click on Next

The next screen prompts you to enter your name, company name and the program's serial number (located on the software package). You must enter the serial number before you can continue:

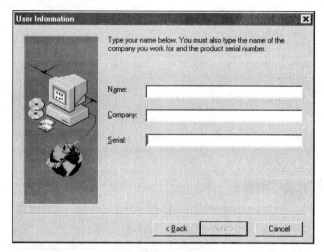

Type the required information. Press ⌷tab⌷ to advance to the next field.

Click on Next. When prompted, confirm that you entered the information correctly,

Click on Yes to continue with the installation. Your next decision concerns the location of your program files as shown:

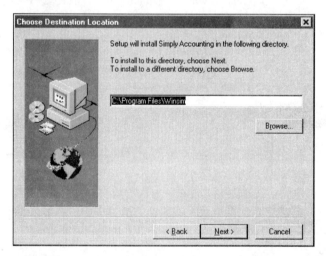

You can accept the default location, choose another folder from the pop-up list provided when you click on Browse, or type in an alternate location.

Click on Next to continue with the selection of program components to install:

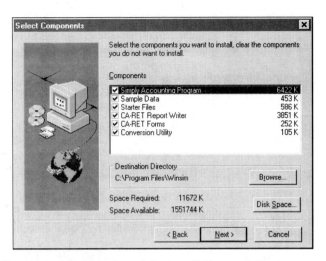

By default, all components are selected for installation, as follows:

- **Simply Accounting Program**: the Simply Accounting program that you will need to perform the accounting transactions for your company. It will be placed in the main WINSIM folder under the Program Files folder.

- **Sample Data**: complete company records for the companies described in the user's manual (Universal Construction and Universal Crustacean Farm). They will be placed in the folder under WINSIM called SAMDATA if you install them. (They are not needed to complete the applications in this workbook, so you do not need to install them.)

- **Starter Files**: predefined charts of accounts to use as starter files for creating company records for the setup applications in this workbook or to create your own company files. You do need these files. These files will be stored in a folder under WINSIM called SAMDATA, with the Sample Data files. The install program creates this folder for you automatically.

- **CA-RET Report Writer**: the program to access and customize the CA-RET forms. The CA-RET program, if installed, will be placed in its own folder under WINSIM called CARET. CA-RET is described in Appendix E. (You do not need this program for the applications in the workbook.)

- **CA-RET Forms**: a variety of commonly used business forms that you can customize to suit your own business needs. They will be placed in a folder under WINSIM called FORMS. Their use is described in Appendix E. (They are not used in this workbook.)

- **Conversion Utility**: a program that can be used to convert accounting records that were created using non-Windows versions of the Bedford and Simply Accounting programs into a form that can be used with the Simply Accounting Windows version. The conversion program is also placed in the main WINSIM folder. (You do not need this program to complete the applications in this workbook, so you do not need to install this program.)

Click on any component to deselect it and remove the ✔ so that it will not be installed. Click on it again to select it.

Click on Next. You will also be asked to choose the name of the program as you want it to appear on the Programs list. By default, the name will be Simply Accounting. You may accept this name or type in another name such as Simply Accounting Version 5.0.

Follow the instructions to proceed with the installation.

The Install program creates the folders for all the components described above — the main WINSIM folder with the SAMDATA, CARET and FORMS folders under it. There is an additional folder, WINSIM\DATA, that is empty initially. We will use this folder to store the data files for the applications in the workbook.

In addition, the installation procedure adds:
- names in the Programs list for the Simply Accounting program and for the Conversion program if it is installed (or icons if you display programs by icon)
- the CA_APPSW folder that holds DLL files shared by all the parts of the Simply Accounting program. Do not remove these shared files when you are removing an earlier version of the program.

After the installation is complete, you may see a brief Readme file with recent announcements of program changes. Please read this information. After you have read the file, click on ☒ to close the window.

If you are using disks, after the programs on the first disk are installed, you will be prompted to change disks. Follow the prompts to change disks as required.

If you have previously installed versions of the software, you will be asked whether or not you want to replace individual program files. You can choose to replace them all, or decide on a one-by-one basis.

Restart your computer before using the Simply Accounting program.

BACKING UP YOUR DATA DISK

Before you begin the applications, you must make a backup copy of the Data Disk to work with. This way you will have the original for future use if you need to begin again.

Copying Your Data Disk Using Floppies

Disks, folders and files may be copied from the My Computer window; folders and files may also be copied using Windows Explorer. You should be in the Windows 95 opening screen and the Data Disk that came with this book should be in drive A:, your floppy disk drive. To make a copy of the Data Disk using another floppy disk, use the My Computer control window.

To use the Copy Disk command, your floppy must be the same size and type as the Data Disk packaged with the workbook, a double-sided, high density 3 1/2 disk (HD). We also recommend using HD disks because you will be less likely to encounter "disk full errors" that can result from the large number of files created while completing the workbook.

Double click on the **My Computer icon,** [My Computer] to open the My Computer window.

Click on the **3 1/2 Floppy (A:) icon,** to highlight it.

Choose Copy Disk from the pull-down menu under **File.** Your window should look like the one shown here:

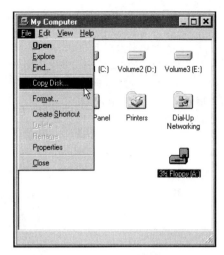

The Copy Disk window appears:

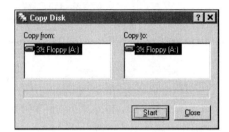

Click on Start. When instructed to do so, insert your new blank formatted disk in drive A:.

Click on Close or ☒ when the copying is completed.

Copying your Data Files onto your Hard Disk

To make a copy of the data files on your hard disk, use the Windows Explorer program.

Click on Start

Choose (point to) **Programs** and then **click on Windows Explorer** (usually the last program in the list).

Click on the disk drive icon or name for **3 1/2 Floppy (A:)** so that the contents of the Data Disk — the 12 folders, appear on the Contents side of the window.

Scroll down the All Folders side to the Program Files folder. Click on the ⊞ beside the folder to see the folders under Program Files. Now click on the ⊞ beside the Winsim folder to list the folders under Winsim. The Data folder should be visible.

Click on Brides, the first folder in the Contents list. Now **press** ⎗shift and **click on Setup**, the last folder in the Contents list. Or, you can choose Select All from the pull-down menu under Edit. This will highlight all the folders on the Data Disk.

Drag the **highlighted folders to** the **Program Files\Winsim\Data folder** (click on the list and while holding the mouse button down point to Data). As soon as the Data folder is highlighted, as shown here, release the mouse:

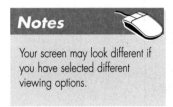
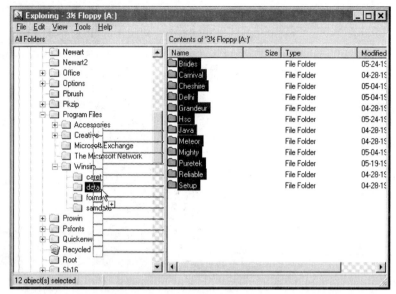

Your screen will show the files being copied. When the copying is complete, all the folders and files from A: will be copied to the Data folder under Winsim that was created during installation. When you click on the ⊞ beside Data, you will see the new list of data folders.

Click on ☒ to close the Explorer window.

If you want to copy only the files for a single application, click on the folder for the application you want, e.g., Reliable, under A:\ to highlight it. Drag the single folder to the new location to complete the copy as you would for the entire disk.

STARTING SIMPLY ACCOUNTING AND ACCESSING DATA FILES

From your Windows 95 opening screen,

Click on Start

Point to Programs. Hold the mouse on Programs until the list of programs appears.

Point to Simply Accounting (or the name you entered for the Simply Accounting program when you installed it. In the list shown below, it is named Simply Accounting 5.0 because there are other versions of the program installed as well). Hold the mouse on Simply Accounting until its program list appears.

Click on Simply Accounting. You should follow the path illustrated here:

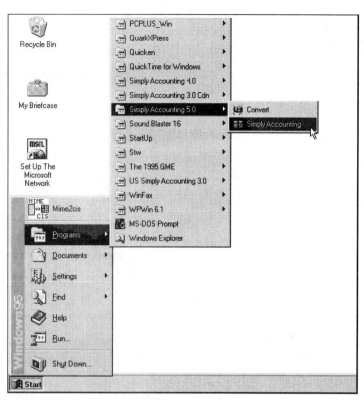

The Simply Accounting Open File window appears next with the most recently used file selected. Therefore the File name you see on your screen may be different from the one shown below.

Click on the **Look in field** to see the folder path for the file selected:

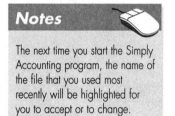

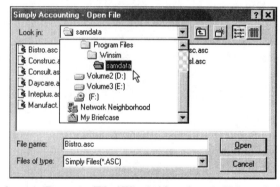

The path shown here is Program Files\Winsim\Samdata in Volume1 (C:). The following instructions will access the data stored in the Winsim\Data folder.

Click on the **Winsim folder** to select it and list the four folders under Winsim in the larger files list in the centre of the window. The Look in field now displays Winsim as the folder name:

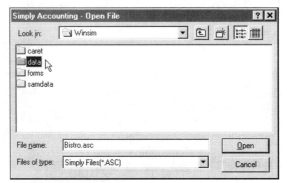

Click on the **Data folder** to select it as shown above.

Click on Open to list the 12 folders containing your workbook data. The folder name Data now appears in the Look in field.

Click on the **Reliable folder** to select it.

Click on Open to list the Simply Accounting data files contained in this folder and to display the name Reliable in the Look in field. There should be just one file listed, reliable.asc (or reliable).

Click on reliable.asc to select it and add this name to the File name field as shown:

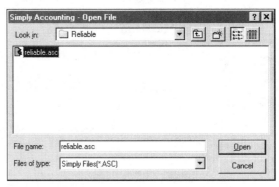

Click on Open to see the following screen prompting you to accept or change the using date:

For now you should accept the date shown. Click on OK and you will see the Simply Accounting Home window.

Substitute the appropriate drive and path or folders for your own setup to access the Simply Accounting Home window.

For other applications, substitute the appropriate folder and file name for reliable and reliable.asc above.

Accessing Data Files from Floppy Disks

If you are using floppy disks for your working files, you can click on the Look in field, scroll up and click on 3 1/2 Floppy (A:). This will list the folders on the Data Disk as shown:

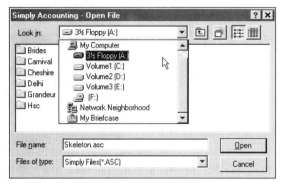

Click on the **Reliable folder**

Click on **Open**.

Click on the file **reliable.asc**

Click on **Open** again to display the using date window.

Click on **OK** to accept the date and continue.

For other applications, substitute the appropriate folder and file name for reliable and reliable.asc above.

You should now see the Simply Accounting Home window:

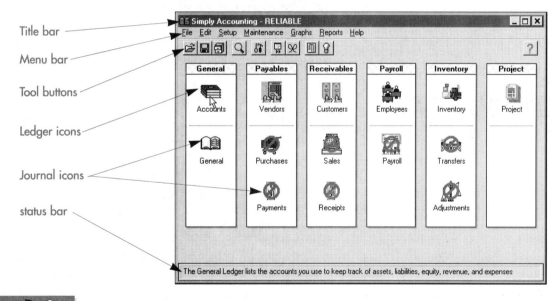

The Home window is organized as follows: the title bar with the program and file names, control menu icon and size buttons are on top; the main menu bar comes next with the tool bar buttons below. The tool buttons permit an alternative and quick access to commonly used menu items. Different Simply Accounting windows have different buttons on the tool bar. The six ledger names come next with their respective icons filling up the major part of the window — six ledgers in the top row below the ledger or module name, journal icons under their respective ledgers in the middle two icon rows of the window. Below the journal icons, the status bar describes the purpose of the General Ledger because the pointer is on the Accounts icon.

SIMPLY ACCOUNTING HELP FEATURES

Simply Accounting provides program assistance in a number of different ways. You can display or print **Help** information on a number of topics in Simply Accounting. General accounting information, advice topics and Simply Accounting software assistance are included. You can access Help from the menu bar in the Home window, from the Help tool button ? in the Home window or by pressing f1 .

The most immediate form of help comes from the Status Bar at the bottom of many program windows that offers a one line description about the icon or field that the mouse is pointing to. As you move the mouse around the screen, the status bar information changes accordingly. The message in the status bar is connected to the mouse position only. This may not be the same as the position of the cursor or insertion point, which is located wherever the mouse was when you last clicked the mouse button. The status bar can be turned off if it is not needed.

The general help menu can be accessed in several ways: by pressing f1 , by choosing Contents from the pull-down menu under Help from the main menu bar or by clicking on the Help button ? .

The "book" menu is shown here:

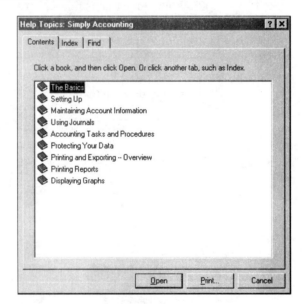

Click on a "book" title and then Click on Open to see the list of topics under that heading (or double click on the book). Click on a topic and then click on Display to get the complete information on that subject (or double click on the topic). Included under the title, The Basics, is the topic "Using Help." This is a good place to begin if you have not used Windows programs' Help features before.

When you access the Help menu from within one of the Simply Accounting ledger windows, you will get Help information related to that specific ledger.

Also available from the Help window on any topic is an extensive glossary of general accounting and Simply Accounting terms. Click on the Glossary tab and then click on a glossary topic to see the explanation or definition.

Click on the Advice tool button ? in Simply Accounting's Home window to access the main Advice menu shown here:

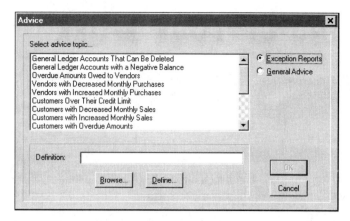

The default list of topics is the list of Exception Reports. Click on the report or advice topic you want and then click on OK to see the report (or double click on the topic). Rather than providing general information, these reports relate specifically to the company data set that is in use at the time. The reports combine the company data with forms and reports provided through CA-RET. If you have not installed CA-RET and CA-RET Forms, these reports will not be available.

Click on General Advice to see the list of topics that provide other helpful suggestions about accounting practices in general. These same two lists of advice topics are available when you choose Advice from the pull-down menu under Help.

A final set of general assistance is available as automatic advice. Again this is a feature that can be turned off if it is not needed. When it is turned on, the Simply Accounting program will provide warning statements, as for example, when a sale will cause inventory to drop below the re-order point, or when year-end is approaching and it is time to complete year-end adjustments. The following screen shows a sample of an advice screen warning that a customer sale will cause the customer to exceed the credit limit:

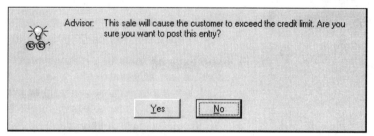

To proceed, you must close an advice screen. In the example shown here, you can click on Yes if you want to proceed with the sale, or on No if you want to make a change (perhaps asking for a deposit). Sometimes the advisor is just a statement that you have to close by clicking on the advisor icon (the message "click here to close" will be part of these screens).

BACKING UP YOUR WORK

Simply Accounting saves your work automatically at various stages when you are working with the program. For example, when you display or print reports, Simply Accounting writes all the journal transactions to your disk in order to compile the report you want. When you exit from the program properly, Simply Accounting also saves all your work. At any time while working in Simply Accounting, you can save your work.

Click on the **Save button** 💾 on the tool bar or **choose Save** from the pull-down menu under **File**.

On a regular basis, you should also save a backup copy of your files.

Make a folder on your backup disk to contain the company data files. You can make all the backup folders you need before beginning — one folder for each application — or you can make folders as you need them in the Save As window.

Making Folders

It is a good practice to keep backup copies on a separate disk from your working copy so that if your working disk is damaged, you can continue your work without starting over.

You will need to make folders to work with the applications in this workbook. For the four setup applications — CISV, Maverick, Hearth House and Serene Sailing — you need to make new folders. In addition, you will need to make folders for backing up individual applications using the Save As command described below. If you are working on floppies, you must use a separate folder for each application because the large number of files in each application's data set will result in "disk full errors." You can make folders from the Save As window.

From the Simply Accounting Home window,

Choose Save As from the pull-down menu under **File**. This will open the Save As window. Be sure that you are in the appropriate folder before you create the new folder. Select the folder that you want to use for your backup file by clicking on the Save in field, and successively opening the folders you need. You can check the path by clicking on the Save in field again.

Now point to an empty part of the central section of the window and **click the right mouse button**. If you click on a folder or folder name, you will see a different menu when you click the right mouse button.

Point to New and then **click on Folder** as shown in the following screen:

You will create a folder titled New Folder with the name highlighted so you can rename the folder immediately.

Type   `Reliable.bak`

Reliable Backup appears as the name for the folder but it is still highlighted. Then click somewhere else on the screen to save the name change.

Double click on the **File name field** to highlight the contents.

Type   `rely-bak.asc`

Click on Save

If you are replacing a previous backup copy with the same name, you will be asked to confirm that you want to replace the previous copy.

Click on Yes to confirm the replacement, or **click on No** and then change the file name.

A new Home window appears with RELY-BAK as the new file name.

Choose Open File from the pull-down menu under **File** to select your original working data file to continue with entering transactions. (If a journal or ledger icon is selected, you will open it instead of accessing the Open File window.) Confirm that you are finished with the current data set by clicking on Yes.

If you are working with floppies, the simplest way to back up your work is to use the Copy Disk command. (Refer to page 10.)

FINISHING A SESSION

Choose Close from the pull-down menu under the control menu icon or click on ☒ to close the journal input form or display window you are working in.

You will return to the main Home window.

Choose Close from the pull-down menu under the control menu icon, click on ☒ or choose Exit from the pull-down menu under File to close the Home window.

Your work will be saved automatically again when you complete this step.

You should now be in the Windows 95 opening screen.

Close any other programs that you have open.

Click on Start

Click on Shut Down

Click on Yes to confirm your choice.

You may now turn off your computer.

The Goods and Services Tax

Upon completion of
this chapter, you
will be able to:

OBJECTIVES

- *understand* the terms relevant to the federal Goods and Services Tax
- *understand* the different methods of calculating the GST
- *understand* how to file for remittance or refund
- *understand* Harmonized Sales Tax and other provincial taxes in relation to GST

GENERAL ACCOUNTING INFORMATION

Definition of GST

The Goods and Services Tax is a compulsory tax, levied by the federal government on most goods and services in Canada. It replaces the old federal sales tax (regular and construction), which was applied mainly at the wholesale level to manufacturing and construction goods and built into the final consumer price. The present Goods and Services Tax rate of 7 percent applies at all levels. Retailers pay the GST to wholesalers and other vendors, but are allowed to deduct it from GST collected from customers. They remit GST owing to the Receiver General of Canada or claim a refund on a monthly or quarterly basis.

Provinces may or may not include GST in the price on which they calculate Provincial Sales Tax (PST). Provincial tax rates vary from province to province.

GST Registration

A business with annual sales exceeding $30 000 per year **must** register to apply the Goods and Services Tax. Registration is optional for those businesses whose annual sales are less than $30 000. Registration allows a business to recover any GST paid on purchases made.

Collecting the GST

The business must collect GST for those goods and services sold that are not zero-rated or tax exempt. GST collected on sales is reduced by the GST on sales returns. The business must remit GST at regular intervals, filing GST returns monthly, quarterly or annually with quarterly installments, depending on annual income and GST owing.

Zero-Rated Goods and Services

Zero-rated goods and services are those on which the tax rate is zero. These goods include basic groceries, prescribed medical instruments and devices, prescribed drugs, exported goods and services, agricultural products and fish products. A business selling only zero-rated goods and services is not able to collect GST from customers, but it can still claim a refund for GST paid for any purchases made for selling these zero-rated goods and services.

Tax-Exempted Goods and Services

Tax-exempted goods and services are those on which tax is not collected. These goods and services include health care, dental care, day care services and rents on residences. Most educational and financial services are also included in this group. These businesses are not able to claim refunds for GST paid for any business purchases made for selling tax-exempted goods and services.

Paying the GST

The business must pay GST for purchases made specifically for business purposes unless the goods or services purchased are zero-rated or tax exempt. The business can use the GST paid as an **input tax credit** by subtracting the amount of GST paid from the amount of GST collected and remitting GST owing or claiming a refund. The input tax credit is reduced by the amount of GST for purchases returned. Purchases for personal use do not qualify as input tax credits.

Bank and Financial Institution Services

Most bank products and services are not taxable. Exceptions include safety deposit box rentals, custodial and safekeeping services, personalized cheques, fees for self-administrated registered savings plans, payroll services, rentals of night depository, rentals of credit card imprinters and reconciliation of cheques. Banks must remit the full amount of GST they collect from customers. They cannot claim input tax credits for GST they pay on business-related purchases.

Administering the GST

The federal government has approved different methods of administering the GST; the regular method and the quick method are the most common.

The Regular Method

The regular method of administering the GST requires the business to keep track of all GST paid for goods and services purchased from vendors (less returns) and of all GST collected for goods and services sold to customers (less returns). It then deducts the GST paid from the GST collected and files for a refund or remits the balance owing to the Receiver General on a monthly or quarterly basis.

Accounting Examples Using the Regular Method (without PST)

SALES INVOICE

Sold goods on account to customer for $200 plus $14 GST collected. Invoice total, $214.

Date	Particulars	Ref.	Debit	Credit
xx/xx	Accounts Receivable		214.00	
	GST Charged on Sales			14.00
	Revenue from Sales			200.00

PURCHASE INVOICE

Purchased supplies on account from vendor for $300 plus $21 GST paid. Invoice total, $321.

Date	Particulars	Ref.	Debit	Credit
xx/xx	Supplies		300.00	
	GST Paid on Purchases		21.00	
	Accounts Payable			321.00

The GST owing is further reduced by any GST adjustments — for example, GST that applies to bad debts that are written off. If the debt is later recovered, the GST liability is also restored as an input tax credit adjustment.

Simplified Accounting Methods

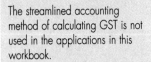

Notes

The streamlined accounting method of calculating GST is not used in the applications in this workbook.

Certain small businesses may be eligible to use a simplified method of calculating their GST refunds and remittances that does not require them to keep a separate record for GST on each individual purchase or sale.

The Streamlined Accounting Method is available only to some grocery and convenience stores. The Quick Method is available to a wider range of businesses.

The Quick Method

Some small businesses may opt to remit a flat tax payment ranging from 1 percent to 5 percent of their sales. This simplified system is available to manufacturers and retailers with sales up to a maximum of $200 000 per year, to grocery and convenience stores with sales up to $500 000 per year and to some service businesses. The GST is calculated by multiplying the total sales for the filing period (monthly or quarterly) by the flat tax rate for the type of business under consideration. A business is still able to deduct any GST paid on **capital expenditures** from the GST liability calculated using the flat tax rate. Capital expenditures include purchases of plant and equipment such as cash registers, furniture, computers and other depreciable assets.

The quick method described above is not available to legal, accounting or financial consulting businesses. Businesses allowed by Revenue Canada to use the quick method may change methods from year to year.

Accounting Examples Using the Quick Method (without PST)

CASH SALES OVER THE COUNTER

Cash register tapes in a café for one week total $3 200 including GST collected for goods and services.

Date	Particulars	Ref.	Debit	Credit
xx/xx	Cash in Bank		3 200.00	
	Revenue from Services			3 200.00

PURCHASE INVOICES

1. Food Inventory
   Purchased basic groceries for café services from vendor for $1 000 on account. Basic groceries are zero-rated goods.

Date	Particulars	Ref.	Debit	Credit
xx/xx	Food Inventory		1 000.00	
	Accounts Payable			1 000.00

2. Non-Capital Expenditures
   Purchased gasoline, oil and repair services for delivery van from vendor on account for $428, including $28 GST.

Date	Particulars	Ref.	Debit	Credit
xx/xx	Van Maintenance		428.00	
	Accounts Payable			428.00

3. Capital Expenditures
   Purchased pizza oven for café from vendor on account for $2 000 plus $140 GST paid. Invoice total, $2 140.

Date	Particulars	Ref.	Debit	Credit
xx/xx	Cafeteria Equipment		2 000.00	
	GST Paid on Capital Goods		140.00	
	Accounts Payable			2 140.00

Calculating GST Refunds or Remittances

The following examples are for a retailer who is filing quarterly and has maximum annual sales of $200 000.

The Regular Method

Quarterly Total Sales	$50 000.00	
Quarterly Total Purchases	29 700.00	
GST Charged on Sales		$3 500.00
Less: GST Paid on Purchases		
Cash Register (cost $1 000)	70.00	
Inventory (cost $25 000)	1 750.00	
Supplies (cost $500)	35.00	
Payroll Services (cost $200)	14.00	
Store Lease (cost $3 000)	210.00	
Total GST Paid		− 2 079.00
GST Remittance		$1 421.00

The Quick Method with a flat rate of 3 percent

Quarterly Total Sales	$50 000.00	
Multiply by 3%		$1 500.00
Less: GST Paid on Capital Goods		
Cash Register (cost $1 000)		− 70.00
GST Remittance		$1 430.00

Generally the flat rate is set so that there is very little difference between using the regular and quick methods. The quick method can save time if the business has a large number of purchases for small amounts.

GST Remittances and Refunds

GST Collected on Sales	>	GST Paid on Purchases	=	GST Owing	
GST Collected on Sales	<	GST Paid on Purchases	=	GST Refund	

The business must file a statement periodically that summarizes the amount of GST it has collected and the amount of GST it has paid. The business may file monthly, quarterly or yearly with quarterly installments.

Accounting Examples for Remittances and Refunds

Remittances

Most of the time a business will make GST remittances since sales usually exceed expenses — the business operates at a profit. The example below shows how the GST accounts are cleared and a liability (*Accounts Payable* account) is set up to remit GST owing to the Receiver General of Canada. In this case, the usual one, the Receiver General becomes a vendor for the business so that the liability can be entered and the payment made.

Date	Particulars	Ref.	Debit	Credit
03/31	GST Charged on Sales		2 500.00	
	GST Paid on Purchases			700.00
	A/P - Receiver General			1 800.00
03/31	A/P - Receiver General		1 800.00	
	Cash in Bank			1 800.00

Refunds

The example below shows how the GST accounts are cleared and a current asset account (*Accounts Receivable* account) is set up for a GST refund from the Receiver General of Canada. In this case, the Receiver General owes money to the business; that is, it acts like a customer. A customer record is set up for the Receiver General to record and collect the amount receivable.

Date	Particulars	Ref.	Debit	Credit
03/31	GST Charged on Sales		1 500.00	
	A/R - Receiver General		500.00	
	GST Paid on Purchases			2 000.00
04/15	Cash in Bank		500.00	
	A/R - Receiver General			500.00

GST and Provincial Sales Taxes

The rules governing provincial sales taxes vary from province to province, in terms of the rates of taxation, the goods and services that are taxed, and whether or not PST is applied to the GST as well as the base purchase price. The examples that follow assume that the item sold has both GST and PST applied.

For the province of Alberta, there is no provincial sales tax. The examples provided above, without PST, illustrate the application of GST for this province.

PST in Ontario, Manitoba, Saskatchewan and British Columbia

The provinces west of Quebec apply PST to the base price of the sale, the amount without GST included.

ONTARIO

Sold goods on account to customer for $500. GST charged is 7% and PST charged is 8%.

GST = (0.07 * 500) = $35
PST = (0.08 * 500) = $40
Total amount of invoice = $500 + $35 + $40 = $575

Date	Particulars	Ref.	Debit	Credit
xx/xx	Accounts Receivable		575.00	
	GST Charged on Sales			35.00
	PST Payable			40.00
	Revenue from Sales			500.00

The full amount of PST collected on sales is remitted to the provincial treasurer (less any applicable sales tax commissions).

Harmonized Sales Tax — Nova Scotia, Newfoundland, New Brunswick and Labrador

Notes

The harmonized sales tax model adopted in these Atlantic provinces is the one that the Federal Government would like to apply across all provinces in Canada.

In these Atlantic provinces, the GST and PST are harmonized at a single rate of 15 percent. The full 15 percent Harmonized Sales Tax (HST) operates much like the basic GST, with HST remittances equal to HST collected on sales less HST paid on purchases. Prices shown to customers must have the HST included (tax-inclusive pricing), with separate information showing either the rate of HST or the amount of HST included in the price.

NEW BRUNSWICK

Sold goods on account to customer for $575, including HST at 15% ($500 base price).

HST = (0.15 * 500) = $75
Total amount of invoice = $575

Date	Particulars	Ref.	Debit	Credit
xx/xx	Accounts Receivable		575.00	
	HST Charged on Sales			75.00
	Revenue from Sales			500.00

A single remittance for the full 15 percent is made to the Receiver General; the provincial portion of the HST is not remitted separately. The administration of the HST may be taken over by the provincial governments in the future.

Quebec Sales Tax (QST)

Provincial sales taxes in Quebec (QST) are also combined with the GST in that the provincial tax rate was reduced in order to apply it to a broader base of goods and services, like the base that has GST applied. The QST is calculated on the base amount of the sale plus the GST. That is, QST is applied to GST — a piggy-backed tax or a tax on a tax.

QUEBEC

Sold goods on account to customer for $500. GST charged is 7% and QST charged is 6.5%.

GST = (0.07 * 500) = $35
QST = (0.065 * 535) = $34.78
Total amount of invoice = $500.00 + $35.00 + $34.78 = $569.78

Date	Particulars	Ref.	Debit	Credit
xx/xx	Accounts Receivable		569.78	
	GST Charged on Sales			35.00
	QST Charged on Sales			34.78
	Revenue from Sales			500.00

QST is remitted to the provincial treasurer, separately from GST. However, part of the QST is refundable and businesses can deduct some of the QST they pay on their purchases from the QST they collect on sales. The QST paid on items that are inputs to the business is refundable, the rest is not. Therefore, QST paid must be designated as refundable or non-refundable at the time of the purchase and when the purchase is recorded.

PST in Prince Edward Island

Provincial sales taxes in PEI are applied to the base sale price plus GST. However, unlike Quebec, and like Ontario, some items have GST only applied, and some have both GST and PST applied.

PRINCE EDWARD ISLAND

Sold goods on account to customer for $500. GST charged is 7% and PST charged is 10%.

GST = (0.07 * 500) = $35
PST = (0.10 * 535) = $53.50
Total amount of invoice = $500.00 + $35.00 + $53.50 = $588.50

Date	Particulars	Ref.	Debit	Credit
xx/xx	Accounts Receivable		588.50	
	GST Charged on Sales			35.00
	PST Payable			53.50
	Revenue from Sales			500.00

The full amount of PST collected on sales is remitted to the provincial treasurer (less any applicable sales tax commissions).

PART 2

APPLICATIONS

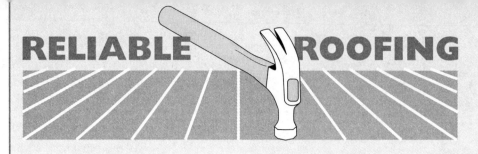

CHAPTER THREE

RELIABLE ROOFING

Upon completion of this chapter, you will be able to:

OBJECTIVES

- *access* the Simply Accounting program
- *access* the data files for the business
- *open* the General Journal
- *enter* transactions in the General Journal
- *edit* and *review* General Journal transactions
- *post* transactions
- *create* new General Ledger accounts
- *display* General Ledger and General Journal reports
- *print* General Ledger and General Journal reports
- *graph* General Ledger reports
- *display* and *print* comparative financial reports
- *back up* your data files
- *advance* the using date
- *finish* an accounting session

COMPANY INFORMATION

Company Profile

Reliable Roofing, owned by Albert Dresden, has operated successfully in Red Deer, Alberta, for the past six years. Dresden works alone most of the time, replacing and repairing roofs in the Red Deer area. For larger projects, or for tighter deadlines, he hires an assistant on a day-to-day contractual basis. Dresden's friendly manner and his work guarantees — five years for roof replacement work and one year for repair work — have developed for him a community reputation for reliability, honesty and friendly service.

Albert Dresden keeps up with the changing trends and roof styles. The majority of Reliable Roofing's customers still request the traditional asphalt roof shingles. However, an increasing number are replacing old asphalt shingle roofs with cedar or slate shingles, with Marlee or clay tiles or with copper. These homeowners believe that the greater expense is justified because the roof will last longer and make their house more attractive. Dresden's mobile unit is specially equipped for working with the traditional as well as the specialty roofing materials.

Since Dresden is on a job most of the time, he relies on his answering machine, pager and cellular telephone to arrange appointments for work estimates or to schedule work. Individual homeowners, most of Reliable Roofing's customers, generally settle their accounts as soon as the work is completed, but Dresden sometimes extends the payment period for up to one month. When Dresden replaces or repairs roofs on townhouse and apartment complexes, he deals directly with the property management companies rather than the owners or tenants. These companies have set up accounts with Reliable Roofing and are expected to pay for completed work within thirty days.

For an annual fee, Peter Lacklustre, an accountant, records and manages all the financial transactions for Reliable Roofing. Mr. Lacklustre is gradually converting the accounts for all his clients to Simply Accounting, because the program is well suited for small businesses. He converted the accounts for Reliable Roofing on July 1, 1999, using the following information:

- Chart of Accounts
- Trial Balance
- Accounting Procedures

Notes

The Chart of Accounts includes only postable accounts and the Net Income or Current Earnings account. Simply Accounting uses the Net Income account for the income statement to calculate the difference between revenue and expenses before closing the books.

**RELIABLE ROOFING
CHART OF ACCOUNTS**

ASSETS
1080 Cash in Bank
1200 A/R - Toller Properties
1220 A/R - Lakeside Co-op
1240 A/R - M. DeZwager
1320 Prepaid Insurance
1340 Supplies: Computer
1360 Supplies: Roofing
1540 Portable Computer
1550 Computer Peripherals
1560 Power Tools
1580 Mobile Roofing Unit

LIABILITIES
2100 A/P - Space for You
2120 A/P - Ads On-Line
2130 A/P - Alberta Hydro
2140 A/P - Alberta Telephone
2160 A/P - Dominion Building Supplies
2190 A/P - Summit Scaffold
2650 GST Charged on Services
2670 GST Paid on Purchases

EQUITY
3100 A. Dresden, Capital
3150 A. Dresden, Drawings
3600 Net Income

REVENUE
4100 Revenue from Roofing
4200 Interest Revenue

EXPENSES
5050 Advertising
5080 Bank Charges
5130 Hydro Expense
5150 Interest Expense
5200 Mobile Unit Maintenance
5250 Rent
5280 Telephone Expense
5500 Wages Expense

```
RELIABLE ROOFING
TRIAL BALANCE

June 30, 1999

1080 Cash in Bank                          $16 250.50
1200 A/R - Toller Properties                 3 210.00
1240 A/R - M. DeZwager                       1 070.00
1320 Prepaid Insurance                       1 200.00
1340 Supplies: Computer                        500.00
1360 Supplies: Roofing                       2 800.00
1540 Portable Computer                         800.00
1550 Computer Peripherals                    2 000.00
1560 Power Tools                             3 200.00
1580 Mobile Roofing Unit                    35 000.00
2160 A/P - Dominion Building Supplies                       457.50
2650 GST Charged on Services                               560.00
2670 GST Paid on Purchases                    105.00
3100 A. Dresden, Capital                                59 700.00
3150 A. Dresden, Drawings                     750.00
4100 Revenue from Roofing                                8 000.00
5050 Advertising                               75.00
5080 Bank Charges                              32.00
5200 Mobile Unit Maintenance                  175.00
5250 Rent                                   1 000.00
5280 Telephone Expense                         50.00
5500 Wages Expense                            500.00
                                          _____    _____
                                          $ 68 717.50    $ 68 717.50
```

Accounting Procedures

GST Remittances

Dresden has chosen the regular method for remittance of the Goods and Services Tax (GST). He will record the GST collected from customers as a liability (credit) in the *GST Charged on Services* account. He records GST that he pays to vendors in the *GST Paid on Purchases* account as a decrease (debit) to his liability to Revenue Canada. His GST remittance or refund is calculated automatically in the *GST Owing (Refund)* subtotal. You can see these accounts when you display or print the Balance Sheet. Dresden files his GST remittances or requests for refunds with the Receiver General of Canada on the last day of each fiscal quarter. (For details, please read Chapter 2 on the Goods and Services Tax.)

INSTRUCTIONS

1. Using the Chart of Accounts and Trial Balance for Reliable Roofing, enter the source documents for July using the General Journal in Simply Accounting. The procedures for entering each new type of transaction for this application are outlined step by step in the keystroke section following the source documents. These transactions have a ✔ in the check box and the page number on which the relevant keystrokes begin immediately below the check box.

2. After you have completed your entries, print the reports and graphs indicated on the printing form below. Keystrokes for reports begin on page 45.

SOURCE DOCUMENTS

USING DATE — July 6

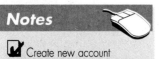

Notes

Remember that the ✔ and the number beneath it indicate that keystroke instructions for this entry begin on page 35.

Notes

☑ Create new account
41 2200 Bank Loan. (See Keystrokes on page 41.)

☑
35
Sales Invoice #RR-99001
Dated July 2, 1999
To Georg Johanssen, $650 for replacement of garage shingle roof plus GST charged $45.50. Sales Invoice total $695.50. Payment received in cash on completion of work.

☐ Bank Credit Memo #WCU-2264
Dated July 3, 1999
From Workers' Credit Union, $8 000 bank loan deposited in bank account.

☐ Purchase Invoice #DBS-7643
Dated July 3, 1999
From Dominion Building Supplies, $850 for roofing supplies (tar paper and shingles) plus GST paid $59.50. Purchase Invoice total $909.50. Terms: 2/15 net 30 days.

☐ Sales Invoice #RR-99002
Dated July 3, 1999
To Maryke DeZwager, $380 for roof repair work completed plus GST charged $26.60. Sales Invoice total $406.60. Terms: net 30 days.

☐ Cheque Copy #501
Dated July 3, 1999
To Dominion Building Supplies, $457.50 in full payment of invoice #DBS-6199.

Purchase Invoice #AOL-431
Dated July 5, 1999
From Ads On-Line Inc., $1 800 to design a Web page for advertising of roofing services plus GST paid $126. Purchase Invoice total $1 926. Terms: net 20 days.

Bank Debit Memo #WCU-3181
Dated July 5, 1999
From Workers' Credit Union, $35.50 for bank service charges.

Cash Receipt #45
Dated July 6, 1999
From Toller Properties, $3 210 in full payment of account.

Cash Receipt #46
Dated July 6, 1999
From Maryke DeZwager, $1 070 in payment of account.

Notes

See Keystrokes on Advancing the Using Date, page 43.

USING DATE — July 13

Utility Statement #AT-44318
Dated July 9, 1999
From Alberta Telephone, $240.00 for office and cellular telephone services plus GST paid $16.80. Purchase Invoice total $256.80. Terms: cash on receipt of invoice.

Cheque Copy #502
Dated July 10, 1999
To Alberta Telephone, $256.80 in full payment of account.

Purchase Invoice #DBS-8763
Dated July 10, 1999
From Dominion Building Supplies, $250 for roofing supplies (tar, tar paper and nails) plus GST paid $17.50. Purchase Invoice total $267.50. Terms: 2/15 net 30 days.

Bank Credit Memo #WCU-7101
Dated July 11, 1999
From Workers' Credit Union, $312 for interest on bank account.

Sales Invoice #RR-99003
Dated July 12, 1999
To Toller Properties Management, $3 000 for reshingling roof on two townhouse units plus GST charged $210. Sales Invoice total $3 210. Terms: 50% due on completion of work, balance in 30 days.

Cash Receipt #47
Dated July 12, 1999
From Toller Properties Management, $1 605 in payment of account.

Purchase Invoice #ME-64299
Dated July 13, 1999
From Micron Equipment, $4 800 for Pentium 166 MHZ Micron portable computer with active matrix screen, plus GST paid $336. Purchase Invoice total $5 136. Terms: C.O.D.

Notes

☐ Create a new account, 2170 A/P - Micron Equipment.

☐ Cheque Copy #503
Dated July 13, 1999
To Micron Equipment, $5 136 in full payment of account.

KEYSTROKES

Opening Data Files

Using the instructions for accessing a data file in Chapter 1, page 12, open the Reliable Roofing application.

The following screen appears, asking (prompting) you to enter the using date for this work session:

Notes

Many screens include a cancel button. If you click on Cancel, you will return to your previous screen without entering any changes.

The using date is the date of your work session, the date on which you are recording the accounting transactions on the computer. A business with a large number of transactions may record these transactions at the end of each day. One with fewer transactions may enter them once a week. In this workbook, transactions are entered once a week so the using date is updated by one week at a time. The using date may or may not be the same as the date on which the transaction actually took place, but obviously it cannot be earlier.

The using date for your session is July 6, 1999. Since this date is not shown by default on the screen, you must change the date. You can enter dates using the following alternative formats. Note that they all use the same order of month, day and year:

Notes

- The using date must be between the previous using date and the end of the fiscal period.
- You cannot enter transactions for dates later than the using date you have entered.
- The section Advancing the Using Date on page 43 will explain how to work with later dates.
- The format of the date that shows on your screen is controlled by the Regional Settings in the Control Panel of your Windows program, not by the format you use to enter the date. Refer to your Windows manual for further information.

- 07-06-99
- 07/06/99
- 07 06 99
- 07 06
- July 6, 1999

- 7-6-99
- 7/6/99
- 7 6 99
- 7 6 (The year is filled in by the program.)

- other non-alpha or non-numeric separating characters may also be accepted by the program

For consistency, we will use the first of these date formats (07-06-99) throughout this workbook.

Type   07-06-99

Click on OK

Your screen shows the following Home window:

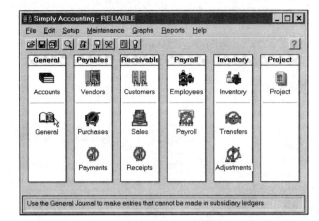

Notes

Only the General Journal can be accessed for this file. The no entry symbol on the remaining journal icons indicates that these have not been set up, are not ready to use and cannot be accessed.

The Home window is divided as follows: the title bar with the program and file names, control menu icon and size icons are on top; the main menu bar comes next followed by the tool bar with tool buttons that permit an alternative and quick access to commonly used menu items. The Home window tool buttons from left to right (with their alternative pull-down menu locations) are: Open File, Save and Backup (File menu), Find ledger record (Edit menu), Setup (Setup menu), Advance Using Date and To Do Lists (Maintenance menu), Display reports (Reports menu), Advice and Help (Help menu).

The six ledger names with their respective icons fill up the major part of the window — six ledgers in the top row below the ledger or module name, journal icons below the line under their respective ledgers in the next two icon rows of the window. Ledgers contain the records for accounts, customers, vendors, employees, inventory items and their balances. Journals are used to enter accounting transactions.

Below the journal icons, the status bar describes the purpose of the General Journal because the pointer is on the General icon. Point to different parts of the Home Window to observe the changes in the status bar message.

Entering General Journal Transactions

All transactions for Reliable Roofing are entered in the General Journal, indicated by the arrow pointer in the following screen:

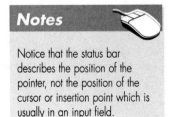

Notes

Notice that the status bar describes the position of the pointer, not the position of the cursor or insertion point which is usually in an input field.

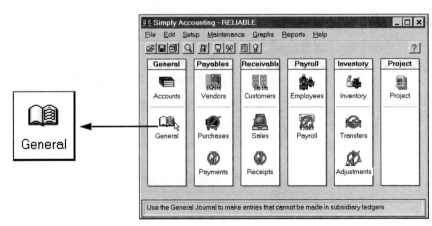

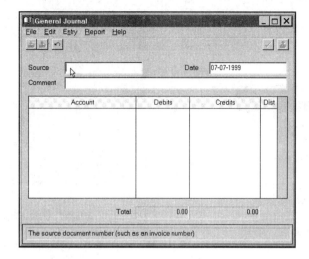

Double click on the **General icon** from the middle portion of the Home window to open the General Journal. The General Journal input form shown below appears on your screen:

You are now ready to enter the first transaction in the General Journal input screen. The cursor, a flashing vertical line, is blinking in the Source field ready to receive information. The Source field identifies the reference document from which you obtain the information for a transaction. In this transaction, the source is the invoice number.

Type   RR-99001

Press   (tab)

The cursor advances to the next field, the Date field. Here you should enter the transaction date. The program enters the using date by default for all journal entries. It is highlighted, ready to be accepted or changed. Because the work was completed on July 2, 1999, the using date of July 6 is incorrect and must be changed.

Type   07-02-99

Press   (tab)

The cursor advances to the Comment field, where you can enter a description of the transaction to make the permanent record more meaningful. You may enter up to 39 characters, including spaces.

Type   Johanssen garage roof replacement

Press   (tab)

The cursor moves forward to the first line of the Account field, creating a dotted box for the first account. Following usual accounting practice, enter the account to be debited first.

Simply Accounting organizes accounts into categories using the following boundaries for numbering:

• 1000 – 1999 Assets
• 2000 – 2999 Liabilities
• 3000 – 3999 Equity
• 4000 – 4999 Revenue
• 5000 – 5999 Expense

This system makes it easy to remember the first digit of an account. Pressing (enter) when the cursor is in the Account field will display the list of accounts. By typing the first digit of an account then pressing (enter) while the cursor is flashing in any account field, the program will advance the list to the accounts beginning with that digit.

Type   1

Press   (enter)

The following list of accounts appears:

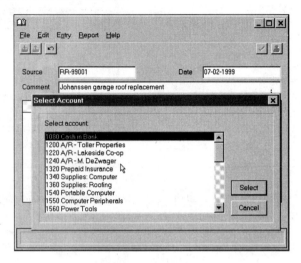

Because *1080 Cash in Bank* is the first account and the first 1000 level account, it is already highlighted or selected. The list includes only postable accounts, those which can be debited or credited in journal entries.

Click on the darkened or highlighted **Select** button. (The box framing the button is darker.) Notice that the account number and name have now been added to your input form so you can easily see if you have selected the correct account. If the screen does not display the entire account title, you can see the rest of the account title by clicking anywhere on the part that is showing.

Your cursor is now positioned in the Debits field. The amount is selected, ready to be changed.

Type   695.50

Press   (tab)

Your input form should now appear as follows:

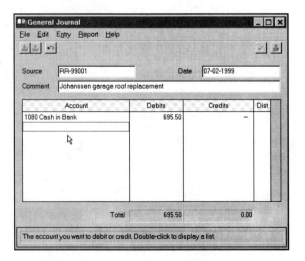

The cursor has advanced to the next line of the Account field, creating a new dotted box so you can enter the first account to be credited for this transaction: the liability account, *GST Charged on Services*. Remember, liability accounts start with "2". However, we will type 3 in order to advance to the end of the 2000 level accounts.

Type   3

Press [enter] to advance your list to the 3000 accounts as shown:

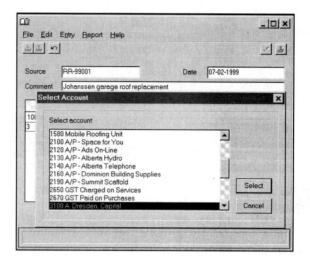

Click on 2650 GST Charged on Services from the displayed list to highlight it. If necessary, click on the scroll arrow to move through the account list to include 2650 in the display.

Click on Select

Again, the account number and name have been added to your transaction form. The cursor has advanced to the Credits field, which shows $695.50 as the default amount because this amount will balance the entry. The amount is highlighted to indicate that you may edit it. Because this is a compound entry, you must change the amount to separate the GST and revenue.

Type   45.50

Press [tab]

The cursor moves to the next line in the Account field.

Type   4

Press [enter] to advance your list to the 4000 accounts.

Click on 4100 Revenue from Roofing from the displayed list.

Click on Select. The cursor advances to the Credits field again, where the remaining balance of $650 is shown by default. This time the amount is correct, so you can accept it.

Press   [tab]

The cursor advances to the next line in the Account field. Your completed input form should appear as follows:

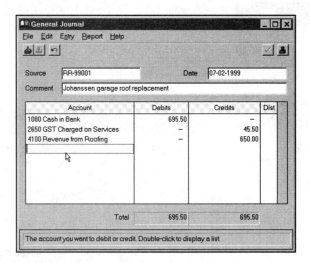

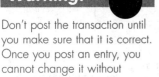
Until the debits and credits of a transaction are equal, you cannot post an entry and the Post button will remain dim. It is now darkened to show that the entry is complete, balanced and can be posted. The Store button, for recurring entries, is also darkened. We will use the store button in the following application, Java Jean's (Chapter 4). Before you store or post an entry, you should review the transaction.

Reviewing the General Journal Entry

Choose **Display General Journal Entry** from the pull-down menu under **Report** as shown:

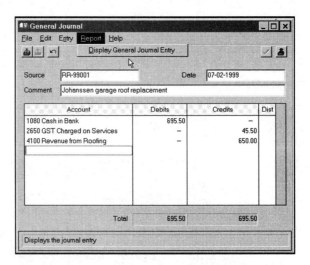

The transaction is displayed as follows:

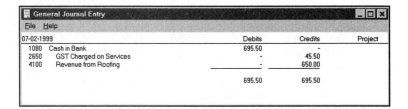

Clicking on the maximize button ⬜ to change your display to full screen size or use the scroll arrows to see more of the display if your transaction does not fit completely on the screen. To return to your input form,

Click on ☒ or **choose** Close from the pull-down menu under the control menu icon.

CORRECTING THE GENERAL JOURNAL ENTRY BEFORE POSTING

Press (tab) to advance to the field that has the error. To move to a previous field, **press** (shift) and (tab) together (that is, while holding down (shift), **press** (tab)). The field will be highlighted, ready for editing. **Type** the correct information and **press** (tab) to enter it.

You can also use the mouse to point to a field and drag through the incorrect information to highlight it. You can highlight a single number or letter or the entire field. **Type** the correct information and **press** (tab) to enter it.

To correct an account number, **click on** the incorrect account number (or name) to select the field. **Press** (enter) to display the list of accounts. **Click on** the correct account. **Click on Select**; and **press** (tab) to advance to the next line and enter the correction.

To correct an amount, **click on** it to highlight it. **Type** the correct amount and **press** (tab).

To discard the entry and begin again, **click on** ☒ or ↶ (on the tool bar). When Simply Accounting asks if you want to discard the entry, **click on Yes** to confirm your decision.

Posting

Once you are sure that all the information is correct, you are ready to post the transaction.

Click on the **post button** 🖼 in the General Journal tool bar (the one that looks like a stamp) or choose Post from the pull-down menu under Entry.

A new General Journal input form appears for you to enter the next transaction for this using date.

Adding a New Account

The bank credit memo on July 3 uses an account that is not listed in your Chart of Accounts. Often a company will need to create new accounts as it expands or changes direction. These future needs are not always foreseen when the accounts are first set up. You must add the account *2200 Bank Loan* in order to enter the bank credit memo transaction.

Click on the **minimize button** ⬓ to reduce the General Journal to the task bar at the bottom of you screen. If you wish, you may close the Journal window, but this is not necessary.

New accounts are entered in the General Ledger using the Accounts icon under General, the one with the arrow pointer on it in the Home window displayed here:

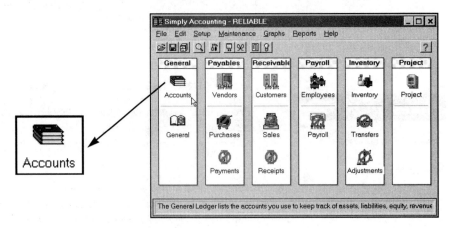

Double click on the **Accounts icon** to open the Accounts window. All accounts may be represented by their icons or listed numerically as shown here:

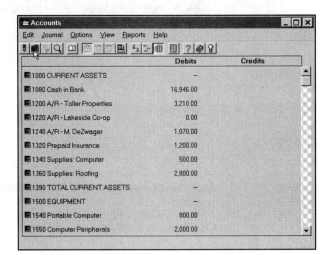

Again, the set of tool buttons in the Accounts window has changed. Hold the mouse pointer on each one briefly to see its name or purpose.

Click on the **Create button** ▣ on the tool bar at the top of the Accounts window (the button that looks like an open ledger book) or **choose** Create from the pull-down menu under **Edit** to see the General Ledger window — the new account information form:

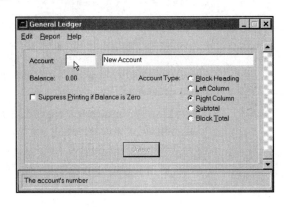

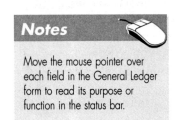

Move the mouse pointer over each field in the General Ledger form to read its purpose or function in the status bar.

The cursor is in the account number part of the Account field.

Type   2200

Press `tab`

The cursor advances to the name part of the Account field. New Account is highlighted, ready to be changed.

Type `Bank Loan`

Press `tab`

Account type set at "Right column" means that this is a postable account and its balance will be printed in the right-hand column of the liabilities section of the Balance Sheet. This default setting is correct. The use of different account types will be explained in the CISV application (Chapter 6), where you will set up the accounting records for a company from scratch.

You should turn on the **Suppress Printing if Balance is Zero** option. This choice means that if the balance in this account is zero, the account will not be included in your financial statements. If you leave this box unchecked, the account will be printed, even if it has a balance of zero. Some accounts, such as *Cash in Bank*, should always be printed in financial statements.

Click on **Suppress Printing if Balance is Zero** to turn the option on.

Check your work. Make any corrections necessary by highlighting the incorrect information and retyping it. When all of the information is correct, you need to save the new account information.

Click on **Create**

Another new account form opens so you can create additional accounts.

Click on ⊠ or **choose** **Close** from the pull-down menu under the control menu icon to close the General Ledger new account information window and return to the Accounts window.

Click on ⊠ or **choose** **Close** from the pull-down menu under the control menu icon to close the Accounts window and return to the Home window.

Double click on the **General icon** in the Home window to restore the General Journal. If you were in the middle of entering a transaction, you can continue from where you left off.

When you press `enter` in an Account field or display your Chart of Accounts, you will see that the Simply Accounting program has added the Bank Loan account to the list.

Advancing the Using Date

When you have finished making all the entries for the July 6 using date, the date for the next transaction is later than July 6. Therefore you must advance the using date before you can continue. Before taking this step, however, this is a good time to save and back up your work because you have already completed one week of transactions. Although Simply Accounting saves automatically each time you display a report or exit the program, it is important to know how you save and back up your work directly.

Click on ⊠ or **choose** **Close** from the pull-down menu under the control menu icon to close the General Journal.

Click on 🖫 on the tool bar or **choose** **Save** from the pull-down menu under **File**.

The data files for this workbook have been prepared with the default warning to back up your work weekly. Since we also advance the using date by one week at a time, you will be reminded to back up each time you advance the using date. You are now ready to advance the using date to July 13.

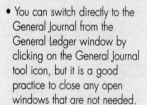

Choose Advance Using Date from the pull-down menu under **Maintenance** as shown:

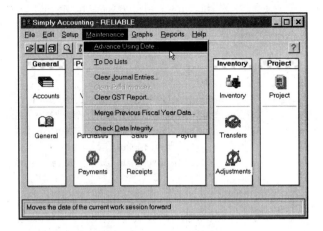

Notes

You can also make backups by using the Simply Accounting Save As command. Refer to Chapter 1, page 18 if you need help with or instructions on using the Save As command.

The following dialogue box appears, advising you that you have not yet backed up your work:

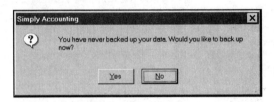

Click on Yes to proceed with the backup. The next screen asks for a file name for the backup:

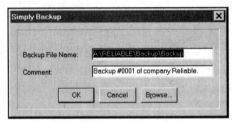

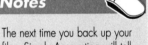

Notes

The next time you back up your files, Simply Accounting will tell you the date of your most recent backup and will provide the same location that you used before. The backup number in the comment will be updated.

Simply Accounting will create a default directory named backup under the folder that contains your working data files. You can edit the file name and comment if you wish. If you want to change the location of the backup, click on Browse, select a folder and file name and click on Save. The backup file is different from the one you create by copying or using the Save As command. The Copy and Save As commands create a complete working copy of your data that you can access with the Simply Accounting program directly. Backup creates a special format file that must first be restored before you can use it to enter transactions.

Notes

If your working files are lost or damaged, you can restore the backup files by choosing Restore from the pull-down menu under File. Follow the on-screen instructions to locate the backup and choose a file name for the restored data files.

Click on OK to accept the file name and proceed with the backup. After a brief period, you will see the following message that the backup is complete:

Click on OK to proceed to the Advance Using Date dialogue box with the current using date highlighted:

Type 07-13-99

Click on OK to accept the new date. You may now enter the remaining transactions for this exercise.

Displaying General Reports

A key advantage to using Simply Accounting rather than a manual system is the ability to produce financial reports quickly for any date or time period. Reports that are provided for a specific date, such as the Balance Sheet, can be produced for any date from the time the accounting records were converted to the computerized system up to the most recent using date. Reports that summarize a financial period, such as the income statement can be produced from the beginning of the fiscal period up to any date after the conversion took place.

Displaying the Balance Sheet

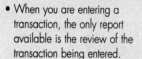

• When you are entering a transaction, the only report available is the review of the transaction being entered.
• When the Accounts window is open, all General Reports are available from the pull-down menu under Reports.

You can display the Balance Sheet at any time except when you are entering a transaction. In the Home window,

Choose Financials and then **Balance Sheet** from the pull-down menu under **Reports** (click on Reports in the menu bar, point to Financials, then move the pointer across to Balance Sheet and click) as shown:

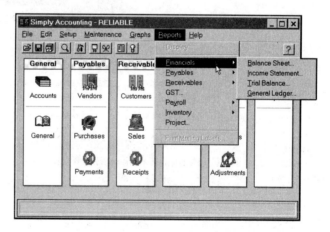

Your screen now includes the following Balance Sheet Options window:

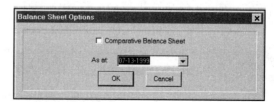

One of the options is to show the balance sheet for two different dates at the same time, the Comparative Balance Sheet.

Click on **Comparative Balance Sheet** to select this style of report and expand the report options as follows:

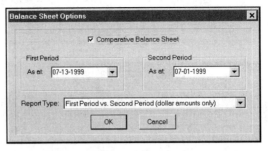

Your most recent using date is displayed in the first date field. The second date is the date on which the files were converted to Simply Accounting. Press ⌐tab⌐ to highlight the first date if you want to change it. If you click on the drop-down list arrow to the right of the Date (As at) field, you can see some alternative dates for the Balance Sheet. Choose from this list or type in the date you want using one of the accepted formats given earlier.

Press ⌐tab⌐

Type in the second date or choose from the list.

Click on the **Report Type field** to display the types in the drop-down list as shown:

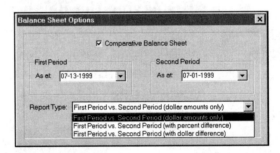

Choose Dollar Amounts if you want only the dollar balances for both dates. Choose Percent Difference if you want the dollar balances as well as the percentage increase from the second period amount to the first; and choose Dollar Difference if you want the dollar balances together with the difference between them in dollars. The second period amount is subtracted from the first to calculate the difference.

Click on the **report type** you want.

Click on **OK** to display the Balance Sheet.

Click on ☒ when you have finished to return to the screen or window you were last working with.

Displaying the Trial Balance

You can display the Trial Balance at any time while working with the software, except when you are actually entering a transaction.

Choose **Financials** and then **Trial Balance** from the pull-down menu under **Reports**. The using date is once again highlighted.

Type the date for which you want the Trial Balance or choose from the options given with the drop-down list arrow.

Click on **OK** to display the Trial Balance.

Click on ☒ to leave the display and return to the previous screen or window.

Displaying the Income Statement

You can view the Income Statement at any time, except when you are actually entering a transaction.

Choose Financials and then Income Statement from the pull-down menu under Reports to display the following Income Statement Options window with Start and Finish date fields:

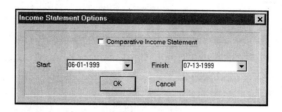

The Income Statement also has a comparative report option, allowing comparisons between two different time periods. You might want to compare the income for two different months, quarters or years. The report types are the same as for the balance sheet.

Click on Comparative Income Statement to select this option.

By default, the beginning of the fiscal period and the current using date are provided as the start and finish dates (for both periods if you have selected the comparative report). You must enter the beginning and ending dates for the period (or periods) you wish your Income Statement to cover. Again, you may choose one of the dates offered from the drop-down list or you may type in the dates.

Type the date on which your Income Statement period begins.

Press (tab)

Type the date on which your Income Statement period ends.

Type the start and finish dates for the second period and choose a report type if your report is comparative.

Click on OK

Close the display window when you are finished.

Displaying General Ledger Reports

You can display the General Ledger at any time unless you are entering a transaction.

Choose Financials and then General Ledger from the pull-down menu under Reports to display the following report options:

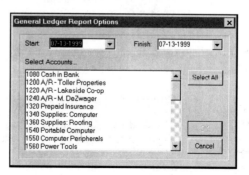

Type the starting date for your General Ledger report, or choose a date from the drop-down list selections.

Press `tab`

Type the ending date for your General Ledger report.

Click on the account or accounts you wish to display. Use the scroll arrow to see more accounts if the one you want is not visible. If you want to include all the accounts in the display, click on **Select All**.

Close the display window when you have finished viewing it.

Tool Bar Report Button

Reports related directly to ledger and journal icons in the Home window are available from the Report button on the tool bar. These include lists related to the ledgers such as the Chart of Accounts, and customer, vendor and employee lists as well as all journal reports. The Report button works in one of three ways.

- If a ledger or journal icon is highlighted or selected but not open, the report for that item or its options window is displayed immediately when you click on the Report button.

- If no icon is highlighted, clicking on the Report button produces a list of all journal reports and ledger lists. Choose from this list to display the report or its options window.

- When the Accounts window is open, clicking on the Report button provides a list of all General Ledger reports. Choose from this list to display the report or its options window. From other ledger windows, the report list will include the reports related to that ledger.

To view these same reports from the Reports menu in the Home window, you must first highlight, but not open the corresponding ledger or journal. You can do this by

- clicking on the ledger or journal

- using arrow keys to move from a selected icon to the one you need if any icon is already highlighted, or

- pressing `alt` twice and then pressing arrow keys to begin highlighting the icons.

The Report button provides a simple method of displaying reports.

Displaying the Chart of Accounts

Click on the **Accounts icon** to select it.

Click on the **Report button** 🖼 on the tool bar or **choose** **Display Chart of Accounts** from the pull-down menu under **Reports**. The report will be displayed immediately.

Close the display when you are finished.

Displaying the General Journal

Click on the **General icon** to select it.

Click on the **Report button** 🖼 on the tool bar or **choose** **Display General Journal** from the pull-down menu under **Reports**. The following report options will be displayed:

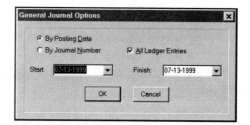

You may display journals either by the posting date of the journal entries or by journal entry number. All reports in this workbook are requested by posting date — the default setting, so leave this option unchanged.

The latest using date is given by default for the period of the report, with the starting date highlighted for editing.

Type the beginning date for which you want the journal entries printed.

Press `tab`

Type the ending date of the period for your journal report.

Click on OK

Close the display when you are finished.

Displaying Reports from Other Reports

Some reports can be accessed from other reports that you have open or displayed. These cross-referenced reports are available whenever the pointer changes to a magnifying glass icon with a plus sign inside it. As you move the mouse pointer over various items in the first report, the type of second report available may change. The name of the second report will appear in the status bar. Double click while the magnifying glass icon is visible to display the second report immediately. The first report stays open in the background.

The General Ledger Report for a specific account can be accessed from the Balance Sheet, Income Statement, Trial Balance, Chart of Accounts or General Journal when you double click on an account number, name or balance amount. The General Ledger record for an account can be accessed from the General Ledger Report.

While you have the additional report displayed, you may print it. (See Printing General Reports below.)

Close the second report and then close the first report when you are finished viewing them.

Printing General Reports

Display the report you wish to print by following the instructions in the previous section on Displaying General Reports.

Choose Print from the pull-down menu under File.

Wait for the printing information displayed to clear from the screen, then close the displayed report.

Graphing General Reports

Graphs are available only from the Home window.

Expenses and Net Profits as a % of Revenue

Choose Expenses and Net Profit as a % of Revenue from the pull-down menu under Graphs to display the following report options:

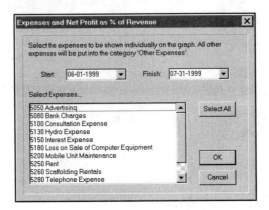

Type the beginning date for which you want the graph.

Press (tab)

Type the ending date of the period for your graph.

Click on each expense account you want included in the graph or click on Select All to include all the accounts in the graph.

Click on OK

The graph will be displayed. The pie chart graph shown here, including all accounts for the period from June 1 to July 31, is a form of the income statement:

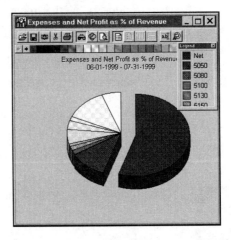

You have a number of different options regarding the graph at this stage. The tool bar options are the same for all graphs. By selecting the appropriate button on the tool bar, you can import a graph, export the displayed graph, copy it to the clipboard as a bitmap or a text file, print the graph, change the view from 3-D to 2-D, hide the legend, edit or add titles, etc. Hold the mouse pointer over a tool button for a few seconds to see a brief description of the tool's purpose. Most tool buttons lead to an additional option or control window requiring your input.

In addition, you can change colours by dragging the colour you want to the pie section you want to change; expand or shrink the legend by dragging its bottom border down or up respectively; pull out a section of the pie chart by dragging it away from the rest of the chart. The graph displayed has the Net Profit portion pulled out for emphasis.

Close the graph when you are finished.

Revenues by Account

Choose Revenues by Account from the pull-down menu under **Graphs** to display the following report options:

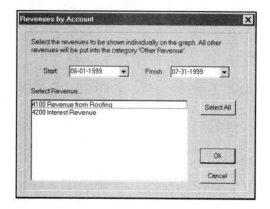

Type the beginning date for which you want the graph.

Press ⟨tab⟩

Type the ending date of the period for your graph.

Click on each revenue account you want included in the graph or click on **Select All** to include all the accounts in the graph.

Click on OK to display the pie chart graph as shown:

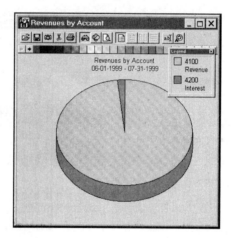

The pie chart graph has each revenue account represented by a different piece of the pie. You can see that almost all of the revenue comes from roofing work.

You have the same options for the graph as you did for the Expenses and Net Profit as % of Revenue.

Close the graph when you are finished.

Expenses by Account

Choose Expenses by Account from the pull-down menu under **Graphs** to display the following report options:

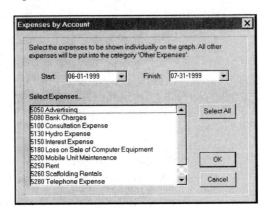

Type the beginning date for which you want the graph.

Press [tab]

Type the ending date of the period for your graph.

Click on each expense account you want included in the graph or click on **Select All** to include all the accounts in the graph.

Click on OK to see the pie chart graph:

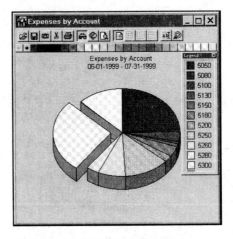

Each expense account that was selected is represented as a separate piece of the pie. The accounts not selected are grouped together in the other category. The expenses graph makes it easy to identify at a glance the items that account for the largest share of expenses.

Close the graph when you are finished.

Finishing a Session

Finish the last transaction you are working on for this session.

Close the transaction window (such as journal input or display) to return to the Home window.

Close the Home window. The Simply Accounting program will automatically save your work when you finish your session and exit properly.

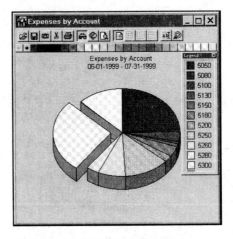

Notes

Alternatively, you could choose Exit from the pull-down menu under File.

Click on Start in the Windows opening screen.

Click on Shut Down

Be sure that the option to Shut Down the Computer is selected.

Click on Yes to confirm your intention to turn off the computer.

CASE PROBLEMS

Case One

At the end of March 1999, when Dresden received his bank statement, he completed the manual journal entries as follows:

Date	Ref.	Accounts	Debit	Credit
Mar. 31	Mar. Bk Stmt.	Bank	400	
		Interest Revenue		400
Mar. 31	Mar. Bk Stmt.	Service Charges	30	
		Bank		30
Mar. 31	Mar. Bk Stmt.	NSF Charges	15	
		Bank		15

Manually show the single journal entry in Simply Accounting that represents the same information?

How is the Simply Accounting method of entering journal transactions different from the manual accounting procedures? What are the advantages of using Simply Accounting?

Case Two

Enter the following source documents using the General Journal in Simply Accounting. Advance the using date to July 21, July 28 and July 31 as required.

Notes

☐ You will need to create the following new accounts in order to complete these realistic source documents:
5180 Loss on Sale of
    Computer Equipment
5100 Consultation Expense
2180 A/P - InfraRed
    Diagnostics
5260 Scaffolding Rentals
2185 A/P - Prairie Roof
    Equipment
1250 A/R - Premier Ballet
    School
5300 Supplies Used

RELIABLE ROOFING

456 The Skyway
Red Deer
Alberta T4P 7C2
Tel.: 403-776-8866 or 403-776-6632
Fax.: 403-776-7521

Invoice: __RR-99004__

To: Lakeside Co-op
55 Lakeside Drive
Red Deer, Alberta T4N 1T6

Date: July 15, 1999

Description of Work Completed	Amount
Roof repair work on condominium units	750.00
All work guaranteed for 1 year	
Terms: Net 30 days	**Subtotal** 750.00
GST # 554333789 RT	**GST** 52.50
Customer Signature *Myrtle Watters*	**Total** 802.50

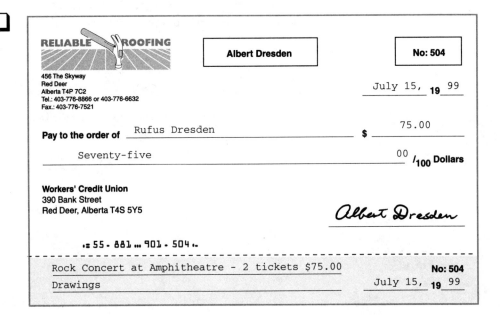

RELIABLE ROOFING

456 The Skyway
Red Deer
Alberta T4P 7C2
Tel.: 403-776-8866 or 403-776-6632
Fax.: 403-776-7521

Albert Dresden

No: 504

July 15, 19 99

Pay to the order of Rufus Dresden $ 75.00

Seventy-five 00 /100 **Dollars**

Workers' Credit Union
390 Bank Street
Red Deer, Alberta T4S 5Y5

Albert Dresden

·⑆ 55 · 881 ⑈ 901 · 504 ·⑈

Rock Concert at Amphitheatre - 2 tickets $75.00   **No: 504**

Drawings   July 15, 19 99

Student Credit Union
110 College Street
Red Deer
Alberta T4P 4T7

No: 250

July 16, 19 99

Pay to the order of ___Reliable Roofing___ $ ___500.00___

___Five hundred___ 00 /100 **Dollars**

Lynn Roth
McKinley Hall, U of C
Calgary, Alberta T1Y 5H6

Lynn Roth

⑆ 449 ⋅ 7 ⑆ 8811 ⋅ 250 ⑈

Purchase used portable computer from

Reliable Roofing for $500

No: 250

July 16, 19 99

InfraRed Diagnostics
340 Rouge Valley Road
Red Deer
Alberta T4R 9J1
Tel.: 403-465-1751
Fax.: 403-465-1755

No: ___ID 61086___

To: Reliable Roofing
456 The Skyway
Red Deer
Alberta T4P 7C2

Date: July 17, 1999

Description of Service	Amount
Roof consultation on building requiring roof work. Use of infra-red heat seeking device to estimate thermal efficiency.	300.00

Terms: Cash on Receipt	**Subtotal** 300.00
GST # 561066631 RT	21.00
Signature _Albert Dresden_	**Total** 321.00

RELIABLE ROOFING

Albert Dresden

No: 505

456 The Skyway
Red Deer
Alberta T4P 7C2
Tel.: 403-776-8866 or 403-776-6632
Fax.: 403-776-7521

July 18, 19 99

Pay to the order of InfraRed Diagnostics $ 321.00

Three hundred twenty-one   00 /100 **Dollars**

Workers' Credit Union
390 Bank Street
Red Deer, Alberta T4S 5Y5

Albert Dresden

⑆55-881⑈901-505⑉

InfraRed Diagnostics - Consultation Service   **No: 505**
roof consultation $300 + $21 GST   July 18, 19 99

Dominion Building Supplies
800 Ash Avenue, Red Deer, Alberta T4N 4V2.   Tel: 403-349-5176   Fax: 403-344-5910

No: _____ DBS 9541   Date: July 18, 1999

Sold To:

Reliable Roofing
456 The Skyway
Red Deer
Alberta T4P 7C2

Deliver to:

same

Deliver Date:

Customer pick up

Qty	Description	Amount
	Roofing supplies	400.00

Terms: 2/15, Net 30	**Subtotal**	400.00
GST # 461877290	**GST**	28.00
Signed *Albert Dresden*	**Total**	428.00

Summit Scaffold

56 Hilife Cres., Red Deer, Alberta T4S 8B5   Tel:(403)752-8861   Fax:(403)752-8888

No: _____ SS 66312 _____   Invoice Date: July 19, 1999

To: Reliable Roofing | rental period:

           456 The Skyway |
           Red Deer | July 19 - July 26
           Alberta T4P 7C2 |

description	amt
scaffolding: frames, braces, guardposts, platforms & wheels	600.00

terms: Net 30 days	#: 442197610	gst	42.00
Customer: *Albert Dresden*		total	642.00

Invoice: _____ 99-61247 _____

Date: July 22, 1999

Prairie Roof Equipment

8500 Cannon Heights, Red Deer, Alberta T4R 1P8 Tel:(403) 556-3491 Fax: (403) 556-4980

Customer: Albert Dresden - Reliable Roofing

Address: 456 The Skyway
            Red Deer
            Alberta T4P 7C2

Item Description	Qty	Amount
Mobile Roofing Unit Equipment	1	2100.00

Terms: Net 30 days	Sub	2100.00
Reg#: 410277188 RT	GST	147.00
Customer: *Albert Dresden*	Total	2247.00

Lakeside Co-op
55 Lakeside Drive
Red Deer, Alberta T4N 1T6

No: 308

July 24, 19 99

Pay to the order of ___Reliable Roofing___ $ ___802.50___

___Eight hundred two___ 50 /100 **Dollars**

Royalty Trust
1201 Queen Street
Red Deer, Alberta T4P 3M3

Myrtle Watters

.: 3331 - 3366 ... 97112 - 308 .·

Payment of invoice # RR 99004 **No: 308**

Reliable Roofing –$802.50 July 24, 19 99

ALBERTA HYDRO

No: ___6119961___

444 GENERATOR COURT, RED DEER, ALBERTA

Account: ___2290 000 91000 1___ Statement Date: ___July 25, 1999___

Reliable Roofing
456 The Skyway, Red Deer, Alberta T4P 7C2

Description	Billing Period	Rate/KwH	Energy Consumption	Amount
Minimum Business rate	20/05-20/07			60.00
GST (#220876177)				4.20
			Total due	64.20
Business office: (403) 777-6193			If paid after 01/08/99	70.20

RELIABLE ROOFING

456 The Skyway
Red Deer
Alberta T4P 7C2
Tel.: 403-776-8866 or 403-776-6632
Fax.: 403-776-7521

Invoice: RR-99005

To: Premier Ballet School
106 Classic Blvd.
Red Deer,
Alberta T4P 3L5

Date: July 26, 1999

Description of Work Completed	Amount
Replace school roof - shingle	4000.00
All work guaranteed for 5 years	

Terms: Net 30 days	**Subtotal**	4000.00
GST # 554333789 RT	**GST**	280.00
Customer Signature *Nadia Kaumanski*	**Total**	4280.00

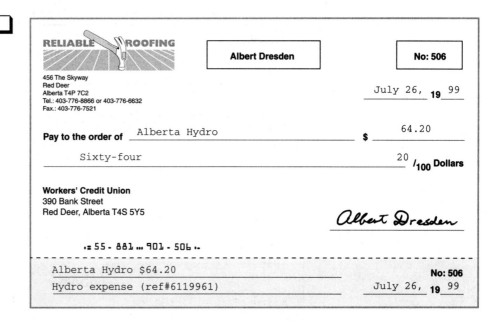

RELIABLE ROOFING

456 The Skyway
Red Deer
Alberta T4P 7C2
Tel.: 403-776-8866 or 403-776-6632
Fax.: 403-776-7521

Albert Dresden

No: 506

July 26, 19 99

Pay to the order of Alberta Hydro $ 64.20

Sixty-four   20 /100 Dollars

Workers' Credit Union
390 Bank Street
Red Deer, Alberta T4S 5Y5

Albert Dresden

.: 55 - 881 ... 901 - 506 .·

Alberta Hydro $64.20   **No: 506**
Hydro expense (ref#6119961)   July 26, 19 99

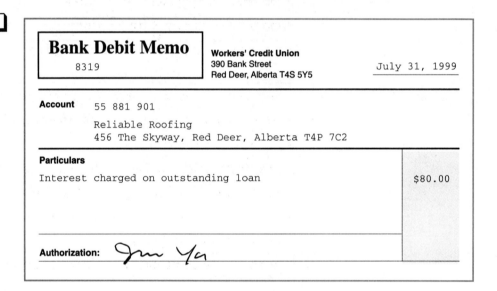

RELIABLE ROOFING

456 The Skyway
Red Deer
Alberta T4P 7C2
Tel.: 403-776-8866 or 403-776-6632
Fax.: 403-776-7521

Albert Dresden

No: 507

July 30, **19** 99

Pay to the order of Sal Skywalker $ 500.00

Five hundred   00 /**100** **Dollars**

Workers' Credit Union
390 Bank Street
Red Deer, Alberta T4S 5Y5

Albert Dresden

⑆55·881⑆901-507⑆

- -

Sal Skywalker re: wages $500   **No: 507**

Assist-Premier Ballet School   July 30, **19** 99

Bank Debit Memo
8319

Workers' Credit Union
390 Bank Street
Red Deer, Alberta T4S 5Y5

July 31, 1999

Account   55 881 901

Reliable Roofing
456 The Skyway, Red Deer, Alberta T4P 7C2

Particulars

Interest charged on outstanding loan $80.00

Authorization:

MEMO

From: A. Dresden

Date: July 31/99

Roofing supplies used for work completed in July were valued at $2 100. This amount should be charged to expense account, 5300 Supplies Used. Asset account 1360 Supplies: Roofing should be reduced (credited) by this amount.

OBJECTIVES

Upon completion of
this chapter, you
will be able to:

- *open* the General and Payables journals
- *enter* vendor-related purchase transactions
- *enter* vendor-related payment transactions
- *enter* partial payments to vendors
- *enter* cash purchase transactions
- *store* recurring purchase transactions
- *add* a new vendor account
- *edit* and *review* transactions in the journals
- *recall, use* and *edit* stored purchase transactions
- *place* and *fill* purchase orders
- *post* transactions in each of the journals
- *understand* Payables Ledger integration accounts
- *display* and *print* payables transactions and reports
- *graph* payables reports
- *advance* the using date and *finish* an accounting session

COMPANY INFORMATION

Company Profile

Java Jean's Coffee Emporium is a small coffee and pastry shop owned and
operated by Jean Yankelovich. Since opening the store two years ago, Jean
expanded her business by buying an adjacent store, using the additional space to
create a seating area for about twenty customers. Situated in the busy downtown
business and entertainment section of Calgary, Alberta, most of the take-out business

comes from clients on their way to work while the in-store customers enjoy the stimulating atmosphere at lunchtime or after-theatre events.

Although she offers a wide selection of teas and hot chocolate, Jean's specialty coffees, roasted directly in the store, and her home-baked pastries are the main source of the Emporium's success. To provide this variety, she has fully equipped the store with coffee makers, espresso machines and cappuccino makers, as well as coffee roasting ovens and regular baking ovens. She also sells some merchandise items, an assortment of specialty coffees in 500-gram packages and a selection of coffee mugs designed by Canadian artists.

Her latest expansion project is the outdoor patio. Sliding patio doors connect the patio to the indoor seating area and a retractable awning ensures that, even on most rainy days, the customers can sit comfortably outdoors. She has obtained the permit and the renovations have begun.

All food and merchandise sales are cash only; weekly summary entries are made from cash register tapes. A small number of vendors make regular deliveries — coffee and chocolate every second week and baking supplies weekly. Jean has set up accounts with these suppliers, as well as other vendors who provide services or products to the Emporium.

Jean employs four university students, including her eldest daughter Judy, on a part-time basis to help run the store. Judy, a business student, plans to open her own coffee emporium, Java Judy's, after she graduates next year. With her business and computer training, her experience in her mother's store and her mother's guidance, she is well-prepared for the entrepreneurial experience. She is currently managing all the accounting records for the Emporium and has just finished converting the manual records to Simply Accounting using the following:

- Chart of Accounts
- Post-Closing Trial Balance
- Vendor Information
- Accounting Procedures

JAVA JEAN'S COFFEE EMPORIUM
CHART OF ACCOUNTS

ASSETS
1080 Bank Account
1220 Packaged Coffee
1240 Coffee Mugs
1260 Coffee & Chocolate
1280 Tea
1300 Baking Goods
1330 Cappuccino Maker
1350 Chairs & Tables
1370 Computerized Cash Register
1390 Coffee Makers
1410 Coffee Roasting Oven
1430 Coffee Mill/Grinder
1450 Cutlery & Dishes
1470 Espresso Machine
1490 Kitchen Equipment
1600 Coffee Emporium

LIABILITIES
2100 Bank Loan
2200 Accounts Payable
2650 GST Charged
2670 GST Paid on Capital Expenditures
2850 Mortgage Payable

EQUITY
3100 J. Yankelovich, Capital
3200 J. Yankelovich, Drawings
3600 Net Income

REVENUE
4100 Revenue from Sales

EXPENSES
5100 Baking Goods
5120 Coffee & Chocolate
5140 Cost of Goods Sold
5160 Tea
5200 Advertising & Promotion
5220 Bank Charges
5240 Hydro Expense
5260 Loan Interest Expense
5280 Maintenance & Repairs
5300 Miscellaneous Expenses
5350 Mortgage Interest
5380 Telephone Expense
5500 Wages Expense
5600 Washroom Supplies Expense

JAVA JEAN'S COFFEE EMPORIUM
POST-CLOSING TRIAL BALANCE

May 31, 1999

1080 Bank Account	$10 250.00	
1220 Packaged Coffee	2 500.00	
1240 Coffee Mugs	1 500.00	
1260 Coffee & Chocolate	600.00	
1280 Tea	200.00	
1300 Baking Goods	400.00	
1330 Cappuccino Maker	800.00	
1350 Chairs & Tables	2 000.00	
1370 Computerized Cash Register	3 000.00	
1390 Coffee Makers	1 200.00	
1410 Coffee Roasting Oven	900.00	
1430 Coffee Mill/Grinder	500.00	
1450 Cutlery & Dishes	2 000.00	
1470 Espresso Machine	800.00	
1490 Kitchen Equipment	15 000.00	
1600 Coffee Emporium	50 000.00	
2100 Bank Loan		$ 5 000.00
2200 Accounts Payable		3 700.00
2650 GST Charged		700.00
2670 GST Paid on Capital Expenditures	210.00	
2850 Mortgage Payable		45 000.00
3100 J. Yankelovich, Capital		37 460.00
	$91 860.00	$91 860.00

JAVA JEAN'S COFFEE EMPORIUM
VENDOR INFORMATION

Vendor Name (Contact)	Address Phone & Fax	Invoice Terms	Invoice Date	Invoice/ Cheque No.	Outstanding Balance
AA Cleaning Services (Katie Klenzer)	10 Bleech Circle Calgary, Alberta T2M 7Y1 Tel: 712-5611 Fax: 712-6481	N/1(Payment on Receipt of Invoice)			
Alberta Telephone (Kiepa Tokkin)	556 Connexion Blvd. Calgary, Alberta T2P 1X2 Tel: 834-7120 Fax: 834-7668	N/1			
Baking Supplies Wholesalers (Alix Fuda)	7 Cherry Lane Calgary, Alberta T2R 6B2 Tel: 611-4423 Fax: 611-6892	N/15	05/26/99	BS-1121	$200.00
Blue Mountain Mugs (Art Isan)	699 Pottery Rd. Beaumont, Alberta T4X 4V3 Tel: 403-779-6188	N/30	05/25/99	BM-411	$800.00
Ceylon Tea Co. (Bev Ridges)	200 Tannin Ave. Vancouver, B.C. V5L 4L8 Tel: 1-800-662-8619	N/15			
Columbia House (Lax Kaffine)	111 Rue Hautbois Montreal, Quebec H6T 9B2 Tel: 1-800-552-9641	N/30	05/06/99 05/20/99	CH-505 CH-512	$450.00 $450.00 $900.00
Equipment Suppliers	28 Coolcrest Rd. Calgary, Alberta T2G 8N8 Tel: 529-7624 Fax: 529-8261	N/30	05/05/99 05/05/99 05/31/99	ES-133 CHQ#623 ES-169	$1 800.00 −$1 000.00 $1 000.00 $1 800.00
International Coffee (I. M. Porter)	688 Colonial Ct. Halifax, N.S. B3R 7Y1 Tel: 1-800-618-6173	N/30			
Maintenance Services Inc. (Ken Fixet)	92 Carpenter St. Calgary, Alberta T2S 2R3 Tel: 881-8811 Fax: 719-7700	N/30			
Western Hydro (Les Power)	45 Uranium Cres. Calgary, Alberta T3P 3X1 Tel: 771-9911 Fax: 778-8800	N/1			
				Grand Total	$3 700.00

Accounting Procedures

The Goods and Services Tax (GST)

Java Jean's uses the **quick method** for calculating and remitting the GST. All items sold in the café are priced to include the GST, and a sign is posted so that customers are aware that they are paying the GST. At the end of each quarter, a flat tax rate of 5 percent on revenue from sales will be calculated and charged to the *GST Charged* account. This flat rate GST liability to the Receiver General is reduced by any GST paid to vendors on capital expenditures, such as equipment, cash registers, capital improvements to the emporium, and furniture and fixtures. These amounts are input tax credits recorded in the *GST Paid on Capital Expenditures* account. GST paid on supplies and services is not included as a decrease in the GST liability to the Receiver General under the quick method. GST is included in the purchase price for these non-capital items. Java Jean's account, *GST Owing (Refund)*, shows the amount of GST that is to be remitted to the Receiver General of Canada on the last day of each quarter. (For details please read Chapter 2 on the Goods and Services Tax.)

Open-Invoice Accounting for Payables

The open-invoice method of accounting for invoices issued to a business allows a business to keep track of each individual invoice and partial payment made against the invoice. This is in contrast to methods that keep track only of the outstanding balance by combining all invoice balances owed to a vendor. Simply Accounting uses the open-invoice method. When an invoice is fully paid, you can either retain the invoice or remove (clear) it.

Purchase of Inventory Items

Inventory items purchased are immediately recorded in the appropriate inventory or supplies asset account. The items in stock are also manually recorded on inventory cards for periodic updating.

Cost of Goods Sold

Periodically, the food inventory on hand is counted. The manager then calculates the cost price of the inventory or food supplies sold and issues a memo to reduce the inventory or supplies asset account and to charge the cost price to the corresponding expense account. For example, at the end of each month, the *Coffee & Chocolate* asset account (*1260*) is reduced (credited) and the *Coffee & Chocolate* expense account (*5120*) is increased (debited) by the cost price of the amount sold.

Notes

- In some source documents that follow, such as purchase invoices for non-capital expenditures and cash receipts from cash register tapes, GST is included in the total amount. Do not record GST separately for these source documents.
- Beverages and food items are zero-rated goods.
- Most bank and other financial institution services are exempted from GST charges. Bank payroll services are subject to GST charges.
- Provincial sales tax is not levied in the province of Alberta. It will be introduced in a later application.

INSTRUCTIONS

1. Using the Chart of Accounts, Trial Balance, Vendor Information and Accounting Procedures for Java Jean's, enter the source documents for the month of June using Simply Accounting. The procedures for entering each new type of transaction for this application are outlined step by step in the keystroke section following the source documents. These transactions have a ✔ in the check box and below the box is the page number where the related keystrokes begin.

2. Print the reports and graphs indicated on the printing form below after you have completed your entries. Printing instructions begin on page 88.

REPORTS

Lists
- ☐ Chart of Accounts
- ☐ Vendor List

Financials
- ☐ Balance Sheet
- ☑ Income Statement
  from June 1 to June 30
- ☑ Trial Balance
  date: June 30
- ☑ General Ledger
  accounts: 1300 4100 5100
  from June 1 to June 30

Mailing Labels
- ☐ Labels

Journals
- ☑ General (by posting date)
  from June 1 to June 30
- ☑ Purchases (by posting date)
  from June 1 to June 30
- ☑ Payments (by posting date)
  from June 1 to June 30

Payables
- ☑ Vendor Aged
  Detail Report
- ☐ Aged Overdue Payables
- ☐ Pending Purchase Orders

GRAPHS

- ☑ Payables by Aging Period
- ☐ Revenues by Account
- ☐ Expenses & Net Profit as % of Revenue
- ☐ Payables by Vendor
- ☐ Expenses by Account
- ☐ Current Revenue vs Last Year

SOURCE DOCUMENTS

USING DATE — June 7

Purchase Invoice #BS-1274
Dated June 1/99
70
From Baking Supplies Wholesalers, regular weekly supplies of baking goods, $200. Terms: n/15. Store this entry because it is a recurring weekly entry.

Cheque Copy #638
Dated June 2/99
75
To Equipment Suppliers, $800 in payment of account. Reference invoice #ES-133.

☑ Outdoor Contractors
78 (Contact Pierre Slate)
is located at
447 Stones Ave.
Calgary, Alberta
T3N 8J5
Tel: 291-8907

☑ Purchase Order #1
81 Dated June 2/99
From Outdoor Contractors (new vendor), $3 000 for granite patio stones for coffee emporium's outdoor patio, plus $210 GST Paid on Capital Expenditures. Patio stones to be shipped and installed on June 9. Purchase invoice total $3 210. Terms: net 30 days.

☐ Purchase Invoice #CH-601
Dated June 3/99
From Columbia House, $450 for bi-weekly purchase of coffee and hot chocolate. (Store as recurring bi-weekly entry.) Terms: net 30 days.

☐ Cheque Copy #639
Dated June 4/99
To Columbia House, $900 in payment of account. Reference invoices #CH-505 and CH-512.

☐ Cheque Copy #640
Dated June 4/99
To Blue Mountain Mugs, $400 in partial payment of account. Reference invoice #BM-411.

☐ Cheque Copy #641
Dated June 7/99
To Baking Supplies Wholesalers, $200 in payment of account. Reference invoice #BS-1121.

☐ Cash Receipt #31
Dated June 7/99
From cash register tapes (no. 3491 to 4193), $3 600 including GST collected for sale of food and merchandise. Amount deposited in bank.

USING DATE — June 14

☑ Purchase Invoice #BS-1396
84 Dated June 8/99
From Baking Supplies Wholesalers, $200 for weekly baking supplies delivery. (Recall stored entry.) Terms n/15.

☑ Cash Purchase: Utility Statement #WH-611
85 Dated June 9/99
From Western Hydro, $149.50 for hydro service including GST. Terms: cash on receipt of invoice.
Issued cheque #642 in full payment.

☑ Purchase Invoice #6127-OC
86 Dated June 9/99
Filled purchase order from Outdoor Contractors, installation of granite patio stones for coffee emporium's outdoor patio completed. Purchase invoice total $3 210. Terms: net 30 days.

☐ Purchase Invoice #IC-642PC
Dated June 10/99
From International Coffee, $400 for pre-packaged flavoured coffees for resale (Packaged Coffee merchandise.) Terms: net 30 days.

☐ Bank Credit Memo #AT-75119
Dated June 11/99
From Alberta Trust, $5 000 loan secured for upcoming purchase of new refrigeration unit.

☐ Purchase Order #2
Dated June 12/99
From Patio Warehouse (new vendor), $400 for 40 new patio chairs and $400 for 10 patio tables (Capital Expenditure: Chairs & Tables account) plus $56 GST paid. Invoice total $856. All items to be shipped on June 16. Terms net/30.

☐ Memo #101
Dated June 13/99
From Store Manager, $55 cash plus coupon book to compensate customer for soiled shirt — employee spilled coffee. Charge to Miscellaneous Expenses.

☐ Cash Purchase Invoice #KR-53196
Dated June 13/99
From Koolhouse Refrigeration (one-time vendor), $4 800 for new outdoor refrigeration unit (Capital Expenditure: Kitchen Equipment) for patio, plus $336 GST paid. Invoice total $5 136. Terms: cash on receipt and installation. Issued cheque #643 in full payment.

☐ Cash Receipt #32
Dated June 14/99
From cash register tapes (no. 4194 to 5124), $3 500 including GST collected for sales of food and merchandise. Amount deposited in bank.

USING DATE — June 21

☑ Purchase Invoice #BS-1739
87 Dated June 15/99
From Baking Supplies Wholesalers, $250 for weekly baking supplies delivery. (Recall the stored entry and edit the amount.) Terms n/15.

☐ Cash Purchase Invoice #PA-472
Dated June 16/99
From Prairie Advertising (new vendor), for advertising flyers for coffee house, $107 including GST. Terms: cash on receipt.
Issued cheque #644 in full payment.

☐ Purchase Invoice # PW-710
Dated June 16/99
Filled purchase order from Patio Warehouse for 40 patio chairs and 10 tables. Invoice total $856. Terms net/30.

☐ Cheque Copy #645
Dated June 17/99
To Baking Supplies Wholesalers, $200 in payment of account. Reference invoice #BS-1274.

☐ Purchase Invoice #CH-825
Dated June 17/99
From Columbia House, for bi-weekly purchase of coffee and hot chocolate supplies, $450. (Recall stored entry.) Terms: n/30.

Notes

☐ Patio Warehouse
(Contact Patti Owens)
is located at
1100 Flagstone Ct.
Calgary, Alberta
T1P 1T2
Tel: 712-8611

Notes

☐ Prairie Advertising
(Contact Lila Adze)
is located at
150 Flatland Blvd.
Calgary, Alberta
T2P 6F4
Tel: 775-6109
Fax: 771-7111

☐ Purchase Invoice #CTC-614
Dated June 19/99
From Ceylon Tea Co., for the purchase of a variety of teas, $100. Terms: n/15.

☐ Cash Receipt #33
Dated June 21/99
From cash register tapes (no. 5125 to 5998), $3 750 including GST collected for sales of food and merchandise. Amount deposited in bank.

USING DATE — June 28

☐ Purchase Invoice #BS-2136
Dated June 22/99
From Baking Supplies Wholesalers, $250 for weekly baking supplies delivery. (Recall stored entry.) Terms n/15.

☐ Cheque Copy #646
Dated June 23/99
To Baking Supplies Wholesalers, $200 in payment of account. Reference invoice #BS-1396.

☐ Purchase Invoice #BM-599
Dated June 24/99
From Blue Mountain Mugs, $500 for 130 designer mugs. Terms: net 30 days.

☐ Cash Purchase - Utility Statement #ATC-311904
Dated June 25/99
From Alberta Telephone, $73 for monthly telephone services, including GST. Terms: cash on receipt.
Issued cheque #647 in full payment.

☐ Cheque Copy #648
Dated June 26/99
To Ceylon Tea Co., $100 in full payment of account. Reference invoice #CTC-614.

☐ Bank Debit Memo #AT-5295
Dated June 28/99
From Alberta Trust, $3 250 for wages to part-time employees, including GST on payroll services.

☐ Cash Receipt #34
Dated June 28/99
From cash register tapes (no. 5999 to 7011), $3 800 including GST collected for sales of food and merchandise. Amount deposited in bank.

USING DATE — June 30

☐ Cash Purchase Invoice #AA-191
Dated June 29/99
From AA Cleaning Services, $428 for cleaning services provided during June, GST included. Terms: cash on receipt. Issued cheque #649 in full payment.

☐ Purchase Invoice #BS-2416
Dated June 29/99
From Baking Supplies Wholesalers, $250 for weekly baking supplies delivery.
(Recall stored entry.) Terms n/15.

☐ Bank Debit Memo #AT-6125
Dated June 30/99
From Alberta Trust, $72 for interest expense on bank loan.

☐ Memo #102
Dated June 30/99
From Store Manager: Based on end-of-the-month inventory count, make
adjusting entries to account for supplies used and inventory sold in June.

From (Inventory)	To (Expense)	Amount Used/Sold
Baking Goods (1300)	Baking Goods (5100)	$1 025
Coffee & Chocolate (1260)	Coffee & Chocolate (5120)	$875
Tea (1280)	Tea (5160)	$150
Packaged Coffee (1220)	Cost of Goods Sold (5140)	$1 100
Coffee Mugs (1240)	Cost of Goods Sold (5140)	$800

KEYSTROKES

Opening Data Files

Using the instructions for accessing data files in Chapter 1, page 12, open the data
files for Java Jean's. You are prompted to enter the first using date, June 7, 1999, for
this application.

Type   06-07-99

Click on OK to enter the first using date for this application. The familiar Home
window appears.

Accounting for Purchases

Purchases from vendors are entered in the Purchases Journal indicated by the arrow
pointer as follows:

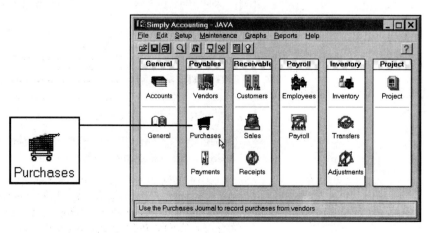

Double click on the **Purchases icon** to open the Purchases Journal. The Purchases Journal input form appears on the screen as follows:

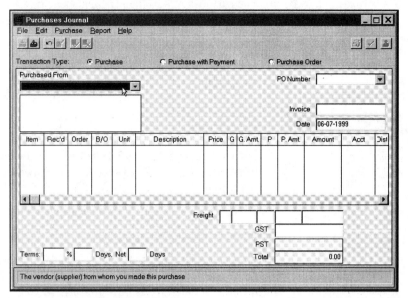

Purchase, selected initially by default, is correct as the Transaction Type because this is a normal credit purchase invoice. The Adjust invoice, Fill Backordered quantities, Cancel backordered quantities and Print tool buttons have been added to the Purchases Journal window. Each tool is discussed when it is used. The Vendor (Purchased From) field is darkened, ready to receive information.

Click on the **Vendor field** or **its drop-down list arrow** to obtain the list of vendors as shown:

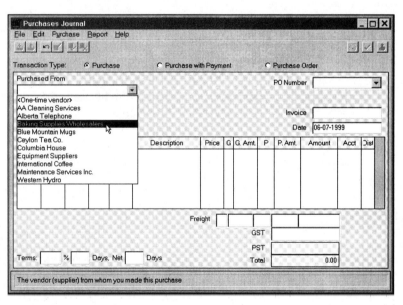

Whenever you see this arrow beside a field, a selection list is available to choose from. You can type the first letter to advance to the names beginning with that letter.

Click on Baking Supplies Wholesalers, the vendor for this purchase, to select and enter it.

Notice that the vendor's name and address have been added to your input form, making it easy to check whether you have selected the correct vendor. The payment terms for the vendor are also included. If you have made an error in your selection, click on the Vendor field and start again. If you have selected correctly,

Notes

Purchase Order Numbers are used when the goods purchased will be received at a later date.

Notes

You can also click on the Invoice field directly to move to this field.

Notes

You will use the tax fields when you enter the next purchase and the inventory-related fields will be explained in a later application.

Notes

Double clicking on the dotted box in the Account field also provides the list of accounts. Notice that you cannot access the Accounts Payable account from this list. Simply Accounting completes this portion of the journal entry automatically.

Press

The cursor moves to the PO Number field, where you would type the Number from Java's purchase order form. This field does not apply so you should skip it.

Press

The cursor moves to the Invoice field, where you should type in the alphanumeric invoice number.

Type BS-1274

Press

The cursor moves to the Date field. Enter the date on which the transaction took place, June 1, 1999. The using date appears automatically by default. It is highlighted, ready to be accepted or changed. You need to change the date.

Type 06-01-99

Press

The cursor advances to the Item field. The next fields pertain to inventory items. Because we are not using the Inventory Ledger for this application, you can ignore the inventory-related fields. Any information you type in these fields does not appear on the journal report or the printed cheque/invoice.

Click on the **first line of the Amount field**, where you will enter the total amount for this purchase. Because the business is using the quick method for administering the GST, purchases of non-capital expenditures, such as supplies and services, will be recorded with the GST included. Since food inventory is zero-rated, it will not include any GST. There is also no PST charged on food purchases. Review the Accounting Procedures section on page 65 for more information if necessary.

Type 200

Press

The cursor moves to the Account field. The Account field for this purchase refers to the debit part of the journal entry, normally the acquisition of an asset or the incurring of an expense. It could also be used to decrease a liability account or to decrease an equity account if the purchase were made for the owner's personal use. When you work in the subsidiary Payables journal, your *Accounts Payable* control account in the General Ledger will automatically be credited for the purchase. In fact, you cannot access the *Accounts Payable* account directly once the Payables Ledger has been set up and integrated.

In this example, the business has acquired an asset, so you need to enter the asset account to which the purchase should be debited.

Type 1

Press enter

The familiar list of accounts appears with the first asset account highlighted.

Click on 1300 Baking Goods to highlight it.

Click on Select to enter the account to your Purchases Journal form. Your screen should now resemble the following:

The account name may not fit in the account column if the column is very narrow. You can change the width of the columns. Make the journal window wider by dragging the side frame. Point to the column dividing line beside the column title. When the pointer changes to a double-sided arrow drag the line to the new location.

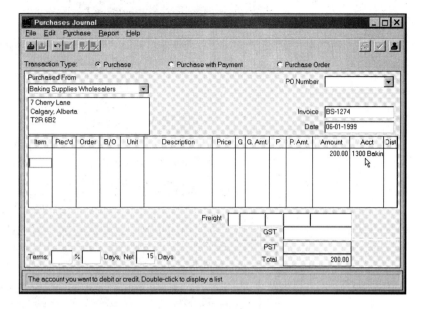

The cursor is flashing in the Item field on the second line so that you can enter additional purchases from this vendor. The payment terms have been set up as defaults for this vendor and are entered automatically. They can be edited if necessary for specific purchases but in this case they are correct. There is no discount and full payment is due in 15 days.

The entries for this transaction are now complete, so you are ready to review your transaction.

Reviewing the Purchases Journal Entry

Choose Display Purchases Journal Entry from the pull-down menu under Report to display the transaction you have entered on the screen:

Purchases Journal Entry			
File Help			
06-01-1999	Debits	Credits	Project
1300 Baking Goods	200.00	-	
2200 Accounts Payable	-	200.00	
	200.00	200.00	

Other integration accounts for the Payables Ledger include a GST Paid account, a bank account, a freight expense account and a purchase discounts account. Each integration account will be explained when it is used in this workbook.

By reviewing the journal entry, you can check for mistakes. Note that the Simply Accounting program automatically updates the *Accounts Payable* control account because the Payables and General Ledgers are linked or fully integrated. Even though you did not enter account 2200, Simply Accounting uses it because it has been defined as the integration account to which all purchases should be credited. Using the Purchases Journal instead of the General Journal to enter purchase transactions is faster because you need to enter only half of the journal entry, the program provides a credit directly to the account of the selected vendor and it prevents you from choosing an incorrect payables account. In the next purchase example, you will see that the GST account is also integrated.

Close the display to return to the Purchases Journal input screen.

Storing the Recurring Journal Entry

Businesses often have transactions that are repeated on a regular basis. For example, loan payments, bank charges and rent payments usually occur on the same day each month; supplies may be ordered more frequently, insurance payments may occur less frequently but nonetheless regularly. Java Jean's has store food supplies delivered on a regular basis. By storing the entry, and indicating the frequency, the entry can be recalled the next time it is needed, without re-entering all the information.

Click on the Store button 🖪 on the tool bar or choose Store from the pull-down menu under Purchase to open the following recurring entry dialogue box:

Simply Accounting has entered the name of the vendor and Monthly as the default name and frequency for the entry. The name is highlighted, so it can be changed if needed. You can type in another descriptive name if you want. Be sure to use one that you will recognize easily as belonging to this entry. The default frequency is incorrect since the food items are purchased weekly.

Click on Monthly to display the list of choices for the recurring frequency:

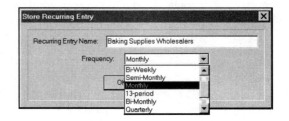

> **Notes** 🖱
>
> The procedure for storing an entry is the same for all journals where the option is available. After choosing Store, you assign a name to the entry, then you choose a frequency.

> **Notes** 🖱
>
> The frequency options are: Random (for irregular purchases) Weekly, Bi-Weekly, Semi-Monthly, Monthly, 13 times per year, Bi-Monthly, Quarterly, Semi-Annually and Annually. Simply Accounting advances the default journal date when you recall the stored entry according to the frequency selected. The using date is entered if the random frequency is chosen.

Scroll (click on the up scroll arrow) if necessary so that the frequency Weekly is included in the viewing area.

Click on Weekly.

Click on OK to return to the Purchases Journal window. Notice that the Recall button is now darkened and can be selected because you have stored a journal entry.

If you notice an error in the stored journal entry before posting, you must first correct the journal entry in the Purchases Journal window, then click on Store. When asked to confirm that you want to overwrite or replace the previous version, click on Yes.

Posting

When you are certain that you have entered all the information correctly, and you have stored the entry if it is a repeating one, you must post the transaction to save it. Notice that the Post button is no longer dimmed.

Click on the Post button 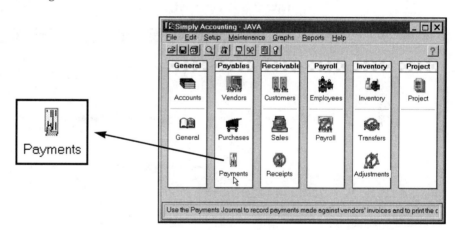 or choose Post from the pull-down menu under Purchase to save your transaction.

A new blank Purchases Journal form appears on the screen. Our next transaction is a payment, however, not a purchase.

Close the Purchases Journal window to return to the Home window.

Accounting for Payments

Payments are made in the Payments Journal indicated by the arrow pointer in the following screen:

If you edit the journal entry after storing it, Simply Accounting will warn you that the entry has changed. Click on Yes to proceed.

Double click on the **Payments Journal icon** to open the journal. The following blank Payments Journal input screen appears:

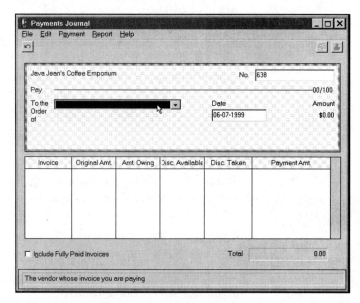

The Vendor (To the Order of) field is darkened, ready to receive information.

Click on the **Vendor field** or **its drop-down list arrow** to see the familiar list of vendors displayed in alphabetical order.

Click on Equipment Suppliers to choose and enter the vendor to whom the payment is made. As shown, the vendor's name, address and outstanding invoice(s) have been added automatically to your input form, making it easy to see whether you have selected correctly:

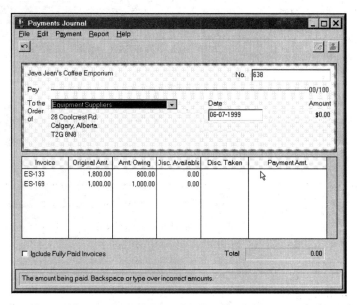

If you need to change the vendor, click on the Vendor field again to select from the vendor list. When you have the correct vendor,

Press `tab`

The cursor advances to the No. field, where the cheque number is entered. By default, the next cheque number according to the defaults set up for the company appears. It is correct, so you can accept it.

Press `tab`

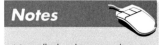

Normally the cheque number should be correct. It can be edited, if necessary, for reversing or correcting entries.

The cursor moves to the Date field, where the using date appears by default. Because it is highlighted, you can change it as required for this transaction.

Type   06-02-99

Press   [tab]

The cursor moves to the Invoice field. All outstanding invoices, including both the amount of the original invoice and the balance owing for the vendor selected are listed on the screen.

Press   [tab]

The cursor advances to the Disc. Taken (Discount Taken) field. Since there is no discount available, skip this field.

Press [tab] . The amount outstanding for the selected invoice is highlighted as the payment amount. You can accept a highlighted amount, or type in an exact amount for a partial payment. To confirm that this invoice is being paid,

Press [tab] to advance the cursor to the Discount Taken field for the next invoice.

The amount for the next invoice should not be highlighted. Since this invoice is not being paid, if its amount is highlighted or entered, you must delete it by **pressing** [del] and then **pressing** [tab] .

Your completed Payments Journal form should now appear as follows:

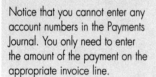

Notes

Check the option to Include Fully Paid Invoices if you need to make a reversing entry for a payment that was posted incorrectly. The Payments Journal will then display all paid and unpaid invoices for the selected vendor.

Notes

Notice that you cannot enter any account numbers in the Payments Journal. You only need to enter the amount of the payment on the appropriate invoice line.

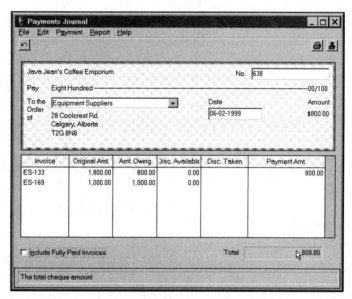

Notice that the upper cheque portion of the form is also complete.

As you work in the subsidiary Payments Journal, you do not enter any accounts. Simply Accounting chooses the default integration accounts defined for the Payables Ledger to create the journal entry. The *Accounts Payable* control account in the General Ledger will automatically be debited for the payment and the *Bank Account* will be credited.

The entries for this transaction are complete, so you are ready to review and post your transaction.

Notes

If you want to print the cheque, you should do this before posting the journal entry. Be sure that the information is correct before you print and that your printer is turned on; then click on the Print button.

Reviewing the Payments Journal Entry

Choose **Display Payments Journal Entry** from the pull-down menu under **Report** to display the transaction you have entered:

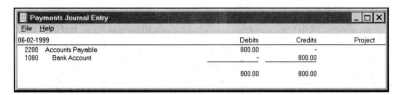

You can see that the Simply Accounting program automatically creates a related journal entry when you complete a Payments Journal entry. The program updates the *Accounts Payable* and *Bank Account* accounts because the Payables and General Ledgers are fully integrated. *Bank Account* has been defined as the Payables integration account to which payments are credited. The payment is also recorded to the vendor's account to reduce the balance owing.

Close the display to return to the Payments Journal input screen.

Notes

To correct errors after posting, refer to Appendix C.

CORRECTING THE PAYMENTS JOURNAL ENTRY BEFORE POSTING

Move to the field that has the error. **Press** `tab` to move forward through the fields or **press** `shift` and `tab` together to move back to a previous field. This will highlight the field information so you can change it. **Type** the correct information and **press** `tab` to enter it.

You can also use the mouse to point to a field and drag through the incorrect information to highlight it. **Type** the correct information and **press** `tab` to enter it.

Click on an incorrect amount to highlight it. **Type** in the correct amount or **press** `del` if this invoice is not being paid.

If the vendor is incorrect, **click on** `↰` or `X` to undo the entry or reselect from the vendor list by **clicking on** the vendor field. **Click on** the name of the correct vendor. You will be asked to confirm that you want to discard the current transaction. **Click on** **Yes** to discard the incorrect vendor entry and display the outstanding invoices for the correct vendor. Re-enter the payment information for this vendor.

Notes

To complete transactions involving the General Journal, you must exit to the Home window and follow the keystroke instructions for the General Journal from the Reliable Roofing application.

Posting

When you are certain that you have entered all the information correctly, you must post the transaction to save it. Notice that the Post button is no longer dimmed.

Click on the **Post button** 🔲 or choose Post from the pull-down menu under Payment to save your transaction.

Adding a New Vendor

The next transaction on June 2 involves a purchase from a company that is not listed as a vendor. You must add *Outdoor Contractors* to the vendor list in order to record the transaction.

Vendors are added through the Payables Ledger, indicated by the Vendors icon as shown below:

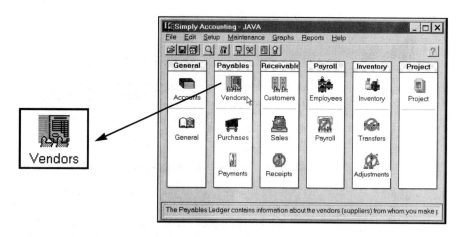

Notes

If the Purchases Journal is already open, you can minimize it to return to the Home window and add the vendor. After creating the new vendor, close the Payables Ledger, then close the Vendors window to return to the Home window. Click on the Purchases Journal icon to restore the journal window, and continue with the journal entry. The new vendor should be included in the vendor list.

Double click on the Vendors icon to open the Vendors window:

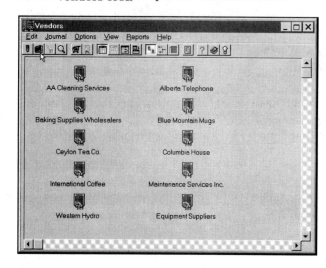

Notes

If you need to edit a vendor record, click on the vendor's icon in the Vendors window to select the vendor. Then click on the Edit tool button (the pencil icon) or choose Edit from the pull-down menu under Edit to open the Payables Ledger record for the selected vendor. (Or, you can double click on the vendor's icon in the Vendors window to open the ledger.) Make the necessary changes and close the Payables Ledger.

The vendor accounts screen appears. Vendors are represented by their icons as shown here or may be listed alphabetically by name. (Choose Name from the pull-down menu under View to change the way the vendors are displayed.)

Click on the Create button on the tool bar of the Vendors window, or **choose** Create from the pull-down menu under Edit to display the Payables Ledger or new vendor input screen:

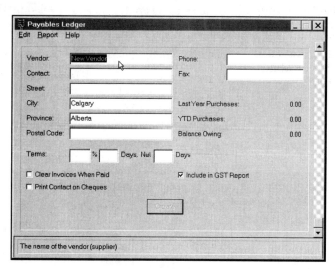

You are ready to enter the new vendor. The Vendor field is highlighted, ready to receive new information.

Type   Outdoor Contractors

Press   [tab]

The cursor advances to the Contact field, where you enter the name of Java Jean's contact person at Outdoor Contractors. This field can also be used to enter additional address information if the single street line is insufficient. It may be left blank by **pressing** [tab] .

Type   Pierre Slate

Press   [tab]

The cursor moves to the Street field.

Type   447 Stones Ave.

Press   [tab]

The cursor moves to the City field. By default, the program has entered the name of the city and province in which Java Jean's is located. You can accept these defaults because they are correct for Outdoor Contractors as well.

Press   [tab]

Press   [tab]

The cursor moves to the Postal Code field. You do not need to use capital letters, and you do not need to leave a space within the postal code. The program will make these adjustments for you.

Type   t3n8j5

Press   [tab]

Notice that the format of the postal code has been corrected automatically. The cursor moves to the Phone field. You do not need to insert a dash when you enter a telephone number.

Type   2918907

Press   [tab]

Notice that the format for the telephone number has been corrected automatically. The cursor advances to the Fax field. Outdoor Contractors does not have a fax number, so ignore this field by **pressing** [tab] .

The cursor now advances to the payment terms section of the ledger, starting in the discount field. The terms stated in the source document are net 30 days. There is no discount offered for early payment, so you should skip to the Net ___ Days field.

Press [tab] twice to advance the cursor.

Type   30

Three other fields appear on this form as check boxes: Clear Invoices When Paid, Print Contact on Cheques and Include in GST Report. The Clear Invoices option is used to remove invoices that are fully paid. Choose not to clear the invoices so that you can keep a record of all purchases and payments. Leave the box unchecked.

Selecting Print Contact on Cheques will add the name of the contact person to the cheque written to the vendor. If the contact field contains address information, check this box, otherwise leave it unchecked.

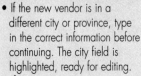

Notes

- If the new vendor is in a different city or province, type in the correct information before continuing. The city field is highlighted, ready for editing.
- If you are missing any information for a vendor, you can leave the field blank.

Notes

Telephone and fax numbers may be entered with or without the area code.

Any vendor supplying goods or services that qualify as input tax credits should be included in GST reports and have this box checked. Since Java Jean's uses the quick method, only vendors supplying capital goods would fall into this category. Outdoor Contractors does supply capital goods, so you should leave the option on.

Your completed new vendor input screen now appears as follows:

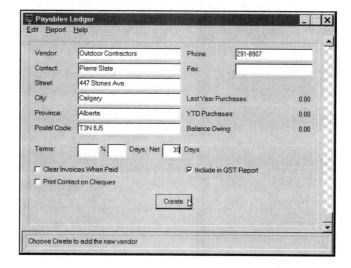

Saving a New Vendor Account

When you are certain that all of the information is correct, you must save the newly created vendor and add it to the current list.

Click on Create to save the new vendor information.

A new Payables Ledger vendor information form appears. Close the Payables Ledger window.

The new vendor has been added to the Vendors accounts screen. Close the Vendors window to return to the Home window and enter the purchase order transaction for the new vendor, using the keystrokes that follow. You will see the new vendor added when you display the vendor list.

Placing a Purchase Order

The purchase from Outdoor Contractors is an order for the patio stones and work to be completed the following week. This is a purchase order rather than a purchase invoice. Purchase orders are entered in the Purchases Journal. When the order is received, or work is completed, the order is filled and the purchase is completed.

Double click on the **Purchases icon** in the Home window to open the Purchases Journal.

Select the new vendor, **Outdoor Contractors**, to add it to your invoice.

Click on Purchase Order as the Transaction Type (just above the main body of the invoice form) to select this option. The Purchases Journal invoice becomes the order form as shown here:

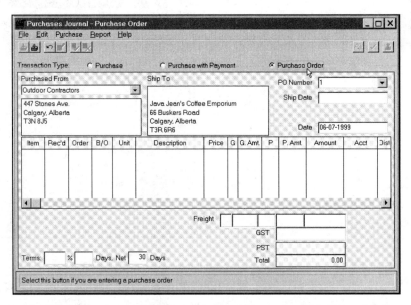

Java Jean's address has been added for shipping information, together with the next available purchase order number (PO Number) and a field for the expected shipping date. The PO number is correct. It can be edited if necessary.

Click on the **Ship Date field** to advance the cursor. This is the date on which the work is to be completed or the order is to be received.

Type   06-09-99

Press (tab) to advance to the Date field where you should enter the date that the order was placed.

Type   06-02-99

Press (tab) twice to move the cursor to the Order field. The Item field refers to the code for inventory items and the Rec'd (quantity received with this purchase) field is skipped because no items are included with the order. However you must enter the number of units that are ordered. You cannot leave the Order field blank. Since this is a contract job order, we will enter one as the quantity.

Type   1

Press (tab) to advance to the B/O (back order) field where you should enter the number of units that are backordered. Usually this number is the same as the quantity ordered. By default, the program enters the order quantity and it is correct. You cannot leave the back order field blank.

Press (tab) twice to advance to the Description field. We can skip the Unit field because it also relates to inventory purchases.

Type   Granite Patio Stones

Press (tab) advance to the Price field. This field refers to the unit price of the items.

Type   3000

Press `tab` to advance to the G (GST code) field. Here you must enter the GST code for the purchase because this is a capital expenditure. Notice that the program has calculated and entered the amount of the purchase as the number of items ordered times the price.

Press `enter` to see the following list of available GST codes provided by the program:

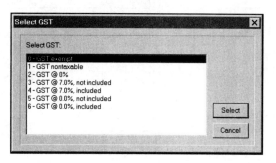

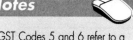

Notes

- GST Codes 5 and 6 refer to a second GST rate, should the government decide to apply a separate rate for different items. The second rate is set to zero and does not apply here.
- If the Include in GST Report option was not selected in the Vendor Ledger, you will see only GST Codes 0 and 1.

Notes

When sales tax is applied, type the tax rate in the P field. For example, if the sales tax rate is 8%, you would type 8 in the P field. The program will calculate the amount of the tax.

Some goods and services are tax-exempt or zero-rated and will not have GST applied. You would select **codes 0** or **2** respectively for these items. **Code 1** applies to non-taxable items. You would use this code for discounts. Some imported goods would also fall into this category. **Code 3** is used if the GST is not already included in the price. This option is used for most applications in this workbook. **Code 4** would be selected if the GST were already included in the price, as it is in the next application, Grandeur Graphics.

Click on **3 - GST @ 7.0%, not included** because GST has not yet been included in the purchase price.

Click on **Select**

The code is added to the purchase order form, and the amount of GST is calculated and added to the G. Amt. (GST Amount) field.

There is no Provincial Sales Tax in Alberta, so the next two fields for the sales tax rate (P) and the amount of sales tax (P. Amt.) do not apply to purchases for Java Jean's.

Click on the **Acct (Account) field** to advance the cursor.

Press `enter` to see the list of accounts.

Click on **1600 Coffee Emporium**

Click on **Select** to add the account number to the order form. The cursor advances to the next invoice line.

Your order form is now complete. Check your work carefully and make any corrections necessary. Refer to page 74 if you need help with correcting the entry. When you display the Purchases Journal entry, you will see that there is no journal entry associated with the order. The related journal entry will be completed when the order is filled.

Your order form should now look like the following:

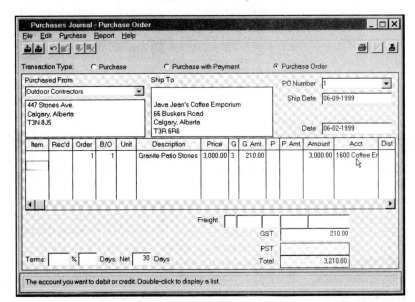

Notes

Again, you may not be able to see the entire contents of a field if the columns are narrow. You can change the width of a column by dragging its border in the title line of the column.

When you are sure that the entry is correct,

Click on the **Post button** or choose Record from the pull-down menu under Purchase to save your transaction.

Recalling a Stored Entry

The first journal entry for the June 14 using date is the recurring purchase from Baking Supplies Wholesalers. Since we have stored this purchase, we do not need to re-enter all the information.

Double click on the **Purchases icon** in the Home window to open the Purchases Journal.

Click on the **Recall button** in the tool bar or choose Recall from the pull-down menu under Purchase to display the Recall Recurring Entry dialogue box as shown here:

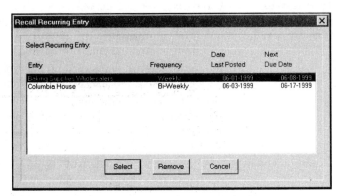

Notes

• From the Recall Stored Entry dialogue box, you can remove an entry that is incorrect or no longer needed. Click on Remove and then click on Yes to confirm that you wish to delete the entry.
• The stored entries are listed in order according to the next date that they will be repeated.

Baking Supplies Wholesalers, the name of the entry we wish to use, should be selected because it is the next recurring entry that is due. (If it is not already selected, click on Baking Supplies Wholesalers.)

Click on **Select** to return to the Purchases Journal.

The entry we stored is displayed just as we entered it the first time, except that the date has been changed to one week past the previous posting date, as needed, and the

Invoice field is blank so we can enter the new invoice number. Remember that Simply Accounting does not accept duplicate invoice numbers.

Click on the Invoice field to move the cursor.

Type   BS-1396

The entry is now complete. You should review it before posting.

Choose Display Purchases Journal Entry from the pull-down menu under Reports.

Close the display when you are finished and make any necessary corrections.

Click on the Post button ![post button icon]. Leave the Purchases Journal open.

Entering Cash Purchases

The Hydro statement on June 9 is to be paid immediately on receipt of the invoice. Instead of recording a separate payment in the Payments Journal, you can record the payment with the purchase in the Purchases Journal. The Purchases Journal should be open.

Choose Western Hydro from the vendor list.

Click on Purchase with Payment to select this Transaction Type. The Cheque field opens with the next available cheque number entered by default as shown:

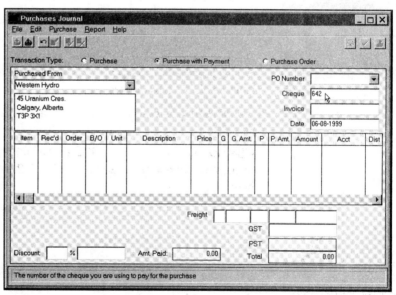

Click on the Invoice field to advance to the Invoice field. Complete the rest of the invoice in the same way you completed the credit purchases earlier. Refer to the keystrokes on page 70 if you need assistance. When you have finished, review the entry.

Choose Display Purchases Journal Entry from the pull-down menu under Report. Your display should look like the following:

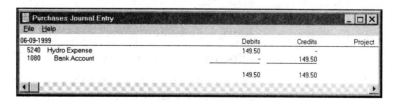

Notice that the program has automatically credited the *Bank Account*, the Payables integration bank account, instead of the *Accounts Payable* account because we indicated that payment was included with the purchase.

Close the display when you are finished and make any corrections necessary. If this is not a cash purchase, that is, the payment is not included with the purchase, click on Purchase to change the transaction type. The Cheque number field will be removed.

Post the entry when you are certain that it is correct. Leave the Purchases Journal open.

Filling a Purchase Order

When an ordered item is received, or work is completed, you must complete a purchase invoice entry to record the receipt. The Purchases Journal should still be open.

Click on **Purchase** as the Transaction Type to indicate that this is neither a cash purchase nor a purchase order.

Click on the **PO Number** drop-down list arrow to display the numbers for all unfilled purchase orders.

Click on **1** (it is the only order number available at this time).

Press ⌷tab⌷. You will see the following purchase order that was completed on June 2:

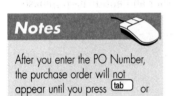

After you enter the PO Number, the purchase order will <u>not</u> appear until you press ⌷tab⌷ or advance to another field.

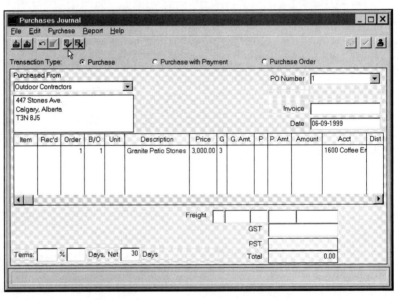

Click on the **Invoice field** to move the cursor to the Invoice field.

Type   6127-OC

Click on the **Fill backordered quantities button** 📥 in the tool bar or choose Fill Purchase Order from the pull-down menu under Purchase. Your invoice now is completed as shown here:

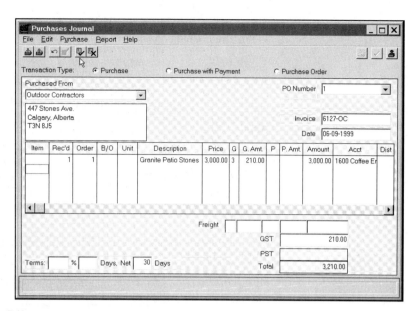

The B/O quantity has been moved to the Rec'd column to reflect the completion of the order. Check the entry carefully to be sure that it is correct.

If it is not correct, undo the journal entry (click on ⤺). Confirm that you want to discard the entry by clicking on Yes. Click on Purchase Order and enter the purchase order number in the PO Number field. Press (tab). Choose Adjust Purchase Order from the pull-down menu under Purchase. You can now edit the purchase order as needed. Post the revised purchase order. Click on Yes when asked to confirm that you want to overwrite the original purchase order. Then complete a purchase entry to fill the purchase order.

Choose Display Purchases Journal Entry from the pull-down menu under **Report**. You can see that this is a normal journal entry.

Close the display. When the information is correct,

Click on the **Post button** ▣ or choose Post from the pull-down menu under Purchase.

You will see the following warning message:

Click on OK to display a new Purchases Journal invoice form.

Changing a Stored Entry

The first entry on the June 21 using date is the weekly purchase from Baking Supplies Wholesalers. However the amount of the purchase has changed and we need to update the stored entry.

Double click on the **Purchases icon** in the Home window to open the Purchases Journal.

Click on the **Recall button** ▣ on the tool bar or choose Recall from the pull-down menu under Purchase to display the Recall Recurring Entry dialogue box.

Notes

If the change is for a single purchase and will not be repeated, edit the entry after recalling it but do not store the entry again.

Click on Baking Supplies Wholesalers, the name of the entry we wish to use (if it is not already highlighted).

Click on Select to display the purchase journal entry with the new date. Add the new invoice number.

Click on the Amount to highlight it so that you can edit it.

Type 250

Press [tab] to enter the change.

Review the journal entry as usual to make sure that it is correct before proceeding.

Click on the Store button ⬛ or choose Store from the pull-down menu under Purchase.

Click on OK to accept the name and frequency without changes. The following warning appears:

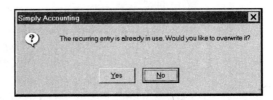

Click on Yes to confirm that you want to replace the previous stored version and return to the Purchases Journal.

Click on the Post button ⬛ to save the journal entry.

Displaying Vendor Reports

All vendor-related reports can be displayed or printed from the Vendors window.

Double click on the Vendors icon in the Home window to open the Vendors window. The Reports menu list now contains only vendor reports. You can select the report you want from this list and follow the instructions below to choose report options.

Displaying Vendor Lists

You should be in the Home window.

Click on the Vendors icon in the Home window to select it.

Click on the Report button ⬛ on the tool bar or choose Display Vendor List from the pull-down menu under Reports. The report will be displayed immediately. Maximize the display and scroll as necessary to see vendors outside the screen viewing area.

Close the display when you have finished viewing the report.

Displaying Vendor Aged Reports

You can display Vendor Aged reports at any time except when you are entering a transaction.

Choose Payables and then Vendor Aged from the menu under Reports in the Home window. The following window appears with several options for your display:

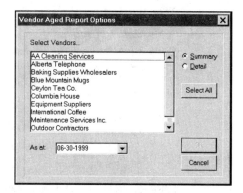

The **Summary** option provides the total balance owing to each vendor. It displays an alphabetic list of vendors with outstanding total balances organized into aged columns. By default, the program selects this option.

Select the **Detail** option if you wish to see individual outstanding invoices and payments made to vendors. This more descriptive report is also aged. Management can use it to make payment decisions. Click on Detail to choose this option. With the Detail option, you can also choose to add vendor payment terms by clicking on Terms.

Click on the **name** or **names in the vendor list** to select the vendors for whom you want to see the report. If you want the report to include all vendors, click on **Select All**.

Type the date you want for the report, choose a date from the drop-down list or accept the using date given by default. After you have indicated all of the options,

Click on **OK** to see the report.

Close the displayed report when you have finished.

Displaying Aged Overdue Payables Reports

You can display Aged Overdue Payables reports at any time except when you are entering a transaction.

Choose **Payables** and then **Aged Overdue Payables** from the menu under **Reports** in the Home window. The following report options window appears:

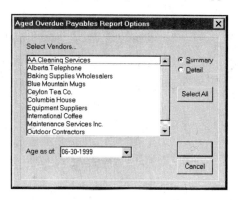

The Aged Overdue Payables report includes the same information as the Vendor Aged reports but it adds a column for the invoice amounts that are overdue.

Choose **Summary** or **Detail**.

Click on the **name** or **names in the vendor list** to select the vendors for whom you want to see the report. If you want to include all vendors, click on **Select All**.

Type the date you want for the report, choose a date from the drop-down list or accept the using date given by default. After you have indicated all of the options,

Click on OK to see the report.

Close the displayed report when you have finished.

Displaying Pending Purchase Orders Reports

You can display Pending Purchase Orders reports at any time except when you are entering a transaction.

Choose Payables and then **Pending Purchase Orders** from the menu under Reports in the Home window. The report options window appears:

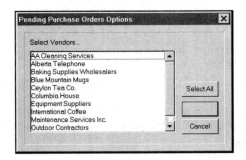

Click on the name or **names in the vendor list** to select the vendors for whom you want to see the report of unfilled purchase orders, organized by the selected vendors. If you want the report to include all vendors, click on **Select All**

Click on OK to see the report.

Close the displayed report when you have finished.

Displaying the Purchases Journal

Click on the Purchases icon in the Home window to select it.

Click on the Report button 🖳 on the tool bar or choose Display Purchases Journal from the pull-down menu under Reports. You will see the report options screen:

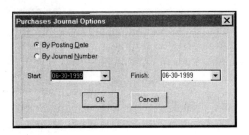

The Purchases Journal can be displayed by posting date or by journal entry number. By default, the By Posting Date option is selected. Since all reports in this workbook use this option, leave the selection unchanged.

Type the beginning date for the journal transactions you want to display.

Press ⟨tab⟩

Type the ending date for the transaction period you want to see.

Click on OK to see the report.

Notes

If no icons are selected in the Home window, Purchases and Payments Journal reports are available from the list when you click on the Report tool button.

Notes

You can display Vendor Aged Reports and General Ledger Reports from the Purchases Journal or the Payments Journal Report.

Close the display when you have finished.

Displaying the Payments Journal

Click on the **Payments icon** in the Home window to select it.

Click on the **Report button** 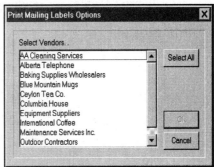 on the tool bar or choose Display Vendor List from the pull-down menu under Reports to see the report options screen.

The Payments Journal has the same choices as the Purchase Journal report. You can display the report by posting date, the default setting, or by journal entry number.

Type the beginning date for the journal transactions you want to display.

Press tab

Type the ending date for the transaction period you want to display.

Click on OK to see the report.

Close the display when you are finished.

Printing Vendor Reports

To print vendor reports, display the report you want to print.

Choose Print from the pull-down menu under **File**. Make sure that the print options have been set correctly before you print.

Printing Mailing Labels

Click on the **Vendors icon** to select or highlight it in the Home window, or with the Vendors window open,

Choose Print Mailing Labels from the pull-down menu under **Reports**:

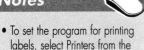
Print Mailing Labels Options

Select Vendors. .

AA Cleaning Services
Alberta Telephone
Baking Supplies Wholesalers
Blue Mountain Mugs
Ceylon Tea Co.
Columbia House
Equipment Suppliers
International Coffee
Maintenance Services Inc.
Outdoor Contractors

Select All

OK

Cancel

The menu option refers to the selected ledger. If the Customers or Employees icon is selected, their mailing labels will be printed. Click on the names of the vendors to include in your list, or click on Select All to include all the vendors.

Make sure that the print options have been set correctly before you print and that your printer is turned on and has the correct labels paper.

Click on OK

Graphing Vendor Reports

You must be in the Home window to display graphs.

Payables by Aging Period Charts

Choose Payables by Aging Period from the pull-down menu under Graphs to display the pie chart graph immediately:

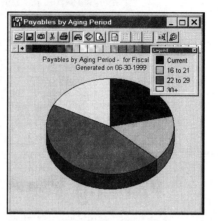

Your graph will show all vendors combined with the aging periods selected in the company setup options providing a quick visual reference for payment obligations. (The aging periods were changed for this graph.) The Tool bar options, and the control of the colour and the legend is the same as for other graphs. Refer to page 50 for a review of these features.

Close the graph when you are finished.

Payables by Vendors Charts

Choose Payables by Vendors from the pull-down menu under Graphs to display the pie chart options:

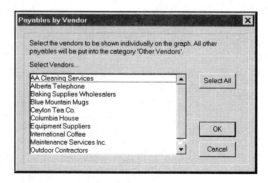

Click on the names of the vendors to include in your pie chart, or click on Select All to include all the vendors.

Click on OK to display the graph:

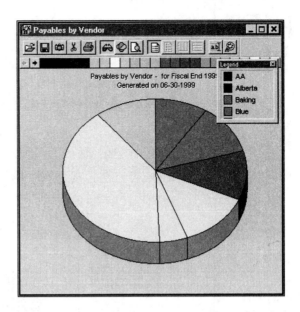

The graph shows the proportion of the total payables that is owed to each selected vendor. The Tool bar options, and the control of the colour and the legend is the same as for the other graphs.

Close the graph when you are finished.

CASE PROBLEMS

Case One

On July 14, Java Jean's purchased additional dishes for the new patio from a new vendor, Eternity Porcelains. Judy entered the purchase incorrectly as a purchase from Equipment Suppliers. She did not discover the error until two weeks later when the invoice was due. When she tried to make the payment in the Payments journal, Eternal Porcelains did not appear in the vendor list, so she could not make the payment. At that time, Judy was certain that she had entered the purchase, but did not remember exactly how she had entered it.

How could she find the original entry? In detail, describe how she would make the necessary corrections in order to complete the payment.

Case Two

At the end of September 1999, Java Jean's has the following balances for the quarter:

Revenue from Sales	CR	$58 600
GST Paid on Capital Goods	DR	$670

Manually show the journal entries to reflect the GST liability incurred from Emporium sales for the quarterly period and the remittance of the balance owing to the Receiver General. Assume that the flat tax rate is 5 percent.

CHAPTER FIVE

OBJECTIVES

Upon completion of this chapter, you will be able to:

- *open* the Sales and Receipts journals
- *enter* customer-related sale transactions
- *enter* customer-related receipt transactions
- *enter* transactions including harmonized sales tax (HST)
- *store* and *recall* recurring entries
- *enter* partial payments made by customers
- *add* a new customer account
- *handle* an NSF cheque from a customer
- *edit* and *review* journal transactions
- *post* transactions in the Sales and Receipts journals
- *display, print* and *graph* customer reports
- *understand* Receivables Ledger integration accounts

COMPANY INFORMATION

Company Profile

Grandeur Graphics, owned and operated by Kathy Grandeur provides a wide range of graphics, designing and desktopping services to the business community in Halifax, Nova Scotia. After completing a graphics design program at a community college in Montreal, and working for a large publishing company in Toronto, Grandeur decided to return to Halifax, her home town, to start her own business. Building on her old connections and her reputation for creativity and reliability, she steadily acquired more work and made her business successful.

Grandeur now employs two full-time assistants. The senior designer assists with magazine layouts and with designing advertising and promotional material. The recently hired junior designer inputs material for text intensive projects such as newspapers or company training manuals, and assists with layout on some other projects. Grandeur herself prepares initial design sketches and business proposals and oversees all the work. Since she particularly enjoys creative design, she sometimes completes projects by herself, being careful to delegate not only the more routine assignments, but also the interesting and challenging work. Over time she wants to increase the number of repeat customers or regular contracts and hire additional assistants.

In the past few months, Grandeur has completed accounting for small business courses including an introduction to Simply Accounting. She is now ready to use the software for her business needs. She will continue to use the bank's payroll services for the time being, knowing that she can easily add her employees to the accounting files when she is more familiar with the program. She has gathered the following records to convert her manual accounting system:

- Chart of Accounts
- Post-Closing Trial Balance
- Vendor Information
- Customer Information
- Accounting Procedures

GRANDEUR GRAPHICS
CHART OF ACCOUNTS

ASSETS
1080 Cash in Bank
1200 Accounts Receivable
1240 Software Library
1280 Office Supplies
1300 Desktop Supplies
1340 Prepaid Insurance
1380 Computers
1400 Monitors
1420 Fax
1440 Scanner
1480 Laser Colour Printers
1500 LCD Projector
1610 Furniture & Equipment
1650 Automobile
1690 Office Condominium

LIABILITIES
2100 Bank Loan
2200 Accounts Payable
2650 HST Charged on Services
2670 HST Paid on Purchases
2850 Mortgage Payable

EQUITY
3560 K. Grandeur, Capital
3600 Net Income

REVENUE
4100 Revenue from Design
4140 Revenue from Desktop Services
4180 Revenue from Consulting
4200 Sales Allowances

EXPENSES
5200 Advertising
5250 Bank Charges
5300 General Expense
5360 Interest Expense
5400 Hydro Expense
5425 Payroll Service Charges
5450 Salaries
5610 Telephone Expense
5650 Wages

GRANDEUR GRAPHICS
POST-CLOSING TRIAL BALANCE

March 31, 1999

1080 Cash in Bank	$ 22 310.00	
1200 Accounts Receivable	2 000.00	
1240 Software Library	3 600.00	
1280 Office Supplies	600.00	
1300 Desktop Supplies	450.00	
1340 Prepaid Insurance	840.00	
1380 Computers	6 400.00	
1400 Monitors	3 200.00	
1420 Fax	500.00	
1440 Scanner	1 600.00	
1480 Laser Colour Printers	4 200.00	
1500 LCD Projector	2 100.00	
1610 Furniture & Equipment	4 200.00	
1650 Automobile	25 000.00	
1690 Office Condominium	175 000.00	
2100 Bank Loan		$ 8 000.00
2200 Accounts Payable		4 000.00
2850 Mortgage Payable		150 000.00
3560 K. Grandeur, Capital		90 000.00
	$252 000.00	$252 000.00

Vendor Name (Contact)	Address Phone & Fax	Invoice Terms	Invoice Date	Invoice/ Cheque No.	Outstanding Balance
Custom Office Furniture (Tori Carpenter)	22 Sawdust Rd. Halifax, NS B3R 7T1 Tel: (902) 661-3412 Fax: (902) 661-5910	N/30	3/10/99 3/10/99	CF-15981 Chq 588 Balance	$2 500.00 −1 000.00 $1 500.00
Eastern Bell (Ella Tokmore)	600 Seaforth St. Halifax, NS B3L 1E3 Tel: (902) 662-3998 Fax: (902) 662-4120	N/1 (Payment on Receipt of Invoice)			
Expressions Inc. (Yvan Temper)	75 Agricola Lane Halifax, NS B3J 9P1 Tel: (902) 486-5127 Fax: (902) 486-9125	N/15			
Language Resources Inc. (Foorin Tung)	510 White Dove Crt. Halifax, NS B3N 8N2 Tel: (902) 598-8227 Fax: (902) 598-5101	N/15			
Nova Scotia Hydro (Thor Lektrik)	59 Wildwood Ave. Halifax, NS B3N 6W9 Tel: (902) 596-5197 Fax: (902) 596-5100	N/1			
Sentinel Software Insurance (Chip Garde)	1 Sentinel Sq. Halifax, NS B3K 2F5 Tel: (902) 662-6197 Fax: (902) 662-7100	N/15			
Telecompute Inc. (Ram Gazer)	45 Terminal Rd. Halifax, NS B3J 4D3 Tel: (902) 664-6619 Fax: (902) 664-6699	N/30	3/16/99 3/16/99	TI-673 Chq 592 Balance	$3 000.00 −500.00 $2 500.00
				Grand Total	$4 000.00

GRANDEUR GRAPHICS
CUSTOMER INFORMATION

Customer Name (Contact)	Address Phone & Fax	Invoice Terms	Invoice Date	Invoice/ Cheque No.	Outstanding Balance
Atlantic Business Cards, Inc. (Sandi Beech)	33 Pacific St. Halifax, NS B3K 7Y4 Tel: (902) 488-9137 Fax: (902) 488-8120	N/15	3/15/99	GG-1201	$450.00
Cabot Trail Guides (Amy Walker)	1200 Clearview St. Halifax, NS B3R 3F3 Tel: (902) 662-9484 Fax: (902) 662-9400	N/15			
Coastal Corporation (Crystal Waters)	48 Heron Walk Halifax, NS B3K 5R2 Tel: (902) 598-1123 Fax: (902) 598-1000	N/15			
Fundy Corporation (Rocky Shore)	29 Herring Cove Rd. Halifax, NS B3R 6T9 Tel: (902) 662-7291 Fax: (902) 662-7900	N/15			
Halifax Gazette (Lois Lane)	6 Jubilee Rd. Halifax, NS B3H 8U5 Tel: (902) 594-6199 Fax: (902) 594-5200	N/15	3/5/99 3/15/99	GG-1179 Chq 87 Balance	$1 500.00 −1 000.00 $ 500.00
Nova Publishing House (Jill Harlequin)	70 Drumdonald Rd. Halifax, NS B3P 1M2 Tel: (902) 666-1299 Fax: (902) 666-1111	N/15	3/21/99 3/24/99	GG-1269 GG-1275 Total	$ 800.00 $ 250.00 $1 050.00
				Grand Total	$2 000.00

Accounting Procedures

Open-Invoice Accounting for Receivables

The open-invoice method of accounting for invoices issued by a business allows the business to keep track of each individual invoice and of any partial payments made against it. In contrast, other methods only keep track of the outstanding balance by combining all invoice balances owed by a customer. Simply Accounting uses the open-invoice method. When an invoice is fully paid, you can either retain the invoice or remove (clear) it.

NSF Cheques

If a cheque is deposited from an account that does not have enough money to cover it, the bank may return it to the depositor as NSF (Non-Sufficient Funds). The treatment of an NSF cheque from a customer requires a reversing entry in the Receipts Journal. (See Keystrokes, page 119.) In most companies, the accounting department notifies the customer who wrote the NSF cheque to explain that the debt remains unpaid. Many companies charge an additional fee to the customer to recover their bank charges for the NSF cheque. A separate sales invoice should be prepared for the additional charge.

The Harmonized Sales Tax (HST)

Grandeur Graphics is a service business using the regular method of calculating HST, the Harmonized Sales Tax. The HST combines and replaces the separate GST and PST at a single rate of 15%. The HST is included in all prices quoted to customers. The harmonized HST charged and collected from customers will be recorded as a liability in the *HST Charged on Services* account. HST paid to vendors will be recorded in the *HST Paid on Purchases* account as a decrease in tax liability. Like the GST, the balance owing is the difference between the HST charged and HST paid.

The harmonized tax is administered by the Federal Government and the balance to be remitted or the request for a refund will be sent to the Receiver General of Canada by the last day of the month for the previous quarterly period. The Federal Government forwards to the province the provincial sales tax portion of the amount remitted by the business. Refer to Chapter 2 for further details.

Cash Sales of Services

Cash transactions for services rendered are a normal occurrence in most service businesses. The Simply Accounting program's Sales Journal has a cash sale option to handle cash transactions. (See Keystrokes, page 118.) When you choose this option, the program will debit the *Cash in Bank* account instead of the *Accounts Receivable* control account. All other accounts for this transaction will be debited or credited in the same way as they would be for credit sale transactions.

Sales Allowances and Credits

When a customer is dissatisfied with the service provided, Grandeur Graphics may offer a reduction in the price paid for the work. If the customer has not yet paid for the work, you can issue a negative sales invoice. Enter the allowance as a *negative* amount in the amount field and use the *Sales Allowances* account. Treat the allowance as non-taxable by entering the HST non-taxable code (Code 1) in the HST field. When payment is received, remember to "pay" the allowance invoice. If the customer has paid for the work, make a cash purchase journal entry to provide the refund. Again, the allowance should be non-taxable.

Purchases with Down Payments

When a purchase is accompanied by a partial payment, or a down payment, you should post a Purchases Journal entry for the full amount of the invoice followed by a Payments Journal entry for the amount of the down payment. Thus, two separate entries are required.

Notes

- Bank and other financial institution services are exempted from HST collection.
- The name of the tax has been changed from GST to HST in the default settings for this application.
- HST is also sometimes called Blended Sales Tax or BST.
- The Harmonized Sales Tax as used in the Atlantic provinces is the tax model the Federal Government would like to see adopted by all provinces.

Notes

The sales tax rules for credits, allowances and discounts are complex, and may vary from province to province and for federal taxes. Simply Accounting does not include the sales tax components when it calculates sales discounts, so adjusting General Journal entries would be required to adjust the amount of tax owing and calculate the tax remittance. Therefore we have chosen to leave out the tax component for transactions of this type.

INSTRUCTIONS

1. Using the Chart of Accounts, Vendor Information, Customer Information and Accounting Procedures for Grandeur Graphics, record entries for the source documents in Simply Accounting. The procedures for entering each new type of transaction in this application are outlined step by step in the keystroke section following the source documents. These transactions are indicated with a ✔ in the completion box beside the source document. The page on which the relevant keystrokes begin is printed immediately below the check box.

2. After you have finished making your entries, print the reports and graphs indicated on the following printing form. Printing instructions begin on page 122.

REPORTS

Lists
- ☐ Chart of Accounts
- ☐ Vendor List
- ☐ Customer List

Financials
- ☑ Balance Sheet
  date: April 30
- ☑ Income Statement
  from April 1 to April 30
- ☐ Trial Balance
- ☑ General Ledger
  accounts: 1200 2650 4100 4140
  from April 1 to April 30

HST
- ☑ HST Summary Report

Mailing Labels
- ☐ Labels

Journals
- ☑ General (by posting date)
  from April 1 to April 30
- ☐ Purchases
- ☐ Payments
- ☑ Sales (by posting date)
  from April 1 to April 30
- ☑ Receipts (by posting date)
  from April 1 to April 30

Payables
- ☐ Vendor Aged
- ☐ Aged Overdue Payables
- ☐ Pending Purchase Orders

Receivables
- ☑ Customer Aged
  Detail Report
- ☐ Aged Overdue Receivables
- ☑ Customer Statement
  for Halifax Gazette

GRAPHS

- ☐ Payables by Aging Period
- ☑ Receivables by Aging Period
- ☑ Sales vs Receivables (all revenue accts)
- ☐ Revenues by Account
- ☐ Expenses & Net Profit as % of Revenue

- ☐ Payables by Vendor
- ☐ Receivables by Customer
- ☐ Receivables Due vs Payables Due
- ☐ Expenses by Account
- ☐ Current Revenue vs Last Year

SOURCE DOCUMENTS

USING DATE — April 8

Notes

Refer to Keystrokes, page 105.

☑ **105** Sales Invoice #GG-1300
Dated April 2/99
To Coastal Corporation, $1 380 for completion of desktopping services contract.
15% HST included. Terms: net 15 days.

☑ **110** Cash Receipt #101
Dated April 3/99
From Halifax Gazette, cheque #121, $500 in full payment of account. Reference
invoice #GG-1179.

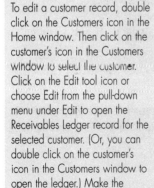

Notes

☑ **114** Artworks Inc.
(Contact Joan Miro)
is located at
33 Abinaki Rd.
Truro, NS B2N 8T1
Tel: 902-771-9831
Fax: 902-771-8136
Credit Limit: $2 000

☐ Sales Invoice #GG-1301
Dated April 3/99
To Artworks Inc. (new customer), $1 725 for designing toy box lid. 15% HST
included. Terms: net 15 days.

☑ **118** Cash Sales Invoice #GG-1302
Dated April 4/99
To David Manga, $460 for design work for Canadian Trivia game. 15% HST
included. Full payment received in cash.

☑ **119** Sales Invoice #GG-1303
Dated April 4/99
To Halifax Gazette, $460 for desktopping services for weekly paper. 15% HST
included. Store as recurring weekly entry. Terms: net 15 days.

☑ **119** Bank Debit Memo #SB-7911
Dated April 4/99
From Scotia Bank, $500 for NSF cheque from Halifax Gazette. Reference invoice
#GG-1179 and cheque #121. The Gazette has been notified of the unpaid
account.

☐ Cash Receipt #102
Dated April 5/99
From Halifax Gazette, certified cheque #255 for $500 with letter of apology, in
full payment of account. Reference Bank Debit Memo #SB-7911 and invoice
#GG-1179.

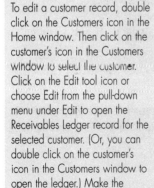

Notes

To edit a customer record, double
click on the Customers icon in the
Home window. Then click on the
customer's icon in the Customers
window to select the customer.
Click on the Edit tool icon or
choose Edit from the pull-down
menu under Edit to open the
Receivables Ledger record for the
selected customer. (Or, you can
double click on the customer's
icon in the Customers window to
open the ledger.) Make the
necessary changes and close the
Receivables Ledger.

☐ Memo # 1
Dated April 5/99
From Owner: Edit all existing customer records to include a credit limit of
$5 000. The credit limit for new customers will be $2 000.

☐ Cheque Copy #601
Dated April 5/99
To Custom Office Furniture, $1 500 in full payment of account. Reference
invoice #CF-15981.

☐ Purchase Invoice #EI-4172
Dated April 5/99
From Expressions Inc., $690 for advertising in graphics magazine including $90
HST. Charge to advertising expense. Terms: N/15 days.

Cash Sales customers are One-time customers unless identified as new customers.

☐ Vision Camera
  (Contact Polly Lenz)
  is located at
  390 Kodak Cres.
  Halifax, NS B3P 5T4
  Tel: (902) 668-7191
  Fax: (902) 668-7109
☐ Create new account::
  1390 Digital Cameras

☐ Cash Sales Invoice #GG-1304
Dated April 6/99
To Malin Andersson, $287.50 for consulting services. 15% HST included.
Received money order #3121.

☐ Purchase Invoice #VC-414
Dated April 6/99
From Vision Camera (new vendor), $2 760 for a new digital camera (new account) including $360 HST. Terms: N/30 days.

☐ Sales Invoice #GG-1305
Dated April 8/99
To Nova Publishing House, $3 450 for design on three book covers. 15% HST included. Terms: net 30 days.

☐ Cash Receipt #103
Dated April 8/99
From Nova Publishing House, cheque #884 for $800 in payment of account.
Reference invoice #GG-1269.

USING DATE — April 14

☐ Cheque Copy #602
Dated April 9/99
To Telecompute Inc., $2 500 in full payment of account. Reference invoice #TI-673.

☐ Purchase Invoice #SS-14219
Dated April 10/99
From Sentinel Software Insurance, $1 104 for insurance on software for one year including $144 HST. Terms: net 15 days.

☐ Sales Invoice #GG-1306
Dated April 10/99
To Cabot Trail Guides, $1 265 for desktopping work. 15% HST included. Terms: net 30 days.

☐ Bank Credit Memo #SB-62514
Dated April 10/99
From Scotia Bank, $3 000 six month loan granted to purchase LCD projector.

☑ Sales Invoice #GG-1307
121 Dated April 11/99
To Halifax Gazette, $460 for weekly desktopping assignment. 15% HST included. Recall recurring weekly entry. Terms: net 15 days.

☐☐ Purchase Invoice #TI-818
Dated April 11/99
From Telecompute Inc., $5 750 for a new LCD projector for workshops and demonstrations including $750 HST. Paid $3 000 with cheque #603, and balance on terms. Terms: net 30 days.

The computer purchase with partial payment requires two journal entries — first a purchase and then a payment. Refer to Accounting Procedures.

☐ Cash Receipt #104
Dated April 12/99
From Nova Publishing House, cheque #1007 for $250 in payment of account.
Reference invoice #GG-1275.

Cash Receipt #105
Dated April 13/99
From Coastal Corporation, cheque #73 for $1 380 in full payment of account.
Reference invoice #GG-1300.

Cash Sales Invoice #GG-1308
Dated April 14/99
To Swedish Design Inc., $575 for consulting services. 15% HST included.
Received cheque #4321.

USING DATE — April 21

Sales Invoice #GG-1309
Dated April 15/99
To Atlantic Business Cards, Inc., $575 for design work. 15% HST included.
Terms: net 30 days.

Sales Invoice #GG-1310
Dated April 15/99
To Lobster Hut (new customer), $690 for design of menu for restaurant. 15%
HST included. Terms: net 15 days.

Cash Sales Invoice #GG-1311
Dated April 16/99
To Goodbar Law Firm, $460 for desktopping task. 15% HST included. Payment
by Visa #4444 340 512 569.

Cash Utility Purchase Invoice #NSH-33437
Dated April 16/99
From Nova Scotia Hydro, $230 for hydro services including $30 HST. Terms:
cash on receipt. Issued cheque #604 in full payment.

Memo #2
Dated April 17/99
From Owner: Give Coastal Corporation an allowance of $100 for errors that
required corrections by Coastal Corporation staff. Issued cheque #605 together
with a letter of apology.

Cheque Copy #606
Dated April 17/99
To Expressions Inc., $690 in full payment of account. Reference invoice
#EI-4172.

Sales Invoice #GG-1312
Dated April 18/99
To Halifax Gazette, $920 for weekly desktopping assignment plus work on
annual supplement. 15% HST included. Edit the recurring weekly entry but do
not store the changes. Terms: net 15 days.

Cash Utility Purchase Invoice #EB-67212
Dated April 18/99
From Eastern Bell, $172.50 for telephone services including $22.50 HST. Terms:
cash on receipt. Issued cheque #607 in full payment.

☐ Cash Receipt #106
Dated April 18/99
From Artworks Inc., cheque #312 for $1 725 in full payment of account.
Reference invoice #GG-1301.

☐ Purchase Invoice #TI-982
Dated April 19/99
From Telecompute Inc., $345 for two rechargeable ni-cad batteries for portable computer including $45 HST. Terms: net 30 days. (Use Computers asset account.)

☐ Cash Sales Invoice #GG-1313
Dated April 20/99
To Carol Andonova, design artist, $287.50 for consultation services. 15% HST included. Payment by Visa # 4919 559 971 346.

☐ Cash Receipt #107
Dated April 20/99
From Atlantic Business Cards, Inc., cheque #387 for $450 in payment of account. Reference Invoice #GG-1201.

USING DATE — April 28

☐ Sales Invoice #GG-1314
Dated April 22/99
To Fundy Corporation, $4 830 for desktop work on Training Manual for corporation employees. 15% HST included. Terms: net 30 days.

☐ Bank Debit Memo #SB-10901
Dated April 23/99
From Scotia Bank, $46 for bank services charges, including charge for NSF cheque.

☐ Purchase Invoice #LR-679
Dated April 23/99
From Language Resources Inc., $345 for language fonts (Software Library account) required for special publishing project including $45 HST. Terms: N/15.

☐ Bank Debit Memo #SB-11004
Dated April 24/99
From Scotia Bank, $80 interest charges on outstanding loan.

☐ Cheque Copy #608
Dated April 24/99
To Sentinel Software Insurance, $1 104 in full payment of account. Reference invoice #SS-14219.

Notes

☐ Maritime Biscuit Co.
(Contact Ivan McCain)
is located at
80 Strawberry Hill
Halifax NS B3K 6G6
Tel: (902) 488-7199
Fax: (902) 488-7001

☐ Sales Invoice #GG-1315
Dated April 24/99
To Maritime Biscuit Co. (new customer), $1 725 for cookie box design. 15% HST included. Terms: net 15 days.

☐ Sales Invoice #GG-1316
Dated April 25/99
To Halifax Gazette, $460 for weekly desktopping assignment. 15% HST included. Use recurring weekly entry. Terms: net 15 days.

☐ Purchase Invoice #CF-16213
Dated April 26/99
From Custom Office Furniture, $920 for new design table required for extra
workload including $120 HST. Terms: net 30 days.

☐ Cash Sales Invoice #GG-1317
Dated April 27/99
To Terry Geroche, $460 for design work. 15% HST included. Paid in cash.

☐ Cash Sales Invoice #GG-1318
Dated April 28/99
To Lila Read, $287.50 for consulting services. 15% HST included. Cheque #332
received in payment.

USING DATE — April 30

☐ Bank Debit Memo #SB-13129
Dated April 29/99
From Scotia Bank, monthly payroll and payroll services

Wages	$2 100.00
Salaries	3 200.00
Payroll Services	650.00
HST @ 15%	97.50
Total	$6 047.50

☐☐ Sales Invoice #GG-1319
Dated April 30/99
To Halifax Art School (new customer), $1 380 with taxes included for sale of old
LCD projector valued at $2 100. Sale price of projector is $1 200. Charge loss to
new account, 5390 Loss on Sale of Peripherals. (Complete a Sales Journal entry
for the sale and a General Journal entry for the loss.)

Notes

☐ Halifax Art School
(Contact Joyce Kane)
is located at
5000 Gainsborough Pl.
Halifax NS B3K 2K8
Tel: (902) 596-6129
Fax: (902) 596-6200

KEYSTROKES

Opening Data Files

Using the instructions for accessing data files in Chapter 1, page 12, open the data
files for Grandeur Graphics. Enter the first using date, April 8, 1999, for this
application.

Type   04-08-99

Click on OK

You are shown the following warning statement:

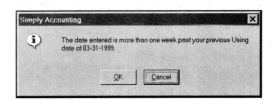

Normally a business would update its accounting records more frequently. If you have
entered the correct date,

Click on OK to accept the date entered and display the familiar Home window.

Accounting for Sales

Sales are entered in the Sales Journal indicated in the following screen:

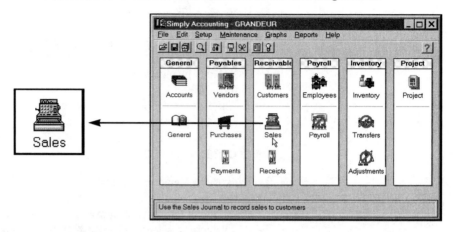

Double click on the Sales icon to open the Sales Journal. The Sales Journal input form appears on the screen as follows:

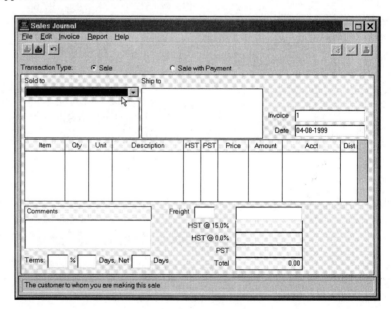

Notes

Most of the tool bar buttons in the Sales Journal are the same as those in the General Journal — Store, Recall, Undo, Distribute and Post. A Print button is added because you can print an invoice directly from the journal before you post an entry in order to provide a customer or store copy of the sales invoice.

The Sale option is selected initially by default as the Transaction Type. Since this is a regular sale, leave this selection unchanged.

The Customer (Sold to) field is darkened, ready to receive information.

Click on the **Customer field** or its **drop-down list arrow** to obtain the list of customers as shown on the following screen:

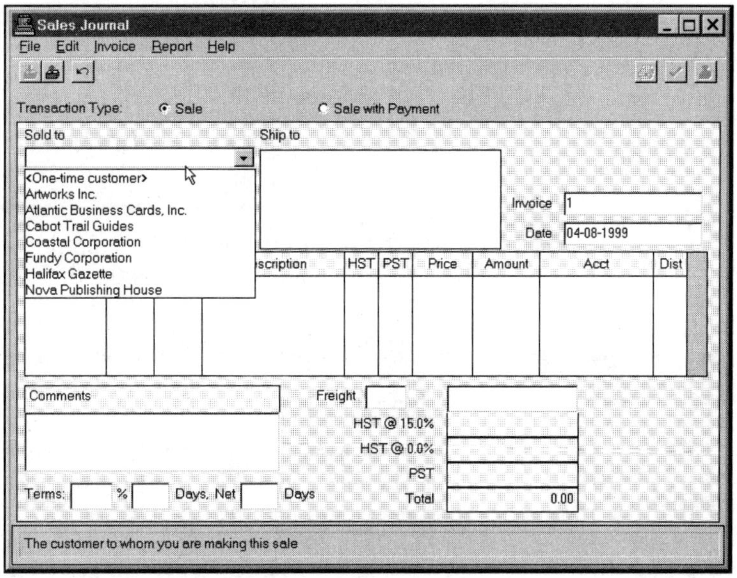

Click on **Coastal Corporation**, the customer in the first source document, to select and enter it.

Notice that the customer's name and address have been added to your input form. If you have made an error in your selection, click on the customer list arrow and start again. By default, the Sold to and the Ship to fields are the same. If a customer has more than one business location and a different shipping address, you can edit the information in the Ship to field. If you have selected correctly, you can skip over the shipping information for this customer. You can also skip over the Cash Sale field because this is a credit sale.

Press tab repeatedly until the Invoice field is highlighted.

Type `GG-1300`

Press tab

The cursor moves to the Date field. The using date appears automatically by default. It is highlighted, ready to be accepted or changed. You need to change the date. Enter the date on which the transaction took place, April 2, 1997.

Type `04-02-99`

Press tab

The cursor advances to the Item field. Because we are not using the Inventory Ledger for this application, ignore this field and the next two.

Click on the first line of the **Description field**. The Description field is used to enter a description or comment concerning the sale.

Type `Desktop services contract`

Press tab

The cursor is now positioned in the HST field. We will use this field to enter the HST which replaces GST in Nova Scotia.

Press enter to display the following HST codes on your screen:

Notes

- You can also double click on the Invoice field to move the cursor and highlight the default information, then type in the invoice number.
- You can press tab repeatedly until you are in the Description field.
- If you wish, you can enter the quantity (one for services, in this case), enter the price per unit in the price field and let the program calculate the amount by multiplying the two together. You can use this method if you are selling more than one item that is not an inventory item.

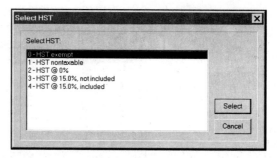

You may select from this list the appropriate HST code for the company. Since the invoice amount already includes the HST, you should choose Code 4 - HST @ 15%, Included.

Click on 4 - HST @ 15.0%, included to highlight it.

Click on Select to enter the code.

The cursor is now in the Price field. Since the provincial and federal retail sales taxes are harmonized, and there is no separate entry for PST, the PST rate is set at 0% and the cursor skips over this field. When PST is applicable and is set up in the defaults for the company, the program will not skip over the PST field. The Price field also refers to inventory items with unit prices; it is not applicable to Grandeur Graphics.

Press `tab`

The cursor should now be positioned in the Amount field, where you will enter the total amount for this invoice, with the HST included.

Type 1380

Press `tab`

The Account field in a sales invoice refers to the credit portion of the journal entry, usually a revenue account. Again, you cannot access the *Accounts Receivable* integration account directly. The software will automatically debit the *Accounts Receivable* control account in the General Ledger.

In the Account field, you can see the list of accounts. To see revenue accounts, type the first digit for the revenue accounts.

Type 4

Press `enter`

Scroll down until the other revenue accounts are included in the viewing area.

Click on 4140 Revenue from Desktop Services to highlight it.

Click on Select to add it to your input form.

The cursor is now placed in the Item field of line 2, ready for additional sale items if necessary.

The Comments box can be used for a default comment for the business so that it appears on all invoices, or you can enter a comment at the time of the sale. You can add to or change a default comment if you want. We will add the comment that HST is included in all prices.

Click in the Comments field.

Type HST @ 15% is included in all prices.

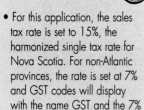

Notes

- For this application, the sales tax rate is set to 15%, the harmonized single tax rate for Nova Scotia. For non-Atlantic provinces, the rate is set at 7% and GST codes will display with the name GST and the 7% rate.
- Code 3, HST not included, is used when HST must be added to the sale price. HST codes 0, 1 and 2 are used for exempt, non-taxable and zero-rated goods.

The transaction is now complete, and your invoice should resemble the following:

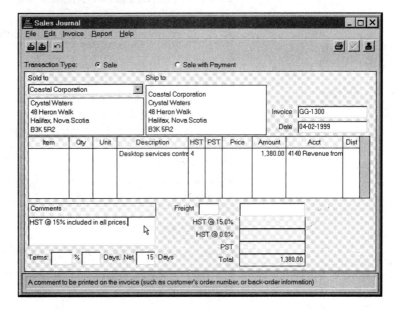

The payment terms have been set up as defaults for all customers as net 15 days. There is no discount. Terms can be changed for individual customers or on individual sales invoices.

Before storing, posting or printing a sales journal entry, you should review it carefully.

Reviewing the Sales Journal Entry

Choose Display Sales Journal Entry from the pull-down menu under **Report** to display the transaction you have entered as shown:

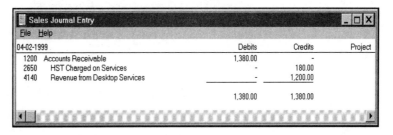

Review the journal entry to check for mistakes. You can see that the *Accounts Receivable* control account has been updated automatically by the Simply Accounting program because the Receivables and General Ledgers are fully integrated. *Accounts Receivable* has been set up as the default Receivables Ledger integration to which all sales are debited. The *HST Charged on Services* account has also been updated correctly because of the HST code you entered and because *HST Charged on Services* was defined as the HST integration account for the Receivables Ledger. You did not need to enter either of these two accounts directly in the Sales Journal. The balance owing by this customer is also directly updated as a result of the Sales Journal entry.

Close the display to return to the Sales Journal input screen.

CORRECTING THE SALES JOURNAL ENTRY BEFORE POSTING

Move to the field that has the error. **Press** (tab) to move forward through the fields or **press** (shift) and (tab) together to move back to a previous field. This will highlight the field information so you can change it. **Type** the correct information and **press** (tab) to enter it.

You can also use the mouse to point to a field and drag through the incorrect information to highlight it. **Type** the correct information and **press** (tab) to enter it.

If the customer is incorrect, re-select from the customer list by **clicking on** the customer field. **Click on** the name of the correct customer.

Click on an incorrect description, HST code, amount or account to highlight the incorrect entry. **Type** the correct information and **press** (tab). Or, in the HST and Account fields, **press** (enter) to display the selection list. **Click on** the correct entry, **click on Select**, then **press** (tab) to enter the change.

You can discard the entire entry. Click on ⟲ to leave the Sales Journal open or ☒ to close the Sales Journal. Simply Accounting will prompt you to confirm that you want to discard the entry.

Posting

When you are certain that you have entered all the information correctly, you must post the transaction to save it. Notice that the Post button is no longer dimmed.

Click on the **Post button** 🔲 on the tool bar or choose Post from the pull-down menu under Invoice to save your transaction.

A new blank Sales Journal form appears on the screen. The next transaction is a receipt, however, so we must exit from the Sales Journal.

Close the Sales Journal input form to return to the Home window.

Accounting for Receipts

Receipts are entered in the Receipts Journal indicated by the arrow pointer as follows:

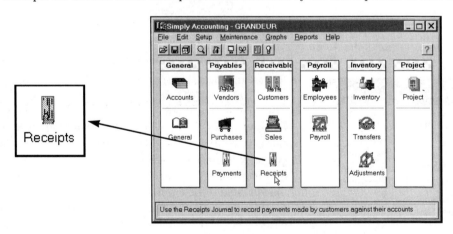

Double click on the **Receipts icon** to open the Receipts Journal. The following blank Receipts Journal input screen appears:

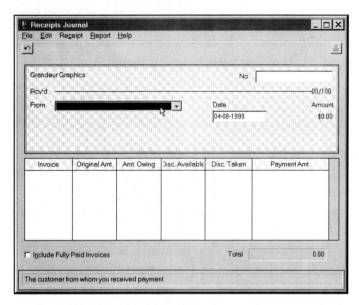

The Customer (Rcv'd From) field is darkened, ready to receive information.

Click on the **Customer field** or its **drop-down list arrow** to display the familiar customer list as shown:

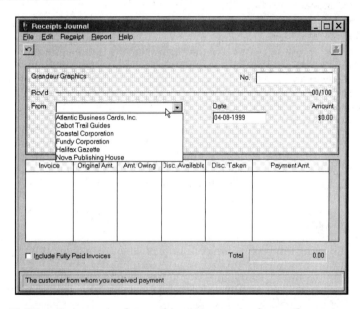

Click on Halifax Gazette to choose this customer. As shown, the customer's name and address have been added to your input form, together with all outstanding invoices for Halifax Gazette:

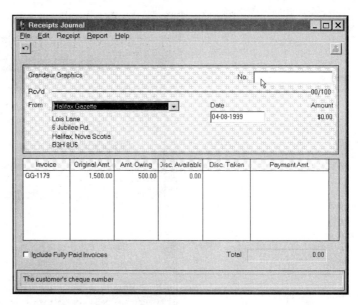

If you have chosen the wrong customer, display the list again and click on the correct customer. If you have selected correctly,

Press [tab]

The cursor advances to the No. field, where you should enter the cheque number.

Type 121

Press [tab]

The cursor moves to the Date field. Replace the using date with the date for this transaction.

Type 04-03-99

Press [tab]

The cursor moves to the Invoice field.

Press [tab] to advance to the Disc. Taken field. Since Grandeur Graphics does not offer customer discounts, we can skip this field.

Press [tab] to advance to the Payment Amt. field. By default, the amount owing on the first invoice is shown and highlighted. All outstanding invoices are listed on the screen. You can accept a highlighted amount, or type in an exact amount for a partial payment. In this case, there is only one invoice and the full amount is being paid so you can accept the default.

Press [tab] to accept the amount in the Payment Amt. field. When there is more than one outstanding invoice, the cursor will advance to the Disc. Taken field for the next invoice.

Notes

As with payments to vendors, you cannot enter account numbers in the Receipts Journal. You need only to enter the amount paid on the appropriate invoice line. The program automatically creates the journal entry.

Notes

When an invoice amount is highlighted and it is not being paid, press [del] to remove the amount from the total, and press [tab] to update the total.

The completed Receipts form should now appear as follows:

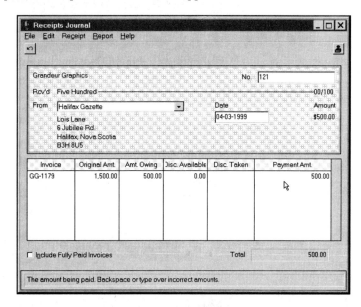

Notice that the upper cheque portion of the form has also been completed. In making Receipts Journal entries, you do not need to enter any accounts because Simply Accounting chooses the default integration accounts defined for the Receivables Ledger to create the journal entry. The *Cash in Bank* account will be debited automatically and the *Accounts Receivable* account will be credited.

You have made all the entries for this transaction, so you are ready to review and post your transaction.

Reviewing the Receipts Journal Entry

Choose Display Receipts Journal Entry from the pull-down menu under Report to display the transaction you have entered as follows:

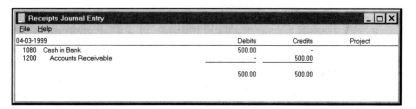

Here you can see the related journal entry created by Simply Accounting when you complete a Receipts Journal entry. The program updates the *Accounts Receivable* control account in the General Ledger and the *Cash in Bank* account because the Receivables and General ledgers are fully integrated. *Cash in Bank* is defined as the Receivables bank integration account as well as the Payables bank integration account because Grandeur Graphics has only one bank account. The receipt will also be credited directly to the customer's account in the Receivables Ledger to reduce the balance owing.

Close the display to return to the Receipts Journal input screen.

CORRECTING THE RECEIPTS JOURNAL ENTRY BEFORE POSTING

Move to the field that has the error. **Press** `tab` to move forward through the fields or **press** `shift` and `tab` together to move back to a previous field. This will highlight the field information so you can change it. **Type** the correct information and **press** `tab` to enter it.

You can also use the mouse to point to a field and drag through the incorrect information to highlight it. **Type** the correct information and **press** `tab` to enter it.

If the customer is incorrect, re-select from the customer list by **clicking on** the arrow beside this field. **Click on** the name of the correct customer. You will be asked to confirm that you want to discard the current transaction. **Click on Yes** to discard the incorrect entry and display the outstanding invoices for the correct customer. **Type** the receipt information for this customer.

You can also discard the entry by clicking on ☒ or ↩ and then clicking on **Yes** to confirm.

Posting

When you are certain that you have entered all the information correctly, you must post the transaction to save it. Notice that the Post button is no longer dimmed.

Click on the **Post button** 🛐 on the tool bar or choose Post from the pull-down menu under Receipt to save your transaction.

Adding a New Customer

On April 3, a new customer is listed in the source documents and must be added to your list.

Customers are added in the Receivables Ledger, indicated by the Customers icon shown:

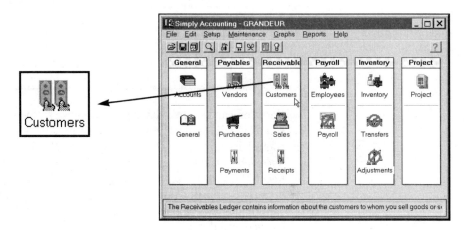

> **Notes**
>
> Click on ▭ to minimize the Sales Journal if it is open and return to the Home window to add the vendor. After creating the new vendor, close the Receivables Ledger, then close the Customers window to return to the Home window. Click on the Sales Journal icon to restore that journal window, and continue with the journal entry. The new customer should be included in the customer list.

Double click on the **Customers icon** to open the the Customers accounts screen:

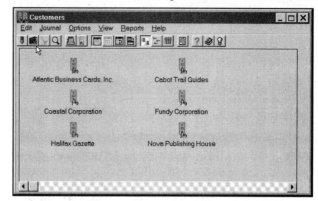

All customers are listed alphabetically or represented by their icons, depending on the viewing option selected.

Click on the **Create button**  on the tool bar in the Customers window or **choose Create** from the pull-down menu under **Edit** to display the following new customer input screen:

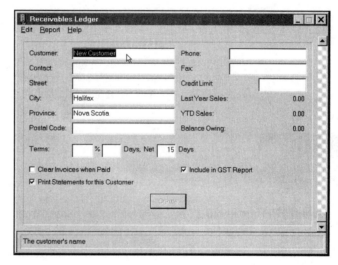

Notes

If you need to edit a customer record, click on the customer's icon in the Customers window to select the customer. Then click on the Edit tool icon or choose Edit from the pull-down menu under Edit to open the Receivables Ledger record for the selected customer. (Or, you can double click on the customer's icon in the Customers window to open the ledger.) Make the necessary changes and close the Receivables Ledger.

You are ready to enter your new customer. The Customer field is highlighted, ready to receive new information.

Type   `Artworks Inc.`

Press   `tab`

The cursor moves to the Contact field. If Grandeur Graphics normally deals with a particular individual at Artworks Inc. (e.g., the owner or the accountant), enter that person's name here.

Type   `Joan Miro`

Press   `tab`

The cursor moves to the Street field.

Type   `33 Abinaki Rd.`

Press   `tab`

The cursor moves to the City field. Notice that the city and province in which Grandeur Graphics is located have been entered by default. The province is correct but you must change the city.

Type   Truro

Press (tab) to advance to the Province field.

Press (tab) to skip the Province field.

The cursor moves to the Postal Code field. You do not need to use capital letters or to leave a space within the postal code. The program will make these adjustments for you.

Type   b2n8t1

Press   (tab)

Notice that the format of the postal code is corrected automatically. The cursor moves to the Phone field. You do not need to insert a dash when you enter a telephone number.

Type   9027719831

Press (tab) to advance to the Fax field.

Type   9027718136

Press (tab) to advance to the Credit Limit field.

Notice that the format for the telephone and fax numbers are corrected automatically. In the next field, the Credit Limit field, you can enter the upper credit limit for a particular customer to help keep bad debts to a minimum. Customers who have previously defaulted on making their payments could be placed on a cash-only basis by setting their credit limits at zero. Grandeur Graphics is presently analyzing customer payment trends to add this feature. The limit will be set at $2 000 on a trial basis.

Type   2000

Press   (tab)

The cursor advances to the Terms fields. The payment terms have been set up for all customers in the company defaults at net 15 days with no discount. They can be edited if necessary for individual customers.

Three other options are available for customer records. The default settings for these options are correct, so do not change them. You can change these settings at any time.

The Clear Invoices When Paid option removes invoices that are fully paid. Choose not to remove paid invoices by leaving this box empty. This way you can keep a record of all purchases and payments made by this customer.

You may also choose the Print Statements for this Customer option. You should use the correct statement forms, but you could also print statements on ordinary printer paper.

The Include in HST Report option should also be left checked so that sales to this customer become part of the permanent HST or GST record.

Notes

Telephone and fax numbers may be entered with or without the area code.

Notes

When a customer exceeds the credit limit, the program will warn you before you can post the sale. You can accept the over-the-limit sale, or ask for a deposit to avoid exceeding the limit. Customers should be notified of changes in policy.

Notes

Unless you have checked *Include in HST Report* for a customer, the HST fields and codes will not be available in the Sales Journal for that customer. Applications for other provinces will display this option as Include in GST Report.

Your completed customer information form now appears as follows:

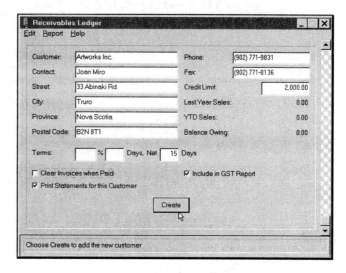

CORRECTING A NEW CUSTOMER ACCOUNT

Move to the field that contains the error by **pressing** (tab) to move forward or (shift) and (tab) to go back to the previous field. **Type** the correct information.

You can also highlight the incorrect information by dragging the cursor through it. You can now **type** the correct information.

After you have corrected a field, **press** (tab) to enter the correction.

Saving a New Customer Account

When you are certain that all of the information is correct, you must save the newly created customer account and add it to the current list.

Click on Create to save the new customer information.

You can now return to the Sales Journal and enter the sale transaction for the new customer by following the procedures outlined earlier.

Close the Receivables Ledger window and then close the Customers window.

When you display the customer list in the Sales Journal, note that the new customer has been added to it.

Notes

If the customer icons in the Customers window are out of order, choose Re-sort Icons from the pull-down menu under Options to restore the alphabetic order.

Entering Cash Sales

Open the Sales Journal from the Home window.

Click on the **Sale with Payment** option immediately above the invoice portion of the Journal.

Your sales invoice changes as shown here:

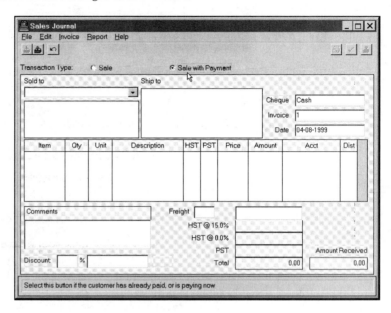

Choose <One-time customer> from the drop-down list of customers because David Manga is not a regular customer.

Press (tab)

The Cheque (number) field opens with the default entry Cash. To make a cash sale to a regular customer, choose the customer's name from the list and click on Sale with Payment to open the Cheque (number) field.

The cursor should be in the Customer Address field. You can type the customer's name and address in the Customer Address field so that it will appear on the printed invoice. If you include the name, it will appear on the journal report as well.

Type David Manga

Since David Manga is paying in cash, leave the default Cheque field entry unchanged.

Complete the rest of the invoice in the usual manner. Refer to the keystroke instructions on page 106 if you need help. You can add "Thank you" or "Paid in full" to the comment in the Comments field.

Choose Display Sales Journal Entry from the pull-down menu under **Report**. Your display should look like the one shown here:

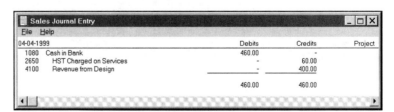

Notice that the *Cash in Bank* account is debited automatically instead of the *Accounts Receivable* account because we selected Sale with Payment as the

Transaction Type. Close the display when you are finished. Make corrections if necessary.

Click on the **Post button** 🖳 to save the entry.

Storing a Recurring Entry

Completing and storing a recurring entry in the Sales Journal is similar to storing a Purchases Journal entry. Complete and review the invoice in the usual way.

When you are certain that the invoice is correct,

Click on the **Store button** 🖳 on the tool bar or choose Store from the pull-down menu under Invoice.

The familiar Store Recurring Entry window appears:

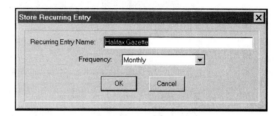

The customer name appears as the entry name, and the default frequency, Monthly is selected. If you wish, you can change the entry name to a more descriptive one that will help you identify the entry when you need to recall it.

Click on Monthly to display the frequency options.

Click on the **up scroll arrow** until Weekly is in view.

Click on Weekly to select this frequency.

Click on OK to save the entry and return to the Sales Journal. Notice that the Recall button is now available.

Click on the **Post button** 🖳 to save the entry.

Reversing a Payment (NSF Cheques)

When a cheque is returned by the bank as NSF, you need to record the fact that the invoice is still outstanding. You can do this in the Receipts Journal by entering a negative payment.

Open the Receipts Journal from the Home window.

Choose Halifax Gazette from the customer list to display outstanding invoices for this customer:

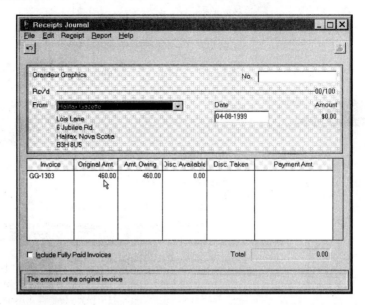

You can see that the only invoice displayed is the recurring entry just posted.

Click on the No. field to move the cursor. To indicate that the original cheque is NSF and is being reversed, add NSF to the cheque number, or enter the bank memo number for reference.

Type   NSF-121

Press ⌈tab⌉. In the Date field, enter the date of the bank memo.

Type   04-04-99

Click on Include Fully Paid Invoices to include the invoices that were paid as shown here:

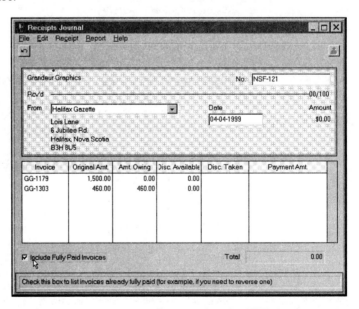

Notes

Or, you can click in the Payment Amt. field on the line for invoice GG-1179.

Click on invoice number GG-1179, the one that the NSF cheque was issued against.

Press ⌈tab⌉ twice to advance to the Payment Amt. field for this invoice line.

Notice that the Payment Amount field is still blank because no balance is owing. Enter the amount of the cheque as a negative amount to indicate the amount of the NSF cheque.

Type −500

Press (tab)

The cursor advances to the Discount Taken field for the next invoice.

Review the Receipts Journal entry. It should look like the one shown here:

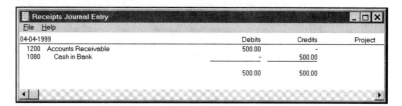

Notice that the same two integration accounts are used to create the reversing journal entry as the regular Receipts Journal entry. However, this time, the *Cash in Bank* account is credited and the *Accounts Receivable* account is debited because we entered a negative amount instead of a positive amount for the payment. This is a reversing entry of the payment.

Close the display when you are finished.

Click on the **Post button** 📇 to display a new Payments Journal.

Choose Halifax Gazette from the Customer list. The unpaid invoice is added to the outstanding invoices and you can proceed with the payment.

Recalling a Stored Entry

On April 11, Grandeur Graphics completed the second of its weekly jobs for Halifax Gazette.

Open the Sales Journal from the Home window.

Click on the **Recall button** 📇 or choose Recall from the pull-down menu under Invoice to display the Recall Recurring Entry window:

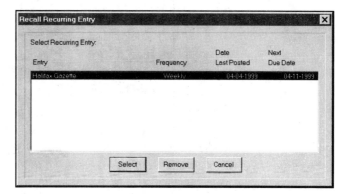

Since only one entry — the one for Halifax Gazette — is stored, it is selected.

Click on Select to display the following copy of the entry posted on April 4:

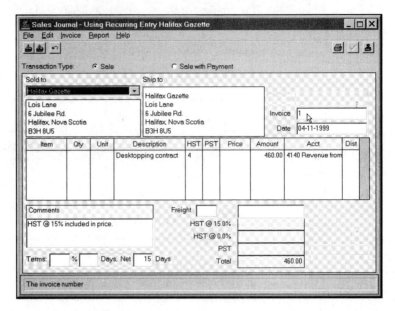

The default date is exactly one week past the previous posting date because we chose weekly as the frequency. Only the Invoice field needs to be updated because a new invoice number is required.

Double click on the Invoice field to advance the cursor and highlight the contents.

Type   GG-1307

Review the entry to be certain that it is correct.

Click on the Post button 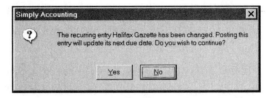 to save the entry. Simply Accounting may display the following warning:

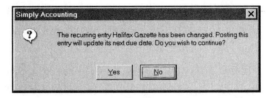

Click on Yes to accept the change and continue with posting the journal entry.

Displaying Customer Reports

All customer-related reports can be displayed or printed from the Home window or the Customers window.

Double click on the Customers icon in the Home window to open the Customers window. The Reports menu list now contains only customer reports. You can select the report you want from this list and follow the instructions below to choose report options. Customer-related graphs are not available from the Customers window.

Displaying Customer Lists

You should be in the Home window.

Click on the Customers icon to select it.

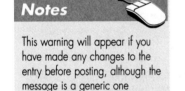

Notes

This warning will appear if you have made any changes to the entry before posting, although the message is a generic one referring only to the posting date.

Notes

You can display the Customer Aged Report from the Customer List.

Click on the Report button  on the tool bar, or choose Display Customer List from the pull-down menu under Reports. The report will be displayed immediately. Maximize the display and scroll as necessary to see customers outside the screen viewing area.

Close the display when you have finished viewing it.

Displaying Customer Aged Reports

Choose Receivables and then Customer Aged from the pull-down menu under Reports at any time except when you are entering a transaction. The following window will appear, showing several options for your display:

Type the date for the report, choose a date from the drop-down list in the As at field or accept the default using date.

Click on the appropriate name or names in the customer list. If you want the report to include all customers, click on **Select All**.

The **Summary** option will display an alphabetic list of the selected customers with outstanding total balances owing, organized into aging period columns, according to the defaults set up for the company. By default, the program selects this option.

Select the **Detail** option if you wish to see individual outstanding invoices and payments made by customers. This more descriptive report is also aged. Management can use it to make credit decisions. Click on Detail to choose this option.

After you have indicated all of the options you want,

Click on OK to see the report.

Close the displayed report when you have finished.

Notes

- To display journal reports from the Reports menu in the Home window you must first highlight the corresponding journal icon. Click on an icon to select it.
- Sales and Receipts Journal reports are also available from the list when you click on the Report tool icon.

Notes

You can display the Customer Ledger from the Customer Aged Report.

Displaying Aged Overdue Receivables Reports

Choose Receivables and then Aged Overdue Receivables from the pull-down menu under Reports at any time except when you are entering a transaction. The following window will appear, showing the options for your display:

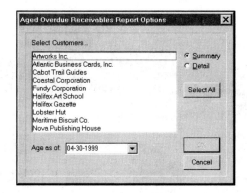

Type the date for the report, choose a date from the drop-down list in the Age as at field or accept the default using date.

Click on the appropriate name or names in the customer list. If you want the report to include all customers, click on Select All.

The Summary option will display an alphabetic list of the selected customers with outstanding total balances owing, organized into aging period columns, with an additional column for the amount that is overdue.

Select the Detail option if you wish to see individual outstanding invoices, due dates, payments and overdue amounts for the selected customers. Click on Detail to choose this option.

After you have indicated all of the options you want,

Click on OK to see the report.

Close the displayed report when you have finished.

Displaying the Sales Journal

Click on the Sales icon in the Home window.

Click on the Report button 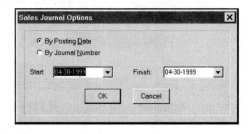 or choose Display Sales Journal from the pull-down menu under Reports to see the report options for the Sales Journal:

You can display the Sales Journal by posting date or by journal entry number. The default setting, the By Posting Date option, is the one used for all reports in this workbook, so leave the selection unchanged.

Type the beginning date for the journal transactions you want to display.

Press [tab]

Type the ending date for the transaction period you want to see.

Click on OK to see the report.

Close the display when you are finished.

Displaying the Receipts Journal

Click on the **Receipts icon** in the Home window.

Click on the **Report button** or choose Display Receipts Journal from the pull-down menu under Reports to see the report options for the Receipts Journal.

The Receipts Journal, like the Sales Journal, can also be displayed by posting date or by journal entry number. The default setting, the By Posting Date option, is the one requested for all reports in this workbook, so leave the selection unchanged.

Type the beginning date for the journal transactions you want to display.

Press ⌐tab⌐

Type the ending date for the transaction period you want to see.

Click on OK to see the report.

Close the display when you are finished.

Displaying the HST (GST) Report

Choose HST from the pull-down menu under **Reports** in the Home window. The following dialogue window appears:

Type the date for which you want the report.

The default setting at **Summary** includes only the totals for the purchases, GST/HST Paid on Purchases, taxable sales and GST/HST Charged on Services.

Click on **Detail** if you want a detailed breakdown of individual customer and vendor transactions that included GST/HST. Totals are also provided.

Once you have set the options as you wish,

Click on OK to see the report.

Close the display window when you are finished

Printing Customer Reports

To print customer reports, display the report you want to print.

Choose Print from the pull-down menu under File. Since printing will begin immediately, make sure that you have set the print options correctly.

Notes

You can display the Customer Aged Report and the General Ledger Report from the Receipts Journal.

Notes

In applications for other provinces, the report is named GST report. Only the GST/HST transactions that were entered through the Sales Journal or the Purchases Journal will be included in this report. Furthermore, only customers and vendors for whom *Include in GST/HST Report* was checked will be included. GST/HST-related transactions completed in the General Journal will not be included. Therefore, the amounts shown in the GST report may differ from the balances in the General Ledger GST/HST accounts that include all GST/HST transactions. You should use the General Ledger accounts to determine the balance owing (or refund) and then make adjustments in the report as necessary.

Printing Customer Statements

Choose Receivables and then **Print Customer Statements** from the pull-down menu under **Reports** to see the following options:

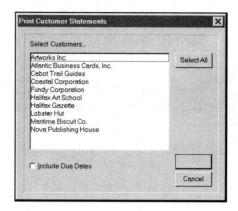

Click on the customer for whom you want to print the statement or click on **Select All** to include all customers.

Click on Include Due Dates if you want to add the date on which payment for each invoice is due.

Click on OK

Printing will begin immediately, so be sure your printer is set up with the correct forms before you begin.

Printing Customer Mailing Labels

Click on the **Customers icon** in the Home window. The Customers icon must be selected so that the mailing labels report option will refer to customers. If the Vendors icon is selected, Vendor labels will be printed. If no icon is selected, the report option will be dimmed.

Choose Print Mailing Labels from the pull-down menu under **Reports** to see the following options:

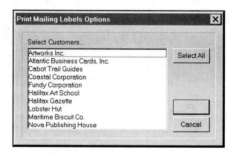

Click on the customer for whom you want to print the labels or click on **Select All** to include all customers.

Click on OK

Printing will begin immediately, so be sure that the print options have been set correctly before you print and that your printer is turned on and has the correct labels paper.

Notes

- To set the program for printing labels, select Printers from the pull-down menu under Setup in the Home window.
- Click on Labels.
- Enter the appropriate details for the labels you are using.
- Click on OK to return to the Home window.

Graphing Customer Reports

The customer-related graphs are available from the Home window.

Receivables by Aging Period Graph

Choose **Receivables by Aging Period** from the pull-down menu under **Graphs**.

Again the pie chart is displayed immediately showing the total receivables divided according to the aging intervals set up in the company defaults. You have the same Tool bar options, and colour and legend control choices that you have for the Expenses and Net Profit as % of Revenue graph. Refer to page 50 for a review of these features if you need further assistance.

Close the graph when you are finished.

Receivables by Customer Graph

Choose **Receivables by Customer** from the pull-down menu under **Graphs** to see the following options:

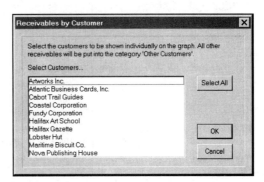

Click on the customer you want individually on the chart or click on **Select All** to include all customers.

Click on **OK** to display the chart:

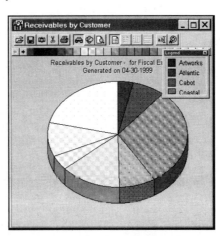

The amount owed by each customer, represented by a different colour in the pie chart, is shown as a proportion of the total receivables. Again the options for displaying, editing, printing and exporting the graph are the same as for other graphs.

Close the display when you are finished.

Notes

- Double click on a portion of a graph to see the aging period, the dollar amount and the percentage of the total.
- Click on the legend to make it larger. Double click on the expanded legend to reduce it.

Notes

- Double click on a portion of a graph to see the customer, the dollar amount and the percentage of the total.
- Click on the legend to make it large and add the customer names. Double click on the expanded legend to reduce it.

Sales vs Receivables Graph

Choose Sales vs Receivables from the pull-down menu under Graphs to see the following options:

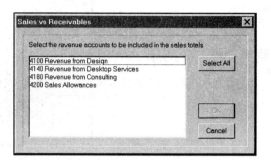

Click on the revenue accounts that you want to include in the graph or click on Select All to include all revenue accounts.

Click on OK to display the following bar chart for the end of April:

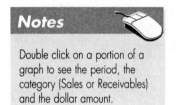
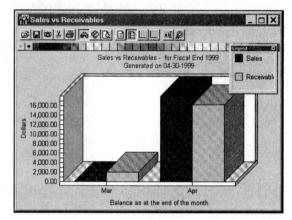

Although this is not a pie chart, you have the same options for exporting, copying, changing the display, and so on that you do for other graphs.

Close the graph when you are finished.

Receivables Due vs Payables Due Graph

Choose Receivables Due vs Payables Due from the pull-down menu under Graphs to see the following options:

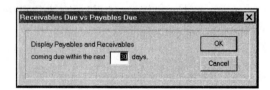

Type the number of days that you want the graph to include. All Receivables and Payables that become due in this number of days will be added to the chart totals.

Click on OK to display the bar chart:

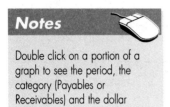
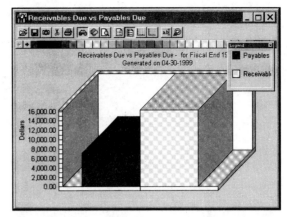

The graph shows the total amounts for receivables and payables due in the selected time period.

For this bar chart too, you have the same options for exporting, copying, changing the display and so on that you do for other graphs.

Close the graph when you are finished.

CASE PROBLEMS

Case One

For one of the regular customers, a credit sale of $230 was recorded with the HST Code 3 - HST not included in price. Therefore the customer was overcharged by 15%. The error was not noticed until after the customer had made the full payment for the overcharged amount. What options does Grandeur Graphics have to correct this error,

a. If the payment was not yet recorded?

b. If the payment has been recorded?

Case Two

Entering a purchase with a deposit required a Purchases Journal entry together with a separate Payments Journal entry. In the same way, a sale with a down payment will require separate Sales and Receipts Journal entries. Explain why this is so. (Hint: You may want to try to enter the transaction entirely in the Sales Journal to observe how the software treats the information and why it demands separate entries.)

CHAPTER SIX

Children's International Summer Villages TORONTO VILLAGE

Upon completion of this chapter, you will be able to:

OBJECTIVES

- *plan* and *design* an accounting system for a non-profit organization
- *prepare* a conversion procedure from manual records
- *understand* the objectives of a computerized accounting system
- *create* company files using the skeleton starter file for a non-profit organization
- *set up* the organization's accounts using Setup Input Forms
- *make* the accounting system ready for operation
- *enter* transactions using the General Journal
- *display* and *print* reports

COMPANY INFORMATION

Company Profile

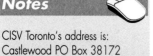

Children's International Summer Villages (CISV) is a worldwide organization promoting international peace, education and cross-cultural friendship. Doris Allen created CISV in 1951 because she believed that helping the world's young people "to live amicably with one another as friends" would contribute to a peaceful future. Today, over 70 countries are members of CISV. In Canada alone there are ten chapters with a total of over 3 000 members.

To accomplish its goals, CISV offers a number of programs for children between the ages of 10 and 18. Eleven-year-old boys and girls from 12 different countries come together for four weeks in "Villages" to share their cultures through sports, social activities and cooperative games, learning to communicate even without a common language. Twelve- to fifteen-year-olds can participate in Summer Camps, a village-like experience for older children, or in family-oriented Interchanges with a single other country. All groups of children who travel are accompanied by an adult leader. Older children (16 through 18) have many opportunities to develop their leadership skills in

> **Notes**
>
> CISV Toronto's address is:
> Castlewood PO Box 38172
> 550 Eglinton Ave. W.
> Toronto, Ontario M5N 3A8
> Business No.: 5643 87694

Notes

CISV exists as a real organization. Its goals and programs are as described in this chapter. The accounting information, although realistic, has been simplified for this application and the source documents are simulated. CISV International is independent of any government, political party, religious organization or umbrella organization. It is administered by an International Board of Directors and has a permanent International Office in England. Similarly, CISV Canada is administered by a National Board of Directors and has a permanent National Office in Ottawa. CISV is a non-profit charitable organization.

Notes

Participants in each program pay international and national fees. Similarly, each Chapter pays fees to the national office to cover insurance, administration and other expenses.

the organization. They can serve as Junior Counsellors, assisting leaders in the planning and running of villages. They can also participate in Seminar Camps and Youth Meetings where international and intercultural issues are explored through activities and discussion. And finally, on an ongoing basis, they plan and organize year-round educational and social activities for all junior members of their local chapter — the Junior Branch. Through these and planned local work programs, the whole family can participate in the CISV experience.

As a non-profit, volunteer organization, CISV relies strongly on its members to volunteer for its regular activities as well as a variety of fund-raising events. Member fees, donations which are fully receipted for income tax purposes, support the day-to-day operational expenses of the chapter. Money from fund-raising activities is used to support operations, programs and special events. Each Chapter is expected to host a Village every two or three years in return for sending delegates to Villages elsewhere. All the costs of running the Village, except for the travel expenses of the children and leaders attending, are borne by CISV Toronto. Similarly, a chapter will periodically host a Summer Camp or a Seminar Camp. Interchanges are generally paid for by the members who participate in them, with the interchange group itself, rather than the entire chapter, organizing special fund-raising activities.

A separate bank account is set up for the Village funds. When the Village is in operation, it sets up its own accounting system, and the summary expense is consolidated into the Chapter's books. It operates as if it were a wholly owned subsidiary company. The Junior Branch also has its own accounting records and supports its own activities financially.

This application deals with the accounting for a four-week Village.

The Toronto Chapter has decided to use Simply Accounting to keep the accounting records for the Village in July 1999. They currently use only General Ledger accounts. The Chapter itself uses the Receivables Ledger to keep track of memberships and the Payables Ledger for regular vendor accounts. To set up the accounts using the General Ledger, they will use the following information:

- Chart of Accounts
- Income Statement
- Balance Sheet
- Trial Balance
- Accounting Procedures

CISV TORONTO VILLAGE
CHART OF ACCOUNTS

ASSETS
1020 Cash in Bank - Village
1100 Cash on Hand
1200 Arts & Crafts Supplies
1300 Food Supplies
1320 Office Supplies
1360 Village T-shirts for Sale
1450 Computer
1500 Fax/Answering Machine

LIABILITIES
2200 A/P - Designs U Wear
2300 A/P - Quiq Kopy
2350 A/P - Sleeptight Cots
2400 A/P - Travel in Comfort
2670 GST Paid on Purchases

CISV EQUITY
3560 Surplus Funds
3600 Net Income

REVENUE
4020 Revenue from Bingo
4080 Interest Revenue
4120 Other Revenue

EXPENSE
5020 Caretaking Expense
5050 Cost of T-shirts
5080 Cots & Linen Rental
5180 Food Expense
5200 General Expense
5250 Office Supplies Used
5280 Non-refundable GST
5300 Postage Expense
5320 Printing & Copying
5350 Publicity
5400 Telephone Expense
5420 Wages - Cook
5500 Crafts Supplies Used
5550 Entertainment Expenses
5600 Transportation

CISV TORONTO VILLAGE
INCOME STATEMENT

For the Six Months Ending June 30, 1999

Revenue
4000 REVENUE

4020 Revenue from Bingo	$9 200.00
4080 Interest Revenue	240.00
4120 Other Revenue	100.00
4390 TOTAL REVENUE	$9 540.00
TOTAL REVENUE	$9 540.00

Expense
5000 OPERATING & ADMIN EXPENSES

5020 Caretaking Expense	0.00
5050 Cost of T-shirts	0.00
5080 Cots & Linen Rental	6 100.00
5180 Food Expense	0.00
5200 General Expense	0.00
5250 Office Supplies Used	0.00
5280 Non-refundable GST	0.00
5300 Postage Expense	70.00
5320 Printing & Copying	150.00
5350 Publicity	0.00
5400 Telephone Expense	0.00
5420 Wages - Cook	0.00
5440 TOTAL OPERATING & ADMIN EXPENSES	$6 320.00

5450 PROGRAM & ACTIVITY EXPENSES	
5500 Crafts Supplies Used	0.00
5550 Entertainment Expenses	0.00
5600 Transportation	200.00
5690 TOTAL PROGRAM & ACTIVITY EXPENSES	$ 200.00
TOTAL EXPENSE	$6 520.00
NET INCOME (LOSS)	$3 020.00

CISV TORONTO VILLAGE
BALANCE SHEET

July 1, 1999

Assets
1000 CURRENT ASSETS

1020 Cash in Bank - Village	$49 550.00	
1100 Cash on Hand	1 000.00	
1150 Total Cash		$50 550.00
1200 Arts & Crafts Supplies		500.00
1300 Food Supplies		2 300.00
1320 Office Supplies		400.00
1360 Village T-shirts for Sale		800.00
1390 TOTAL CURRENT ASSETS		$54 550.00

1400 EQUIPMENT		
1450 Computer		$ 1 500.00
1500 Fax/Answering Machine		500.00
1590 TOTAL EQUIPMENT		$ 2 000.00
TOTAL ASSETS		$56 550.00

Liabilities
2000 CURRENT LIABILITIES

2200 A/P - Designs U Wear	$ 800.00
2300 A/P - Quiq Kopy	150.00
2350 A/P - Sleeptight Cots	3 050.00
2400 A/P - Travel in Comfort	200.00
2670 GST Paid on Purchases	−385.00
2690 TOTAL CURRENT LIABILITIES	$ 3 815.00
TOTAL LIABILITIES	$ 3 815.00

Equity
3000 CISV EQUITY

3560 Surplus Funds	$49 715.00
3600 Net Income	3 020.00
3690 TOTAL CISV EQUITY	$52 735.00
TOTAL EQUITY	$52 735.00
LIABILITIES AND EQUITY	$56 550.00

```
CISV TORONTO VILLAGE
TRIAL BALANCE

July 1, 1999

1020 Cash in Bank - Village        $49 550.00
1100 Cash on Hand                    1 000.00
1200 Arts & Crafts Supplies            500.00
1300 Food Supplies                   2 300.00
1320 Office Supplies                   400.00
1360 Village T-shirts for Sale         800.00
1450 Computer                        1 500.00
1500 Fax/Answering Machine             500.00
2200 A/P - Designs U Wear                            $     800.00
2300 A/P - Quiq Kopy                                       150.00
2350 A/P - Sleeptight Cots                               3 050.00
2400 A/P - Travel in Comfort                              200.00
2670 GST Paid on Purchases             385.00
3560 Surplus Funds                                      49 715.00
4020 Revenue from Bingo                                  9 200.00
4080 Interest Revenue                                      240.00
4120 Other Revenue                                         100.00
5080 Cots & Linen Rental             6 100.00
5300 Postage Expense                    70.00
5320 Printing & Copying                150.00
5600 Transportation                    200.00
                                   _____          _____
                                   $63 455.00           $63 455.00
                                   ===========          ===========
```

Accounting Procedures

GST

As a registered charity, CISV has two options with respect to the GST. Like regular for-profit businesses, it can register to apply the GST, charge its members GST on their membership fees and claim all GST paid as input tax credits to reduce the liability to the Receiver General of Canada. Not wanting to subject the members to an increase in fees, CISV has not chosen this option. Instead it has chosen the second option that does not require registration or collection of GST but does permit a partial rebate of GST paid. CISV submits an application for refunds quarterly, listing the total of all GST paid toward its operating expenses. Fifty percent of this amount is eligible for the rebate. Therefore, CISV records all purchases as compound General Journal entries, separating the amount paid for GST from the total and entering this amount into the *GST Paid on Purchases* account. Every quarter, this account is cleared as the application for a rebate is submitted. The remaining 50 percent of the GST paid is charged to the *Non-refundable GST* expense account.

Bank Accounts

The proceeds from the weekly Bingo night fund-raising event are entered into the Village bank account. They are reserved exclusively for the Village expenses and are not used for operational expenses of the Chapter as a whole. A separate bank account, not included here, is used for Chapter expenses. During the Village, a *Cash on Hand* account is set up for day-to-day expenses incurred by the Village staff. Regular transfers are made from the *Cash in Bank - Village* account to *Cash on Hand*.

Chapter Operating Expenses

All day-to-day operational expenses for the Chapter as a whole are itemized separately from the Village expenses. Membership fees are deposited in the main Chapter bank account to support the operational expenses. A summary of village expenses is recorded in the main chapter statements after the Village has ended.

INSTRUCTIONS

Notes

If you prefer to enter the source documents before setting up the data files, you can use the CISV.ASC file in the SETUP folder on the Data Disk. In this way, you will become familiar with the account structure and the setup may be easier to complete.

1. Using all of the information provided in this application, set up the company accounts for CISV Toronto using only the General Ledger. Detailed keystroke instructions follow.

2. Using the Chart of Accounts and other information provided, enter the source documents that begin on page 157 using the General Journal in Simply Accounting.

3. After you have completed your entries, print the following reports:

   a. General Journal from July 1 - July 31
   b. Balance Sheet as at July 31, 1999
   c. Income Statement for the period Jan. 1, 1999, to July 31, 1999.

KEYSTROKES FOR SETUP

Notes

Using subsequent versions of the Simply Accounting program may result in different screens and keystrokes from those described in this application.

There are four key stages in preparing the Simply Accounting program for use by a company:

1. creating company files
2. preparing the system
3. preparing the ledgers
4. backing up your files and making the program ready.

The following keystroke instructions are written for a stand-alone IBM-PC or compatible with a hard disk system and single or dual floppy disk drives. The keystroke instructions provided in this application demonstrate one approach to setting up company accounts. Always refer to your Simply Accounting user's guide and DOS and Windows manuals for further details.

Creating Company Files

Notes

• When working through this application, save your work frequently by choosing Save from the pull-down menu under File. You will also save your work by finishing your session properly. You may finish your session at any time while completing the setup. Simply continue the next time from where you left off.

• Use Save As or Backup frequently while setting up your files to update your backup files.

The following instructions assume that you have the Simply Accounting program correctly installed on your hard disk in drive C: in the Program Files\WINSIM folder .

Simply Accounting provides a set of starter files to make it easier to create files for a new company. These starter files contain different sets of accounts that match the needs of different kinds of businesses. By starting with one of these files, you eliminate the need to create all of the accounts for your business from scratch. You should work with a copy of these files so that you can use the original starter files for future applications. Simply Accounting includes the following starter files:

• Bistro
• Construction
• Consulting
• Daycare
• Integration Plus
• Manufacturing

• Medical
• Office
• Property
• Retail
• Service
• Skeleton

Most of starter files are suited to the type of business named by the files. The Manufacturing starter files are tailored to a merchandising business that sells manufactured goods. The Skeleton starter has only General Ledger accounts whereas the Integration Plus starter is suitable for a variety of business types because it has the basic integration accounts for all the ledgers. Display or print the Chart of Accounts from any of the starter files if you want to see the differences between them.

You will have to customize any of these starter files to your particular company. Rarely are accounts identical for any two businesses. The files that most closely match the Chart of Accounts for CISV are the Skeleton starter files (skeleton.asc). These files contain only a few General Ledger accounts, Headings and Totals. They contain no integration accounts that link General Ledger accounts to accounts in the subsidiary ledgers. This is appropriate for the CISV Village because they use only the General Ledger.

The starter files are located in the folder called samdata in the Winsim folder, which also contains your Simply Accounting program. If you accepted the default installation location, they should be in the folder named Program Files in Volume 1 (drive C:) on your hard disk. These starter files were created when you installed the program.

Start the Simply Accounting program.

If you were previously working with files in the Data folder under Winsim,

Click on the **Up One Level folder icon** ⬆ beside the Look in field to go the Winsim folder level. You should see the four folders under the Winsim folder.

Double click on samdata to open it or click on samdata to highlight it and then click on Open.

You should now see the list of starter files as shown:

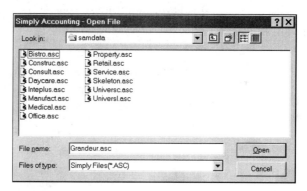

Click on Skeleton.asc

Click on Open to access the Skeleton starter files.

The familiar Home window appears. You are now ready to make a copy of these files to store your records for CISV. Always work with a backup copy of the starter files so that you will have the original to use when creating other company records.

Choose Save As from the pull-down menu under **File** to display the following dialogue box:

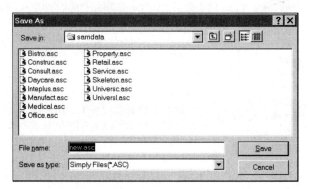

Click on the Up One Level folder icon [image] to return to the Winsim folder level.

Double click on the data folder to open it (double click on A: in the Save in field if you are using floppy disks to store your data files).

Create a new folder for the CISV company files called CISV. Click the right mouse button and choose New and then Folder from the displayed menu. Type the new folder name, CISV.

Double click on the CISV folder to open it.

Double click on new.asc, the file name, to prepare the field for editing.

Type cisv.asc to change the file name for the CISV files.

Click on Save

You have now created a copy of the Skeleton starter files in a new folder and under the new name in the data folder (or on the floppy disk) where you stored your other data files. Several files were created in this procedure, all of which are necessary to work in Simply Accounting. The .asc file is the only one displayed on your file list because it is the one that you open to get started. If the other files are not in the same folder, you will not be able to access your data. Using the Save As command automatically puts all the necessary files together.

When you return to the Home window, the name CISV appears at the top of the window as shown:

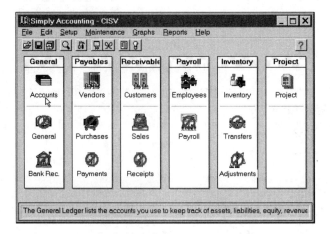

All journals icons are currently locked. A no entry symbol appears on each journal icon. You must enter all of the necessary company information and make the ledgers ready before you can enter journal transactions.

Preparing the System

Before entering financial records for a new company, you must prepare the system for operation. This involves changing the defaults that were set up when the CISV company files were created. For the General Ledger, these defaults include the company name and address, fiscal dates, screen display preferences, and the Chart of Accounts. When you set up other ledgers, there will be additional default information. Some of the defaults will not be suitable for CISV. You must also provide other information, such as the printer(s) that you will be using and printing formats. This process of adding, deleting and modifying information is called *customizing the system*.

You should change the defaults to suit your own work environment, such as choosing a printer or adding information for a second printer.

Setup Input Forms

Each stage of the setup is shown with an input form for that stage. We use these forms to show the information that you must enter at each stage and will discuss each of the different setup input forms as it is used. You may choose not to use the setup forms in the Appendix, using the Company Information at the beginning of this application to enter the company details directly into the computer.

The setup input form, Form SYS-1 profiles the company and gives information about CISV computer equipment:

SYSTEM PREPARATION

Form SYS-1
Page 1 of 1

COMPANY INFORMATION

Name: CISV Toronto

Street: Castlewood PO Box 38172

City: Toronto

Province: Ontario

Postal Code: M5N 3A8

Business No.: 564387694

Fiscal Start: 01-01-99 (mm-dd-yy)

Fiscal End: 12-31-99 (mm-dd-yy)

Conversion: 07-01-99 (mm-dd-yy)

PRINTER NAMES

	Form/Paper Size	Margins TOP	LEFT
Reports/Graphs: HP LaserJet		.50	.50
Cheques:			
Invoices:			
Other:			

	Number across page	Height	Width
Labels:			

Changing Defaults

Entering Company Information

Choose Company Information from the pull-down menu under Setup. You will see the following screen:

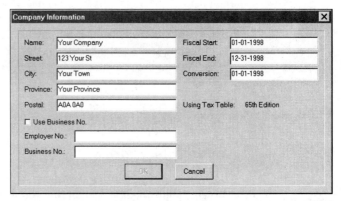

The cursor is in the Name field. This field contains the information "Your Company" to let you know that this is where you should enter the name of your company. Drag the cursor through the contents of the field so that you can edit the field. When the field is completely highlighted,

Type   CISV Toronto

Press   [tab]

The cursor moves to the Street field, the first address field. You can enter the address immediately because the current contents are already highlighted.

Type   Castlewood PO Box 38172

Press   [tab]

The cursor advances to and highlights the contents of the City field.

Type   Toronto

Press   [tab]

The cursor advances to the Province field. It, too, is ready for editing.

Type   Ontario

Press   [tab]

The cursor is now placed at the highlighted Postal (postal code) field. Remember you do not have to type the capitals or spaces in postal codes. The program automatically corrects the postal code format.

Type   m5n3a8

Press   [tab]

Beginning in 1997, all companies must use a single Revenue Canada registration number to replace the Employer and GST registration numbers. When you choose to use the Business Number, the employer number and GST registration number fields are removed. For most businesses, the GST registration number becomes the single business registration number.

Click on Use Business No. to open the Business No. field.

Click on the **Business No. field** to move the cursor.

Type   564387694

Simply Accounting will accept dates between January 1, 1900 and December 31, 2027. Since you can store up to two years of accounting records, you should not start with dates past the year 2025.

Press ⌷tab⌷ to advance to the Fiscal Start field. This date field contains the date at which the current fiscal year begins. This is usually the date used to define the beginning of the fiscal year for income tax purposes. As usual, the date format is mm-dd-yy (month, day, year).

Type   01-01-99

Press ⌷tab⌷. The cursor moves to the Fiscal End field. This is the date at which the company closes its books, usually one year after the fiscal start, and the end of the fiscal year used for income tax reporting purposes.

Type   12-31-99

Press   ⌷tab⌷

The cursor is now placed in the Conversion field. This is the date on which the company converts its manual accounting records to the computerized system. The date must not be earlier than the fiscal start, and not later than the fiscal end. The conversion date will be the first using date when you are ready to enter journal transactions. Simply Accounting automatically advances the conversion date when you start a new fiscal year and when you clear journal entries. Transaction dates must fall between the conversion date and the fiscal end.

Type   07-01-99

Check your work. Conversion dates cannot be changed once you have made the program ready and have started to enter journal transactions. Return to any field with errors and correct the mistakes. Other company information can be edited at any time.

Click on OK to save the new company information.

Changing the Printer Defaults

The Printers section on input form SYS-1 shows the settings for reports. Since CISV does not have customer or vendor information, the remaining sections are blank.

Choose Printers from the pull-down menu under **Setup** to show this screen:

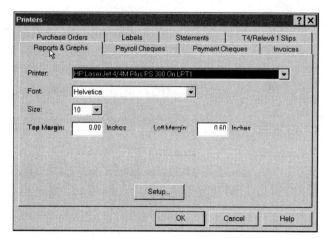

You can see that Simply Accounting allows you to set different printers for reports and graphs, cheques, invoices, labels, statements, purchase orders and T4s/Relevé 1s. Many companies use one printer for their reports and another for various preprinted

Notes

When you use dates in the year 2000 or later, you must enter all four digits for the year so that the program will recognize the date correctly. Once you have entered the fiscal start, end, and conversion dates, the program will correctly fill in the dates when you type in the last two digits, or leave out the year because the using date must fall between the conversion and end dates.

Notes

It is possible for a company to use a fiscal period less than one year for reporting purposes and to close its books more frequently, but the most common period is one year.

Notes

The Names option in the Setup menu refers to other ledgers. It will be introduced in a later application.

Notes

The default printer you selected for your other Windows programs will be selected initially.

forms and invoices. Once you choose printer settings, Simply Accounting will apply them to all of your Simply Accounting files.

The printer setting options for reports and graphs are given. Choose the printer you will be using for reports from the list provided using the arrow beside the field. All printers that are attached to your computer and were installed under Windows should be on the list. Change the margins if necessary. Choose a font and type size from the lists available when you click on the arrows beside these fields. You may have to experiment with fonts and type sizes to find the combination that will fit the reports neatly on the page.

To modify the printer setup for other outputs, click on the relevant tab at the top of the settings screen. You can modify printer setup information any time by returning to this screen.

The specific options will vary from one printer to another. To change additional settings,

Click on Setup to display the following screen:

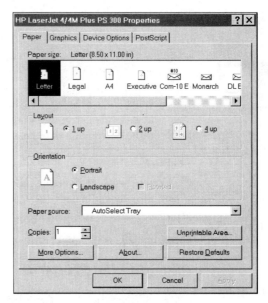

Your options at this stage are to modify the source of the paper, the paper size, orientation and number of copies. Remember that companies generally print at least two copies of invoices and customer statements.

Additional control over your printed copy may be available from this screen by clicking on the tabs for Graphics, Device Options or PostScript, or on the More Options button. Each one will give you additional printing options. The sequence of screens and options will vary from printer to printer.

Click on OK to leave each dialogue box and save the changes or

Click on Cancel to exit without making changes and return to the Home window.

Changing Default Settings

Form SYS-2 shows the first group of settings that you need to modify for CISV.

SYSTEM PREPARATION

SETTINGS : Display

Display Font : `Helvetica`   Size : `10`

Hide Modules

Payables: Y ___ , N ✔

Receivables: Y ___ , N ✔

Payroll: Y ___ , N ✔

Inventory: Y ___ , N ✔

Project: Y ___ , N ✔

Display To Do Lists: At Startup   Y ✔ , N ___   After Advancing Using Date   Y ✔ , N ___

Home Window Background: `Windows default`

Show Status Bar: Y ✔ , N ___

SETTINGS : System

Track Inventory Turnover: Y ___ , N ✔

Store Invoice Lookup Details: Y ___ , N ✔

Cash Basis Accounting: Y ___ , N ✔   Date _____

Use Cheque No. as Source Code: Y ___ , N ✔

Auto Advice: On ✔ , Off ___

Backup frequency: ___ `Weekly` ___

SETTINGS : General

Skip Accounts Icon Window: Y ___ , N ✔

Budget: Y ___ , N ✔   Budget Period _____

Bank Reconciliation: Y ___ , N ✔

Changing Display Defaults

Choose Settings from the pull-down menu under **Setup**. The Display options are shown:

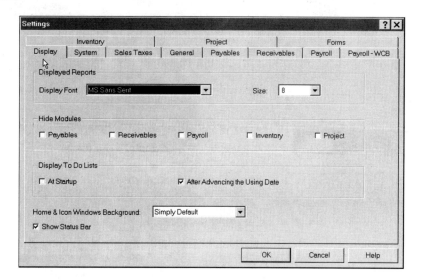

From this screen, you can change the appearance of the Home window and the ledger screens. You can choose to hide, that is, not to display the icons for ledgers that you are not using by clicking on their check boxes. If you choose to display them again, click on the same boxes to reveal the icons. The General ledger and journal icons cannot be removed. Simply Accounting offers reminders about upcoming activities such as payments that are due, discounts available and recurring entries. You can choose to be reminded of these activities each time you start the program, each time you advance the using date, or both. The default is to show the "To Do List" when the using date is advanced. Click on At Startup to add the reminders each time you start the program as well.

You can also alter the background of the Home window if you wish by choosing from the drop-down list. The screen displays in this workbook were prepared with the Windows Default background setting.

You should enter a display font and size in the appropriate fields by choosing from the drop-down lists. These entries control the way your reports appear on your screen. The printing font is controlled by the choices you made in the Printer Setup. You can turn off the Status Bar at the bottom of many windows by clicking on its check box. The status bar explains the role of the field containing the mouse.

All of these settings can be altered at any time while you are using the Simply Accounting program.

Setting System Defaults

Further options for changing the method of accounting and the appearance of the ledger windows are available from the System settings.

Click on the **System tab** at the top of the Settings screen. The System options are displayed:

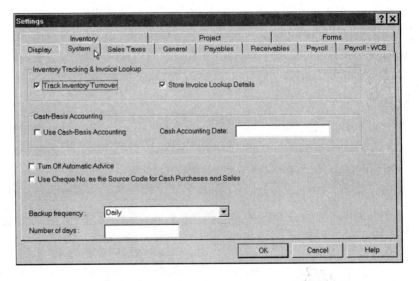

Notes

Inventory Tracking and Invoice Lookup are used in the Meteor Mountain Bike Shop application.

One of the System settings refers to the inventory tracking option. If you want to prepare additional inventory reports, you must turn on the option to Track Inventory Turnover. In some starter files, this option is turned on by default — there is a ✔ in the check box. Clicking on the Track Inventory Turnover option will change the setting. The second option in this group is to Store Invoice Lookup Data, allowing you to display, print and store invoices that have already been posted. To do this, you must first turn on the inventory tracking option. If you try to turn on the lookup option first, Simply Accounting will warn you and then turn on the inventory tracking feature at the same time when you proceed. Again, the option is turned on, or selected when the ✔ appears in the check box. CISV does not need these features because they refer to Sales and Purchases journal invoices, so leave the options turned off. Selecting these options also increases the size of your data files, so you will need additional disk space.

From this same window, you can indicate whether the business is using the cash-basis of accounting instead of the default, accrual-based accounting. To indicate the change, click on the check box and enter the date on which the change is to take effect. Do not change this setting for CISV.

Automatic advice can be turned off by clicking on its check box. This will prevent advisory messages from appearing automatically while you are entering transactions, as, for example, when customers exceed credit limits.

The next option relates to the use of the cheque number as the source code for cash purchases and sales in bank reconciliation. Since CISV uses only the General Ledger, this does not apply. When you are using the Payables and Receivables Ledgers, you should turn on the option.

The final option refers to the frequency with which you back up your data. Since we advance the using date on a weekly basis, we will choose that as the backup frequency as well. Choose Weekly from the drop-down list for the Backup frequency field. If you wish, you can choose a specific number of days instead as the interval between backups by typing the number in the Number of days field.

Setting General Defaults

To change the settings for the General Ledger for CISV,

Click on the **General tab** from the top of the Settings screen to display the options:

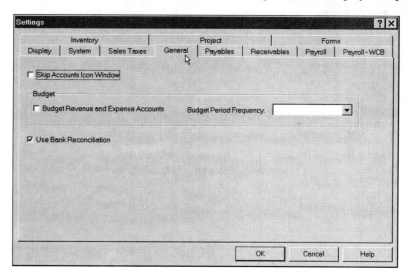

You can Skip the Accounts Icon Window by clicking on the check box. When you select the Home window Accounts icon with this option turned on, account information for the first account will be displayed instead of the list of accounts.

If you want the Simply Accounting program to prepare budget reports, click on *Budget Revenue and Expense Accounts* and choose the budget period from the drop-down list. Each revenue and expense account information window will include a *Budget this Account* check box. Click on this box and then enter the budget amounts for the account to include the account automatically in budget reports.

If you want to use Simply Accounting to reconcile your bank statements, you must activate the option from this screen by clicking on Use Bank Reconciliation. This provides access to the setup and use of this feature. When the option is turned on, a

Notes

The cash basis of accounting records revenues and expenses on the date the money is actually received or paid out. In the accrual method, revenues and expenses are recorded on the date of the sale or purchase, taking into account the matching principal. All the applications in this workbook use the accrual basis.

Notes
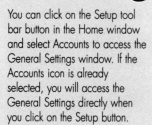

You can click on the Setup tool bar button in the Home window and select Accounts to access the General Settings window. If the Accounts icon is already selected, you will access the General Settings directly when you click on the Setup button.

Warning!

Do not choose to skip the Accounts Icon Window before completing the company setup because you need to see which accounts you have already created.

Bank Reconciliation icon appears under the General Journal icon in the Home window. CISV is not using the budgeting or bank reconciliation features.

Click on Use Bank Reconciliation to remove the ✔ and turn off the feature. Simply Accounting will display the following warning:

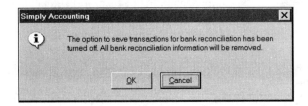

Click on OK to continue.

You can turn on both of these features at any time if you need them.

Since the other ledgers are not used by CISV, you do not need to change any of their settings. You may choose to hide their Home window icons from the Display options.

Click on OK to leave the Settings dialogue box and return to the Home window. Notice that the Bank Reconciliation journal icon has been removed.

You are now ready to make the necessary changes in the General Ledger.

Preparing the Ledgers

The third stage in setting up an accounting system involves preparing each ledger for operation. For CISV, this important stage involves the following steps:

1. organizing all accounting reports and records (this step has already been completed for you)
2. modifying some existing accounts (you will not need to delete any accounts for CISV)
3. creating new accounts
4. entering historical startup information.

Defining the Skeleton Starter Files

When you created the company files for CISV in stage one, Creating Company Files (page 136), a list of preset startup accounts was provided. You can find a complete list of these accounts in Form SKL-1 and the print-out requested earlier.

Form SKL-1 shows that accounts are organized by section, including Assets, Liabilities, Equity, Revenue and Expense. The form also shows the account type, such as Heading (H), Subtotal (S), Total (T), Left Column (L), Right Column (R) and Current Earnings (X). Account type is a method of classifying and organizing accounts within a section or subsection of a report.

Form SKL-1 also provides the Initial Account Number for each account on the list. The accounts are numbered as follows:

- 1000 - 1999   Assets
- 2000 - 2999   Liabilities
- 3000 - 3999   Equity
- 4000 - 4999   Revenue
- 5000 - 5999   Expense

The Chart of Accounts for CISV follows these sectional boundaries.

SKELETON ACCOUNTS - MAINTENANCE

Account Title [Initial]	SECTION	TYPE	Initial Account Number	CODE	Account Title [New]	TYPE	New Account Number
CURRENT ASSETS	A	H	1000	*			
Bank	A	R	1020	M	Cash in Bank - Village	L	1020
Accounts Receivable	A	R	1200	M	Arts & Crafts Supplies	R	1200
TOTAL CURRENT ASSETS	A	T	1390	*			
CURRENT LIABILITIES	L	H	2000	*			
Accounts Payable	L	R	2200	M	A/P - Designs U Wear	R	2200
TOTAL CURRENT LIABILITIES	L	T	2690	*			
EARNINGS	E	H	3000	M	CISV EQUITY	H	3000
Retained Earnings	E	R	3560	M	Surplus Funds	R	3560
Current Earnings	E	X	3600	M	Net Income	X	3600
TOTAL EARNINGS	E	T	3690	M	TOTAL CISV EQUITY	T	3690
REVENUE	R	H	4000	*			
General Revenue	R	R	4020	M	Revenue from Bingo	R	4020
TOTAL REVENUE	R	T	4390	*			
EXPENSES	X	H	5000	M	OPERATING & ADMIN EXPENSES	H	5000
General Expense	X	R	5020	M	Caretaking Expense	R	5020
TOTAL EXPENSES	X	T	5390	M	TOTAL OPERATING & ADMIN EXPENSES	T	5440

SECTION:
A = ASSETS
L = LIABILTIES
E = EQUITY
R = REVENUE
X = EXPENSE

TYPE:
H = Heading
R = Right
L = Left
S = Subtotal
X = Current Earnings
T = Total

CODE:
R = Remove
M = Modify
* = no change

The Format of Financial Statements

When setting up the complete Chart of Accounts for CISV, it is important that you understand the composition and format of financial statements that Simply Accounting will accept.

The Balance Sheet is organized and divided into three sections, each with headings: **Assets**, **Liabilities** and **Equity**. The Income Statement is divided into two sections, each with headings: **Revenue** and **Expense**.

Each section of the financial statements can be further subdivided into blocks. Assets can be divided into blocks such as **CURRENT ASSETS**, **INVENTORY ASSETS** and **PLANT AND EQUIPMENT**. Liabilities can be divided into blocks titled **CURRENT LIABILITIES** and **LONG TERM DEBT**. Equity, Revenue and Expense sections can also be divided.

Simply Accounting requires that all accounts, including block headings, subtotals and block totals, be assigned numbers. This is quite different from a manual accounting system, in which numbers are assigned only to postable accounts. Predefined section headings and section totals (e.g., ASSETS, TOTAL ASSETS and LIABILITIES), however, are not assigned numbers by the program.

Financial Statement Blocks

The following are the Simply Accounting rules concerning financial statement **blocks**:

1. Each block must contain a **block heading (H)**, which will be printed in boldface type. A heading is not considered a postable account, cannot be debited or credited through transaction entries, and cannot have an amount assigned to it.

2. Each block must contain at least one, and possibly more, **postable accounts**. Postable accounts are those that can be debited or credited through journal transaction entries. Postable accounts may have an opening balance.

3. Postable accounts can appear in the **left (L)** or the **right (R)** column.

4. Postable accounts in the left column must be followed by a **subtotal (S)** account. A subtotal is not a postable account and cannot be given an opening balance. The program automatically calculates a subtotal by adding all preceding Left postable account balances that follow the last Right, Subtotal or Heading account. Subtotal balances always appear in the right column. For example, in the previous applications, *GST Charged on Sales* and *GST Paid on Purchases* are Left accounts followed by the Subtotal *GST Owing (Refund)*.

5. Each block must contain a **block total (T)**. All accounts in the right column, both postable and subtotal accounts, are added together to form the block total. A block total is not a postable account. The program automatically calculates it and prints it in boldface type.

ORGANIZATION: BALANCE SHEET ACCOUNTS

ASSETS - [section heading]

TYPE	Account Description	Amount	Amount
H	**CURRENT ASSETS**		
L	Cash in Bank - Village	XXX	
L	Cash on Hand	XXX	
S	Total Cash		XXX
R	Arts & Crafts Supplies		XXX
R	Food Supplies		XXX
	-		
	-		
	-		
T	**TOTAL CURRENT ASSETS**		**XXX**
		Left	Right

TYPE	Account Description	Amount	Amount
H	**EQUIPMENT**		
R	Computer		XXX
R	Fax/Answering Machine		XXX
	-		
	-		
	-		
T	**TOTAL EQUIPMENT**		**XXX**
		Left	Right

Account Description	Amount	Amount
	Left	Right

TOTAL ASSETS - [section total]

LIABILITIES - [section heading]

TYPE	Account Description	Amount	Amount
H	**CURRENT LIABILITIES**		
R	A/P - Designs U Wear		XXX
R	A/P - Quiq Kopy		XXX
	-		
	-		
	-		
T	**TOTAL CURRENT LIABILITIES**		**XXX**
		Left	Right

Account Description	Amount	Amount
	Left	Right

TOTAL LIABILITIES - [section total]

EQUITY - [section heading]

TYPE	Account Description	Amount	Amount
H	**CISV EQUITY**		
R	Surplus Funds		XXX
X	Net Income		XXX
	-		
	-		
	-		
T	**TOTAL CISV EQUITY**		**XXX**
		Left	Right

TOTAL EQUITY - [section total]
LIABILITIES AND EQUITY

ORGANIZATION: INCOME STATEMENT ACCOUNTS

REVENUE - [section heading]

	Account Description	Amount	Amount
T Y P E			
H	**REVENUE**		
R	Revenue from Bingo		XXX
R	Interest Revenue		XXX
		. . .	
		Left	Right
T	**TOTAL REVENUE**		XXX

TOTAL REVENUE - [section total]

EXPENSE - [section heading]

	Account Description	Amount	Amount
T Y P E			
H	**OPERATING & ADMIN EXPENSES**		
R	Caretaking Expense		XXX
R	Cost of T-shirts		XXX
		. . .	
		Left	Right
T	**TOTAL OPERATING & ADMIN EXPENSES**		XXX

	Account Description	Amount	Amount
H	**PROGRAM & ACTIVITY EXPENSES**		
R	Crafts Supplies Used		XXX
R	Entertainment Expenses		XXX
		. . .	
		Left	Right
T	**TOTAL PROGRAM & ACTIVITY EXPENSES**		XXX

TOTAL EXPENSE - [section total]
NET INCOME

Financial Statement Sections

The following are the Simply Accounting rules concerning financial statement **sections**:

1. Each of the financial statement sections described above must have a **total**. A section total is the total of the individual block totals within that section. The five section totals are:

    TOTAL ASSETS
    TOTAL LIABILITIES
    TOTAL EQUITY
    TOTAL REVENUE
    TOTAL EXPENSE

    The user cannot change the titles of the section totals; the program will automatically print them in the financial statement reports.

2. The Liabilities and Equity section totals are also automatically added together. **LIABILITIES AND EQUITY** is the sum of TOTAL LIABILITIES and TOTAL EQUITY. The user cannot change this title.

3. In the Income Statement, the difference between TOTAL REVENUE and TOTAL EXPENSE is automatically calculated as **NET INCOME** and listed under TOTAL EXPENSE. The user cannot change this title.

The Current Earnings (X) Account

There are two integration accounts for the General Ledger — *Retained Earnings* and *Current Earnings*. Both accounts appear under the EQUITY section in the Balance Sheet. You do not need to change the integration settings for these accounts. Their titles will be modified later (see Editing Accounts in the General Ledger, page 154).

It is easy to identify the *Current Earnings* account because it is the only account in the Chart of Accounts whose type is X. This account is calculated as follows:

    Current Earnings = Total Revenue - Total Expense

The *Current Earnings* account is not a postable account and only appears in the right column of the block. It cannot be removed, but its title can be modified. The *Current Earnings* account is updated from any transactions that change revenue and expense accounts. At the end of the fiscal period when closing routines are performed, the balance of this account is added to the *Retained Earnings* account (or a renamed account for *Retained Earnings*) and then it is reset to zero.

For CISV, a charitable organization, the *Retained Earnings* account will be renamed *Surplus Funds*. The *Current Earnings* account will be renamed *Net Income*.

Suppressing Zero Account Balances

At certain times, it may be appropriate to print an account with a zero balance, although usually zero balance accounts do not need to be printed. The user has the option in Simply Accounting to suppress the printing of accounts with zero balances. You may select this option in the General Ledger.

Preparing the General Ledger

Compare the Skeleton Chart of Accounts you have printed out with the CISV Chart of Accounts, Balance Sheet and Income Statement provided in this application. You will see that some of the accounts are the same, and some of the accounts you need are not yet in the program. You have to customize the accounts specifically for CISV.

Changing Skeleton Accounts

The first step, that of identifying the changes needed in the Skeleton preset accounts to match the accounts needed for CISV, is a very important one. Form SKL-1, on page 147, shows the changes that must be made to these preset accounts. On Form SKL-1, the following steps have been done for you:

1. The starter accounts provided by the program that require no changes have been marked with an asterisk (*). The account title, the initial account number and the account type are the same as those given in the financial statements. Those accounts not requiring changes follow:

CURRENT ASSETS	1000	Type H
TOTAL CURRENT ASSETS	1390	Type T
CURRENT LIABILITIES	2000	Type H
TOTAL CURRENT LIABILITIES	2690	Type T
REVENUE	4000	Type H
TOTAL REVENUE	4390	Type T

2. The accounts for which the account title and/or the account type need to be changed have been modified (M) on Form SKL-1. These include:

Bank	1020	Type R
Accounts Receivable	1200	Type R
Accounts Payable	2200	Type R
EARNINGS	3000	Type H
Retained Earnings	3560	Type R
Current Earnings	3600	Type X
TOTAL EARNINGS	3690	Type T
General Revenue	4020	Type R
EXPENSES	5000	Type H
General Expense	5020	Type R

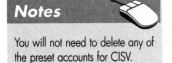

Notes

You will not need to delete any of the preset accounts for CISV.

3. The following account requires changes in both the account title and the number. It has been modified on form SKL-1:

TOTAL EXPENSES	5390	Type T

Creating New Accounts

After identifying the modifications that must be made to the Skeleton accounts, the next step is to identify the accounts that you will need to create or add to the preset accounts. Again, you need to refer to the company Chart of Accounts, Balance Sheet, and Income Statement in this application to complete this step.

The Chart of Accounts Maintenance input form (Form CHA-1) that follows shows the accounts that you will need to create. The chart includes account titles, account numbers, account types and the option to suppress printing zero balances. It lists both postable and non-postable accounts (subtotals, block headings and block totals).

CHART OF ACCOUNTS MAINTENANCE

Code: M = Modify   Type: H = Heading   S = Subtotal   Suppress: Y = Yes
      C = Create   R = Right   X = Current Earnings   N = No
      R = Remove   L = Left   T = Total

Code	Account Title (Maximum 26 Characters)	Account No.	Type	Suppress
C	Cash on Hand	1100	L	N
C	Total Cash	1150	S	–
C	Food Supplies	1300	R	Y
C	Office Supplies	1320	R	Y
C	Village T-shirts for Sale	1360	R	Y
C	EQUIPMENT	1400	H	–
C	Computer	1450	R	N
C	Fax/Answering Machine	1500	R	N
C	TOTAL EQUIPMENT	1590	T	–
C	A/P - Quiq Kopy	2300	R	Y
C	A/P - Sleeptight Cots	2350	R	Y
C	A/P - Travel in Comfort	2400	R	Y
C	GST Paid on Purchases	2670	R	Y
C	Interest Revenue	4080	R	N
C	Other Revenue	4120	R	N
C	Cost of T-shirts	5050	R	Y
C	Cots & Linen Rental	5080	R	Y
C	Food Expense	5180	R	Y
C	General Expense	5200	R	Y
C	Office Supplies Used	5250	R	Y
C	Non-refundable GST	5280	R	Y
C	Postage Expense	5300	R	Y
C	Printing & Copying	5320	R	Y
C	Publicity	5350	R	Y
C	Telephone Expense	5400	R	Y
C	Wages - Cook	5420	R	Y
C	PROGRAM & ACTIVITY EXPENSES	5450	H	–
C	Crafts Supplies Used	5500	R	Y
C	Entertainment Expenses	5550	R	Y
C	Transportation	5600	R	Y
C	TOTAL PROGRAM & ACTIVITY EXPENSES	5690	T	–

You are now ready to enter the account information into the CISV files.

Entering General Ledger Information

Double click on the **Accounts icon** under the General heading in the Home window to open the main Accounts window.

The preset accounts are displayed in Icon form. In this form or view, the icons can be rearranged by dragging so that frequently used accounts appear on top for easier access. New accounts are added at the end but can be moved to the desired location. The same option of moving accounts is available for the Small Icon view. In small icon viewing mode, more accounts can be displayed at the same time. However, for entering new accounts and editing a large number of existing accounts, it is easier to work with the accounts in lists displayed in numeric order. New accounts are inserted in their correct numeric order, providing a better view of the progress during the setup phase. To change the way accounts are displayed,

Choose Name from the pull-down menu under **View** as shown (or click on the Display by name tool bar button):

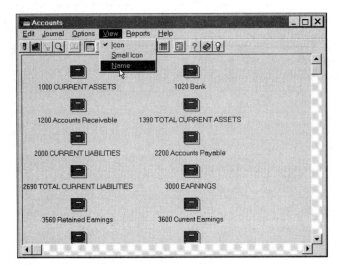

Editing Accounts in the General Ledger

We will change the first account that requires editing, *1020 Bank*.

Open the **Accounts window** if it is not already open. The preset accounts are displayed as shown:

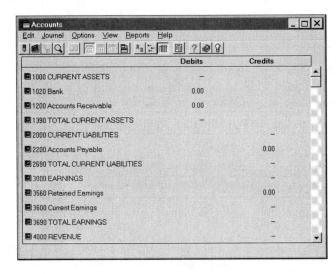

Click on the **icon** or **name of the account 1020 Bank** to highlight or select it.

Notes

Click on ☐ to enlarge the Accounts window to fill up the entire screen. This will allow you to display more accounts and keep the Accounts window in view in the background while you are creating or editing accounts. Return to the normal size window by clicking on ☐ .

Notes

If you wish, you can enter account balances at the same time as you are editing and creating the accounts.

Notes

• Alternatively, you can double click on the account's icon or name to open the account.
• If you choose to skip the Accounts icon window in the General Settings, you will see the General Ledger window for CURRENT ASSETS, the first account, when you double click on the Accounts icon. You can use the scroll arrow or choose Find from the pull-down menu under Edit to find the Bank account.

Click on the **Edit button** on the Accounts window tool bar or **choose** Edit from the pull-down menu under **Edit** to display the account information as shown.

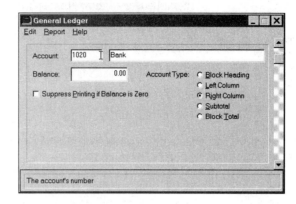

The account window is similar to the new account window you are familiar with from adding new accounts. The balance field, for entering the account balance at the date of conversion can be edited. If you have turned on the Bank Reconciliation feature, Bank Reconciliation check box is also added for asset accounts as shown here:

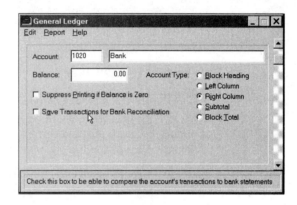

For the bank account, the account number is correct. The balance of this account should always be displayed, so do not change the suppress printing option.

Press ⌖tab⌖ to advance to the name of the account and highlight it.

Type   `Cash in Bank - Village`

The account balance will be added in the next step, Entering Historical Account Balances.

Click on Left Column to change the account type to Left. The two cash accounts together will be subtotalled.

Click on the **down scroll arrow** in the lower right corner of the account ledger window to advance to the next account.

Edit the remaining accounts as required. You may choose to print zero balances or to suppress them.

Creating New Accounts in the General Ledger

You are now ready to enter the information for the first new account, *Cash on Hand*, using Form CHA-1 as your reference. The following keystrokes will enter the account title, number, type and option not to suppress printing a zero balance.

With the main Accounts window open or any individual General Ledger account information window displayed,

Notes

If you have turned on the Bank Reconciliation feature, your General Ledger form will show the option to Save Transactions for Bank Reconciliation. Leave this option turned off. You can turn it on after you have a bank statement and completed transactions, i.e., when you are ready to complete the first reconciliation statement.

Notes

You can close the bank account window to return to the main Accounts window and select the next account to be changed; choose Edit from the pull-down menu under Edit to open the account information window.

Notes

You will also reach a new account form if you continue to scroll down past the last account, TOTAL PROGRAM & ACTIVITY EXPENSES.

Click on the **Create button** on the Accounts window tool bar or **choose Create** from the pull-down menu under **Edit** (in the Accounts window or in the General Ledger window) to display the new account information window shown below:

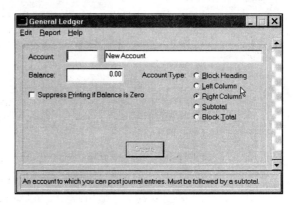

We will create the first account that is not in the preset list, *Cash on Hand*. The cursor is in the Account number field.

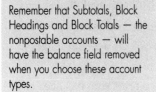
Type   1100

Press (tab) to advance the the account title field.

Type   Cash on Hand

Click on Left Column to change the account type to Left.

Leave the option to suppress printing turned off.

Check your work. Make any necessary corrections by returning to the incorrect field, pressing (tab), typing the correct information, and pressing (tab) if necessary. When the information has been entered correctly, save your work.

Click on Create to save the new account and to advance to another new account information window. Enter the remaining accounts.

Insert the remaining accounts on your Form CHA-1.

Display or print the Chart of Accounts to check the accuracy of your work. If you find mistakes, edit the account information as described above in the section Editing Accounts in the General Ledger.

When you have entered the last account or you want to end your session,

Close the General Ledger account information window.

Close the main Accounts window to return to the Home window.

Entering Historical Account Balances

You are now ready to enter the balance for all postable (type R or L) accounts. The opening historical account balances for CISV can be found in the Trial Balance.

Open the account information form for account *1020 Cash in Bank - Village*.

Press (tab) to advance to the Balance field and highlight it.

Type   49550

Press   (tab)

Click on the **down scroll arrow** to advance to the next ledger account window.

Enter the balances for the remaining accounts.

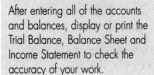

Making the General Ledger Ready
Making a Backup Copy

By having a backup copy of your files before setting the ledgers to ready, you will be able to make changes easily if you find an error, without having to repeat the entire setup from scratch. After the ledger is ready, the program will not permit you to make certain changes, e.g., account balances and fiscal dates. You cannot change the account number for an account after making a journal entry to the account.

You should save your not ready files under a different folder name so that they will be easily identified (e.g., NRCISV) or use a different disk and label it "Data Disk — Not Ready Files."

Choose Save As from the pull-down menu under **File**.

Create a new folder for your backup file. Change the name of the folder. Open the new folder and enter the file name in the File name field.

Click on Save

Close the backup copy of your file and put the disk in a safe place.

Setting the General Ledger to Ready

Open your working copy of the CISV file again. You should be in the Home window.

Click on the **Accounts icon** to select it. If the Accounts icon is not selected, the Set General Ready menu option is not available.

Choose Set General Ready from the pull-down menu under **Setup**.

The following caution appears:

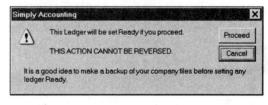

If you have not made a backup copy yet, click on Cancel and do so before proceeding. If you have made your backup copy, you should continue.

Click on Proceed

Notice that the General Journal icon no longer has the No Entry symbol on it.

You can now exit the program or continue by entering the source documents for the month of July. Remember to advance the Using Date.

SOURCE DOCUMENTS

USING DATE — July 7

☐ Purchase Invoice #QK-2252
Dated July 2/99
From Quiq Kopy, $162 (including PST) for photocopying of village participant packages, plus $10.50 GST. Invoice total $172.50. Terms: net 15 days.

☐ Purchase Invoice #BC-10116
Dated July 2/99
From Bell Canada, $324 (including PST) for rental of cellular telephone
equipment, plus $21 GST. Invoice total $345. Deposit required and balance due
at end of month or rental period.

☐ Cheque Copy #167
Dated July 2/99
To Bell Canada, $100 deposit on rental of telephone equipment. Reference
invoice #BC-10116.

☐ Memo #1
Dated July 2/99
From Village Director to Treasurer: Give T-shirt to each Village participant. Cost
of T-shirts given out is $500. Reduce T-shirt asset account and increase Cost of
T-shirts expense account.

☐ Purchase Invoice #QK-2299
Dated July 3/99
From Quiq Kopy, $54 (including PST) for photocopying of invitations to Village
Open House, plus $3.50 GST. Invoice total $57.50. Terms: net 15 days.

☐ Cash Purchase Invoice #CP-1
Dated July 4/99
Postage for mailing out Open House invitations to all members, $60 plus $4.20
GST. Invoice total $64.20. Amount paid from Cash on Hand.

☐ Funds Raised Form: #FR-9926
Dated July 5/99
Collected $350 net from weekly Bingo night. Amount deposited in bank (Cash in
Bank - Village).

☐ Cash Purchase Invoice TTC-1
Dated July 5/99
From TTC, $125.00 for bus tickets for transportation to and from Science
Centre. Paid from Cash on Hand.

☐ Cash Purchase Invoice #OSC-662
Dated July 5/99
From Science Centre, $450 for admission of all participants to Science Centre,
plus $31.50 GST. Invoice total $481.50. Paid from Cash on Hand.

☐ Memo #2
Dated July 7/99
From Village Director to Treasurer: Issue cheque #168 for $1 500 to transfer
funds to Cash on Hand for Village food purchases, and for bus and
entertainment expenses for the week.

☐ Cash Purchase Invoice #SF-2168
Dated July 7/99
From SuperFoods, $916 for food for Village participant meals. Paid from Cash on
Hand.

Notes

In most businesses, the Cash on
Hand balance is usually small
and is used only for paying small
amounts. In this application, we
are using the Cash on Hand
account to pay for any purchases
that normally would require cash
payments. In reality, the village
director, or another staff member,
receives cash advances to cover
these costs.

☐ Cash Purchase Invoice TTC-2
Dated July 8/99
From TTC, $118.00 for bus tickets for transportation to down town Toronto.
Paid from Cash on Hand.

☐ Purchase Invoice #TC-10986
Dated July 8/99
From Travel in Comfort, $600 for bus rental for trip to Niagara Falls, plus $42
GST. Invoice total $642.

☐ Cheque Copy #169
Dated July 9/99
To Travel in Comfort, $842 in full payment of account. Reference invoice
#TC-10986 and previous balance owing, $200.

☐ Cash Purchase Invoice #MM-55231
Dated July 9/99
From Niagara Tours Inc., $320 for group rates on Misty Maid tour, plus $22.40
GST. Invoice total $342.40. Paid from Cash on Hand.

☐ Funds Raised Form: #FR-9927
Dated July 11/99
Collected $650 net from weekly Bingo night. Amount deposited in bank
(Village).

☐ Cheque Copy #170
Dated July 12/99
To Sleeptight Cots, $3 050 in full payment of account. Reference Invoice
#SC-606.

☐ Cash Purchase Invoice #CSS-5566
Dated July 14/99
From City Schools, Permits Department, $3 600 for caretaking expenses on
Village site plus $252 GST. Invoice total $3 852. Terms: cash on receipt of
invoice. Paid by cheque #171.

☐ Memo #3
Dated July 14/99
From Village Director to Treasurer: Issue cheque #172 for $1 500 to transfer
funds to Cash on Hand for Village food purchases, and for bus and
entertainment expenses for the week.

☐ Cash Purchase Invoice #SF-3988
Dated July 14/99
From SuperFoods, $885 for food for Village participant meals. Paid from Cash on
Hand.

☐ Cash Purchase Invoice #QAS-4632
Dated July 14/99
From Quarts Arts Supplies, $216 (including PST) for craft supplies plus $14
GST. Invoice total $230. Paid from Cash on Hand.

☐ Cheque Copy #173
Dated July 15/99
To Sophia Waterman, Village cook, $1 500 for wages for two weeks.

☐ Cheque Copy #174
Dated July 15/99
To Quiq Kopy $380, in full payment of account.

☐ Cheque Copy #175
Dated July 15/99
To Designs U Wear $800, in full payment of account.

☐ Purchase Invoice #TC-14913
Dated July 16/99
From Travel in Comfort, $800 for bus rental for trip to Algonquin Park, plus $56 GST. Invoice total $856.

☐ Cheque Copy #176
Dated July 16/99
To Travel in Comfort, $856 in full payment of account. Reference invoice #TC-14913.

☐ Cash Purchase Invoice #AP-988
Dated July 16/99
From Ontario Parks, $70.10 for park admission for Village participants, plus $4.90 GST. Invoice total $75. Paid from Cash on Hand.

☐ Funds Raised Form: FR-9928
Dated July 18/99
Collected $420 net from weekly Bingo night. Amount deposited in bank (Village).

☐ Cash Purchase Invoice TTC-3
Dated July 20/99
From TTC, $130.00 for bus tickets for transportation to beach. Paid from Cash on Hand.

☐ Memo #4
Dated July 21/99
From Village Director to Treasurer: Issue cheque #177 for $1 500 to transfer funds to Cash on Hand for Village food purchases, and for bus and entertainment expenses for the week.

☐ Cash Purchase Invoice #SF-5217
Dated July 21/99
From SuperFoods, $1 022 for food for Village participant meals and Open House hors d'oeuvres. Paid from Cash on Hand.

USING DATE — July 28

☐ Purchase Invoice #QK-5306
Dated July 22/99
From Quiq Kopy, $108 (including PST) for photocopying of visitor handouts for Village Open House, plus $7 GST. Invoice total $115.00. Terms: net 15 days.

☐ Funds Raised Form #FR-9929A
Dated July 22/99
From sale of T-shirts at Open House, $600 revenue received in cash and deposited in bank. The cost of the T-shirts sold was $300. Reduce the Village T-shirts asset account and increase the Cost of T-shirts expense account for the cost of T-shirts sold.

☐ Cash Purchase Invoice #TTC-4
Dated July 25/99
From TTC, $108.00 for bus tickets for transportation to CN Tower. Paid from Cash on Hand.

☐ Cash Purchase Invoice #CNTower
Dated July 25/99
From CN Tours Inc., $420.56 for admissions to CN Tower, plus $29.44 GST. Invoice total $450. Paid from Cash on Hand.

☐ Funds Raised Form: #FR-9929
Dated July 25/99
Collected $530 net from weekly Bingo night. Amount deposited in bank (Village).

☐ Cash Purchase Invoice #CinOd-1
Dated July 26/99
From Cineplex Odeon theatre, $300 for admissions to movie, plus $21 GST. Invoice total $321. Paid from Cash on Hand.

☐ Cheque Copy #178
Dated July 28/99
To Sophia Waterman, Village cook, $1 500 for wages for two weeks.

☐ Cheque Copy #179
Dated July 28/99
To Quiq Kopy $115, in full payment of account. Reference invoice #QK-5306.

☐ Cash Purchase Invoice #Gifts-1
Dated July 28/99
From Gifts For All Occasions, $162.00 (including PST) for honorarium gifts for Village staff, plus $10.50 GST. Invoice total $172.50. Paid from Cash on Hand. Charge to General Expense.

USING DATE — July 31

☐ Purchase Invoice #QK-6732
Dated July 29/99
From Quiq Kopy, $129.60 (including PST) for colour copies of group Village photo to send to all participants, plus $8.40 GST. Invoice total $138. Terms: net 15 days.

☐ Cheque Copy #180
Dated July 31/99
To Quiq Kopy, $138 in full payment of account. Reference invoice #QK-6732.

At the time of writing this book, CISV Canada had chapters in the following cities:

Fredericton, NB
St. Gregoire, QC
Ottawa, ON
Toronto, ON
Waterloo, ON
London, ON
Saskatoon, SK
Calgary, AB
Vancouver, BC
Victoria, BC

If you want more information about CISV, or to locate the Chapter nearest you, you can contact the National Office at
CISV Canada
5 Dunvegan Road
Ottawa
Ontario K1K 3E7

— or the International Office at
CISV International
MEA House,
Ellison Place
Newcastle Upon Tyne
NE1 8X5 England

Notes

Create new accounts:
5010 Bank Charges
1180 GST Refund Receivable

☐ Cash Purchase Invoice #CP-2
Dated July 31/99
From Canada Post, $40 for postage to mail photographs, plus $2.80 GST. Invoice total $42.80. Paid from Cash on Hand.

☐ Memo #5
Dated July 31/99
From Village Director to Treasurer: A small quantity of supplies were left at the end of the Village. Leftover food supplies have been donated to food banks; craft and office supplies have been donated to the junior branch. Reduce the following asset accounts to zero and increase the corresponding expense accounts to reflect supplies used during village:
Reduce Food Supplies and increase Food Expense by $5 123.
Reduce Arts & Crafts Supplies and increase Crafts Supplies Used by $716.
Reduce Office Supplies and increase Office Supplies Used by $400.

☐ Memo #6
Dated July 31/99
From Village Director to Treasurer: Deposit $16.60 balance of Cash on Hand to bank.

☐ Cheque Copy #181
Dated July 31/99
To Bell Canada, $245, in full payment of account. Reference invoice #BC-10116 and cheque #167.

☐ Bank Credit Memo #CT-53197
Dated July 31/99
From Canada Trust, $63 interest paid on bank account.

☐ Bank Debit Memo #CT-3881
Dated July 31/99
From Canada Trust, $21.50 in bank charges for cheques and statement preparation.

☐ Memo #7
Dated July 31/99
From Treasurer: Apply for GST rebate, record 50% of GST Paid on Purchases as GST Refund Receivable, the other 50% as Non-refundable GST expense.

CASE PROBLEMS

1. A friend who had extensive experience using Simply Accounting advised the Treasurer for CISV to number the accounts with gaps between successive accounts, e.g. 1000, 1020, 1040, 1060, etc.

   a. Explain why this may be helpful.
   b. How is this different from a manual accounting system?

2. Some time later, two new accounts were needed to represent more accurately the list of expenses. Unfortunately, in order to maintain the correct sequence of accounts and to have the correct subtotal, the new accounts had to be placed between the accounts that were presently numbered 5050 and 5051. Discuss ways that you could resolve this problem?

CHAPTER SEVEN

OBJECTIVES

Upon completion of this chapter, you will be able to:

- *open* the Payroll Journal
- *enter* employee-related payroll transactions
- *understand* automatic payroll deductions
- *post* payroll transactions
- *understand* Payroll Ledger integration accounts
- *edit* and *review* payroll transactions
- *adjust* Payroll Journal invoices that have been posted
- *use* To Do Lists to make journal entries
- *display* and *print* payroll reports

COMPANY INFORMATION

Company Profile

Carnival Catering, owned and managed by Susie Sardinha in the city of Victoria, British Columbia, provides a variety of menus for all occasions. Sardinha's excellent international cuisine appeals to people from different cultures so that her reputation and business have grown steadily. She now handles weddings, anniversaries, retirements, funerals, birthdays, business meetings, conferences or any other special event for any size group.

Sardinha started a catering business alone two years ago, occasionally bringing in assistants when needed. Recently she has consistently been getting larger contracts and has bought out an old catering business from a friend who wanted to retire. She took over some of the old assets, purchased additional equipment including a computer and hired a full-time staff to work with her.

Sardinha manages the business but also takes an active role in the day-to-day work. She actively seeks out new business and negotiates the contracts with her clients, basing the price on the size of the group, the complexity of the menu and the number of hours involved in the actual event. She then works out the menu details with the chef, gets final client approval and obtains an advance from the client. The advance is used to purchase food for the special event. The chefs then purchase all the food required from the city market, butcher shops, delicatessen and supermarkets. With some of these stores, Sardinha has arranged for weekly deliveries. The two full-time cooks, under the supervision of the chef, complete most of the food preparation. Three waiters make up the rest of the staff, setting up the tables at the catered event, serving food and cleaning up afterwards.

Sardinha's business and food sciences education have prepared her not only for the menu planning part of her job, but also for the business management aspects. Her solid grasp of accounting principles has enabled her to set up all of her accounting records in Simply Accounting using the following:

- Chart of Accounts
- Post-Closing Trial Balance
- Vendor Information
- Customer Information
- Employee Information
- Employee Profiles and TD1 Information
- Accounting Procedures

**CARNIVAL CATERING
CHART OF ACCOUNTS**

ASSETS
1080 Cash
1200 Accounts Receivable
1240 Advances Receivable
1260 Food Inventory
1280 Liquor & Wine Inventory
1300 Catering Supplies
1360 Appliances & Equipment
1380 Chairs & Tables
1400 Computers & Peripherals
1420 Cutlery & Dishes
1460 Delivery Truck
1480 Shop

LIABILITIES
2100 Bank Loan
2200 Accounts Payable
2300 Vacation Payable
2310 EI Payable
2320 CPP Payable
2330 Income Tax Payable
2400 Medical Payable
2410 RRS-Plan Payable
2460 WCB Payable
2640 PST Payable
2650 GST Charged on Services
2670 GST Paid on Purchases
2940 Mortgage Payable

EQUITY
3560 S. Sardinha, Capital
3580 S. Sardinha, Drawings
3600 Net Income

REVENUE
4020 Revenue from Catering

EXPENSES
5020 Advertising & Promotion
5040 Bank Charges
5060 Hydro Expense
5080 Telephone Expense
5100 Truck Expenses
5200 Food Used for Catering
5220 Liquor Used for Catering
5240 Catering Supplies Used
5300 Wages
5310 EI Expense
5320 CPP Expense
5330 WCB Expense

CARNIVAL CATERING
POST-CLOSING TRIAL BALANCE

June 1, 1999

1080 Cash	$ 30 000.00	
1200 Accounts Receivable		$ 9 000.00
1260 Food Inventory	1 500.00	
1280 Liquor & Wine Inventory	5 000.00	
1300 Catering Supplies	200.00	
1360 Appliances & Equipment	24 000.00	
1380 Chairs & Tables	2 500.00	
1400 Computers & Peripherals	4 000.00	
1420 Cutlery & Dishes	4 000.00	
1460 Delivery Truck	30 000.00	
1480 Shop	250 000.00	
2100 Bank Loan		25 000.00
2200 Accounts Payable		6 450.00
2670 GST Paid on Purchases	450.00	
2940 Mortgage Payable		225 000.00
3560 S. Sardinha, Capital		86 200.00
	$351 650.00	$351 650.00

CARNIVAL CATERING
VENDOR INFORMATION

Vendor Name (Contact)	Address Phone & Fax	Invoice Terms	Invoice Date	Invoice/ Cheque No.	Outstanding Balance
Caterers Suppliers (Sue Plyers)	62 Providence Ave. Victoria, BC V9U 8H1 Tel: (250) 883-7735 Fax: (250) 883-1922	Net 30			
Coastal Fish Wholesalers (Marina Pesce)	21 Salmon Ave. Victoria, BC V8T 2R4 Tel: (250) 888-7163 Fax: (250) 888-7299	Net 15			
Commercial Cutlery Ltd. (Mac LeCouteau)	88 Ontario St. Vancouver, BC V7U 1A2 Tel: (604) 266-9013 Fax: (604) 266-9001	Net 30	May 28/99	CC-4321	$1 150.00
David's Fresh Produce (David Appleton)	44 Pears Ave. Victoria, BC V8M 6M1 Tel: (250) 892-7844 Fax: (250) 892-5611	Net 15			
European Smoked Meats (Antoine Jambon)	6 Alpine Court Victoria, BC V8B 2T7 Tel: (250) 891-7199 Fax: (250) 891-5191	Net 15			

Vendor Name (Contact)	Address Phone & Fax	Invoice Terms	Invoice Date	Invoice/ Cheque No.	Outstanding Balance
House of Spirits (Al Cool)	91 Moonshine Lane Victoria, BC V8T 5R2 Tel: (250) 896-6639 Fax: (250) 896-0111	(Payment with Purchase)			
Hydro BC (Manny Lighter)	67 Energy Rd. Victoria, BC V8R 1H4 Tel: (250) 896-2345	Net 1 (Payment on receipt of invoice)			
Ideal Equipment (Ivory Range)	181 Brunswick Rd. Vancouver, BC V7U 2D4 Tel: (604) 775-6370 Fax: (604) 775-6666	Net 30	May 29/99	IE-6374	$5 300.00
Pacific Telephone (M.A. Bell)	55 Signal Rd. Victoria, BC V9P 3K9 Tel: (250) 895-5617 Fax: (250) 895-5600	Net 1			
Reliable Food Supplies (Thon Visser)	366 Orange Grove Victoria, BC V8S 4L5 Tel: (250) 889-7190 Fax: (250) 889-7199	Net 15			
Valu Petroleum (Val Petro)	79 Gasoline Alley Victoria, BC V8D 7B2 Tel: (250) 893-5286 Fax: (250) 893-5211	Net 1			

Grand Total $6 450.00

CARNIVAL CATERING
CUSTOMER INFORMATION

Customer Name (Contact)	Address Phone & Fax	Invoice Terms (Credit Limit)	Invoice Date	Invoice/ Cheque No.	Advances Paid Balance
Coastal Corporation (Emery Lighthouse)	33 Seaside Cr. Victoria, BC V9X 2E7 Tel: (250) 882-8166 Fax: (250) 882-6210	Net 1	June 1/99	CR-1	–$3 000.00
Ministry of Environment (Vicki Greene)	BC Government 660 Parliament Rd. Victoria, BC V9B 6R6 Tel: (250) 884-7182 Fax: (250) 884-7110	Net 1	June 1/99	CR-2	–$6 000.00
Victoria Ladies Bridge Club (Victoria Bridge)	54 Gambler Rd. Victoria, BC V8C 7E3 Tel: (250) 896-8610 Fax: (250) 896-8011	Net 30 ($3 000)			Grand Total –$9 000.00

CARNIVAL CATERING
EMPLOYEE INFORMATION SHEET

Employee Name Position Social Insurance Number	Susie Sardinha Owner/Exec chef 419 910 983	Louie Perch Chef 477 732 750	Peter Terkee Sous Chef 469 412 400	Sera Suflay Cook 571 628 649
Address & Telephone	31 Bawssey Cres. Victoria, BC V8R 1S4 (250) 882-7100	711 Bass Rd. Victoria, BC V7P 2R1 (250) 883-6108	60 Fowler Blvd. Victoria, BC V9Z 3M2 (250) 895-8262	53 Omlet St. Victoria, BC V8M 4B3 (250) 892-6173
Date of Birth (dd-mm-yy)	14-6-64	21-2-58	25-12-66	1-10-70
Tax Exemption (TD-1)				
Basic Personal	$6 456	$6 456	$6 456	$6 456
Spouse		$5 380	$5 380	$5 380
Children under 18		2	1	
Disability				$5 816
Education & Tuition				
Other				
Total Exemptions	$6 456	$11 836	$11 836	$17 652
Employee Earnings				
Regular Wage Rate				$18.00/hour
Overtime Wage Rate				$27.00/hour
Regular Salary	$2 000.00/month	$4 000.00/month	$3 200.00/month	
Commission		1% catering revenue	1/2% catering revenue	
Vacation		4 weeks	3 weeks	6%
Employee Deductions				
Medical/pay period	$75.00	$75.00	$75.00	$18.75
RRSP/pay period	$200.00	$200.00	$200.00	
Additional Income Tax/pay period		$80.00		
EI, CPP and Income Tax	calculations built into the Simply Accounting program			

Employee Name	Ben Branjil	Sylvia Mellon	Adrian Poppi	Aziz Atta
Position	Cook	Waitress	Waiter	Waiter
Social Insurance Number	721 971 634	618 932 635	552 846 820	492 746 542
Address & Telephone	47 Aubergine St. Victoria, BC V7N 2L2 (250) 889-6291	9 Orchardview Ct. Victoria, BC V8K 4K2 (250) 893-7595	50 Seed St. #322 Victoria, BC V9B 4C1 (250) 881-8138	63 Peppertree Ave. Victoria, BC V8U 1X3 (250) 888-6353
Date of Birth (dd-mm-yy)	31-7-69	15-8-75	3-11-72	6-8-62
Tax Exemption (TD-1)				
Basic Personal	$6 456	$6 456	$6 456	$6 456
Spouse				
Children under 18				
Disability				
Education & Tuition				
Other				
Total Exemptions	$6 456	$6 456	$6 456	$6 456
Employee Earnings				
Regular Wage Rate	$18.00	$10.00	$10.00	$10.00
Overtime Wage Rate	$27.00	$15.00	$15.00	$15.00
Regular Salary				
Commission				
Vacation	6%	4%	4%	4%
Employee Deductions				
Medical/pay period	$18.75	$20.00	$20.00	$20.00
RRSP/pay period	$25.00			
Additional Income Tax/pay period		$20.00		
EI, CPP and Income Tax	calculations built into the Simply Accounting program			

Employee Profiles and TD1 Information

Susie Sardinha is the owner and executive chef for Carnival Catering. She negotiates all contracts with clients, plans menus, hires the staff and performs general management duties. In addition to the company's profits, she draws a monthly salary of $2 000. She is married but claims a single tax exemption. Through the payroll, she pays her medical premiums and makes regular RRSP contributions. As an owner, she is not eligible for EI and does not make EI contributions.

Louie Perch, the chef at Carnival Catering, works closely with the owner, planning and writing menus and scheduling the work of other staff for all events. He is also responsible for food purchases. Perch receives $4 000 per month in salary plus a 1 percent commission on the revenue from catering. He is entitled to take four weeks vacation each year. Perch is married and fully supports his wife and two children who have no income, and therefore he pays the family rate for medical premiums. In addition, he has elected to make RRSP contributions through payroll deductions and to pay additional income tax each month to offset the tax on his investment income.

Peter Terkee, the sous chef, assists the chef in all aspects of the work, carries out his orders with respect to food preparation and supervises the cooks. His monthly salary of $3 200 is supplemented by a commission of 0.5 percent of the revenue from catering. His vacation entitlement is three weeks per year. Terkee fully supports his wife and two children who have no income. His regular pay deductions include the family rate for medical insurance premiums and RRSP contributions.

Sera Suflay works as one of the two cooks for Carnival Catering. Her primary responsibility is to prepare food for the catered events. She is paid weekly at the rate of $18 per hour for regular work and $27 per hour for overtime work. Her vacation pay is calculated at 6 percent. She is the sole supporter for her infirm brother for whom she claims the spousal equivalent and disability tax credit amounts. Her payroll deductions include the family rate for medical premiums.

Ben Branjil, the second cook at Carnival Catering, has the same job responsibilities and wages as Sera Suflay. He is married but his wife earns a full-time salary. He pays the married medical insurance premium for his family and makes weekly RRSP contributions through payroll.

Sylvia Mellon works as one of three waiters for Carnival Catering. Her job is to help set up, serve food, and clean up at all catered events. She is paid bi-weekly at $10 per hour for regular work and $15 for overtime work, and vacation pay is calculated at 4 percent. She is single and self-supporting and pays the single rate for medical premiums. She also makes regular RRSP contributions through payroll and has elected to pay additional income tax.

Adrian Poppi, the second waiter, shares the job with Sylvia Mellon and Aziz Atta. His wages and vacation pay are also the same as Mellon's. He is single and self-supporting and pays the single rate for medical premiums.

Aziz Atta is the third waiter and has the same job responsibilities and wages as Sylvia Mellon and Adrian Poppi. He is single and self-supporting and pays the single rate for medical premiums.

Additional Payroll Information

1. The owner, chef and sous chef are paid monthly, cooks are paid weekly and waiters are paid biweekly.

2. EI, CPP and income taxes withheld are remitted to the Receiver General of Canada monthly.

3. Medical payments are remitted to the Provincial Treasurer monthly.

4. Participation in the Registered Retirement Savings Plan (RRSP) is voluntary.

5. The employer's contributions include
    *   CPP contributions equal to employee contributions
    *   EI (formerly called UI) factor of 1.4
    *   WCB rate of 1.09

Accounting Procedures

The Goods and Services Tax: Remittances

Carnival Catering uses the **regular method** for remittance of the Goods and Services Tax. It will record the GST collected from customers as a liability in the *GST Charged on Sales* account. GST paid by vendors will be recorded in the *GST Paid on Purchases* account as a decrease in the liability to Revenue Canada. The GST quarterly refund or remittance will be calculated automatically in the *GST Owing (Refund)* subtotal account. You will see this balance when you display or print the Balance Sheet. Susie Sardinha will file for a refund or remit the balance owing to the Receiver General of Canada by the last day of the month for the previous quarterly period.

Food is zero-rated with respect to GST. Vendors who supply food also sell taxable goods; therefore the option to include them in GST reports is turned on so that the

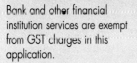

Notes

Bank and other financial institution services are exempt from GST charges in this application.

GST field is available when needed. You should enter GST Code 0 when the GST amount paid is zero.

PST

Provincial Sales Tax at 7 percent is charged on all food services provided. This amount is set up in the defaults for the company. However, because the Inventory Ledger is not set up, the program does not enter the PST rate automatically. You must type 7 in the PST field. Simply Accounting will then automatically calculate the amount of tax and credit the *PST Payable* account.

PST at the rate of 7 percent is also paid on non-food purchases.

Advances from Customers

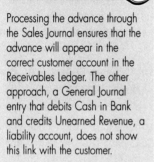

Notes

Processing the advance through the Sales Journal ensures that the advance will appear in the correct customer account in the Receivables Ledger. The other approach, a General Journal entry that debits Cash in Bank and credits Unearned Revenue, a liability account, does not show this link with the customer.

All clients are asked for an advance of between 25 and 30 percent of the total contracted price when the contract is signed, usually one to two weeks before the catered event. The advance is entered in the Sales Journal as a **negative invoice**. That is, the amount is entered with a minus sign. The GST code is 1 (non-taxable) and no PST is included in the advance. Enter the *Cash in Bank* account in the account field. This entry will credit the *Accounts Receivable* account for the customer. When the catering services are performed, complete a Sales Journal entry for the full amount of the contract, with the appropriate taxes and revenue account. When the customer pays the balance of the invoice, the invoice for both the advance and the full contract price should be marked as paid. In this way, the balance owing will match the amount of the cheque. Customers are expected to settle their accounts as soon as the catered event is finished.

Because customers pay a non-refundable advance, the credit limit option is not used. The exception is for the Bridge Club, which has negotiated with Carnival Catering to provide hors d'oeuvres and beverages for its weekly bridge tournaments. The Bridge Club settles its accounts at the end of each month. This is a normal open account customer.

INSTRUCTIONS

1. Using the instructions for accessing data files on page 12, open the application for Carnival Catering. Using Simply Accounting and the Chart of Accounts, Vendor, Customer and Employee Information, enter the transactions for the June 7 using date up to the payroll entries. (Refer to the keystroke instructions covered earlier in this workbook.)

   The procedures for entering each new transaction for this application are outlined step by step in the keystroke section following the source documents. These transaction have a ✔ in the check box and the page number where the keystrokes begin appears immediately below the check box.

2. After you have finished making your entries, print the reports and graphs indicated on the printing form below. Keystrokes for payroll reports begin on page 189.

REPORTS

Lists
☐ Chart of Accounts
☐ Vendor List
☐ Customer List
☑ Employee List

Financials
☐ Balance Sheet
☑ Income Statement
   from June 1 to June 30
☑ Trial Balance
   date: June 30
☑ General Ledger
   accounts: 2310 2320 2330 5300
   from June 1 to June 30

GST
☐ GST Report

Payroll
☑ Employee Summary
☑ Employee Detail
   include all details for all employees
☐ T-4 Slips
☐ Relevé-1 Slips

Mailing Labels
☐ Labels

Journals
☑ General (by posting date)
   from June 1 to June 30
☐ Purchases
☐ Payments
☑ Sales (by posting date)
   from June 1 to June 30
☐ Receipts
☑ Payroll (by posting date)
   from June 1 to June 30

Payables
☐ Vendor Aged
☐ Aged Overdue Payables
☐ Pending Purchase Orders

Receivables
☐ Customer Aged
☐ Aged Overdue Receivables
☐ Customer Statements

GRAPHS

☐ Payables by Aging Period
☐ Receivables by Aging Period
☐ Sales vs Receivables
☐ Revenues by Account
☑ Expenses & Net Profit as % of Revenue

☐ Payables by Vendor
☐ Receivables by Customer
☐ Receivables Due vs Payables Due
☐ Expenses by Account
☐ Current Revenue vs Last Year

SOURCE DOCUMENTS

USING DATE — June 7

Notes

Remember to choose the GST Code 0 and enter PST at 0% for food purchases.

☐ Purchase Invoice #RF-411
Dated June 1/99
From Reliable Foods, $2 000 for delivery of basic grocery items for catering services. This is a weekly recurring purchase as agreed. Terms: N/15 days.

Purchase Invoice #ESM-1712
Dated June 1/99
From European Smoked Meats, $1 000 for delivery of cheeses and deli meats for catering services. This is a weekly recurring purchase. Terms: N/15 days.

Cheque Copy #11
Dated June 2/99
To Commercial Cutlery, $1 150 in full payment of account. Reference invoice #CC-4321.

Purchase Invoice #DP-1793
Dated June 3/99
From David's Fresh Produce, $500 for delivery of fresh fruits and vegetables for catering services. This is a weekly recurring purchase. Terms: N/15 days.

Purchase Invoice #CF-976
Dated June 3/99
From Coastal Fish Wholesalers, $1 000 for delivery of shrimp, lobster and assorted fresh fish for catering services. Terms: N/15 days.

Notes

Choose GST Code 3 and type 7 in the PST rate field for purchases and sales to record the taxes paid and received.

Cash Purchase Invoice #VP-11234
Dated June 5/99
From Valu Petroleum, $80 plus 7% PST and 7% GST for gas and oil change to delivery truck. Invoice total $91.20. Paid by cheque #12.

Sales Invoice #CC-1
Dated June 5/99
To Ministry of Environment, $20 000 plus 7% GST and 7% PST for catering contract completed. Invoice total $22 800. Terms: cash on receipt of invoice.

Cash Receipt #CR-3
Dated June 6/99
From Ministry of Environment, cheque #1371 for $16 800 in full payment of account. Reference invoices #CR-2 & CC-1.

Notes

☐ Liza Haskett is located at
555 Honeymooners Lane
Victoria, BC
V8T 4W2
Tel: (250) 882-7499

Cash Receipt #CR-4
Dated June 6/99
From Liza Haskett (new customer), cheque #271 for $4 500 advance payment toward wedding reception.

Sales Invoice #CC-2
Dated June 6/99
To Victoria Ladies Bridge Club, $500 plus 7% GST and 7% PST for weekly contracted catering services. Invoice total $570. Terms: net 30 days. Store this entry as a weekly recurring sale.

Sales Invoice #CC-3
Dated June 7/99
To Coastal Corporation, $10 000 plus 7% GST and 7% PST for catering contract completed. Invoice total $11 400. Terms: cash on receipt of invoice.

EMPLOYEE TIME SUMMARY SHEET #1

(pay period ending June 7, 1999)

Name of Employee	Regular Hours	Overtime Hours
☑ 179 Sera Suflay	40	2
☐ Ben Branjil	40	–

a. Using Employee Time Summary Sheet #1 and Employee Information Sheet, complete payroll for weekly paid employees.
b. Sera Suflay will receive an advance of $240 for emergency car repairs. Her next four paycheques will each have $60 deducted to pay back the advance.
c. Issue cheques #13 and #14.

☐ Purchase Invoice #CS-9114
Dated June 7/99
From Caterers Suppliers, $200 plus 7% PST and 7% GST for regular weekly delivery of catering supplies. Invoice total $228. This is a weekly recurring purchase. Terms: net 30 days.

USING DATE − June 14

☑ Memo #1
183
Dated June 8/99
From Manager: Adjust paycheque for Sera Suflay (cheque #13) to include 4 hours overtime. Suflay has returned the original cheque.

☐ Cash Receipt #CR-5
Dated June 8/99
From Coastal Corporation, cheque #194 for $8 400 in full payment of account. Reference invoices #CR-1 & CC-3.

Notes

Remember to use the stored entries for recurring purchases and sales.

☐ Purchase Invoice #RF-507
Dated June 8/99
From Reliable Foods, $2 000 for regular weekly delivery of basic grocery items for catering services. Terms: N/15 days.

☐ Purchase Invoice #ESM-2027
Dated June 8/99
From European Smoked Meats, $1 000 for regular weekly delivery of cheeses and deli meats for catering services. Terms: N/15 days.

☐ Purchase Invoice #DP-1993
Dated June 10/99
From David's Fresh Produce, $500 for regular weekly delivery of fresh fruits and vegetables for catering services. Terms: N/15 days.

☐ Cheque Copy #15
Dated June 10/99
To Ideal Equipment, $5 300 in full payment of account. Reference invoice #IE-6374.

Notes

Gloria Vitale is located at
88 Bridal Path
Victoria, BC V8P 9H4
Tel: (250) 893-7014
Fax: (250) 893-7711

Cash Receipt #CR-6
Dated June 10/99
From Gloria Vitale (new customer), cheque #37 for $3 600 advance payment toward wedding reception.

Sales Invoice #CC-4
Dated June 13/99
To Victoria Ladies Bridge Club, $500 plus 7% GST and 7% PST for weekly contracted catering services. Invoice total $570. Terms: net 30 days.

Purchase Invoice #CF-1211
Dated June 13/99
From Coastal Fish Wholesalers, $500 for fresh fish for wedding catering contract. Terms: N/15 days.

Sales Invoice #CC-5
Dated June 14/99
To Liza Haskett, $15 000 plus 7% GST and 7% PST for completion of wedding catering contract. Invoice total $17 100. Terms: Cash on receipt of invoice.

Notes

Sean O'Casey is located at
120 Wakefield Rd.
Victoria, BC
V8E 6G9
Tel: (250) 895-7397
Fax: (250) 895-7399

Cash Receipt #CR-7
Dated June 14/99
From Sean O'Casey (new customer), cheque #631 for $1 000 advance payment for catering wake.

Cash Purchase Invoice #HS-75200
Dated June 14/99
From House of Spirits, $1 500 for wine and liquor plus $105 GST. Invoice total $1 605. Terms: Cash. Issued cheque #16.

Purchase Invoice #CS-9327
Dated June 14/99
From Caterers Suppliers, $200 plus 7% PST and 7% GST for regular weekly delivery of catering supplies. Invoice total $228. Terms: net 30 days.

EMPLOYEE TIME SUMMARY SHEET #2

(pay period ending June 14, 1999)

Name of Employee	Week 1 Hours	Week 2 Hours	Regular Hours	Overtime Hours
Sera Suflay	N/A	42	40	2
Ben Branjil	N/A	40	40	–
Sylvia Mellon	40	40	80	–
Adrian Poppi	40	42	80	2
Aziz Atta	40	40	80	–

a. Using Employee Time Summary Sheet #2 and Employee Information Sheet, complete payroll for all hourly employees.
b. Recover $60 advance from Sera Suflay. Remember to change the amount in the Advance field from -240 to -60.
c. Issue cheques #17 through #21.

☐ Cash Receipt #CR-8
Dated June 15/99
From Liza Haskett, cheque #288 for $12 600 in full payment of account.
Reference invoice #CR-4 & CC-5.

☐ Purchase Invoice #RF-611
Dated June 15/99
From Reliable Foods, $2 000 for regular weekly delivery of basic grocery items
for catering services. Terms: N/15 days.

☐ Purchase Invoice #ESM-2410
Dated June 15/99
From European Smoked Meats, $1 000 for regular weekly delivery of cheeses
and deli meats for catering services. Terms: N/15 days.

☐ Cheque Copy #22
Dated June 16/99
To Reliable Foods, $2 000 in payment of account. Reference invoice #RF-411.

☐ Cheque Copy #23
Dated June 16/99
To European Smoked Meats, $1 000 in payment of account. Reference invoice
#ESM-1712.

☐ Purchase Invoice #DP-2114
Dated June 17/99
From David's Fresh Produce, $500 for regular weekly delivery of fresh fruits and
vegetables for catering services. Terms: N/15 days.

☐ Cash Receipt #CR-9
Dated June 17/99
From Pringle Estate (new customer), cheque #5991 for $2 400 advance payment
on anniversary party catering contract.

☐ Sales Invoice #CC-6
Dated June 17/99
To Sean O'Casey, $4 000 plus 7% GST and 7% PST for catering services
completed. Invoice total $4 560. Terms: Cash on receipt of invoice.

☐ Cheque Copy #24
Dated June 18/99
To David's Fresh Produce, $500 in payment of account. Reference invoice
#DP-1793.

☐ Cash Receipt #CR-10
Dated June 18/99
From Sean O'Casey, cheque #649 for $3 560 in full payment of account.
Reference invoice #CR-7 & CC-6.

☐ Cash Receipt #CR-11
Dated June 18/99
From Pacific College (new customer), cheque #4581 for $2 400 advance
payment on retirement catering contract.

Notes

☐ Pringle Estate
(contact Molly Pringle)
is located at
1 Pringle Circle
Victoria, BC
V9B 6F7
Tel: (250) 891-7492
Fax: (250) 891-7000

Notes

☐ Pacific College
(contact Alana Teutor)
is located at
777 Scholars Rd.
Victoria, BC
V8N 4D1
Tel: (250) 885-8101
Fax: (250) 885-8800

☐ Sales Invoice #CC-7
Dated June 20/99
To Victoria Ladies Bridge Club, $500 plus 7% GST and 7% PST for weekly
contracted catering services. Invoice total $570. Terms: net 30 days.

☐ Cash Purchase Invoice #IM-6119
Dated June 20/99
From Island Motors, $400 plus 7% PST and 7% GST for new tires for delivery
truck. Invoice total $456. Terms: cash on receipt. Issued cheque #25. (Use Truck
Expenses account.)

☐ Sales Invoice #CC-8
Dated June 21/99
To Gloria Vitale, $12 000 plus 7% GST and 7% PST for catering services. Invoice
total $13 680. Terms: Cash on receipt of invoice.

☐ Purchase Invoice #CS-10107
Dated June 21/99
From Caterers Suppliers, $200 plus 7% PST and 7% GST for regular weekly
delivery of catering supplies. Invoice total $228. Terms: net 30 days.

EMPLOYEE TIME SUMMARY SHEET #3

(pay period ending June 21, 1999)

Name of Employee	Regular Hours	Overtime Hours
☐ Sera Suflay	40	2
☐ Ben Branjil	40	–

a. Using Employee Time Summary Sheet #3 and Employee Information Sheet,
complete payroll for weekly paid employees.
b. Recover $60 advance from Sera Suflay.
c. Issue cheques #26 and #27.

USING DATE – June 28

☐ Cash Receipt #CR-12
Dated June 22/99
From G. Vitale, cheque #61 for $10 080 in full payment of account. Reference
invoice #CR-6 & CC-8.

☐ Purchase Invoice #RF-724
Dated June 22/99
From Reliable Foods, $2 000 for regular weekly delivery of basic grocery items
for catering services. Terms: N/15 days.

☐ Purchase Invoice #ESM-2719
Dated June 22/99
From European Smoked Meats, $1 000 for regular weekly delivery of cheeses
and deli meats for catering services. Terms: N/15 days.

Cheque Copy #28
Dated June 22/99
To Reliable Foods, $2 000 in payment of account. Reference invoice #RF-507.

Cheque Copy #29
Dated June 22/99
To European Smoked Meats, $1 000 in payment of account. Reference invoice #ESM-2027.

Cheque Copy #30
Dated June 23/99
To David's Fresh Produce, $500 in payment of account. Reference invoice #DP-1993.

Notes

☐ Create a new account for the labour expenses, 5280 Personnel Services Expense.

Cash Purchase Invoice #KPS-4010
Dated June 23/99
From Kwik Personnel Services, $1 500 for labour supplied for catering contracts. Terms: Payment on completion of contract. Issued cheque #31.

Purchase Invoice #DP-2302
Dated June 24/99
From David's Fresh Produce, $500 for regular weekly delivery of fresh fruits and vegetables for catering services. Terms: N/15 days.

Purchase Invoice #IE-6931
Dated June 24/99
From Ideal Equipment, $2 500 for new appliances plus 7% PST and 7% GST. Invoice total $2 850. Terms: net 30 days.

Sales Invoice #CC-9
Dated June 24/99
To Pringle Estate, $8 000 plus 7% GST and 7% PST for anniversary catering contract completed. Invoice total $9 120. Terms: Cash on receipt of invoice.

Cash Purchase Invoice #HS-88620
Dated June 25/99
From House of Spirits, $1 200 for wine and liquor plus $84 GST. Invoice total $1 284. Terms: Cash. Issued cheque #32.

Cash Receipt #CR-13
Dated June 27/99
From Pringle Estate, cheque #6113 for $6 720 in full payment of account. Reference invoice #CR-9 & CC-9.

Sales Invoice #CC-10
Dated June 27/99
To Victoria Ladies Bridge Club, $500 plus 7% GST and 7% PST for weekly contracted catering services. Invoice total $570. Terms: net 30 days.

Notes

☐ Vancouver Island Cadets (contact Gunnel Cannon) are located at 48 Archer St. Victoria, BC V8R 5B8 Tel: (250) 881-7014 Fax: (250) 881-6215

Cash Receipt #CR-14
Dated June 27/99
From Vancouver Island Cadets (new customer), cheque #721 for $3 000 advance for graduation ceremony catering contract.

☐ Sales Invoice #CC-11
Dated June 28/99
To Pacific College, $8 000 plus 7% GST and 7% PST for retirement catering contract completed. Invoice total $9 120. Terms: Cash on receipt of invoice.

☐ Purchase Invoice #CS-11191
Dated June 28/99
From Caterers Suppliers, $200 plus 7% PST and 7% GST for regular weekly delivery of catering supplies. Invoice total $228. Terms: net 30 days.

EMPLOYEE TIME SUMMARY SHEET #4

(pay period ending June 28, 1999)

Name of Employee	Week 3 Hours	Week 4 Hours	Regular Hours	Overtime Hours
☐ Sera Suflay	N/A	42	40	2
☐ Ben Branjil	N/A	40	40	–
☐ Sylvia Mellon	40	42	80	2
☐ Adrian Poppi	42	40	80	2
☐ Aziz Atta	40	40	80	–

a. Using Employee Time Summary Sheet #4 and Employee Information Sheet, complete payroll for all hourly employees.
b. Recover $60 advance from Sera Suflay.
c. Issue cheques #33 through #37.

USING DATE — June 30

☐ Cash Receipt #CR-15
Dated June 29/99
From Pacific College, cheque #4688 for $6 720 in full payment of account. Reference invoices #CR-11 & CC-11.

☐ Cheque Copy #38
Dated June 29/99
To Reliable Foods, $2 000 in payment of account. Reference invoice #RF-611.

☐ Cheque Copy #39
Dated June 29/99
To European Smoked Meats, $1 000 in payment of account. Reference invoice #ESM-2410.

☑ Memo #2
Dated June 29/99
From Owner: Check all To Do Lists. Complete the following entries that are due:

☑ Recurring Purchase: Invoice #ESM-3162
From European Smoked Meats, $1 000 for regular weekly delivery of cheeses and deli meats for catering services. Terms: N/15 days.

☑ Recurring Purchase: Invoice #RF-863
From Reliable Foods, $2 000 for regular weekly delivery of basic grocery items for catering services. Terms: N/15 days.

☑ Pay Cheque #40 for $1 500 to settle Coastal Fish Wholesalers account.

Notes

185

Keystrokes for all entries resulting from the To Do Lists begin on page 185.

Notes

Create two new accounts for the bank memo transaction:
5140 Loan Interest
5160 Mortgage Interest.

Bank Debit Memo PT-555111
Dated June 30/99
From Pacific Trust: authorized withdrawals
$40 for monthly bank service charges
$850 monthly loan payment, including $210 interest and $640 principle
$2 250 monthly mortgage payment, including $2 025 interest and $225 principle

Memo #3
Dated June 30/99
From Owner: Pay the owner and salaried employees, Susie Sardinha, Louie Perch and Peter Terkee. Issue cheques #41 to #43. Perch's commission for June is $790 and Terkee's is $395.

Memo #4
Dated June 30/99
From Owner: Adjust the inventory and supplies accounts for amounts used in catering contracts for the month of June as follows:
Charge $15 800 from Food Inventory to Food Used for Catering account.
Charge $4 200 from Liquor & Wine Inventory to Liquor Used for Catering.
Charge $890 from Catering Supplies to Catering Supplies Used.

KEYSTROKES

Entering Payroll Transactions

Payroll transactions are entered in the Payroll Journal indicated by the arrow pointer in the following screen:

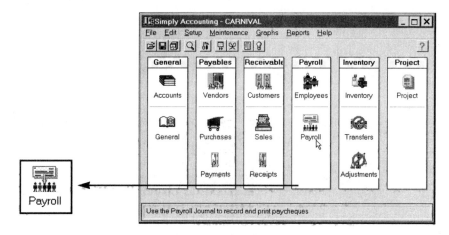

Double click on the **Payroll Journal icon** to open it and display the following Payroll Journal input form:

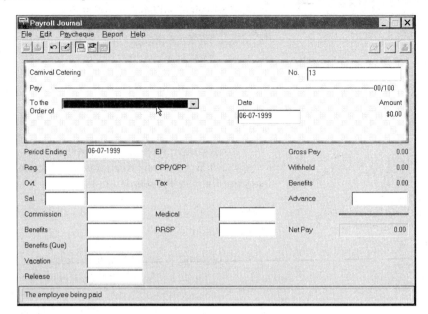

The cursor is in the Employee (To the Order of) field.

Click on the **Employee field** or **its arrow** to see the list of employees as follows:

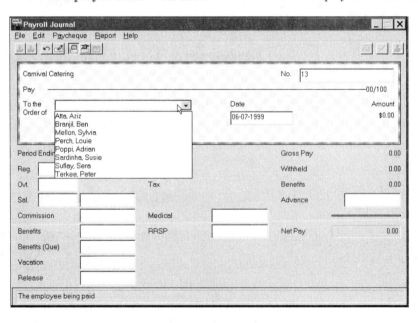

Click on Suflay, Sera to select this employee and add her name to the input form. If you have not chosen correctly, return to the employee list. Otherwise

Press `tab`

The cursor is now in the Cheque (No.) field. The employee's address has been added to the form. The cheque number, 13, should be correct because we have set up the number to advance automatically. If the number is incorrect, you can change it.

Press `tab`

The cursor moves to the Date field, where you should enter the date of payment. As usual, the using date, June 7 has been entered by default. Unlike other journals, where changing the date in the journal also changes the posting date, Payroll Journal entries always use the using date as the posting date. In this case, the using date, June 7, is correct so you should accept this date.

Press

The cursor advances to the Period Ending field. This refers to the last day of the pay period for the employee. It may be later or earlier than the cheque date. In this case, the using date is also the same as the pay period ending date, so you can accept the default date again.

Press

The cursor advances to the Regular hours (Reg.) field. This field contains the number of regular hours an employee has worked for the regular pay rate during the pay period.

Type 40

Press (tab)

Notice that many of the remaining fields have been calculated automatically. The cursor advances to the Overtime (Ovt.) field. This field contains the number of overtime hours an employee has worked during the pay period.

Type 2

Press (tab)

Notice that the remaining fields have been recalculated to include the additional pay. The cursor advances to the Salary field. This and the next several fields do not apply to this employee. The Salary field is used only for salaried employees. Since Sera Suflay is not a salaried employee, ignore this field.

The Commission field is used for employees who earn a commission to be paid in this pay period. For employees who receive commissions, you will have to calculate manually the amount of the commission and enter it in this field. Since Sera Suflay does not receive a commission, ignore this field.

The Benefits field is used to enter the total amount of taxable benefits a business offers to its employees, such as health insurance or dental plans. Carnival Catering does not offer any employee benefits, so ignore this field.

The Simply Accounting program automatically calculates an amount in the Vacation pay field and displays it as a default. This default amount is calculated at the vacation pay rate of 6 percent entered for this employee and will be retained by the business (*Vacation Payable* account) until the employee takes a vacation or leaves the employ of the business. (See the Employee Information Sheet.) You should accept the default.

The Release field is used to release the accumulated vacation pay retained for an employee. The amount to be released appears as a default when you turn off the option to retain vacation. For this application, none of the employees are taking vacations or leaving the business, so ignore this field.

Notice that the medical deduction is entered automatically because the amounts were entered as part of the setup. If necessary, the amount can be edited, just like any other field, except EI, CPP and Tax.

Click on the **Advance field** to move the cursor.

The Advance field is used to enter an amount advanced to an employee in addition to his or her normal pay from wages or salary. Advances are given for emergencies and other personal reasons upon approval by management. An advance offered to an employee is shown as a positive amount. An advance recovered on a regular basis is indicated as a negative amount in this same field. An advance of $240 for Sera Suflay has been approved.

Type 240

Press (tab)

Notice that the upper cheque portion of your input form window has been updated continuously as you added information about deductions or pay. Your complete payroll form should look like the one shown below:

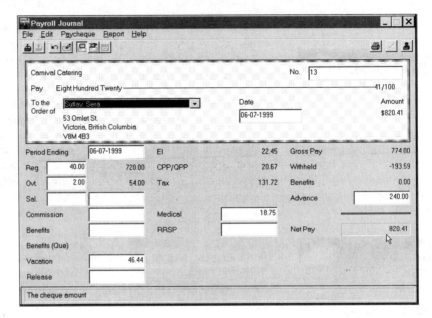

Notes

If you are using a later version of the Simply Accounting program, your amounts may be different from those shown because different tax tables are used.

Reviewing the Payroll Journal Transaction

When you have completed entering all the information, you should review the completed transaction before posting.

Choose Display Payroll Journal Entry from the pull-down menu under **Report**. The transaction you have just completed appears as follows:

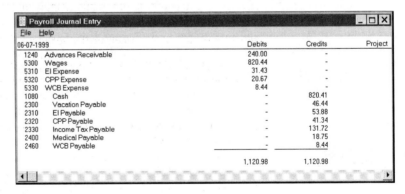

Notice that all the relevant wage expense accounts have been debited. In addition, all the wage-related liability accounts and the *Cash* account have been updated automatically because the Payroll Ledger is integrated with the General Ledger. All the accounts shown in the journal entry have all been defined as integration accounts for the Payroll Ledger so you do not enter part of the journal entry or any account numbers directly.

Notes

Payroll expense accounts reflect the employer's share of payroll tax obligations. The liabilities reflect the amounts that the owner must remit to the appropriate agencies and include both the employer's share of these tax liabilities and the employee's share (deductions withheld). For example, CPP contributions by the employee are matched by the employer. Therefore, the CPP Expense (employer's share) is one-half of the CPP Payable amount (employee and employer's share). WCB is paid entirely by the employer (the expense amount is the same as the liability amount) while Medical is paid entirely by the employee so there is no expense amount. For EI, the employer's share is 1.4 times the employee's share. Vacation pay is part of the Wages expense.

Simply Accounting uses the Revenue Canada tax formulas to calculate the deduction amounts for CPP, EI and Income Tax. These formulas are updated every six months. The remaining deductions are determined from Employee Ledger entries, if different rates apply to different employees (WCB, vacation pay rate and Medical), or from Payroll Ledger settings if the same rate applies to all employees (EI factor of 1.4).

Close the display to return to the Payroll Journal input screen.

CORRECTING THE PAYROLL JOURNAL ENTRY BEFORE POSTING

Move the cursor to the field that contains the error. **Press** `tab` to move forward through the fields or **press** `shift` and `tab` together to move back to a previous field. This will highlight the field information so that you can change it. **Type** the correct information and **press** `tab` to enter the change.

You can also use the mouse to point to a field and drag through the incorrect information to highlight it. **Type** the correct information. **Press** `tab` to save the corrections.

You can discard the entry by clicking on ☒ or ↶ or return to the employee list by **clicking on** a different employee name. **Click on** the name of the correct employee and **press** `tab`. When prompted, confirm that you wish to discard the incorrect entry. **Click on Yes**, and start again from the beginning.

Posting

When all the information in your journal entry is correct,

Click on Post 👤 to save your work.

The following caution is displayed when the dates of the transaction are different from the dates of the tax tables in your Simply Accounting program:

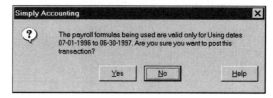

Click on Yes, unless you have made a mistake. A new blank Payroll Journal input screen appears for you to enter the next payroll transaction.

To complete transactions involving other ledgers, you must close the Payroll Journal input form window to return to the Home window.

Adjusting Payroll Entries

On June 8, Sera Suflay returned with her paycheque to ask for a correction because she worked four hours overtime instead of the two she was paid for. Simply Accounting no longer requires you to make reversing and correcting entries for situations like these. Instead you can complete a paycheque adjustment in the Payroll Journal.

Double click on the **Payroll Journal icon** to open the Payroll Journal.

Notes

Payroll Journal entries may be stored as recurring entries before posting. Follow the same steps as you would for recurring sales or purchases.

Click on the **Adjust Cheque button** 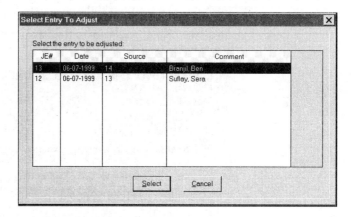 on the Payroll Journal tool bar or choose Adjust Cheque from the pull-down menu under Paycheque to access the list of payroll entries posted:

Click on JE #12 Suflay, Sera to select the Payroll Journal entry for Suflay.

Click on Select to display the entry that was posted. First, Simply Accounting offers the following reminder about recalculating taxes for an adjustment:

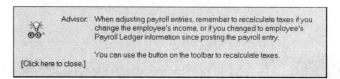

The program is advising you that the tax recalculation will not be automatic if you change an amount on the payroll entry.

Click on the **advisor icon** to close the warning and display the payroll journal entry:

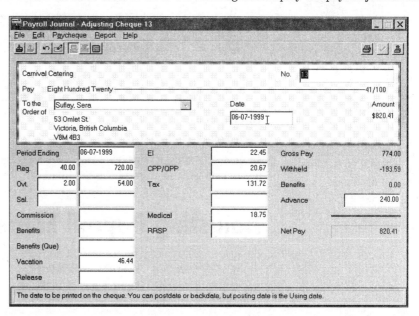

This is a duplicate of the payroll entry. All the fields can be edited with the exception of the employee name. The cheque number is highlighted because normally you would prepare a new cheque. However, Suflay has not cashed the cheque so we could use the same number. We need to change the number of overtime hours.

Double click on the **Ovt. field** (Overtime hours) to highlight the current entry.

Type   4

Press   tab   to enter the change and update the amounts. Notice that the deduction amounts have not changed yet.

Click on the **Recalculate taxes button** 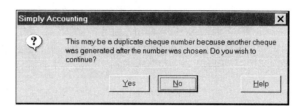 on the Payroll Journal tool bar or choose Recalculate Taxes from the pull-down menu under Paycheque. All the deduction amounts are updated for the new number of work hours.

Review the Payroll Journal entry, and close the display when you have finished. Make corrections if necessary.

Click on the **Post button** to save the adjustment. Simply Accounting displays the following warning when you do not change the cheque number:

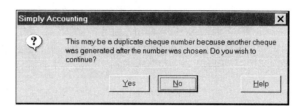

If you want to change the cheque number, click on No, make the change, then post. If you want to proceed with the duplicate cheque number, because Suflay returned the original,

Click on Yes to display the Payroll Journal input screen.

Close the Payroll Journal to return to the Home window .

When you display the Payroll Journal, you will see three journal entries for Suflay, the original entry, the reversing adjusting entry and the final correct entry.

Displaying To Do Lists

Simply Accounting helps a business monitor its performance and cash flow through several of the reports that you have seen so far. It also keeps track of recurring transactions, and payments and receipts due in the form of To Do Lists. These lists offer an additional method of internal control.

You must be in the Home window to access the To Do Lists.

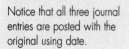

Notice that all three journal entries are posted with the original using date.

You can include Display Settings to show To Do Lists automatically each time you advance the using date, each time you start the program or both. Choose Settings from the Setup menu and click on the Display tab. Menu and tool bar access to the lists is always available from the Home window.

Click on the **To Do Lists button** 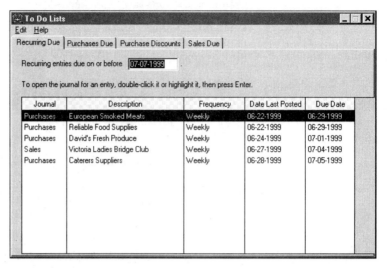 or choose To Do Lists from the pull-down menu under Maintenance to see the following list:

By default, Simply Accounting chooses a date that is one week past the current using date for its To Do Lists. The date can be edited like any other date field by typing in a new date and pressing `tab`. All recurring entries that will be due by the date shown are listed with the original journal used for the entry, the entry name and its recurring frequency. The most recent posting date and the due date are also included. The entries are listed according to the due date, with earliest date at the top of the list.

You can see that two entries — the purchases from European Smoked Meats and Reliable Food Supplies — are due today, June 29. As indicated by the message above the list, you can open the journal for these entries directly from the To Do List. Since these are the next two purchases in our source documents, we will complete the journal entries from the To Do Lists screen.

Double click on the **European Smoked Meats** entry that is selected or highlighted to display the Purchases Journal entry for this item:

Notes

You can double click on any part of the line for the entry you want to recall to open the journal.

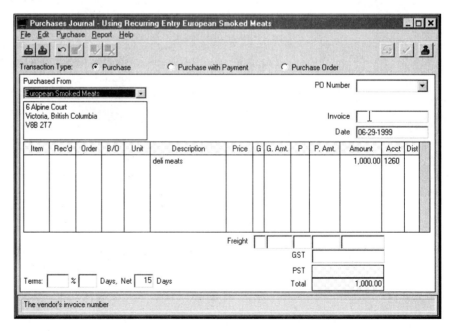

Enter the new invoice number, ESM-3162, according to the source document to complete the journal entry.

Click on the **Post button** 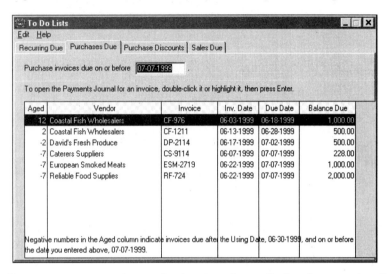 to save the entry. Close the Purchases Journal to return to the To Do Lists screen. The European Smoked Meats entry is now at the end of the list. You can now enter the purchase from Reliable Food Supplies.

Double click on the **Reliable Food Supplies** entry. Complete this invoice by entering the new invoice number, RF-863. Post the entry and close the journal to return to the To Do Lists screen. Again the list has been updated. The remaining list items are not due before the end of the month, so we can proceed to the next part of the To Do Lists.

Click on the **Purchases Due tab** to see all outstanding purchase invoices that should be paid before the date above the list, one week past the using date:

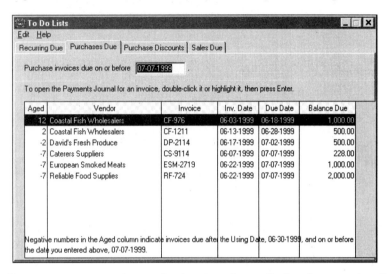

Again, if you want, you can change the date in order to display, for example, all invoices that should be paid within the next month. You might use this list to plan a payment schedule.

The columns of this list repeat journal information, including the vendor, invoice number, invoice date and balance due. The due date is calculated from the posting date and the payment terms on the invoice. The Aged column is calculated as the number of days from the current using date. Positive numbers in the Aged column indicate overdue accounts and negative numbers indicate that payment is due after the using date. You can see that the two invoices from Coastal Fish Wholesalers are overdue. Although there is no interest penalty for late payments, these invoices should be paid immediately in order to maintain good business relations with the vendor. Again, you can access the Payments Journal for this vendor directly from the To Do Lists screen.

Double click on the **Coastal Fish Wholesalers** entry that is selected or highlighted to display the Payments Journal for this vendor:

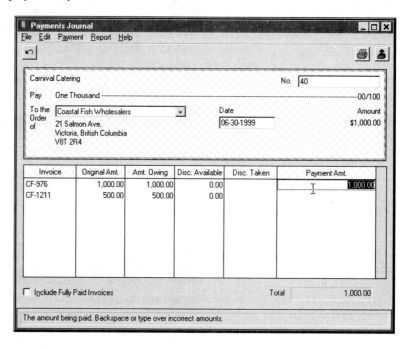

Complete the payment dated June 29, for $1 500 to cover both outstanding invoices.

Click on the **Post button** ![post] to save the entry. Close the Payments Journal to return to the To Do Lists screen. The Coastal Fish Wholesalers entries have been removed from the list.

Close the Payments Journal to return to the To Do Lists screen.

Click on the **Purchase Discounts tab** to see all outstanding purchase invoices that are eligible for discounts if paid on time:

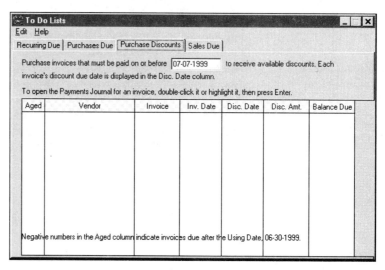

Because none of Carnival Catering's vendors offer discounts for early payment, this list is blank. You can see that it is very similar to the Purchases Due list with the addition of the Disc. (Discount) Date and Disc. Amt. (Discount Amount) columns. These items tell you the last day that the invoice will be eligible for discount and the amount of the discount. Again, you would use this information to plan payment schedules. For example, a business could choose to pass up a discount for a small amount in order to take advantage of larger discounts if there were insufficient cash for both payments.

Click on the **Sales Due tab** to see all outstanding sales invoices due by the date shown:

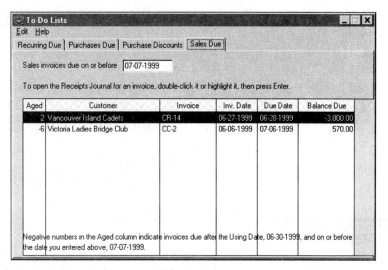

This list is the customer equivalent of the Purchases Due list. Positive numbers in the Aged column show overdue accounts and indicate that reminder notices should be sent to customers. The two invoices displayed here are the deposit from Vancouver Island Cadets and the recurring sale to Victoria Bridge Club. You can change the date to include a different time frame just as you can for other To Do Lists.

Click on ☒ to return to the Home window. Continue with the remaining entries for the June 30 using date to finish the application.

Displaying Payroll Reports

You can access all payroll reports from the Reports menu in the Employees window. Double click on the Employees icon to open the Employees window.

Displaying Employee Lists

You should be in the Home window.

Click on the **Employees icon** to select it.

Click on the **Report button** 🔳 or choose Display Employee List from the pull-down menu under Reports. The report will display a list of all current employees, together with their addresses and telephone numbers.

Close the display when you are finished.

Displaying Employee Reports

You should be in the Home window.

Choose **Payroll** and then **Employee** from the pull-down menu under **Reports** to see the following Employee Report Options window:

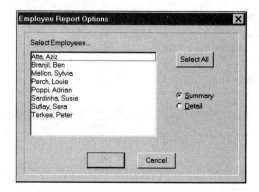

Click on the **employee(s)** for whom you want the report, or click on **Select All** to include all employees in the report.

The **Summary** option allows you to see an employee's payroll report in summary form. The summary report will give you the accumulated totals only for all deductions and payments, which are updated each pay period. You will not be able to see earlier summary reports unless you have a backup copy for that specific time period (i.e., using date) or if you have a hard copy of the summary output.

The **Detail** option will give you the following payroll items to choose from:

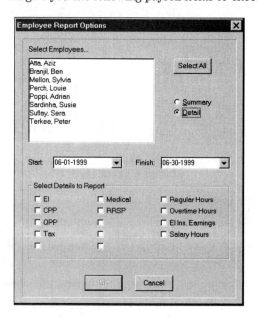

Type the beginning date for the report you want to see in the Start field.

Press (tab)

Type the ending date for the report you want to see.

Click on all of the details you wish to include in the report. The amount for each detail you choose will be listed for each payroll period for the selected employees, with the totals for the period selected.

Once you have selected your employees and report options,

Click on OK

Close the display when you are finished.

Displaying the Payroll Journal

You should be in the Home window.

Click on the **Payroll Journal icon** to select it.

Click on the **Report button** 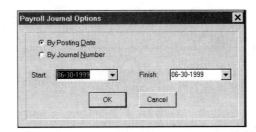 or choose Display Payroll Journal from the pull-down menu under Reports. Your screen will display the following Payroll Journal Options window:

Notes

You can display the Employee Detail Report and the General Ledger Report from the Payroll Journal.

By default, the By Posting Date option is selected. This option is used for all reports in this application. Your latest using date appears by default in both the Start and Finish date fields. The start date is highlighted, ready for editing.

Type the beginning date for the report you want to see.

Press `tab`

Type the ending date for the report you want to see.

Click on OK

Close the display when you are finished.

Printing Payroll Reports

Choose **Print** from the pull-down menu under **File** while you are displaying any of the reports listed in the section Displaying Payroll Reports.

Printing T4s

Notes

Relevé 1 slips are used only in the province of Quebec. The report options are similar to those for the T4 Slips.

You can also print two reports that are not available for display: **T4 Slips** and **Relevé 1 Slips**. The **T4** option will allow you to print T4 slips, which are compulsory for employees for income tax return filing. You should have the proper tax statement forms from Revenue Canada to take full advantage of this option. You should retain payroll information for employees who leave during the year so that you can prepare T4 slips to mail to them.

Choose **Payroll** and then **Print T4 Slips** (or **Print Relevé 1 Slips**) from the pull-down menu under **Reports** to display the following options:

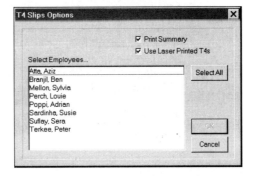

Click on **Select All** or on the names of the employees for whom you want the report printed. Notice that you may use a laser printer for the forms and include a printed summary of the amounts on the T4.

Click on OK

Printing will begin immediately, so be sure that you have set up your printer correctly before you begin.

Print Employee Mailing Labels

Click on the **Employees icon** in the Home window to select it.

Choose **Mailing Labels** from the pull-down menu under **Reports** to display the list of employee names.

Click on the **Employees names** or **click on Select All**.

Click on OK to start printing.

CASE PROBLEMS

Case One

After several months of successful operation, Susie Sardinha realized how large a role her cooks play in the success of her catering business, so she decided to include a commission with their regular wages.

a. What must she do to the setup of the Simply Accounting program and in the regular Payroll Journal entries to add the commissions?

b. Before making the commitment to the employees, what information should she consider, and how should she determine the basis or amount of the commission?

Case Two

During the fall when her father was ill, Sardinha was away from Victoria for four weeks to take care of him. She left her chef in charge of the business. On her return, she was extremely pleased to learn that the business had run smoothly and the chef had successfully negotiated some new contracts with only minimal telephone assistance from Sardinha. She wanted to show her appreciation to the staff by adding a significant bonus to their next paycheques.

Sardinha knew that if she added the bonus directly in the next Payroll Journal entry, the taxes would be overpaid because the program assumes that the pay for the period selected is the regular rate of pay. She needed to turn off the automatic payroll deductions feature before she could edit the tax amounts that the program calculates automatically. However, she still needed to know how much tax should be deducted. In the manual approach, she would divide the bonus evenly over the entire year, calculate the amount of tax increase for each pay period, then multiply this amount by the number of pay periods. This way, the entire tax amount is paid at the time of the bonus, but the amount is based on the yearly increase in income.

Describe how Sardinha can use the software to perform these calculations.

CHAPTER EIGHT

Meteor Mountain Bike Shop

OBJECTIVES

Upon completion of this chapter, you will be able to:

- *enter* inventory-related purchase transactions
- *enter* inventory-related credit sale transactions of goods and services
- *enter* inventory-related cash sale transactions of goods and services
- *make* inventory adjustments
- *record* sales discounts for early payments
- *understand* the integration of the Inventory Ledger with the Payables, Receivables and General ledgers
- *enter* new inventory items
- *look up* invoices that have been posted
- *adjust* invoices that have been posted
- *display* and *print* inventory reports

COMPANY INFORMATION

Company Profile

Meteor Mountain Bike Shop in Collingwood, Ontario serves the cottage country area by selling bicycles and bicycle accessories, and by renting, servicing and repairing bicycles. The shop, owned and operated by Tom and Betsy Trycykel, carries a small inventory of popular bicycle models and basic accessories. In addition, the shop carries a few bicycles for rentals on a daily or weekly basis to individuals, clubs and resorts in the area. A few clubs and resorts that purchase regularly from Meteor Mountain Bike Shop have opened accounts. The Trycykels recommend annual spring bicycle tune-ups to all their customers.

Based on the spring to fall season for biking and cottage use, the Trycykels decided to restrict their business to May through October each year. With this schedule, they are free to participate in the local opportunities for skiing in the winter.

Because the shop is small, the Trycykels are able to manage most of the work themselves. Occasionally, however, such as during summer long weekends, they engage the help of local students who work as needed on a casual hourly basis. One of these students helped Tom Trycykel to convert the manual accounting records to Simply Accounting. On May 31, 1999, the books were closed and the following information was used to set up the Simply Accounting files:

- Chart of Accounts
- Post-Closing Trial Balance
- Vendor Information
- Customer Information
- Inventory Information
- Accounting Procedures

METEOR MOUNTAIN BIKE SHOP
CHART OF ACCOUNTS

ASSETS
1080 Cash in Bank
1200 Accounts Receivable
1220 Bicycle Repair Parts
1240 Prepaid Insurance
1260 Rental Bicycles
1280 Store Supplies
1300 Accessories
1320 Helmets
1340 Mountain Bicycles
1360 Services
1420 Cash Register
1440 Computers & Peripherals
1480 Display Fixtures
1500 Fax Machine
1520 Shop
1540 Tools & Equipment

LIABILITIES
2100 Bank Loan
2200 Accounts Payable
2640 PST Payable
2650 GST Charged on Sales
2670 GST Paid on Purchases
2850 Mortgage Payable

EQUITY
3560 Trycykels, Capital
3580 Trycykels, Drawings
3600 Net Income

REVENUE
4020 Revenue from Sales
4030 Sales Allowances & Discounts
4040 Revenue from Services
4100 Sales Tax Commission
4200 Freight Revenue

EXPENSES
5020 Advertising & Promotion
5040 Bank Charges
5060 Cost of Goods Sold
5080 Purchases Returns
5100 Damaged Inventory
5200 Freight Expense
5220 Interest Expense
5260 Telephone Expense
5300 Temporary Services

METEOR MOUNTAIN BIKE SHOP
POST-CLOSING TRIAL BALANCE

May 31, 1999

1080 Cash in Bank	$ 8 350.00	
1200 Accounts Receivable	460.00	
1220 Bicycle Repair Parts	2 000.00	
1240 Prepaid Insurance	500.00	
1260 Rental Bicycles	3 000.00	
1280 Store Supplies	200.00	
1300 Accessories	1 960.00	
1320 Helmets	830.00	
1340 Mountain Bicycles	15 700.00	
1420 Cash Register	1 000.00	
1440 Computers & Peripherals	2 800.00	
1480 Display Fixtures	1 200.00	
1500 Fax Machine	400.00	
1520 Shop	72 000.00	
1540 Tools & Equipment	2 400.00	
2100 Bank Loan		$ 5 000.00
2200 Accounts Payable		4 025.00
2640 PST Payable		1 280.00
2650 GST Charged on Sales		1 120.00
2670 GST Paid on Purchases	560.00	
2850 Mortgage Payable		60 000.00
3560 Trycykels, Capital		41 935.00
	$113 360.00	$113 360.00

METEOR MOUNTAIN BIKE SHOP
VENDOR INFORMATION

Vendor Name (Contact)	Address Phone & Fax	Invoice Terms	Invoice Date	Invoice/ Cheque No.	Outstanding Balance
Bell Canada (Dessy Bell)	13 Sonic St. Collingwood, ON L9Y 8T2 Tel: (705) 711-7483 Fax: (705) 711-8100	Net 1			
Cycling Equipment Inc. (Petal Spokes)	62 Cyclo Dr. North York, ON M9Y 7H3 Tel: (416) 488-6190 Fax: (416) 488-9000	Net 30	5/11/99	CE-714	$575.00
Global Cyclists (Norma Ryder)	710 Touring Cr. Toronto, ON M4P 2M9 Tel: (416) 932-7401 Fax: (416) 932-6222	Net 30	5/6/99	GC-1543	$3 450.00
Ontario Hydro (Atam Powers)	201 Generator Rd. Collingwood, ON L9Y 5B7 Tel: (705) 714-9733	Net 1			

METEOR MOUNTAIN BIKE SHOP
VENDOR INFORMATION CONTINUED

Vendor Name (Contact)	Address Phone & Fax	Invoice Terms	Invoice Date	Invoice/ Cheque No.	Outstanding Balance
Receiver General of Canada	Summerside Tax Centre Summerside, PE C1N 6L2 Tel: (902) 821-8186	Net 1			
Trail Canada Accessories & Parts (Helmut Locke)	18 Woodlands Trail Waterloo, ON N2L 6F2 Tel: (519) 886-6321 Fax: (519) 886-7191	Net 30			
Treasurer of Ontario	Box 620 33 King St. W. Oshawa, ON L1H 8H5 Tel: (905) 965-8470	Net 1			
Wheeler & Shield Co. (Lawrence Shields)	75 Raleigh Ct. Hamilton, ON L8H 4B8 Tel: (905) 522-6123 Fax: (905) 522-9210	Net 15			
				Grand Total	$4 025.00

METEOR MOUNTAIN BIKE SHOP
CUSTOMER INFORMATION

Customer Name (Contact)	Address Phone & Fax	Invoice Terms (Credit Limit)	Invoice Date	Invoice/ Cheque No.	Outstanding Balance
Bay Land Bikers (Kyle Wheeling)	72 Bayview Ave. Collingwood, ON L9Y 4D3 Tel: (705) 713-4567 Fax: (705) 713-6285	2/10, Net 15 ($4 000)			
Blue Mountain Lodge (Ceram Potter)	95 Ridgewood Dr. Collingwood, ON L9Y 6V1 Tel: (705) 711-4723 Fax: (705) 711-4111	2/10, Net 15 ($4 000)	5/21/99	53	$287.50
Lakeland Mountain Bike Club (Sylva Lake)	811 Highland Cr. Meaford, ON N4L 1E3 Tel: (519) 653-8016 Fax: (519) 653-9054	2/10, Net 15 ($4 000)			
Teehani Summer Resort (Edward Bassige)	4 Seasons Rd. Meaford, ON N4L 1C8 Tel: (519) 655-3478 Fax: (519) 655-5522	2/10, Net 15 ($4 000)	5/28/99	59	$172.50
				Grand Total	$460.00

```
METEOR MOUNTAIN BIKE SHOP
INVENTORY INFORMATION
```

Code	Description	Selling Price	Qty on Hand	Amt (Cost)	Min Stock Level
Accessories					
ACC-BS1	Bell - steel	$ 6	10	$30	2
ACC-CL1	Cable Lock - heavy duty	30	15	150	3
ACC-LH1	Light - halogen clamp style	20	10	100	2
ACC-PA1	Pump - lightweight aluminum	20	10	100	2
ACC-SD1	Speedometer - digital deluxe	40	10	200	2
ACC-SD2	Speedometer - digital standard	30	10	150	2
ACC-SG1	Seat - gel extra cushioning	20	20	200	4
ACC-TK1	Toolkit - multi-function	40	10	100	2
ACC-TR1	Tires - 26″ mountain	20	20	200	4
ACC-TR2	Tires - 24″ mountain	16	20	160	4
ACC-TR3	Tires - 20″ mountain	12	20	120	4
ACC-UL1	U-Lock - heavy duty	40	10	200	2
ACC-UL2	U-Lock - heavy duty, centre lock	50	10	250	2
				$1 960	
Helmets					
HMT-11A	Charm - 11 vent aerodynamic in-line	$25	10	150	2
HMT-11B	Tuff - 11 vent super lock-tech	40	10	250	2
HMT-21A	Myti - 21 vent adjustable in-line	40	10	250	2
HMT-21B	Excel - 21 vent lightweight	30	10	180	2
				$830	
Mountain Bicycles (1-21 speed)					
MTB-A241	Brava - 18sp Shimano SIS alum alloy	$ 500	5	1500	1
MTB-A242	Brava - 18sp high tensile steel	250	5	700	1
MTB-A261	Maxim - 18sp Shimano alloy rim/hub	400	10	2 500	2
MTB-A262	Maxim - 15sp high tens steel hybrid	160	10	800	2
MTB-A263	Summit - 18sp STX Alvio A-frame	800	3	1500	0
MTB-A264	Summit - 18sp Alvio drivetrain chr	600	10	4 000	2
MTB-A265	Summit - 21sp Shimano XT/LE Al. DB	1 600	2	2 000	0
MTB-Y201	BMC - 1sp deluxe high tensile	150	5	400	1
MTB-Y202	Trac - 5sp chromoly hybrid	300	10	1 800	2
MTB-YU20	Trac - 5sp steel frame twist shift	200	5	500	1
				$15 700	
Services					
SRV-RTD	Daily rental per bicycle	$15/day	1 500		
SRV-RTW	Weekly rental per bicycle	50/wk	225		
SRV-TU	Tune-up per bicycle	30	500		

Accounting Procedures

The Goods and Services Tax: Remittances

Meteor Mountain Bike Shop uses the regular method for remittance of the Goods and Services Tax. GST collected from customers is recorded as a liability in the *GST Charged on Sales* account. GST paid to vendors is recorded in the *GST Paid on Purchases* account as a decrease in liability to Revenue Canada. The Trycykels file their return to the Receiver General of Canada by the last day of the month for the previous quarterly period, either requesting a refund or remitting the balance owing.

GST remittances are recorded in the Purchases Journal. Select the Receiver General as the vendor. Enter the GST charged as a **positive** amount in the Amount field with the *GST Charged on Sales* account in the Account field. On the next line, enter the GST paid as a **negative** amount in the Amount field with the *GST Paid on Purchases* account in the Account field. This will debit the GST charged account and credit the GST paid account. Make the payment in the Payments Journal, or as a cash purchase.

Provincial Sales Tax (PST)

Provincial sales tax of 8 percent is applied to all cash and credit sales of goods and services in the province of Ontario and remitted monthly to the Provincial Treasurer. Set up a liability owing to the vendor, Provincial Treasurer, in the Purchases Journal, using the General Ledger balance in the *PST Payable* account for the end of the previous month to determine the balance owing. A 5 percent sales tax commission is earned for prompt payment and reduces the liability to the Provincial Treasurer.

PST at the rate of 8 percent is also paid on purchases that are not inventory items for resale. PST paid is not allocated to a separate account. It is charged to the asset or expense account associated with the purchase.

Sales Invoices

If you want to print the sales invoice through the program, complete the Sales Journal transaction as you would otherwise. Before posting the transaction, choose Print from the pull-down menu under File or click on the Print button on the tool bar for the invoice form. Printing will begin immediately, so be sure you have the correct forms for your printer before you begin.

Cash Sales and Purchases

The keystrokes for cash inventory transactions are similar to those for other credit cash sales and purchases. When you choose the One-time customer (or vendor) and press (tab), Sale (or Purchase) with Payment is chosen as the transaction type and the Cheque field opens. When you choose a regular customer (or vendor), click on the Sale (or Purchase) with Payment option to open the Cheque field.

Freight Expenses and Charges

When a business purchases inventory items, the cost of any freight that cannot be directly allocated to a specific item must be charged to the *Freight Expense* account. This amount will be regarded as an expense rather than being charged to an inventory asset account.

Freight or delivery charges to customers are allocated to a *Freight Revenue* account.

Sales Discounts

Discounts may be offered to encourage customers to settle their accounts early. Meteor offers its account customers a 2 percent discount if they pay their accounts within ten days. Discounts are entered in the Receipts Journal and are calculated automatically by the program when the payment terms are set up and the customer is eligible to receive the discount. Refer to Keystroke section, page 222.

INSTRUCTIONS

1. Using the Chart of Accounts, Trial Balance, Vendor Information, Customer Information and Inventory Information provided, record entries for the source documents for June 1999 using Simply Accounting. The procedures for entering each new type of transaction are outlined step by step in the keystroke section that follows the source documents. These transactions have a ✔ in the check box and the page number where the keystrokes begin is printed below the check box.

2. After you have finished making your entries, print the reports indicated on the following printing form. Instructions for printing inventory reports begin on page 225.

REPORTS

Lists
- ☐ Chart of Accounts
- ☐ Vendor List
- ☐ Customer List
- ☐ Inventory List

Financials
- ☑ Comparative Balance Sheet
  dates: June 1 & June 14
  With Dollar Difference
- ☑ Income Statement
  from June 1 to June 14
- ☑ Trial Balance
  date: June 14
- ☑ General Ledger
  accounts: 1300 5060
  from June 1 to June 14

GST
- ☑ GST Detail Report
  date: June 14

Inventory
- ☑ Inventory Detail
  all details for Bags & Accessories
- ☑ Inventory Sales Detail
  for Accessories
  from June 1 to June 14
- ☑ Inventory Activity Detail
  for Mountain Bikes
  from June 1 to June 14

Journals
- ☑ General (by posting date)
  from June 1 to June 14
- ☐ Purchases
- ☐ Payments
- ☐ Sales
- ☐ Receipts
- ☐ Transfers
- ☑ Adjustments (by posting date)
  from June 1 to June 14

Payables
- ☐ Vendor Aged
- ☐ Aged Overdue Payables
- ☑ Vendor Purchases Summary
  for all vendors, all items
  from June 1 to June 14
- ☐ Pending Purchase Orders

Receivables
- ☐ Customer Aged
- ☐ Aged Overdue Receivables
- ☐ Customer Sales
- ☐ Customer Statements

Mailing Labels
- ☐ Labels

GRAPHS

- ☐ Payables by Aging Period
- ☐ Receivables by Aging Period
- ☐ Sales vs Receivables
- ☐ Revenues by Account
- ☐ Expenses & Net Profit as % of Revenue

- ☐ Payables by Vendor
- ☐ Receivables by Customer
- ☐ Receivables Due vs Payables Due
- ☐ Expenses by Account
- ☐ Current Revenue vs Last Year

SOURCE DOCUMENTS

USING DATE — June 7

206

Sales Invoice #61
Dated June 1/99
To Bay Land Bikers

two MTB-A261 Maxim - 18sp Shimano alloy rim/hub	$400 each
two MTB-Y202 Trac - 5sp chromoly hybrid	300 each
one MTB-A264 Summit - 18sp Alvio drivetrain chr	600
two HMT-21A Myti - 21 vent adjustable in-line	40 each
two ACC-UL1 U-Lock - heavy duty	40 each
three ACC-CL1 Cable Lock - heavy duty	30 each
Delivery charge	50
Goods & Services Tax	7%
Provincial Sales Tax	8%

Terms: 2/10, n/15 days.

210

Purchase Invoice #WS-1217
Dated June 1/99
From Wheeler & Shield Co.

five ACC-CL1 Cable Lock - heavy duty	$ 50.00
five ACC-UL1 U-Lock - heavy duty	100.00
five ACC-UL2 U-Lock - heavy duty, centre lock	125.00
GST Paid	19.25
Invoice Total	$294.25

Terms: n/15 days

214

Memo #1
Dated June 2/99
From Owner: Adjust inventory records for one Speedometer - digital deluxe valued at $20. The speedometer was accidentally dropped and damaged beyond repair. Charge to Damaged Inventory account.

Memo #2
Dated June 2/99

216

From Owner: Create a new asset account in the General Ledger, 1310 Bags
              Add the following inventory records in the Inventory Ledger

Code	Description	Price	Min.
BAG-N1	Saddle Bags - ballistic nylon light	$35 each	1
BAG-L1	Saddle Bags - leather split cowhide	$75 each	1

Asset account:	1310 Bags (New account)	
Revenue account:	4020 Revenue from Sales	
Expense account:	5060 Cost of Goods Sold	

Purchase Invoice #GSB-8218
Dated June 2/99
From Guelph Saddle & Bags (new vendor)

five BAG-L1 Saddle Bags - leather split cowhide	$200.00
five BAG-N1 Saddle Bags - ballistic nylon light	100.00
GST Paid	21.00
Invoice Total	$321.00

Terms: n/15 days

Notes

☐ Guelph Saddle & Bags
(Contact JoAnn Baggett)
is located at
RR #3 Guelph
N2P 8H6
Tel: (519) 821-6344
Fax: (519) 821-6211

Memo #3

220

Dated June 3/99
From Owner: Adjust the purchase invoice from Guelph Saddle & Bags to include $20 for freight charges plus 7% GST. Invoice total to increase by $21.40.

Cash Sales Invoice #62
Dated June 3/99
To Gus Farouk

one MTB-A263 Summit - 18sp STX Alvio A-frame	$800
one ACC-UL2 U-Lock - heavy duty, centre lock	50
one ACC-PA1 Pump - lightweight aluminum	20
one ACC-TK1 Toolkit - multi-function	40
Goods & Services Tax	7%
Provincial Sales Tax	8%

Paid by Visa #4504 562 918 731

Cash Sales Invoice #63
Dated June 4/99
To Chris Chihrin

one MTB-A265 Summit - 21sp Shimano XT/LE Al. DB	$1 600
Goods & Services Tax	7%
Provincial Sales Tax	8%

Paid by MasterCard #9215 4421 3361 7712

Cash Sales Invoice #64
Dated June 4/99
To Vinoo Manga

one SRV-TU Tune-up	$30
one day SRV-RTD Daily rental	15
Goods & Services Tax	7%
Provincial Sales Tax	8%

Paid in cash.

Cash Receipt #50
Dated June 4/99
From Blue Mountain Lodge, cheque #2994 for $287.50 in full payment of account. Reference invoice #53.

Cash Purchase Invoice #CG-662
Dated June 5/99
From Collingwood Graphics, $250 for business cards and flyers for business promotion, plus $17.50 GST(7%) and $20 PST (8%). Invoice total $287.50. Terms: Cash on receipt of invoice. Issued cheque #44 in payment.

Cheque Copy #45
Dated June 5/99
To Global Cyclists, $3 450 in full payment of account. Reference invoice #GC-1543.

Notes

You must add the GST code and the PST rate for non-inventory purchases. They are not entered automatically. The PST amount paid is added to the expense account for the purchase.

Sales Invoice #65
Dated June 6/99
To Lakeland Mountain Bike Club

two MTB-A241 Brava - 18sp Shimano SIS alum alloy	$ 500 each
two MTB-A261 Maxim - 18sp Shimano alloy rim/hub	400 each
four ACC-BS1 Bells - steel	6 each
four ACC-LH1 Lights - halogen clamp style	20 each
four ACC-SG1 Seats - gel extra cushioning	20 each
four ACC-SD2 Speedometers - digital standard	30 each
four HMT-11B Tuff - 11 vent super lock-tech	40 each
three SRV-TU Tune-ups	30 each
Delivery charge	50
Goods & Services Tax	7%
Provincial Sales Tax	8%

Terms: 2/10, n/15 days.

Cash Sales Invoice #66
Dated June 6/99
To Ikuko Hashimi

two ACC-TR1 Tires - 26" mountain	$20 each
one BAG-L1 Saddle Bags - leather split cowhide	75
one HMT-21A Myti - 21 vent adjustable in-line	40
one SRV-TU Tune-up	30
Goods & Services Tax	7%
Provincial Sales Tax	8%

Paid by certified cheque #221.

Sales Invoice #67
Dated June 7/99
To Collingwood Kiwanis Youth Centre (new customer)

five MTB-Y202 Trac - 5sp chromoly hybrid	$300 each
five HMT-21B Excel - 21 vent lightweight	30 each
five ACC-CL1 Cable Lock - heavy duty	30 each
Delivery charge	50
Goods & Services Tax	7%
Provincial Sales Tax	8%

Terms: 2/10, n/15 days.

Sales Invoice #68
Dated June 7/99
To Teehani Summer Resort

six SRV-RTW Weekly rentals	$50 each
Goods & Services Tax	7%
Provincial Sales Tax	8%

Terms: 2/10, n/15.

USING DATE — June 14

Cash Receipt #51
Dated June 8/99
222
From Bay Land Bikers, cheque #411 for $2 588.18 in full payment of account, including $52.82 (2%) discount taken for early payment of account. Reference invoice #61.

Memo # 4

223

Dated June 8/99

From Owner: Teehani Summer Resort has decided to rent 6 bicycles per week for the rest of the summer with an option to purchase at the end of the summer. Look up the original invoice and store it as a weekly recurring entry.

Purchase Invoice #TC-7141

Dated June 8/99

From Trail Canada Accessories & Parts, $150 for bicycle repair parts, plus $10.50 GST(7%) and $12 PST (8%). Invoice total $172.50. Terms: net 30 days.

Cash Sales Invoice #69

Dated June 8/99

To Jasmine Traynor

two MTB-A242 Brava - 18sp high tensile steel	$250 each
two HMT-11B Tuff - 11 vent super lock-tech	40 each
two ACC-UL2 U-Lock - heavy duty, centre lock	50 each
Goods & Services Tax	7%
Provincial Sales Tax	8%

Paid by Visa #4510 733 002 118

Purchase Order #1

Dated June 8/99

Shipping Date June 12/99

From Global Cyclists

five MTB-Y202 Trac - 5sp chromoly hybrid	$ 900.00
four MTB-A261 Maxim - 18sp Shimano alloy rim/hub	1 000.00
two MTB-A241 Brava - 18sp Shimano SIS alum alloy	600.00
two MTB-A264 Summit - 18sp Alvio drivetrain chr	800.00
GST Paid	231.00
Invoice total	$3 531.00

Sales Invoice #70

Dated June 9/99

To Muskoka Seniors Club (new customer)

two MTB-A262 Maxim - 15sp high tens steel hybrid	$160 each
two HMT-11A Charm - 11 vent aerodynamic in-line	25 each
two ACC-SG1 Seats - gel extra cushioning	20 each
two BAG-N1 Saddle Bags - ballistic nylon light	35 each
Goods & Services Tax	7%
Provincial Sales Tax	8%

Terms: 2/10, n/15 days.

Cash Sales Invoice #71

Dated June 10/99

To Grygori Ryder

one MTB-A264 Summit - 18sp Alvio drivetrain chr	$600.00
one ACC-SD1 Speedometer - digital deluxe	40
two ACC-TR2 Tires - 24" mountain	16 each
Goods & Services Tax	7%
Provincial Sales Tax	8%

Paid by Visa #4421 649 720 035

Notes

Muskoka Seniors Club (Contact Hendrik Oude) is located at
4 Everyoung Circle
Collingwood, ON
L9Y 3B9
Tel: (705) 711-4926
Fax: (705) 711-4998
Credit Limit: $4 000

Cheque Copy #46
Dated June 10/99
To Cycling Equipment Inc., $575 in full payment of account. Reference invoice #CE-714.

Memo #5
Dated June 11/99
Record the PST Payable account balance for May 31, 1999 as a liability owing to the Treasurer of Ontario. The liability must be reduced by the sales tax commission earned of 5% on the PST Payable account balance ($1 280 * .05 = $64). Recognize $64 as the Sales Tax Commission earned.

Cheque Copy #47
Dated June 11/99
To the Treasurer of Ontario, $1 216 for the payment of PST Payable for the previous month.

Memo #6
Dated June 11/99
Refer to the May 31 General Ledger balances to record the liability for GST to the Receiver General for May 1999.

Cheque Copy #48
Dated June 11/99
To the Receiver General, $560 for the payment of GST for the previous month.

Cash Sales Invoice #72
Dated June 11/99
To Jon Ming
one MTB-YU20 Trac - 5sp steel frame twist shift	$200
Goods & Services Tax	7%
Provincial Sales Tax	8%
Paid by MasterCard #9123 6154 3491 6101

Memo #7
Dated June 11/99
From Owner: Issue Cheque #49 for $50 to Jay Ruby for assisting with sales in store for a few hours. Charge to Temporary Services account.

Cash Receipt #52
Dated June 11/99
From Teehani Summer Resort, cheque #34 for $510.60 in payment of account (including 2% discount taken on invoice #68). Reference invoices #59 and 68.

Purchase Invoice #CE-918
Dated June 12/99
From Cycling Equipment Inc.
Cycling Equipment included a notice of a price increase for Excel helmets.
five HMT-21B Excel - 21 vent lightweight	$ 100.00
five ACC-SG1 Seats - gel extra cushioning	50.00
five ACC-SD2 Speedometers - digital standard	75.00
GST Paid	15.75
Invoice total	$240.75
Terms: net 30 days.
Increase the selling price of Excel helmets (HMT-21B) to $35 in the Inventory Ledger.

Cash Sales Invoice #73
Dated June 12/99
To Bonni Peddler

one MTB-Y201 BMC - 1sp deluxe high tensile	$150
one ACC-PA1 Pump - lightweight aluminum	20
one ACC-SD2 Speedometer - digital standard	30
one BAG-L1 Saddle Bags - leather split cowhide	75
Goods & Services Tax	7%
Provincial Sales Tax	8%

Paid by Visa #4503 671990 013

Purchase Invoice #GC-1871
Dated June 12/99
Received from Global Cyclists to fill purchase order #1

five MTB-Y202 Trac - 5sp chromoly hybrid	$ 900.00
four MTB-A261 Maxim - 18sp Shimano alloy rim/hub	1 000.00
two MTB-A241 Brava - 18sp Shimano SIS alum alloy	600.00
two MTB-A264 Summit - 18sp Alvio drivetrain chr	800.00
GST Paid	231.00
Invoice total	$3 531.00

Terms: net 30 days.

Memo #8
Dated June 13/99
From Owner: The following youth bicycles will be used for rental. For internal control purposes, prepare an inventory adjustment entry and debit the Rental Bicycles asset account instead of the default Damaged Inventory account.

one MTB-Y201 BMC - 1sp deluxe high tensile	$ 80
one MTB-YU20 Trac - 5sp steel frame twist shift	100

Notes

Enter a negative quantity for the return.

Purchase Return #GC-1871R
Dated June 13/99
To Global Cyclists

one MTB-Y202 Trac - 5sp chromoly hybrid	$180.00
GST Paid	12.60
Total Credit amount	$192.60

Cash Receipt #53
Dated June 13/99
From Lakeland Mountain Bike Club, cheque #4272 for $2 705.39 in payment of account (including $55.21 discount taken). Reference invoice # 65.

Sales Invoice #74
Dated June 14/99
To Blue Mountain Lodge

five SRV-RTW Weekly rentals	$50 each
Goods & Services Tax	7%
Provincial Sales Tax	8%

Terms: 2/10, n/15.

Sales Invoice #75
Dated June 14/99
To Teehani Summer Resort, $300 plus $24 PST and $21 GST for regular weekly rental of six bicycles as agreed. Invoice total $345. Terms: 2/10, n/15. Recall stored entry.

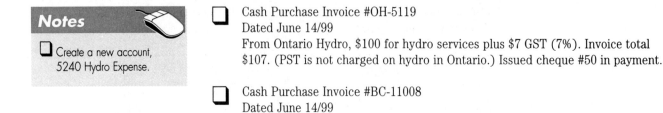
☐ Cash Purchase Invoice #OH-5119
Dated June 14/99
From Ontario Hydro, $100 for hydro services plus $7 GST (7%). Invoice total
$107. (PST is not charged on hydro in Ontario.) Issued cheque #50 in payment.

☐ Cash Purchase Invoice #BC-11008
Dated June 14/99
From Bell Canada, $80 for telephone services plus $5.60 GST (7%) and $6.40
PST (8%). Invoice total $92. Issued cheque #51 in payment.

KEYSTROKES

Accounting for Inventory Sales

Using the instructions for accessing data files in Chapter 1, page 12, open the files for
Meteor Mountain Bike Shop.

Type   06-07-99

This will enter the using date June 7, 1999. The familiar Home window appears.

Double click on the **Sales Journal icon** to open and display the familiar Sales
Journal input screen:

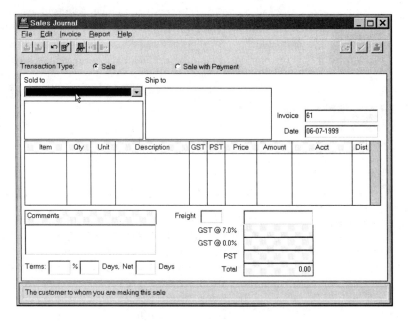

Notice that there are four additional buttons on the tool bar: Adjust invoice, Look up a
posted invoice, Look up previous invoice and Look up next invoice. These are included
because the inventory tracking and invoice lookup options have been turned on. We
will use these buttons later in this application.

The first transaction involves the sale of inventory items. Many of the steps are
identical to those you used for sales in previous applications. You will be using the
inventory database and all of the input form fields to complete this transaction.

The Customer (Sold To) field is darkened, ready for you to enter the information and
Sale is selected as the type of transaction.

Click on the **Customer field** to display the list of customers.

Click on Bay Land Bikers to enter the customer's name and address on the form. If you have selected an incorrect customer, return to the customer list and select again. If you have selected correctly, you should enter the invoice number.

You can skip over the Ship to fields because the default information is correct. The Invoice number is correct because the numeric invoice sequence has been set up in the defaults. If necessary, you can edit the invoice number.

Double click on the Date field to advance the cursor and highlight the contents. Here you must enter the source document date because the default using date is incorrect.

Type   06-01-99

Press   (tab)

The cursor advances to the first line of the Item field. One line is used for each different inventory item or service sold by the business. A separate line would also be used to enter returns and allowances made.

Press   (enter)

The following inventory list appears:

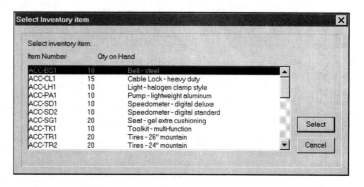

All inventory items the business offers are listed in order according to the item number or code. Quantities available are also included in this display to prevent the company from overselling an item. Scroll down the list.

Click on MTB-A261 Maxim - 18sp Shimano alloy rim/hub from the list.

Click on Select to add the inventory item to your form.

The cursor moves to the Quantity field. If you try to enter a quantity greater than the available stock, the program warns you before you can continue. (You may want to continue with the order if the customer is purchasing inventory stock that is back-ordered.) If you have made an incorrect selection, return to the Item field and re-select from the inventory list. Then enter the number of units of this item sold.

Type   2

Press (tab) repeatedly to advance to the GST field. Notice that the program adds information in each of the fields automatically, based on the inventory record information. Since it is correct, you do not need to change it.

Press (enter) to see the familiar list of available GST codes. These are the same codes we have seen for previous sales journal entries.

Click on 3 - GST @ 7.0%, not included because GST has not yet been included in the selling price.

Click on Select

The cursor advances to the PST field. The PST rate, set up at 8 percent for the company, is entered by default for inventory sales. The rate can be edited if necessary, or deleted if the item is non-taxable. The rate is correct.

Press (tab) to advance through the remaining fields until you reach the next line, or click on the second line, because the default information based on the records is correct. If you need to change the selling price for a particular item or customer, you can edit this field. The program automatically calculates an amount based on the selling price per unit. This figure appears in the Amount field.

The default revenue account appears but can be accepted or changed. You would change the account for returns and allowances or unusual entries. Press (enter) while in the Account field to obtain a list of accounts. Accept the default revenue account for this sale.

You may now enter the second and remaining sale items using the same steps that you used to enter the first item. Notice that all the information except quantity and amount is added by default as soon as you enter the inventory item number. GST codes match the entry on line one. As you complete each line and advance to the next, the totals and tax amounts at the bottom of the form are updated to include the last item entered.

If there are no further items on your input form to enter, the next step is to enter the delivery or freight charges to the customer. There are two Freight fields, just below the section for inventory items. The first Freight field, the small box, contains the GST code that applies to freight charges. The second field contains the amount of freight.

Click on the first Freight field

The default GST code is 3, because that is the code you chose for the inventory sales. The code can be edited if necessary. Press (enter) while in this field to obtain the familiar list of GST code options. However, the code is correct, so you can continue.

Press (tab) to advance to the second Freight field, where you should enter the amount of the freight or delivery charges.

Type 50

Press (tab) to accept the amount and update the totals. Notice that the GST amount is updated as well. Since there is no PST on freight, the PST amount does not change.

Your completed invoice should look like the one shown here:

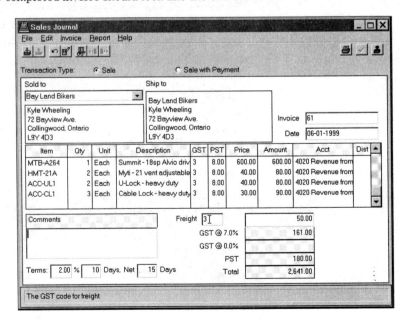

Notes

• You can use a short cut when the default information is correct. Select the inventory item, type the quantity, then click on the next line in the item field. The previous line will then be updated.

• When you complete the last displayed line on the sales invoice, press (tab) in the Account field to add a new invoice line.

Reviewing the Inventory Sales Journal Transaction

Choose Display Sales Journal Entry from the pull-down menu under Report to display the transaction you have entered:

Sales Journal Entry			
File Help			
06-01-1999	Debits	Credits	Project
1200 Accounts Receivable	2,641.00	-	
5060 Cost of Goods Sold	1,380.00		
1300 Accessories	-	70.00	
1320 Helmets	-	50.00	
1340 Mountain Bicycles	-	1,260.00	
2640 PST Payable	-	180.00	
2650 GST Charged on Sales	-	161.00	
4020 Revenue from Sales	-	2,250.00	
4200 Freight Revenue	-	50.00	
	4,021.00	4,021.00	

Notice that all relevant accounts have been updated automatically because the Inventory and Receivables ledgers are integrated with the General Ledger. Therefore, the integrated asset, revenue and expense accounts defined for each inventory item have been debited or credited as required. In addition, the integration accounts we saw earlier for the Receivables Ledger — PST and GST liability accounts and *Accounts Receivable*, together with an additional integration account, *Freight Revenue* — are used. The inventory database and customer record are also updated.

Close the display to return to the journal input screen.

If this is a recurring inventory sale, you can store it just like other sales.

CORRECTING THE INVENTORY SALES ENTRY BEFORE POSTING

Move to the field that has the error. **Press** (tab) to move forward through the fields or **press** (shift) and (tab) together to move back to a previous field. This will highlight the field information so you can change it. **Type** the correct information and **press** (tab) to enter it.

You can also use the mouse to point to a field and drag through the incorrect information to highlight it. **Type** the correct information and **press** (tab) to enter it.

To correct any item on the inventory line, **click on** the incorrect field to move the cursor and highlight the contents of this field. **Press** (enter) to display the list of inventory items, GST codes or accounts. **Click on** the correct selection to highlight it, then **click on** Select. For the remaining fields, **type** the correct information. **Press** (tab) to enter the change.

If you change the inventory item, you must re-enter the quantity sold and **press** (tab). The totals will be updated correctly if you follow this procedure.

If the customer is incorrect, re-select from the customer list by **clicking on** the arrow beside this field. **Click on** the name of the correct customer.

If you have forgotten a complete line of the invoice, **click on** the line below the one you have forgotten. **Choose** Insert Line from the pull-down menu under Edit to add a blank invoice line to your form. To remove a complete line, **click on** the line you want to delete and **choose** Remove Line from the pull-down menu under Edit.

Click on ↶ or ☒ to remove the entire invoice and start over or **choose** Undo Entry from the pull-down menu under Edit. You will be asked to confirm that this is what you want to do.

Posting

When all the information in your journal entry is correct, you must post the transaction to save your work.

Click on Post ![icon] to save the transaction.

The next transaction is an inventory purchase, not a sale. Close the Sales Journal window to exit to the Home window.

Accounting for Inventory Purchases

The second transaction involves the purchase of inventory items. Many of the steps in completing this entry are the same as those you have been using for other credit purchase transactions. Now you will be completing all the parts of this form, using the inventory database for the additional information.

Double click on the **Purchases Journal icon** in the Home window to display the familiar Purchases Journal input form window:

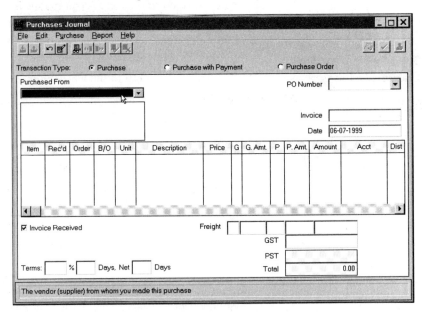

You are now ready to enter the second transaction on the input screen. The Vendor (Purchased from) field is darkened, ready for you to enter the information and Purchase is selected as the type of transaction.

Click on the **Vendor (Purchased From) field** to display the list of vendors.

Click on **Wheeler & Shield Co.** from the list to add it to your input form. You now have the opportunity to check your selection. If you have selected an incorrect vendor, select again from the vendor list. If you have selected correctly, proceed by entering the invoice number.

Press (tab) twice to skip the PO Number field and advance to the Invoice field.

Type WS-1217

Press (tab)

The cursor advances to the Date field. Here you should enter the source document date, unless it is the same as the default using date.

Type 06-01-99

The cursor advances to the Item field.

Press (enter) to see the list of inventory items.

Click on ACC-CL1 Cable Lock - heavy duty from the list to highlight it.

Click on Select

The cursor advances to the Rec'd field (quantity received). The Description field should now show the name, **Cable Lock - heavy duty**. If you have made an incorrect selection, return to the Item field and select again. The default price contained in the inventory records is entered automatically. Now enter the quantity for this item.

Type 5

Press (tab)

The cursor advances to the Unit field, skipping the Order and B/O (back order) fields because this is not a purchase order.

Press (tab) twice because the Unit and Description are correct based on inventory ledger records.

The cursor advances to the Price field, which is used to record the unit price paid for the purchase of the inventory items. This amount should not include any GST paid that can be used as an input tax credit, or PST paid on the purchase. The default information, based on previous purchases, is correct so do not change it. If it is incorrect because the price has changed, you can edit the amount shown by default.

Press (tab) to advance to the GST code field. The correct code is entered by default. If it is not,

Press (enter) if you need to see the list of GST codes.

Click on 3 - GST @ 7% not included to highlight it.

Click on Select

The cursor advances to the GST Amount field. The amount is correct so **press** (tab) to advance to the P (PST rate) field. No PST is paid for inventory purchases.

Press (del) to remove the default entry of 8%.

Press (tab) repeatedly to advance to the next line, with the cursor blinking in the Item field again. Notice that the Account field was skipped over, because you cannot change the entry for inventory purchases. The Asset account for the inventory purchase is defined in the inventory ledger as the integration account for purchases and sales.

Enter the remaining items on the source document, using the same steps that you used to record the first item.

The Freight fields are used to enter any freight charges that cannot be allocated to a specific item purchased and to enter the taxes paid on the freight charges. There are five Freight fields: GST code, GST amount, PST rate, PST amount and finally the base amount of the freight charge. Because GST is paid on freight you must enter GST information if the vendor charges freight. Click on the first Freight field. **Press** (enter) to see the list of GST codes and select the correct one. You do not need to enter amounts for the taxes; they are calculated as soon as you enter the amount of freight charged. **Press** (tab) twice to advance to the PST rate field. If provincial taxes are applied to freight, enter the tax rate in the third Freight field. In the final Freight field, type the base amount of freight and **press** (tab) . Simply Accounting calculates the amount of GST and PST, and updates all the totals.

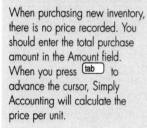

Notes

When purchasing new inventory, there is no price recorded. You should enter the total purchase amount in the Amount field. When you press (tab) to advance the cursor, Simply Accounting will calculate the price per unit.

There are no freight charges for this entry so you can skip the freight fields. Your input form is completed and should appear as follows:

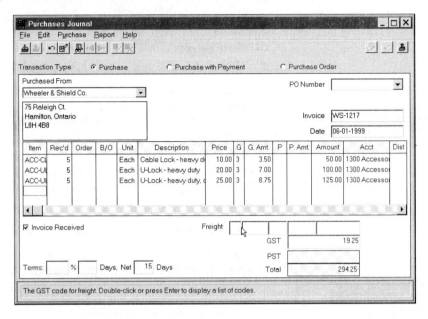

Reviewing the Inventory Purchases Journal Transaction

Choose Display Purchases Journal Entry from the pull-down menu under **Report** to display the transaction you have entered as shown:

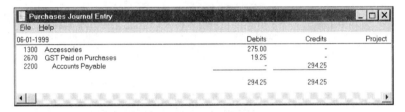

You can see that the Simply Accounting program has automatically updated all accounts relevant to this transaction. The appropriate inventory asset account (*Accessories*), *Accounts Payable* and *GST Paid on Purchases* accounts have been updated as required because the ledgers are integrated. The inventory database and the vendor record are also updated.

Close the display to return to the Purchases Journal input screen.

If this is a recurring purchase, you can store the entry, just like other recurring purchases.

Warning!

Please be careful when reviewing your transaction to make sure you have entered the correct information.

Move to the field that has the error. **Press** (tab) to move forward through the fields or **press** (shift) and (tab) together to move back to a previous field. This will highlight the field information so you can change it. **Type** the correct information and **press** (tab) to enter it.

You can also use the mouse to point to a field and drag through the incorrect information to highlight it. **Type** the correct information and **press** (tab) to enter it.

If the inventory item is incorrect, re-select from the inventory list by pressing (enter) while in this field. **Click on Select** to add the item to your form. **Type** the quantity purchased and **press** (tab) repeatedly to advance to the next line in order to update the totals.

If the vendor is incorrect, re-select from the vendor list by **clicking on** the Vendor field. **Click on** the name of the correct vendor and **press** (tab) .

Account numbers cannot be changed on the purchase invoice for inventory items. They must be edited in the Inventory ledger.

If you have forgotten a complete line of the invoice, **click on** the line below the one you have forgotten. **Choose Insert Line** from the pull-down menu under **Edit** to add a blank invoice line to your form. To remove a complete line, **click on** the line you want to delete and **choose Remove Line** from the pull-down menu under **Edit**.

Click on 🔄 or ❌ to remove the entire invoice and start over or **choose Undo Entry** from the pull-down menu under **Edit**. You will be asked to confirm that this is what you want to do.

Posting

When all the information in your journal entry is correct, you must post the transaction to save your work.

Click on Post 📥

The next transaction is an inventory adjustment. Close the Purchases Journal to exit to the Home window.

Placing a Purchase Order

Placing a purchase order for inventory items is the same as a purchase order for non-inventory items.

Choose Purchase Order as the Transaction Type.

Enter the PO Number and Shipping Date.

Then complete the selection of inventory items as you would for an inventory purchase. Instead of filling in the Rec'd field, however, you will complete the Order and B/O fields.

When the goods are received, fill the purchase order. Refer to Chapter 4, page 81 if you need to review purchase orders.

Making Inventory Adjustments

Inventory adjustments are made in the Adjustments Journal indicated in the Home window shown here:

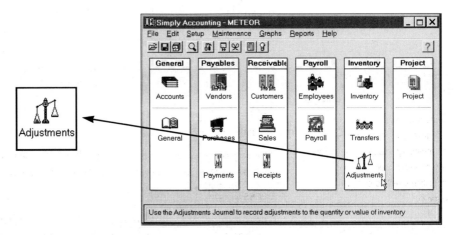

Double click on the **Adjustments Journal icon** to display the blank inventory Adjustments Journal input screen:

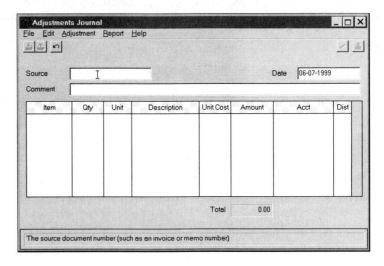

The cursor is in the Source field. The source for an adjustment will normally be a memo from a manager or owner.

Type   Memo 1

Press   (tab)

The cursor is now in the Date field, with the using date entered and highlighted as usual.

Type   06-02-99

Press   (tab)

The cursor is now in the Comment field, where you can enter a brief explanation for this transaction.

Type   Speedometer damaged beyond repair

Press   (tab)

The cursor is now in the Item field.

Press (enter) to display the familiar inventory list. Notice that the quantities have been updated to include the previous sale and purchase.

Click on **ACC-SD1 Speedometer - digital deluxe** from the list to highlight it.

Click on **Select** to enter it onto the form.

The item name, *Speedometer - digital deluxe*, the unit, the unit cost and the account have been added automatically. The cursor advances to the Quantity field. You need to indicate that the inventory has been reduced because of the damaged item. You do this by typing a negative number in the field.

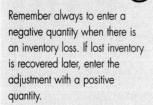

Notes

Remember always to enter a negative quantity when there is an inventory loss. If lost inventory is recovered later, enter the adjustment with a positive quantity.

Notes

If you need to choose another account, press (enter) to display the list of accounts and select the account as usual.

Type -1

Press (tab)

The cursor advances to the Amount field. A negative amount, reflecting the inventory loss, automatically appears as a default. Choose the default.

Press (tab)

The cursor advances to the Account field. *Damaged Inventory*, the default integration account for inventory losses appears automatically for this entry. This is the correct account.

The Dist field for project allocations is not used by Meteor Mountain Bike Shop, so ignore it. We will discuss it in a later application.

Press (tab) to advance the cursor to the next line.

Your entry is complete as shown and you are ready to review it:

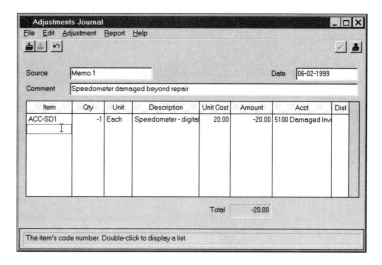

Reviewing the Adjustments Journal Entry

Choose **Display Adjustments Journal Entry** from the pull-down menu under **Report** to display the transaction you have entered as shown here:

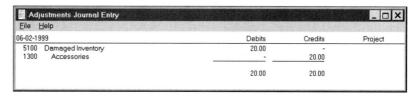

You can see that the Simply Accounting program has automatically updated all the relevant accounts for this transaction. The appropriate inventory asset defined for this inventory item, *Accessories*, and the inventory database have also been updated. The *Damaged Inventory* account, the Inventory integration expense account that was defined for inventory losses or adjustments, has also been updated.

Close the display to return to the Adjustments Journal input screen.

CORRECTING THE ADJUSTMENTS JOURNAL ENTRY

Move to the field that has the error. **Press** (tab) to move forward through the fields or **press** (shift) and (tab) together to move back to a previous field. This will highlight the field information so you can change it. **Type** the correct information and **press** (tab) to enter it.

You can also use the mouse to point to a field and drag through the incorrect information to highlight it. **Type** the correct information and **press** (tab) to enter it.

If the inventory item is incorrect, re-select from the inventory list by pressing (enter) while in this field. **Click on Select** to add the item to your form. **Type** the quantity and **press** (tab). If you have changed any information on an inventory item line, you must **press** (tab) to update the totals.

Click on ↺ or ✕ to remove the entire invoice and start over or **choose Undo Entry** from the pull-down menu under **Edit**. You will be asked to confirm that this is what you want to do.

Posting

When all the information in your journal entry is correct, you must post the transaction to save your work.

Click on Post 📤

The next keystroke transaction is a purchase of new inventory items.

Adding a New Inventory Item

The source document, Memo #2, on June 2 requires you to add Saddle Bags as a new inventory item to the current list. When you check the Chart of Accounts, you can see that saddle bags do not belong in any of the existing inventory asset accounts. Therefore you must create a new asset account called **Bags** and give it a new account number, **1310**.

The keystrokes for inserting a new General Ledger account are provided in the Reliable Roofing application.

Inventory items are added in the Inventory Ledger indicated in the following screen:

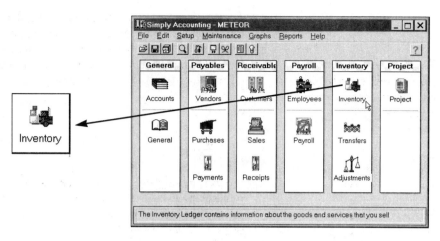

Double click on the **Inventory icon** on the Home window to open it and display the Inventory window with inventory items listed by name:

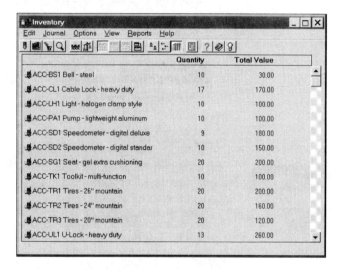

Click on the **Create button** on the tool bar in the Inventory window, or choose Create from the pull-down menu under Edit, to provide the following Inventory Ledger input screen:

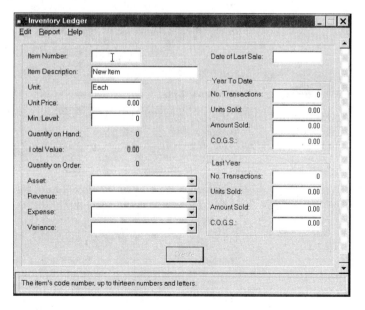

The cursor is flashing in the Item Number field, ready for you to enter information. From your source document information, you must enter the item code and description. The first Item field contains the code or number of the inventory item; the second Item field contains the description or item name.

Type   BAG-N1

Press   (tab) to advance to the Item Description field.

Type   Saddle Bags - ballistic nylon light

Press   (tab)

The cursor advances to the Unit field, which shows the way in which goods are sold (e.g., by the dozen, by the tonne or by item). The default entry, Each is correct.

Press   (tab)

The cursor advances to the Unit Price field. Here you must enter the selling price of the item.

Type   35

Press   (tab)

The cursor advances to the Minimum Level field. Here you must enter the stock level at which you wish to reorder the item in question. When you print out inventory reports, items that have fallen below the minimum level will be flagged.

Type   1

Press   (tab)

The cursor advances to the Asset field. Here you must enter the number of the integration asset account affected by purchases and sales of this item. You must enter the number of the asset account you created for this item from the account list provided when you click on the arrow to the right of the field.

Click on 1310 Bags from this list to enter it on your form.

Press   (tab)

The cursor advances to the Revenue field. Here you must enter the integration revenue account that will be credited when this inventory item is sold.

Click on 4020 Revenue from Sales from the list of revenue accounts provided when you click on the arrow beside the field and enter it on your form.

Press   (tab)

The cursor advances to the Expense field. Here you must enter the integration expense account that will be debited when this inventory item is sold.

Click on 5060 Cost of Goods Sold from the list of expense accounts displayed when you click on the arrow beside the field and enter it on your form.

Press   (tab)

The cursor advances to the Variance field. The integration variance expense account is used when the inventory sold is on order, before the goods are in stock. At the time of the sale, the *Cost of Goods Sold* account is debited for the average cost of the inventory based on previous purchases. When the goods are received, the actual purchase price may be different from this historical average cost. The price difference is charged to the variance account. Meteor does not use this field so you can skip it.

Press   (tab)

Notes

The setup option chosen for inventory is to sort the items by code or number. Therefore the number field is the first item field. When you choose to sort by description, the longer description field will come first.

Notes

• Only asset accounts are available in the list for the Asset field.
• Only revenue accounts are available in the list for the Revenue field.
• Only expense accounts are available in the lists for the Expense field and the Variance field.
• Variance accounts are used in the Hearth House application.

Notes

Integration accounts are defined for each item in the Inventory Ledger because each inventory item can be related to separate asset, revenue, expense and variance accounts. For other ledgers, the integration accounts are defined for the entire ledger. For example, there is only one Accounts Receivable account.

The cursor advances to the Date of Last Sale field. This field refers to historical information — the most recent date that this item was sold. Use an accepted date format. Since this is a new inventory item, there are no previous sales.

Press [tab]

The cursor advances to No. Transactions, the first field in the Year To Date section. This section and the one below it refer to historical information for the current fiscal period, and for the previous year because Simply Accounting allows you to store two years of transactions.

The No. (number of) Transactions refers to the total number of times the item was sold. For example, if one customer bought the item on three separate dates, there would be three transactions. If four customers bought the item on one day, there would be four transactions. If one customer bought four of the same item at one time, there would be one transaction. The Units Sold counts the total number of items that were sold on all occasions to all customers in the relevant time period. In the Amount Sold field you would enter the total sale price of all items sold in the time period, and in the C.O.G.S. (cost of goods sold) field, enter the total purchase price of all the items sold.

Once again, because there are no prior sales of this inventory item, leave the entries at zero. Your form is now complete and is shown as follows:

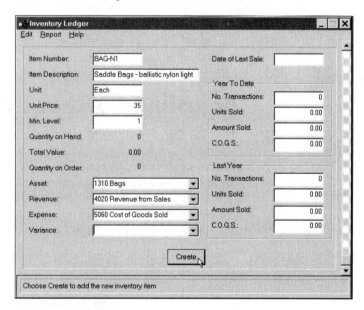

Correct the information if necessary by returning to the field that contains the error. Highlight the error and type the correct information.

Press [tab] to enter the correction.

When all the information is correct, you must save your information.

Click on Create to save the new record and add it to your list of inventory items.

Repeat the procedures above for the second new inventory item in the source document. You should use the same asset, revenue and expense accounts that you used for the first new inventory item. Save your information and proceed to record the purchase invoice, using the keystroke instructions provided earlier in this application.

Close the Inventory Ledger window.

Close the Inventory window to return to the Home window. Enter the new vendor and then complete the inventory purchase entry.

When the Inventory Tracking option is turned off in the System setup, the Inventory Ledger does not include any historical information fields. That is, the Date of Last Sale, the Year To Date and Last Year fields are omitted as shown here:

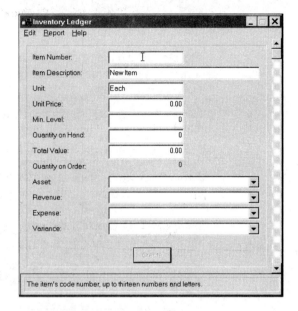

The rest of the fields are identical and the reduced form is completed in the same way as indicated in the steps provided above for Adding Inventory.

Adjusting Purchase Invoices

Notes

Inventory Tracking and Invoice Lookup can be activated in the System Settings under the Setup menu from the Home window.

When the Inventory Tracking and Invoice Lookup features are turned on, Simply Accounting keeps a copy of all purchase and sales invoices so that you can look at them at any time after posting. You can also use the Adjust Invoice feature to correct mistakes in previously posted entries. Adjusting a purchase entry is similar to adjusting a payroll entry. We will adjust the purchase from Guelph Saddle & Bags to add the freight charges.

Open the Purchases Journal.

Click on the **Adjust invoice button** 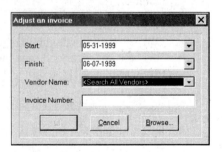 or choose Adjust Invoice from the pull-down menu under Purchase to display the following dialogue box:

You can search through all invoices for the fiscal year to date, or enter a narrower range of dates, search invoices for all vendors or for a specific vendor, or if you know the invoice number, you can enter it.

Click on the **Vendor Name** field to see the list of vendors.

Click on Guelph Saddle & Bags to select this vendor.

Click on Browse to display the purchases from this vendor.

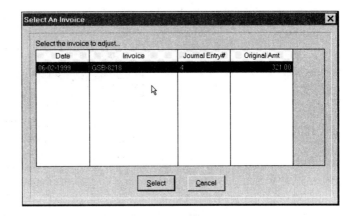

The only purchase from this vendor is selected.

Click on Select to display the original invoice that we posted:

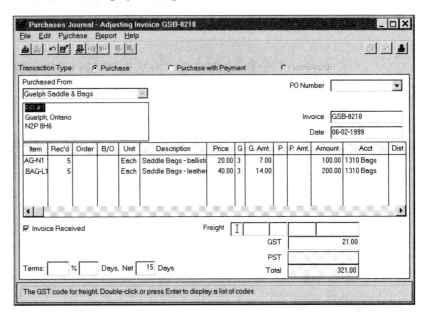

All the fields except the vendor name can be edited. We need only to add freight and GST paid on freight.

Click on the **first Freight field**, the one for the GST code.

Press (enter)

Click on 3- GST @ 7%, not included

Click on Select to add the code to the invoice. We can skip the two Freight fields that relate to PST because PST is not charged on freight.

Click on the **final Freight field**

Type 20

Press (tab) to update the GST amount field and all the totals.

Review the journal entry. It is the entry for the adjusted invoice. Close the display. When you are certain that the invoice is correct,

Click on Post [icon]

Close the Purchases Journal.

Display the Purchases Journal entry for June 2. It should look like the following:

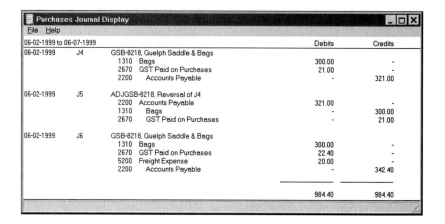

Notice that there are three entries relating to the purchase from Guelph Saddle & Bags — the original one, a reversing entry and the final correct entry with GST and freight updated. Close the display when you are finished.

Entering Sales Discounts

The early payment by Bay Land Bikers is eligible for the 2 percent discount.

Open the Receipts Journal.

Choose the vendor Bay Land Bikers and add it to the receipt. Invoice #61 is outstanding and no discount is shown as available:

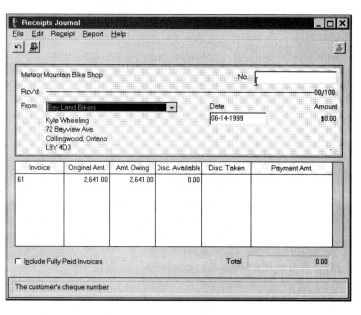

Notes

Double click on the Invoice number (e.g., 61) if you want to see the sales invoice previously posted. You can also look up purchase invoices from the Payments Journal by clicking on an invoice number. This feature is available only when Invoice Lookup is turned on.

Press [tab] to advance to the cheque No. field.

Type 411

Press [tab] to advance to the Date field.

Type 06-08-99

Press [tab] to advance to the Invoice field. The invoice line changes as shown here:

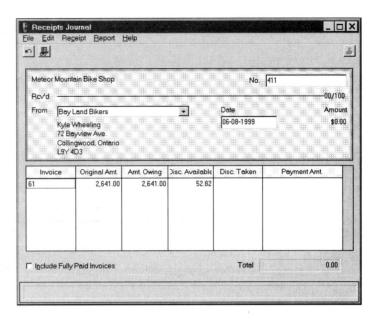

Because the date of the payment is now within ten days of the sale, the customer is eligible for a discount. It is calculated and displayed in the Disc. Available field.

Press [tab] to advance to the Disc. (Discount) Taken field. The amount is highlighted and it is correct.

Press [tab] again to advance to the Payment Amt. (Amount) field. The amount is correct, the discount amount is subtracted from the original total invoice amount.

Press [tab] once more to accept the amount. The entry is complete.

Display the Receipts Journal entry. It should look like the one shown here:

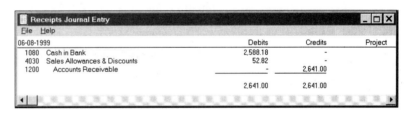

Enter purchases discounts in the Payments Journal in the same way that you enter sales discounts in the Receipts Journal. If the time for the discount has not passed, the discount will show as available.

Simply Accounting has automatically charged the discount to the *Sales Allowances & Discounts* account, the account defined for the Receivables Ledger as the sales discount integration account. This part of the journal entry is added to the regular Receipts Journal entry we have seen previously.

Close the display when you are finished. Make corrections if necessary.

Post the receipt.

Looking up Invoices

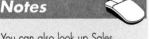

You can also look up Sales invoices from the Receipts Journal window and Purchase invoices from the Payments Journal window.

Lookup provides an exact copy of the posted invoice that you can store or print if you have forgotten to do so before posting. It may also be useful if a customer has an enquiry about a purchase or needs a copy of the invoice. Obviously these features demand extra storage space on your hard or floppy disk.

Open the Sales Journal.

Click on the **Look up a posted invoice button** 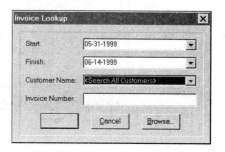 or choose Look up Invoice from the pull-down menu under Invoice to display the following dialogue box:

You can search through all invoices for the fiscal year to date, or enter a narrower range of dates, search for all customer invoices or for a specific customer, or search for a specific invoice number. Your search strategy will depend on how much information you have before you begin the search and how many invoices there are altogether.

Notes

If you know the invoice number, enter it in the Invoice Number field and click OK.

By default, the program enters as the Start date either the beginning of the Fiscal period or the date on which the records were converted to Simply Accounting, whichever comes later. The Finish date is the most recent using date. You can change these dates to narrow the search, just as you would edit any other date fields.

The Customer Name option allows you to Search All Customers, the default setting, or a specific Customer's invoices.

Click on the **Customer Name field** or its **drop-down list arrow** to display the list of customers and click on the name you need. Notice that you can also look up the invoices for One-time customers. In this case we will look at all invoices so choose the default to Search All Customers.

Click on Browse to display the list of invoices that meet the search conditions of date and customers:

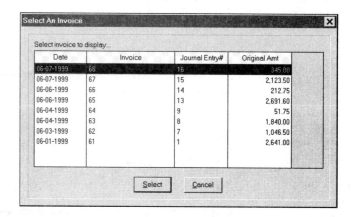

Invoice #68, the invoice we want to see is already selected because it is the last one we posted.

Click on Select. The requested invoice will be displayed as follows:

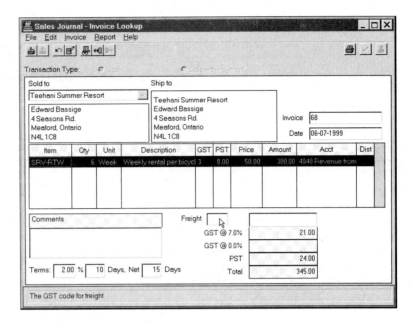

Notice that this is an exact copy of the original invoice, except that you cannot post it. You can however store it or print it.

Click on Look up next invoice [image] or Look up previous invoice [image] if you want to access other invoices from this one.

Click on Store as a recurring entry [image]. Follow the usual procedure to store the invoice as a recurring weekly entry. Refer to Chapter 5, page 119 if you need help.

You can look up purchase invoices in the same way as you look up sales invoices. Open the Purchases Journal, click on Look up a posted invoice, decide whether you want to restrict the search dates or vendors, and click on Browse. Choose an invoice from the displayed list and click on Select. Again, if you know the invoice number you can enter it directly, click on OK and display the requested invoice immediately.

Displaying Inventory Reports

Most inventory reports can be displayed from the pull-down menu under Reports in the Inventory window.

Displaying Inventory Lists

In the Home window,

Click on the **Inventory icon** to select it.

Click on the **Report button** [image] or **choose Display Inventory List** from the pull-down menu under **Reports**. You will see the list immediately.

Close the display when you are finished.

Displaying the Adjustments Journal

In the Home window,

Click on the **Adjustments Journal icon** to select it.

Click on the **Report button** [image] or **choose Display Adjustments Journal** from the pull-down menu under **Reports**.

You will see the following screen asking for the dates for your report:

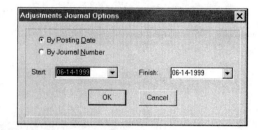

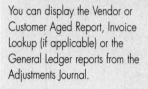
As usual, the using date and the By Posting Date option are provided by default.

Type the beginning date for the report you want.

Press [tab]

Type the ending date for the report.

Click on OK

Close the display when you are finished.

Displaying Inventory Reports

Choose Inventory and then Inventory from the pull-down menu under Reports to display the following report options:

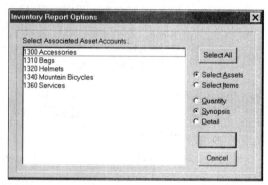

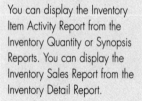
The Select Assets option will provide information for all inventory items in the asset group(s) chosen.

The Select Items option will provide information for the inventory items selected. When you click on Select Items, the boxed list will contain all inventory items by name.

You can obtain information for all items through either option by choosing Select All.

Inventory reports can be displayed with three types of information, quantity, synopsis or detail.

The Quantity option provides current information about the quantity on hand, the minimum stock levels and whether the item has fallen below the minimum level and needs to be re-ordered. The information is given for the items requested or for all items in the asset group(s), according to the option you selected.

The Synopsis option lists selling price, quantity on hand, the cost of the inventory on hand, the total value of inventory on hand and the profit margin for the items requested or for all items in the asset group(s), according to the option you selected. Total value of the inventory in an asset group is also given if you choose Select Assets.

Choose the options you need for your report.

Click on the names of all the items or asset groups you want included in the report.

Click on OK

The Detail option is available only when Inventory Tracking is turned on.

Click on Detail to see the following expanded set of options:

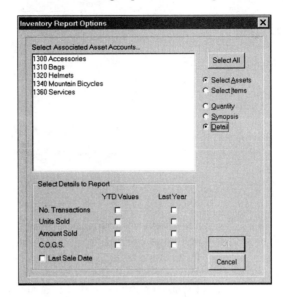

Click on the names of all the items or asset groups you want included in the report.

Click on all the details you wish to have information on for the current fiscal year to date and the last (previous) year. The categories (No. Transactions, Units Sold, Amount Sold, C.O.G.S. and Last Sale Date) are the same as those in the Inventory Ledger. Refer to page 219 for a description of these details.

Click on OK

Close the display when you are finished.

Displaying Inventory Tracking Reports

When Inventory Tracking is turned on, there are four additional reports that you can display or print. All of these reports provide information about the turnover of inventory products.

Notes

When invoice lookup and inventory tracking are turned on, additional inventory-related reports become available from the displayed reports described earlier for the other ledgers.

Vendor Purchases Reports

Notes

You can display the Inventory Detail Report from the Purchases Summary Report. You can display the Vendor Aged, Invoice Lookup and Journal Report from the Purchases Detail Report.

Choose Payables and then **Vendor Purchases** from the pull-down menu under Reports to display the following report options:

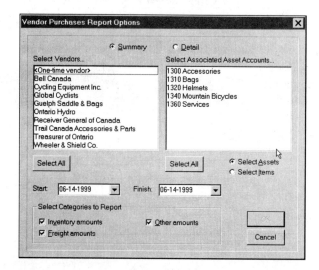

The Summary option, selected by default, includes totals for the selected categories and items or asset group, organized by vendor. The Detail option provides the same information by individual journal entry, including the source document numbers and journal entry numbers. The report includes details on the number of transactions (Summary option only), the quantity of items sold, the cost per item and the total cost of the purchase. Non-inventory purchases, such as telephone services, are listed as Other. **Click on** Detail to choose the Detail option.

Click on one or more of the asset groups to include them in the report, or click on the Select All button below the list to include all inventory items in the report. Selecting an asset group will include all the inventory items in that group in the report.

Click on Select Items to include individual inventory items in the report. The box contents will change to display the inventory item list.

Click on one or more items to include them in the report, or click on Select All to include all inventory items in the report.

Click on one or more of the Vendor names to include them in the report, or click on the Select All button below the list to include all Vendors in the report.

Notes

Once a category is not selected you can click on it again to select it.

Type the starting date for the report in the Start field and the ending date for the report in the Finish field. By default, the latest using date appears in both fields.

By default, all categories will be included in the report. Click on any category to remove the ✔ and deselect it. You can choose to include purchases of inventory items, non-inventory purchases (other) and freight charges for the selected vendor and item transactions.

Click on OK

Close the display when you are finished.

Customer Sales Reports

Choose Receivables and then **Customer Sales** from the pull-down menu under **Reports** to display the following report options:

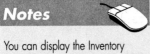
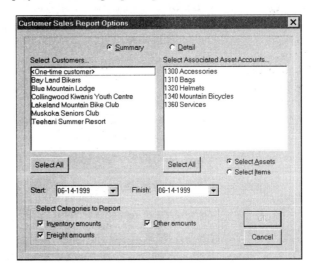

The **Summary** option, selected by default, includes totals for the selected categories and items or asset groups, organized by customer. The **Detail** option provides the same information listed by individual journal entry, including the source document numbers and journal entry numbers. The report includes details on the number of transactions (Summary option only), the quantity of items sold, the revenue per item, the cost of goods sold and the profit on each sale transaction. Non-inventory sales, such as discounts, are listed as Other. **Click on** Detail to choose the Detail option.

Select items or assets, customers, dates and categories as you do for Vendor Purchases reports.

Click on OK

Close the display when you are finished.

Inventory Sales Reports

Choose Inventory and then **Inventory Sales** from the pull-down menu under **Reports** to display the following report options:

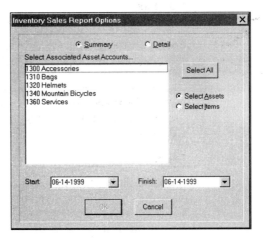

The **Summary** option, selected by default, includes totals for the selected inventory items organized by item. The **Detail** option provides the same information listed by individual journal entry, including the source document numbers and journal entry numbers. The report includes details on the number of transactions (Summary option only), the quantity of items sold, the revenue per item, the cost of goods sold and the profit on each sale transaction. Non-inventory sales are not included. **Click on Detail** to choose the Detail option.

Click on one or more of the asset groups to include them in the report, or click on Select All to include all inventory items in the report. Selecting an asset group will include all the inventory items in that group in the report.

Click on Select Items to include individual inventory items in the report. **Click on one or more items** to include them in the report, or click on Select All to include all inventory items in the report.

Type the starting date for the report in the Start field and the ending date for the report in the Finish field. By default, the latest using date appears in both fields.

Click on OK

Close the display when you are finished.

Inventory Activity Reports

Choose Inventory and then **Inventory Activity** from the pull-down menu under **Reports** to display the following report options:

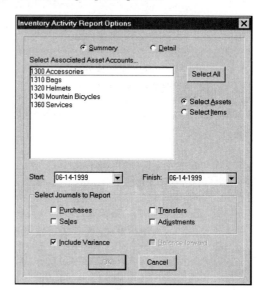

The **Summary** option, selected by default, includes totals for the selected inventory items organized by item. The **Detail** option provides the same information listed by individual journal entry, including the source document numbers and journal entry numbers. The report includes details on the number of transactions (Summary option only), the Quantity In (increases to inventory) and Out (decreases in inventory) and the Amount In and Out (cost price) for each item in each of the selected journals.

Click on Detail to choose the Detail option.

Click on one or more of the asset groups to include them in the report, or click on Select All to include all inventory items in the report. Selecting an asset group will include all the inventory items in that group.

Click on Select Items to include individual inventory items in the report. **Click on one or more items** to include them in the report, or click on Select All to include all inventory items in the report.

Type the starting date for the report in the Start field and the ending date for the report in the Finish field. By default, the latest using date appears in both fields.

Click on the journals to include in the report.

Click on Balance Forward to include opening and closing balances for each item.

Click on OK

Close the display when you are finished.

Printing Inventory Reports

To print an inventory report, first display the report. Then,

Choose Print from the pull-down menu under **File**.

CASE PROBLEM

Examine the sale of new items — saddle bags — and determine how successful they have been relative to other items. What information should Meteor Mountain Bike Shop use to decide whether or not to continue selling these items?

How is the decision to continue providing a service different from the decision to carry inventory items?

Why might a store continue to sell inventory items or provide a service even if they were not selling well?

Upon completion of
this chapter, you
will be able to:

OBJECTIVE

- *enter* year-end adjustments using the General Journal in Simply
  Accounting

COMPANY INFORMATION

Company Profile

Mighty Mack Service Centre in Winnipeg, Manitoba, is owned and operated by Siobhan Mackenzie, an experienced and licensed auto mechanic. When she was young, no one could pronounce her first name so she quickly became known as Mack. After a college diploma, an apprenticeship, and several years experience in a car repair and body shop, she opened her own service centre in 1999.

The service centre repairs small trucks and cars. Mackenzie works by herself but subcontracts some work for big repair jobs. Most of the time she has two or three vehicles to work on at the same time. She earns additional income from leasing automobiles as replacement vehicles to customers whose cars she repairs, and from renting the apartment above the service centre.

At the end of 1999, she has completed all the day-to-day journal entries, but still needs to make the end of year adjustments in preparation for closing the books and beginning a new fiscal year. She has been using the General Ledger in Simply Accounting for her record keeping but she may add Receivables and Payables information at the beginning of the new year. For now, the following information is available to complete the adjustments using Simply Accounting:

- Chart of Accounts
- Trial Balance

MIGHTY MACK SERVICE CENTRE
CHART OF ACCOUNTS

ASSETS
1080 Cash in Bank
1150 Marketable Securities
1200 Accounts Receivable
1220 Notes Receivable
1240 Interest Receivable
1260 Allowance for Doubtful Accounts
1280 Parts Inventory
1300 Prepaid Advertising
1320 Prepaid Insurance
1400 Land
1420 Machinery & Tools
1440 Accum Deprec: Mach & Tools
1480 Service Centre
1500 Accum Deprec: Serv Ctr
1540 Towing Vehicle
1560 Accum Deprec: Tow Veh
1600 Truck
1620 Accum Deprec: Truck

LIABILITIES
2100 Bank Loan
2200 Accounts Payable
2220 Advance from Leasing
2240 Advance from Rentals
2650 GST Charged on Services
2670 GST Paid on Purchases
2800 Interest Accrued: Bank Loan
2820 Interest Accrued: Mortgage
2860 Subcontracting Fees Payable
2940 Mortgage Payable

EQUITY
3560 S. Mackenzie, Capital
3580 S. Mackenzie, Drawings
3600 Current Earnings

REVENUE
4020 Interest Revenue
4040 Leasing Revenue
4060 Rental Revenue
4100 Service Revenue

EXPENSE
5020 Advertising Expense
5040 Bank Charges
5060 Doubtful Accounts Expense
5100 Depreciation: Mach & Tools
5120 Depreciation: Serv Ctr
5140 Depreciation: Tow Veh
5160 Depreciation: Truck
5200 Hydro Expense
5220 Interest Expense: Bank Loan
5240 Interest Expense: Mortgage
5280 Insurance Expense
5300 Parts Inventory Used
5320 Subcontracting Fees
5380 Telephone Expense

MIGHTY MACK SERVICE CENTRE
TRIAL BALANCE

December 30, 1999

1080 Cash in Bank	$ 6 293.00	
1150 Marketable Securities	10 000.00	
1200 Accounts Receivable	12 800.00	
1220 Notes Receivable	2 400.00	
1260 Allowance for Doubtful Accounts		$ 150.00
1280 Parts Inventory	14 200.00	
1300 Prepaid Advertising	450.00	
1320 Prepaid Insurance	1 800.00	
1400 Land	30 000.00	
1420 Machinery & Tools	20 000.00	
1480 Service Centre	120 000.00	
1540 Towing Vehicle	25 000.00	
1600 Truck	20 000.00	
2100 Bank Loan		10 000.00
2200 Accounts Payable		6 850.00
2220 Advance from Leasing		900.00
2240 Advance from Rentals		1 500.00
2940 Mortgage Payable		100 000.00
3560 S. Mackenzie, Capital		80 000.00
4040 Leasing Revenue		2 200.00
4060 Rental Revenue		3 000.00
4100 Service Revenue		74 800.00
5040 Bank Charges	142.00	
5200 Hydro Expense	1 480.00	
5220 Interest Expense: Bank Loan	990.00	
5240 Interest Expense: Mortgage	11 250.00	
5280 Insurance Expense	450.00	
5320 Subcontracting Fees	1 620.00	
5380 Telephone Expense	525.00	
	$279 400.00	$279 400.00

INSTRUCTIONS

1. Using the Source Transactions provided, record the adjusting entries using the General Journal in Simply Accounting. Since no source document numbers are provided, you may enter ADJ1, ADJ2, etc., or ADJUST-A, ADJUST-B, etc., in the Source field. The using date is December 31, 1999.

2. After you have finished making your entries, print the following reports:

    • Balance Sheet as at December 31

    • Trial Balance as at December 31

    • Income Statement for January 1 to December 31

    • General Journal by posting date December 31

SOURCE TRANSACTIONS

☐ The truck was leased to a client on December 1, 1999 for $900 for a three-month period ending February 29, 2000. The client paid for the lease in advance. Adjust and record revenue earned for one month.

☐ A university student leased the small apartment on the second floor of the service centre for a five-month period beginning on September 1, 1999, paying the full $1 500 rental costs in advance. Calculate and record the earned portion of the rent on December 31, 1999.

☐ The aging of accounts receivables indicates that the estimate for the Allowance for Doubtful Accounts should be increased to $500 for the coming year. Remember to take into consideration any existing balance in the allowance account. This is the Balance Sheet approach to estimating uncollectible accounts.

☐ Mighty Mack purchased a regular weekly advertisement on November 1, 1999 to run in a local paper for three months. Two months of this prepaid account has expired.

☐ The business purchased insurance coverage on June 1, 1999 when the old policy expired. The insurance was prepaid for two years. Calculate and charge the expired portion on December 31, 1999.

☐ The amount of Parts Inventory on hand, based on a physical count on December 31, 1999, was $4 600.

☐ Mighty Mack's accumulated unpaid interest on its bank loan is $90 on December 31, 1999.

☐ Mighty Mack's accumulated unpaid interest on its mortgage is $750 on December 31, 1999.

☐ The Marketable Securities purchased by the business early in the year have earned and accrued interest revenue of $442 as of December 31, 1999.

☐ The Notes Receivable outstanding of $2 400 was drawn on October 1, 1999 for a six-month period at 10 percent interest per annum. Calculate interest earned and accrued at the end of December 31, 1999.

☐ On December 15, 1999, a client required a new transmission and a remanufactured engine installed in her car for a contract price of $4 000. The work was estimated to continue into the new year because of a delay on ordered parts. On December 31, the work was 75 percent completed. No advance or deposit was requested as the client was a family friend.

☐ Mighty Mack subcontracted a truck for repairs for a client at a neighbouring service specialty shop. Subcontracting fees of $1 200 have accrued and should be charged to expenses on December 31, 1999.

☐ The business purchased the machinery and tools on January 1, 1999. The capital cost allowance rate for this class of equipment for tax purposes is 20 percent.

Notes

Do not use the half-year convention to calculate the depreciation expenses for Mighty Mack Service Centre.

☐ The towing vehicle was purchased on April 1, 1999. The capital cost allowance rate for this class of equipment for tax purposes is 30 percent.

☐ The truck leased out to clients on a monthly basis was acquired on March 1, 1999. The capital cost allowance rate for this class of equipment for tax purposes is 30 percent.

☐ The service centre, purchased on January 1, 1999, has a capital cost allowance rate for tax purposes of 5 percent.

CASE PROBLEM

While entering the regular end-of-period adjustments, Mackenzie noticed that she had entered an invoice for a series of ads three months earlier as an expense. At the end of the year, when the ads were still scheduled to run for another six months, she realized that she should have set up a prepaid expense account.

a. How can she make the adjusting entries now, before closing the books for the year?

b. Why is it important to make the correction?

c. Would it make a difference in correcting the error if the amount spent was $600 or $60?

OBJECTIVES

Upon completion of
this chapter, you
will be able to:

- *plan and design* an accounting system for a small business
- *prepare* procedures for converting from a manual system
- *understand* the objectives of a computerized system
- *create* company files
- *observe* and *understand* integration accounts
- *create* integration accounts
- *set up* the General, Payables and Receivables ledgers using setup input forms
- *make* the accounting system ready for operation
- *enter* vendor- and customer-related transactions
- *edit, review* and *post* transactions from each journal
- *display* and *print* vendor and customer reports

COMPANY INFORMATION

Company Profile

Notes

Maverick Micro Solutions is located at
17 Turbo Lane
Calgary, Alberta
T3B 4U2
Business No.: 98233 2812

Maverick Micro Solutions is a sole proprietorship owned and run by James Maverick in Calgary, Alberta. Maverick graduated from the computer engineering program at Calgary College several years ago. After working as a computer technician for several years with a large computer company in Winnipeg, he returned to Calgary and started his own business in January, 1999.

Maverick provides on-site service to a few large firms and colleges in the Calgary district. These account customers have a credit limit of $5 000, are offered a 1 percent discount for payment within five days and are requested to settle their accounts in 20 days. After 30 days, Maverick charges 1 percent interest per month on amounts overdue and accounts are aged accordingly. Customer statements are sent every 30 days or monthly.

Maverick designed, printed and distributed a promotional brochure at the beginning of the year. In it he described the variety of services that he offers to businesses that use computers as an integral part of their day-to-day operation. Currently, Maverick is able to set up new computer systems and networks, install memory chips, circuit boards, modems, backup drives and hard disks as equipment upgrades, install and test software protection and other programs, recover damaged or deleted data files and convert PC data files to TV format. Maverick also repairs computers, printers, monitors, digital cameras, projection panels or other related components. His fee for these services is always negotiated before he begins the work. In addition to these services, Maverick provides technical training in his machine shop to interested individuals. For training, he charges on an hourly basis.

By dealing with both the software and hardware needs of his clients, Maverick has been able to expand his customer base more quickly. He estimates that in the near future, he will require a full-time assistant. For now, he works alone most of the time. Whenever he has a large contract with tight deadlines, he brings in, as assistants, some of the advanced students from the evening class he teaches at Calgary College.

Just last month, the editor from a popular computer magazine approached Maverick to ask him to contribute to their reviews and tests of new hardware and software. Even though he was already very busy with the other aspects of his work, he accepted because it would provide further opportunity for keeping up with the rapid changes in industry standards, and for increased recognition and professional credibility.

At the start of his business, he also set up accounts with a few suppliers of computer and related equipment. These vendors, as well as other regular vendors, will be included as Maverick's vendor accounts. Vendor accounts are aged at 15-day intervals.

Maverick Micro Solutions has its bank account, bank loan and mortgage with Alberta Trust. As an incentive to new high tech firms locating in Calgary, the bank has provided a waiver on mortgage interest for the first six months on long-term mortgages. In July, Maverick will begin to make regular monthly mortgage payments of $1 550.

Although Maverick could have set up his business records in Simply Accounting at the beginning of January, he chose to wait until he had a more accurate picture of his ongoing accounting profile. After closing his books on March 31, he is ready to make the conversion from the manual to the computerized accounting system for his next fiscal quarter beginning on April 1, 1999, using the following information:

- Chart of Accounts
- Income Statement
- Balance Sheet
- Post-Closing Trial Balance
- Vendor Information
- Customer Information
- Accounting Procedures

MAVERICK MICRO SOLUTIONS
CHART OF ACCOUNTS

ASSETS
1080 Cash in Bank
1200 Accounts Receivable
1240 Parts Inventory
1300 Office Supplies
1420 Furniture & Fixtures
1460 Machinery & Equipment
1490 Machine Shop
1520 Motor Vehicles
1550 Specialty Tools

LIABILITIES
2100 Bank Loan
2200 Accounts Payable
2650 GST Charged on Services
2670 GST Paid on Purchases
2850 Mortgage Payable

EQUITY
3560 J. Maverick, Capital
3580 J. Maverick, Drawings
3600 Net Income

REVENUE
4020 Revenue from Services
4080 Revenue from Training
4100 Sales Discounts
4120 Interest Earned

EXPENSE
5020 Bank Charges
5040 Hydro Expenses
5060 Purchase Discounts
5080 Damaged Inventory
5100 Delivery Expenses
5120 Parts Used
5140 Telephone Expenses
5200 Temporary Services

MAVERICK MICRO SOLUTIONS
INCOME STATEMENT

For the Quarter Ending March 31, 1999

Revenue	
4000 REVENUE	
4020 Revenue from Services	$10 500.00
4080 Revenue from Training	560.00
4100 Sales Discounts	0.00
4120 Interest Earned	40.00
4390 TOTAL REVENUE	$11 100.00
TOTAL REVENUE	$11 100.00
Expense	
5000 OPERATING EXPENSES	
5020 Bank Charges	50.00
5040 Hydro Expenses	180.00
5060 Purchase Discounts	0.00
5080 Damaged Inventory	70.00
5100 Delivery Expenses	60.00
5120 Parts Used	770.00
5140 Telephone Expenses	65.00
5200 Temporary Services	300.00
5690 TOTAL OPERATING EXPENSES	$ 1 495.00
TOTAL EXPENSE	$ 1 495.00
NET INCOME	$ 9 605.00

MAVERICK MICRO SOLUTIONS
BALANCE SHEET

March 31, 1999

Assets
1000 CURRENT ASSETS
1080 Cash in Bank $ 36 580.00
1200 Accounts Receivable   5 340.00
1240 Parts Inventory   3 000.00
1300 Office Supplies   200.00
1390 TOTAL CURRENT ASSETS $ 45 120.00

1400 PLANT & EQUIPMENT
1420 Furniture & Fixtures   1 800.00
1460 Machinery & Equipment   48 000.00
1490 Machine Shop   165 000.00
1520 Motor Vehicles   25 000.00
1550 Specialty Tools   20 000.00
1590 TOTAL PLANT & EQUIPMENT $259 800.00

TOTAL ASSETS $304 920.00

Liabilities
2000 CURRENT LIABILITIES
2100 Bank Loan   25 000.00
2200 Accounts Payable   4 500.00
2650 GST Charged on Services $840.00
2670 GST Paid on Purchases   −420.00
2750 GST Owing (Refund)   420.00
2790 TOTAL CURRENT LIABILITIES $29 920.00

2800 LONG TERM DEBT
2850 Mortgage Payable   150 000.00
2890 TOTAL LONG TERM DEBT $150 000.00

TOTAL LIABILITIES $179 920.00

Equity
3000 OWNER'S EQUITY
3560 J. Maverick, Capital   115 395.00
3600 Net Income   9 605.00
3690 TOTAL OWNER'S EQUITY $125 000.00

TOTAL EQUITY $125 000.00

LIABILITIES AND EQUITY $304 920.00

```
MAVERICK MICRO SOLUTIONS
POST-CLOSING TRIAL BALANCE

March 31, 1999

    1080 Cash in Bank              $ 36 580.00
    1200 Accounts Receivable          5 340.00
    1240 Parts Inventory              3 000.00
    1300 Office Supplies                200.00
    1420 Furniture & Fixtures         1 800.00
    1460 Machinery & Equipment       48 000.00
    1490 Machine Shop               165 000.00
    1520 Motor Vehicles             25 000.00
    1550 Specialty Tools            20 000.00
    2100 Bank Loan                                  $  25 000.00
    2200 Accounts Payable                               4 500.00
    2650 GST Charged on Services                          840.00
    2670 GST Paid on Purchases          420.00
    2850 Mortgage Payable                             150 000.00
    3560 J. Maverick, Capital                         125 000.00
                                   _____       _____
                                   $305 340.00       $305 340.00
                                   ===========       ===========
```

MAVERICK MICRO SOLUTIONS
VENDOR INFORMATION

Vendor Name (Contact)	Address Phone & Fax	Invoice Terms	Invoice Date	Invoice/ Cheque No.	Amount/ Balance
Alberta Hydro (Nida Power)	49 Glowing Lights Rd. Calgary, AB T3P 4X2 Tel: (403) 771-8877 Fax: (403) 771-2900	Net 1			
Alberta Telephone (Mora Noys)	344 A. G. Bell Way Calgary, AB T2T 7N8 Tel: (403) 775-6644 Fax: (403) 775-8102	Net 1			
Cybertek Systems (Colm Peuter)	586 Pentium Alley Calgary, AB T2E 7D3 Tel: (403) 778-6188 Fax: (403) 778-6100	2/5, N/20	03/28/99 03/28/99	CS-4211 Chq 189 Balance	$1 000 −500 $ 500
Flextech Products (Mike Roechip)	42 Intell Blvd. Calgary, AB T1S 5C8 Tel: (403) 522-1817 Fax: (403) 522-1899	1/10, N/30	03/24/99 03/24/99	FP-95 Chq 181 Balance	$3 400 −1 000 $2 400
Microtek Corporation (Meg A. Herz)	486 Memory Lane Calgary, AB T3K 2H5 Tel: (403) 528-7365 Fax: (403) 528-7433	Net 30	03/21/99	MC-721	$1 600

MAVERICK MICRO SOLUTIONS
VENDOR INFORMATION CONTINUED

Vendor Name (Contact)	Address Phone & Fax	Invoice Terms	Invoice Date	Invoice/ Cheque No.	Amount/ Balance
Receiver General of Canada	Summerside Tax Centre Summerside, PE C1N 6L2 Tel: (902) 821-8186	Net 1			
Vision Technologies (Ram Sites)	10 Nuview Cr. Edmonton, AB T6J 9G2 Tel: (403) 489-3921 Fax: (403) 489-3376	Net 20		Grand Total	$4 500

MAVERICK MICRO SOLUTIONS
CUSTOMER INFORMATION

Customer Name (Contact)	Address Phone & Fax	Invoice Terms (Credit Limit)	Invoice Date	Invoice/ Cheque No.	Amount/ Balance
Alberta Insurance Co. (Joel Careless)	571 Litty Gate Calgary, AB T2B 1A6 Tel: (403) 773-0208 Fax: (403) 773-0100	1/5, N/20 ($5 000)			
Calgary College (Jan Booker)	54 University Ave. Calgary, AB T3D 6B1 Tel: (403) 525-4412 Fax: (403) 525-7100	1/5, N/20 ($5 000)	03/28/99 03/28/99	52 Chq#187 Balance	$4 210 −1 000 $3 210
Performance Technical School (Arch I. Tektur)	19 Scholastic Rd. Calgary, AB T1W 4R1 Tel: (403) 774-8135 Fax: (403) 774-7200	1/5, N/20 ($5 000)			
Prairie Finance Company (Andy Bluitt)	131 Bond St. Calgary, AB T2V 5F8 Tel: (403) 526-6101 Fax: (403) 526-1919	1/5 ,N/20 ($5 000)	03/25/99	49	$2 130
Western Home Security (Marlie Safer)	9 Vigilance Blvd. Calgary, AB T1B 8R2 Tel: (403) 771-7711 Fax: (403) 771-6292	1/5, N/20 ($5 000)		Grand Total	$5 340

Accounting Procedures

Open-Invoice Accounting for Payables and Receivables

The open-invoice method of accounting for invoices obtained from vendors or issued by a business to customers allows the business to keep track of each individual invoice and any partial payments made against it. This is in contrast to methods that only keep track of the outstanding balance by combining all invoice balances owed to a vendor or by a customer. Simply Accounting uses the open-invoice method. When an invoice is fully paid, it becomes optional either to retain the invoice or to remove (clear) it.

The Goods and Services Tax: Remittances

Maverick Micro Solutions uses the regular method for remittance of the Goods and Services Tax. GST collected from customers is recorded as a liability in the *GST Charged on Services* account. GST paid to vendors is recorded in the *GST Paid on Purchases* account as a decrease in the liability to Revenue Canada. The balance, or request for refund, is remitted to the Receiver General of Canada by the last day of the month for the previous month.

Cash Sales of Services

Cash transactions for services and training are handled through the Sales Journal. You enter the cash transaction for services in the same way as you would enter any credit sale transaction for services and membership to customers, with the following changes. Choose <One-time customer> from the customer list and type the name of the customer in the address field. Or choose a regular customer from the list and click on the Sale with Payment option. Then enter the customer's cheque number in the Cheque field or leave the default entry as Cash.

The program will then generate an entry that will debit the *Cash in Bank* account instead of the *Accounts Receivable* control account. All other entries for this transaction will be appropriately debited and credited.

Cash Purchases

Cash purchases will be handled through the Purchases Journal. You enter the cash transaction for purchases in the same way as you would enter any credit purchase transaction with the following changes. Choose <One-time vendor> from the vendor list and type the vendor's name in the address field. Or choose a regular vendor from the list and click on the Purchase with Payment option. Then enter the cheque number in the Cheque field.

The program will then generate an entry that will credit the *Cash in Bank* account instead of the *Accounts Payable* control account. All other entries for this transaction will be appropriately debited and credited.

Discounts

Maverick offers a 1 percent discount to his account customers if they settle their accounts within five days. Full payment is requested within 20 days. These payment terms are set up as defaults. When the receipt is entered, and the discount is still available, the program will show the amount of the discount and the net amount owing automatically.

Some vendors also offer discounts for early settlement of accounts. Again, when the terms are entered for the vendor, and payment is made before the discount offer expires, the program will display the discount as available and automatically calculate a net balance owing. Payment terms vary from vendor to vendor.

Notes

- Provincial sales taxes are not levied in Alberta.
- Most bank and other financial institution services are exempt from GST collection.

INSTRUCTIONS

1. Using the Chart of Accounts, Balance Sheet, Income Statement, Trial Balance and Vendor and Customer Information provided above for March 31, 1999, set up the company accounts. If you wish, you can use the setup input forms provided in Appendix A. Detailed instructions to assist you in setting up the company accounts follow. Source documents begin on page 270 after the setup instructions.

2. Using the Chart of Accounts, Vendor Information, Customer Information and Accounting Procedures, enter the transactions beginning on page 270 using Simply Accounting.

3. After you have completed your entries, print the reports and graphs indicated on the following printing form:

REPORTS

Lists
- ❏ Chart of Accounts
- ❏ Vendor List
- ❏ Customer List

Financials
- ☑ Comparative Balance Sheet
  dates: April 1 & April 28
  With Dollar Difference
- ☑ Income Statement
  from April 1 to April 28
- ❏ Trial Balance
- ❏ General Ledger

GST
- ☑ GST Detail Report
  date: April 28

Mailing Labels
- ❏ Labels

Journals
- ☑ General (by posting date)
  all ledger entries
  from April 1 to April 28
- ❏ Purchases
- ❏ Payments
- ❏ Sales
- ❏ Receipts

Payables
- ☑ Vendor Aged Detail
  for all vendors
- ❏ Aged Overdue Payables
- ❏ Pending Purchase Orders

Receivables
- ☑ Customer Aged Detail
  for all customers
- ❏ Aged Overdue Receivables
- ❏ Customer Statements

GRAPHS

- ❏ Payables by Aging Period
- ❏ Receivables by Aging Period
- ☑ Sales vs Receivables (all revenue accounts)
- ❏ Revenues by Account
- ❏ Expenses & Net Profit as % of Revenue

- ❏ Payables by Vendor
- ❏ Receivables by Customer
- ❏ Receivables Due vs Payables Due
- ❏ Expenses by Account
- ❏ Current Revenue vs Last Year

KEYSTROKES FOR SETUP

Creating Company Files

For Maverick Micro Solutions, we will create the company files from scratch rather than use one of the starter files. Once we create the files and define the defaults, we will add the accounts, define integration accounts for the General, Payables and Receivables ledgers and create vendor and customer records.

Start the Simply Accounting program.

At the Simply Accounting - Open File window, create a new folder called MAVERICK to contain the company files. You should create this folder inside the same DATA folder, or on the same floppy disk, where your other Simply Accounting company data files are stored. Refer to Chapter 1, page 18 if you need further assistance.

Then select the MAVERICK folder you just created. No file names are listed in the File name list box because the folder contains no files yet. The File name field may contain the name of the last file that you were working with in Simply Accounting as shown here:

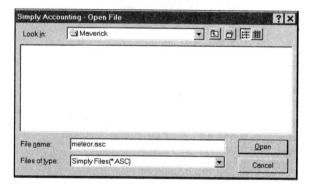

Double click in the File name field to move the cursor and highlight the file name if necessary, or if a file name is already highlighted,

Type   maverick.asc

Click on Open

You will see the following warning message:

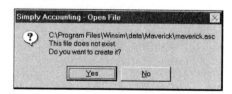

Simply Accounting is warning you that the file you named does not yet exist. Since you want to create it,

Click on Yes

You will see the following Setup Wizard starting screen:

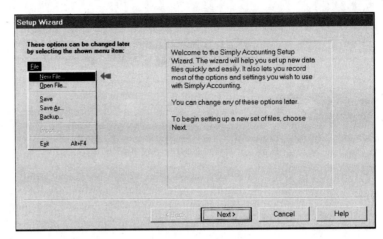

This screen is an invitation to use the Setup Wizard to begin the setup of company files. We will choose not to use the wizard because we want to see all the options available for each stage.

Click on **Cancel** to leave the Wizard and open the Company Dates window:

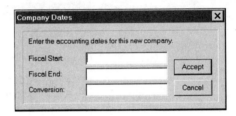

These company fiscal dates are like the ones you entered for CISV (Chapter 6) as part of the Company Information setup. The cursor is in the Fiscal Start field. This is the date on which the business begins its fiscal year. For Maverick Micro Solutions, the fiscal start date is the same as the date the business is converting to Simply Accounting because the books were closed before the conversion.

Type 04-01-99

Press (tab)

The cursor advances to the Fiscal End field for the date on which Maverick Micro Solutions ends its fiscal period and closes its books.

Type 06-30-99

Press (tab)

The program now advances to the Conversion date field. This is the date on which the business is changing from a manual accounting system to a computerized accounting system.

Press (tab)

Type 04-01-99

Click on **Accept** to save the date information. The familiar Home Window appears with the name Maverick at the top of the window.

All of the journal icons are locked because the files are not ready for you to enter transactions.

Display the Chart of Accounts. You will see that the only account provided by default is the type X account, the General Ledger integration account, *Current Earnings*.

Preparing the System

The next step is to enter all of the necessary company information to customize the files for Maverick Micro Solutions. You begin by preparing the system and changing the defaults.

You should change the defaults to suit your own work environment if you have more than one printer or if you are using forms for cheques, invoices or statements. The instructions for computer-generated cheques, invoices and statements are provided.

Changing Defaults

Use the Company Information to enter the defaults and computer equipment on setup input forms Form SYS-1 and Form SYS-2. Form SYS-1 profiles the company and gives information about Maverick Micro Solutions' computer equipment. Form SYS-2 shows the defaults for Maverick Micro Solutions for each of the accounting ledgers. Page 2 of Form SYS-2, shown on page 248, includes the settings that are being introduced for the first time in this application. Other SYS forms were shown in the CISV application.

Changing Company Information

Use Form SYS-1 to complete this step.

Choose Company Information from the pull-down menu under **Setup** to display the company information screen.

Notice that the name and address fields are blank and that the fiscal dates you entered in the previous stage are provided. You can edit these if you made a mistake.

The cursor is in the Name field.

Type   Maverick Micro Solutions
Press `tab`
Type   17 Turbo Lane
Press `tab`
Type   Calgary
Press `tab`
Type   Alberta
Press `tab`
Type   t3b 4u2

The Use Business Number option is already checked.

Click on the Business No. field to move the cursor to the field.

Type   98233 2812

Check the information you have just entered and make any necessary corrections.

Click on OK to save the new information and return to the Home window.

You can return to the Company Information screen at any time to make changes. The program will set up defaults for the using date and for the city and province fields for customers and vendors based on the information you have just entered.

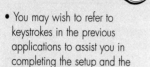

SYSTEM PREPARATION

SETTINGS: Payables

Skip Vendors Icon Window: Y ___ , N ✔

Aging: _1 5_ , _3 0_ , _4 5_ (days)

SETTINGS: Receivables

Skip Customers Icon Window: Y ___ , N ✔

Aging: _5_ , _20_ , _30_ (days)

Interest Charges: _1.0_   Y ✔ , N ___ Over _30_ days

Include Invoices Paid in Last: _31_ Days

Terms: _1_ % _5_ Days, Net _20_ Days

Apply terms to all customers: Y ✔ , N ___

SETTINGS: Sales Taxes

GST Rate 1:   _7.0_ %

GST Rate 2:   _0.0_ %

Use Quebec Tax: Y ___ , N ✔

PST Rate: _0.0_ %

Apply PST to Freight: Y ___ , N ✔

Apply PST to GST: Y ___ , N ✔

SETTINGS: Forms

Next Invoice Number: _60_

Next PO Number: _1001_

Next Payables Cheque Number: _201_

Next Payroll Cheque Number: _____

Confirm Printing   For Invoices: Y ✔ , N ___

For POs: Y ✔ , N ___

For Cheques: Y ✔ , N ___

Print address: On Invoices: Y ✔ , N ___

On POs: Y ✔ , N ___

On Statements: Y ✔ , N ___

On Cheques: Y ✔ , N ___

Default Invoice Comment: _Interest at 1% per month charged on accounts_
over 30 days.

Changing the Printer Defaults

Use Form SYS-1 to enter information about your printer setup.

Choose Printers from the pull-down menu under **Setup**.

The printer setting options for reports and graphs are given. Most of the default settings should be correct, but you may wish to change the margins, font and size for your reports. When all the settings are correct,

Click on OK to save the new information or click on Cancel if you have not made any changes and return to the Home window. You can change the printer settings at any time.

Changing Appearance Defaults

Use Form SYS-2 to enter information about your appearance settings.

Choose Settings from the pull-down menu under **Setup** to display the default settings for the Display.

Choose Windows Default from the drop-down list for **Home & Icon Windows Background**.

The status bar for the Home window and other windows is turned on by default as we want.

Decide whether you want to display To Do Lists each time you open a file, each time you advance the using date, or both. By default both options are selected.

Use this screen to adjust the other aspects of the appearance of the program to suit your needs.

Changing System Defaults

Use Form SYS-2 to enter information about your system settings.

Click on the System tab at the top of the Settings screen.

The Inventory Tracking and Invoice Lookup options are selected. These settings are correct for Maverick Micro Solutions. Even though we are not using the Inventory module, we want to be able to use the Lookup feature.

Choose Weekly as the Backup frequency.

The remaining settings are also correct.

Notes

- If you choose Settings when a ledger icon is selected, you will display the settings for the selected ledger.
- If you click on the Setup tool bar button when a ledger icon is selected, you will display the Settings for the selected ledger.
- If you click on the Setup tool icon when no ledger or journal icon is selected, select the ledger for which you want to display the settings from the list.

Changing Sales Taxes Defaults

The settings for Sales Taxes for Maverick are shown on the SYS-2 Page 2 input form (page 248).

Click on the Sales Taxes tab at the top of the Settings screen to display the default tax settings:

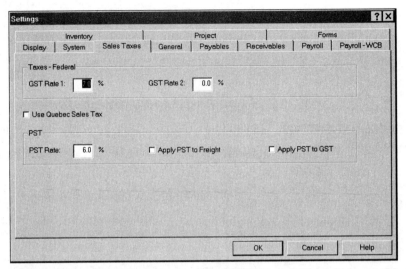

The GST Rates at 7% and 0% are correct. The GST Rate 2 field might be used in the future if different tax rates were applied to different types of goods or services. At present, however, there is no second rate for GST, so you can leave 0.0% unchanged. Since we do not need to use the Quebec Sales Tax, this default is also correctly set.

No PST is applied in the province of Alberta so you must change the PST rate.

Double click on the PST Rate field to highlight the contents.

Type 0

Two other options concern the application of PST. Leave the boxes unchecked for Maverick Micro Solutions because PST is not applied to freight charges or on GST. For Prince Edward Island, you would choose to apply PST to GST. If at any time the regulations in a province changed, you could return to this screen and change the settings.

Changing General Defaults

If you are using the input forms, use Form SYS-2 to enter information about the General Ledger settings.

Click on the General tab.

These settings are correct for Maverick Micro Solutions. The first option, to skip the accounts window will bypass the General Ledger screen that shows all of the accounts by icon or in numerical order by name. Do not select this option before completing the setup because the icon window allows easy access to accounts that you need to edit. For now, Maverick will not be using the budgeting or bank reconciliation features.

Payables Default Settings

The setting for the Payables Ledger are shown on the SYS-2 input form.

Click on the Payables tab on the Settings screen to display the default settings:

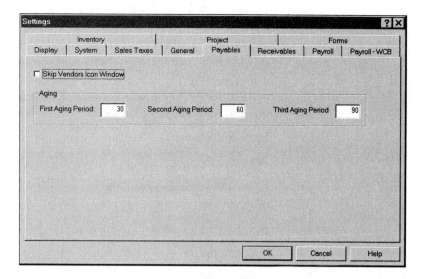

The option for the Payables Ledger concerning the aging of accounts is preset at 30, 60 and 90 days. We will change these for Maverick to reflect the payment terms most commonly used by Maverick's vendors.

Double click on 30 in the First Aging Period field so you can change this number.

Type 15

Press (tab) to advance to the Second Aging Period field and select it.

Type 30

Press (tab) to advance to the Third Aging Period field.

Type 45

Again, choose not to skip the Vendors Icon Window before completing the setup of Vendor accounts. This introductory vendors ledger window shows all vendors by icon (or by name) and allows you to monitor your progress more easily as you add new vendors.

Receivables Default Settings

Input form SYS-2 shows the settings for the Receivables Ledger.

Click on the **Receivables tab** to display the following Receivables Ledger choices:

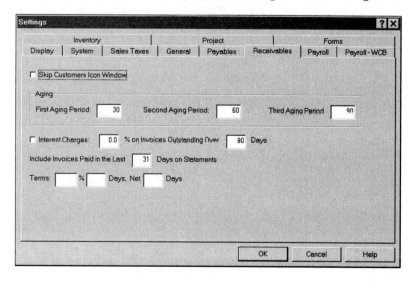

Again you should choose not to skip the introductory Customers Icon Window. This introductory ledger window shows all customers by icon (or by name) and allows you to monitor your progress more easily as you add new customers.

Maverick Micro Solutions offers a 1 percent discount if customers pay within 5 days, and expects full payment within 20 days. After 30 days, customers are charged 1 percent interest per month on the overdue accounts. Therefore the aging periods are set at 5, 20 and 30 days and we must change the default settings.

Double click on 30 in the First Aging Period field to highlight the amount.

Type   5

Press `tab` to advance to the Second Aging Period field.

Type   20

Press `tab` to advance to the Third Aging Period field.

Type   30

Click on Interest Charges to select this feature.

Press `tab` to advance to and highlight the contents of the Interest Rate field for editing.

Type   1.0

Press `tab` to advance to and highlight the contents of the Days field for editing.

Type   30

The next option relates to printing historic information on invoices. The maximum setting is 999 days. For Maverick Micro Solutions, the period should be 31 days because they send customer statements every month. Any invoices paid in the past 31 days will be included in the statements. Unpaid invoices are automatically included on statements. The default setting is correct. Next we must enter the account customer payment terms, 1 percent discount if the account is paid in the first 5 days, and net payment due in 20 days.

Click on the **first Terms field**, the % field, to advance the cursor.

Type   1.0

Press `tab` to advance to the Days field.

Type   5

Press `tab` to advance to the Net Days field.

Type   20

Changing Forms Default Settings

The settings for Forms are shown on form SYS-2.

Click on the **Forms tab**. Before advancing to the next group of settings, Simply Accounting shows you the following warning:

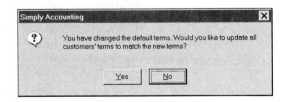

Simply Accounting gives you the option to add the customer payment terms you just entered as a default for all customers. The alternatives are to set the terms for each customer record or sales invoice individually. We want to use the same terms for all customers. Individual customer records or invoices can still be modified if needed.

Click on Yes. The Settings screen for Forms now appears:

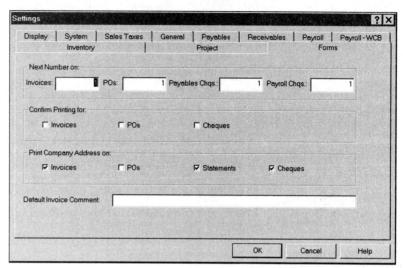

This window allows you to set up the automatic invoice, purchase order and cheque numbering sequences.

The Invoices number field is ready for editing.

Type   60

Press (tab) or double click on the **POs (Purchase Orders) field** to highlight the contents.

Type   1001

Press (tab) or double click on the **Payables Chq field** to highlight the contents.

Type   201

We do not need to change the Payroll Cheque number because Maverick is not using the Payroll ledger.

We do want to add a default comment that will appear on every customer invoice. The comment may include payment terms, company motto, notice of an upcoming sale or, in this case, a warning about interest charges. Remember that you can change the default message any time you want. You can also edit it for a particular invoice when you are completing the invoice.

Click on the **Default Invoice Comment field** to move the cursor.

Type   Interest at 1% per month charged on accounts over 30 days.

From this Settings window you can set the options for the remaining ledgers. Since Maverick does not use them, you can leave them unchanged. They are explained in the Hearth House application.

Click on OK to return to the Home window.

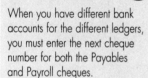

When you have different bank accounts for the different ledgers, you must enter the next cheque number for both the Payables and Payroll cheques.

Three of the company address options are turned on by default. You should turn on the printing confirmation if you are printing invoices, purchase orders and cheques from the software. Click on them to add a ✔ to the check box. The program will then remind you to print invoices before posting.

Preparing the Ledgers

The third stage in setting up an accounting system involves preparing each ledger for operation. This stage involves the following steps:

1. organizing all accounting reports and records (this step has already been completed for you)
2. modifying the *Current Earnings* account
3. creating new accounts
4. defining integration accounts
5. inserting vendor and customer information
6. entering historical startup information.

Preparing the General Ledger

Accounts are organized by section, including Assets, Liabilities, Equity, Revenue and Expense. The account type, such as Heading (H), Subtotal (S), Total (T), Left Column (L), Right Column (R) and Current Earnings (X), is a method of classifying and organizing accounts within a section or subsection of a report.

The accounts follow the same pattern described previously:

- 1000 - 1999   Assets
- 2000 - 2999   Liabilities
- 3000 - 3999   Equity
- 4000 - 4999   Revenue
- 5000 - 5999   Expense

Use the Chart of Accounts, Income Statement and Balance Sheet to enter all the accounts you need to create. Remember to include all Block Headings, Totals and Subtotals in addition to postable accounts, and remember to add the type of account and whether you wish to suppress the printing of zero balances. The first block of asset accounts that you will enter are shown here on Form CHA-1 (complete the remaining accounts on your own):

CHART OF ACCOUNTS MAINTENANCE

GENERAL LEDGER
Form CHA-1
Page __1_ of ___

Code: M = Modify   Type: H = Heading   S = Subtotal   Suppress: Y = Yes
      C = Create   R = Right   X = Current Earnings   N = No
      R = Remove   L = Left   T = Total

Code	Account Title (Maximum 26 Characters)	Account No.	Type	Suppress
C	CURRENT ASSETS	1000	H	–
C	Cash in Bank	1080	R	N
C	Accounts Receivable	1200	R	N
C	Parts Inventory	1240	R	N
C	Office Supplies	1300	R	N
C	TOTAL CURRENT ASSETS	1390	T	–

Modifying Accounts in the General Ledger

The following keystrokes will modify the *Current Earnings* account in the General Ledger to match the account name defined in the Chart of Accounts.

In the Home window,

Double click on the Accounts icon to open the main Accounts window.

Choose Name from the pull-down menu under View in the Accounts window to display the accounts in numeric order by name.

Double click on 3600 Current Earnings to display its ledger form.

Press (tab) to advance to the Account name field and highlight it.

Type   Net Income

The account types are dimmed because the Current Earnings account type must remain as type X. Only the account number and account title can be edited. You cannot enter a balance because the program automatically calculates the amount as the net difference between the total revenue and expense account balances.

Close the General Ledger account window. Close the Accounts icon window to return to the Home window unless you want to continue to the next step, which also involves working in the General Ledger.

Creating New Accounts in the General Ledger

With the Accounts window open, or any account information window on display,

Click on the Create tool bar button ▦ in the Accounts window or choose Create from the pull-down menu under Edit.

Enter account information for the accounts that you listed on Form CHA-1. Remember, you cannot use duplicate account numbers.

Type the account number.

Press   (tab)

Type the account title or name.

Press   (tab)

The cursor advances to the Balance field. Ignore this field for now; you will enter the account balances in the next stage.

Click on the Account type for the account.

If this is a postable account, indicate whether you want to suppress the printing of this account if its balance is zero.

When all the information is entered correctly, you must save your account.

Click on Create or press (enter) to save the new account and advance to a new blank ledger account window.

Repeat these procedures to create the other accounts marked for creation on Form CHA-1.

Close the General Ledger account window. Close the Accounts icon window to return to the Home window unless you want to continue to the next step, which also involves working in the General Ledger.

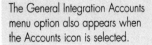

Notes

- Accounts that decrease the total in a block or section (e.g., GST Paid on Purchases) must be entered as negative numbers. These account balances are indicated with a (–) minus sign in the Balance Sheet.
- After entering all account balances, you may wish to display or print your Balance Sheet and Trial Balance to check for accuracy.
- You may wish to save your work and finish your session. This will give you an opportunity to read the next section.

Notes

In the setup for Hearth House, we will use the Integration Plus starter files which have a full set of integration accounts already defined. In that application, you will modify and delete integration accounts to customize them for the company.

Entering Historical Account Balances

The opening historical balances for Maverick Micro Solutions can be found in the Trial Balance dated March 31, 1999. You cannot enter balances for headings, totals or subtotals (i.e., for the non-postable accounts). The Accounts window should be open.

Open the General Ledger account information window for the first account that has a balance, *Cash in Bank 1080*.

Press [tab] until you advance to the Balance field and highlight its contents.

Type the balance.

Correct the information if necessary by repeating the above steps.

Click on **the down scroll arrow** in the ledger window to advance to the next account information form. Repeat the above procedures to enter the balances for the remaining accounts as indicated in the Trial Balance.

Return to the Home window when you are finished.

Integration Accounts

Integration Accounts are accounts in the General Ledger that are affected by changes resulting from entries in other journals. For example, an entry to record a credit sale in the Sales Journal will cause automatic changes in several General Ledger accounts. In the General Ledger, the *Accounts Receivable* [+], *Revenue from Sales* [+], *GST Charged on Sales* [+], and *PST Payable* [+] accounts will all be affected by the sale. The type of change, increase [+] or decrease [-], is indicated in the brackets. The program must know which account numbers are to be used for posting journal entries in any of the journals. It is this interconnection of account numbers and information between ledgers that makes Simply Accounting fully integrated.

Since the only integration account already defined is *Current Earnings* in the General Ledger, we must identify the remaining integration accounts for the General, Payables and Receivables ledgers.

Setup Tool Button

The Setup button on the tool bar 🔧 works very much like the Report button. Select a journal icon and click on the Setup button to see the integration accounts window for the corresponding ledger. If no icon is selected, choose the journal name from the Setup button's list to display the integration accounts for the corresponding ledger. If a ledger icon is selected, clicking on the Setup tool button displays the Settings window for that ledger.

Defining the General Integration Accounts

Click on the **General journal icon** in the Home window to select it. (Do not double click because you cannot open the journal and you do not want to open it.)

Click on the **Setup tool bar button** 🔧 or choose General Integration Accounts from the pull-down menu under Setup to display the General Integration accounts window with the cursor in the Retained earnings field:

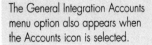

Notes

The General Integration Accounts menu option also appears when the Accounts icon is selected.

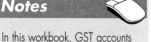
The Retained Earnings account is the Capital account to which expense and revenue accounts are closed at the end of the fiscal period.

Type   3560   to enter the account number, or

Click on the **drop-down list arrow beside the field**. All available postable capital accounts are listed.

Click on 3560 J. Maverick, Capital.

The Current Earnings account is correctly defined and cannot be changed, although as you saw earlier, you can modify the account number and account title.

Click on OK to close the General Integration Accounts window to return to the Home window.

Defining the Payables Integration Accounts

To enter the Payables Ledger integration accounts,

Click on the **Purchases** or **Payments Journal icon** in the Home window to select it.

Click on the **Setup tool bar button** or choose Payables Integration Accounts from the pull-down menu under Setup to display the integration accounts window:

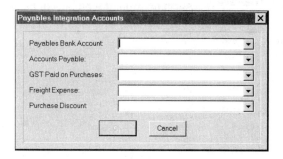

We need to identify the General Ledger bank account used to make payments to vendors. Cash transactions in the Payments Journal will automatically be posted to this General Ledger account when journal entries are made. You can see the list of available accounts by clicking on the drop-down list arrow. Only asset accounts may be used in this field. You can select the bank account, *Cash in Bank*, from this list or

Type   1080

Press (tab) to enter the account number. The cursor advances to the Accounts Payable field. This account is used to record the amounts owing to vendors whenever a credit Purchases Journal entry is completed. The balance in this account reflects the total owing to all vendors. You must use a liability account in this field. Select the *Accounts Payable* control account from the drop-down list, or

Type   2200

Press (tab) to enter the account number. The cursor advances to the GST Paid on Purchases field. This account records the totals of amounts entered in the GST field in the Purchases Journal whenever a purchase is made. You may choose an asset or a liability account. Choose the *GST Paid on Purchases* account from the drop-down list, or

Type   2670

Press (tab) to enter the account number. The cursor advances to the Freight Expense field. This account is used to record the delivery or freight charges associated with purchases. Only freight charged by the vendor should be entered using this account. Since Maverick's vendors do not charge for delivery, you should leave this field blank.

Press (tab) twice to advance to the Purchase Discount field. This account is used to record any vendor discounts taken for early payments. Choose *Purchase Discounts* from the drop-down list, or

Type   5060

Press   (tab)

Check the integration accounts carefully. To delete an integration account, highlight it and press (del) . To select a different account, highlight the one that is incorrect and type in the correct number, or select from the drop-down list.

Click on OK to close the Payables Integration Accounts window to return to the Home window.

Defining the Receivables Integration Accounts

To enter the Receivables Ledger integration accounts,

Click on the **Sales** or **Receipts journal icon** in the Home window.

Click on the **Setup tool bar button** 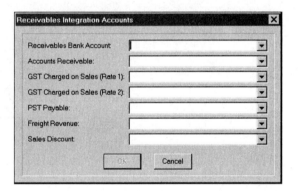 or choose Receivables Integration Accounts from the pull-down menu under Setup to display the integration accounts window:

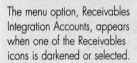
We need to identify the General Ledger bank account used to receive payments from customers. Cash transactions in the Sales and Receipts Journals will automatically be posted to this General Ledger account when journal entries are made. You can see the list of available asset accounts by clicking on the drop-down list arrow. Maverick has only one bank account, *Cash in Bank*. Select the bank account from the list or

Type   1080

Press (tab) to enter the account number. The cursor advances to the Accounts Receivable field. This account records the amounts owed to Maverick by its customers whenever a credit Sales Journal entry is completed. The balance in this account reflects the total owed by all customers. You must use an asset account in this field. Select the *Accounts Receivable* control account from the drop-down list, or

Type   1200

Press (tab) to enter the account number. The cursor advances to the GST Charged on Sales (Rate 1) field. This account records the totals of amounts entered in the GST field in the Sales Journal whenever a sale is made. You may use an asset or a liability account. Choose the *GST Charged on Services* account from the drop-down list, or

Type   2650

Press `tab` to enter the account number. The cursor advances to the GST Charged on Sales (Rate 2) field. Since there is currently only one GST rate, leave this field blank. Similarly, the next two fields should be left blank. PST is not applied in Alberta and Maverick does not collect Freight Revenue because it does not charge for deliveries.

Press `tab` until the cursor is in the Sales Discount field. This field is used to record the discounts that customers receive for early settlement of their accounts. Choose Sales Discounts from the drop-down list, or

Type   4100

Press `tab`

Click on OK to close the Receivables Integration Accounts window to return to the Home window.

Since Maverick does not use the Payroll or Inventory Ledgers, you do not need to define integration accounts for them.

Preparing the Payables Ledger

Using the Vendor Information for Maverick Micro Solutions and forms VEN-1 and VEN-2 provided in Appendix A, you should complete the following steps:

1. Complete the Vendor Maintenance form, Form VEN-1. Form VEN-1 profiles the vendor. For the first vendor, the form is completed as follows:

VENDOR MAINTENANCE

PAYABLES LEDGER
Form VEN-1
Page _1_ of ___

Code	C **Code : M = Modify C = Create R = Remove**
Vendor Name	Alberta Hydro
Contact	Nida Power
Street Address	49 Glowing Lights Rd.
City	Calgary
Province	Alberta

			Yes/No
Postal Code	T3P 4X2	Clear Invoices When Paid	N
Phone Number	4037718877	Include in GST Report	Y
Fax Number	4037712900	Print Contact on Cheques	N
Terms	____ % ____ Days, Net _1_ Days		

---

2. Next you should complete the Vendor Transactions (Historical) form, Form VEN-2. Form VEN-2 records all transactions with a vendor prior to conversion. The transactions for the first vendor with outstanding invoices are completed as follows:

VENDOR TRANSACTIONS (HISTORICAL)

PAYABLES LEDGER
Form VEN-2
Page _1_ of ___

Code: 1 = Purchase   2 = Payment

Code	Vendor	Invoice/ Chq. No.	Date (mm-dd-yy)	Amount	Cheque
1	Cybertek Systems	CS-4211	03-28-99	$1000	
2	Cybertek Systems	189	03-28-99		$500

Entering Vendor Accounts

The following keystrokes will enter the information for **Alberta Hydro**, a vendor of Maverick Micro Solutions, using Form VEN-1.

Double click on the **Vendors icon** in the Home window to display the Vendors icon window. The window is empty because there are no vendors on file yet for Maverick.

Click on the **Create tool bar button** 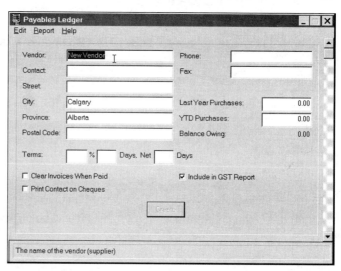 in the Vendors window or choose Create from the pull-down menu under Edit to display the following vendor input screen:

The Vendor field is highlighted, ready for you to enter information.

Type   Alberta Hydro

Press   [tab]

The cursor advances to the Contact field. Here you should enter the name of the person (or department) at Alberta Hydro with whom Maverick Micro Solutions will be dealing. This information will enable a company to make enquiries more professionally and effectively. For a small business, the owner's name may appear in this field.

Type   Nida Power

Press [tab]

The cursor advances to the Street field.

Type 49 Glowing Lights Rd.

Press [tab]

The cursor advances to the City field. Calgary has been entered by default because it is the city in which Maverick Micro Solutions is located. Since it is correct, you can accept it.

Press [tab]

The cursor advances to the Province field. Again, the default information is correct.

Press [tab]

The cursor advances to the Postal Code field.

Type t3p4x2

Press [tab]

The program corrects the format of the previous field, and the cursor advances to the Phone field. You can enter phone and fax numbers with or without the area code.

Type 4037718877

Press [tab]

The program corrects the format of the previous field, and advances the cursor to the Fax field.

Type 4037712900

The next two fields refer to previous purchases. Maverick Micro Solutions will not enter the historical summary information of total purchases for the previous and current year. Maverick will enter only outstanding invoices and the balance field will be completed automatically by the program once you have entered these historical invoices in the following section.

We now need to add the payment terms for this vendor in the Terms fields. Alberta Hydro expects payment immediately on receipt of invoices, terms that we will enter as Net 1 Day. Since there is no discount, skip to the third Terms field.

Click on the **Net Days field**.

Type 1

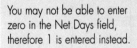

Notes

You may not be able to enter zero in the Net Days field, therefore 1 is entered instead.

Indicate that you want to retain all invoices for this vendor by leaving the box beside Clear Invoices When Paid unchecked. Do not turn on the option to Print Contact on Cheques because the contact field does not contain address information.

Indicate that purchases from this vendor are eligible for GST input credits and should be included in GST reports by leaving this box checked. All vendors for Maverick Micro Solutions, except the Receiver General, should be included in GST reports. Vendors such as the Receiver General of Canada, who do not supply goods or services eligible for input tax credits, should not be included in GST reports.

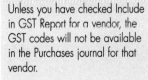

Notes

Unless you have checked Include in GST Report for a vendor, the GST codes will not be available in the Purchases journal for that vendor.

Correct any errors by returning to the field with the mistake, highlighting the errors and entering the correct information.

When all the information is entered correctly, you must save your vendor information.

Click on Create to save the vendor information and display a blank new vendor screen. Notice that Simply Accounting has created a vendor icon for Alberta Hydro in the Vendors window.

Repeat these procedures to enter the remaining vendors.

Close the vendor information window after entering the last vendor to return to the Vendors icon window.

Entering Historical Vendor Information

The following keystrokes will enter the historical information for Cybertek Systems, the first vendor with outstanding invoices. Use Form VEN-2 as your input form.

With the Vendors icon window open,

Double click on Cybertek Systems to display the ledger form for this vendor as shown here:

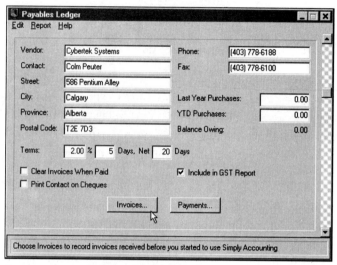

Notice that the screen now has two additional options: *Invoices* and *Payments*. You should select the **Invoices** option to record the outstanding invoices. Use the **Payments** option to record prior payments that you want to keep on record after entering the invoices.

Click on Invoices to see the following input screen:

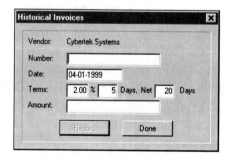

The cursor is in the Number field so you can enter the first invoice number from Form VEN-2 for Cybertek Systems.

Type   CS-4211

Press   tab

The cursor advances to the Date field. Enter the invoice date for the first invoice on Form VEN-2 to replace the default conversion date (the using date).

Type   03-28-99

The Terms are entered from the Vendor record and are correct although they can be edited if necessary. You should enter the amount for the first invoice on Form VEN-2.

Click on the **Amount field** to advance the cursor.

Type   1000

You may correct any errors by pressing ⌊tab⌋ to return to the field with the error and highlight it. Then, enter the correct information.

Be sure that all the information is entered correctly before you save your vendor account balance. If you save incorrect invoice information, and you want to change it, you must first delete the vendor, re-enter all the vendor information, and then re-enter the invoice.

Click on Record to save the information and to display another blank invoice for this vendor.

Repeat these procedures to enter the remaining invoices for the vendor if there are any.

When you have recorded all outstanding invoices for a vendor,

Click on Done to return to the vendor information form. Notice that the invoice you have just entered has been added to the Balance field. Now you can enter the historical payment information for this vendor.

Click on Payments to display the payments form:

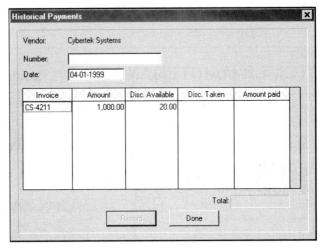

All outstanding invoices that you entered are displayed. Entering historical payments is very much like entering current payments in the Payments Journal.

Click on the **Number field** to move the cursor to the cheque number field.

Type   189

Press   ⌊tab⌋

The cursor advances to the Date field. Enter the cheque date for the first payment towards invoice #CS-4211 to replace the default conversion date (the using date).

Type   03-28-99

Click on the **Amount paid column on the line for invoice #CS-4211** because the full amount is not being paid so the discount does not apply.

The full invoice amount is displayed as the default, and highlighted so you can edit it.

Type   500

Press `tab`

Check your information carefully before you proceed and make corrections if necessary.

Click on Record to save the information and to display another payment form for this vendor in case there are additional payments to record. Notice that the amount owing has been updated to include the payment entry just completed.

Repeat these procedures to enter any other payments to this vendor.

When you have recorded all outstanding payments to a vendor,

Click on Done to return to the vendor information form. Notice that the payment you entered has been included to reduce the amount of the balance owing.

Repeat these procedures to enter historical transactions for other vendors.

Close the vendor display and Vendors icon window to return to the Home window.

Notes

You may wish to display or print a Vendor Detail Report to check it for accuracy.

Preparing the Receivables Ledger

Using the Customer Information chart for Maverick Micro Solutions and forms CUS-1 and CUS-2 provided in Appendix A, you should complete the following steps:

1. Complete the Customer Maintenance form, Form CUS-1. Form CUS-1 profiles Maverick Micro Solutions' customers. For the first customer, the form is completed as follows:

CUSTOMER MAINTENANCE

RECEIVABLES LEDGER
Form CUS-1
Page __1__ of ___

Code	_C_ Code : **M = Modify** **C = Create** **R = Remove**
Customer Name	Alberta Insurance Co.
Contact	Joel Careless
Street Address	571 Litty Gate
City	Calgary
Province	Alberta
Postal Code	T2B 1A6
Phone Number	4037730208
Fax Number	4037730100
Credit Limit	5000
Terms	__1__ % __5__ Days, Net __20__ Days

Yes/No

Clear Invoices When Paid	N
Include in GST Report	Y
Print Statement for Customer	Y

2. Next, you should complete the Customer Transactions (Historical) form, Form CUS-2. Form CUS-2 records all transactions with a customer prior to conversion. The transactions for the first customer with an outstanding balance follow:

CUSTOMER TRANSACTIONS (HISTORICAL)

RECEIVABLES LEDGER
Form CUS-2
Page 1 of ___

Code: 1 = Sale   2 = Receipt

Code	Customer	Invoice/ Chq. No.	Date (mm-dd-yy)	Amount	Cheque
1	Calgary College	52	03-28-99	$4210	
2	Calgary College	187	03-28-99		$1000

Entering Customer Accounts

The following keystrokes will enter the information for **Alberta Insurance Co.**, a customer of Maverick Micro Solutions, using Form CUS-1.

Double click on the **Customers icon** in the Home window to display the Customers icon window. The window is empty because there are no customers on file yet for Maverick.

Click on the **Create tool bar button** in the Customers window or choose Create from the pull-down menu under Edit to display the customer input screen:

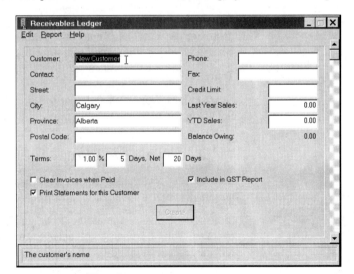
The Customer field is highlighted, ready for you to enter information.

Type   Alberta Insurance Co.

Press   [tab]

The cursor advances to the Contact field. Enter the name of the primary person or department who should be contacted by Maverick Micro Solutions about any sale.

Type   Joel Careless

Press [tab]

The cursor advances to the Street field.

Type   571 Litty Gate

Press [tab]

The cursor advances to the City field, where Calgary is entered by default because it is the city in which Maverick Micro Solutions is situated. You should accept this entry.

Press [tab]

The cursor advances to the Province field. Again, the default entry is correct.

Press [tab]

The cursor advances to the Postal Code field.

Type   t2b1a6

Press [tab]

The program corrects the format of the previous field and advances the cursor to the Phone number field.

Type   4037730208

Press [tab]

The program corrects the format of the previous field and advances the cursor to the Fax field. You should enter the customer's fax number or skip this field if there is none.

Type   4037730100

Press [tab]

The cursor is now in the Credit Limit field. You should type in the amount that the customer can purchase on account before payments are required. If the customer goes beyond its credit limit, the program will issue a warning before accepting an invoice.

Type   5000

Skip the Last Year Sales and Year to Date (YTD) Sales fields because Maverick Micro Solutions has not kept this historical information on record. Balances will be included automatically once you have provided the outstanding invoice information.

The payment terms are correctly entered based on the defaults for Maverick.

Indicate that you want to retain all invoices by leaving the Clear Invoices When Paid box unchecked.

Indicate that this customer should be included in GST reports by leaving this box checked. The GST charged on sales to this customer will now automatically be included in the detailed GST reports.

Indicate that you want a statement to be printed for this customer by leaving this box checked.

You may correct any errors by returning to the field with the error, highlighting the error and entering the correct information. When all the information is entered correctly, you must save your customer information.

Click on Create to save the information and advance to the next new customer input screen. Notice that Simply Accounting has created an icon for Alberta Insurance Co. in the Customers window.

Notes

Unless you have checked Include in GST Report for a customer, the GST fields and codes will not be available in the Sales journal for that customer.

Repeat these procedures to enter the remaining customers. Close the new customer ledger when you have entered all customers.

Entering Historical Customer Information

The following keystrokes will enter the historical information for Calgary College using Form CUS-2.

With the Customers icon window open,

Double click on Calgary College to display the information for this customer as follows:

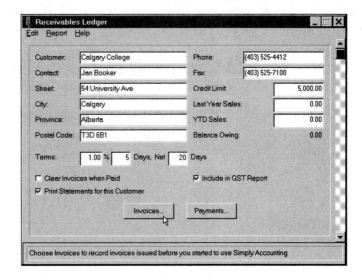

Notice that two new options are available: Invoices and Payments. You can use the Payments option to record any payments against previous invoices that you want to keep on record.

Click on Invoices to display the following input form:

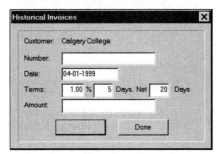

The cursor is in the Invoice (Number) field so you can enter the first invoice number on Form CUS-2.

Type   52

Press   [tab]

The cursor advances to the Date field, ready for you to replace the using date with the date for the first invoice on Form CUS-2.

Type   03-28-99

Click on the Amount field because the payment terms are correctly entered.

Type   4210

You may correct any errors by returning to the field with the error, highlighting the error and entering the correct information.

Check the information carefully before you save your customer account balance. Incorrect invoices can be changed only by deleting the customers, re-entering the customer information and then re-entering the invoices.

Click on Record to save the invoice and to display the next blank invoice form for this customer.

Repeat these procedures to enter the remaining invoices for this customer, if any.

After all invoices for a customer have been entered,

Click on Done to return to the customer's information window. Notice that the program has added the customer's balance. You are now ready to record the payment made by Calgary College against this invoice.

Click on Payments to display the customer payments form:

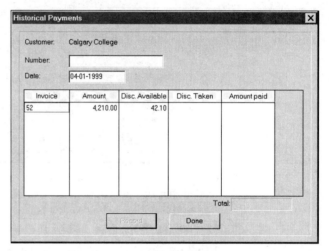

All outstanding invoices that you entered are displayed. Entering historical customer payments is very much like entering current receipts in the Receipts journal.

Click on the **Number field** to move the cursor to the cheque number field.

Type   187

Press   [tab]

The cursor advances to the Date field. Enter the date for the first cheque on Form CUS-2 to replace the default conversion date information (the using date).

Type   03-28-99

Discounts can be taken only when the full payment is made before the due date, so we must skip the Discount fields.

Click on the **Amount paid column on the line for invoice #52**.

The full invoice amount is displayed as the default, and highlighted so you can edit it.

Type   1000

Check your information carefully before you proceed and make corrections if necessary.

Click on Record to save the information and to display another payment form for this customer in case there are additional payments to record. Notice that the amount owing has been updated to include the payment entry just completed.

Repeat these procedures to enter other payments by this customer if there are any.

When you have recorded all outstanding payments by a customer,

Click on Done to return to the customer information form. Notice that the payment you entered has been included to reduce the amount of the balance owing.

Repeat these procedures to enter historical transactions for other customers.

Close the customer display and the Customers icon window to return to the Home window.

Making the Program Ready

The last stage in setting up the accounting system involves making each ledger "Ready." You must complete this final sequence of steps before you can proceed with journalizing transactions. The status of each ledger must be changed from a Not Ready to a Ready state. In the Not Ready state, the ledgers are not integrated so you can change historical information in one ledger without affecting any other ledger, making it easy to correct mistakes.

Making a Backup of the Company Files

Choose Save As from the pull-down menu under File.

Place the disk labelled Data Disk Not Ready Files in drive A. Create a new folder called NR-MAVE on this backup data disk to store the not ready version of your data files. In the File name field,

Type `a:\nr-mave\maverick.asc`

Click on Save

This command will create a copy of the files for Maverick Micro Solutions. The "NR" designates files as not ready to distinguish them from the ones you will work with to enter journal transactions. Put this backup disk in a safe place. Close the new backup file and open your working copy of the Maverick data file again.

Changing the Status of the Ledgers

Each ledger must be set to Ready before you can begin to enter journal transactions.

Highlight the Accounts icon in the Home window.

Choose Set General Ready from the pull-down menu under Setup. You are being warned that this step cannot be reversed.

Click on Proceed if you have already backed up your files.

Repeat this procedure for the Payables and Receivables ledgers, highlighting the Vendors and Customers icons in turn and choosing the corresponding Set Ready command.

When the program is Ready, all your ledgers are integrated and any journal entry you make henceforth will change the General Ledger accounts. Certain restrictions, outlined in the Simply Accounting user's guide, apply when you are operating the program in its Ready state. Please be aware of these restrictions.

Notes

You may wish to display or print a Customer Detail Report to check it for accuracy.

Warning!

Make a back-up copy before proceeding. In this way, if you set the General Ledger to Ready and discover that the historical balances do not match the control account balance, you can correct the error without re-entering all the information.

Notes

Substitute the appropriate drive and folders for the location of your files.

Notes

• The Set General Ready option is available only when the Accounts icon is highlighted in the Home window.
• As you select each ledger icon, the Setup menu option changes to name the selected ledger.

The Maverick Micro Solutions' files are now ready for you to enter transactions. Notice that the no entry symbols are removed from the General, Payables and Receivables journal icons on the Home window.

You can now exit the program or continue by entering the transactions that follow. Remember to advance the using date.

SOURCE DOCUMENTS

☐ Sales Invoice #60
Dated April 2/99
To Alberta Insurance Co., $3 000 for installation of new hardware drives on company computers, plus $210 GST charged. Sales invoice total $3 210. Terms: 1/5, net 20 days.

☐ Cash Receipt #100
Dated April 2/99
From Calgary College, cheque #209 for $3 167.90 in full payment of account including $42.10 discount taken for early payment. Reference invoice #52.

☐ Cheque Copy #201
Dated April 2/99
To Cybertek Systems, $480 in payment of account including 2% discount taken for early payment. Reference invoice #CS-4211.

☐ Cheque Copy #202
Dated April 3/99
To Flextech Products, $2 366 in full payment of account including 1% discount for early payment. Reference invoice #FP-95.

☐ Bank Debit Memo #142723
Dated April 4/99
From Alberta Trust, $48 for service charges.

☐ Purchase Invoice #VT-397
Dated April 5/99
From Vision Technologies, $600 for a new projection panel circuit board (Parts Inventory), plus $42 GST paid. Purchase invoice total $642. Terms: net 20 days. The board, a replacement part for a repair job, will be shipped express at our expense.

☐ Cash Purchase Invoice #UPS-1142
Dated April 5/99
From UPS Delivery, $20 for delivery charges, plus $1.40 GST paid. Purchase invoice total $21.40. Terms: Cash on receipt. Paid by cheque #203.

☐ Memo #1
Dated April 6/99
From the owner: Withdrew $450 from the business for personal use. Paid by cheque #204.

Notes

Although the owner's withdrawal is a cash purchase, you should create a vendor record for the owner because he will make further withdrawals. Do not include the owner in GST reports.

❏ Memo #2
Dated April 8/99
From the owner: 5 memory chips (Parts Inventory) were accidentally crushed and damaged beyond repair. Charge the $125 cost of the chips to the Damaged Inventory expense account.

❏ Purchase Invoice #FP-121
Dated April 9/99
From Flextech Products, $1 200 for data recovery equipment, plus $84 GST paid. Purchase invoice total $1 284. Terms: 1/10, net 30 days.

❏ Purchase Invoice #CS-4440
Dated April 10/99
From Cybertek Systems, $400 for a specialized micro-computer tool set, plus $28 GST. Purchase invoice total $428. Terms: 2/5, net 20 days.

❏ Sales Invoice #61
Dated April 11/99
To Performance Technical School, $2 000 for repairs, installation, and PC to TV conversion, plus $140 GST charged. Sales invoice total $2 140. Terms: 1/5, net 20 days.

❏ Cash Receipt #101
Dated April 13/99
From Prairie Finance Company, cheque #642 for $2 130 in full payment of account. Reference invoice #49.

❏ Bank Debit Memo #142993
Dated April 14/99
From Alberta Trust, $1 200 for reduction of bank loan principal.

❏ Cheque Copy #205
Dated April 14/99
To Cybertek Systems, $419.44 in payment of account including 2% discount taken for early payment. Reference invoice #CS-4440.

Notes
You can process the GST remittance as a cash purchase from the Receiver General.

❏ Memo #3
Dated April 14/99
From the owner: Remit GST payment to the Receiver General for the month of March. Refer to the April 1 general ledger account balances to determine the amount owing, and issue cheque #206 in payment.

❏ Cash Receipt #102
Dated April 14/99
From Performance Technical School, cheque #2615 for $2 118.60 in full payment of account including $21.40 discount for early payment. Reference invoice #61.

❏ Sales Invoice #62
Dated April 16/99
To Western Home Security, $800 for installation of software protection program and projection panel repair work, plus $56 GST charged. Sales invoice total $856. Terms: 1/5, net 20 days.

☐ Sales Invoice #63
Dated April 17/99
To Calgary College, $3 600 for memory upgrades on computers, and repairs to monitors and digital cameras, plus $252 GST charged. Sales invoice total $3 852. Terms: 1/5, net 20 days.

☐ Cheque Copy #207
Dated April 18/99
To Microtek Corporation, $1 600 in full payment of account. Reference invoice #MC-721.

☐ Cheque Copy #208
Dated April 18/99
To Flextech Products, $1 271.16 in full payment of account including 1% discount for early payment. Reference invoice #FP-121.

☐ Cash Sales Invoice #64
Dated April 19/99
To Michael Salerno, $275 for personal training on computer technology, plus $19.25 GST charged. Sales invoice total $294.25. Received certified cheque #RB2742 for $294.25 in full payment.

☐ Cheque Copy #209
Dated April 20/99
To Celine Jocelyn, $200 for assistance in completing the work for Calgary College. Charge to Temporary Services expense account.

☐ Cash Receipt #103
Dated April 21/99
From Calgary College, cheque #1104 for $3 813.48 in full payment of account including $38.52 discount for early payment. Reference invoice #63.

USING DATE — April 28

☐ Cash Receipt #104
Dated April 22/99
From Alberta Insurance Co., cheque #613 for $3 210 in full payment of account. Reference invoice #60.

☐ Cheque Copy #210
Dated April 23/99
To Vision Technologies, $642 in full payment of account. Reference invoice #VT-397.

☐ Cash Purchase Invoice #AH-61421
Dated April 24/99
From Alberta Hydro, $100 for hydro services, plus $7 GST paid. Purchase invoice total $107. Terms: Cash on receipt. Paid by cheque #211.

☐ Cash Purchase Invoice #AT-21417
Dated April 25/99
From Alberta Telephone, $50 for telephone services, plus $3.50 GST paid. Purchase invoice total $53.50. Terms: Cash on receipt. Paid by cheque #212.

☐ Purchase Invoice #MC-912
Dated April 26/99
From Microtek Corporation, $500 for memory chips (Parts Inventory), plus $35 GST paid. Purchase invoice total $535. Terms: net 30 days.

☐ Sales Invoice #65
Dated April 27/99
To Performance Technical School, $1 200 for installation of memory chips and new disk drives, plus $84 GST charged. Sales invoice total $1 284. Terms: 1/5, net 20 days.

☐ Sales Invoice #66
Dated April 28/99
To Calgary College, $800 for repairs and maintenance to college micro computers, plus $56 GST charged. Sales invoice total $856. Terms: 1/5, net 20 days.

☐ Memo #4
Dated April 28/99
From Owner: Charge $1 300 for parts used for customer repairs and installations from Parts Inventory supplies account to Parts Used expense account.

CASE PROBLEM

A new vendor for Maverick Micro Solutions routinely adds freight charges to the purchase invoices. However, Maverick does not have a Freight Expense account. How can Maverick enter the freight charges in the Purchases Journal? What must he do if he wants to use the Freight Expense integration account?

Puretek
Paving &
Stoneworks

OBJECTIVES

Upon completion of
this chapter, you
will be able to:

- *enter* transactions in all journals
- *distribute* revenues and expenses in the General, Sales, Purchases and Payroll Journals
- *create* new projects
- *transfer* inventory items to reserve them for projects
- *display* and *print* transactions with project details
- *display* and *print* project reports

COMPANY INFORMATION

Company Profile

Puretek Paving & Stoneworks operates in the Hamilton area, laying brick and stone walkways and driveways, building stone retaining walls for gardens, and paving driveways. Some concrete work is involved, but the majority of customers use Puretek for their excellent stone work.

Rochi Stoanfayce, the owner, started Puretek four years ago, after an apprenticeship and several years of masonry experience. Since 90 percent of his business falls within the spring to autumn season, he decided to make the business a seasonal one, closing down each winter. In March, he purchased new inventory and supplies with the bank loan he secured, and negotiated some contracts with new customers. In April, when he opens the store and brings back his staff, they can be fully employed immediately. Clients pay a 20 percent cash advance when they sign a contract, ensuring no cash flow problems for Stoanfayce. By mid-November, he starts to shut down for the winter, and does not negotiate any new contracts to begin before the following spring.

Most projects take one to two weeks to complete, and employees are scheduled to work on projects in the most efficient way. Employees are not at the same project every day, but are moved from job to job according to the PERT and CPM schedules that Stoanfayce and the field manager draw up each time a new project is negotiated in order to minimize unnecessary delays. Weather, yet to be controlled or even accurately predicted, remains the principle cause of delays.

Stoanfayce also manages the store himself with the help of an assistant who takes charge of the sale of store and yard inventory and has accounting and other clerical responsibilities. The rest of the staff are primarily occupied as stone workers on the construction projects under the supervision of the field manager who is an engineer by training. Although Stoanfayce is active in the business, he has chosen not to draw a regular salary, withdrawing money from the business as needed. His store assistant and manager are salaried while the other five employees are paid on an hourly basis.

For each contract, a separate project is set up when the contract is signed. Project costs are allocated on the basis of time spent and materials used as a percentage of the totals. The field manager keeps track of these breakdowns. In addition, the operation of the store is defined as an ongoing project.

As soon as a contract is signed, the necessary inventory is requisitioned and reserved. Other construction materials are requisitioned as needed, keeping records of the actual usage for each project for accurate costing and inventory control.

With the assistance of Joanna Severino, a business teacher, Ashikaya, the accounting and store assistant for Puretek, have together compiled the following records and used them to set up the business in Simply Accounting:

- Chart of Accounts
- Post-Closing Trial Balance
- Vendor Information
- Customer Information
- Employee Information
- Employee Profiles and TD-1 Information
- Inventory Information
- Project Information
- Accounting Procedures

PURETEK PAVING & STONEWORKS
CHART OF ACCOUNTS

ASSETS
Current Assets
1080 Cash in Bank
1200 Accounts Receivable
1220 Advances Receivable
1240 Construction Materials
1260 Office Supplies

Inventory Assets
1360 Base Materials
1380 Cobble Pavestones
1400 Edging Stone Blocks
1420 Patio Stone Blocks
1440 Paver Slabs
1460 Stone Slabs
1480 Wall Building Blocks

Plant & Equipment
1760 Cash Register
1780 Computers & Peripherals
1820 Construction Equipment
1840 Delivery Truck
1860 Furniture & Fixtures
1880 Loading Equipment
1940 Warehouse
1960 Yard

LIABILITIES
Current Liabilities
2100 Bank Loan
2200 Accounts Payable
2300 Vacation Payable
2310 EI Payable
2320 CPP Payable
2330 Income Tax Payable
2390 EHT Payable
2400 CSB Plan Payable
2460 WCB Payable
2640 PST Payable
2650 GST Charged on Sales
2670 GST Paid on Purchases

Long Term Liabilities
2850 Mortgage Payable

EQUITY
Owner's Equity
3560 R. Stoanfayce, Capital
3580 R. Stoanfayce, Drawings
3600 Current Earnings

REVENUE
Revenue
4020 Revenue from Store Sales
4040 Revenue from Contracting
4080 Sales Returns & Allowances
4100 Returns Policy Revenue
4150 Other Revenue

EXPENSES
Operating Expenses
5020 Advertising & Promotion
5040 Bank Charges
5060 Construction Materials Used
5080 Cost of Goods Sold
5100 Delivery Expense
5120 Freight Expense
5140 Hydro Expense
5150 Interest Expense - Loan
5160 Interest Expense - Mortgage
5180 Inventory Adjustment
5200 Legal Expenses
5220 Repairs & Maintenance
5260 Telephone Expense
5280 Transfer Costs

Payroll Expenses
5300 Wages
5310 EI Expense
5320 CPP Expense
5330 WCB Expense
5360 EHT Expense

PURETEK PAVING & STONEWORKS
POST-CLOSING TRIAL BALANCE

March 31, 1999

1080 Cash in Bank	$54 895.00	
1200 Accounts Receivable		$9 500.00
1240 Construction Materials	2 800.00	
1360 Base Materials	6 500.00	
1380 Cobble Pavestones	10 145.00	
1400 Edging Stone Blocks	1 950.00	
1420 Patio Stone Blocks	6 600.00	
1440 Paver Slabs	4 380.00	
1460 Stone Slabs	13 900.00	
1480 Wall Building Blocks	9 000.00	
1760 Cash Register	1 200.00	
1780 Computers & Peripherals	3 800.00	
1820 Construction Equipment	45 000.00	
1840 Delivery Truck	50 000.00	
1860 Furniture & Fixtures	3 000.00	
1880 Loading Equipment	25 000.00	
1940 Warehouse	150 000.00	
1960 Yard	100 000.00	
2100 Bank Loan		40 000.00
2200 Accounts Payable		20 330.00
2670 GST Paid on Purchases	1 330.00	
2850 Mortgage Payable		200 000.00
3560 R. Stoanfayce, Capital		219 670.00
	$489 500.00	$489 500.00

PURETEK PAVING & STONEWORKS
VENDOR INFORMATION

Vendor Name (Contact)	Address Phone & Fax	Invoice Terms	Invoice Date	Invoice/ Cheque No.	Outstanding Balance
Bell Telephone (Colin Yu)	88 Sounder Ave. Hamilton, ON L8M 9T3 Tel: (905) 525-6100 Fax: (905) 525-6000	Net 1			
Castillo & Maturi, Lawyers (Vito Castillo)	44 Barton St. Hamilton, ON L9P 6F1 Tel: (905) 822-8320 Fax: (905) 822-8321	Net 10			
Dundas Concrete Works (C. Mentor)	642 Dundas St. Dundas, ON L8P 7C9 Tel: (905) 592-7299 Fax: (905) 592-8234	Net 20	3/21/99	DC-1472	$2 140
Groundfos Machinery (Max Groundfos)	96 Caterpiller Rd. Hamilton, ON L8R 4D7 Tel: (905) 524-8124 Fax: (905) 524-8221	Net 15	3/18/99	GM-677	$10 700

Vendor Name (Contact)	Address Phone & Fax	Invoice Terms	Invoice Date	Invoice/ Cheque No.	Outstanding Balance
Hamilton Hydro (Electra Deau)	27 Utility St. Hamilton, ON L8T 3V7 Tel: (905) 788-9245 Fax: (905) 788-8101	Net 1			
Hamilton Mountain Quarry (Stoney Quartz)	RR #2 Hamilton, ON L9N 5S3 Tel: (905) 522-5724 Fax: (905) 522-6267	Net 20	3/20/99	HMQ-614	$3 210
Hamilton Spectator (Nuse Worthy)	5 Readers Den Hamilton, ON L8P 6H3 Tel: (905) 633-5839 Fax: (905) 633-5889	Net 30			
Manitoulin Flagstone & Slate (Peter Cutter)	Mindemoya Manitoulin Island, ON P0P 1S0 Tel: (705) 736-8542 Fax: (705) 736-5377	Net 15			
Receiver General of Canada	Summerside Tax Centre Summerside, PE C1N 6L2 Tel: (902) 821-8186	Net 1			
Stoanfayce, R. Drawings		N/A			
Stoneycreek Cement Co. (Conn Kreat)	59 Sandfield Rd. Stoney Creek, ON L8J 5E1 Tel: (905) 664-6644 Fax: (905) 664-8993	Net 30			
Sudbury Granite (Jem Stone)	38 Blackstone Cr. Sudbury, ON P3A 7N2 Tel: (705) 594-7428 Fax: (705) 594-7654	Net 30			
Waterloo Pavestone Ltd. (Crystal Slater)	66 Rockcliff St. Waterloo, ON N2T 3V2 Tel: (519) 663-7373 Fax: (519) 663-7711	Net 20	3/21/99	WP-3124	$4 280
				Grand Total	$20 330

PURETEK PAVING & STONEWORKS
CUSTOMER INFORMATION

Customer Name (Contact)	Address Phone & Fax	Invoice Terms	Invoice Date	Invoice/ Cheque No.	Credit Balance
Akonta, Wisdom	359 Forest Glen Blvd. Hamilton, ON L8N 5W2 Tel: (905) 788-8234	Net 1	3/27/99	CR-1	−$2 000
MacGregor, Cameron	101 Chaplin Cres. Hamilton, ON L9R 2S6 Tel: (905) 622-7351 Fax: (905) 622-1199	Net 1	3/28/99	CR-2	−$3 000
Omand, Jim	222 Briar Hill Ave. Hamilton, ON L8P 4B8 Tel: (905) 488-6126 Fax: (905) 488-8221	Net 1	3/30/99	CR-3	−$2 000
Payne, Mark	43 Sherwood Dr. Dundas, ON L9T 3E2 Tel: (905) 522-1369	Net 1	3/31/99	CR-4	−$2 500
				Grand Total	−$9 500

PURETEK PAVING & STONEWORKS
EMPLOYEE INFORMATION SHEET

Employee Name Position Social Insurance Number	Alana Gascon Field Engineer/Mgr 593 821 645	Michael Arturo Stone Cutter 621 534 966	Hans Bekker Bricklayer 499 634 526	Dimitri Valios Bricklayer 512 523 545
Address & Telephone	12 Rockland Ave. Hamilton, ON L8W 3B7 (905) 583-1020	62 Stonegate Dr. Ancaster, ON L9G 3P3 (905) 413-6021	77 Rockcliffe Rd. Dundas, ON L9H 7H5 (905) 734-9209	6 Mountain Ave. Hamilton, ON L8P 4E9 (905) 522-8165
Date of Birth (dd-mm-yy)	21-6-55	15-3-60	11-11-49	10-8-51
Tax Exemption (TD-1)				
Basic Personal	$6 456	$6 456	$6 456	$6 456
Spouse	$5 380	$5 380		
Children under 18		one		
Disability				
Education & Tuition				
Other				
Total Exemptions	$11 836	$11 836	$6 456	$6 456
Employee Earnings				
Regular Wage Rate		$18.00	$18.00	$16.00
Overtime Wage Rate		$27.00	$27.00	$24.00
Regular Salary	$4 000/mo			
Commission	2% (Contracts)			
Vacation	3 weeks	6%	6%	6%
Employee Deductions				
Canada Savings Bond (CSB)	$200	$100	$50	$50
EI, CPP & Income Tax	calculations built into Simply Accounting program			
Additional Income Tax	$50	$25		

Employee Name	Mita Ashikaya	Evelyn Nicols	Max Matthias
Position	Clerk/Accountant	Part-time	Part-time
Social Insurance Number	477 527 691	514 825 633	412 645 965
Address & Telephone	58 Highridge Ave.	32 Stonecliffe Crt.	66 Mountain Brow Blvd.
	Hamilton, ON	Hamilton, ON	Hamilton, ON
	L8E 2S2	L9C 7G3	L8T 1A4
	(905) 889-3465	(905) 421-8313	(905) 782-3429
Date of Birth (dd-mm-yy)	31-7-62	29-4-72	2-12-75
Tax Exemption (TD-1)			
Basic Personal	$6 456	$6 456	$6 456
Spouse	$5 380		
Children under 18			
Disability			
Education & Tuition		$4 200	$3 200
Other			
Total Exemptions	$11 836	$10 656	$9 656
Employee Earnings			
Regular Wage Rate		$14.00	$12.00
Overtime Wage Rate		$21.00	$18.00
Regular Salary	$2 500/mo		
Commission	1% (Sales - Returns)		
Vacation	3 weeks	4%	4%
Employee Deductions			
Canada Savings Bond (CSB)	$100		
EI, CPP & Income Tax	calculations built into Simply Accounting program		
Additional Income Tax	$20		

Employee Profiles and TD1 Information

Alana Gascon, as the field manager and engineer for Puretek, plans and designs the stonework for all projects, and schedules and oversees the field workers. She is single and supports her father for whom she claims the spousal equivalent tax exemption. She contributes $200 to the Canada Savings Bond payroll deduction plan each month and has elected to have additional income tax deducted from her pay. Her monthly salary of $4 000, paid on the last day of each month, is supplemented by a commission of 2 percent of contract revenue. Gascon is entitled to three weeks vacation with pay.

Michael Arturo is a stonecutter by training. He is married and fully supports his wife and 12-year-old child who have no income. Every two weeks he receives $18 per hour for the first 40 hours of work per week and $27 for each hour of overtime work. He makes bi-weekly payroll contributions of $100 to the Canada Savings Bond plan, and has additional income tax deducted from each pay. Arturo's vacation pay, at the rate of 6 percent, is retained until he takes vacation time.

Hans Bekker is employed as a bricklayer and general handyperson. He is single and self-supporting, and participates in the Savings Bond plan, paying $50 every bi-weekly pay period. He earns $18 per hour for regular work and $27 for overtime hours. Bekker's vacation pay, at the rate of 6 percent, is retained until he takes vacation time.

Dimitri Valios assists with bricklaying and operates the machinery. He is single and self-supporting. He has chosen to participate in the payroll savings plan, deducting $50 for Canada Savings Bond purchases. He is paid bi-weekly, earning $16 per hour for regular work and $24 for overtime work. Valios' vacation pay, at the rate of 6 percent, is retained until he takes vacation time.

Mita Ashikaya works in the store, performing clerical, sales and accounting tasks. She is single and supports fully her younger sister. Since her sister has no income, Ashikaya is entitled to the spousal equivalent tax claim for her sister. She contributes $100 each month to purchase Canada Savings Bonds and pays additional income tax from her $2 500 monthly salary. As an additional incentive, she receives a commission of 1 percent of store sales, net of returns and taxes. Ashikaya receives three weeks vacation with pay each year.

Evelyn Nicols works wherever she is needed most, either in the store or on projects. Nicols is a single, self-supporting university student who claims her $3 000 tuition fees and $150 per month education deduction for the eight-month school year. She is paid weekly, earning $14 per hour for regular hours and $21 for overtime work, and she does not participate in the Savings Bond plan. Her vacation pay at 4 percent is retained.

Max Matthias also assists as needed with a project or store work. He too is single and self-supporting while he attends college. His $2 000 in tuition fees and his $1 200 educational deduction are claimed as tax exemptions. He earns $12 per hour for regular work and $18 for overtime work, receives his pay weekly, and does not participate in the Canada Savings Bond plan. His vacation pay at 4 percent is retained.

Additional Payroll Information

Employees have the following pay periods:
• salaried employees are paid on the last day of each month
• part-time employees are paid weekly
• the remaining full-time hourly workers are paid bi-weekly.

The employer's contributions include the following:
• CPP contributions equal to employee contributions
• EI contributions at 1.4 times the employee contributions
• WCB rate for Ashikaya is 1.52
  WCB rate for all other employees is 7.87
• EHT rate is 0.98

Notes

Remember that EI is the new name for UI.

PURETEK PAVING & STONEWORKS
INVENTORY INFORMATION

Code	Description	Selling Price /Unit	Qty on Hand	Amt (Cost)	Min Stock
Base materials					
BM-1	Base Material: Gravel 3/4 crushed	$30.00/ton	100	$1 800	10
BM-2	Base Material: Gravel 3/4 smooth	32.00/ton	100	2 000	10
BM-3	Base Material: Sand	25.00/ton	100	1 500	10
BM-4	Base Material: Screening	22.00/ton	100	1 200	10
				$6 500	
Cobble Pavestones					
CP-1	Cobblestone: Berlin circular 4x8	$1.80/sqft	1 000	$1 000	100
CP-2	Cobblestone: Cordoba textured 4x8	1.60/sqft	1 200	960	120
CP-3	Cobblestone: Goteberg random 4x8	1.60/sqft	1 200	960	120
CP-4	Cobblestone: Haarlem octagonal 4x8	1.50/sqft	1 000	750	100
CP-5	Cobblestone: Leeds texture reg. 4x8	1.40/sqft	1 500	1 050	150
CP-6	Cobblestone: Madrid hexagon 4x8	1.40/sqft	1 500	1 050	150
CP-7	Cobblestone: Verona classic 4x8	1.50/sqft	1 500	1 125	150
CP-8	Cobblestone: Ypress Roman 9x18	3.95 each	500	1 250	50
CP-9	Cobblestone: Zurich grid 18x18	6.95 each	500	2 000	50
				$10 145	
Edging Stone Blocks					
ES-1	Edging Stone: Crv scalloped 2ft	$3.00 each	250	$450	25
ES-2	Edging Stone: Crv scalloped 3ft	4.50 each	250	750	25
ES-3	Edging Stone: Str scalloped 2ft	2.00 each	250	300	25
ES-4	Edging Stone: Str scalloped 3ft	3.00 each	250	450	25
				$1 950	
Patio Stone Blocks					
PTS-1	Patio Block: Deck concrete 24x24	$6.00 each	500	$2 000	50
PTS-2	Patio Block: Diamond natural 24x30	8.00 each	300	1 500	30
PTS-3	Patio Block: Diamond non-slip 18x18	3.00 each	300	600	30
PTS-4	Patio Block: Diamond non-slip 24x24	5.00 each	300	900	30
PTS-5	Patio Block: Red brick litewt 24x24	6.00 each	400	1 600	40
				$6 600	
Paver Slabs					
PVS-1	Paver Slab: Natural expose 18x16	$1.00 each	1 000	$500	100
PVS-2	Paver Slab: Natural pattern 18x16	1.50 each	800	800	80
PVS-3	Paver Slab: Red expose 18x16	1.20 each	800	640	80
PVS-4	Paver Slab: Red pattern 18x16	1.80 each	1 000	1 000	100
PVS-5	Paver Slab: Texture non-slip 12x12	2.00 each	1 200	1 440	80
				$4 380	
Stone Slabs					
SF-1	Stone Slab: Flagstone irregular	$160.00/ton	25	$2 500	5
SF-2	Stone Slab: Flagstone prem. square	12.00/sqft	300	2 400	30
SF-3	Stone Slab: Granite irregular	180.00/ton	25	3 000	5
SF-4	Stone Slab: Granite premium square	14.00/sqft	250	2 000	25
SF-5	Stone Slab: Slate irregular	140.00/ton	25	2 000	5
SF-6	Stone Slab: Slate premium square	10.00/sqft	400	2 000	40
				$13 900	
Wall Building Blocks					
WB-1	Wall Block: Retaining basic	$6.00 each	1 000	$4 000	100
WB-2	Wall Block: Retaining curvable	9.00 each	500	2 500	50
WB-3	Wall Block: Retaining step plus	8.00 each	500	2 500	50
				$9 000	

Project Information

Puretek uses a separate project for each new contract. At the beginning of April, there are four contracts to be set up as projects: Briar Hill, Chaplin Estates, Forest Glen, and Sherwood. In addition, Store Operations, is an ongoing project. The field manager keeps track of the percentage of time each worker spends on each project. Because these times vary from project to project and from week to week, the percentage allocation is included with each source document that follows. Revenue allocations are also included with the source documents.

Accounting Procedures

The Employer Health Tax (EHT)

The Employer Health Tax (EHT) is paid by all employers in Ontario who pay remuneration to employees who report to work. It also includes employees who are not required to report for work as long as an employer-employee relationship exists. The EHT is based on the total annual remuneration paid to employees. The EHT rate ranges from 0.98 percent to 1.95 percent. The lowest rate (0.98 percent) applies if the total remuneration is under $200 000. The highest rate (1.95 percent) applies to employers paying total remuneration exceeding $400 000.

Simply Accounting will calculate the employer's liability to the Provincial Treasurer automatically once the information is set up correctly in the payroll defaults and integration accounts. A later application, Hearth House, will provide you with the keystrokes necessary for setting up the EHT information. The EHT can be remitted monthly or quarterly.

The Goods and Services Tax: Remittances

Puretek Paving & Stoneworks uses the regular method for remittance of the Goods and Services Tax. GST collected from customers is recorded as a liability in the *GST Charged on Sales* account. GST paid to vendors is recorded in the *GST Paid on Purchases* account as a decrease in liability to Revenue Canada. The report is filed with the Receiver General of Canada by the last day of the month for the previous quarterly period, either including the balance owing or requesting a refund.

Normally the business makes GST remittances, and the Receiver General is listed as a vendor. However, since business purchases were made in March, before the business opened for the season, Puretek has a debit balance and will file for a refund in the month of April. Refunds are processed through the Sales Journal. The Receiver General must be added as a customer and then selected to process the request for a refund. When the refund is received, it is processed as a customer receipt.

Advances on Projects

When customers sign a contract, they pay an advance of 20 percent of the negotiated price (before taxes). The advance is entered in the Sales Journal for the customer as a negative invoice. That is, the amount is entered with a minus sign, no PST or GST is charged and the *Cash in Bank* account is entered in the account field. The *Accounts Receivable* account will automatically be credited for the amount of the advance for the selected customer, and *Cash in Bank* will be debited. When the project is completed, make a Sales Journal entry for the full amount of the contract, including relevant taxes. When the customer settles the account, mark the invoice for both the advance and the full amount as paid. The balance owing in the Receipts Journal should then match the amount of the customer's cheque.

Because several customers paid their advances in March for work to be completed in April, the *Accounts Receivable* account has an opening credit balance.

NSF Cheques

When a bank returns a customer's cheque because there were insufficient funds in the

Notes

Processing the advance through the Sales Journal ensures that the advance will appear in the correct customer account in the Receivables Ledger. The other approach, a General Journal entry that debits Cash in Bank and credits Unearned Revenue, a liability account, does not show this link with the customer.

customer's bank account to cover the cheque, the payment must be reversed. If the payment was processed through the Payments Journal, the reversal should also be processed through the Payments Journal by including fully paid invoices on the screen. If the sale was a cash sale, the reversal must be processed through the Sales Journal. Create a customer record for the customer and process a credit sale for the amount of the NSF cheque. Choose Code 1 for GST and leave the PST field blank to indicate the amount is non-taxable because taxes for the sale were recorded at the time of the original sale. Enter the amount as a positive amount in the amount field and enter the *Cash in Bank* account in the account field. On a separate invoice line, enter the amount of the handling charge for the NSF cheque in the amount field with the *Other Revenue* account in the account field. Again, the handling charge is non-taxable.

Returns

When customers return merchandise, they are charged a 20 percent handling charge. In the Sales Journal, enter the quantity returned with a **minus** sign at the full sale price with taxes, and enter the *Sales Returns & Allowances* account in the account field. The amounts will automatically be negative because of the minus sign in the quantity field, so that *Accounts Receivable* will be credited automatically as well. On a separate invoice line, enter the amount withheld, the handling charge, as a **positive** amount with no GST or PST and credit the *Returns Policy Revenue* account. Treat this revenue as non-taxable. *Accounts Receivable* will be debited automatically for the amount of the handling charge.

If the original sale was a credit sale, and the account is not yet paid, the return should also be entered as a credit sale so that the *Accounts Receivable* account will be credited. If the original sale was paid in cash, or the account has been paid, the return should be entered as a cash sale so that the *Cash in Bank* account will be credited.

Reserved Inventory for Projects

When customers sign a contract, the inventory items needed to complete the project are set aside or reserved by transferring them through the software to a designated account. In this way, these items cannot be sold to other customers because the inventory quantities are already reduced. The minimum stock level for reserved inventory will be zero. Refer to the Keystrokes section, page 306.

Cash Sales and Purchases

Cash transactions for goods and services occur normally in most types of businesses. The Simply Accounting program handles cash transactions through the Sales Journal. Choose <One-time customer> from the customer list if this is not a regular customer and press (tab). The Sale with Payment option is marked and the Cheque field opens with the default entry "Cash." Enter the name and address of the customer in the Address field. You can also choose a customer from the customer list and then click on Sale with Payment. Type the cheque number if payment is by cheque. For credit card sales, type Visa or MC in the cheque number field.

Enter the remainder of the cash transaction in the same way you would enter any credit sale transaction for services to customers.

The program will debit the *Cash in Bank* account instead of the *Accounts Receivable* control account. All the other accounts for this transaction will be appropriately debited or credited.

For cash purchases, choose <One-time vendor> from the vendor list and press (tab). The Purchase with Payment option is marked and the Cheque field opens. Enter the name and address of the vendor in the Address field. You can also choose a vendor from the vendor list and then click on Purchase with Payment. Type the cheque number in the Cheque field and complete the remainder of the cash transaction in the same way you would enter a credit purchase transaction.

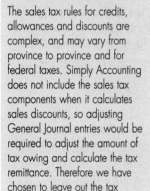

Notes

The sales tax rules for credits, allowances and discounts are complex, and may vary from province to province and for federal taxes. Simply Accounting does not include the sales tax components when it calculates sales discounts, so adjusting General Journal entries would be required to adjust the amount of tax owing and calculate the tax remittance. Therefore we have chosen to leave out the tax component for transactions of this type.

The program will debit the *Cash in Bank* account instead of the *Accounts Payable* control account. All the other accounts for this transaction will be appropriately debited or credited.

Freight Expense
When a business purchases inventory items, the cost of any freight that cannot be directly allocated to a specific item must be charged to the *Freight Expense* account. This amount will be regarded as an expense rather than being charged to any inventory asset account.

PST
The province of Ontario has ruled that PST is calculated on the base amount of the invoice, which does not include the GST. In this application, provincial sales taxes of 8 percent are applied to cash and credit sales of paving materials and to construction work.

Sales Invoices
If you want to print the sales invoice through the program, complete the Sales Journal transaction as you would otherwise. Before posting the transaction, choose Print from the pull-down menu under File or click on the Print button on the tool bar for the invoice form. Printing will begin immediately, so be sure you have the correct forms for your printer before you begin.

Materials Summary Form
Construction materials are requisitioned for projects as needed. These requisition forms are summarized twice a month in a Materials Summary Form. When this form is completed, an adjusting entry must be made in the General Journal to reduce the *Construction Materials* asset account and increase the *Construction Materials Used* expense account.

INSTRUCTIONS

1. Using the Chart of Accounts, Trial Balance and other information, record entries for the source documents for April 1999 using Simply Accounting. The procedures for entering each new type of transaction are outlined step by step in the keystroke section that follows the source documents. A ✔ in the source document completion check box indicates that keystrokes are provided. The page number immediately below the check box is where these keystroke instructions begin.

2. After you have finished making your entries, print the reports and graphs indicated on the following printing form.

REPORTS

Lists
- ☐ Chart of Accounts
- ☐ Vendor List
- ☐ Customer List
- ☐ Employee List
- ☐ Inventory List
- ☐ Project List

Financials
- ☑ Comparative Balance Sheet
  dates: April 1 & April 30
  With Percent Difference
- ☑ Income Statement
  from April 1 to April 30
- ☑ Trial Balance
  date: April 30
- ☑ General Ledger
  accounts: 1380 4020 4040
  from April 1 to April 30

GST
- ☐ GST Report

Payroll
- ☑ Employee Summary
  for all employees
- ☐ T-4 Slips

Project
- ☑ Project Summary
  for all projects, all accounts
  from April 1 to April 30

Mailing Labels
- ☐ Labels

Journals
- ☑ General (by posting date)
  from April 1 to April 30
  With project distributions
- ☐ Purchases
- ☐ Payments
- ☐ Sales
- ☐ Receipts
- ☐ Payroll
- ☑ Transfers (by posting date)
  from April 1 to April 30
- ☐ Adjustments

Payables
- ☐ Vendor Aged
- ☐ Aged Overdue Payables
- ☐ Vendor Purchases
- ☐ Pending Purchase Orders

Receivables
- ☐ Customer Aged
- ☐ Aged Overdue Receivables
- ☐ Customer Sales
- ☐ Customer Statements

Inventory
- ☐ Inventory
- ☑ Inventory Sales Summary
  for Base Materials
  from April 1 to April 30
- ☑ Inventory Activity Summary
  for Patio Blocks, all journals
  from April 1 to April 30

GRAPHS

- ☐ Payables by Aging Period
- ☐ Receivables by Aging Period
- ☐ Sales vs Receivables
- ☐ Revenues by Account
- ☑ Expenses & Net Profit as % of Revenue

- ☐ Payables by Vendor
- ☐ Receivables by Customer
- ☐ Receivables Due vs Payables Due
- ☐ Expenses by Account
- ☐ Current Revenue vs Last Year

SOURCE DOCUMENTS

USING DATE — April 7

Keystrokes begin on page 298.

298 Project Setup
Dated April 1, 1999
Create the following projects for the store and the construction projects:
Briar Hill Project
Chaplin Estates Project
Forest Glen Project
Sherwood Project
Store Operations

300 Legal Statement #CM-67
Dated April 1, 1999
From Castillo & Maturi, Lawyers, $200 to draw up contracts for clients, plus $14
GST. Purchase invoice total $214. Terms: net 10 days. Charge expense at 25% to
each project excluding Store Operations.

306 Inventory Transfer Form #IT-1001
Dated April 1/99
Reserve inventory for Briar Hill Project with minimum level set at zero.
Create a new inventory asset account, 1500 Reserved Inventory for Projects.
Create the new inventory record in the inventory ledger for the project:
Item Number: BH-1   Item Description: Briar Hill Project: reserved
Price = $2 415/project
Asset Account: 1500   Revenue Account: 4040   Expense Account: 5080
Transfer the following inventory to the reserved inventory BH-1 at cost price.
10 tons Base Material: Gravel 3/4 crushed
5 tons Base Material: Sand
5 tons Base Material: Screening
60 sqft Stone Slabs: Flagstone prem. square
600 sqft Cobblestone: Cordoba textured 4x8
100 Edging Stones: Str scalloped 2ft

Notes

Be very careful in making transfer
entries. Because they are
compound entries, they are
difficult to reverse. Therefore
keystrokes are included for storing
the entry so you will have a copy
on record if reversing is
necessary.

Cash Sales Invoice #100
Dated April 2/99
To Carol Jasenko

100 Wall Blocks: Retaining basic	$6.00 each
Goods & Services Tax	7%
Provincial Sales Tax	8%

Paid by certified cheque #RB-6143. Allocate 100% of revenue and costs to Store
Operations.

Memo #1
Dated April 2/99
From Owner: File Goods and Services Tax return for March. Create a Customer
record for the Receiver General and complete a Sales Journal entry to file for
the refund of $1 330. Refer to the General Ledger GST account balances for
March 31.

Enter a positive amount for GST
Paid on Purchases in the Sales
Journal to credit this account. Use
Memo 1 as the invoice number.
Refer to Accounting Procedures
and Chapter 2 on GST if you
need more information about
GST refunds.

Cheque Copy #55
Dated April 3/99
To Groundfos Machinery, $10 700 in full payment of account. Reference invoice
#GM-677.

Purchase Invoice #HS-6927
Dated April 3/99
From Hamilton Spectator, $400 for weekly ad in newspaper, plus $28 GST.
Purchase invoice total $428. Terms: net 30 days. Charge expense at 20% to each
project.

Cash Sales Invoice #101
Dated April 4/99
To Brian Wilkinson

400 Cobblestone: Berlin circular 4x8	$1.80 /sqft
200 Cobblestone: Verona classic 4x8	1.50 /sqft
25 Paver Slabs: Texture non-slip 12x12	2.00 each
Goods & Services Tax	7%
Provincial Sales Tax	8%

Paid by Master Card #7432 6634 9810 1231. Allocate 100% of revenue and costs
to Store Operations.

Purchase Invoice #MFS-541
Dated April 4/99
From Manitoulin Flagstone & Slate

100 sqft Stone Slabs: Flagstone prem. square	$ 800.00
100 sqft Stone Slabs: Slate premium square	500.00
GST Paid	91.00
Invoice Total	$1 391.00

Terms: n/15 days

Cash Sales Invoice #102
Dated April 4/99
To Mergim Shena

10 Patio Blocks: Deck concrete 24x24	$6.00 each
10 Edging Stones: Crv scalloped 3ft	4.50 each
Goods & Services Tax	7%
Provincial Sales Tax	8%

Paid by cheque #44. Allocate 100% of revenue and costs to Store Operations.

Purchase Invoice #MD-14171
Dated April 5/99
From Mohawk Office Depot (new vendor), $100 for office supplies plus $7 GST
and $8 PST. Invoice total $115. Terms: net 30 days.

Cash Sales Invoice #103
Dated April 5/99
To Elaine Sivcoski

5 tons Stone Slabs: Granite irregular	$180.00 /ton
50 sqft Stone Slabs: Granite premium square	14.00 /sqft
Goods & Services Tax	7%
Provincial Sales Tax	8%

Paid by Visa #4714 553197623. Allocate 100% of revenue and costs to Store
Operations.

Bank Debit Memo #671431
Dated April 6/99
From National Bank, $120.75 for NSF cheque #44 from Mergim Shena.
Reference invoice #102. Mr. Shena has been notified by owner of the
outstanding balance plus a $15 charge for issuing the NSF cheque. Other
Revenue is assigned to Store Operations.

Cash Receipt #5
Dated April 7/99
From Mergim Shena, certified cheque #NB-1421 for $135.75 in full payment of account including $15 NSF handling charges. Reference invoices #102 and Bank Debit Memo #671431. Mr. Shena apologized for the error.

Cash Refund Receipt #1
Dated April 7/99
To Carol Jasenko for return of 100 Wall Blocks: Retaining basic purchased on April 2/99. Invoice total was $690. Issued $552 cash and retained $138 as Returns Policy Revenue. Reference invoice #100. Allocate 100% of revenue and costs to Store Operations.

Notes

Remember to use the Sales Returns & Allowances account for the return. Use Ret-100 as the invoice number. See Accounting Procedures.

EMPLOYEE TIME SUMMARY SHEET #1

(pay period ending April 7, 1999)

Name of Employee	Regular Hours	Overtime Hours
Matthias, Max	30	–
Nicols, Evelyn	32	–

a. Using Employee Time Summary Sheet #1 and Employee Information Sheet, complete payroll for weekly paid employees.
b. Charge payroll expenses at 60% to Store Operations and 40% to Briar Hill project for both employees.
c. Issue cheques #56 and #57.

Purchase Invoice #SG-1352
Dated April 7/99
From Sudbury Granite

20 tons Stone Slabs: Flagstone irregular	$2 000.00
150 sqft Stone Slabs: Flagstone prem. square	1 200.00
Freight	200.00
GST Paid	238.00
Invoice Total	$3 638.00

Terms: n/30 days

USING DATE — April 14

Inventory Transfer Form #IT-1002
Dated April 8/99
Reserve inventory for Chaplin Estates Project
Create the new inventory record for the project in the inventory ledger:
Item Number: CE-1   Item Description: Chaplin Estates Project: reserved
Price = $4 885/project
Asset Account: 1500   Revenue Account: 4040   Expense Account: 5080
Transfer out the following inventory at cost price into the reserved inventory for Chaplin Estates (CE-1).
10 tons Stone Slabs: Flagstone irregular
100 sqft Stone Slabs: Flagstone prem. square
300 Cobblestone: Zurich grid 18x18

☐ Sales Invoice #104
Dated April 8/99
To Jim Omand, completion of Briar Hill Project

1 BH-1 Briar Hill Project: reserved	$2 415.00
1 contracting services	7 585.00
Goods & Services Tax	7%
Provincial Sales Tax	8%

Terms: Cash on receipt of invoice. Allocate 100% of revenue and costs to Briar Hill Project.

☐ Cash Receipt #6
Dated April 8/99
From Jim Omand, cheque #72 for $9 500 in full payment of account. Reference invoices #104 and CR-3.

☐ Purchase Invoice #SC-1117
Dated April 8/99
From Stoneycreek Cement Co., $500 for bi-weekly delivery of construction materials plus $35 GST. Invoice total $535. Terms: net 30 days.
Store this purchase as a bi-weekly recurring entry.

☐ Cash Sales Invoice #105
Dated April 9/99
To Bruce McCallum

5 tons Base Material: Gravel 3/4 smooth	$32.00 /ton
5 tons Base Material: Sand	25.00 /ton
Goods & Services Tax	7%
Provincial Sales Tax	8%

Paid by certified cheque #TD-4321. Allocate 100% of revenue and costs to Store Operations.

☐ Cheque Copy #58
Dated April 9/99
To Hamilton Mountain Quarry, $3 210 in full payment of account. Reference invoice #HMQ-614.

☐ Purchase Invoice #HMQ-769
Dated April 10/99
From Hamilton Mountain Quarry

10 tons Base Material: Gravel 3/4 crushed	$180.00
10 tons Base Material: Gravel 3/4 smooth	200.00
10 tons Base Material: Sand	150.00
10 tons Base Material: Screening	120.00
Freight Expense	50.00
GST Paid	49.00
Invoice Total	$749.00

Terms: n/20 days

Cash Sales Invoice #106
Dated April 10/99
To Karen Afante

10 tons Base Material: Sand	$25.00 /ton
10 tons Base Material: Screening	22.00 /ton
200 Cobblestone: Ypress Roman 9x18	3.95 each
Goods & Services Tax	7%
Provincial Sales Tax	8%

Paid by Visa #4502 753122764. Allocate 100% of revenue and costs to Store Operations.

Cheque Copy #59
Dated April 11/99
To Waterloo Pavestone Ltd., $4 280 in full payment of account. Reference invoice #WP-3124.

Cheque Copy #60
Dated April 12/99
To Castillo & Maturi, $214 in full payment of account. Reference invoice #CM-67.

Purchase Invoice #WM-1912
Dated April 12/99
From Westdale Machinery (new vendor), $500 for repairs to machinery and equipment plus $35 GST. Invoice total $535. Terms: net 30 days. Charge repairs at 50% to Store Operations, 25% to Briar Hill Project, and 25% to Chaplin Estates Project.

Cash Sales Invoice #107
Dated April 13/99
To Mark Lyne

100 Wall Blocks: Retaining curvable	$ 9.00 each
10 tons Stone Slabs: Flagstone irregular	160.00 /ton
Goods & Services Tax	7%
Provincial Sales Tax	8%

Paid by cheque #465. Allocate 100% of revenue and costs to Store Operations.

Cash Purchase Invoice #HH-42142
Dated April 13/99
To Hamilton Hydro, $200 for hydro services plus $14 GST. Invoice total $214. Issued cheque #61 in payment. Charge full hydro expense to Store Operations.

Cash Purchase Invoice #BC-43179
Dated April 13/99
To Bell Canada, $80 for telephone services plus $5.60 GST and $6.40 PST. Invoice total $92. Issued cheque #62 in payment. Charge complete telephone expense to Store Operations.

Purchase Invoice #WP-3857
Dated April 14/99
From Waterloo Pavestone

400 sqft Cobblestone: Berlin circular 4x8	$400.00
400 sqft Cobblestone: Cordoba textured 4x8	320.00
400 sqft Cobblestone: Verona classic 4x8	300.00
400 sqft Cobblestone: Zurich grid 18x18	1 600.00
GST Paid	183.40
Invoice Total	$2 803.40

Terms: n/20 days

Notes

Westdale Machinery
(Contact Dale West)
is located at
35 Sterling St.
Hamilton, ON
L8S 4H6
Tel: (905) 528-6992
Fax: (905) 528-8921

(pay period ending April 14, 1999)

Name of Employee	Week 1 Hours	Week 2 Hours	Regular Hours	Overtime Hours
☐ Arturo, Michael	40	42	80	2
☐ Bekker, Hans	40	40	80	–
☐ Matthias, Max	n/a	42	40	2
☐ Nicols, Evelyn	n/a	40	40	–
☐ Valios, Dimitri	40	42	80	2

a. Using Employee Time Summary Sheet #2 and Employee Information Sheet, complete payroll for all hourly employees.

b. For Arturo, Bekker and Valios, charge payroll expenses at 50% to Briar Hill Project and 50% to Chaplin Estates Project.

c. For Matthias and Nicols, charge payroll expenses at 60% to Store Operations and 40% to Chaplin Estates Project.

d. Issue cheques #63 through #67.

USING DATE — April 21

☐ Materials Summary Form #1
Dated April 15/99
From Owner: Charge $1 000 to Construction Materials Used account and reduce the Construction Materials asset account for the mid-month adjustment. Charge 60% of the materials cost to the Briar Hill Project and 40% to the Chaplin Estates Project.

☐ Inventory Transfer Form #IT-1003
Dated April 15/99
Reserve inventory for Forest Glen Project
Create the new inventory record for the project in the inventory ledger:
   Item Number: FG-1   Item Description: Forest Glen Project: reserved
   Price = $3 020/project
   Asset Account: 1500   Revenue Account: 4040   Expense Account: 5080
Transfer out the following inventory at cost price into the reserved inventory for Forest Glen (FG-1).
   10 tons Base Material: Gravel 3/4 crushed
   10 tons Base Material: Sand
   10 tons Base Material: Screening
   1000 sqft Cobblestone: Madrid hexagon 4x8
   100 Edging Stones: Crv scalloped 3ft
   200 Paver Slabs: Texture non-slip 12x12

☐ Sales Invoice #108
Dated April 15/99
To Cameron MacGregor, completion of Chaplin Estates Project
   1 CE-1 Chaplin Estates Project: reserved $ 4 885.00
   1 contracting services   10 115.00
   Goods & Services Tax   7%
   Provincial Sales Tax   8%
Terms: Cash on receipt of invoice. Allocate 100% of revenue and costs to Chaplin Estates Project.

☐ Cash Receipt #7
Dated April 15/99
From Cameron MacGregor, cheque #121 for $14 250 in full payment of account.
Reference invoices #108 and CR-2.

☐ Cheque Copy #68
Dated April 15/99
To Dundas Concrete Works, $2 140 in full payment of account. Reference invoice
#DC-1472.

☐ Cash Sales Invoice #109
Dated April 16/99
To Lou Sialtsis
    200 Wall Blocks: Retaining step plus $ 8.00 each
    5 tons Base Material: Gravel 3/4 smooth   32.00 /ton
    Goods & Services Tax   7%
    Provincial Sales Tax   8%
Paid by Visa #4510 341630972. Allocate 100% of revenue and costs to Store
Operations.

☐ Purchase Invoice #DC-2599
Dated April 16/99
From Dundas Concrete Works
    100 Wall Blocks: Retaining basic $400.00
    100 Wall Blocks: Retaining curvable   500.00
    100 Wall Blocks: Retaining step plus   500.00
    GST Paid   98.00
    Invoice Total $1 498.00
Terms: n/20 days

☐ Cheque Copy #69
Dated April 18/99
To Manitoulin Flagstone & Slate, $1 391 in full payment of account. Reference
invoice #MFS-541.

☐ Cash Sales Invoice #110
Dated April 18/99
To John Pissaris
    50 sqft Stone Slabs: Granite premium square $14.00 /sqft
    Goods & Services Tax   7%
    Provincial Sales Tax   8%
Paid by Master Card #7430 7491 8752 2784. Allocate 100% of revenue and costs
to Store Operations.

☐ Purchase Invoice #GM-719
Dated April 18/99
From Groundfos Machinery, $8 500 for new loading machinery plus $595 GST.
Purchase invoice total $9 095. Terms: net 15 days

☐ Cash Sales Invoice #111
Dated April 19/99
To Elena Cannatelli

600 Cobblestone: Goteberg random 4x8	$1.60 /sqft
200 Paver Slabs: Red pattern 18x16	1.80 each
Goods & Services Tax	7%
Provincial Sales Tax	8%

Paid by Visa #4514 667346102. Allocate 100% of revenue and costs to Store Operations.

☐ Purchase Invoice #NT-611
Dated April 20/99
From Niagara Transport (new vendor), $200 for emergency delivery to Forest Glen project plus $14 GST and $16 PST. Invoice total $230. Terms: N/15 days. Charge 100% of the cost to Forest Glen Project.

☐ Sales Invoice #112
Dated April 21/99
To Wisdom Akonta, completion of Forest Glen Project

1 FG-1 Forest Glen Project: reserved	$3 020.00
1 Contracting Services	6 980.00
Goods & Services Tax	7%
Provincial Sales Tax	8%

Terms: Cash on receipt of invoice. Allocate 100% of revenue and costs to Forest Glen Project.

☐ Cash Receipt #8
Dated April 21/99
From Wisdom Akonta, certified cheque #SB-81214 for $9 500 in full payment of account. Reference invoices #112 and CR-1.

Notes

☐ Niagara Transport (Contact Water Fallis) is located at 699 Niagara St. Hamilton, ON L8L 6A7 Tel: (905) 527-1353 Fax: (905) 527-5221

EMPLOYEE TIME SUMMARY SHEET #3

(pay period ending April 21, 1999)

Name of Employee	Regular Hours	Overtime Hours
☐ Matthias, Max	40	–
☐ Nicols, Evelyn	40	–

a. Using Employee Time Summary Sheet #3 and Employee Information Sheet, complete payroll for weekly paid employees.
b. Charge payroll expenses at 75% to Store Operations and 25% to Forest Glen Project for both employees.
c. Issue cheques #70 and #71.

☐ Inventory Transfer Form #IT-1004
Dated April 22/99
Reserve inventory for Sherwood Project
Create the new inventory record for the project in the inventory ledger:
    Item Number: SH-1   Item Description: Sherwood Project: reserved
    Price = $3 910/project
    Asset Account: 1500   Revenue Account: 4040   Expense Account: 5080
Transfer out the following inventory at cost price into the reserved inventory for Sherwood (SH-1).
    10 tons Base Material: Gravel 3/4 crushed
    10 tons Base Material: Sand
    10 tons Base Material: Screening
    600 sqft Cobblestone: Leeds texture reg. 4x8
    100 sqft Stone Slabs: Granite premium square
    5 tons Stone Slabs: Granite irregular

☐ Purchase Invoice #SC-1194
Dated April 22/99
From Stoneycreek Cement Co., $500 for construction materials plus $35 GST.
Purchase invoice total $535. Terms: net 30 days. Recall stored entry.

☐ Cash Sales Invoice #113
Dated April 23/99
To Karlene Mistry

50 Patio Blocks: Red brick litewt 24x24	$6.00 each
50 Paver Slabs: Red pattern 18x16	1.80 each
Goods & Services Tax	7%
Provincial Sales Tax	8%

Paid by certified cheque #TD-8918. Allocate 100% of revenue and costs to Store Operations.

☐ Purchase Invoice #MP-614
Dated April 24/99
From McMaster Paintworks (new vendor), $1 000 for painting logo on delivery truck plus $70 GST. Invoice total $1 070. Terms: net 30 days. Capitalize this cost to the Delivery Truck account.

☐ Purchase Invoice #WP-3996
Dated April 24/99
From Waterloo Pavestone Ltd.

400 sqft Cobblestone: Goteberg random 4x8	$320.00
400 sqft Cobblestone: Haarlem octagonal 4x8	300.00
400 sqft Cobblestone: Madrid hexagon 4x8	280.00
GST Paid	63.00
Invoice Total	$963.00

Terms: n/20 days

Notes

☐ McMaster Paintworks
(Contact Art Paynter)
is located at
42 McMaster Ave.
Dundas, ON
L9H 4M7
Tel: (905) 588-7129
Fax: (905) 588-2101

Sales Invoice #114
Dated April 24/99
To Renaissance Renovations (new customer)

10 tons Base Material: Gravel 3/4 smooth	$32.00 /ton
10 tons Base Material: Sand	25.00 /ton
10 tons Base Material: Screening	22.00 /ton
500 Cobblestone: Haarlem octagonal 4x8	1.50 /sqft
100 Patio Blocks: Diamond non-slip 24x24	5.00 each
Goods & Services Tax	7%
Provincial Sales Tax	8%

Terms: 2/10, N/15 days. Allocate 100% of revenue and costs to Store Operations.

Cash Sales Invoice #115
Dated April 25/99
To Manek Singh

50 sqft Stone Slabs: Flagstone prem. square	$12.00 /sqft
Goods & Services Tax	7%
Provincial Sales Tax	8%

Paid by money order #RB-67214. Allocate 100% of revenue and costs to Store Operations.

Cash Sales Invoice #116
Dated April 26/99
To Lori Christoffer

3 tons Base Material: Sand	$25.00 /ton
100 Cobblestone: Zurich grid 18x18	6.95 each
Goods & Services Tax	7%
Provincial Sales Tax	8%

Paid by Visa #4502 812365003. Allocate 100% of revenue and costs to Store Operations.

Sales Invoice #117
Dated April 27/99
To Renaissance Renovations (returns and exchange)

– 100 Patio Blocks: Diamond non-slip 24x24	$ 5.00 each
100 Patio Blocks: Diamond natural 24x30	8.00 each
Returns Policy handling charge (no GST or PST)	115.00
Goods & Services Tax	7%
Provincial Sales Tax	8%

Terms: 2/10, N/15 days. Allocate 100% of revenue and costs to Store Operations.

EMPLOYEE TIME SUMMARY SHEET #4

(pay period ending April 28, 1999)

	Name of Employee	Week 1 Hours	Week 2 Hours	Regular Hours	Overtime Hours
❑	Arturo, Michael	42	40	80	2
❑	Bekker, Hans	42	40	80	2
❑	Matthias, Max	n/a	40	40	–
❑	Nicols, Evelyn	n/a	40	40	–
❑	Valios, Dimitri	42	40	80	2

a. Using Employee Time Summary Sheet #4 and Employee Information Sheet, complete payroll for all hourly employees.
b. For Arturo, Bekker and Valios, charge payroll expenses at 50% to Forest Glen Project and 50% to Sherwood Project.
c. For Matthias and Nicols, charge payroll expenses at 75% to Store Operations and 25% to Sherwood Project.
d. Issue cheques #72 through #76.

USING DATE — April 30

❑ Sales Invoice #118
Dated April 29/99
To Mark Payne for completion of Sherwood Project

SH-1 Sherwood Project: reserved	$3 910.00 /project
1 Contracting Services	8 590.00 each
Goods & Services Tax	7%
Provincial Sales Tax	8%

Terms: Cash on Receipt of invoice. Allocate 100% of revenue and costs to Sherwood Project.

❑ Cash Receipt #9
Dated April 29/99
From Mark Payne, certified cheque #BM-54821 for $11 875 in full payment of account. Reference invoices #118 and CR-4

❑ Cash Receipt #10
Dated April 29/99
From Nora Nesbitt (new customer), cheque #167 for $2 000 received in advance on the negotiated Nesbitt House contract. Work to be completed in May.

❑❑ Memo #2
Dated April 30/99
From Owner: Complete payroll for salaried employees. Issue cheques #77 and #78. Employee commissions of $950 (2% of Contracting Revenue) for Alana Gascon, and $147 (1% of Store Sales less Returns) for Mita Ashikaya should be included in their paycheques. Charge Gascon's payroll expenses at 20% to each project. Charge Ashikaya's payroll expenses fully to Store Operations project.

❑ Memo #3
Dated April 30/99
From Owner: For audit and internal control purposes, set up a liability for withdrawal of $2 000 from the business for personal use. Issue cheque #79 to R. Stoanfayce.

Notes

❑ Nora Nesbitt
is located at
677 Victoria Ave.
Hamilton, ON
L8L 8B3
Tel: (905) 525-3745

Notes

Treat the withdrawal as a cash purchase by the owner. The Drawings account should be debited.

Bank Debit Memo #924793
Dated April 30/99
From Royal Bank

Bank charges	$ 32.00
Interest on 3 yr bank loan	240.00
Bank loan principal reduced	160.00
Interest on Mortgage	1 900.00
Mortgage principal reduced	100.00

Allocate 100% of costs to Store Operations.

Cash Receipt #11
Dated April 30/99
From Receiver General of Canada, cheque #2114321 for $1 330 for GST refund filed earlier in the month.

Materials Summary Form #2
Dated April 30/99
From Owner: Charge $1 200 to Construction Materials Used account and reduce the Construction Materials asset account for the end-of-month adjustment. Charge 50% of the materials cost to the Forest Glen Project and 50% to the Sherwood Project.

Cheque Copy #80
Dated April 30/99
To Hamilton Mountain Quarry, $749 in full payment of account. Reference invoice #HMQ-769.

Memo #4
Dated April 30/99
From Owner: Create a new project for the Nesbitt House work.

KEYSTROKES

Creating New Projects

Before entering any transactions with cost or revenue distributions, you must create the projects.

Open the files for Puretek Paving & Stoneworks.

Type   04-07-99

Click on OK

This will enter the using date, April 7, 1999. The Home window appears.

Double click on the **Project ledger icon** shown on the following screen:

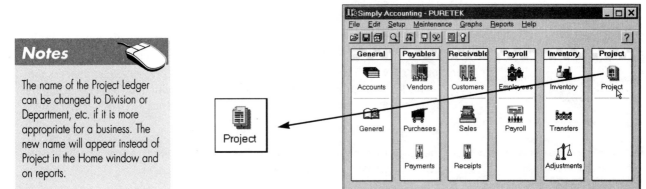

The Project window that follows should appear on your screen:

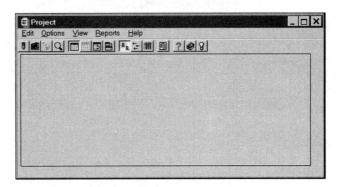

The Project window is empty because we have not yet created any projects.

Click on the **Create button** [icon] in the Project window or choose Create from the pull-down menu under Edit. The following new Project Ledger screen appears:

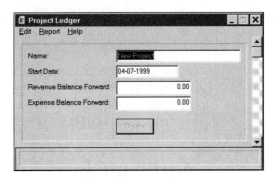

The cursor is in the Name field with the contents highlighted, ready to be edited. You must enter the name of the first project.

Type   Briar Hill Project

Press   ⟮tab⟯

The cursor moves to the Start Date field. Enter the date on which you want to begin recording project information, April 1, 1999. The using date appears automatically by default, ready to be accepted. You need to change the date.

Type   04-01-99

Press   ⟮tab⟯

The cursor moves to the Revenue Balance Forward field. This field and the next, Expense Balance Forward, can be used to enter historical information for the project, the amount of revenue and expense generated by the project before the starting date entered. The balances are zero for Puretek because a new fiscal year is just beginning. The project information is complete.

Click on Create to save the new project. Another blank project ledger appears for you to enter the next project on the list. Enter the remaining four projects, using the steps described above for the Briar Hill Project, and the April 1, 1999 starting date.

When you have entered and saved all five projects,

Close the Project Ledger to return to the Project window. Notice that Simply Accounting has created an icon for each project.

Close the main Project window to return to the Home window. Leave the Project icon selected.

Click on the **Setup button** or choose Settings from the pull-down menu under Setup to display the Settings window. Because the Project icon was selected, you will see the Project Settings immediately as shown here:

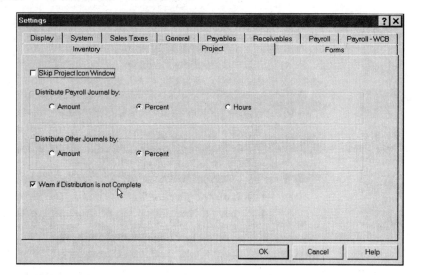

Click on Warn if Distribution is not Complete if this option is not already selected. This will allow the program to warn you before you post an entry that has not been fully allocated. The remaining default settings, to distribute expenses by percentage, are correct.

Entering Cost Distributions

Costs or expenses, and revenues are distributed after the regular journal entry is completed but before it is posted. Whenever the project ledger is set up, and a revenue or expense account is used in the journal entry, the distribution option is available.

Double click on the Purchases icon as shown here:

Notes

You can re-sort the project icons if they are out of order by choosing Re-sort Items from the pull-down menu under Options. You can list the projects by name in the Project window by choosing By Name from the pull-down menu under View.

Notes

If the Project icon is not selected, choose Project from the Setup button drop-down list. Or choose Settings from the pull-down menu under Setup and click on the Project tab.

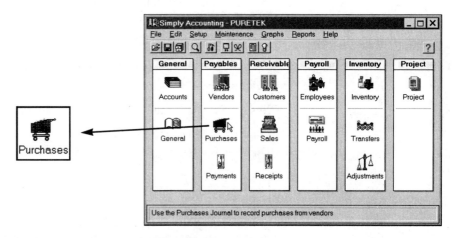

The familiar Purchases Journal input form opens:

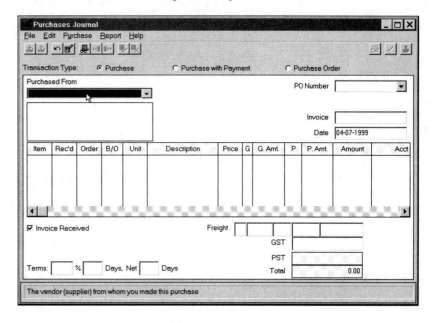

The first transaction does not involve the purchase of inventory items so you will not use the inventory database to complete this transaction.

The cursor is flashing in the Vendor field, ready to receive information. From the list of vendors,

Click on Castillo & Maturi, Lawyers

Press ⌷tab⌷

The cursor moves to the PO Number field.

Press ⌷tab⌷ to advance to the Invoice field so you can enter the alphanumeric invoice number.

Type CM-67

Press ⌷tab⌷

The cursor moves to the Date field. Enter the date on which the transaction took place, April 1, 1999. The using date appears automatically by default, ready to be accepted. You need to change the date.

Type 04-01-99

Press ⌷tab⌷

The cursor moves to the Item field.

Press (tab) repeatedly to advance to the G (GST code) field.

Press (enter) to display the list of GST codes.

Notes

Alternatively, you could click on the first line of the G (GST code) field to move the cursor.

Click on 3 from the selection list.

Click on Select to add the code to the input form.

Press (tab) repeatedly to advance to the Amount field because there is no PST charged on the service. Enter the amount of the invoice, excluding any taxes.

Type 200

Press (tab)

The cursor moves to the Account field. When you are working in a subsidiary ledger, your *Accounts Payable* control account in the General Ledger will automatically be credited for purchases you enter. You must enter the expense or debit part of this entry.

Press (enter) to display the list of accounts.

Click on 5200 Legal Expenses

Click on Select to add the account to the input form.

Notice that the Distribute button is no longer dimmed.

Click on the **Distribute button** or double click on the Dist. column beside the account to see the Project Distribution window for the Purchases Journal as follows:

Notes

If the cursor has advanced to the next line of the invoice, the Distribute button will be dimmed and unavailable. Click on the invoice line for the amount you want to distribute to activate the Distribute option. Only Expense and Revenue accounts will activate the Distribute option.

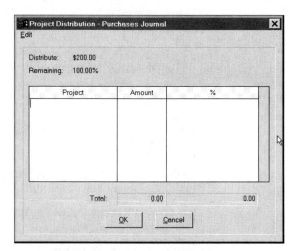

The cursor is in the Project field. The full amount to be distributed, $200, is shown at the top for reference together with the proportion remaining to be distributed, 100%. Amounts can be distributed by percentage or by actual amount. This choice is made in the Project Settings window (choose Settings from the pull-down menu under Setup). The setting can be changed as needed. Puretek uses the percentage allocation method as indicated in the Project Information.

Press (enter)

The following list of Projects is displayed in alphabetic order:

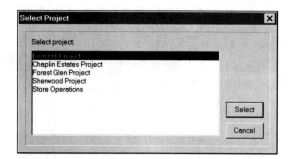

The first project is Briar Hill, which incurs 25% of the total legal expense according to the source document information.

The Briar Hill Project, the first one we need, is highlighted.

Click on Select to enter it on your form.

The cursor advances to the percentage field. By default the unallocated amount is indicated in this field.

Type   25

Press   [tab]

The program calculates the dollar amount for this project automatically based on the percentage entered. The percentage remaining at the top of the input form has been updated to 75%. The cursor moves to the next line in the Project field. Now you are ready to enter the amounts for the other projects, 25% each. You need to repeat the steps outlined above in order to allocate the remainder of the expense.

Press   [enter]

Click on Chaplin Estates Project

Click on Select

The cursor is in the Percentage field again, with the default amount shown as 75%.

Type   25

Press   [tab]

The cursor returns to the Project field so that you can enter the amount for the next project.

Press [enter] to display the list of projects.

Click on Forest Glen Project

Click on Select

The cursor is in the Percentage field again, with the default amount shown as 50%.

Type   25

Press   [tab]

The cursor returns to the Project field.

Press [enter] to display the list of projects.

Sherwood Project is highlighted as the next project unused in this transaction.

Click on Select to enter it on your form and advance to the percentage field.

The final percentage is correct.

Press [tab] to enter it and complete the distribution.

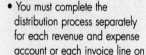

Click on OK to return to the Purchases Journal. Your form is now complete as shown below, and you are ready to review your work:

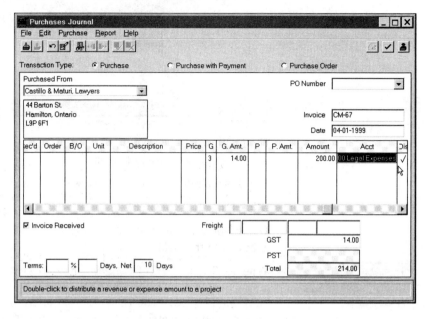

The ✔ in the Dist column indicates that the amount has been distributed.

Reviewing the Purchases Journal Distribution

Choose Display Purchases Journal Entry from the pull-down menu under **Report** to display the transaction you have entered:

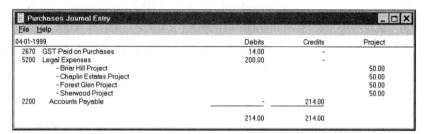

You may need to scroll to see all of the information. Notice that the Simply Accounting program has automatically updated the *Accounts Payable* control account because the Payables and General ledgers are fully integrated. Notice also that the legal expense has been distributed among the four projects.

Close the display to return to the Purchases Journal input screen.

Posting

When you are certain that you have entered all the information correctly,

Post the transaction to save it.

Distributing Revenue and Expenses in Other Journals

Use the same principles outlined above to distribute revenues and expenses in the Sales Journal, the General Journal or the Payroll Journal to projects, departments or profit centres. You can change the setup to make distributions by dollar amounts or by percentage.

Once you have entered the journal information, the Distribute button on the tool bar will be darkened. Use it to enter the distribution information as you did for the Purchases Journal. In the Payroll Journal, the total payroll expense, including employer contributions, such as EI, CPP, WCB and EHT, not the net pay, is being distributed. In the setup for Payroll distributions, you also have the option of distributing the expenses according to the number of hours worked on each project.

When you review the journal entry, you will see that all of the payroll-related expenses are divided among the projects according to the percentages you entered. They are shown under the Project column. You may have to scroll the display to see all of the information.

Entering Inventory Transfers

Puretek uses the inventory Transfers Journal in Simply Accounting to ensure that the inventory to complete a project will be available when needed. The necessary items are taken out of their regular inventory account and transferred to a special reserve account. When requested under the usual inventory names, they appear not to be there because those quantities are reduced, but they will appear in the new account.

You must create the required new asset account, *1500 Reserved Inventory for Projects* and the inventory ledger item, *BH-1 Briar Hill Project: reserved*, before beginning the transfer.

Inventory transfers are completed in the Transfers Journal indicated below:

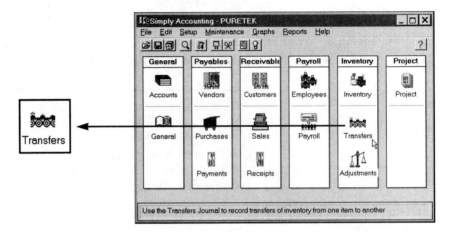

Double click on the Transfers icon to open the Transfers Journal shown:

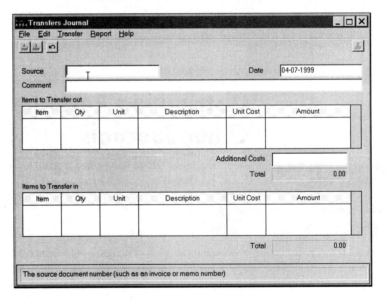

The cursor is in the Source field where you should enter the invoice number.

Type   IT-1001

Press [tab] to advance to the Date field. Enter the date of the transfer.

Type   04-01-99

Press [tab] to advance to the Comment field.

Type   Inventory required for Briar Hill

Press tab to advance to the first line of the Item field in the Items to Transfer out section. This section refers to the items that are being removed from inventory, the "from" part of the transfer. These items are being reserved for the project.

Press enter to display the familiar inventory selection list.

Click on BM-1 Base Material: Gravel 3/4 crushed to select the first item needed for the Briar Hill Project.

Click on Select to add the item to the transfer form and advance to the Quantity (Qty) field.

Type 10

Press tab to advance the cursor to the Unit cost field and to update the amount. The cost is correct but can be edited if necessary.

Click on the next line in the Item column.

Select the next inventory item to be transferred, enter the quantity and then continue to enter the remaining inventory for the Briar Hill Project.

At this stage, your screen should look like the one shown here:

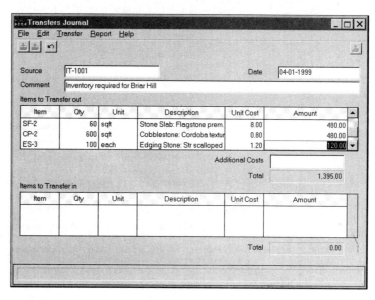

The middle part of the transfers form contains two fields, Additional Costs and the Total. Additional costs may be incurred with transfers if there are shipping or packaging costs involved with moving or transferring the inventory. These costs should be entered into the Additional Costs field. The Total is calculated automatically by Simply Accounting to include the individual costs of all items transferred plus any additional costs. There are no additional costs in this transfer.

Click on the first line in the Item column of the Items to Transfer In section. This section refers to the new or reserved inventory — in this case, the "to" part of the transfer.

Press enter to display the familiar inventory selection list.

Click on BH-1 Briar Hill Project: reserved to select the new inventory ledger item created for the Briar Hill Project.

Click on Select to add the item to the transfer form and advance to the Quantity (Qty) field. We will enter the reserved inventory as a group into the single ledger item or category.

Type   1

Press (tab) to advance the cursor to the Unit Cost field. Because all items were transferred at cost and the quantity is one, the unit cost is the Total amount listed under the transfer out section.

Type   1395

Press (tab) to enter the cost and update the amount. The Totals in the two parts of the transfer form should be the same. If they are not, you will be unable to post the entry. Your completed form should now resemble the following:

Notes

The unit cost of the items to transfer in is the total cost of the items transferred out divided by the quantity or number of units transferred in. It may be simpler to enter the quantity and the amount, the total of the costs in the transfer out portion in the top half of the form, and then let Simply Accounting calculate the unit cost.

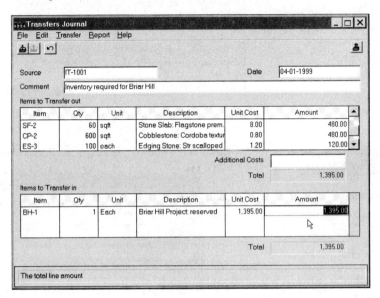

Reviewing the Transfers Journal Entry

Choose **Display Transfers Journal Entry** from the pull-down menu under **Report** to display the transaction you have entered:

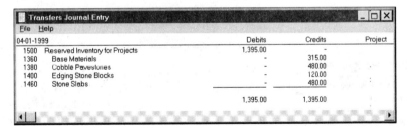

You may need to scroll to see all of the information. Notice that the Simply Accounting program has moved the inventory items from their original asset account to the new reserved inventory asset account. When you display inventory selection lists or quantity reports, you will see that all the quantities for the items involved have been updated.

Close the display to return to the Transfers Journal input screen.

Because the transfer entry is a complex one, it is very easy to make a mistake, so check your work carefully. You may also want to store the original entry. If you discover later that you have made an error, you can recall the entry, jot down the details and use them to make a reversing entry.

Click on the **Store button** [icon] to display the familiar Store Recurring Entry screen.

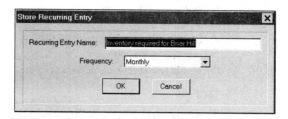

Notes

Choosing the Random frequency
for recurring entries enters the
using date as the date when you
recall the journal entry.

Click on Monthly to display the Frequency options. Because this is not a regular recurring transaction, we will use the Random frequency.

Scroll up until the Random frequency is in view.

Click on Random to select this frequency.

Click on OK to save the entry and return to the Transfers Journal. Notice that the Recall button is now active.

CORRECTING THE TRANSFERS JOURNAL ENTRY

Move to the field that has the error. **Press** (tab) to move forward through the fields or **press** (shift) and (tab) together to move back to a previous field. This will highlight the field information so you can change it. **Type** the correct information and **press** (tab) to enter it. You must advance the cursor to the next invoice line to enter a change.

You can also use the mouse to point to a field and drag through the incorrect information to highlight it. **Type** the correct information and **press** (tab) to enter it.

If an inventory item is incorrect, **press** (enter) to display the appropriate list. **Click on** the correct selection to highlight it and **click on** Select to enter the change. Then re-enter the quantity.

Posting

When you are certain that you have entered all the information correctly, you must post the transaction to save it.

Post the transaction.

Displaying Project Reports
Displaying the Project List

Notes

You can display the Project Detail
Report from the Project List.

Click on the Project icon to select it.

Click on the Report button  or choose Display Project List from the pull-down menu under Reports.

Close the display when you are finished viewing it.

To include project information in any journal reports, click on Project Distributions in the Journal Report options window.

Displaying Project Reports

Choose Project from the pull-down menu under **Reports** to display the following Project Report Options window:

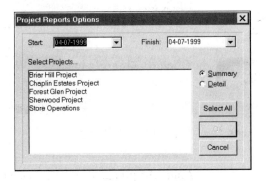

As usual, the program gives the using date as the default.

Type the beginning date for the report you want.

Press (tab)

Type the ending date for the report.

Click on Select All to include all the projects in the report or choose a single project by clicking on its name.

Leave the **Summary** option, the one selected by default, if you want your report to show summary information for each account selected for each project. The **Detail** option provides complete journal information for each account for each project selected, including the names of all customers, vendors and employees, as well as the reference document number, journal entry number and date. Both options provide a calculation for revenue minus expense.

After you have indicated which options you want,

Click on OK

The program then asks you to select the particular revenue or expense account that you want the report for, as in the following window:

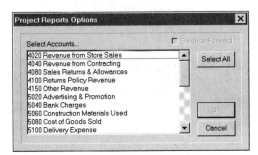

Click on Select All or on the specific accounts you want.

Click on OK to display the report.

Close the display when you are finished.

Notes

You can display the Project Detail Report from the Project Summary Report. You can display the Project Ledger, General Ledger, Invoice Lookup, Customer or Vendor Aged or Employee Report (if applicable) from the Project Detail Report.

Displaying the Transfers Journal Report

Click on the Transfers icon to select it.

Click on the Report button 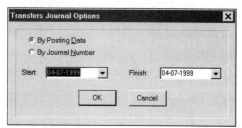 or choose Display Transfers Journal from the pull-down menu under Reports to display the report options:

Again, the program gives the using date as the default.

Type the beginning date for the report you want.

Press (tab)

Type the ending date for the report.

Click on OK to display the report.

Close the display when you are finished.

Printing Reports

Display the report you want on the screen by following the instructions above.

Choose Print from the pull-down menu under File.

CASE PROBLEM

Puretek has been advised that the stock of several styles of cobblestone is being discontinued. Since they will be unable to replace the current stock when it runs out, they have decided to clear it at sale prices.

a. How should they record the sales of the items with reduced prices in the Sales Journal?

b. What changes should they make in the inventory ledger in the Simply Accounting program to build in the price changes?

c. If they decide to offer additional volume discounts, how should the changes be made in Simply Accounting?

d. What should they do if they decide to bundle several different kinds of cobblestones at special sale prices?

CHAPTER TWELVE

![BONNIE BRIDES — BRIDAL GOWNS, FORMAL GOWNS & ACCESSORIES]

OBJECTIVES

Upon completion of this chapter, you will be able to:

- *turn on* the budgeting feature in Simply Accounting
- *determine* budgeting periods and amounts
- *allocate* budget amounts to revenue and expense accounts
- *enter* inventory-related credit purchase and sale transactions
- *enter* transactions involving Quebec Sales Tax
- *enter* inventory adjustments
- *enter* customer deposits
- *display* and *print* income statements with budget comparisons
- *analyze* budget reports

COMPANY INFORMATION

Company Profile

Bonnie Brides, a small bridal boutique owned and operated by Bonnie Brioche, has been in business for about two years in Montreal. The store sells a small but carefully selected range of moderately priced designer bridal gowns and bridal accessories as well as gowns for the other members of the bridal party, bridesmaids and mothers. Some of the attendants' gowns are specifically designed to complement the bride's gowns. The rest of the store's revenue comes from custom-made gowns whose designs are chosen from a specialized pattern catalogue or adapted from photographs in bridal magazines. The custom work is completed by Sylvie Couturier, Brioche's cousin. Couturier, who had previously worked from her home designing a variety of business and formal wear for women, joined the business in January after repeated enquiries from customers about such work. The change was a relatively easy one to make because Brioche already had the sewing machines for alteration work.

Notes

Bonnie Brides is located at Rue Simard, 1650 Montreal, QC H2H 2K8. Its Revenue Canada business number is 58123 0458.

Since most weddings are planned for the summer, most brides choose their gowns at the beginning of the year, making January and February the busiest months. Although Brioche requests that customers pay for their gowns immediately, she offers to store them until just before the wedding when final fittings and alterations are made. As a service to her clients, Brioche provides free alterations on all regularly priced merchandise.

Custom-made gowns take about two weeks full time to complete. Dress fabrics are purchased immediately after the dress is ordered and measurements are taken. Although a small supply of beads, pearls, buttons and lace is kept on hand at the store, most dresses require a special order of these items as well. Therefore customers pay a 25 percent non-refundable deposit to allow the store to purchase the necessary materials. The balance is paid when the dress is completed. Couturier is paid a commission only for her work, at the rate of 25 percent of revenue from design work.

Bonnie Brides keeps two sets of customer mailing lists. All custom-order customers are entered into the Simply Accounting program Receivables Ledger. Brioche maintains a second customer list in a mail merge program in order to send information about the store's new line of gowns or about promotions. Vendors who are regular suppliers are entered into the Payables Ledger in the Simply Accounting program.

Bonnie Brides has entered all its manual accounting records into the Simply Accounting program at the end of December 1998 in preparation for the new fiscal year. Brioche has also decided to use the budgeting feature based on the previous year's income statement and projections for the new design part of the business. She set up the company files with the help of Lori Christoffer who studied with her at McGill University. They used the following information for the conversion:

- Chart of Accounts
- Income Statement
- Post-Closing Trial Balance
- Vendor Information
- Customer Information
- Employee Information
- Inventory Information
- Accounting Procedures

BONNIE BRIDES
CHART OF ACCOUNTS

ASSETS
1080 Cash in Bank
1100 Marketable Securities
1200 Accounts Receivable
1220 Fabrics
1240 Dressmaking Supplies
1260 Prepaid Insurance
1280 Store Supplies
1300 Accessories
1320 Bridal Gowns
1340 Bridesmaids' Gowns
1360 Hats and Veils
1380 Mothers' Gowns
1420 Cash Register
1440 Computers & Peripherals
1480 Display Fixtures
1500 Sewing Machines & Sergers
1520 Shop

LIABILITIES
2200 Accounts Payable
2310 EI Payable
2330 Income Tax Payable
2350 QPP Payable
2360 Quebec Income Tax Payable
2370 QHIP Payable
2460 WCB Payable
2650 GST Charged on Sales
2670 GST Paid on Purchases
2800 Refundable QST Paid
2810 QST Charged on Sales
2950 Mortgage Payable

EQUITY
3560 Bonnie Brioche, Capital
3580 Bonnie Brioche, Drawings
3600 Current Earnings

REVENUE
4020 Revenue from Sales
4040 Sales Discount
4100 Revenue from Design
4200 Interest Revenue

EXPENSES
5020 Advertising & Promotion
5040 Bank Charges
5060 Cost of Goods Sold
5070 Fabrics Used
5080 Dressmaking Supplies Used
5100 Damaged Inventory
5150 Delivery Expense
5160 Freight Expense
5170 Hydro Expense
5180 Insurance Expense
5200 Interest Expense
5240 Store Supplies Used
5260 Telephone Expense
5300 Commissions
5310 EI Expense
5330 WCB Expense
5340 QPP Expense
5350 QHIP Expense
5380 Subcontractors' Fees

Notes

The accounts PST Payable, CPP Payable and CPP Expense appear in the Chart of Accounts on the Data Disk because they are necessary for the program to be set to ready. They are not used in the province of Quebec, their balances will remain at zero. CPP Expenses will therefore not be part of the budget.

BONNIE BRIDES
INCOME STATEMENT

FOR THE YEAR ENDING DECEMBER 31, 1998

REVENUE
4020 Revenue from Sales	$112 650.00	
4040 Sales Discount	– 1 179.00	
4080 Net Sales		$111 471.00
4200 Interest Revenue		7 500.00
TOTAL REVENUE		$118 971.00

EXPENSES
5020 Advertising & Promotion	2 160.00
5040 Bank Charges	360.00
5060 Cost of Goods Sold	57 560.00
5070 Fabrics Used	500.00
5080 Dressmaking Supplies Used	300.00
5100 Damaged Inventory	955.00
5150 Delivery Expense	720.00
5160 Freight Expense	405.00
5170 Hydro Expense	1 283.40
5180 Insurance Expense	800.00
5200 Interest Expense	10 098.00
5240 Store Supplies Used	1 620.00
5260 Telephone Expense	872.76
TOTAL EXPENSE	$ 77 634.16

NET INCOME $ 41 336.84

BONNIE BRIDES
POST-CLOSING TRIAL BALANCE

December 31, 1998

1080 Cash in Bank	$ 20 197.45	
1100 Marketable Securities	50 000.00	
1200 Accounts Receivable	1 139.55	
1220 Fabrics	3 000.00	
1240 Dressmaking Supplies	1 000.00	
1280 Store Supplies	650.00	
1300 Accessories	7 265.00	
1320 Bridal Gowns	28 950.00	
1340 Bridesmaids' Gowns	3 680.00	
1360 Hats and Veils	2 440.00	
1380 Mothers' Gowns	2 170.00	
1420 Cash Register	1 200.00	
1440 Computers & Peripherals	3 000.00	
1480 Display Fixtures	1 500.00	
1500 Sewing Machines & Sergers	7 200.00	
1520 Shop	100 000.00	
2200 Accounts Payable		$ 2 782.00
2650 GST Charged on Sales		2 450.00
2670 GST Paid on Purchases	840.00	
2950 Mortgage Payable		84 000.00
3560 Bonnie Brioche, Capital		145 000.00
	$234 232.00	$234 232.00

BONNIE BRIDES
VENDOR INFORMATION

Vendor Name (Contact)	Address Phone & Fax	Invoice Terms	Invoice Date	Invoice Number	Outstanding Balance
Beads & Threads (Louise Fabricant)	Rue Laperle, 10823 Montreal, QC H2C 3C6 Tel: (514) 476-8109 Fax: (514) 476-8225	Net 10			
Bell Quebec	Rue Alouette, 8180 Montreal, QC H9A 3G8 Tel: (514) 573-7102 Fax: (514) 573-7211	Net 1			
Bridal Originals Ltd. (Yves Rodier)	Ch De Mariee, 505 Montreal, QC H3F 2S3 Tel: (514) 386-5199 Fax: (514) 385-2926	Net 20	12/15/98	BO-1347	$2 140
Bridal Xpress Delivery	Av Chamionnage, 4021 Montreal, QC H1G 5B2 Tel: (514) 622-5372 Fax: (514) 622-5710	Net 10			
Kristin Couture (Kristin Couture)	Rue Carriere, 6022 Montreal, QC H1B 3X5 Tel: (514) 782-7493 Fax: (514) 782-7408	Net 1			
Paris Import Fabrics (Emilie Paquin)	Av Paris, 3010 Montreal, QC H4G 3C6 Tel: (514) 477-3117 Fax: (514) 477-3911	Net 15	12/20/98	PI-642	$642
Quebec Hydro	Rue Fullum, 300 Montreal, QC H2K 4R4 Tel: (514) 566-8224 Fax: (514) 566-8210	Net 1			
Quebec Minister of Finance	Boul De Maisonneuve E, 400 Montreal, QC H2L 5A1 Tel: (514) 829-6201 Fax: (514) 829-0900	Net 1			
Receiver General of Canada	Summerside Tax Centre Summerside, PE C1N 6L2 Tel: (902) 821-8186	Net 1			

Grand Total $2 782

BONNIE BRIDES
CUSTOMER INFORMATION

Customer Name (Contact)	Address Phone & Fax	Invoice Terms	Invoice Date	Invoice Number	Outstanding Balance
Josee Drouin	Rue Camille, 56 Montreal, QC H8R 1G4 Tel: (514) 622-6197	Net 1	12/29/98	98-169	$1 139.55

BONNIE BRIDES
EMPLOYEE INFORMATION SHEET

Employee Name	Sylvie Couturier
Position	Designer/Dressmaker
Social Insurance Number	414 243 643
Address & Telephone	Rue Carillon, 5020 Dorval, QC H9A 2K5 (514) 687-2104
Date of Birth (dd-mm-yy)	21-04-69
Tax Exemption (TD-1)	
Basic Personal	$6 456
Quebec Tax Claim	$5 900
Employee Earnings	
Commission	25% of Revenue from Design
Vacation	3 weeks
Employee Deductions	
EI, QPP and QHIP,	calculations built into Simply Accounting program
Quebec Tax and Income Tax	calculations built into Simply Accounting program
Additional Income Tax	

Employee Profile and TD-1 Information

Sylvie Couturier began working for Bonnie Brides on January 1, 1999 as a designer and dressmaker. She is married and self-supporting. At the end of each month, she is paid a 25 percent commission based on the design revenue. She receives no vacation pay or employee benefits, but expects to take about three weeks off during the less busy time of the year.

Additional Payroll Information

The employer's contributions include the following:

- QPP contributions equal to employee contributions
- EI factor of 1.4
- Workers Compensation Board (WCB) rate is 3.82

BONNIE BRIDES
INVENTORY INFORMATION

Code	Description	Sell Price /Unit	Qty on Hand	Amt (Cost)	Min Stock
Accessories					
AC01	Capes: brocade full length	$700 each	2	$ 800	1
AC02	Capes: velvet full length	800 each	2	900	1
AC03	Earrings: diamond studs	200/pair	10	1 000	2
AC04	Earrings: pearl studs	70/pair	15	450	5
AC05	Earrings: pearl tear drop	110/pair	10	500	2
AC06	Garters: blue, var designs S/M/L	30 each	12	240	6
AC07	Muffs: imitation fur	60 each	4	120	1
AC08	Shoes: peau-de-soie/satin/leather	110/pair	60	3 000	12
AC09	Stockings: sheer white/almnd/taupe	10/pair	30	150	5
AC10	Stockings: lace white/almond	15/pair	15	105	3
				$7 265	
Bridal Gowns: various sizes each					
BG01	Ari empire line antique ivory lace	$1 100 each	2	$1 100	1
BG02	Arezzo peau-de-soie A-line fl lace	1 050 each	5	2 500	2
BG03	Ferrucci embr silk satn sheer slv	1 500 each	5	3 750	2
BG04	Lagar matte satn/halter top/roses	1 200 each	5	3 000	2
BG05	Miyaki matte organza/chapel train	1 400 each	5	3 500	1
BG06	Paolo poly-satn fit/flare prl clus	950 each	5	2 250	2
BG07	Raffaelli full tulle/basque waist	1 000 each	5	2 500	2
BG08	Rojas peau-de-soie slvless/prl bttn	800 each	5	2 000	1
BG09	Shijo silk satn slvless/prl bodice	1 250 each	5	3 100	2
BG10	Vasari silk satn roses/cathed train	2 500 each	1	1 250	1
BG11	Vernet nat'l silk/lace/sweep train	1 600 each	4	4 000	1
				$28 950	
Bridesmaids' Gowns: various colours and sizes					
BMG01	Ferrucci velvet/satn fit/flare	$250 each	4	$500	2
BMG02	Lagar velvet/chiffon skirt/empire	225 each	8	900	2
BMG03	Miyaki cut velvet/crepe flared skrt	200 each	8	800	2
BMG04	Rojas poly-satn drop waist skirt	160 each	8	640	2
BMG05	Shijo crepe sweetheart neckline	180 each	6	540	2
BMG06	Vernet short floral pattern skirt	150 each	4	300	2
				$3 680	
Hats and Veils					
HV01	Hats: ostriche w/chenille dot veil	$140 each	2	$140	0
HV02	Hats: sheer organza w/silk bow	150 each	2	150	1
HV03	Headband: silk satn rosettes	50 each	6	150	2
HV04	Veil: lace cath embroid w/sequins	200 each	4	400	1
HV05	Veil: lace chapel w/pearl bead edge	170 each	4	320	1
HV06	Veil: silk cathedral w/prl clusters	180 each	4	360	1
HV07	Veil: tulle full asymetric scallopd	150 each	8	600	2
HV08	Veil: tulle plain chapel length	80 each	8	320	2
				$2 440	
Mothers' Gowns: various sizes each					
MG01	Ari crepe sand 2pce suit	$200 each	3	$300	1
MG02	Paolo ivory crepe empire line gown	140 each	4	280	1
MG03	Raffaelli gold khaki gown w/lace	175 each	2	170	1
MG04	Rojas 2pce suit w/lace overlay	225 each	4	440	1
MG05	Vasari black satn w/gold embroid	210 each	3	300	1
MG06	Vernet silk sarong w/gold bead	195 each	2	180	1
MG07	Vezeley pink crepe w/cord lace jckt	190 each	5	500	1
				$2 170	

Accounting Procedures

The Goods and Services Tax: Remittances

Bonnie Brides uses the regular method for remittance of the Goods and Services Tax. GST collected from customers is recorded as a liability in the *GST Charged on Sales* account. GST paid to vendors is recorded in the *GST Paid on Purchases* account as a decrease in the liability to Revenue Canada. Brioche files her return to the Receiver General of Canada by the last day of the month for the previous quarterly period, either requesting a refund or remitting the balance owing.

Quebec Sales Tax (QST)

Provincial sales tax (QST) of 6.5 percent is applied to all cash and credit sales of goods and services in the province of Quebec. At the time this workbook was written, the province of Quebec ruled that the provincial sales tax would apply to the amount of the invoice with GST included. This is often referred to as a "tax on a tax" or a "piggy-backed" tax. The defaults for this application are set so that the program will automatically calculate the QST rate on the amount with GST included. Accounting examples for sales taxes in different provinces are provided in Chapter 2.

Refundable and Non-refundable QST

Some purchases qualify for refundable QST credits to reduce the QST owing in much the same way as the GST owing is calculated. Generally QST is refundable if the purchase consists of inputs to the items sold, for example, the QST on fabrics that are used to make dresses for sale. QST on sales are similarly divided into refundable and non-refundable taxes. The codes for QST available in the QST field (press (enter) when the cursor is in the tax field) therefore include a refundable and non-refundable division as follows:

A - QST exempt
B - QST nontaxable
C - QST @ 0%
D - QST @ 6.5%, not included (refundable)
E - QST @ 6.5%, not included, non-refundable
F - QST @ 6.5%, included (refundable)
G - QST @ 6.5%, included, non-refundable

Only businesses qualify for refunds on QST paid. Since customers of Bonnie Brides purchase items for personal use, Code E is used for all sales — the QST is not included and is non-refundable. In this application, Codes D and E are used for purchases. Any purchases that qualify for the refundable tax credits are clearly indicated in the source documents.

QST owing (*QST Charged on Sales* less *Refundable QST Paid*) must be remitted quarterly to the Provincial Treasurer.

When Quebec Sales Taxes are included in the company setup, the Reports menu item GST Reports is no longer displayed. A new option, Taxes Report, replaces GST Reports because both GST and QST reports can be displayed and printed. Detail and summary forms are available.

Deposits on Custom Orders

When customers order a custom-made gown, they pay an advance of 25 percent of the negotiated price (before taxes). The advance is entered in the Sales Journal for the customer as a negative invoice. That is, the amount is entered with a minus sign, no QST or GST is charged and the *Cash in Bank* account is entered in the account field. The *Accounts Receivable* account will be credited for the amount of the advance for the selected customer, and *Cash in Bank* will be debited. When the work is completed, make a Sales Journal entry for the full amount of the contract, including relevant taxes. When the customer settles the account, mark the invoice for both the

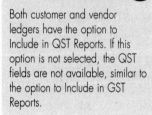
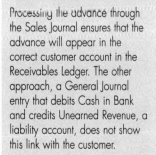

advance and the full amount as paid. The balance owing in the Receipts Journal should then match the amount of the customer's cheque.

Sales Discounts
Bonnie Brides occasionally offers customer discounts at the time of sale. These discounts are like a negative invoice line attached to the original sales invoice. Discounts are recorded in the Sales Journal at the time of the sale as follows:

- Choose the customer and click on Sale with Payment or choose <One-time customer> and enter the cheque number, invoice and date.
- Enter all items sold to the customer as usual, one item per invoice line.
- Click on the discount field (%) in the Terms section at the bottom of the invoice.
- Enter the percentage discount and press (tab)

The invoice total is reduced by the discount amount and the GST and QST are reduced.

Freight Expenses
When a business purchases inventory items, the cost of freight that cannot be directly allocated to a specific item of purchase must be charged to the *Freight Expense* account. This amount will be regarded as an expense and will not be part of the costs of any inventory asset account.

Sales Invoices
If you want to print the sales invoice through the program, complete the Sales Journal transaction as you would otherwise. Before posting the transaction, click on Print or choose Print from the pull-down menu under File. Printing will begin immediately, so be sure you have the correct forms for your printer before you begin.

INSTRUCTIONS

1. Set up the budget for Bonnie Brides on January 1, 1999, using Simply Accounting. Detailed keystrokes follow the instructions to assist you.

2. Using the Chart of Accounts, the Trial Balance, Vendor, Customer, Payroll and Inventory Information provided, enter the source documents for January 1999 in Simply Accounting. Source documents begin on page 329, following the keystrokes.

3. Print the following reports and graphs:

    - Balance Sheet as at Jan. 31

    - General Journal with all ledger entries by posting date from Jan. 1 to Jan 31

    - Inventory Sales Detail Report for Bridal Gowns

    - Income Statement, Budget Percentage Difference Report for Jan. 1 to Jan. 31

    - Sales vs Budget graph for accounts 4020 and 4100

    - Expenses vs Budget graph for accounts 5060, 5070 and 5080

KEYSTROKES FOR BUDGET SETUP

It is important for a business to gauge its performance against some standards. These standards can be provided through comparisons with other companies that are in the same kind of business or by comparing the same company over several time periods. It is common for a business to set goals for future performance based on the past. For example, there may be an expectation that profits will increase by 10 percent over the previous year, or that expenses will be reduced because of the introduction of new cost reduction methods. If a business waits till the end of the year to assess its progress towards its goals, it may be too late to make necessary corrections if things are not proceeding according to plan. Budgets serve this purpose of offering a realistic financial plan for the future that can be used as a standard for assessing performance.

Before analyzing a budget report, you must turn on the option and enter the budget amounts for the relevant accounts.

Turning on the Budgeting Feature

Open the data files for Bonnie Brides. Do not advance the Using Date until you have finished the budget setup.

Choose Settings from the pull-down menu under Setup in the Home window.

Click on the General tab in the Settings window to display the following setup options for the General ledger:

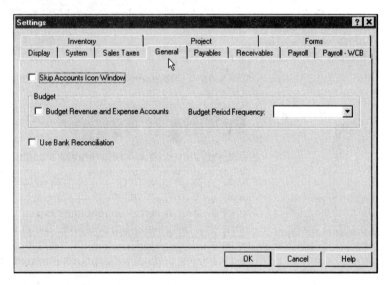

Click on Budget Revenue and Expense Accounts to turn on the budgeting feature.

The first decision after choosing the budgeting feature involves a budget period. Whether a business chooses to budget amounts on a yearly, quarterly or monthly basis depends on the needs and nature of the business. Monthly budget reports will be appropriate if the business cycle of buying and selling is short but not appropriate if long term projects are involved. The period chosen must provide meaningful feedback about performance. If the periods are too short, there may be insufficient information to judge performance; if the periods are too long, there may be no opportunity to correct problems because they are not detected soon enough. Bonnie Brides will use monthly budget periods, at least initially, because Bonnie Brioche wants frequent progress reports.

Click on the **Budget Period Frequency field** to see the drop-down list of period options:

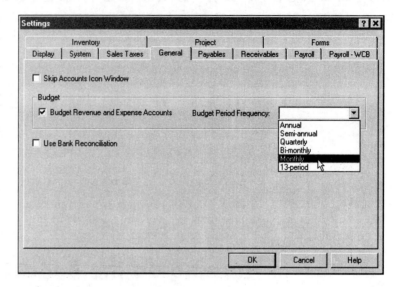

Click on Monthly

Click on OK. Before changing the budget settings, Simply Accounting shows you the following warning:

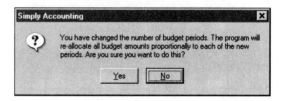

Click on Yes to return to the Home window and save the settings.

Setting a Budget

The next step is to enter the budget amounts for all expense and revenue accounts.

Budgets can be determined in several different ways. The most common methods are zero-based and incremental budgeting. With the zero-based method, a forecast is made for each revenue and expense account based on expectations about specific planned activities and expenditures. Each budget item must usually be justified. More commonly, last year's budgets and income statements are used as the starting point and a specific percentage change is included. Thus, a company might expect to improve its performance over last year by 5 percent, either by increasing sales or by decreasing expenses. Planned special events such as annual month-long sales, new customer drives, peak Christmas periods or slow periods for the product can be built into the changes in budgeted amounts from one period to the next. Whatever method is used, it is important that the budget be realistic.

Bonnie Brioche's approach is to examine her previous income statements and business practices to see where she can make improvements and get a realistic forecast. She has observed that her business is growing at about 10 percent. The corresponding expenses, sales discounts, cost of goods sold, etc. will also increase by the same amount. Sales are not divided evenly throughout the 12-month period. Most brides purchase their gowns about six months before the wedding date, and spring and summer are the most popular choices for weddings. This results in January and

February being the busiest months for the shop, followed by March through June in preparation for fall through Christmas weddings.

This pattern has led Brioche to expect 15 percent of her year's sales to occur each month in January and February, 10 percent each month in March through June, and 5 percent each month in July through December. Her addition of custom-design dresses is based on her best guess, taking into account the seasonal pattern. Her estimate of twelve gowns per year is a conservative one, but she does not want to promise her cousin work that she cannot deliver. During the busiest months, she expects to use assistants to complete the work in a timely fashion.

Her detailed forecast is presented in the following chart:

BONNIE BRIDES
BUDGET FORECAST FOR 1999

	12 Months	Jan/Feb each month	Mar - Jun each month	Jul - Dec each month
Revenue				
Revenue from Sales	$122 000	$18 300	$12 200	$ 6 100
Sales Discount	– 1 220	–183	–122	–61
Revenue from Design	108 000	16 200	10 800	5 400
Interest Revenue	7 500	625	625	625
Total Revenue	$236 280	$34 942	$23 503	$12 064
Expenses				
Advertising & Promotion	$ 2 400	$ 200	$ 200	$ 200
Bank Charges	360	30	30	30
Cost of Goods Sold	61 000	9 150	6 100	3 050
Fabrics Used	27 000	4 050	2 700	1 350
Dressmaking Supplies Used	5 400	810	540	270
Damaged Inventory	1 220	183	122	61
Delivery Expense	600	90	60	30
Freight Expense	600	90	60	30
Hydro Expense	1 280	110	110	110
Insurance Expense	800	70	70	70
Interest Expense	9 600	800	800	800
Store Supplies Used	1 500	125	125	125
Telephone Expense	900	75	75	75
Commissions	27 125	4 050	2 700	1 350
EI Expense	800	120	80	40
WCB Expense	1 040	156	104	52
QPP Expense	850	127	85	42
QHIP Expense	1 200	180	120	60
Subcontractors' Fees	1 600	800	0	0
Total Expense	$145 275	$21 216	$14 081	$ 7 745
Net Income	$ 91 005	$13 726	$ 9 422	$ 4 319

She has based these amounts on the following estimates for the year's activities:

Sales: January 15% of year's sales, February 15%, March 10%, April 10%, May 10%, June 10%, July 5%, August 5%, September 5%, October 5%, November 5%, December 5%

Sales Revenue: increase by 10% over previous year

Sales Discount: expect about 1% on average, most sales are not discounted

Revenue from Design: make 12 dresses at an average price of $9 000

Interest Revenue: constant monthly income, same as previous year

Cost of Goods Sold: 50% of net sales

Damaged Inventory: 2% of Cost of Goods Sold

Delivery and Freight: average at about 1% of sales

Fabrics Used: mostly for custom made gowns — estimated at 25% of finished price

Dressmaking Supplies Used: some for alterations, most for custom made gowns — estimated at 5% of finished price of gowns (Revenue from Design)

Commissions: will pay 25% of finished price of gowns (Revenue from Design)

EI, QPP, WCB and QHIP: straight percentage of commissions

Subcontractors' Fees: assistance with four gowns at $400 each, Jan and Feb only

Interest Expense: small decrease each year as loan principal is reduced

Other Expenses: constant each month, no change over last year

Entering Budget Amounts in the General Ledger

Double click on the **Accounts icon** in the Home window to open the Accounts Window.

Click on Revenue from Sales to highlight this first revenue account.

Click on the **Edit button** 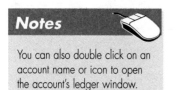 or choose Edit from the pull-down menu under Edit to open the account ledger window as shown:

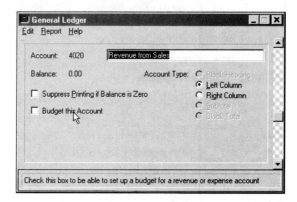

Notice that a new option has been added for budgeting. This option will appear only for postable revenue and expense accounts.

Click on Budget this Account to select the option and reveal the Budget options button as shown:

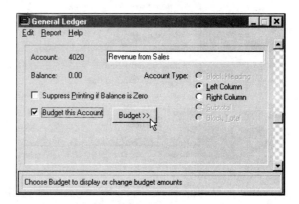

Click on Budget>> to display the expanded budget information input window:

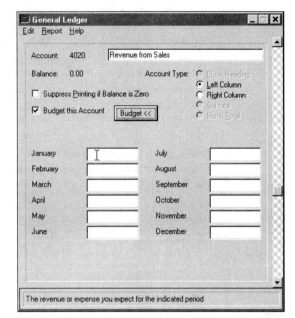

The budget periods displayed at this stage match the period frequency selected in the setup stage. Because we selected Monthly, a 12-month calendar is given, beginning with the first month of the fiscal year as entered in the company setup window. If we had selected quarterly, the quarterly input calendar would be provided for the account. You can enter the budget amounts for one or more months now, if the information is available. For Bonnie Brides, we will enter the amounts for each month as determined earlier.

Click on the **January field** to move the cursor.

Type   18300

Press   [tab]

The cursor advances to the February field. Enter the amounts for the remaining 11 months according to the budget forecast by typing the amount and pressing [tab] to move to the next month. When you have entered the amounts for each month,

Click on Budget<< to close the expanded budget details.

Budget amounts can be updated if needed based on feedback from earlier budget reports. They should not of course be changed without good reason.

Close the account information window.

Continue to enter budget information for the remaining revenue and expense accounts by following the steps outlined above. Use the amounts determined previously for each account.

Enter the transactions as usual for the month.

Updating Budget Amounts

If you discover that your budget forecasts are incorrect, you can update the amounts. You can do this in two ways: editing the amounts individually for each account, repeating the process described above for entering initial budget amounts or globally updating all amounts by a fixed percentage.

To update the amounts globally, choose Update Budget Amounts from the pull-down menu under Maintenance in the Home window. You will see the following Update Budget window:

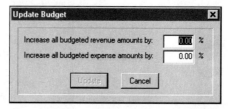

You can change the budgets for revenue and expense accounts separately. Type in the percentage change that you want to apply, typing a negative number for decreases. Click on Update. The screen that follows asks you to confirm that you want to update the budget. Click on Yes to apply the changes and return to the Home window. When you review the account's budget information in the account ledger, you will see that the change has been applied.

Budget Reports

The effective use of budget reports involves more than merely observing whether budgeted targets were met or not. Sometimes more information is gained when targets are not met because the differences can lead to asking important questions:

- Were the targets realistic? What items were not on target and why?
- If performance exceeds the targets, how can we repeat the success?
- If performance did not meet the targets, were there factors that we failed to anticipate?
- Should we revise future budgets based on the new information?

In other words, the problem-solving cycle is set in motion. Even an income statement that is on target should be reviewed carefully. There may be room for improvements if the budget was a conservative estimate. There may be new information that will affect future performance that was unknown when the budget was drawn up.

Displaying Budget Reports

Choose Financials and then **Income Statement** from the pull-down menu under **Reports** in the Home window to display the Income Statement options window:

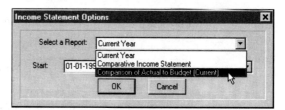

A budget-related option has been added in the Select a Report drop-down list.

Click on Comparison of Actual to Budget to select this option and open the Report Type field.

Click on Report Type to show the options in the drop-down list as follows:

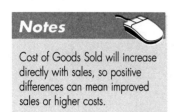
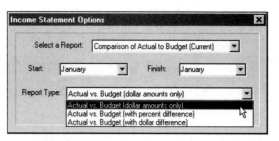

Three types of reports are available. The first, Actual vs. Budget (dollar amounts only), lists the amounts that were budgeted for the revenue and expense accounts for the time period indicated and the revenues and expenses actually obtained for the same period. The second, Actual vs. Budget (with percent difference), gives these two amounts as well as the percentage that the actual amount is above or below the budgeted amount. The third option, Actual vs. Budget (with dollar difference) provides the same two base amounts, budget and actual as well as the difference between them as a dollar amount.

For the dollar difference and the percent difference reports, a positive difference means that the budget was exceeded, a negative difference indicates that the results came in under budget. Remember that for revenues, a positive difference means results were better than expected but for expenses, a positive difference means that results were poorer than expected (expenses were higher than budgeted).

Printing Budget Reports

Display the report you want to print.

Choose Print from the pull-down menu under File.

Close the displayed report when you are finished.

Graphing Budget Reports

When the Budgeting option is activated and set up, two additional graphs are available from the Graphs menu, Sales vs Budget and Expenses vs Budget.

Sales vs Budget Graphs

Choose Sales vs Budget from the pull-down menu under Graphs in the Home window to display the set of revenue accounts:

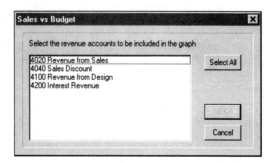

Click on the accounts you want to include in the graph or click on Select All.

Click on OK to display the bar chart graph:

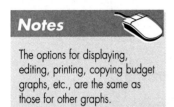
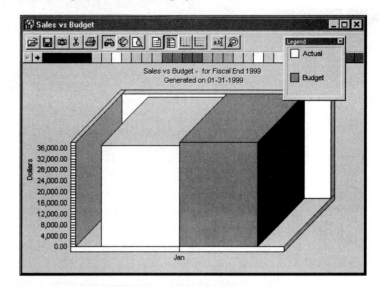

The displayed graph includes the Revenue from Sales and the Revenue from Design account before the 10 percent budget increase at the end of the January. The amounts for the two revenue accounts are added together in the single bar labelled Actual. The other bar represents the budgeted amount for the two accounts together.

Close the displayed graph when you are finished.

Expenses vs Budget Graphs

Choose **Expenses vs Budget** from the pull-down menu under **Graphs** in the Home window to display the set of expense accounts:

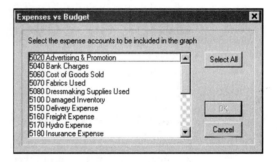

Click on the accounts you want to include in the graph or click on Select All.

Click on OK to display the bar chart graph:

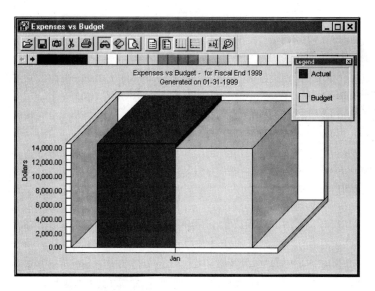

The displayed graph includes three expense accounts, *Cost of Goods Sold*, *Fabrics Used* and *Dressmaking Supplies Used*, before the 10 percent budget increase at the end of the January. The expense accounts are added together in the bar labelled Actual. The other bar represents the budgeted amount for the three accounts.

Close the displayed graph when you are finished.

SOURCE DOCUMENTS

USING DATE — January 7

☐ Cash Purchase Invoice #SL-43216
Dated Jan. 2/99
From Sunlife Insurance Co., $800 for a one-year insurance policy. Paid by cheque #100.

☐ Cash Receipt #1
Dated Jan. 2/99
From Deanne Demarais (new customer), cheque #45 for $2 000 for deposit on custom design silk and satin gown plus cathedral length train with floral lace and sequin embroidery details. Balance to be paid on delivery.

☐ Cash Receipt #2
Dated Jan. 2/99
From Josee Drouin, cheque #32 for $1 139.55 in full payment of account. Reference invoice #98-169.

☐ Cheque Copy #101
Dated Jan. 3/99
To Bridal Originals Ltd., $2 140 in full payment of account. Reference invoice #BO-1347.

Notes

☐ Deanne Demarais
is located at
Av De L'Eglise, 450
Montreal, QC
H4E 1G3
Tel: (514) 583-5437
Fax:(514) 583-7501
Include in GST and QST
Reports

Cash Sales Invoice #99-001
Dated Jan. 3/99
To Jocelyn Carnot

one BG05 Miyaki matte organza/chapel train	$1 400
two BMG02 Lagar velvet/chiffon skirt/empire	225 each
one HV05 Veil: lace chapel w/pearl bead edge	170
one pr AC03 Earrings: diamond studs	200
three pr AC08 Shoes: peau-de-soie	110 /pair
Goods & Services Tax	7.0%
Quebec Sales Tax	6.5%

Paid by MasterCard #6453 9104 6832 4015

Purchase Invoice #BT-804
Dated Jan. 3/99
From Beads & Threads, $200 for lace, sequins and other supplies for Deanne Demerais gown plus $14 GST and $13.91 refundable QST. Purchase Invoice total $227.91. Terms: net 10 days.

Purchase Invoice #PI-5391
Dated Jan. 3/99
From Paris Import Fabrics, $1 800 for silk and satin fabrics required for Deanne Demarais gown plus $126 GST and $125.19 refundable QST. Purchase Invoice total $2 051.19. Terms: net 15 days.

Cash Sales Invoice #99-002
Dated Jan. 5/99
To Simone Villeneuve

one BG11 Vernet nat'l silk/lace w/sweep train	$1 600
one HV03 Headband: silk satn rosettes	50
four BMG04 Rojas poly-satn drop waist skirt	160 each
one pr AC04 Earrings: pearl studs	70
one AC06 Garter: blue, M	30
Goods & Services Tax	7.0%
Quebec Sales Tax	6.5%

Paid by Visa #4510 569 612 592

Cheque Copy #102
Dated Jan. 5/99
To Paris Import Fabrics, $642 in payment of account. Reference invoice #PI-642.

Memo #1
Dated Jan. 7/99
From owner: Adjust inventory for one Headband: silk satn rosettes ripped on the display fixtures and damaged beyond repair. Charge to Damaged Inventory account.

Notes

Allow inventory to drop below re-order point.

☐ Cash Sales Invoice #99-003
Dated Jan. 8/99
To Renee Gilles

one BG03 Ferrucci embr silk satn sheer slv	$1 500
three BMG01 Ferrucci velvet/satn fit/flare	250 each
one MG04 Rojas 2pce suit w/lace overlay	225
one AC06 Garter: blue, S	30
one HV07 Veil: tulle full asymetric scallopd	150
Goods & Services Tax	7.0%
Quebec Sales Tax	6.5%

Paid by Visa #4502 399 573 218

Notes

Use QST Code E, QST @ 6.5%, not included, non-refundable.

☐ Cash Purchase Invoice #MS-314
Dated Jan. 9/99
From Montreal Sewing Centre, $120 for servicing sewing machines and sergers plus $8.40 GST and $8.35 non-refundable QST. Purchase Invoice total $136.75. Paid by cheque #103. Create a new expense account, 5220 Maintenance & Repairs, and budget $100 per month for this expense.

☐ Cash Purchase Invoice #WB-13121
Dated Jan. 10/99
From Wedding Bells Magazine, $200 for promotional ads plus $14 GST and $13.91 non-refundable QST. Purchase Invoice total $227.91. Paid by cheque #104.

Notes

Enter 10 in the % field of the Terms section of the invoice. Refer to the Accounting Procedures for the Sales Discount.

☐ Cash Sales Invoice #99-004
Dated Jan. 12/99
To Julie Therieaux

one BG01 Ari empire line antique ivory lace	$1 100
two BMG06 Vernet short floral pattern skirt	150 each
one MG07 Vezeley pink crepe w/cord lace jckt	190
three pr AC08 Shoes: leather	110 /pair
three pr AC10 Stockings: lace almond	15 /pair
Sales Discount	10.0%
Goods & Services Tax	7.0%
Quebec Sales Tax	6.5%

Paid by Visa #4610 821 457 391

☐ Cash Purchase Invoice #QH-67120
Dated Jan. 13/99
From Quebec Hydro, $100 for hydro service in store plus $7 GST and $6.95 non-refundable QST. Purchase Invoice total $113.95. Paid by cheque #105.

☐ Cheque Copy #106
Dated Jan. 13/99
To Beads & Threads, $227.91 in full payment of account. Reference invoice #BT-804.

☐ Cheque Copy #107
Dated Jan. 13/99
To Paris Import Fabrics, $2 051.19 in full payment of account. Reference invoice #PI-5391.

Sales Invoice #99-005
Dated Jan. 14/99
To Deanne Demarais, $8 000 for completion of custom bridal gown plus $560 GST and $556.40 QST. Sales invoice total $9 116.40. Allocate to Revenue from Design. Terms: Cash on Receipt.

Cash Receipt #3
Dated Jan. 14/99
From Deanne Demarais, cheque #58 for $7 116.40 in full payment of account. Reference invoices #99-005 and CR-1.

Memo #2
Dated Jan. 14/99
Paid cheque #108 for $500 to Kristin Couture for subcontracting work on Deanne Demarais gown.

USING DATE – January 21

Purchase Invoice #BX-956
Dated Jan. 15/99
From Bridal Xpress Delivery, $60 for delivery of gowns and other inventory to customers plus $4.20 GST and $4.17 non-refundable QST. Purchase Invoice total $68.37. Terms: net 10 days.

Cash Receipt #4
Dated Jan. 15/99
From Catherine Rothchild (new customer), cheque #385 for $2 500 for deposit on custom design full lace and organza gown with genuine pearl buttons and bead embroidery. Balance to be paid on delivery.

Cash Purchase Invoice #BQ-13459
Dated Jan. 16/99
From Bell Quebec, $68 for telephone services plus $4.76 GST and $4.73 non-refundable QST. Purchase Invoice total $77.49. Issued cheque #109.

Purchase Invoice #BT-1022
Dated Jan. 16/99
From Beads & Threads, $250 for pearls, beads and other supplies for Catherine Rothchild gown plus $17.50 GST and $17.39 refundable QST. Purchase Invoice total $284.89. Terms: net 10 days.

Purchase Invoice #PI-6205
Dated Jan. 18/99
From Paris Import Fabrics, $2 400 for organza and lace fabrics required for Catherine Rothchild gown plus $168 GST and $166.92 refundable QST. Purchase Invoice total $2 734.92. Terms: net 15 days.

☐ Cash Sales Invoice #99-006
Dated Jan. 19/99
To Genevieve Thibault

one BG10 Vasari silk satn roses/cathed train	$2 500
one HV04 Veil: lace cath embroid w/sequins	200
one pr AC08 Shoes: satin	110
one pr AC03 Earrings: diamond studs	200
one AC02 Cape: velvet full length	800
Goods & Services Tax	7.0%
Quebec Sales Tax	6.5%

Paid by MasterCard #5319 6492 3880 4765

☐ Cash Sales Invoice #99-007
Dated Jan. 20/99
To Monique Ranier

one BG09 Shijo silk satn slvless/prl bodice	$1 250
four BMG05 Shijo crepe sweetheart neckline	180 each
four pr AC08 Shoes: leather	110 /pair
four pr AC05 Earrings: pearl tear drop	110 /pair
four pr AC09 Stockings: sheer white	10 /pair
Goods & Services Tax	7.0%
Quebec Sales Tax	6.5%

Paid by Visa #4300 732 191 836

USING DATE — January 28

☐ Cash Sales Invoice #99-008
Dated Jan. 25/99
To Andre Villone

one BG07 Raffaelli full tulle/basque waist	$1 000
four BMG04 Rojas poly-satn drop waist skirt	160 each
one MG03 Raffaelli gold khaki gown w/lace	175
five pr AC08 Shoes: peau de soie	110 /pair
one HV02 Hat: sheer organza w/silk bow	150
Goods & Services Tax	7.0%
Quebec Sales Tax	6.5%

Paid by Visa #4510 417 181 537

☐ Cheque Copy #110
Dated Jan. 25/99
To Bridal Xpress Delivery, $68.37 in full payment of account. Reference invoice #BX-956.

☐ Sales Invoice #99-009
Dated Jan. 28/99
To Catherine Rothchild, $10 000 for completion of custom bridal gown plus $700 GST and $695.50 QST. Sales invoice total $11 395.50. Terms: Cash on receipt.

☐ Cash Receipt #5
Dated Jan. 28/99
From Catherine Rothchild, cheque #481 for $8 895.50 in full payment of account. Reference invoices #99-009 and CR-4.

☐ Purchase Invoice #BX-1021
Dated Jan. 29/99
From Bridal Xpress Delivery, $60 for delivery of gowns and other inventory to customers plus $4.20 GST and $4.17 non-refundable QST. Purchase Invoice total $68.37. Terms: net 10 days.

Notes

Enter the payment for subcontracting work as a cash purchase.

☐ Memo #3
Dated Jan. 30/99
Paid cheque #111 for $500 to Kamala Srivina for subcontracting work on Catherine Rothchild gown.

☐ Bank Debit Memo #6432193
Dated Jan. 31/99
For monthly bank service charges, $30.

☐ Bank Debit Memo #6432194
Dated Jan. 31/99
For mortgage payment, $850, including $765 for interest and $85 for reduction of principal.

☐ Bank Credit Memo #3214721
Dated Jan. 31/99
For interest on bank account and securities, $625 deposited to account.

☐ Memo #4
Dated Jan. 31/99
Prepare payroll for Sylvie Couturier. Couturier earned $4 500 in commissions for custom design and tailoring work. Issue cheque #112.

☐ Memo #5
Dated Jan. 31/99
From owner: Make entries to record the following adjustments:
   Physical count shows the following inventory on hand
      Fabrics $2 800
      Dressmaking Supplies $800
      Store Supplies $500
   One month of insurance has expired.

Notes

Refer to Updating Budgets in the Keystrokes section on page 325.

☑ Memo #6
Dated Jan. 31/99
325
From owner: Increase all revenue budget amounts by 10% to allow for expected increases in sales as a result of the closing of a nearby competitor.

CASE PROBLEMS

Case One

At the end of February, a custom-made gown costing $8 000 was completed but not picked up by the customer. Inquiries revealed that she had cancelled her wedding plans and did not intend to take possession of her dress, even though the store reminded her that her $2 000 deposit was not refundable.

a. How should the store record the accounting transactions for this situation?

b. How should Brioche process the inventory setup for the special item?

c. What factors should Brioche consider in setting the selling price for the special order gown? For example, would the dress size and style of the gown influence the pricing decision in any way?

Case Two

At the end of February, Bonnie Brioche printed her monthly income statement. Individual items that differed by more than 10 percent from her updated budget forecasts are shown in the following Income Statement. Items that did not differ from the forecast are combined into the Other Expenses category. (All amounts are rounded to the nearest $10.)

SUMMARY OF EXCEPTIONAL BUDGET ITEMS – FEBRUARY 1999

	Actual	Budget
Revenue		
Revenue from Sales	$24 000	$20 130
Sales Discount	– 50	-200
Revenue from Design	27 500	17 820
Interest Revenue	430	690
Total Revenue	$51 880	$38 440
Operating Expenses		
Cost of Goods Sold	$14 400	$9 150
Fabrics Used	6 750	4 050
Dressmaking Supplies Used	1 400	810
Delivery Expense	240	90
Wages	6 880	4 050
Other Payroll Expenses	940	580
Subcontractors' Fees	1 620	800
Other Expenses	1 810	1 790
Total Expenses	$34 040	$21 320
Net Income	$17 840	$17 100

Explain some of the reasons why these differences may have occurred. You may wish to review the rationale notes for the preliminary budget on page 323.

CHAPTER THIRTEEN

OBJECTIVES

Upon completion of this chapter, you will be able to:

- *plan and design* an accounting system for a small business
- *prepare* procedures for converting from a manual system
- *understand* the objectives of a computerized system
- *create* company files
- *set up* company accounts using setup input forms
- *make* the accounting system ready for operation
- *enter* journal transactions using Simply Accounting
- *insert* new vendors, customers and employees as required
- *add* new accounts as required
- *display* and *print* reports
- *export* reports
- *use* spreadsheets for analyzing, planning and decision making
- *enter* transactions that result in inventory variances
- *enter* end-of-accounting-period adjustments
- *perform* end-of-accounting-period closing routines
- *analyze and interpret* case studies
- *develop* further group interpersonal skills
- *develop* further oral and written skills

INTRODUCTION

This application provides a complete accounting cycle for a merchandising business. It is a comprehensive application covering a three-month fiscal period. You will use Simply Accounting to convert a manual accounting system to a computerized accounting system and then enter transactions for each month. The routines in this application are part of the demands of many small businesses, so you should find them useful. The information in this application reflects the business realities of Ontario in July 1997.

You may substitute information relevant to other provinces or the latest payroll and tax regulations wherever it is appropriate to do so. Rules for the application of the federal Goods and Services Tax (GST), provincial sales taxes and payroll may vary from one province to another.

Because of the length of the application, instructions for working with the source documents are presented with those documents, on page 394.

Because of the length of the Hearth House application, group work is encouraged in setting up error-free company files and completing the transactions.

Notes

COMPANY INFORMATION

Company Profile

Hearth House, owned by Amber Ashe, is situated in the Beaches area of Toronto. Ashe has built up her business steadily since graduating from Ryerson, beginning with freelance contract work installing and renovating all types of fireplaces. She opened her retail business two years ago, selling a variety of fireplaces and related products, and providing design consultation and installation services for her customers.

Most of the customers for Hearth House own homes and are adding a fireplace, or want to replace existing woodburning fireplaces with the newer, cleaner, more efficient gas burning units. People frequently install more than one fireplace in their home. These homeowners pay cash on delivery of the fireplace, or on completion of the installation. In addition, Hearth House installs fireplaces in the lobbies and lounges of clubs, apartment buildings, and other businesses. These customers, who have accounts with Hearth House, can take a 1 percent discount if they settle their account within five days. Full payment is requested in ten days.

Hearth House has credit accounts with several suppliers of fireplaces, related products and other business supplies. Some of these suppliers offer discounts for early payment. Other vendors that Hearth House deals with on a regular cash basis are also included in the list of vendors.

Amber Ashe has three full-time employees to assist her: the manager assists with contract negotiations and supervises store sales and installation work; the installer, an experienced gas-fitter, completes most of the installation work, assisted by the manager on difficult projects; the store assistant handles store sales and accounting work. Ashe is still active in her business, but mostly with design consultation, purchases, and contract negotiations. If there is additional work that the current staff cannot complete or that requires special skills, Hearth House will subcontract to another installer, a former employee who now works independently.

Ashe wanted to computerize her accounting records and asked the manager and store assistant to research the available software. They recommended Simply Accounting for Windows, outlining their reasons in the following report.

Notes

Hearth House is located at
44 Warmley Road
Toronto, Ontario
M6R 2P6
Business No.: 20736 5818

MANAGER'S REPORT

1. Using Simply Accounting would allow the business to process all source documents in a timely fashion. It would automatically prepare both single period and comparative accounting reports for planning, making decisions and controlling operations within the business.

2. The software would eliminate some of the time-consuming clerical functions that are performed manually. For example, it can automatically prepare invoices, cheques and statements, and can perform all the necessary arithmetic calculations. Being freed from these chores, the accountant could extend his or her role to assume a much higher level of responsibility. For example, the accountant would have more time to spend analyzing reports with the owner and could work more directly with the owner in making business decisions.

3. Simply Accounting can easily export reports to spreadsheets for further analysis or link with other software programs for interactive data exchange. When combined with the graphing, bank reconciliation and budgeting features, these reports would permit the owner to analyze past trends and to make better predictions about the future behaviour of the business.

4. As the business grows, the manager could divide work more meaningfully among new accounting personnel. Since Simply Accounting provides subsidiary ledgers, which are integrated to control accounts in the General Ledger, it could automatically co-ordinate accounting work performed by different individuals.

5. It would allow the owner to exercise business controls in a number of areas:

In General

- Access to confidential accounting records and editing capability can be restricted to authorized personnel by using passwords.
- Mechanical errors can be virtually eliminated, since journal transactions with unequal debits and credits cannot be posted. Customer, vendor, employee, inventory and jobcost names appear in full on the journal entry input forms, making errors less likely.
- The ability to store recurring entries and look up posted invoices makes it possible to double check invoices in response to customer and vendor inquiries.
- Errors in Sales, Purchases and Payroll journal entries can be corrected as adjustments. The software automatically creates and posts the reversing entries.
- Simply Accounting provides an audit trail for all journals.
- To Do Lists provide reminders of upcoming discounts and recurring entries.

General Ledger

- The software provides a directory of accounts used by the business, including all the integration accounts for the other ledgers in Simply Accounting. The information in these accounts can be used to prepare and analyze financial reports such as the Balance Sheet and Income Statement.
- Simply Accounting provides an audit trail for all types of journal transactions.

Receivables Ledger

- Simply Accounting provides a directory of customers and mailing labels.
- Credit limit entries for each customer should reduce the losses from non-payment of accounts. Customers with poor payment histories can have their credit limits reduced or their credit purchase privileges removed.
- Accounts receivable can be aged, and each customer's payment behaviour can be analyzed. This allows for the accurate calculation of provisions for bad debts.

Payables Ledger

- Simply Accounting provides a directory of vendors and mailing labels.
- The information from the review of transactions with vendors and from the accounts payable aged analysis can be combined to make payment decisions. Simply Accounting helps to predict short-term cash needs in order to establish priorities for making payments and to schedule payments to vendors.
- Simply Accounting provides an audit trail for the Payables journals.
- The GST remittance or refund is calculated automatically because of the integration of the GST accounts in the Payables and Receivables ledgers.
- Simply Accounting permits Purchase Order entries that result in an automatic Purchases Journal entry when the order is filled.

The manager found an application called Artistic Interiors in an older Simply Accounting textbook. It appeared similar in complexity and structure to Hearth House and even included complete instructions for setting up a computerized accounting system in Simply Accounting. She and the store assistant used this for practice before converting the books for Hearth House. They then prepared the following reports to assist with the conversion:

- Chart of Accounts
- Income Statement
- Balance Sheet
- Post-Closing Trial Balance
- Vendor Information
- Customer Information
- Employee Information
- Inventory Information
- Accounting Procedures

Notes

The Chart of Accounts does not include account names or numbers for headings, totals or subtotals. These are included in the financial statements that follow.

HEARTH HOUSE
CHART OF ACCOUNTS

ASSETS
Current Assets
1080 Cash in Bank
1200 Accounts Receivable
1220 Allowance for Doubtful Accounts
1240 Advances Receivable
1260 Interest Receivable
1280 Prepaid Advertising
1300 Prepaid Insurance
1320 Supplies: Office
1340 Supplies: Insulation
1360 Supplies: Fireplace Hardware

Inventory
1400 Accessories
1410 Ceramic Gas Logs
1420 Glass Doors
1430 Grills
1440 Fireplaces and Inserts
1450 Mantels and Surrounds
1460 Remote Control Units
1470 Space Heaters
1480 Services

Plant & Equipment
1510 Computers
1520 Accum Deprec: Computers
1530 Installation Equipment
1540 Accum Deprec: Install Equip
1560 Shop Centre
1570 Accum Deprec: Shop Centre
1590 Transport Vehicles
1600 Accum Deprec: Trans Vehicles

LIABILITIES
Current Liabilities
2100 Bank Loan
2200 Accounts Payable
2300 Vacation Payable
2310 EI Payable
2320 CPP Payable
2330 Income Tax Payable
2390 EHT Payable
2400 RRS-Plan Payable
2410 CSB-Plan Payable
2420 Group Insurance Payable
2460 WCB Payable
2500 Business Income Tax Payable
2640 PST Payable
2650 GST Charged on Sales
2670 GST Paid on Purchases
2690 GST Payroll Deductions
2710 GST Adjustments
2730 ITC Adjustments

Long Term Liabilities
2850 Mortgage Payable

EQUITY
Owner's Equity
3560 AA, Capital
3600 Current Earnings

REVENUE
General Revenue
4020 Revenue from Sales
4040 Revenue from Services
4060 Sales Returns & Allowances
4070 Sales Discount
4100 Interest Earned
4120 Sales Tax Commission

EXPENSES
Operating Expenses
5020 Advertising & Promotion
5040 Bank Charges
5050 Cost of Goods Sold
5060 Purchase Discounts
5070 Purchases Returns & Allowances
5080 Damaged Inventory
5085 Depreciation: Computers
5090 Depreciation: Install Equip
5095 Depreciation: Shop Centre
5100 Depreciation: Transport Vehicles
5110 Delivery Expenses
5120 Freight Expense
5130 Hydro Expense
5150 Insurance Expense
5160 Interest on Loan
5165 Interest on Mortgage
5170 Maintenance and Repairs
5180 Property Taxes
5200 Supplies Used: Office
5230 Supplies Used: Insulation
5240 Supplies Used: FP Hardware
5250 Uncollectable Accounts Expense
5260 Telephone Expense

Payroll Expenses
5300 Wages
5310 EI Expense
5320 CPP Expense
5330 WCB Expense
5360 EHT Expense

Income Tax Expense
5540 Business Income Tax Expense

**HEARTH HOUSE
INCOME STATEMENT**

For the quarter ending September 30, 1999

REVENUE
4000 GENERAL REVENUE

4020 Revenue from Sales	$157 500.00	
4040 Revenue from Services	22 500.00	
4060 Sales Returns & Allowances	0.00	
4070 Sales Discount	0.00	
4080 Net Sales		$180 000.00
4100 Interest Earned		340.00
4120 Sales Tax Commission		480.00
4390 TOTAL GENERAL REVENUE		$180 820.00
TOTAL REVENUE		$180 820.00

EXPENSE
5000 OPERATING EXPENSES

5020 Advertising & Promotion		$ 250.00
5040 Bank Charges		75.00
5050 Cost of Goods Sold	94 500.00	
5060 Purchase Discounts	−450.00	
5070 Purchases Returns & Allowances	0.00	
5075 Net Cost of Goods Sold		94 050.00
5080 Damaged Inventory		0.00
5085 Depreciation: Computers		500.00
5090 Depreciation: Install Equip		250.00
5095 Depreciation: Shop Centre		3 000.00
5100 Depreciation: Transport Vehicles		1 000.00
5110 Delivery Expenses		800.00
5120 Freight Expense		300.00
5130 Hydro Expense		360.00
5150 Insurance Expense		300.00
5160 Interest on Loan		800.00
5165 Interest on Mortgage		6 100.00
5170 Maintenance and Repairs		250.00
5180 Property Taxes		750.00
5200 Supplies Used: Office		150.00
5230 Supplies Used: Insulation		1 200.00
5240 Supplies Used: FP Hardware		300.00
5250 Uncollectable Accounts Expense		900.00
5260 Telephone Expense		160.00
5290 TOTAL OPERATING EXPENSES		$111 495.00

5295 PAYROLL EXPENSES

5300 Wages		33 772.00
5310 EI Expense		1 183.26
5320 CPP Expense		684.15
5330 WCB Expense		889.52
5360 EHT Expense		324.38
5390 TOTAL PAYROLL EXPENSES		$36 853.31

5500 INCOME TAX EXPENSE

5540 Business Income Tax Expense		7 500.00
5590 TOTAL INCOME TAX EXPENSE		$7 500.00
TOTAL EXPENSE		$155 848.31
NET INCOME		$ 24 971.69

HEARTH HOUSE
BALANCE SHEET

September 30, 1999

ASSETS
1000 CURRENT ASSETS
1080 Cash in Bank | | $42 000.50
1200 Accounts Receivable | $9 200.00 |
1220 Allowance for Doubtful Accounts | − 900.00 |
1240 Advances Receivable | 0.00 |
1260 Interest Receivable | 340.00 |
1270 Net Receivables | | 8 640.00
1280 Prepaid Advertising | | 250.00
1300 Prepaid Insurance | | 1 500.00
1320 Supplies: Office | | 200.00
1340 Supplies: Insulation | | 600.00
1360 Supplies: Fireplace Hardware | | 500.00
1380 TOTAL CURRENT ASSETS | | $53 690.50

1390 INVENTORY ASSETS
1400 Accessories | | 4 490.00
1410 Ceramic Gas Logs | | 4 374.00
1420 Glass Doors | | 5 640.00
1430 Grills | | 2 880.00
1440 Fireplaces and Inserts | | 30 180.00
1450 Mantels and Surrounds | | 5 760.00
1460 Remote Control Units | | 900.00
1470 Space Heaters | | 5 040.00
1480 Services | | 0.00
1490 TOTAL INVENTORY ASSETS | | $59 264.00

1500 PLANT & EQUIPMENT
1510 Computers | 6 000.00 |
1520 Accum Deprec: Computers | − 1 500.00 |
1525 Net Computers | | 4 500.00
1530 Installation Equipment | 15 000.00 |
1540 Accum Deprec: Install Equip | − 750.00 |
1545 Net Install Equipment | | 14 250.00
1560 Shop Centre | 300 000.00 |
1570 Accum Deprec: Shop Centre | − 9 000.00 |
1575 Net Shop Centre | | 291 000.00
1590 Transport Vehicles | 40 000.00 |
1600 Accum Deprec: Trans Vehicles | − 3 000.00 |
1610 Net Transport Vehicles | | 37 000.00
1690 TOTAL PLANT & EQUIPMENT | | $346 750.00

TOTAL ASSETS | | $459 704.50

continued...

HEARTH HOUSE
BALANCE SHEET CONTINUED

September 30, 1999

LIABILITIES

2000 CURRENT LIABILITIES
2100 Bank Loan		$75 000.00
2200 Accounts Payable		9 309.00
2300 Vacation Payable		1 860.00
2310 EI Payable	$ 746.95	
2320 CPP Payable	386.66	
2330 Income Tax Payable	2 521.30	
2340 Receiver General Payable		3 654.91
2390 EHT Payable		324.38
2400 RRS-Plan Payable		450.00
2410 CSB-Plan Payable		450.00
2420 Group Insurance Payable		35.00
2460 WCB Payable		889.52
2500 Business Income Tax Payable		0.00
2640 PST Payable		4 800.00
2650 GST Charged on Sales	4 200.00	
2670 GST Paid on Purchases	− 2 520.00	
2690 GST Payroll Deductions	0.00	
2710 GST Adjustments	0.00	
2730 ITC Adjustments	0.00	
2750 GST Owing (Refund)		1 680.00
2790 TOTAL CURRENT LIABILITIES		$98 452.81
2800 LONG TERM LIABILITIES		
2850 Mortgage Payable		248 800.00
2890 TOTAL LONG TERM LIABILITIES		$248 800.00
TOTAL LIABILITIES		$347 252.81

EQUITY

3000 OWNER'S EQUITY		
3560 AA, Capital		87 480.00
3600 Current Earnings		24 971.69
3690 UPDATED CAPITAL		$112 451.69
TOTAL EQUITY		$112 451.69
LIABILITIES AND EQUITY		$459 704.50

HEARTH HOUSE
POST-CLOSING TRIAL BALANCE

September 30, 1999

1080 Cash in Bank	$42 000.50	
1200 Accounts Receivable	9 200.00	
1220 Allowance for Doubtful Accounts		900.00
1260 Interest Receivable	340.00	
1280 Prepaid Advertising	250.00	
1300 Prepaid Insurance	1 500.00	
1320 Supplies: Office	200.00	
1340 Supplies: Insulation	600.00	
1360 Supplies: Fireplace Hardware	500.00	
1400 Accessories	4 490.00	
1410 Ceramic Gas Logs	4 374.00	
1420 Glass Doors	5 640.00	
1430 Grills	2 880.00	
1440 Fireplaces and Inserts	30 180.00	
1450 Mantels and Surrounds	5 760.00	
1460 Remote Control Units	900.00	
1470 Space Heaters	5 040.00	
1510 Computers	6 000.00	
1520 Accum Deprec: Computers		1 500.00
1530 Installation Equipment	15 000.00	
1540 Accum Deprec: Install Equip		750.00
1560 Shop Centre	300 000.00	
1570 Accum Deprec: Shop Centre		9 000.00
1590 Transport Vehicles	40 000.00	
1600 Accum Deprec: Trans Vehicles		3 000.00
2100 Bank Loan		75 000.00
2200 Accounts Payable		9 309.00
2300 Vacation Payable		1 860.00
2310 EI Payable		746.95
2320 CPP Payable		386.66
2330 Income Tax Payable		2 521.30
2390 EHT Payable		324.38
2400 RRS-Plan Payable		450.00
2410 CSB-Plan Payable		450.00
2420 Group Insurance Payable		35.00
2460 WCB Payable		889.52
2640 PST Payable		4 800.00
2650 GST Charged on Sales		4 200.00
2670 GST Paid on Purchases	2 520.00	
2850 Mortgage Payable		248 800.00
3560 AA, Capital		112 451.69
	$477 374.50	$477 374.50

HEARTH HOUSE
VENDOR INFORMATION

Vendor Name (Contact)	Address Phone & Fax	Invoice Terms	Invoice Date	Invoice/ Cheque No.	Outstanding Balance
Bell Canada (Maisie Speaker)	88 Holler St. Toronto, ON M6R 3F2 Tel: (416) 588-7290 Fax: (416)588-9001	Net 1			
Cambridge Castings (Blackie Smith)	210 Ironside Rd. Toronto, ON M2Y 7B3 Tel: (416) 922-9871 Fax: (416) 922-9911	2/10, N/15	09/24/99	CC-818	$4 237.20
City Treasurer (Business Dept.)	100 Queen St. W. Toronto, ON M5H 2N1 Tel: (416) 393-6101 Fax: (416) 393-1000	End of Month (15 days)			
Matchless Flame (Ashleigh Burns)	552 Igniter Ct. Hamilton, ON L8V 5N8 Tel: (905) 525-6774 Fax: (905) 525-8108	Net 15	09/24/99 09/24/99	MF-1201 CHQ#281 Balance	$3 210.00 −1 070.00 $2 140.00
Overload Office Supplies (Nellie Stapler)	48 Paper Ave. Toronto, ON M4T 2W1 Tel: (416) 788-1074 Fax: (416) 788-6198	Net 10			
Penguin Insulating Co. (Rob Warme)	386 Vermiculite St. Mississauga, ON L6B 3D5 Tel: (905) 773-5924 Fax: (905) 775-6111	Net 15	09/30/99	PI-901	$428.00
Power Hardware (Shaina Toole)	92 Power St. North York, ON M3H 7E9 Tel: (416) 748-7291 Fax: (416) 748-8282	Net 10			
Receiver General of Canada	Summerside Tax Centre Summerside, PE C1N 6L2 Tel: (902) 821-8186	Net 1			
Standard Insurance Co. (Nevva Smoke)	234 Carefree Blvd. Toronto, ON M3G 5X5 Tel: (416) 489-2935 Fax: (416) 489-2900	Net 1			

Vendor Name (Contact)	Address Phone & Fax	Invoice Terms	Invoice Date	Invoice/ Cheque No.	Outstanding Balance
Starfire Fireplaces (Cindy Heatlie)	355 Sparks St. Scarborough, ON M2F 6M4 Tel: (416) 529-6185 Fax: (416) 529-8100	Net 20			
Telecompute Computers (N. T. Windows)	95 Processor Ave. Etobicoke, ON M8B 2W6 Tel: (416) 630- 6291 Fax: (416) 633-6222	Net 15			
Therma Glow (Margo Flamer)	183 Bright St. Windsor, ON N8N 5F4 Tel: (519) 422-4587 Fax: (519) 423-9464	2/10, N/20	09/28/99	TG-1421	$1 797.60
Toronto Hydro	14 Carlton St. Toronto, ON M5B 1K5 Tel: (416) 599-0735 Fax: (416) 599-6000	Net 1			
Toronto Star	1 Yonge St. Toronto, ON M5E 1E6 Tel: (416) 368-3611 Fax: (416) 368-1000	Net 1			
Transcend Investment Co. (Rich Better)	10 Stocks St. Toronto, ON M6H 4R7 Tel: (416) 663-7401 Fax: (416) 663-7400	Net 15			
Treasurer of Ontario	Box 620 33 King St. W. Oshawa, ON L1H 8H5 Tel: (905) 965-8470	Net 1			
Vulcan Stove Co. (Bryan Stokes)	45 Firestone Cr. Barrie, ON L4N 4C3 Tel: (705) 611-6191 Fax: (705) 611-8101	Net 30	09/27/99	VS-699	$706.20
Workers' Compensation Board	1033 Bay St. Toronto, ON M5T 1D3 Tel: (416) 925-7176 Fax: (416) 925-7222	Net 1		Grand Total	$9 309.00

HEARTH HOUSE
CUSTOMER INFORMATION

Customer Name (Contact)	Address Phone & Fax	Invoice Terms (Credit Limit)	Invoice Date	Invoice/ Cheque No.	Outstanding Balance
Brookhaven Funeral Home (Grim Reaper)	11 Spirits Ave. Toronto, ON M6F 3K2 Tel: (416) 838-5757 Fax: (416) 838-0903	1/5, N/10 ($10 000)	09/21/99 09/21/99	HH-110 CHQ#51 Balance	$4 600 −1 150 $3 450
Lakeshore Condos (Liv Intown)	550 Beach Ave. Toronto, ON M7H 4L4 Tel: (416) 363-6336 Fax: (416) 366-5554	1/5, N/10 ($10 000)			
Rosedale Estates (Dale Rosewood)	75 Crescent Rd. Toronto, ON M1B 3X9 Tel: (416) 488-3939 Fax: (416) 488-9211	1/5, N/10 ($10 000)	09/27/99	HH-115	$3 680
Scarlett Road Condos (Rhett Butler)	450 O'Hara Rd. Toronto, ON M7T 2F5 Tel: (416) 784-5632 Fax: (416) 784-6021	1/5, N/10 ($15 000)			
University Alumni House (Izzy Dunskule)	540 Spadina Ave. Toronto, ON M5J 4E3 Tel: (416) 528-8642 Fax: (416) 528-7201	1/5, N/10 ($15 000)	09/28/99	HH-117	$2 070
Walden Apartments (E. Thoreau)	488 Walden Pond Rd. Toronto, ON M4S 7N2 Tel: (416) 393-0987 Fax: (416) 393-9731	1/5, N/10 ($10 000)			
York Seniors' Club (Nonny Genarian)	129 York Blvd. Toronto, ON M8B 2R3 Tel: (416) 528-5522 Fax: (416) 528-6001	1/5, N/10 ($10 000)		Grand Total	$9 200

HEARTH HOUSE
EMPLOYEE INFORMATION SHEET

Employee Name	Ella Cinder	Kris Kindl	Dana Damper
Position	Manager	Installer	Store Assistant
Social Insurance Number	494 663 481	482 876 340	442 552 771
Address & Telephone	921 Fireside Dr.	82 Mantle St.	588 Hotspur Rd
	Scarborough, ON	Toronto, ON	North York, On
	M1B 2C9	M5B 6D1	M6A 1X6
	(416) 578-7291	(416) 779-7299	(416) 482-6234
Date of Birth (dd-mm-yy)	25-12-71	14-02-68	01-04-78

Tax Exemption (TD-1)

Basic Personal	$6 456	$6 456	$6 456
Spouse/Equivalent	$5 380	$5 380	$5 380
Children under 18	one		
Disability			
Education & Tuition			
Other			$3 482
Total Exemptions	$11 836	$11 836	$15 318

Employee Earnings

Regular Wage Rate		$20.00	
Overtime Wage Rate		$30.00	
Regular Salary	$4 500		$1 400
Commission			
Vacation	4 weeks	6%	3 weeks

Employee Deductions

Registered Retirement Savings (RRS) Plan	$200	$50	$50
Canada Savings Bond (CSB)	$200	$50	$50
Group Insurance	$10	$5	$5
EI, CPP and Income Tax	calculations built into Simply Accounting program		
Additional Income Tax		$20	

Employee Profiles and TD-1 Information

Ella Cinder, the manager at Hearth House, manages the day-to-day store operations, schedules and manages installation projects, assists with difficult installations and assists the owner in decision making. She is married and fully supports her husband and two children under twelve. Her salary, $4 500 per month for a normal month of 140 hours, is paid at the end of each month. She is entitled to four weeks vacation with pay each year. Through payroll deductions, she contributes to a Registered Retirement Savings Plan, a Canada Savings Bond Plan, and to a Group Insurance Plan that provides a basic level of term life insurance. There are no company benefits. She began working for Hearth House on January 1, 1999.

Kris Kindl installs fireplaces for Hearth House, and is responsible for shipping and receiving. He is married and fully supports his wife but has no other dependents. Kindl is paid every 2 weeks (26 pay periods) and earns $20 regularly per hour. After 40 hours in the week he receives $30 per hour as his overtime wage rate. His vacation pay, at the rate of 6 percent, is retained. Kindl has not yet taken vacation time this year. He makes regular payroll contributions to a Registered Retirement Savings Plan, a Canada Savings Bond Plan and to a Group Insurance Plan. There are no company benefits. He started working for Hearth House on January 12, 1999.

Dana Damper works in the store as salesperson and office/accounting assistant. Damper is single and fully supports her father for whom she claims spousal equivalence as well as the age deductions because he is over 65. Her salary of $1 400 is paid semi-monthly (24 pay periods of 70 hours each), and she takes three weeks vacation each year with pay. She contributes to a Registered Retirement Savings Plan, a Canada Savings Bond Plan and to a Group Insurance Plan. There are no company benefits. She began working for Hearth House on January 1, 1999.

Additional Payroll Information

The CSB-Plan is administered by Transcend Investment Co., and the RRS-Plan and Group Insurance plan are administered by Standard Insurance Co. Deductions withheld from employee paycheques are remitted to the proper agencies monthly.

In Ontario, the maximum amount of assessable earnings for Workers' Compensation Board is $55 600.

The employer's contributions include the following:

- CPP contributions equal to employee contributions
- EI factor of 1.4
- EHT rate of .98
- Workers' Compensation Board (WCB) rates for this type of business:
  4.97 for employees who complete installations – Kindl and Cinder
  1.52 for store salesworkers – Damper

HEARTH HOUSE
HISTORICAL PAYROLL INFORMATION

Pay Period Ending September 30, 1999 (Nine months)

Employee Name	Ella Cinder	Kris Kindl	Dana Damper
Regular		$30 400.00	
Overtime		600.00	
Salary	$40 500.00		$25 200.00
Commission			
Benefits			
Vacation Paid			
Gross	$40 500.00	$31 000.00	$25 200.00
EI Ins Earnings	$29 250.00	$28 500.00	$25 200.00
EI	862.92	840.75	743.40
CPP	893.20	796.37	632.16
Income Tax	10 135.08	6 669.74	3 435.48
RRSP	1 800.00	950.00	900.00
CSB	1 800.00	950.00	900.00
Group Insurance	90.00	$95.00	90.00
Withheld	$15 581.20	$10 301.86	6 701.04
Net Pay	$24 918.80	$20 698.14	$18 498.96
Advance Paid			
Vacation Owed		$1 860.00	

HEARTH HOUSE
INVENTORY INFORMATION

Code	Description	Sell Price /Unit	Qty on Hand	Amt (Cost)	Min Stock
Accessories & Tools					
AC01	Andirons: cast iron	$ 100/set	5	$250	1
AC02	Firescreen: brass accent rect	200 each	3	300	1
AC03	Firescreen: brass arch shape	250 each	3	375	1
AC04	Firescreen: iron black accent rect	150 each	3	225	1
AC05	Grate: cast iron black	150 each	4	240	1
AC06	Thermostat: standard	140 each	6	420	1
AC07	Toolset: brass handle solid	300/set	4	720	1
AC08	Toolset: cast iron/black enamel	200/set	5	600	1
AC09	Toolset: glass handle/cast iron	400/set	4	960	1
AC10	Woodholder: oak/mhg/walnut	80 each	10	400	2
				$4 490	
Ceramic Gas Logs					
CL01	Ceram Log: Algonquin Maple AMF5	$500/set	3	$ 900	0
CL02	Ceram Log: Birdseye Maple BMF5	550/set	3	1 050	0
CL03	Ceram Log: Georgian Oak GOF4	450/set	3	810	0
CL04	Ceram Log: Laurentian Birch LBF4	400/set	3	750	0
CL05	Ceram Log: Tobermory Ash TAF5	480/set	3	864	0
				$4 374	
Fireplaces and Inserts					
FI01	CC: Fireplace coal CC200FS	$1 800 each	2	$ 2 160	0
FI02	CC: Fireplace free-std gas DV30DVT	3 000 each	2	3 600	0
FI03	CC: Fireplace gas ins DV32HET	2 800 each	2	3 360	0
FI04	CC: Fireplace wood WC100FS	1 800 each	2	2 160	0
FI05	MF: Fireplace gas ins DV27TVT	1 950 each	2	2 340	0
FI06	MF: Fireplace gas ins DV30HE	2 000 each	2	2 400	0
FI07	MF: Fireplace gas ins slim DV20SL	1 200 each	2	1 440	0
FI08	SF: Fireplace gas ins bay DV30BWT	1 800 each	2	2 160	0
FI09	SF: Fireplace gas ins tp-vnt DV30TV	1 500 each	2	1 800	0
FI10	TG: Fireplace gas ins bay BVDV30T	2 300 each	2	2 760	0
FI11	TG: Fireplace gas ins multi MSDV45T	2 800 each	2	3 360	0
FI12	VS: Fireplace pellet stove VPS1000	2 200 each	2	2 640	0
				$30 180	
Glass Doors					
GD01	Door: Apparition w/damper 2.5wf	$800 each	2	$ 960	0
GD02	Door: Charade w/damper 1wf	600 each	2	720	0
GD03	Door: Mirage w/damper 2.75wf	900 each	2	1 080	0
GD04	Door: Pinnacle Arch w/damper 2wf	1 000 each	2	1 200	0
GD05	Door: Quest w/damper custom 2wf	750 each	2	900	0
GD06	Door: Viewzone w/damper 1.5wf	650 each	2	780	0
				$5 640	
Grills (Barbeque)					
GR01	Grill: mobile/side burner DL-60	$1 100 each	2	$1 320	0
GR02	Grill: rotisserie & spit DX80	1 300 each	2	1 560	0
				$2 880	

continued...

HEARTH HOUSE
INVENTORY INFORMATION CONTINUED

Code	Description	Sell Price /Unit	Qty on Hand	Amt (Cost)	Min Stock
Mantels & Surrounds					
MS01	Mantel: cherry MC-DVT40 kit	$1 200/kit	2	$1 440	0
MS02	Mantel: marble MM-DVT40 kit	1 800/kit	2	2 160	0
MS03	Mantel: oak MO-DVT30 kit	1 000/kit	2	1 200	0
MS04	Mantel: tile MT-DVT30 kit	800/kit	2	960	0
				$5 760	
Remote Control Units					
RC01	Remote control: economy RCE-100	$120 each	6	$360	1
RC02	Remote control: luxury RCL-1000	180 each	6	540	1
				$900	
Space Heaters					
SH01	Heater: vintage 20,000BTU ADVSH-20	$500 each	4	$1 200	1
SH02	Heater: vintage 30,000BTU ADVSH-30	750 each	4	1 800	1
SH03	Heater: vintage 50,000BTU ADVSH-50	850 each	4	2 040	1
				$5 040	
Services					
SV01	Basic installation	$450/job	150	0	0
SV02	Basic installation - plus	500/job	150	0	0
SV03	Customizing inserts	300/job	50	0	0
SV04	Insulating chimney	100/job	50	0	0

Accounting Procedures

The Goods and Service Tax

GST at the rate of 7 percent is applied to all goods and services offered by Hearth House. Hearth House uses the **regular method** for remittance of the Goods and Services Tax. GST collected from customers is recorded as a liability in the *GST Charged on Sales* account. GST paid to vendors is recorded in the *GST Paid on Purchases* account as a decrease in liability to Revenue Canada.

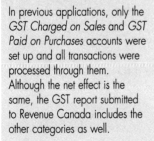

Notes

In previous applications, only the *GST Charged on Sales* and *GST Paid on Purchases* accounts were set up and all transactions were processed through them. Although the net effect is the same, the GST report submitted to Revenue Canada includes the other categories as well.

The accounts, *GST Adjustments* and *ITC (Input Tax Credit) Adjustments* are used to adjust for changes in GST owing, for example, as a result of bad debts. When a bad debt is written off, the GST liability should be reduced because GST was part of the original invoice. Remove the GST portion of the invoice from GST owing by debiting the *ITC Adjustments* account for this amount. If the debt is later recovered, the GST liability should be restored as well. Record the recovery of GST as a credit to the *GST Adjustments* account.

A fifth postable GST account, *Payroll Adjustments*, is provided by the program to record the GST portion of taxable employee benefits that the employer withholds. Although it is not currently used by Hearth House, because there are no benefits, the account will be retained for future use.

These five postable accounts are added together in the subtotal account, *GST Owing (Refund)*. The balance of GST to be remitted or the request for a refund is sent to the Receiver General of Canada by the last day of the current month for the previous month.

Only the GST transactions that were entered through the Sales Journal or the Purchases Journal will be included in the GST report available from the pull-down menu under **Reports**. GST-related transactions completed in the General Journal will not be included. Therefore, the amounts shown in the GST report may differ from the balances in the General Ledger GST accounts, which include all GST transactions. Use the General Ledger accounts to determine the balance owing (or refund due) and make adjustments manually to the report as necessary.

After the report is filed, clear the GST report by choosing **Clear GST Report** from the pull-down menu under **Maintenance**. Enter the last day of the previous month as the date for clearing. Be sure to make a backup copy of your files before clearing the GST report.

Provincial Sales Tax (PST)

Provincial sales tax of 8 percent is applied to all cash and credit sales of goods and services provided by Hearth House. It is applied to the amount of the sale without GST included, and is not applied to freight. The PST collected must be remitted monthly to the Provincial Treasurer. Provincial sales taxes to be remitted must be set up as a liability owing to the vendor, The Treasurer of Ontario, in the Purchases Journal. The *PST Payable* account for the ending date of the previous month will provide you with the total owing. You may display or print this account for reference. A 5 percent sales tax commission is earned for prompt payment. Remittance must be made by the 23rd of the current month for the previous month.

Business Income Tax

Hearth House pays income tax in quarterly installments to the Receiver General based on its previous year's net income.

The Employer Health Tax (EHT)

The Employer Health Tax (EHT) is paid by all employers permanently established in the province of Ontario to pay for the Ontario Health Insurance Plan coverage for all eligible Ontario residents. The EHT is based on the total annual remuneration paid to employees. The EHT rate ranges from 0.98 percent to 1.95 percent. The lowest rate (0.98) is based on total remuneration under $200 000. The highest rate (1.95) is based on total remuneration exceeding $400 000.

In this application, EHT Payable will be remitted quarterly. The EHT Payable account must be set up as a liability owing to the vendor, The Treasurer of Ontario. The account balance in the General Ledger for the last day of the previous three months will provide you with the liability owing to the treasurer.

Aging of Accounts

Hearth House uses aging periods that reflect the payment terms that it provides to customers and that it receives from vendors. For customers, this will be 5, 10 and 30 days, and for vendors, 15, 30 and 45 days. Currently, it does not charge interest on overdue accounts.

Discounts

Hearth House offers a 1 percent discount to account customers if they settle their accounts within 5 days. Full payment is requested within 10 days. These payment terms are set up as defaults. When the receipt is entered, and the discount is still available, the program will show the amount of the discount and the net amount owing automatically.

Some vendors also offer discounts for early settlement of accounts. Again, when the terms are entered for the vendor, and payment is made before the discount period expires, the program will display the discount as available and automatically calculate a net balance owing. Payment terms vary from vendor to vendor.

Freight Expense

When a business purchases inventory items, the cost of any freight that cannot be directly allocated to a specific item must be charged to the *Freight Expense* account. This amount will be regarded as a general expense rather than being charged to the costs of any inventory asset account. Customers are not charged for delivery.

Sales Invoices

To print invoices, click on the Print button before posting the invoice. If you have already posted the invoice, use Look up to restore a copy of the invoice on-screen, and then print it.

Purchase Returns and Allowances

A business will sometimes return inventory items to vendors due to damage, poor quality or shipment of the wrong items. Usually a business records these returns after it receives a credit note from a vendor. The return of inventory is entered in the Purchases Journal as an inventory purchase:

- Select the item in the Item field and enter the quantity returned as a **negative** amount in the Quantity field. The program will automatically calculate a negative amount as a default in the Amount field.
- Accept the default amount and enter other items returned to the vendor.
- When there are no further items, enter any freight charges as a **negative** amount.
- Enter the appropriate GST codes and PST rates for each item returned and for freight.

The program will create a negative invoice to reduce the balance owing to the vendor and will reduce the applicable inventory assets, the freight accounts, the *GST Paid on Purchases* account and the quantity of items in the Inventory Ledger database.

Purchase allowances for damaged merchandise that is not returned are entered as non-inventory negative purchase invoices. Enter the amount of the allowance as a negative amount in the Amount field and leave the tax fields blank (i.e. treat as non-taxable). Enter the *Purchases Returns and Allowances* account in the Account field.

Sales Returns and Allowances

Sometimes customers will return inventory items. Usually a business records the return after it has issued a credit note. The return is entered in the Sales Journal as a negative inventory sale for the customer:

- Select the appropriate item in the Item field.
- Enter the quantity returned as a **negative** amount in the Quantity field.
- The price of the item appears as a positive number in the Price field, and the Amount field is calculated automatically as a negative amount that should be correct. If it is not, you can change it.
- Enter the applicable GST code, PST rate and the account number for *Sales Returns & Allowances*.
- If there were freight charges, enter them as **negative** amounts with the appropriate GST code.

The program will create a negative invoice to reduce the balance owing by the customer, the *Cost of Goods Sold* account, the *GST Charged on Sales* account and the *PST Payable* account. The applicable inventory asset accounts and the quantity of items in the Inventory Ledger database will be increased.

GST Adjustments for Bad Debt

Most businesses set up an allowance for doubtful accounts or bad debts, knowing that some of their customers will fail to pay. When the allowance is set up, a bad debts or uncollectable accounts expense account is debited. When a business is certain that a customer will not pay its account, the debt should be written off. In the past, the business would do this by crediting the *Accounts Receivable* account and debiting the *Allowance for Doubtful Accounts* account. When GST applies, an extra step is required. Part of the original sales invoice was entered as a credit (increase) to *GST Charged on Sales*. The amount of the GST liability can be reduced by the portion of the unpaid debt that was GST. A special GST account, *ITC Adjustments*, is used to record the GST for this transaction. The procedure for entering the transaction in Simply Accounting is to record the write-off of the debt in the Sales Journal using the following steps:

- Select the customer whose debt will not be paid.
- Enter a source document number to identify the transaction (e.g., memo).
- Enter the amount of the unpaid invoice **minus GST** in the Amount field as a **negative** amount.
- Enter the *Allowance for Doubtful Accounts* account number in the Account field.
- Advance to the next line of the invoice.
- Enter the amount of GST that was charged on the invoice in the Amount field as a **negative** amount.
- Enter the *ITC Adjustments* account number in the Account field.

Review the transaction. The *Accounts Receivable* account is credited (reduced) by the full amount of the invoice to remove the balance owing by this customer. The *Allowance for Doubtful Accounts* account has been debited (reduced) by the amount of the invoice minus GST. The *ITC Adjustments* account has been debited for the GST portion of the invoice in order to reduce the liability to the Receiver General.

Manually you would complete the entry as follows:

	Set up the Allowance for Bad Debts.				
Date	Particulars	Ref.	Debit		Credit
xx/xx	Uncollectable Accounts Expense		1 000.00		
	Allowance for Doubtful Accounts				1 000.00

Customer G. Bell declares bankruptcy. Write off outstanding balance, $214, including GST.

Date	Particulars	Ref.	Debit	Credit
xx/xx	Allowance for Doubtful Accounts		200.00	
	ITC Adjustments		14.00	
	Accounts Receivable, G. Bell			214.00

Occasionally, a bad debt is recovered after it has been written off. When this occurs, the above procedure is reversed and the GST liability must also be restored. Another special GST account, *GST Adjustments*, is used to record the increase in the liability to the Receiver General. The recovery is entered as a non-inventory sale in the Sales Journal using the following steps:

- Select the customer and enter the date and source document number.
- Type an appropriate comment such as "Debt recovered" in the Description field.
- Enter the amount of the invoice **minus GST** in the Amount field as a **positive** amount.
- Enter the *Allowance for Doubtful Accounts* account number in the Account field.
- Advance to the next line of the invoice.
- Enter the amount of GST that was charged on the original invoice as a **positive** amount in the Amount field.
- Enter the *GST Adjustments* account number in the Account field.

Review the transaction. You will see that the *Accounts Receivable* account has been debited for the full amount of the invoice. The *Allowance for Doubtful Accounts* account has been credited for the amount of the invoice minus GST. The *GST Adjustments* account has been credited for the amount of the GST to record the increase in the liability to the Receiver General.

As the final step, record the customer's payment using the Payments Journal as you would record any other customer payment.

NSF Cheques

If a cheque is deposited from an account that does not have enough money to cover it, the bank may return it to the depositor as NSF (Non-Sufficient Funds). If the cheque was in payment for a cash sale, you must process the NSF cheque through the Sales Journal because there was no Receipts Journal entry. Create a customer record if necessary and enter a **positive** amount for the amount of the cheque. Choose *Cash in Bank* as the account. If the customer is expected to pay the bank charges, enter these on the second invoice line as a **positive** amount and select the appropriate revenue account.

Hardware and Insulation Supplies

Insulation materials and fireplace hardware supplies are requested as needed for contracts by completing a Materials Request Form. Based on these forms, the inventory used is charged to the appropriate expense accounts each month.

Remittances

The Receiver General of Canada:
Monthly EI, CPP and Income Tax deductions withheld from employees must be paid by the 15th of each month for the previous month.

Monthly GST owing or requests for refunds must be filed by the end of each month for the previous month. The General Ledger GST accounts will provide you with the balance.

Business Income Tax is paid in quarterly installments.

The Treasurer of Ontario:
Quarterly Employer Health Tax (EHT) deductions must be paid by the 15th of April, July, October and January for the previous quarter.

Monthly provincial sales taxes (PST) on revenue from sales must be paid by the 23rd of the month for the previous month. A 5 percent sales tax commission is earned for prompt payment of PST.

The Standard Insurance Company:
Monthly Registered Retirement Savings Plan (RRS-Plan) deductions and group insurance contributions withheld from employees must be paid by the 15th of the month for the previous month. Separate remittances are made because these accounts are separate.

The Transcend Investment Corporation:
Monthly Canada Savings Bond Plan (CSB-Plan) deductions withheld from employees must be paid by the 15th of the month for the previous month.

The Workers' Compensation Board:
Quarterly Workers' Compensation Board (WCB) assessment for employees must be paid by the 15th of the month for the previous quarter.

Notes

Normally a business would make these tax remittances to different federal and provincial tax offices. In this case, you could set up separate vendor accounts for each remittance. For this application, one vendor account and address has been used for the Receiver General and one for the Treasurer of Ontario to reduce the length of the vendor list.

INSTRUCTIONS FOR SETUP

Using the Chart of Accounts, Balance Sheet, Income Statement, Post-Closing Trial Balance and Vendor, Customer, Employee and Inventory Information provided above for September 30, 1999, set up the company accounts. Use the setup input forms provided in Appendix A. Instructions to assist you in setting up the company accounts follow. The setup of the Payroll and Inventory ledgers is given in detail. Abbreviated instructions are included for the remaining steps. Refer to the CISV and the Maverick Micro Solutions applications if you need more detailed explanations.

KEYSTROKES FOR SETUP

Creating Company Files

We will use one of the starter files to begin the setup for Hearth House. The starter files that most closely match the Chart of Accounts are the Integration Plus files (inteplus.asc). This set of accounts is commonly used because it includes integration accounts for all of the ledgers.

Open inteplus.asc in the PROGRAM FILES\WINSIM\SAMDATA folder to access the Integration Plus starter files.

The familiar Home window appears. Make a copy of these files to store your records for Hearth House. Remember always to work with a backup copy of the starter files so that the original is available to create other company records.

Choose Save As from the pull-down menu under **File**.

Click on the Save in field or the Up one level icon  to locate the drive and folder where you want to store the new files and then double click on the folder at each level in the path to open it until you reach the folder that will contain the new folder and files.

Create a new folder for the Hearth House files. Refer to Chapter 1, page 18 if you need help. Replace the highlighted folder name Hearth.

Replace the highlighted file name with the name for the Hearth House files.

Type hearth.asc

Click on Save

Notes

- If you are using an alternative location for your company files, substitute the appropriate path, folder or drive in the example.
- You can also type the complete path in the File name field after creating the new folder —
Type c:\program files\winsim\data\hearth\hearth.asc
(or a:\hearth\hearth.asc if you are using floppy disks).

You have now created a copy of the Integration Plus starter files under the new name. When you return to the Home window, the name Hearth appears at the top of the window. All of the journal icons are locked. You can now begin to enter all of the necessary company information.

Preparing the System

The next step involves changing the defaults that came with the Integration Plus files. Change the defaults to suit your own work environment if you have more than one printer or if you are using forms for cheques, invoices or statements. The keystroke instructions are given for computer-generated cheques, invoices and statements.

Setup Input Forms

Complete the setup input forms, Form SYS-1 and Form SYS-2, to enter changes for the defaults and computer equipment. Use Form SYS-1 to profile the company and give information about computer equipment. Use Form SYS-2 to show the defaults for Hearth House for each of the accounting ledgers. We show the input forms for any information that is being introduced for the first time in this application.

Changing Defaults

Changing Company Information

Choose **Company Information** from the pull-down menu under **Setup**.

The cursor is flashing in the Name field. Highlight the default entry, "Your Company," to prepare the field for editing.

Type	Hearth House
Press	tab

Continue by entering the address.

Type	44 Warmley Road
Press	tab
Type	Toronto
Press	tab
Type	Ontario
Press	tab
Type	m6r2p6
Press	tab

Click on **Use Business No.** to open the new number field.

Click on **the Business Number field** to advance the cursor.

Type	207365818
Press	tab

The fiscal start date is now highlighted. Insert the appropriate fiscal dates for Hearth House as follows:

- Fiscal Start: January 1, 1999
- Fiscal End: December 31, 1999
- Conversion Date: September 30, 1999

Notes

You may choose to complete the setup by working directly from the information provided in the Company Information section rather than using input forms. If you are using the input forms in Appendix A, make additional copies of them as needed.

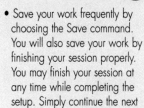

Notes

- Save your work frequently by choosing the Save command. You will also save your work by finishing your session properly. You may finish your session at any time while completing the setup. Simply continue the next time from where you left off.
- Use the Save As feature frequently while setting up your files to update your backup files.

Check the information you have just entered and correct any errors. Remember that you can also correct this information any time before making the system ready. Company name and address information can be changed at any time.

Click on OK to save the new information and return to the Home window.

The program will automatically set up defaults for the using date and for the city and province fields for customers, vendors and employees based on the information you have just entered.

Changing Default Names

The information you need to complete this step is contained in the Names portion of Form SYS-1 as shown here:

SYSTEM PREPARATION

Form SYS-1
Page 1 of 1

NAMES

Tax:	GST	Deduction C:	Gp Insurance
Income A:	Salary	Deduction D:	N/A
Income B:	Commission	Deduction E:	N/A
Deduction A:	RRS-Plan	Prov. Tax:	
Deduction B:	CSB-Plan	Project Title:	

Choose Names from the pull-down menu under **Setup** to display the following screen showing the preset payroll field names:

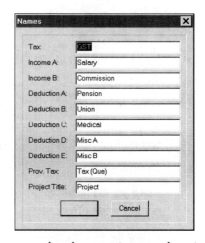

Some of the default names are already correct so you do not need to redefine them. Tax is correctly named GST for the province of Ontario. You can leave Income A and Income B, labelled "Salary" and "Commission," unchanged because Hearth House has salaried employees and is considering sales commissions for the store employees.

Double click on the **Deduction A field**. Each of the deduction field names may have up to 12 characters. Hearth House will use this field for Registered Retirement Savings Plan contributions.

Type   RRS-Plan

Press `tab` to advance to the next field.

The Deduction B field will be used for the Canada Savings Bond Plan that Hearth House offers its employees.

Type   `CSB-Plan`

Press   [tab]

The Deduction C field will be used for the Group Insurance plan that Hearth House offers its employees.

Type   `Gp Insurance`

Press   [tab]

You can ignore the next two name fields because Hearth House does not have other payroll deductions. To indicate that each of these fields is not applicable,

Type   `N/A`

Press   [tab]

The Prov. Tax field is used for Quebec payroll taxes. Since we will not choose Quebec as the province, the program will automatically skip the related payroll fields. The Project ledger will not be used so you can leave it unchanged. The Project name you enter in this window will appear in the Home window as the icon label.

Click on OK to save the new name settings and to return to the Home window.

You should now enter the information about printers you are using.

Changing Printer Settings

Choose Printers from the pull-down menu under **Setup**.

The printer setting options for reports and graphs are given. Choose the printer you will be using for reports. Change the margins if necessary. Choose a suitable font and type size from the lists available.

Click on Setup to set the options for your particular printer if you need to change the paper size and location.

Click on OK to save your settings and return to the previous Printers setting screen.

To set the printer options for cheques, invoices or other forms,

Click on the type of output you are setting the printer for.

As you did for reports, set the margins and select the printer, form or paper size, font and type size to match the forms you are using.

Click on Setup and complete the setting of options if necessary.

Click on OK to save the information.

For printing labels, you need to include the size of the labels and the number that are placed across the page. These fields will become available when you choose Labels.

Click on OK to save the information when all the settings are correct and to return to the Home window. You can change the printer settings at any time.

Changing Appearance Defaults

Form SYS-2 provides information about all the default settings.

Choose Settings from the pull-down menu under **Setup** to display the default settings for the Display. Choose the screen display font and size, and select the appearance settings for the program. Be sure that the option to Show the Status Bar is turned on. You can also choose to display the To Do Lists each time you start the program and when you advance the using date. Click on the check box to change the setting.

The settings for the system and ledgers can be modified at any time by returning to this screen.

Changing System Defaults

Click on the **System tab** to display the default settings for the System. The following options should be turned on:

- Track Inventory Turnover
- Store Invoice Lookup Details
- Use Cheque No. as the Source Code for Cash Purchases and Sales

Choose Weekly as the backup frequency.

These settings can be modified at any time by returning to this screen.

Changing Sales Taxes Defaults

Click on the **Sales Taxes tab** to display the default Sales Taxes settings. The GST rates are correct. The only setting that you must change is the PST rate for Ontario.

Double click on the **PST field** to highlight the contents.

Type   8

Changing General Ledger Defaults

Click on the **General tab** to display the default settings for the General Ledger. You may choose to skip the Accounts icon window, to select the cash accounting method, and to turn on the budgeting and bank reconciliation features. You can turn off bank reconciliation and leave the remaining default settings unchanged. When you turn off Bank Reconciliation, the program warns you that all bank reconciliation information will also be removed. Since there isn't any, click on OK to proceed.

Changing Payables Defaults

Click on the **Payables tab**.

For the Payables Ledger, you can choose to skip the Vendors icon window, and change the settings for the aging of accounts. Since some vendors ask for payment within 15 days, set the aging intervals at 15, 30 and 45 days.

Changing Receivables Defaults

Click on the **Receivables tab** to display the defaults for the Receivables Ledger.

Again you can choose to skip the introductory Customers icon window. You can also decide whether to charge interest on overdue accounts, how long to provide historic information about paid invoices on customer statements, and what aging intervals to use. The remaining settings relate to provincial and federal sales tax rates.

Hearth House offers its account customers payment terms that include a 1 percent discount in the first five days; full payment is due in ten days. Using these terms, set the aging intervals at 5, 10 and 30 days. There are no interest charges for overdue accounts.

Choose to include paid invoices for the past 30 days because statements are mailed every month.

Customers are offered a 1 percent discount if they pay in full withing 5 days, and must remit full payment in 10 days. To enter these terms,

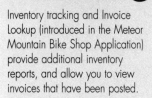

Notes

Inventory tracking and Invoice Lookup (introduced in the Meteor Mountain Bike Shop Application) provide additional inventory reports, and allow you to view invoices that have been posted.

Warning!

Do not skip any ledger icon windows before completing the setup.

Notes

If a ledger icon is selected in the Home window, you will display the Settings for that ledger when you click on the Setup tool bar button. If no ledger icon is highlighted, you can click on the Setup tool icon and select the ledger from the pop-up list to display the ledger's Settings.

Click on the **% field** beside Terms.

Type   1

Press   [tab]

Type   5

Press   [tab]

Type   10

The other Receivables default settings are correct and you do not need to change them.

Changing Default Settings for Forms

Click on the **Forms tab** to display the defaults.

The Forms options relate to the automatic numbering and printing of all cheques and invoices. They apply only to numerical invoices and are very useful for most businesses. Many invoices include the alpha portion of the invoice number on the preprinted invoice form. You could then enter the first number in the numeric portion in the Invoice number field. Alphanumeric invoice numbers cannot be increased automatically by the computer.

If you want to use automatic invoice numbering, type in the next number from the source documents so the automatic numbering system can take over from the manual system. For Hearth House, the next invoice is #HH-120.

The Invoices number field entry is already highlighted, ready to be changed.

Type   120

The PO number is correct. Hearth House will begin the numbering of Purchase Orders with 1. Notice that separate ledgers can have separate bank accounts and cheque numbers. Hearth House has only one bank account, so we need only one number. The next cheque number is 300.

Double click on the **Payables Chqs. field**

Type   300

You can skip the Payroll cheque number.

If you are printing invoices and cheques through the computer, you should turn on the option to confirm printing. The program will then warn you to print before posting a transaction. Remember that if a cheque is printed in error, an appropriate entry or comment should be recorded to explain the discarded cheque or the missing number.

Click on the appropriate boxes to receive the warning.

When printing invoices, statements or cheques, it is good practice to include the company address.

Click on the appropriate boxes to add this feature.

The final option is to add the same comment or notice to all of your invoices. You could use this feature to include payment terms, a company motto or notice of an upcoming sale. Remember that you can change the default message any time you want. You can also edit it for a particular invoice when you are completing the invoice.

Click on the **Default Invoice Comment field**.

Type in the comment you want to see on all your customer invoices.

Payroll Defaults Settings

The portions of Form SYS-2 shown here include the Payroll, Payroll WCB and Inventory settings. These settings are being introduced in this application:

SYSTEM PREPARATION

SETTINGS: Payroll

Skip Employee Icon Window: Y ___ , N ✔

Auto Payroll Deduction: Y ✔ , N ___

RRS-Plan after Tax: Y ___ , N ✔

CSB-Plan after Tax: Y ✔ , N ___

Gp Insurance after Tax: Y ✔ , N ___

Deduction D after Tax: Y ___ , N ___

Deduction E after Tax: Y ___ , N ___

EI Factor: 1.4

EHT Factor : 0.98

Keep Employee Details: 1 year _____ or 2 years _____

SETTINGS: Payroll WCB

Province : Ontario

WCB Maximum Assessable Earnings: 55600

SETTINGS: Inventory

Skip Inventory Icon Window: Y ___ , N ✔

Profit Evaluation: Markup ✔ Margin _____ (Choose one only)

Sort by: Number ✔ Description _____ (Choose one only)

Allow inventory to go below zero: Y ✔ , N ___

Use the Payroll portion of Form SYS-2 to complete this step.

Click on the **Payroll tab** to display the Payroll Ledger settings:

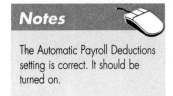

Notes

The Automatic Payroll Deductions setting is correct. It should be turned on.

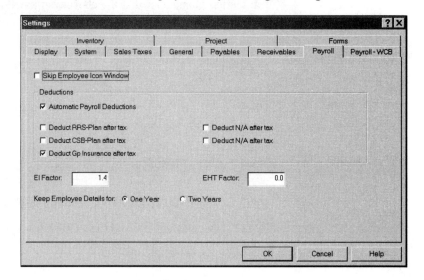

As with the other ledgers, you can skip the icon window, moving directly to the first employee information form window when you open the Payroll Ledger. Do not select this option before completing the setup.

Notice that the deduction names you entered earlier now appear on the screen. Again, most of the information is correct. We want payroll deductions to be calculated automatically so leave this box checked.

The deductions are set by default as either pretax or after tax. The RRS-Plan deduction is already set correctly as a pretax deduction (after tax is not turned on). This means that it qualifies as a tax deduction and will be subtracted from gross income before income tax is calculated.

CSB-Plan is an after-tax deduction, meaning that it is subtracted from income after income tax has been deducted.

Click on Deduct CSB-Plan after tax to change the setting.

Group Insurance is also set correctly as an after-tax deduction.

The remaining fields are not used so you can leave them as they are. You can see that the remaining two deductions are set at pretax by default.

The next two fields refer to the rate at which employer tax obligations are calculated. The factor for Employment Insurance (EI Factor) is correct at 1.4. The employer's contribution is set at 1.4 times the employee's contribution.

Double click on the EHT factor field. This field shows the percentage of payroll costs that the employer contributes to the provincial health plan. Based on the total payroll costs per year, the percentage for Hearth House is 0.98 percent.

Type .98

Notice that you can keep payroll information for two years. Choosing two years will enable you to print employee details for the previous fiscal year when you advance the using date to the next year. The size of your data files will also increase so be sure that your disk storage capacity is large enough before you choose this option.

You have now finished setting the Payroll defaults.

Payroll WCB Defaults

Use the information in the Payroll WCB portion of Form SYS-2 to complete this step.

Click on the Payroll-WCB tab to display the default settings:

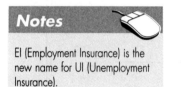

Notes

EI (Employment Insurance) is the new name for UI (Unemployment Insurance).

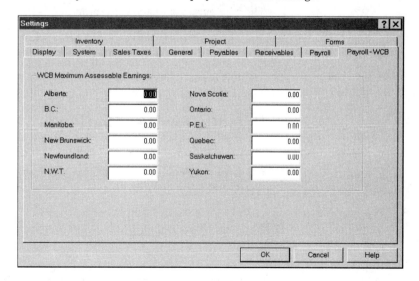

Since all Hearth House employees work in Ontario, you need only enter the maximum assessable earnings amount for Ontario. This is the maximum salary on which the Workers' Compensation Board deduction is calculated and on which any benefits are based.

Double click on the **Ontario field** to move the cursor and highlight the contents.

Type   55600

Changing Defaults for Inventory

The Inventory section on Form SYS-2 provides information about inventory default settings.

Click on the **Inventory tab** to see the options for this ledger:

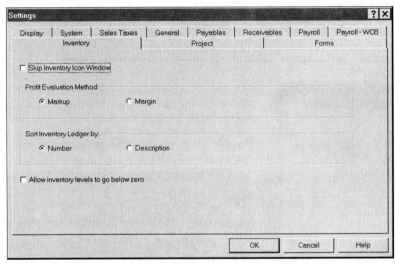

The default setting for the markup method of evaluating the profit on inventory sales is the correct one for Hearth House. Markup is calculated as follows:

Markup = 100% * (Selling Price - Cost Price)/ Cost Price

You may also choose to skip the Inventory icon window and to sort or display the inventory items alphabetically by the description or numerically by the code or number.

The final option is to allow inventory levels to go below zero. Hearth House will choose this option in order to permit customer sales for inventory that is back ordered.

Click on Allow inventory levels to go below zero to select the option.

The remaining default settings are correct.

Defaults for Distributions

Input forms for Distributions settings are included on Form SYS-2 in Appendix A.

Click on the **Project tab** to display the Project settings:

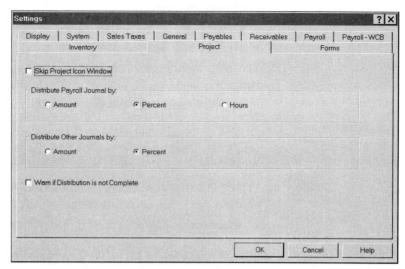

Since Hearth House does not use job costing until December, you do not need to change these settings at this time. You can see that the alternative ways of allocating costs are by percentage (as used in the Puretek application) and by amount. For payroll, the costs may also be distributed according to the number of hours worked. If you are using job costing distributions, you should turn on the warning for incomplete distributions by clicking on its box.

Click on OK to save your new settings and to return to the Home window.

Setting the Security for the System

Simply Accounting allows you to set as many as four passwords. One password controls access to the system or program. The other three control viewing and editing privileges for different ledgers. For example, if different employees work with different accounting records, they can use different passwords.

We strongly advise you not to set passwords for applications used for tutorial purposes. If you set them and forget them, you will be locked out of your data files.

If you want to set passwords, refer to Appendix B and your Simply Accounting manuals before you begin.

Preparing the Ledgers

The third stage in setting up an accounting system involves preparing each ledger for operation. This stage involves:

1. organizing all accounting reports and records (this step has already been completed for you)
2. modifying some existing accounts
3. removing some existing accounts
4. creating new accounts
5. inserting vendor, customer, employee and inventory information
6. entering historical startup information.

Defining the Integration Plus Starter Files

When you created the company files for Hearth House, a list of preset startup accounts was provided in the Integration Plus files. You can find a complete list of

Notes

You may wish to save your work and finish your session. This will give you an opportunity to read the next section.

Notes

Refer to Integration Accounts in the Maverick Micro Solutions application and Format of Financial Statements in the CISV application for a review of these topics if needed.

these accounts and their descriptions in Chapter 3 of the *Simply Accounting Getting Started* manual and on the input Form INT-1 on pages 367-369.

Form INT-1 lists both integration accounts and other accounts for the various ledgers. The integration accounts are printed in bold face and have an entry in the Module (used by) column on Form INT-1. The accounts are organized by section, including Assets, Liabilities, Equity, Revenue and Expense. The form also shows the account type, such as Heading (H), Subtotal (S), Total (T), Left Column (L), Right Column (R) and Current Earnings (X). Account type is a method of classifying and organizing accounts within a section or subsection of a report. The complete list of integration accounts is also presented on page 370.

Form INT-1 also provides the Initial Account Number for each account on the list. The accounts follow the same pattern described previously:

- 1000 - 1999   Assets
- 2000 - 2999   Liabilities
- 3000 - 3999   Equity
- 4000 - 4999   Revenue
- 5000 - 5999   Expense

If necessary, refer to the the CISV application for a review of formats of financial statements and the organization of the Balance Sheet and Income Statement.

Integration Accounts

Integration Accounts are accounts in the General Ledger that are affected by changes resulting from entries in other journals. For example, an entry to record a credit sale of an inventory item in the Sales Journal will cause automatic changes in the Inventory Ledger as well as in several General Ledger accounts. In the General Ledger, the *Accounts Receivable* [+], *Inventory Asset* [-], *Revenue from Sales* [+], *GST Charged on Sales* [+], *PST Payable* [+] and *Cost of Goods Sold* [+] accounts will all be affected by the sale. The type of change, increase [+] or decrease [-], is indicated in the brackets. In the Inventory Ledger, the sale will cause an automatic decrease in the inventory on hand for the items sold. The program must know which account numbers are to be used for posting journal entries in any of the journals. It is this interconnection of account numbers and information between ledgers that makes Simply Accounting fully integrated.

INTEGRATION PLUS ACCOUNTS - MAINTENANCE

Account Title [Initial]	SECTION	TYPE	Module [used by]	Initial Account Number	CODE	Account Title [New]	TYPE	New Account Number
CURRENT ASSETS	A	H	—	1 0 0 0	*			
Bank A - Payable	A	L	A P	1 0 6 0	R			
Bank B - Receivable	A	L	A R	1 0 8 0	M	Cash in Bank	R	1 0 8 0
Bank C - Payroll	A	L	P R	1 1 0 0	R			
Cash - Total	A	S	—	1 1 2 0	R			
Accounts Receivable	A	R	A R	1 2 0 0	M	Accounts Receivable	L	1 2 0 0
Advances Receivable	A	R	P R	1 2 4 0	M	Advances Receivable	L	1 2 4 0
Inventory	A	R	T	1 2 6 0	M	Interest Receivable	L	1 2 6 0
TOTAL CURRENT ASSETS	A	T	T	1 3 9 0	M	TOTAL CURRENT ASSETS	T	1 3 8 0
CURRENT LIABILITIES	L	H	T	2 0 0 0	*			
Accounts Payable	L	R	A P	2 2 0 0	*			
Vacation Payable	L	R	P R	2 3 0 0	*			
EI Payable	L	L	P R	2 3 1 0	*			
CPP Payable	L	L	P R	2 3 2 0	*			
Income Tax Payable	L	L	P R	2 3 3 0	*			
Receiver Genera Payable	L	S	T	2 3 4 0	*			
QPP Payable	L	L	P R	2 3 5 0	R			
Que. Income Tax Payable	L	L	P R	2 3 6 0	R			
QHIP Payable	L	L	P R	2 3 7 0	R			
Que. Minister of Finance	L	S	T	2 3 8 0	R			
EHT Payable	L	R	P R	2 3 9 0	*			

SECTION:
A = ASSETS
L = LIABILITIES
E = EQUITY
R = REVENUE
X = EXPENSE

TYPE:
H = Heading
R = Right
L = Left
S = Subtotal
X = Current Earnings
T = Total

MODULE:
GL = GENERAL
AP = PAYABLES
AR = RECEIVABLES
PR = PAYROLL
IN = INVENTORY

CODE:
R = Remove
M = Modify
* = no change

INTEGRATION PLUS ACCOUNTS - MAINTENANCE

Account Title [Initial]	SECTION	TYPE	Module [used by]	Initial Account Number	CODE	Account Title [New]	TYPE	New Account Number
Deduction A Payable	L	R	P R	2 4 0 0	M	RRS-Plan Payable	R	2 4 0 0
Deduction B Payable	L	R	P R	2 4 1 0	M	CSB-Plan Payable	R	2 4 1 0
Deduction C Payable	L	R	P R	2 4 2 0	M	Group Insurance Payable	R	2 4 2 0
Deduction D Payable	L	R	P R	2 4 3 0	R			
Deduction E Payable	L	R	P R	2 4 4 0	R			
WCB Payable	L	R	P R	2 4 6 0	*			
PST Payable	L	R	A R	2 6 4 0	*			
GST Charged on Sales	L	L	A R	2 6 5 0	*			
GST Paid on Purchases	L	L	A P	2 6 7 0	*			
GST Payroll Deductions	L	L	T	2 6 9 0	*			
GST Adjustments	L	L	T	2 7 1 0	*			
ITC Adjustments	L	L	T	2 7 3 0	*			
GST Owing (Refund)	L	S	T	2 7 5 0	M	LONG TERM LIABILITIES	H	2 8 0 0
Refundable QST Paid	L	L	T	2 8 0 0	R			
QST Charged at Rate 1	L	L	T	2 8 1 0	R			
QST Charged at Rate 2	L	L	T	2 8 2 0	R			
QST Payroll Deductions	L	L	T	2 8 2 5	R			
QST Adjustments	L	L	T	2 8 3 0	R			
ITR Adjustments	L	L	T	2 8 4 0	R			
QST Owing (Refund)	L	S	T	2 8 5 0	M	Mortgage Payable	R	2 8 5 0
TOTAL CURRENT LIABILITIES	L	T	T	2 9 0 0	M	TOTAL CURRENT LIABILITIES	T	2 7 9 0

SECTION:
A = ASSETS
L = LIABILITIES
E = EQUITY
R = REVENUE
X = EXPENSE

TYPE:
H = Heading
R = Right
L = Left
S = Subtotal
X = Current Earnings
T = Total

MODULE:
GL = GENERAL
AP = PAYABLES
AR = RECEIVABLES
PR = PAYROLL
IN = INVENTORY

CODE:
R = Remove
M = Modify
* = no change

INTEGRATION PLUS ACCOUNTS - MAINTENANCE

Account Title [Initial]	SECTION	TYPE	Module [used by]	Initial Account Number	CODE	Account Title [New]	TYPE	New Account Number
EARNINGS	E	H	—	3 0 0	M	OWNER'S EQUITY	H	3 0 0 0
Retained Earnings	E	R	G L	3 5 6 0	M	AA, Capital	R	3 5 6 0
Current Earnings	E	X	G L	3 6 0 0	*			
TOTAL EARNINGS	E	T	—	3 6 9 0	M	UPDATED CAPITAL	T	3 6 9 0
REVENUE	R	H	—	4 0 0 0	M	GENERAL REVENUE	H	4 0 0 0
General Revenue	R	R	—	4 0 2 0	M	Revenue from Sales	R	4 0 2 0
Sales Discounts	R	R	A R	4 1 1 0	M	Sales Discounts	L	4 0 7 0
Freight Revenue	R	R	A R	4 2 0 0	R			
TOTAL REVENUE	R	T	—	4 3 9 0	M	TOTAL GENERAL REVENUE	T	4 3 9 0
ADMINISTRATION	X	H	—	5 0 0 0	M	OPERATING EXPENSES	H	5 0 0 0
General Expense	X	R	—	5 0 2 0	M	Advertising & Promotion	R	5 0 2 0
Adjustment Write-off	X	R	I N	5 0 3 0	M	Damaged Inventory	R	5 0 8 0
Transfer Cos's	X	R	I N	5 0 4 0	M	Bank Charges	R	5 0 4 0
Purchase Discounts	E	R	A P	5 1 1 0	M	Purchase Discounts	L	5 0 6 0
Freight Expense	X	R	A P	5 2 0 0	M	Freight Expense	R	5 1 2 0
Wages	X	R	P R	5 3 0 0	*			
EI Expense	X	R	P R	5 3 1 0	*			
CPP Expense	X	R	P R	5 3 2 0	*			
WCB Expense	X	R	P R	5 3 3 0	*			
QPP Expense	X	R	P R	5 3 4 0	R			
QHIP Expense	X	R	P R	5 3 5 0	R			
EHT Expense	X	R	P R	5 3 6 0	*			
TOTAL ADMINISTRATION	X	T	—	5 3 9 0	M	TOTAL PAYROLL EXPENSES	T	5 3 9 0

SECTION:
A = ASSETS
L = LIABILITIES
E = EQUITY
R = REVENUE
X = EXPENSE

TYPE:
H = Heading
R = Right
L = Left
S = Subtotal
X = Current Earnings
T = Total

MODULE:
GL = GENERAL
AP = PAYABLES
AR = RECEIVABLES
PR = PAYROLL
IN = INVENTORY

CODE:
R = Remove
M = Modify
* = no change

The following chart lists all the integration accounts that are predefined in the Integration Plus starter files. They are organized according to the ledgers that use them:

General		Payroll	
Retained Earnings	3560	Bank C - Payroll	1100
Current Earnings	3600	Advances Receivable	1240
		Vacation Payable	2300
		EI Payable	2310
Payables		CPP Payable	2320
Bank A - Payable	1060	Income Tax Payable	2330
Accounts Payable	2200	QPP Payable	2350
GST Paid on Purchases	2670	Quebec Income Tax Payable	2360
Purchase Discounts	5100	QHIP Payable	2370
Freight Expense	5200	EHT Payable	2390
		Deduction A Payable	2400
		Deduction B Payable	2410
Receivables		Deduction C Payable	2420
Bank B - Receivable	1080	Deduction D Payable	2430
Accounts Receivable	1200	Deduction E Payable	2440
PST Payable	2640	WCB Payable	2460
GST Charged on Sales	2650	Wages	5300
Sales Discounts	4100	EI Expense	5310
Freight Revenue	4200	CPP Expense	5320
		WCB Expense	5330
		QPP Expense	5340
Inventory		QHIP Expense	5350
Adjustment Write-Off	5030	EHT Expense	5360
Transfer Costs	5040		

Preparing the General Ledger

Print the Integration Plus Chart of Accounts from your new Hearth House files and compare it with the Hearth House Chart of Accounts, Balance Sheet and Income Statement provided in this application. As you saw with the CISV application and the Skeleton starter accounts, some of the accounts are the same, some of the accounts you need are not yet in the program, and others that appear on the computer list are not needed for Hearth House. You have to customize the accounts specifically for Hearth House.

Changing Integration Plus Accounts

The first step, that of identifying the changes needed in the Integration Plus preset accounts to match the accounts needed for Hearth House, is a very important one. Form INT-1, on pages 367-369, shows the changes that must be made to these preset accounts. On Form INT-1, the following steps have been done for you:

1. The Integration Plus accounts provided by the program that require no changes have been marked with an asterisk (*). The account title, the initial account number and the account type are the same as those given in the financial statements. Those accounts not requiring changes follow:

CURRENT ASSETS	1000
CURRENT LIABILITIES	2000
Accounts Payable	2200
Vacation Payable	2300
EI Payable	2310
CPP Payable	2320
Income Tax Payable	2330
Receiver General Payable	2340
EHT Payable	2390
WCB Payable	2460
PST Payable	2640
GST Charged on Sales	2650
GST Paid on Purchases	2670
GST Payroll Deductions	2690
GST Adjustments	2710
ITC Adjustments	2730
GST Owing (Refund)	2750
Current Earnings	3600
Wages	5300
EI Expense	5310
CPP Expense	5320
WCB Expense	5330
EHT Expense	5360

2. Account *1080 Cash in Bank* has been identified as the only integrated bank account for the Payables, Receivables and Payroll ledgers. These bank account titles, types and initial account numbers are shown as removed (R) or modified (M) on Form INT-1:

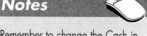

Notes

Remember to change the Cash in Bank account type to Right when you modify the account.

Bank A - Payable	1060	remove (R)
Bank B - Receivable	1080	modify (M) – Cash in Bank Right
Bank C - Payroll	1100	remove (R)

3. The accounts for which only the account type needs to be changed have been identified and modified (M) on Form INT-1. These accounts, for which the initial account numbers and titles are correct but the type is different, include:

Accounts Receivable	1200	modify (M) – Left
Advances Receivable	1240	modify (M) – Left

4. The accounts for which the account number, and possibly the account type need to be changed have been identified and modified (M) on Form INT-1. These accounts, for which the initial account titles are correct include:

TOTAL CURRENT ASSETS	1390	modify (M) – 1380	
TOTAL CURRENT LIABILITIES	2900	modify (M) – 2790	
Sales Discounts	4100	modify (M) – 4070	Left
Purchase Discounts	5100	modify (M) – 5060	Left
Freight Expense	5200	modify (M) – 5120	

5. The accounts for which the account titles and possibly the account type need to be changed have been identified and modified (M) on Form INT-1. These accounts, for which the initial account numbers are correct but the account titles are different, include the following:

For Hearth House, a sole proprietorship, the Retained Earnings account will be renamed "AA, Capital." The Current Earnings account will not be renamed.

Inventory	1260	(M) – Interest Receivable Left
Deduction A Payable	2400	(M) – RRS-Plan Payable
Deduction B Payable	2410	(M) – CSB-Plan Payable
Deduction C Payable	2420	(M) – Group Insurance Payable
Refundable QST Paid	2800	(M) – LONG TERM LIABILITIES Heading
QST Owing (Refund)	2850	(M) – Mortgage Payable Right
EARNINGS	3000	(M) – OWNER'S EQUITY
Retained Earnings	3560	(M) – AA, Capital
TOTAL EARNINGS	3690	(M) – UPDATED CAPITAL
REVENUE	4000	(M) – GENERAL REVENUE
General Revenue	4020	(M) – Revenue from Sales
TOTAL REVENUE	4390	(M) – TOTAL GENERAL REVENUE
ADMINISTRATION	5000	(M) – OPERATING EXPENSES
General Expense	5020	(M) – Advertising & Promotion
Transfer Costs	5040	(M) – Bank Charges
TOTAL ADMINISTRATION	5390	(M) – TOTAL PAYROLL EXPENSES

6. The one account for which the account number and title need to be changed has been identified and modified (M) on Form INT-1. This account, for which only the initial account type is correct is:

Adjustment Write-off	5030	(M) – Damaged Inventory 5080

7. The following accounts that are going to be removed (R) because they are not required for Hearth House have been marked on Form INT-1:

Recall that the two bank accounts that are not needed were marked for removal in Step #2.

Cash - Total	1120
QPP Payable	2350
Quebec Income Tax Payable	2360
QHIP Payable	2370
Quebec Minister of Finance	2380
Deduction D Payable	2430
Deduction E Payable	2440
QST Charged at Rate 1	2810
QST Charged at Rate 2	2820
QST Payroll Deductions	2825
QST Adjustments	2830
ITR Adjustments	2840
Freight Revenue	4200
QPP Expense	5340
QHIP Expense	5350

Creating New Accounts

After identifying the modifications that must be made to the Integration Plus accounts and the accounts that must be removed, the next step is to identify the accounts that you will need to create or add to the preset accounts in the computer. Again, you need to refer to the company Chart of Accounts, Balance Sheet and Income Statement in this application to complete this step.

You should insert (create) each of remaining accounts, including non-postable accounts, on Form CHA-1 provided in Appendix A. Remember to add the type of account and whether you wish to suppress the printing of zero balances.

The accounts you must create are identified below:

Allowance for Doubtful Accounts	1220	Revenue from Services	4040
Net Receivables	1270	Sales Returns & Allowances	4060
Prepaid Advertising	1280	Net Sales	4080
Prepaid Insurance	1300	Interest Earned	4100
Supplies: Office	1320	Sales Tax Commission	4120
Supplies: Insulation	1340		
Supplies: Fireplace Hardware	1360		
INVENTORY ASSETS	1390		
Accessories	1400	Cost of Goods Sold	5050
Ceramic Gas Logs	1410	Purchases Returns & Allowances	5070
Glass Doors	1420	Net Cost of Goods Sold	5075
Grills	1430	Depreciation: Computers	5085
Fireplaces and Inserts	1440	Depreciation: Install Equip	5090
Mantels and Surrounds	1450	Depreciation: Shop Centre	5095
Remote Control Units	1460	Depreciation: Transport Vehicles	5100
Space Heaters	1470	Delivery Expenses	5110
Services	1480	Hydro Expense	5130
TOTAL INVENTORY ASSETS	1490	Insurance Expense	5150
PLANT & EQUIPMENT	1500	Interest on Loan	5160
Computers	1510	Interest on Mortgage	5165
Accum Deprec: Computers	1520	Maintenance and Repairs	5170
Net Computers	1525	Property Taxes	5180
Installation Equipment	1530	Supplies Used: Office	5200
Accum Deprec: Install Equip	1540	Supplies Used: Insulation	5230
Net Install Equipment	1545	Supplies Used: FP Hardware	5240
Shop Centre	1560	Uncollectable Accounts Expense	5250
Accum Deprec: Shop Centre	1570	Telephone Expense	5260
Net Shop Centre	1575	TOTAL OPERATING EXPENSES	5290
Transport Vehicles	1590	PAYROLL EXPENSES	5295
Accum Deprec: Trans Vehicles	1600	INCOME TAX EXPENSE	5500
Net Transport Vehicles	1610	Business Income Tax Expense	5540
TOTAL PLANT & EQUIPMENT	1690	TOTAL INCOME TAX EXPENSE	5590
Bank Loan	2100		
Business Income Tax Payable	2500		
TOTAL LONG TERM LIABILITIES	2890		

You are now ready to enter the account information into the company files.

Modifying Integration Account Settings

Hearth House has only a single bank account, *Cash in Bank*. This account has to be integrated to the subsidiary Payables, Receivables and Payroll ledgers. When the company files were created, Simply Accounting established three default bank integration accounts (see Form INT-1). Access the Hearth House files so you can modify the integration accounts.

Modifying the Payables Integration Settings

To modify the Payables Ledger integration accounts,

Click on the **Purchases journal icon** or the **Payments journal icon** in the Home window to select it.

Click on the **Setup button** 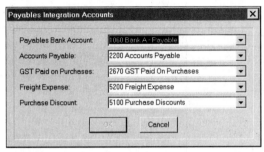 or choose Payables Integration Accounts from the pull-down menu under Setup. The following screen appears with the Payables Bank Account field highlighted and ready to be changed:

You can type in the account number or select the account from the drop-down list.

Type 1080

Press (tab) to enter the new account number.

Cash transactions in the Payments Journal will automatically be posted to this General Ledger account when journal entries are made. The remaining Payables integration accounts are correct, except for the account numbers. You will modify the names and numbers of accounts later. See the section Modifying Accounts in the General Ledger on page 377.

The General Ledger account, *Bank A - Payable*, can now be removed since it is no longer integrated to any ledger. See the section Removing Accounts in the General Ledger on page 376.

Click on OK to save the new account settings and return to the Home window.

Modifying the Payroll Integration Settings

Click on the **Payroll journal icon** in the Home window.

Click on the **Setup tool button** or choose Payroll Integration Accounts from the pull-down menu under Setup to display the Payroll Integration Accounts:

Payroll Integration Accounts

Bank:	1100 Bank C - Payroll	Advances:	1240 Advances Receivable

Payables

Vacation:	2300 Vacation Payable	QPP:	2350 QPP Payable
EI:	2310 EI Payable	QHIP:	2370 QHIP Payable
CPP:	2320 CPP Payable	RRS-Plan:	2400 Deduction A Payable
Tax:	2330 Income Tax Payable	CSB-Plan:	2410 Deduction B Payable
WCB:	2460 WCB Payable	Gp Insurance:	2420 Deduction C Payable
EHT:	2390 EHT Payable	N/A:	2430 Deduction D Payable
Tax (Que):	2360 Quebec Income Tax Paya	N/A:	2440 Deduction E Payable

Expenses

Wage:	5300 Wages	EHT:	5360 EHT Expense
EI:	5310 EI Expense	QPP:	5340 QPP Expense
CPP:	5320 CPP Expense	QHIP:	5350 QHIP Expense
WCB:	5330 WCB Expense		

OK   Cancel

The Bank field is highlighted, ready for you to enter the new account number.

Type   1080

Press   [tab]

You have now identified the single bank account, *1080*, as the bank account for the three ledgers. You will modify the name of the account later. See the section Modifying Accounts in the General Ledger on page 377.

The General Ledger account, *Bank C - Payroll*, can now be removed since it is no longer integrated to any ledger. (See the section Removing Accounts in the General Ledger on page 376).

Leave the Payroll Integration Accounts window open for the next step.

Preparing Integration Accounts for Removal

Removing integration accounts in Simply Accounting involves two stages. The first stage is to turn the integration function off for the account from the appropriate integration accounts window from the Setup tool icon or menu. This action breaks the integration link between General Ledger accounts and the subsidiary ledgers. The second stage involves removing (deleting) the account itself from the Chart of Accounts in the General Ledger. An analogous situation is turning off a circuit breaker or fuse before removing the electrical wiring or connectors.

Some predefined integration accounts are not required as integration accounts. They must therefore be removed as integration accounts. Removing the integration function or status for an account does not remove the account from the General Ledger. That is a separate step. Some accounts will have the titles changed in the General Ledger at a later stage. Refer to Form INT-1.

Warning!

Do not exit yet since you need to prepare to remove additional integration accounts in the Payroll Ledger.

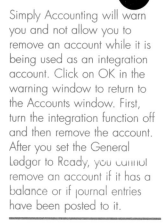

Warning!

Simply Accounting will warn you and not allow you to remove an account while it is being used as an integration account. Click on OK in the warning window to return to the Accounts window. First, turn the integration function off and then remove the account. After you set the General Ledger to Ready, you cannot remove an account if it has a balance or if journal entries have been posted to it.

The following integration accounts can be removed.

Payroll Integration Accounts		Receivables Integration Accounts	
2360	Quebec Income Tax Payable	4200	Freight Revenue
2350	QPP Payable		
2370	QHIP Payable	**Inventory Integration Accounts**	
2430	Deduction D Payable		
2440	Deduction E Payable	5040	Transfer Costs
5340	QPP Expense		
5350	QHIP Expense		

The following keystrokes will prepare the Quebec Income Tax Payable integration account for removal. You should still be in the Payroll Integration Accounts dialogue screen.

Click on 2360 Quebec Income Tax Payable to highlight it.

Press del or the Backspace (<—) key to clear the entry. You have now turned off the integration function for this account.

Press tab to advance to and highlight the next field that should be deleted. Repeat this procedure for all other integration accounts identified for removal in the Payroll Ledger.

Click on OK to save the integration account settings and return to the Home window.

You should now turn off the integration function for the integration accounts identified for removal in the Receivables and Inventory ledgers. Select the Sales or Receipts journal and then click on the Setup tool button to display Receivables Integration Accounts. Click on the Transfers or Adjustments journal icon and click on the Setup tool button to display Inventory Integration Accounts. **Do not forget to complete this step before continuing**.

Removing Accounts in the General Ledger

The following keystrokes will remove the *Bank A - Payable* integration account in the General Ledger.

Double click on the **Accounts icon** to open the Accounts window.

Click on 1060 Bank A - Payable to highlight the account name or icon.

Click on the **Remove tool button** 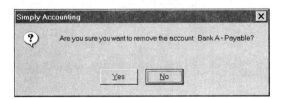 or choose Remove from the pull-down menu under Edit. The following warning message appears, asking for confirmation before the account is removed:

If you have chosen the correct account,

Click on Yes to remove the account.

After you have finished removing the accounts on Form INT-1 designated for removal, you may close the Accounts icon window and exit to the Home window or you may continue directly to the next step, modifying accounts.

Modifying Accounts in the General Ledger

The following keystrokes will modify the *Bank B - Receivable* account in the General Ledger as directed on Form INT-1.

With the General Ledger Accounts window open,

Click on the **Name button** or choose Name from the pull-down menu under View to display the accounts in the Accounts window by name instead of by icon. By keeping the accounts in numerical order and fitting more account names in the Accounts window, this view will make it easier to track your progress as you are editing and creating accounts. You will also see account balances with this view.

Double click on 1080 **Bank B - Receivable** to display it.

Press (tab) to advance to the Account name field and highlight it.

Type Cash in Bank

You must now indicate that the balance of this postable account should appear in the right-hand column of the Current Assets block. (The account's balance will not be part of a subtotal.)

Click on Right Column to change the account type.

Click on the **down scroll arrow** to advance to the next ledger account window.

Repeat this procedure to modify other accounts, changing the account title, type and account number according to Form INT-1.

Close the General Ledger account window and the Accounts icon window to return to the Home window unless you want to continue to the next step, which also involves working in the General Ledger.

Creating New Accounts in the General Ledger

Double click on the **Accounts icon** to open the Accounts window, or with any individual ledger account information window on display,

Click on the **Create button** in the Accounts window or choose Create from the pull-down menu under Edit.

Enter the account number and name for the first account on Form CHA-1.

Press (tab) to advance to the next field.

You will enter the account balances in the next stage.

Click on the **correct account type**. Remember Left-column accounts have the balance on the left-column side in the block and must be followed by a subtotal.

Click on Suppress Printing if Balance is Zero to turn on this option.

When all the information is entered correctly, you must save your account.

Click on Create to save the new account and advance to the next blank ledger account window.

Repeat these procedures to create the other accounts marked for creation on Form CHA-1.

Notes

After modifying an account, you can proceed directly to the next account by clicking once on the down scroll arrow in the lower right corner of the account ledger window.

Notes

Click on ☐ to maximize the Accounts window and drag the ledger account window to a position on the screen so that the Accounts window is still visible. In this way, you should be able to see both the Accounts window and the individual ledger account window.

Close the Accounts window to return to the Home window when you have entered all of the accounts or when you want to end your session.

You may wish to finish your session.

Entering Historical Account Balances

The opening historical balances for Hearth House can be found in the Post-Closing Trial Balance dated September 30, 1999. There are zero balances for Income Statement accounts because the books were closed at the end of the first quarter. Headings, totals and subtotals (i.e., the non-postable accounts) do not have balances.

Open the account information window for the first account requiring a balance.

Press `tab` to advance to the Balance field.

Type the balance in the Balance field.

Correct the information if necessary by repeating the above steps.

Click on the **down scroll arrow** to advance to the next ledger account window.

Repeat the above procedures to enter the balances for the remaining accounts as indicated in the Post-Closing Trial Balance.

Close the ledger account window and then the Accounts window when you want to finish your session and return to the Home window.

Preparing the Payables Ledger

Using Hearth House's Vendor Information and forms VEN-1 and VEN-2 provided in Appendix A, you should complete the following steps:

1. Complete the Vendor Maintenance form, Form VEN-1 to profile the vendors.

2. Next you should complete the Vendor Transactions (Historical) form, Form VEN-2 to record all transactions with a vendor prior to conversion.

Entering Vendor Accounts

Double click on the **Vendors icon** in the Home window to open the Vendors icon window.

Click on the **Create button** ▨ in the Vendors window or choose Create from the pull-down menu under Edit. The Vendor field is highlighted in the Payables Ledger window, ready for you to enter information.

Enter the name, contact, address, phone and fax numbers according to your input Form VEN-1. In the Terms fields, enter the discounts, if there are any, and the number of days in which the net amount is due.

Indicate that you want to retain all invoices for this vendor by leaving the box beside Clear Invoices When Paid unchecked. Check the Print Contact on Cheques option if the contact field contains address information.

Indicate that purchases from this vendor are eligible for GST input credits and should be included in GST reports by leaving this box checked. Remember that vendors such as the City Treasurer, Transcend Investment Co., and others who do not supply goods or services eligible for input tax credits, should not be included in GST reports.

The remaining fields refer to previous purchases; the Balance Owing will be entered automatically by the program once you have entered historical information in the following section.

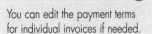

Notes

You may wish to display or print a vendor list to check it for accuracy.

Correct any errors by returning to the field with the mistake, highlighting the errors and entering the correct information.

Click on Create to save the vendor information and display a blank new Payables Ledger screen.

Repeat these procedures to enter the remaining vendors.

Entering Historical Vendor Information

Your completed Form VEN-2 provides the information you need to complete this stage.

Open the Payables Ledger for the first vendor with an outstanding balance. (Double click on the vendor's icon.)

Click on Invoices

Enter the invoice number, date and amount owing for the first invoice.

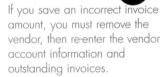

Notes

You can edit the payment terms for individual invoices if needed.

Press (tab) to advance to the next field after entering each piece of information.

When all the information is entered correctly, you must save your vendor invoice.

Click on Record to save the information and to display another blank invoice for this vendor.

Repeat these procedures to enter the remaining invoices for the vendor.

When you have recorded all outstanding invoices for a vendor,

Click on Done to return to the Payables Ledger for the vendor. Notice that the invoices you have just entered have been added to the balance field. Continue by entering historical payments to this vendor, or proceed to the next vendor with outstanding invoices.

Click on Payments

Click on the **Number field**.

Enter the cheque number for the first payment.

Press (tab) and enter the payment date for the first payment. Skip the Discount fields because discounts are taken only when the early payment is a full payment.

Click on the **Amount paid column** (on the line for the invoice being paid).

Enter the payment amount or accept the default.

Warning!

If you save an incorrect invoice amount, you must remove the vendor, then re-enter the vendor account information and outstanding invoices.

Press (tab) to advance to the next invoice if there is one. Delete any amounts or discounts that are not included in the payment.

Click on Record to save the information and to display an updated statement for this vendor.

Repeat these procedures to enter the remaining payments for the vendor.

When you have recorded all outstanding payments for a vendor,

Click on Done to return to the Payables Ledger form for the vendor. Notice that the payments you have just entered have been added to the balance field.

Repeat these procedures to enter historical transactions for other vendors.

Close the vendor ledger and the Vendors icon window to return to the Home window.

Notes

You may wish to display or print a Vendor Detail Report to check it for accuracy.

Preparing the Receivables Ledger

Using Hearth House's Customer Information Chart and forms CUS-1 and CUS-2 provided in Appendix A, you should complete the following steps:

1.   Complete the Customer Maintenance form, Form CUS-1 to profile Hearth House's customers.

2.   Next, you should complete the Customer Transactions (Historical) form, Form CUS-2, to record all transactions with a customer prior to conversion.

Entering Customer Accounts

Double click on the **Customers icon** in the Home window to open the Customers window.

Click on the **Create tool icon** 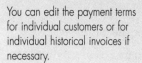 in the Customers window or choose Create from the pull-down menu under Edit. The Customer field in the Receivables Ledger window is highlighted, ready for you to enter information. The payment terms are entered from the default Receivables settings.

Enter the name, contact, address, phone and fax numbers according to your input Form CUS-1.

In the Credit Limit field, type in the amount that the customer can purchase on account before payments are required. If the customer goes beyond the credit limit, the program will issue a warning before posting an invoice.

Indicate that you want to retain all invoices by leaving the Clear Invoices When Paid box unchecked.

Indicate that this customer should be included in GST reports by leaving this box checked. The GST charged on sales to this customer will now automatically be included in the detailed GST reports.

Indicate that you want a statement to be printed for this customer by leaving this box checked.

The balance owing will be included automatically once you have provided the outstanding invoice information.

Click on Create to save the information and advance to the next new Receivables Ledger input screen.

Repeat these procedures to enter the remaining customers.

Entering Historical Customer Information

Your completed Form CUS-2 provides the information you need to complete this stage.

Open the Receivables Ledger for the first customer with an outstanding balance. (Double click on the customer's icon.)

Click on Invoices

Enter the invoice number, date and amount owing for the first invoice.

Press (tab) to advance to the next field after entering each piece of information.

When all the information is entered correctly, you must save your customer invoice.

Click on Record to save the information and to display another blank invoice for this customer.

Repeat these procedures to enter the remaining invoices for the customer, if there are any.

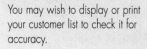

Notes

You can edit the payment terms for individual customers or for individual historical invoices if necessary.

Notes

You may wish to display or print your customer list to check it for accuracy.

Warning!

If you save an incorrect invoice amount, you must remove the customer, then re-enter the customer account information and outstanding invoices.

When you have recorded all outstanding invoices for a customer,

Click on Done to return to the Receivables Ledger window for the customer. Notice that the invoices you have just entered have been added to the Balance field. Continue by entering payments received from this customer, if there are any, or proceed to the next customer with outstanding invoices.

Click on Payments

Click on the **Number field.**

Enter the cheque number for the first payment.

Press $\boxed{\text{tab}}$ and enter the payment date for the first payment. Again, discounts apply only to full payments made before the due dates, so you can skip the Discount fields.

Click on the **Amount paid column** (on the line for the invoice being paid).

Enter the payment amount or accept the default.

Press $\boxed{\text{tab}}$ to advance to the next amount if there are other invoices. Delete any amounts or discounts that will not be included in the payment.

Click on Record to save the information and to display an updated statement for this customer.

Repeat these procedures to enter the remaining payments for the customer.

When you have recorded all outstanding receipts from a customer,

Click on Done to return to the Receivables Ledger window for the customer. Notice that the payments you have just entered have been added to the Balance field.

Repeat these procedures to enter historical transactions for other customers.

Close the customer ledger and Customers window to return to the Home window.

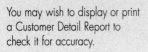

Notes

You may wish to display or print a Customer Detail Report to check it for accuracy.

Preparing the Payroll Ledger

Using the Hearth House Employee Information Sheet, Employee Profiles, Additional Payroll Information, Historical Payroll Information and forms EMP-1 and EMP-2 provided in Appendix A, you should complete the following steps:

1. Complete the Employee Maintenance form, Form EMP-1. Form EMP-1 provides basic personal and tax information about employees. For the first employee, the form is completed as follows:

EMPLOYEE MAINTENANCE

PAYROLL LEDGER
Form EMP-1
Page _1_ of ___

Code	C **Code : M = Modify C = Create R = Remove**
Employee Name	Cinder, Ella
Street Address	921 Fireside Dr.
City	Scarborough
Province	Ontario
Postal Code	M1B 2C9
Phone Number	4165787291
Soc. Ins. Number	494663481
Birth Date	12-25-71 (mm-dd-yy)
Tax Table	Ontario
Pay Periods per Year	12
Federal Claim	11836 dollar amount [TDI – TPD1]
WCB Rate	4.97 (%) WCB = Workers' Compensation Board
EI Eligibility	Y Y = Yes N = No
EI Premium Factor	1.4 (normally 1.4)
Vacation Pay Rate	(%)
Retain Vacation Pay	N Y = Yes N = No
Regular Wage Rate	dollars / hour
Overtime Wage Rate	dollars / hour
Salary per Period	4500 dollars
Salary Hours per Period	140
Hire Date	01-01-99 (mm-dd-yy)

Deductions

RRS-Plan	200	N/A
CSB-Plan	200	N/A
Gp Insurance	10	Additional Fed Tax

---

2. Next you should complete the Employee Records (Historical) form, Form EMP-2. Form EMP-2 is a record of the cumulative year-to-date earnings and deductions for employees. The first employee's record appears as follows:

PAYROLL LEDGER
Form EMP-2
Page _1_ of ___

EMPLOYEE RECORDS (HISTORICAL)

Employee Name	Cinder
Regular Wages	
Overtime Wages	
Salary	40500
Commissions	
Taxable Benefits	
Vacation Pay Paid Out	
CPP Contributions	893.20
QPP Contributions	
EI Ins. Earnings	29250
EI Premiums	862.92
Income Tax	10135.08
Quebec Income Tax	
RRS-Plan	1800
CSB-Plan	1800
Gp Insurance	90
N/A	
N/A	
Net Earnings	24918.80
Advances Paid	
Vacation Pay Owed	

Entering Employee Records

The following keystrokes will enter the information for Hearth House employee, **Ella Cinder**, using Form EMP-1.

Double click on the **Employees icon** in the Home window to open the Employees window:

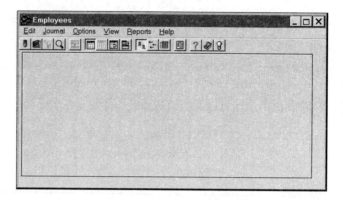

The Employees icon window is blank because no employees are on file at this stage.

Click on the **Create tool icon** in the Employees window or choose Create from the pull-down menu under Edit to display the following Payroll Ledger new employee information form:

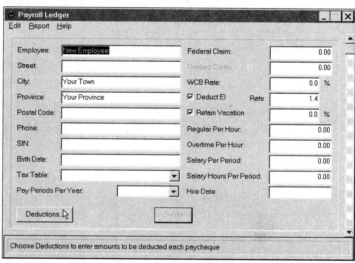

The Employee field is highlighted, ready for you to enter information.

Type   Cinder, Ella

Press   ⌈tab⌋

The cursor advances to the Street field.

Type   921 Fireside Dr.

Press   ⌈tab⌋

The cursor advances to the City field.

Type   Scarborough

Press   ⌈tab⌋

The cursor advances to the Province field. Ontario is the correct entry.

Press   ⌈tab⌋

Notes

If you skip the Employees icon window in the Payroll Settings, you will see the Payroll Ledger window immediately when you click on the Employees icon.

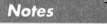

Notes

By entering the surname first, your employee lists will be in correct alphabetic order.

The cursor advances to the Postal Code field.

Type   m1b2c9

Press   [tab]

The program corrects the postal code format and advances the cursor to the Phone field.

Type   4165787291

Press   [tab]

The program corrects the telephone number format and advances the cursor to the Social Insurance Number (SIN) field.

Type   494663481

Press   [tab]

The cursor advances to the Birth Date field. Enter the month, day and year separated by hyphens.

Type   12-25-71

Press   [tab]

The cursor advances to the Tax Table field. A list of provinces appears on the screen when you click on the arrow beside this field.

Click on Ontario, the province of taxation for Hearth House.

Press   [tab]

The cursor advances to the Pay Periods Per Year field. Choose 12 from the list provided when you click on the arrow beside the field, or

Type   12

Press   [tab]

The cursor advances to the Federal Claim field, which holds the total claim for personal tax credits.

Type   11836

Press   [tab]

The cursor skips over the Quebec Claim field because you entered Ontario as the province of taxation. It advances to the WCB Rate field. Here you should enter the applicable Workers' Compensation Board (WCB) rate.

Type   4.97

Press   [tab]

The cursor advances to the Deduct EI field. If an employee is insurable by EI, you must leave the box checked. Then you should enter the EI contribution factor for Hearth House by accepting the default 1.4.

Press   [tab]

Press   [tab]

The cursor advances to the Retain Vacation field. Leave the box checked if you want to retain vacation pay for an employee. You will turn this option off when an employee receives the vacation pay, either when taking a vacation or when leaving the company, or if the employee is salaried and does not receive vacation pay. Cinder is salaried.

Click on Retain Vacation to remove the ✔.

Next, enter the vacation pay rate for an employee who receives vacation pay.

Press (tab) to advance to the vacation rate field. If the employee receives vacation pay, type the rate.

Press (tab) because Cinder is salaried.

The cursor advances to the Regular Per Hour field where you would enter the regular per hour wage for an employee. Skip this field for salaried employees.

Press (tab)

The cursor advances to the Overtime Per Hour field. Enter the per hour overtime earnings for the employee. Again, skip this field since Cinder is a salaried employee.

Press (tab)

The cursor advances to the Salary Per Period field where you can enter the salary Cinder receives every pay period.

Type 4500

Press (tab)

The cursor moves to the Salary Hours Per Period field where you can enter the number of hours the employee normally works in each pay period (e.g., 35 hours per week or 140 hours per month).

Type 140

Press (tab)

The cursor moves to the Hire Date field, which should contain the date when the employee began working for Hearth House.

Type 01-01-99

Press (tab)

The cursor moves to highlight the Deductions button.

Press (enter) to show the optional payroll deductions window for Cinder:

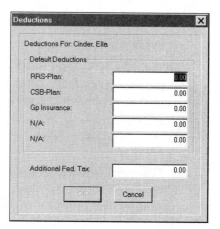

You have the option of entering the deductions here so that they are included automatically on the Payroll Journal input forms or entering them manually in the Journal for each pay period. Since all three employees have chosen to participate in these plans, you can enter the information here so that the deductions are made automatically. You can still edit the amounts in the Payroll Journal if necessary for one-time changes. You should make permanent changes by editing the Employee ledger record.

The cursor is in the RRS-Plan field. You should enter the amount that is to be withheld in each pay period.

Type   200

Press (tab) to advance the cursor to the CSB-Plan field. Enter the amount that is to be withheld in each pay period.

Type   200

Press (tab) to advance the cursor to the Group Insurance field. Enter the amount that is to be withheld in each pay period.

Type   10

Press (tab)

The remaining deductions are not used by Hearth House so they can be ignored.

If an employee has chosen to have additional Federal Income Tax deducted from each paycheque, you can enter the amount of the deduction in the Additional Fed. Tax field. Employees might make this choice if they receive regular additional income from which no tax is deducted. By making this choice, they avoid paying a large amount of tax at the end of the year and possible interest penalties.

When you are certain that you have entered the information correctly,

Click on OK to return to the employee's information window.

Correct any Employee information errors by returning to the field with the error, highlighting the error and entering the correct information.

When all the information is entered correctly, you must save your employee record.

Click on Create to save the record and to move to a new blank employee information form.

Repeat these procedures to enter other employee records.

Entering Historical Employee Information

The following keystrokes will enter the historical information for Ella Cinder using Form EMP-2.

Open the Employees window if it is not already open.

Double click on Cinder, Ella (the icon or name) to display the information for this employee. Notice that a YTD (Year-To-Date) Totals option has been added for entering payroll information up to the conversion date.

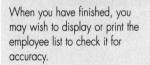

Notes

When you have finished, you may wish to display or print the employee list to check it for accuracy.

Click on YTD Totals to display the following input screen:

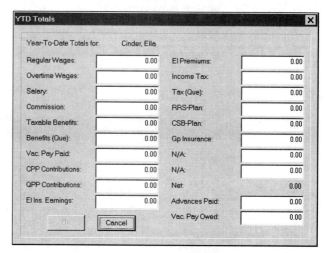

The Regular Wages and the Overtime Wages field do not apply because Cinder is a salaried employee.

Double click on the Salary field.

Type   40500

Press   [tab]

The cursor advances to the Commission field. You can ignore this field and the next two for this employee because they are not applicable. Cinder does not receive a sales commission or company benefits. She takes time off work with pay instead of receiving vacation pay.

Press [tab] until you are in the CPP Contributions field.

Type   893.20

Press   [tab]

The cursor advances to the EI Insurable Earnings field, skipping over the Quebec payroll (QPP) field that is not applicable. You should enter the total salary received to date that is EI insurable. The program will update this total every time you make payroll entries until the maximum salary on which EI is calculated has been reached. At that time, no further EI premiums will be deducted.

Type   29250

Press   [tab]

The cursor advances to the EI Premiums field. Enter the amount of EI paid to date.

Type   862.92

Press   [tab]

The cursor advances to the Income Tax field.

Type   10135.08

Press   [tab]

The cursor advances to the RRS-Plan field, skipping the Quebec tax field.

Type   1800

Press   [tab]

The cursor advances to the CSB-Plan field.

Type 1800

Press [tab]

The cursor advances to the Group Insurance field.

Type 90

Press [tab]

The cursor advances to the N/A field. Skip the N/A fields by pressing [tab].

Advance the cursor to the Advances Paid field. Since Cinder has not received any pay advances, you should skip this field too.

Press [tab]

The cursor advances to the Vacation (Vac.) Pay Owed field. For employees whose vacation pay is retained, you can enter the amount of vacation pay owing. Cinder does not receive vacation pay.

Press [tab]

You may correct any errors by returning to the field with the error, highlighting the incorrect entry and entering the correct information.

When all the information is entered correctly, you must save your employee information.

Click on OK

Repeat these procedures to enter historical payroll information for other employees.

Close the employee ledger and Employees window to return to the Home window.

Notes

You may wish to display or print the Employee Summary to check it for accuracy.

Preparing the Inventory Ledger

Using the Hearth House Inventory Information chart and Form INV-1 provided in Appendix A, you should complete the Inventory Maintenance form, Form INV-1. Form INV-1 records details about the inventory items on hand. The first inventory item is completed as follows:

Item No. Description	Asset Acct.	Rev. Acct.	Exp. Acct.	Var. Acct.	Unit of Sale	Price/ Unit (Sell)	Min. Stk. Lev.	Qty on hand	Total Value (Cost)
AC01 Andirons: cast iron	1400	4020	5050		Set	100	1	5	250

INVENTORY MAINTENANCE

INVENTORY LEDGER
Form INV-1
Page _1_ of ___

Entering Inventory Records

The following keystrokes will enter the information for Hearth House's first inventory item, **Andirons: cast iron**, using Form INV-1.

Double click on the **Inventory icon** in the Home window. Again, with no inventory items on file, the icon window is empty.

Click on the **Create tool icon** 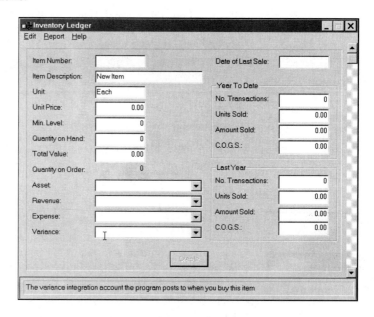 or choose Create from the pull-down menu under Edit to display the Inventory Ledger — the new inventory item input screen that follows:

The cursor is in the Item Number field, where you should enter the inventory number or code for the first item.

Type   AC01

Press   [tab]   to advance to the Item Description field.

Type   Andirons: cast iron

Press   [tab]

The cursor advances to the Unit field. Here you should enter the unit of sale for this item to replace the default entry.

Type   Set

Press   [tab]

The cursor advances to the Unit Price field. Here you should enter the selling price for this inventory item.

Type   100

Press   [tab]

The cursor advances to the Minimum (Min.) Level field. Here you should enter the minimum stock level or re-order point for this inventory item.

Type   1

Press   [tab]

The cursor moves to the Quantity on Hand field, ready for you to enter the opening level of inventory — the actual number of items available for sale.

Type   5

Press   [tab]

The cursor advances to the Total Value field, where you should enter the actual cost of the inventory on hand.

Type   250

Press   tab

The cursor advances to the Asset field. Here you must enter the asset account associated with the sale or purchase of this inventory item. Refer to the Chart of Accounts to find the account number for the inventory asset category Accessories. You can review the list of asset accounts by clicking on the drop-down list arrow beside the field.

Click on 1400

Press   tab

The cursor advances to the Revenue field. Here you must enter the revenue account that will be credited with the sale of this inventory item. Again, you can display the list of revenue accounts by using the drop-down list arrow.

Click on 4020

Press   tab

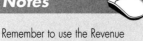

Notes

Remember to use the Revenue from Services account for inventory items that are services. The cost for service inventory items is zero.

The cursor advances to the Expense field. Here you must enter the expense account to be debited with the sale of this inventory item, normally the *Cost of Goods Sold* account. If a company wanted to keep track of each inventory category separately, it could set up different expense accounts for each category and enter them in this field. The appropriate expense account would then be updated automatically when an inventory item was sold. Use the drop-down list arrow beside the field to display the list of available expense accounts.

Click on 5050

Press   tab

Notes

If there are no items on hand at the time of the sale, the average cost is zero and the entire purchase price becomes the variance.

The cursor advances to the Variance field. Simply Accounting uses this account when sales are made of items that are not in stock. If there is a difference between the historical average cost of goods remaining in stock and the actual cost when the new merchandise is received, the price difference is charged to the variance expense account at the time of the purchase. If you have not indicated a variance account, the program will ask you to identify one when you are entering the purchase. Leave the variance field blank for now.

If you have historical information about the sale of the product, you could enter it in the next fields. It would then be added to the inventory tracking information for reports. If you have Inventory Tracking turned off, these fields will not appear in the Inventory Ledger.

The first historical field, the Date of Last Sale, refers to the last date on which the item was sold. The next two sections contain information for the Year To Date and the previous year. Since Hearth House has not kept this information, you can skip these fields. Refer to the description of new inventory items on page 219 in the Meteor Mountain Bike application for a more detailed description of these historical fields.

Correct any errors by returning to the field with the mistake. Highlight the error and enter the correct information.

When all the information is entered correctly, you must save your inventory record.

Notes

You may wish to display or print the Inventory List, Synopsis and Quantity reports to check them for accuracy.

Click on Create to save the record and advance to a new input screen.

Repeat these procedures to enter other inventory records.

Close the inventory information window to return to the Home window.

Making the Program Ready

The last stage in setting up the accounting system involves making each ledger "Ready." You must complete this final sequence of steps before you can proceed with journalizing transactions. The status of each ledger must be changed from a Not Ready to a Ready state.

Making a Backup of the Company Files

With the Hearth House files open,

Choose **Save As** from the pull-down menu under **File**.

Place the disk labelled Data Disk Not Ready Files in drive A:.

Make a new folder, NRHEARTH, for the files on this disk.

Double click on the **File name field**.

Type   a:\nrhearth\hearth.asc

Click on **Save**

This command will create a copy of all the files for Hearth House. The "NR" designates files as not ready to distinguish them from the ones you will work with to enter journal transactions. Put this backup disk in a safe place. Remember to return to your working copy of the file before setting the ledgers Ready.

Changing the Status of the Ledgers

Each ledger must be set to Ready before you can begin to enter journal transactions.

Highlight the **Accounts icon** in the Home window.

Choose **Set General Ready** from the pull-down menu under **Setup** to display the familiar warning.

Click on **Proceed** if you have already backed up your files.

Repeat this procedure for the Payables, Receivables, Payroll and Inventory ledgers, highlighting each ledger icon in turn and choosing the corresponding Set Ready command.

When the program is Ready, all your ledgers are integrated and any journal entry you make will change the General Ledger accounts.

The Hearth House files are now ready for you to enter transactions. Notice that all the journal icons in the Home window are now accessible.

Finish your session and save your work. This gives you the opportunity to read the next section and the instructions before starting the source document transactions.

Exporting Reports

Simply Accounting allows you to export files to a specified drive and path. The files created by the program may then be used by a spreadsheet or wordprocessing program. File formats available for export purposes include Text for a wordprocessing format file, Lotus versions 1 and 2, Symphony, Excel, Supercalc and Comma separated.

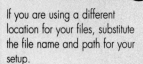
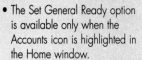

Exporting files will allow you to manipulate and interpret data for reporting purposes. This process of integrating Simply Accounting files with other software is the final step in making the accounting process meaningful.

The following keystrokes will export the opening Balance Sheet for Hearth House to a Lotus Version 2 file.

Display the Balance Sheet.

Choose Export from the pull-down menu under **File** to display the following screen:

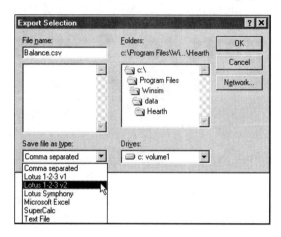

Insert a formatted disk in drive A:.

Click on Lotus 1-2-3 v2 as the type for the Balance Sheet in the Save File as Type field. Use the scroll arrow to display the file type options if necessary.

Click on a: from the list under **Drives** to select drive A:. Double click on a:\ in the Folders section to list the folders on the floppy disk, and then double click on the folder you want to use to store your file.

Accept the default file name, or type in the name you want for your file. Leave the extension of the file name as given by the program so that Lotus will recognize the new file as a Lotus file.

Click on OK

Using the Exported Files with Other Software

Finish the session using Simply Accounting. Start the software program you wish to use with the exported file, referring to the program manuals if necessary. When the blank document or spreadsheet screen appears,

Choose Open from the pull-down menu under **File** if this is a Windows program. Change directories if necessary to locate and then select the exported file. Be sure that the selected file type also matches the format of your exported file (e.g., .txt for a text file).

Click on OK. Your exported file should replace the blank document screen.

Once you have exported a financial statement as a text file, you can include it in a written report prepared with any wordprocessing program. You can then use the features of the wordprocessing software to enhance the appearance of the statement using format styles that are consistent with the remainder of the report. If you have exported a spreadsheet file, you can use the spreadsheet program to perform additional calculations. Then you can save the modified report as a text file to be incorporated in a wordprocessing report.

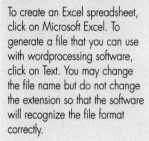

Notes

To create an Excel spreadsheet, click on Microsoft Excel. To generate a file that you can use with wordprocessing software, click on Text. You may change the file name but do not change the extension so that the software will recognize the file format correctly.

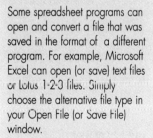

Notes

Some spreadsheet programs can open and convert a file that was saved in the format of a different program. For example, Microsoft Excel can open (or save) text files or Lotus 1-2-3 files. Simply choose the alternative file type in your Open File (or Save File) window.

When working with a spreadsheet program such as Lotus 1-2-3 or Microsoft Excel, you can use the calculation capabilities of the spreadsheet program to make comparisons between statements from different financial periods. You might also want to use the charting or graphing features to prepare presentation materials.

Exporting reports offers advantages over re-creating the statements. Not only do you save the time of re-typing, you also ensure greater accuracy by avoiding errors made while re-typing the numbers and accounts.

INSTRUCTIONS FOR SOURCE DOCUMENTS

Instructions for October

1. Using the Chart of Accounts and other information provided, enter the transactions for the month of October.

2. Print the following:

   a. the General Journal entries for the month of October
   b. the Customer Detail report for all customers for the month of October
   c. the General Ledger account reports for:
      • Cash in Bank
      • Revenue from Sales
      • Sales Returns and Allowances
   d. Vendor Purchases Summary for Cambridge Castings, all categories for October.

3. Export the Balance Sheet as at October 31, 1999 to a spreadsheet application.

4. Calculate the following key ratios in your spreadsheet:
   a. current ratio
   b. quick ratio.

5. Based on expenses and revenues for the month of October, set up a budget for use in November and December.

Instructions for November

1. Using the Chart of Accounts and other information provided, enter the transactions for the month of November.

2. Print the following reports:

   a. the General Journal entries for the month of November
   b. the Vendor Detail Report for all vendors for the month of November
   c. the Employee Summary report for all employees for the pay period ending November 30, 1999
   d. the Inventory Synopsis Report (observe and report items that have not sold well over the two-month period)
   e. Customer Sales Summary (all customers, items and categories) for November.

3. Export the Comparative Balance Sheet for October 31 and November 30, 1999 to a spreadsheet application. You will use these at the end of the year for three-month comparisons.

4. Compare November's performance against October's budget forecast.

Instructions for December

1. Using the Chart of Accounts and other information provided, enter the transactions for the month of December.

2. Print the following reports:

   a. the General Journal entries for the month of December
   b. a Trial Balance, Balance Sheet and Income Statement on December 31
   c. Project Summary report for Highlife Townhouse (all accounts) for December
   d. Inventory Activity report for Fireplaces and Inserts, (all journals) for December.

3. Export the Balance Sheet and Income Statement to a spreadsheet application. Combine the Balance Sheet with the comparative one for October and November. Compare first and second quarter figures, item by item, to assess the performance of Hearth House.

4. Print T4 slips and the cumulative year-to-date 1999 payroll information for each employee.

5. Make a backup copy of your Data Disk before you proceed with this step. Advance the using date to January 1, 2000. Print the Trial Balance, Balance Sheet and Income Statement for January 1, 2000. Compare the end of December and the first of January statements and note the changes that result from Simply Accounting closing the books for the new fiscal period.

Source Documents

USING DATE — October 7

Cash Receipt #100
Dated Oct. 1/99
From Brookhaven Funeral Home, cheque #77 for $3 450 in full payment of account. Reference invoice #HH-110.

Cash Sales Invoice #HH-120
Dated Oct. 2/99
To L. Gien

1 Ceram Log set: Laurentian Birch LBF4	$ 400
1 Firescreen: brass arch shape	250
1 Door: Pinnacle Arch w/damper 2wf	1 000
Goods & Services Tax	7%
Provincial Sales Tax	8%

Paid by Visa #4518 672 881 875.

Cash Receipt #101
Dated Oct. 3/99
From University Alumni House, cheque #337 for $2 049.30 in full payment of account including #20.70 discount for early payment. Reference invoice #HH-117.

Cheque Copy #300
Dated Oct. 3/99
To Cambridge Castings, $4 152.46 in full payment of account, including $84.74 discount taken for early payment. Reference invoice #CC-818.

❑ Stacie's Sports Bar (contact Stacie Ball) is located at:
6 Raptor Cres.
Toronto, ON M4E 3Y6
Tel: (416) 923-6719
Fax: (416) 923-9911
Credit Limit: $10 000

❑ Sales Invoice #HH-121
Dated Oct. 3/99
To Stacie's Sports Bar (new customer)

1 CC: Fireplace gas ins DV32HET	$2 800
1 SF: Fireplace gas ins tp-vnt DV30TV	1 500
2 Basic installation jobs	450 /job
2 Insulating chimney jobs	100 /job
Goods & Services Tax	7%
Provincial Sales Tax	8%

Terms: 1/5, n/10 days.

❑ Purchase Invoice #OS-6431
Dated Oct. 4/99
From Overload Office Supplies, $150 for supplies plus $10.50 GST and $12.00 PST. Purchase invoice total $172.50. Terms: net 10 days.

❑ Cash Sales Invoice #HH-122
Dated Oct. 5/99
To Arlene Hope

1 VS: Fireplace pellet stove VPS1000	$2 200
1 Basic installation job	450
1 Insulating chimney job	100
Goods & Services Tax	7%
Provincial Sales Tax	8%

Paid by MasterCard #5623 7765 7109 3411.

❑ Memo #1
Dated Oct. 6/99
From Manager to Store Assistant: Adjust inventory records for one Thermostat: standard valued at $70 and broken beyond repair. Charge to account 5080 Damaged Inventory.

❑ Cash Receipt #102
Dated Oct. 7/99
From Rosedale Estates, cheque #31 for $3 680 in full payment of account. Reference invoice #HH-115.

USING DATE — October 14

❑ Cheque Copy #301
Dated Oct. 8/99
To Therma Glow, $1 761.65 in full payment of account including $35.95 discount taken for early payment. Reference invoice #TG-1421.

❑ Cheque Copy #302
Dated Oct. 9/99
To Matchless Flame, $2 140 in full payment of account. Reference invoice #MF-1201.

Sales Invoice #HH-123
Dated Oct. 10/99
To Lakeshore Condos

1 CC: Fireplace free-std gas DV30DVT	$3 000
1 TG: Fireplace gas ins bay BVDV30T	2 300
1 Mantel: marble MM-DVT40 kit	1 800
2 Basic installation jobs	450 /job
Goods & Services Tax	7%
Provincial Sales Tax	8%

Terms: 1/5, n/10 days.

Sales Invoice #HH-124
Dated Oct. 12/99
To University Alumni House

3 Remote controls: economy RCE-100	$ 120 each
3 MF: Fireplaces gas ins DV30HE	2 000 each
3 Mantels: oak MO-DVT30 kit	1 000 /kit
3 Basic installation - plus jobs	500 /job
3 Customizing inserts jobs	300 /job
Goods & Services Tax	7%
Provincial Sales Tax	8%

Terms: 1/5, n/10 days.

Purchase Order #1
Dated Oct. 13/99
Shipping Date October 20, 1999
From Vulcan Stove

1 VS: Fireplace pellet stove VPS1000	$1 320.00
2 Mantels: marble MM-DVT40 kits	2 160.00
3 Mantels: oak MO-DVT30 kits	1 950.00
Goods & Services Tax	380.10
	$5 810.10

Purchase Order #2
Dated Oct. 13/99
Shipping Date October 22, 1999
From Matchless Flame

1 MF: Fireplace gas ins slim DV20SL	$ 720.00
2 MF: Fireplace gas ins DV30HE	2 500.00
1 MF: Fireplace gas ins DV27TVT	1 170.00
1 Door: Mirage w/damper 2.75wf	540.00
1 Door: Pinnacle Arch w/damper 2wf	600.00
Goods & Services Tax	387.10
	$5 917.10

Cash Receipt #103
Dated Oct. 13/99
From Stacie's Sports Bar, cheque #103 for $6 210 in full payment of account. Reference invoice #HH-121.

Cheque Copy #303
Dated Oct. 13/99
To Overload Office Supplies, $172.50 in full payment of account. Reference invoice #OS-6431.

EMPLOYEE TIME SUMMARY SHEET #20

(pay period ending October 14, 1999)

Name of Employee	Week 41 Hours	Week 42 Hours	Regular Hours	Overtime Hours
☐ Kris Kindl	40	40	80	–

a. Using Employee Time Summary Sheet #20 and Employee Information Sheet, complete payroll for hourly employee.
b. Kindl will receive an additional $250 advance for emergency purposes. His next five paycheques will recover $50 each for the advance.
c. Issue cheque #304.

USING DATE — October 15

☐ Cheque Copy #305
Dated Oct. 15/99
To Penguin Insulating Co., $428 in payment of account. Reference invoice #PI-901.

☐ Memo #2
Dated Oct. 15/99
From Manager: Using the Employee Information Sheet, prepare payroll for Dana Damper, the store assistant, for the pay period ending October 15, 1999. Issue cheque #306.

Memo #3
Dated Oct. 15/99
From Manager: Refer to September 30 General Ledger balances. For audit and internal control purposes:

Notes

- You may wish to record these payments as cash purchases.
- You may prefer to use the September 30 Balance Sheet to check the amounts for these liabilities.

☐ Record GST Owing for September as a liability owing to the Receiver General of Canada and issue cheque #307 for $1 680 in payment.
☐ Record EI, CPP and Income Tax Payable for September as a liability owing to the Receiver General of Canada and issue cheque #308 for $3 654.91 in payment.
☐ Record EHT Payable for the past three months as a liability owing to the Treasurer of Ontario and issue cheque #309 for $324.38 in payment.
☐ Record PST Payable for September as a liability owing to the Treasurer of Ontario and issue cheque #310 for $4 560 in payment. Remember to reduce PST by 5% sales tax commission.
☐ Record RRS-Plan Payable for September as a liability owing to Standard Insurance Co. and issue cheque #311 for $450 in payment.
☐ Record CSB-Plan Payable for September as a liability owing to Transcend Investment Co. and issue cheque #312 for $450 in payment.
☐ Record Group Insurance Payable for September as a liability owing to Standard Insurance Co. and issue cheque #313 for $35 in payment.
☐ Record WCB Payable for the past three months as a liability owing to the Workers' Compensation Board and issue cheque #314 for $889.52 in payment

☐ Purchase Invoice #PI-1082
Dated Oct. 16/99
From Penguin Insulating Co., $300 for insulation supplies plus $21 GST.
Purchase invoice total $321. Store this entry because it is a standing monthly
order. Terms: net 15 days.

☐ Sales Invoice #HH-125
Dated Oct. 16/99
To Max Polisena (new customer)

1 TG: Fireplace gas ins multi MSDV45T	$2 800
1 CC: Fireplace gas ins DV32HET	2 800
1 Mantel: marble MM-DVT40 kit	1 800
1 Mantel: tile MT-DVT30 kit	800
2 Remote controls: luxury RCL-1000	180 each
2 Basic installation - plus jobs	500 /job
Goods & Services Tax	7%
Provincial Sales Tax	8%

Terms: 1/5, n/10 days.

☐ Cash Receipt #104
Dated Oct. 17/99
From University Alumni House, cheque #378 for $13 388.76 in payment of account
including $135.24 discount for early payment. Reference invoice #HH-124.

☐ Cash Sales Invoice #HH-126
Dated Oct. 17/99
To Maria Andersson

1 CC: Fireplace coal CC200FS	$1 800
1 Mantel: cherry MC-DVT40 kit	1 200
1 Toolset: glass handle/cast iron	400
1 Grate: cast iron black	150
1 Basic installation job	450
Goods & Services Tax	7%
Provincial Sales Tax	8%

Paid by Visa #4104 627 115 825.

☐ Cash Purchase Invoice #TS-31432
Dated Oct. 18/99
From Toronto Star, $400 for advertising over the next twenty weeks plus $28
GST and $32 PST. Purchase invoice total $460. Terms: cash on receipt. Issued
cheque #315 in payment.

☐ Cash Receipt #105
Dated Oct. 20/99
From Lakeshore Condos, cheque #167 for $9 200 in full payment of account.
Reference invoice #HH-123.

Notes

☐ Max Polisena is located at:
45 Fieldstone Rd.
Toronto, ON M3F 4S2
Tel: (416) 662-7165
Fax: (416) 662-6611
Credit Limit: $12 000

Cash Sales Invoice #HH-127
Dated Oct. 21/99
To Terry Fuller

1 MF: Fireplace gas ins DV27TVT	$1 950
1 Mantel: cherry MC-DVT40 kit	1 200
1 Heater: vintage 50,000BTU ADVSH-50	850
3 Basic installation jobs	450 /job
1 Customizing inserts job	300
Goods & Services Tax	7%
Provincial Sales Tax	8%

Paid by certified cheque #SB-6712.

Purchase Invoice #MF-1283
Dated Oct. 21/99
Received from Matchless Flame to fill PO #2

1 MF: Fireplace gas ins slim DV20SL	$ 720.00
2 MF: Fireplace gas ins DV30HE	2 500.00
1 MF: Fireplace gas ins DV27TVT	1 170.00
1 Door: Mirage w/damper 2.75wf	540.00
1 Door: Pinnacle Arch w/damper 2wf	600.00
Goods & Services Tax	387.10
	$5 917.10

Terms: net 15 days.

Notes

☐ Create new account 5055 COGS Variance (Left column). When prompted in the Purchases Journal entry, select this new variance account.

Cash Purchase Invoice #TH-6392
Dated Oct. 21/99
From Toronto Hydro, $110 for hydro services plus $7.70 GST. Purchase invoice total $117.70. Terms: cash on receipt. Issued cheque #316 in payment.

USING DATE — October 28

Cash Sales Invoice #HH-128
Dated Oct. 22/99
To Nicole Harbon

1 Ceram Log: Birdseye Maple set BMF5	$ 550
1 Door: Mirage w/damper 2.75wf	900
1 Toolset: brass handle solid	300
1 Grill: rotisserie & spit DX-80	1 300
1 Thermostat: standard	140
1 Woodholder: mhg	80
Goods & Services Tax	7%
Provincial Sales Tax	8%

Paid by certified cheque #SB-9432.

Cash Purchase Invoice #BC-43293
Dated Oct. 22/99
From Bell Canada, $50 for telephone services plus $3.50 GST and $4.00 PST. Purchase invoice total $57.50. Terms: cash on receipt. Issued cheque #317 in payment.

Notes

When prompted in the Purchases Journal entry, select the variance account 5055.

Purchase Invoice #VS-813
Dated Oct. 22/99
Received from Vulcan Stove to fill PO #1

1 VS: Fireplace pellet stove VPS1000	$1 320.00
2 Mantels: marble MM-DVT40 kits	2 160.00
3 Mantels: oak MO-DVT30 kits	1 950.00
Goods & Services Tax	380.10
	$5 810.10

Terms: net 30 days.

Realty Tax Bill #T1999-4
Dated Oct. 23/99
From City Treasurer, $750 for quarterly property tax assessment. Terms: EOM.

Cash Sales Invoice #HH-129
Dated Oct. 24/99
To Jason Palmer

1 Grill: mobile/side burner DL-60	$1 100
1 Firescreen: brass accent rect	200
2 Andiron sets: cast iron set	100 /set
1 CC: Fireplace wood WC100FS	1 800
1 Toolset: glass handle/cast iron	400
Goods & Services Tax	7%
Provincial Sales Tax	8%

Paid by cheque #39 (certified).

Cash Receipt #106
Dated Oct. 25/99
From Max Polisena, cheque #208 for $10 994 in full payment of account.
Reference invoice #HH-125

Cheque Copy #318
Dated Oct. 26/99
To Vulcan Stove Co., $706.20 in payment of account. Reference invoice #VS-699.

Cheque Copy #319
Dated Oct. 27/99
To City Treasurer, $750 in full payment of property tax assessment. Reference realty bill #T1999-4.

Cash Sales Invoice #HH-130
Dated Oct. 28/99
To Polly Singh

1 SF: Fireplace gas ins bay DV30BWT	$1 800
1 MF: Fireplace gas ins slim DV20SL	1 200
2 Basic installation - plus jobs	500 /job
2 Customizing inserts jobs	300 /job
2 Insulating chimney jobs	100 /job
Goods & Services Tax	7%
Provincial Sales Tax	8%

Paid by MasterCard #4620 6154 2829 4914.

☐ Purchase Invoice #CC-960
Dated Oct. 28/99
From Cambridge Castings

1 CC: Fireplace coal CC200FS	$1 080.00
1 CC: Fireplace free-std gas DV30DVT	1 800.00
2 CC: Fireplace gas ins DV32HET	3 360.00
1 CC: Fireplace wood WC100FS	1 080.00
1 Ceram Log: Birdseye Maple set BMF5	350.00
1 Ceram Log: Georgian Oak set GOF4	270.00
2 Ceram Log: Laurentian Birch sets LBF4	500.00
Freight	50.00
Goods & Services Tax	594.30
	$9 084.30

Terms: 2/10, net 15 days.

EMPLOYEE TIME SUMMARY SHEET #21

(pay period ending October 28, 1999)

Name of Employee	Week 43 Hours	Week 44 Hours	Regular Hours	Overtime Hours
☐ Kris Kindl	42	40	80	2

a. Using Employee Time Summary Sheet #21 and Employee Information Sheet, complete payroll for hourly employee.
b. Remember to recover $50 advance.
c. Issue cheque #320.

USING DATE — October 31

☐ Cash Sales Invoice #HH-131
Dated Oct. 29/99
To Siva Lingam

1 Ceram Log: Georgian Oak set GOF4	$450
1 Ceram Log: Laurentian Birch set LBF4	400
1 Door: Apparition w/damper 2.5wf	800
1 Door: Viewzone w/damper 1.5wf	650
2 Thermostats: standard	140 each
Goods & Services Tax	7%
Provincial Sales Tax	8%

Paid by Visa #4502 629 538 214.

☐ Credit Invoice #HH-127C
Dated Oct. 29/99
To Terry Fuller, $100 allowance for scratched cherry mantel kit. Issued cheque #321.

Notes

Treat the allowance as a cash purchase using Sales Returns & Allowances as the account. This will credit the Cash in Bank account.

☐ Purchase Invoice #TG-1447
Dated Oct. 29/99
From Therma Glow

1 TG: Fireplace gas ins bay BVDV30T	$1 380.00
1 TG: Fireplace gas ins multi MSDV45T	1 680.00
Goods & Services Tax	214.20
	$3 274.20

Terms: 2/10, net 20 days.

☐ Bank Debit Memo #6343172
Dated Oct. 30/99
From Royal Bank, for $2 500. This amount includes $250 for the reduction of principal on mortgage and $2 250 interest.

☐ Bank Debit Memo #6343173
Dated Oct. 30/99
From Royal Bank, for $2 400. This amount includes $2 100 for the reduction of principal on bank loan and $300 interest.

☐ Purchase Invoice #SF-927
Dated Oct. 30/99
From Starfire Fireplaces

1 SF: Fireplace gas ins bay DV30BWT	$1 080.00
1 SF: Fireplace gas ins tp-vnt DV30TV	900.00
1 Grill: mobile/side burner DL-60	660.00
1 Grill: rotisserie & spit DX-80	780.00
Goods & Services Tax	239.40
	$3 659.40

Terms: net 20 days.

☐ Cheque Copy #322
Dated Oct. 31/99
To Penguin Insulating, $321 in full payment of account. Reference invoice #PI-1082

☐☐ Memo #4
Dated Oct. 31/99
From Manager: Using the Employee Information Sheet, prepare payroll for salaried employees, Damper and Cinder, the store assistant and manager, for the pay period ending October 31. Issue cheques #323 and #324.

☐ Materials Summary Form #10
Dated Oct. 31/99
Re: Insulation and Hardware supplies: A physical count of materials inventory used for job orders indicated the following:
    Insulation used $150
    Hardware used $75
Make the necessary asset adjustments and expense charges.

☐ Cash Sales Invoice #HH-132
Dated Nov. 2/99
To Joanna Severino

1 VS: Fireplace pellet stove VPS1000	$2 200
1 Toolset: glass handle/cast iron	400
1 Ceram Log: Tobermory Ash set TAF5	480
1 Door: Apparition w/damper 2.5wf	800
1 Mantel: marble MM-DVT40 kit	1 800
1 Basic installation job	450
Goods & Services Tax	7%
Provincial Sales Tax	8%

Paid by Visa #4164 729 651 641.

☐ Cash Sales Invoice #HH-133
Dated Nov. 3/99
To Crystal Waters

1 Ceram Log: Birdseye Maple set BMF5	$ 550
1 Door: Pinnacle Arch w/damper 2wf	1 000
1 Toolset: brass handle solid	300
1 Thermostat: standard	140
Goods & Services Tax	7%
Provincial Sales Tax	8%

Paid by MasterCard #4398 6101 3725 1846.

Notes

☐ Railside Equipment (Contact Ray Bannister) is located at 444 Railside Drive East York, ON M7T 3V2 Tel: (416) 772-7210 Fax: (416) 772-7100

☐ Purchase Invoice #RE-947
Dated Nov. 4/99
From Railside Equipment (new vendor), $1 000 for new installation equipment plus $70 GST and $80 PST. Purchase invoice total $1 150. Terms: net 30 days.

☐ Purchase Invoice #CC-1005
Dated Nov. 5/99
From Cambridge Castings

4 CC: Fireplace gas ins DV32HET	$6 720.00
Freight	30.00
Goods & Services Tax	472.50
	$7 222.50

Terms: 2/10, net 15 days.

☐ Sales Invoice #HH-134
Dated Nov. 6/99
To Brookhaven Funeral Home

1 TG: Fireplace gas ins multi MSDV45T	$2 800
1 SF: Fireplace gas ins bay DV30BWT	1 800
2 Remote controls: luxury RCL-1000	180 each
2 Basic installation jobs	450 /job
2 Customizing inserts jobs	300 /job
2 Insulating chimney jobs	100 /job
Goods & Services Tax	7%
Provincial Sales Tax	8%

Terms: 1/5, net 10 days.

☐ Cheque Copy #325
Dated Nov. 6/99
To Matchless Flame, $5 917.10 in full payment of account. Reference invoice #MF-1283.

Sales Invoice #HH-135
Dated Nov. 7/99
To Scarlett Road Condos

4 CC: Fireplace gas ins DV32HET	$2 800 each
4 Basic installation jobs	450 /job
4 Insulating chimney jobs	100 /job
Goods & Services Tax	7%
Provincial Sales Tax	8%

Terms: 1/5, net 10 days.

Cheque Copy #326
Dated Nov. 7/99
To Cambridge Castings, $8 902.61 in payment of account including $181.69 discount taken for early payment. Reference invoice #CC-960.

USING DATE — November 11

Insert the following new inventory records:

Code	Item Description	Selling Price	Min Qty
GR03	Grill: stainless steel deluxe M700	$1 400 each	0
GR04	Grill: stainless stl built-in M900	1 750 each	0

Asset account: 1430   Revenue account: 4020   Expense account: 5050
Variance account: 5055

Notes

Hickory Grills (Contact Barb Eekew) is located at:
445 Nutley St.
Toronto, ON M6G 2B6
Tel: (416) 781-5284
Fax: (416) 788-6666

Purchase Invoice #HG-751
Dated Nov. 9/99
From Hickory Grills (new vendor)

1 Grill: stainless steel deluxe M700	$1 000.00
1 Grill: stainless stl built-in M900	1 250.00
Goods & Services Tax	157.50
	$2 407.50

Terms: 2/5, net 10 days.

Cash Receipt #107
Dated Nov. 10/99
From Brookhaven Funeral Home, cheque #123 for $7 582.41 in full payment of account, including $76.59 discount for early payment. Reference invoice #HH-134.

Notes

To issue vacation pay, turn off the Retain Vacation setting in the Payroll Ledger for Kindl before preparing the paycheque (see page 385). Remember to turn on the setting again so that future vacation pay will be retained.

EMPLOYEE TIME SUMMARY SHEET #22

(pay period ending November 11, 1999)

Name of Employee	Week 45 Hours	Week 46 Hours	Regular Hours	Overtime Hours
Kris Kindl	40	40	80	—

a. Using Employee Time Summary Sheet #22 and Employee Information Sheet, complete payroll for hourly employee.
b. Remember to recover $50 advance.
c. Kindl will take a two-week vacation and his vacation pay should be released. Issue a separate cheque for the vacation pay. A new employee will be hired immediately to replace him during vacation and to help with the increasing workload after his return.
d. Issue cheques #327 and #328.

Memo #5
Dated Nov. 11/99
From Manager: Add a new employee record for MyTee Strong
Ms Strong lives at   454 Merlin Cres.
                        Toronto, ON M7T 3R1

Telephone	(416) 569-5612
SIN	499 312 761
Birthdate	Feb. 3, 1959
WCB rate:	4.97

MyTee Strong, an experienced gas fitter and installer, is single and self-supporting (Federal claim amount is $6 456). She will begin work immediately, replacing Kindl who is on vacation, and continue working for the store after Kindl returns since Hearth House expects to be successful in its present bid for work on a new building complex to be completed in December. She will begin working at $18 per hour for regular hours and $27 for overtime work, receiving her pay every two weeks. Her salary will be reviewed after a six month probationary period. Vacation pay at the rate of 6% will be retained until she takes vacation time off. Strong has chosen to participate in the savings and insurance plans that Hearth House offers, paying $50 each pay period for RRSP and CSB contributions and $5 per period for group insurance.

USING DATE — November 15

Cheque Copy #329
Dated Nov. 14/99
To Hickory Grills, $2 359.35 in full payment of account, taking advantage of the $48.15 discount for early payment. Reference invoice #HG-751.

Cash Sales Invoice #HH-136
Dated Nov. 15/99
To Oskar Werner

1 Grill: stainless stl built-in M900	$1 750
1 Ceram Log: Algonquin Maple set AMF5	500
1 Door: Viewzone w/damper 1.5wf	650
Goods & Services Tax	7%
Provincial Sales Tax	8%

Paid by cheque #373.

Memo #6
Dated Nov. 15/99
From Manager: Using the Employee Information Sheet, prepare payroll for Damper for the pay period ending November 15. Issue cheque #330.

Memo #7
Dated Nov. 15/99
From Manager: Refer to previous end-of-month (October 31) General Ledger account balances to record liabilities and payments to the following agencies.

Notes

You may prefer to use the October 31 Balance Sheet to check the amounts for these liabilities.

Issue cheque #331 for GST owing to the Receiver General of Canada.
Issue cheque #332 for EI, CPP and Income Tax Payable owing to the Receiver General of Canada.
Issue cheque #333 for PST Payable owing to the Treasurer of Ontario. Remember to take the 5% sales tax commission.
Issue cheque #334 for RRS-Plan Payable owing to Standard Insurance Co.
Issue cheque #335 for CSB-Plan Payable owing to Transcend Investment Co.
Issue cheque #336 for Group Insurance Payable to Standard Insurance Co.

☐ Cheque Copy #337
Dated Nov. 15/99
To Cambridge Castings, $7 078.05 in full payment of account including $144.45 discount for early payment. Reference invoice #CC-1005.

USING DATE — November 21

☐ Purchase Invoice #PI-1139
Dated Nov. 16/99
From Penguin Insulating Co., $350 for insulation supplies plus $24.50 GST. Purchase invoice total $374.50. Recall and edit the stored entry. Store the new invoice because future purchases will also be for the larger quantity. Terms: net 15 days.

☐ Purchase Invoice #MF-1291
Dated Nov. 17/99
From Matchless Flame

3 MF: Fireplace gas ins slim DV20SL	$2 160.00
Goods & Services Tax	151.20
	$2 311.20

Terms: 2/5, net 10 days.

☐ Sales Invoice #HH-137
Dated Nov. 17/99
To Walden Apartments

3 MF: Fireplace gas ins slim DV20SL	$1 200 each
3 Basic installation jobs	450 /job
3 Customizing inserts jobs	300 /job
3 Insulating chimney jobs	100 /job
Goods & Services Tax	7%
Provincial Sales Tax	8%

Terms: 1/5, net 10 days.

☐ Cash Receipt #108
Dated Nov. 17/99
From Scarlett Road Condos, certified cheque #CIB6431 for $15 410 in full payment of account. Reference invoice #HH-135.

☐ Cheque Copy #338
Dated Nov. 18/99
To Therma Glow, $3 274.20 in payment of account. Reference invoice #TG-1447.

☐ Cheque Copy #339
Dated Nov. 19/99
To Starfire Fireplaces, $3 659.40 in full payment of account. Reference invoice #SF-927.

☐ Cash Purchase Invoice #BC-51239
Dated Nov. 21/99
From Bell Canada, $50 for telephone services plus $3.50 GST and $4.00 PST. Purchase invoice total $57.50. Issued cheque #340 in payment.

☐ Cash Purchase Invoice #TH-8497
Dated Nov. 21/99
From Toronto Hydro, $100 for hydro services plus $7 GST. Purchase invoice total $107. Issued cheque #341 in payment.

◻ Cheque Copy #342
Dated Nov. 21/99
To Vulcan Stove, $5 810.10 in payment of account. Reference invoice #VS-813.

USING DATE — November 25

◻ Cash Sales Invoice #HH-138
Dated Nov. 22/99
To Veronica England

1 MF: Fireplace gas ins DV27TVT	$1 950
1 Mantel: oak MO-DVT30 kit	1 000
1 Customizing inserts job	300
1 Basic installation - plus job	500
Goods & Services Tax	7%
Provincial Sales Tax	8%

Paid by Visa #4502 361 291 642.

◻ Purchase Invoice #PH-36914
Dated Nov. 23/99
From Power Hardware, $150 for installation hardware supplies plus $10.50 GST.
Purchase invoice total $160.50. Terms: net 10 days.

◻ Cash Sales Invoice #HH-139
Dated Nov. 23/99
To Trevor Bullen

1 Mantel: marble MM-DVT40 kit	$1 800
1 Ceram Log: Algonquin Maple set AMF5	500
1 Door: Quest w/damper custom 2wf	750
1 Insulating chimney job	100
1 Grill: rotisserie & spit DX80	1 300
Goods & Services Tax	7%
Provincial Sales Tax	8%

Paid by certified cheque #RB-7726.

◻ Cash Sales Invoice #HH-140
Dated Nov. 24/99
To Gary Tsumura

1 CC: Fireplace coal CC200FS	$1 800
1 Mantel: oak MO-DVT30 kit	1 000
1 Heater: vintage 30,000BTU ADVSH-30	750
1 Firescreen: iron black accent rect	150
Goods & Services Tax	7%
Provincial Sales Tax	8%

Paid by certified cheque #SB-19962.

◻ Purchase Invoice #RS-574
Dated Nov. 24/99
From Rudy's Sunoco (new vendor), $200 for repairs and maintenance on
vehicles plus $14 GST and $16 PST. Purchase invoice total $230. Terms: net
30 days.

◻ Cash Receipt #109
Dated Nov. 25/99
From Walden Apartments, certified cheque #RB-69912 for $7 072.50 in full
payment of account. Reference invoice #HH-137.

Notes

◻ Rudy's Sunoco (Contact
Rudy Mekkanik) is located at
21 Oiler St.
Toronto, ON M4H 3F9
Tel: (416) 822-8101
Fax: (416) 822-8800

EMPLOYEE TIME SUMMARY SHEET #23				
(pay period ending November 25, 1999)				
Name of Employee	Week 47 Hours	Week 48 Hours	Regular Hours	Overtime Hours
☐ MyTee Strong	40	40	80	–

a. Using Employee Time Summary Sheet #23 and Employee Information Sheet, complete payroll for hourly employee.
b. Issue cheque #343.

☐ Purchase Invoice #VS-914
Dated Nov. 25/99
From Vulcan Stove

1 VS: Fireplace pellet stove VPS1000	$1 320.00
2 Mantels: cherry MC-DVT40 kits	1 440.00
2 Mantels: marble MM-DVT40 kits	2 160.00
2 Mantels: oak MO-DVT30 kits	1 300.00
Goods & Services Tax	435.40
	$6 655.40

Terms: net 30 days.

USING DATE — November 30

☐ Cash Sales Invoice #HH-141
Dated Nov. 26/99
To Shereen Ahmed

1 TG: Fireplace gas ins bay BVDV30T	$2 300
1 Heater: vintage 20,000BTU ADVSH-20	500
1 Mantel: marble MM-DVT40 kit	1 800
1 Basic installation job	450
1 Customizing inserts job	300
Subcontracting work on marble	250
Goods & Services Tax	7%
Provincial Sales Tax	8%

Paid by Visa #4110 636 352 188.

Notes

Revenue for subcontracting work should be credited to Revenue from Services.

☐ Cash Purchase Invoice #MM-1347
Dated Nov. 27/99
From Missoni Marbleworks (new vendor), $250 for marble work completed for Shereen Ahmed plus $17.50 GST and $20 PST. Purchase invoice total $287.50. Terms: cash on receipt. Issued cheque #344 in payment.

☐ Purchase Invoice #CC-1320
Dated Nov. 28/99
From Cambridge Castings

1 CC: Fireplace coal CC200FS	$1 080.00
1 CC: Fireplacc free-std gas DV30DVT	1 800.00
2 Ceram Log: Birdseye Maple sets BMF5	700.00
2 Ceram Log: Georgian Oak sets GOF4	540.00
2 Ceram Log: Laurentian Birch sets LBF4	500.00
2 Firescreens: brass accent rect	200.00
Freight	50.00
Goods & Services Tax	340.90
	$5 210.90

Terms: 2/10, net 15 days.

Notes

☐ Missoni Marbleworks
(Contact Petra Missoni)
is located at
67 Stonehenge Ave.
Toronto, ON M8D 1C7
Tel: (416) 923-6291
Fax: (416) 923-0011
☐ Create new account
5380 Subcontracting Fees

☐ Purchase Invoice #MF-1401
   Dated Nov. 28/99
   From Matchless Flame

1 MF: Fireplace gas ins DV27TVT	$1 170.00
2 Doors: Apparition w/damper 2.5wf	960.00
1 Door: Charade w/damper 1wf	360.00
1 Door: Pinnacle Arch w/damper 2wf	600.00
1 Door: Quest w/damper custom 2wf	450.00
2 Doors: Viewzone w/damper 1.5wf	780.00
Goods & Services Tax	302.40
	$4 622.40

Terms: net 15 days.

☐ Purchase Invoice #TG-1601
   Dated Nov. 29/99
   From Therma Glow

1 TG: Fireplace gas ins bay BVDV30T	$1 380.00
1 TG: Fireplace gas ins multi MSDV45T	1 680.00
Goods & Services Tax	214.20
	$3 274.20

Terms: 2/10, net 20 days.

☐ Purchase Invoice #SF-1009
   Dated Nov. 30/99
   From Starfire Fireplaces

1 SF: Fireplace gas ins bay DV30BWT	$1 080.00
1 Grill: mobile/side burner DL-60	660.00
1 Grill: rotisserie & spit DX80	780.00
Goods & Services Tax	176.40
	$2 696.40

Terms: net 20 days.

☐ Bank Debit Memo #7214153
   Dated Nov. 30/99
   From Royal Bank, for $2 400. This amount includes $2 125 for the reduction of
   principal on bank loan and $275 interest.

☐ Bank Debit Memo #7214154
   Dated Nov. 30/99
   From Royal Bank, for $2 500. This amount includes $275 for the reduction of
   principal on mortgage and $2 225 interest.

☐ Cash Sales Invoice #HH-142
   Dated Nov. 30/99
   To Kevin O'Casey

1 Mantel: cherry MC-DVT40 kit	$1 200
1 CC: Fireplace free-std gas DV30DVT	3 000
1 Grill: mobile/side burner DL-60	1 100
Goods & Services Tax	7%
Provincial Sales Tax	8%

   Paid by Visa #4516 779 553 227.

Memo #8
Dated Nov. 30/99
From Manager: Using the Employee Information Sheet, prepare payroll for the salaried employees, Damper and Cinder, for the pay period ending November 30. Issue cheques #345 and #346.

Materials Summary Form #11
Dated Nov. 30/99
Re: Insulation and Hardware supplies: A physical count of materials inventory used for job orders indicated the following:
    Insulation used $500
    Hardware used $100
Make the necessary asset adjustments and expense charges.

Cheque Copy #347
Dated Nov. 30/99
To Penguin Insulating, $374.50 in full payment of account. Reference invoice #PI-1139

Notes

The default Setting, distributing amounts by percentage is correct. Remember to turn on the warning for incomplete distributions in the Distributions Settings. Refer to page 364 if you need further assistance.

Memo #9
Dated Nov. 30/99
The manger of Hearth House has negotiated a project with the management at Highlife Townhouses to install ten new fireplaces in the ten townhouse units. The work will be completed over two weeks in the month of December.
After some discussion, the owner and manager decided to record the revenue and costs of this project separately from the general sales from the store. Create the two projects that are needed for December's revenue and costs:
• General Sales Project for regular store sales and services to customers
• Highlife Townhouse Project for the large contract just negotiated.
A special discount of 10 percent was agreed upon as an incentive to get the Highlife contract. A credit invoice will be issued with each sales invoice (one sales invoice per week) to account for the discount. All revenue and costs will be allocated as indicated in the source document transactions.

USING DATE — December 7

Purchase Invoice #MF-1439
Dated Dec. 1/99
From Matchless Flame

10 MF: Fireplace gas ins DV30HE	$12 500.00
Goods & Services Tax	875.00
	$13 375.00

Terms: net 15 days.

Cheque Copy #348
Dated Dec. 2/99
To Matchless Flame, $2 311.20 in payment of account. Reference invoice #MF-1291.

Cheque Copy #349
Dated Dec. 3/99
To Power Hardware, $160.50 in full payment of account. Reference invoice #PH-36914.

Cheque Copy #350
Dated Dec. 4/99
To Railside Equipment, $1 150 in full payment of account. Reference invoice #RE-947.

Sales Invoice #HH-143
Dated Dec. 5/99
To York Seniors' Club

1 SF: Fireplace gas ins bay DV30BWT	$1 800
1 TG: Fireplace gas ins bay BVDV30T	2 300
2 Mantels: oak MO-DVT30 kits	1 000 /kit
2 Basic installation jobs	450 /job
2 Woodholders: mhg	80 each
Goods & Services Tax	7%
Provincial Sales Tax	8%

Terms: 1/5, net 10 days.
Allocate 100% of revenue and costs to General Sales Project.

Notes

Use the Revenue from Sales account because this is not a return. You may enter this transaction as a negative sale for the two items or as a Sales Adjusting Entry.

Credit Invoice #HH-143C
Dated Dec. 6/99
To York Seniors' Club

–2 Woodholders: mhg	$80 each
Goods & Services Tax	7%
Provincial Sales Tax	8%

The customer did not purchase these items (Woodholders are not required for gas fireplaces). They were incorrectly included in invoice.
Allocate 100% of costs to General Sales Project.

Cheque Copy #351
Dated Dec. 6/99
To Cambridge Castings, $5 106.68 in full payment of account including $104.22 discount taken for early payment. Reference invoice #CC-1320.

Notes

☐ Highlife Townhouses (Contact Marcel Hauteville) is located at
999 Skyview Rd.
Toronto, ON M6R 3F3
Tel: (416) 882-0123
Fax: (416) 882-8888
Credit Limit: $20 000

Sales Invoice #HH-144
Dated Dec. 7/99
To Highlife Townhouses (new customer)

5 MF: Fireplace gas ins DV30HE	$2 000 each
5 Basic installation - plus jobs	500 /job
Goods & Services Tax	7%
Provincial Sales Tax	8%

Terms: 10% discount, cash on receipt of invoice.
Allocate 100% of revenue and costs to Highlife Townhouse Project.
This is a recurring weekly entry.

USING DATE – December 9

Cash Receipt #110
Dated Dec. 8/99
From Highlife Townhouses, certified cheque #NT-37124 for $12 937.50 in full payment of account, including $1 437.50 discount. Reference Invoice #HH-144.

Cash Receipt #111
Dated Dec. 8/99
From York Seniors' Club, cheque #229 for $7 969.50 in full payment of account including $80.50 discount taken for early payment. Reference invoices #HH-143 and HH-143C.

EMPLOYEE TIME SUMMARY SHEET #24

(pay period ending December 9, 1999)

Name of Employee	Week 48 Hours	Week 49 Hours	Regular Hours	Overtime Hours
❏ Kris Kindl	40	40	80	–
❏ MyTee Strong	40	40	80	–

   a. Using Employee Time Summary Sheet #24 and Employee Information Sheet, complete payroll for hourly employees.
   b. Remember to recover $50 advance from Kindl.
   c. Issue cheques #352 and #353.
   d. Allocate 50% of costs to General Sales Project and 50% to Highlife Townhouse Project for each employee.

USING DATE — December 15

❏ Cash Sales Invoice #HH-145
Dated Dec. 10/99
To The Irish Pub

1 TG: Fireplace gas ins multi MSDV45T	$2 800
1 CC: Fireplace free-std gas DV30DVT	3 000
1 Mantel: marble MM-DVT40 kit	1 800
2 Basic installation - plus jobs	500 /job
2 Remote controls: economy RCE-100	120 each
Goods & Services Tax	7%
Provincial Sales Tax	8%

Paid by certified cheque #BM-321431.
Allocate 100% of revenue and costs to General Sales Project.

❏ Cash Purchase Invoice #ST-239
Dated Dec. 11/99
From Speedy Transport, $50 for emergency delivery of gas fireplace inserts to Highlife Townhouses plus $3.50 GST and $4.00 PST. Purchase invoice total $57.50. Terms: cash on receipt of invoice. Issued cheque #354 in payment. Charge 100% of delivery expense to Highlife Townhouse Project.

❏ Cheque Copy #355
Dated Dec. 13/99
To Matchless Flame, $4 622.40 in partial payment of account. Reference invoice #MF-1401.

❏ Sales Invoice #HH-146
Dated Dec. 14/99
To Highlife Townhouses

5 MF: Fireplace gas ins DV30HE	$2 000 each
5 Basic installation - plus jobs	500 /job
Goods & Services Tax	7%
Provincial Sales Tax	8%

Terms: 10% discount, cash on receipt of invoice.
Allocate 100% of revenue and costs to Highlife Townhouse Project.
Recall stored entry.

Memo #10
Dated Dec. 15/99
From Manager: Using the Employee Information Sheet, prepare payroll for Damper for the pay period ending December 15. Allocate 100% of payroll costs to General Sales Project. Issue cheque #356.

Cash Receipt #112
Dated Dec. 15/99
From Highlife Townhouses, certified cheque #NT-38991 for $12 937.50 in full payment of account, including $1 437.50 discount. Reference invoice #HH-146.

Memo #11
Dated Dec. 15/99
From Manager: Issue to the Receiver General of Canada cheque #357 for $7 500 to pay quarterly Business Income Tax installment. Allocate 100% to General Sales Project.

Memo #12
Dated Dec. 15/99
From Manager: Refer to previous end-of-month (November) General Ledger account balances to record liabilities and payments to the following agencies.

Issue cheque #358 for GST owing to the Receiver General of Canada.
Issue cheque #359 for EI, CPP and Income Tax Payable owing to the Receiver General of Canada.
Issue cheque #360 for PST Payable owing to the Treasurer of Ontario. Remember to take the 5% sales tax commission.
Issue cheque #361 for RRS-Plan Payable owing to Standard Insurance Co.
Issue cheque #362 for CSB-Plan Payable owing to Transcend Investment Co.
Issue cheque #363 for Group Insurance Payable to Standard Insurance Co.

USING DATE — December 21

Cash Sales Invoice #HH-147
Dated Dec. 16/99
To Arend Versteeg

1 MF: Fireplace gas ins DV27TVT	$1 950
1 Heater: vintage 50,000BTU ADVSH-50	850
1 Basic installation - plus job	500
Goods & Services Tax	7%
Provincial Sales Tax	8%

Paid by MasterCard #5297 5261 2835 5521.
Allocate 100% of revenue and costs to General Sales Project.

Purchase Invoice #PI-1321
Dated Dec. 16/99
From Penguin Insulating Co., $350 for insulation supplies plus $24.50 GST. Purchase invoice total $374.50. Recall the stored entry. Terms: net 15 days.

Cheque Copy #364
Dated Dec. 16/99
To Matchless Flame, $13 375 in full payment of account. Reference invoice #MF-1439.

Notes

Allocate 100% of the sales tax commission to the General Sales Project.

Purchase Invoice #VS-1002
Dated Dec. 18/99
From Vulcan Stove

2 Toolsets: brass handle solid	$360.00
2 Toolsets: cast iron/black enamel	240.00
2 Toolsets: glass handle/cast iron	480.00
Goods & Services Tax	75.60
	$1 155.60

Terms: net 30 days.

Cash Sales Invoice #HH-148
Dated Dec. 18/99
To Maria's Bed & Breakfast

1 VS: Fireplace pellet stove VPS1000	$2 200
1 CC: Fireplace free-std gas DV30DVT	3 000
2 Basic installation - plus jobs	500 /job
2 Insulating chimney jobs	100 /job
Goods & Services Tax	7%
Provincial Sales Tax	8%

Paid by Visa #4102 371 649 876.
Allocate 100% of revenue and costs to General Sales Project.

Purchase Invoice #VS-1002C
Dated Dec. 18/99
From Vulcan Stove, $120 allowance for damaged Toolset: glass handle/cast iron valued at $240. Reference invoice #VS-1002. Allocate 100% of allowance to General Sales Project.

Cheque Copy #365
Dated Dec. 19/99
To Therma Glow, $3 274.20 in full payment of account. Reference invoice #TG-1601.

Cheque Copy #366
Dated Dec. 19/99
To Starfire Fireplace, $2 696.40 in full payment of account. Reference invoice #SF-1009.

Cheque Copy #367
Dated Dec. 19/99
To Vulcan Stove Co., $6 655.40 in payment of account. Reference invoice #VS-914.

Purchase Invoice #VS-1007
Dated Dec. 19/99
From Vulcan Stove

1 Mantel: cherry MC-DVT40 kit	$ 720.00
3 Mantels: marble MM-DVT40 kits	3 240.00
2 Mantels: oak MO-DVT30 kits	1 300.00
1 Mantel: tile MT-DVT30 kit	480.00
1 VS: Fireplace pellet stove VPS1000	1 320.00
Goods & Services Tax	494.20
	$7 554.20

Terms: net 30 days.

Cash Sales Invoice #HH-149
Dated Dec. 20/99
To Adrian Lee

1 CC: Fireplace gas ins DV32HET	$2 800
1 Mantel: marble MM-DVT40 kit	1 800
1 Basic installation - plus job	500
Subcontracting work on marble	250
Goods & Services Tax	7%
Provincial Sales Tax	8%

Paid by MasterCard #4591 5281 4567 2345.
Allocate 100% of revenue and costs to General Sales Project.

Purchase Invoice #MM-1392
Dated Dec. 21/99
From Missoni Marbleworks, $250 for marble work completed for Adrian Lee plus $17.50 GST and $20 PST. Purchase invoice total $287.50. Terms: cash on receipt. Allocate 100% of expense to General Sales Project.

Cheque Copy #368
Dated Dec. 21/99
To Missoni Marbleworks, $287.50 in full payment of account. Reference invoice #MM-1392.

USING DATE – December 23

Cash Purchase Invoice #TH-11073
Dated Dec. 22/99
From Toronto Hydro, $100 for hydro services plus $7 GST. Purchase invoice total $107. Issued cheque #369 in payment. Allocate 100% of expense to General Sales Project.

Cash Purchase Invoice #BC-52147
Dated Dec. 22/99
From Bell Canada, $50 for telephone services plus $3.50 GST and $4.00 PST. Purchase invoice total $57.50. Issued cheque #370 in payment. Allocate 100% of expense to General Sales Project.

Cash Sales Invoice #HH-150
Dated Dec. 22/99
To Amir Husein

1 Toolset: glass handle/cast iron (Damaged)	$ 200
1 Ceram Log: Birdseye Maple set BMF5	550
1 Door: Pinnacle Arch w/damper 2wf	1 000
1 Grill: rotisserie & spit DX80	1 300
Goods & Services Tax	7%
Provincial Sales Tax	8%

Paid by certified cheque #CB-43228.
Allocate 100% of revenue and costs to General Sales Project.

Cheque Copy #371
Dated Dec. 23/99
To Rudy's Sunoco, $230 in full payment of account. Reference invoice #RS-574.

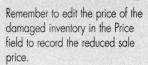

Notes

Remember to edit the price of the damaged inventory in the Price field to record the reduced sale price.

Cash Sales Invoice #HH-151
Dated Dec. 23/99
To Sal Rigger

1 set Andirons: cast iron	$100
Goods & Services Tax	7%
Provincial Sales Tax	8%

Paid by cheque #49. In the rush of pre-Christmas sales fever, no credit check was completed.
Allocate 100% of revenue and costs to General Sales Project.

Memo #13
Dated Dec. 23/99
From owner to accountant: All employees will receive a holiday bonus in addition to their final paycheques for 1999. The amounts of the bonuses will be as follows:

Cinder (Manager)	$800
Damper (Store Assistant)	$500
Kindl (Installer)	$600
Strong (New Installer)	$100

The minimum income tax of 10% should be withheld. Delete the other deductions in the Payroll Journal. (WCB and EHT expenses will still appear in the journal.
Allocate 100% of the cost of the bonus to the General Sales Project for Cinder, Kindle, and Damper. Allocate 100% of the bonus for Strong to the Highlife Townhouse Project. Issue cheques #372 through #375 for the bonuses.

Notes

To issue a bonus cheque, open the Payroll Journal. Click on the Enter taxes manually tool button to turn off the automatic payroll deductions. All the deduction amount fields should now be available for editing. Prepare the paycheque by entering the bonus in the Commission field in the Payroll Journal. Enter the income tax amount (10% of the bonus) to replace the amount in the Income Tax field. Delete all default amounts in the other deduction fields. Remember to click on the Calculate taxes automatically tool button to turn on the automatic payroll deductions immediately after preparing these cheques. (You can also turn automatic payroll deductions off in the Payroll Settings screen. Refer to page 362.)

Warning!

Increase the wage rate in employee record for Strong (Employees icon) before completing the payroll entry.

EMPLOYEE TIME SUMMARY SHEET #25

(pay period ending December 23, 1999)

Name of Employee	Week 50 Hours	Week 51 Hours	Regular Hours	Overtime Hours
Kris Kindl	42	40	80	2
MyTee Strong	42	40	80	2

a. Strong's work has been exceptionally good and the manager is concerned that she may leave because her pay is less than Kindl's. Therefore she will receive a wage increase with this pay. Her new rate is $20 for regular hours and $30 for overtime.
b. Using Employee Time Summary Sheet #25 and Employee Information Sheet, complete payroll for hourly employees.
c. Remember to recover $50 advance from Kindl.
d. Issue cheques #376 and #377 for the paycheques.
e. Allocate 50% of payroll costs to General Sales Project and 50% to Highlife Townhouse Project for each employee.

❏ Cash Sales Invoice #HH-152
Dated Dec. 27/99
To Brian Ames

1 Mantel: cherry MC-DVT40 kit	$1 200
1 Ceram Log: Algonquin Maple set AMF5	500
1 Door: Mirage w/damper 2.75wf	900
1 Woodholder: walnut	80
Goods & Services Tax	7%
Provincial Sales Tax	8%

Paid by Cash.
Allocate 100% of revenue and costs to General Sales Project.

❏ Bank Debit Memo #831214
Dated Dec. 28/99
From Royal Bank, $115 for NSF cheque from Sal Rigger, plus bank service charge of $20 to handle NSF cheque. Set up a customer record for Sal Rigger and charge the full amount to his account. Reference invoice #HH-151 and cheque #49. Allocate 100% of Other Revenue to General Sales Project.

❏ Memo #14
Dated Dec. 29/99
From Manager: Write off the Sal Rigger account because we are unable to collect. His phone number and address are incorrect and attempts to notify him were unsuccessful. Remember to complete credit checks for all customers in future. The amount allocated to the ITC Adjustment account is $7.

❏ Purchase Invoice #CC-1504
Dated Dec. 29/99
From Cambridge Castings

2 CC: Fireplace free-std gas DV30DVT	$3 600.00
1 CC: Fireplace gas ins DV32HET	1 680.00
Goods & Services Tax	369.60
	$5 649.60

Terms: 2/10, net 15 days.

❏ Bank Debit Memo #831419
Dated Dec. 30/99
From Royal Bank, for $2 400. This amount includes $2 150 for the reduction of principal on bank loan and $250 interest. Allocate 100% of expense to General Sales Project.

❏ Bank Debit Memo #831420
Dated Dec. 30/99
From Royal Bank, for $2 500. This amount includes $300 for the reduction of principal on mortgage and $2 200 interest. Allocate 100% of expense to General Sales Project.

❏ Bank Debit Memo #831421
Dated Dec. 30/99
From Royal Bank, for $75 in bank service charges, including NSF charges. Allocate 100% of expense to General Sales Project.

Notes

❏ Sal Rigger is located at
696 Alias Drive
Toronto, ON M4G 2K8
Tel: (416) 482-1938
❏ Create new revenue account:
4200 Other Revenue

Refer to Accounting Procedures for the two transactions relating to Sal Rigger.

☐ Bank Credit Memo #142341
Dated Dec. 31/99
From Royal Bank, for $712 for semi-annual interest on bank account. Remember Interest Receivable $340. Allocate 100% of revenue to General Sales Project.

☐ Cheque Copy #378
Dated Dec. 31/99
To Penguin Insulating Co., $374.50 in full payment of account. Reference invoice #PI-1321.

☐☐ Memo #15
Dated Dec. 31/99
From Manager: Using the Employee Information Sheet, prepare payroll for Damper and Cinder for the pay period ending December 31.
Issue cheques #379 and #380.
Allocate 100% of payroll expense for Damper to General Sales Project. Allocate 70% of payroll expense for Cinder to the General Sales Project and 30% to the Highlife Townhouse Project.

☐ Materials Summary Form #12
Dated Dec. 31/99
Re: Insulation and Hardware supplies: A physical count of materials inventory used for job orders indicated the following:

		Allocations:	
		General Sales	Highlife Townhouse
Insulation used	$300	90%	10%
Hardware used	$180	50%	50%

Make the necessary asset adjustments and expense charges.

Memo #16
Dated Dec. 31/99
From Manager: The following year-end adjustments are required:

☐ The amount of office supplies on hand based on a physical count is $160. Allocate 100% of expense to General Sales Project.

☐ Depreciation for the fiscal quarter ending December 31, 1999 is:

		Allocations:	
		General Sales	Highlife Townhouse
Computers	$500	100%	
Installation Equipment	250	90%	10%
Shop Centre	3 000	100%	
Transport Vehicles	1 000	90%	10%

☐ Payroll liability accrued for hourly employees on December 31, 1999 is:

Kindl	$800
Strong	800
	$1 600

A new account, 2240 Accrued Payroll is required.
Allocate 100% of expense to General Sales Project.

☐ The following amounts of prepaid expenses have expired on December 31:

Prepaid Advertising	$480
Prepaid Insurance	$450

Allocate 100% of expenses to General Sales Project.

CASE PROBLEMS

1. Amber Ashe, the owner, wants to reorganize the Chart of Accounts for Hearth House. The first change is to include Damaged Inventory as part of the subtotal for Net Cost of Goods Sold. However, because the account has had journal entries posted to it, the account number cannot be changed so that it is placed before the subtotal account. How can she resolve this problem?

   Ashe has also decided that she would prefer to have separate costs for each inventory category, a total for the cost of all inventory goods sold and another total for all costs related to the goods sold (i.e., including cost of inventory, discounts and allowances, etc.). Describe in detail the procedures for making this change. What are the advantages of the more detailed accounting for costs? Are there any disadvantages?

2. Hearth House has an opportunity to purchase an adjacent property for its store expansion. Before proceeding, Ashe wants an analysis of how she can include other projects or divisions for the distribution of costs.

   a. What kinds of divisions or projects could a business like Hearth House use?
   b. What advantages are offered by adding project information?
   c. How might the allocation of revenue and expenses be determined for the different projects you are proposing?

3. How does Simply Accounting assist a business that sells inventory items with inventory control? What additional inventory controls can a business put into place to ensure that costs and losses are minimal?

4. The installation services provided by Hearth House are entered into the inventory ledger at zero cost. This is required because the services are not purchased at a real dollar cost from an outside vendor. However, it does mean that there is no information about the actual profitability of providing these services. How might a business like Hearth House establish the profitability of the service side of its operations separate from the profitability of its retail or product sales? What factors should the business take into account in the pricing of its services or the decision to continue to offer them?

CHAPTER FOURTEEN

OBJECTIVES

Upon completion of this chapter, you will be able to:

- *enter* transactions using the General, Receivables, Payables and Inventory Journals
- *print* the General Ledger report for the bank account
- *observe* the differences between a bank statement and the General Ledger report
- *turn on* the bank reconciliation feature
- *create* new accounts for reconciliation
- *integrate* the new reconciliation accounts
- *set up* the bank reconciliation information
- *complete* the bank reconciliation
- *display* and *print* bank reconciliation reports
- *clear* journal entries and paid invoices

COMPANY INFORMATION

Company Profile

HSC School Store is located on the ground floor of High School of Commerce in Toronto, Ontario. It operates for the convenience of the students in the school who can buy their stationery and school supplies at very reasonable prices. Markups on all store goods are very small because the store is not set up to make a profit. The store also carries workbooks that the students must purchase for themselves.

Teachers may also buy from the store. They usually do so to provide a service to their students, buying items that their students are required to have and then reselling them to the students at the same price. This helps reduce line-ups at the store as well. As representatives of a school department, teachers are allowed to buy on credit and customer accounts have been set up for them. The head of each department is the store's contact, but individual teachers are expected to settle their accounts within 15 days. Students pay for all their purchases in cash.

Although supervised by a business department teacher, the store is managed and operated by students in the school who may earn partial credits toward a business course that they are currently taking.

To help the store get started in the fall, the school board provides an interest-free loan because the margins on goods sold are too small to build up a bank account balance large enough to purchase inventory. The store repays the loan at the end of the school year.

September is the busiest month for the school store, followed by October and February, the beginning of the second semester. Store hours are set accordingly. The store is open every day for the first two weeks of September, three days per week until the middle of October and the the first four weeks of the winter term, and two days per week for the rest of the time. During exam periods and summers, the store is closed. The hours of operation, one hour before and after school and during lunch, avoid all conflicts with scheduled classes and makes working in the store equally accessible to all students.

In previous years, all of the record keeping has been performed manually. At the end of August, in keeping with the business department offering Simply Accounting courses and the gift of a used computer, the accounts were set up in Simply Accounting. The following information is available to complete the transactions for October:

- Chart of Accounts
- Trial Balance as at September 30, 1999
- Vendor Information
- Customer Information
- Inventory Information
- Accounting Procedures

Notes

The account 2670 GST Paid on Purchases is required as an integration account for the software to work properly. It is not used in the transactions and will maintain a zero balance.

HSC SCHOOL STORE
CHART OF ACCOUNTS

ASSETS
1080 Cash in Bank
1200 Accounts Receivable
1300 Merchandise Inventory
1400 Computers & Peripherals
1450 Cash Register

LIABILITIES
2100 Loan from Administration
2200 Accounts Payable
2640 PST Payable
2650 GST Charged on Sales
2670 GST Paid on Purchases

EQUITY
3560 School Store Surplus
3600 Current Earnings

REVENUE
4020 Revenue from Sales
4100 Revenue from Textbooks

EXPENSES
5060 Cost of Goods Sold
5100 Damages and Losses
5140 General Expenses

HSC SCHOOL STORE
TRIAL BALANCE

September 30, 1999

1080 Cash in Bank	$ 4 987.51	
1200 Accounts Receivable	642.00	
1300 Merchandise Inventory	7 890.05	
1400 Computers & Peripherals	500.00	
1450 Cash Register	200.00	
2100 Loan from Administration		$ 8 000.00
2200 Accounts Payable		1 921.00
2640 PST Payable		284.21
2650 GST Charged on Sales		441.05
3560 School Store Surplus		2 423.50
4020 Revenue from Sales		3 552.65
4100 Revenue from Textbooks		2 748.00
5060 Cost of Goods Sold	5 150.85	
	$19 370.41	$19 370.41

HSC SCHOOL STORE
VENDOR INFORMATION

Vendor Name (Contact)	Address Phone & Fax	Invoice Terms	Invoice Date	Invoice/ Cheque No.	Outstanding Balance
A.W. Publishers (Wesley Addison)	PO Box 580 Toronto, ON M3C 2T8 Tel: (416) 447-5101	Net 15	8/30/99 9/10/99 9/30/99	AW-334 100 AW-619 Balance owing	$ 600 – 600 1 680 $1 680
Asian Clothing Co.	93 Spadina Ave. Toronto, ON M4R 1K3 Tel: (416) 923-5411	Net 15			
Ling Mfg. Co. (Mi Ling)	395 Queen St. E. Toronto, ON M2P 2T2 Tel: (416) 778-2972	Net 30			
Metro Bookstore (Rhonda Reading)	349 Parliament St. Toronto, ON M3G 6F2 Tel: (416) 672-6219	Net 30			
T.O. School Suppliers (Tori Osborne)	555 Dundas St. W. Toronto, ON M6L 1N4 Tel: (416) 882-7219	Net 15	8/30/99 9/12/99 9/30/99	TSS-642 101 TSS-991 Balance owing	$550 – 550 91 $ 91
Tudor Lock Co. (Mary Q. Scott)	33 Jarvis St. Toronto, ON M4R 1B1 Tel: (416) 528-5119	Net 20	8/30/99 9/15/99 9/30/99	TLC-497 102 TLC-632 Balance owing	$450 – 450 150 $150
				Grand Total	$1 921

HSC SCHOOL STORE
CUSTOMER INFORMATION

Customer Name (Contact)	Address Phone & Fax	Invoice Terms	Invoice Date	Invoice/ Cheque No.	Outstanding Balance
Accounting Dept. (S. Gallo)	H.S.C. 16 Phin Ave. Toronto M3B 9J2 Tel: 393-0230	Net 15	9/3/99 9/10/99 9/11/99 9/26/99 9/22/99	EC-1 Chq 38 EC-7 Chq 103 EC-10	$299.00 −299.00 192.60 −192.60 642.00
				Balance owing	$642.00
Data Processing Dept. (M. Musta)	H.S.C. 16 Phin Ave. Toronto M3B 9J2 Tel: 393-0230	Net 15	9/3/99 9/20/99 9/4/99 9/18/99 9/19/99 9/28/99	EC-2 Chq 23 EC-4 Chq 11 EC-9 Chq 29	$69.00 −69.00 69.00 −69.00 82.80 −82.80
English Dept. (H. Garber)	H.S.C. 16 Phin Ave. Toronto M3B 9J2 Tel: 393-0230	Net 15			
Geography Dept. (D. Little)	H.S.C. 16 Phin Ave. Toronto M3B 9J2 Tel: 393-0230	Net 15			
History Dept. (S. Halloran)	H.S.C. 16 Phin Ave. Toronto M3B 9J2 Tel: 393-0230	Net 15			
Keyboarding Dept. (C. Chihrin)	H.S.C. 16 Phin Ave. Toronto M3B 9J2 Tel: 393-0230	Net 15	9/5/99 9/16/99 9/5/99 9/21/99	EC-5 Chq 15 EC-6 Chq 62	$10.35 −10.35 57.50 −57.50
Math Dept. (W. Erdman)	H.S.C. 16 Phin Ave. Toronto M3B 9J2 Tel: 393-0230	Net 15	9/14/99 9/25/99	EC-8 Chq 33	$46.00 −46.00
Phys. Ed. Dept. (L. Sialtsis)	H.S.C. 16 Phin Ave. Toronto M3B 9J2 Tel: 393-0230	Net 15	9/4/99 9/16/99	EC-3 Chq 31	$331.20 −331.20
Science Dept. (H. Heinola)	H.S.C. 16 Phin Ave. Toronto M3B 9J2 Tel: 393-0230	Net 15			
				Grand Total	$642.00

HSC SCHOOL STORE
INVENTORY INFORMATION

Code	Description	Selling Price /Unit	Qty on Hand	Amt (Cost)	Min Stock
010	ACCO 3 Ring Binder 1" spine	$1.00 each	30	$ 24.00	10
020	ACCO 3 Ring Binder 2" spine	3.00 each	30	75.00	10
030	Accounting Paper - 25 sheets	.75/pkg	20	12.00	5
040	Binder - Blue 3 Ring 2" spine	1.50 each	25	31.25	5
050	Calculator - Basic Math	10.00 each	30	240.00	5
060	Calculator - Scientific	20.00 each	30	480.00	5
070	Clipboard - Acrylic Letter	7.00 each	20	120.00	5
080	Clipboard - Hardwood Letter	1.50 each	40	40.00	10
090	Clipboard - Hardwood Legal	2.00 each	20	30.00	5
100No PST	Dictionary - Pocket Cant/Eng	12.00 each	21	210.00	10
110No PST	Dictionary - Pocket Eng	12.00 each	39	390.00	10
120No PST	Dictionary - Pocket Fr/Eng	12.00 each	14	140.00	2
130No PST	Dictionary - Pocket Punj/Eng	12.00 each	20	200.00	2
140No PST	Dictionary - Pocket Viet/Eng	12.00 each	27	270.00	2
150	Diskettes - DSHD 3.5"	1.00 each	65	32.50	20
160	Dividers - 5 pack	.65/pkg	20	12.00	5
170	Duo Tang Folder	.35 each	30	9.00	5
180	Duo Tang Folders - 4 pack	1.20/pkg	10	10.00	2
190	Eraser	.20 each	50	7.50	10
200	Executive Secretary	3.30 each	10	30.00	2
210	Exercise Book - 4 pack	2.00/pkg	60	105.00	10
220	Glue Stick	1.30 each	50	57.50	5
230	Glue Sticks - 3 pack	4.50/pkg	10	40.00	2
240	Graph Paper - 50 sheets	1.00/pkg	50	40.00	5
250	Gym Bag - HSC Logo	16.00 each	20	240.00	5
260	Index Cards	1.50/pkg	20	25.00	5
270	Knapsack - HSC Logo	20.00 each	20	300.00	5
280	Lock - Combination	4.00 each	80	240.00	30
290	Markers - Self-stick 4 pack	2.00/pkg	20	35.00	2
300	Math Set	5.00/set	40	160.00	5
310	Paper - Blank 50 refill sheets	.60/pkg	50	22.50	10
320	Paper - Lined 200 refill sheets	2.00/pkg	30	48.00	5
330	Paper - Typing 50 full sheets	.65/pkg	40	22.00	5
340	Paper - Typing 50 half sheets	.50/pkg	20	8.00	3
350	Pen - Blue/red	.20 each	50	8.00	10
360	Pen - Blue/red 12 pack	1.20/pkg	10	10.00	2
370	Pen - Solo Cross	10.00 each	10	80.00	2
380	Pencil	.15 each	40	4.80	10
390	Pencil Crayons - 8 pack	1.40/pkg	40	48.00	10
400	Pencil Crayons - 20 pack	$2.50/pkg	30	60.00	5
410	Post-It Notes - 3x3	.60/pad	30	15.00	5
420	Post-it Notes - 3x5	.80/pad	10	6.00	2
430	Portfolio	.30 each	10	2.00	2
440	Reinforcements - Gummed	.40/pkg	20	6.00	2
450	Ruler - 15 cm.	.40 each	20	6.00	5
460	Ruler - 30 cm.	.50 each	20	8.00	2
470	Scissors - 5"	4.00 each	20	60.00	2
480	Scissors - 7"	6.00 each	20	90.00	2
490	Shorthand Coil Notebook	3.00 each	10	20.00	2

continued.......

```
┌────────────────────────────────────────────────────────────────┐
│  HSC SCHOOL STORE                                               │
│  INVENTORY INFORMATION CONTINUED                               │
│                                                                │
│  Code      Description              Selling Price  Qty on   Amt    Min  │
│                                     /Unit          Hand    (Cost)  Stock│
│                                                                │
│  500       Sweatpants - HSC Logo    25.00 each      20    400.00    5   │
│  510       Sweatshirt - HSC Logo    24.00 each      20    360.00    5   │
│  520       Template - Flowchart      1.20 each      10     10.00    2   │
│  530No PST  Workbook - Accounting D'Amico 18.00 each 20   300.00   10   │
│  540No PST  Workbook - Accounting Palmer  18.00 each 30   450.00   10   │
│  550No PST  Workbook - Simply DOS Purbhoo                       │
│                                     30.00 each      40  1 120.00   10   │
│  560No PST  Workbook - Simply Windows Purbhoo                   │
│                                     30.00 each      40  1 120.00   10   │
│                                                        $7 890.05        │
└────────────────────────────────────────────────────────────────┘
```

Accounting Procedures

PST

PST at 8 percent for the province of Ontario is charged on all goods sold by the store, excepts books (workbooks and dictionaries.) All books in inventory have "No PST" included as part of the item code as an additional reminder to the students working in the store not to charge PST on books. That is, they should change the default entry of 8 percent in the PST field to zero. The School Board makes PST remittances centrally based on the store's total sales. Revenue from books is separated to make tax calculations easier.

GST

GST at 7 percent is charged on all goods sold by the store, including books. Again, remittances are handled centrally by the School Board based on total sales. However, educational institutions providing mainly tax exempt services (similar to financial institutions) are not allowed to deduct the GST paid on goods they purchase from the GST charged on sales to calculate the GST owing. They pay all of the GST they collect directly to the Receiver General. Therefore, the GST paid account is not used and GST paid on purchases is added to the purchase price as part of the cost of goods sold.

Cash Sales Summary

Most of the store sales are for small amounts. Therefore, individual sales are recorded on a printed inventory list as they occur. Twice a week, the summaries of these transactions are entered into the accounting program. This saves time because entries for each individual sale are not required. Bank deposits are also made twice a week.

NSF Cheques

If a cheque is deposited from an account that does not have enough money to cover it, the bank may return it to the depositor as NSF (Non-Sufficient Funds). To record the NSF cheque, first reverse the receipt in the Receipts Journal. Turn on the option to Include Fully Paid Invoices and enter a **negative** payment amount. Then enter a Sales Journal invoice for the amount of the handling charge. Refer to Chapter 5, page 119 if you need more help.

If the paid invoices have been cleared, or if the sale was a cash sale, you must process the NSF cheque through the Sales Journal because there is no Receipts Journal entry. Create a customer record if necessary and enter a **positive** amount for the amount of the cheque. Choose *Cash in Bank* as the account. If the customer is expected to pay the bank charges, enter these on the second invoice line as a **positive** amount and select the appropriate revenue account.

INSTRUCTIONS

1. Using the Chart of Accounts, the Trial Balance, Vendor, Customer and Inventory information provided, and using the Keystrokes that follow as a guide, set up and complete the bank reconciliation for HSC School Store for the month of September. The journal transactions for September have been completed for you.

2 Enter the source documents for the month of October including the bank reconciliation. The source documents begin on page 448.

3. After completing your entries, print the reports indicated on the chart below.

REPORTS

Lists
- ☐ Chart of Accounts
- ☐ Vendor List
- ☐ Customer List
- ☐ Inventory List

Financials
- ☑ Comparative Balance Sheet
  dates: September 31 & October 31
  With Dollar Difference
- ☑ Income Statement
  from September 1 to October 31
- ☐ Trial Balance
- ☑ General Ledger
  accounts: 4020 4100
  from September 1 to October 31

GST
- ☐ GST Report

Bank Reconciliation
- ☑ Bank Reconciliation Summary
  from September 1 to September 31
- ☑ Bank Reconciliation Detail
  from October 1 to October 31

Mailing Labels
- ☐ Labels for

Journals
- ☐ General
- ☐ Purchases
- ☐ Payments
- ☑ Sales (by posting date)
  from October 1 to October 31
- ☐ Receipts
- ☐ Transfers
- ☐ Adjustments
- ☑ Bank Reconciliation
  (by posting date)
  from September 1 to October 31

Payables
- ☐ Vendor Aged
- ☐ Aged Overdue Payables
- ☐ Vendor Purchases
- ☐ Pending Purchase Orders

Receivables
- ☑ Customer Aged Detail
  for all customers
- ☐ Aged Overdue Receivables
- ☐ Customer Sales
- ☐ Customer Statements

Inventory
- ☐ Inventory
- ☐ Inventory Sales
- ☐ Inventory Activity

GRAPHS
- ☐ Payables by Aging Period
- ☐ Receivables by Aging Period
- ☐ Sales vs Receivables
- ☐ Revenues by Account
- ☐ Expenses & Net Profit as % of Revenue
- ☐ Payables by Vendor
- ☐ Receivables by Customer
- ☐ Receivables Due vs Payables Due
- ☐ Expenses by Account
- ☐ Current Revenue vs Last Year

KEYSTROKES FOR BANK RECONCILIATION

Bank Reconciliation

For any bank account, the timing of monthly statements is usually not perfectly matched with the accounting entry of the corresponding transaction. Usually some of the cheques written do not appear on the statement, interest earned on the account, or bank charges are not yet recorded because they may be unknown until receipt of the statement. Thus the balance of the bank statement most likely does not match the balance in the cash account. The process of identifying the differences in order to achieve a match is the process of bank reconciliation.

The keystrokes that follow will set up bank reconciliation for the HSC School Store.

Creating Bank Reconciliation General Ledger Accounts

Notes

You can save your work and exit at any time. Any changes you have made will be saved and you can continue from where you left off when you are ready.

Most bank statements include monthly bank charges, loan or mortgage payments and interest on deposits. That is, there are usually some sources of income and some expenses. Normally the only source document for these bank account transactions is the bank statement. In order to use Simply Accounting's bank reconciliation feature, you must first create the accounts that link to these regular bank account transactions. When you examine the September Bank Statement for HSC School Store on page 432 you can see that there is an interest deposit and a withdrawal for service charges. The store does not currently have accounts for either of these items, so you must create them. In addition, you will need an account to enter adjustments related to the reconciliation. The exact role of these accounts will be further explained as we proceed with the bank reconciliation setup.

Open the data files for HSC with September 30 as the using date and open the Accounts window.

Create the following new accounts. All are Right-column accounts.

- Revenue from Interest   4160
- Bank Charges   5020
- Reconciliation Adjustment 5170

These are the accounts that will be linked to the Bank Reconciliation process to identify the bank account related expenses and income.

Before completing the reconciliation procedure, the General Ledger bank accounts required for the bank reconciliation must be identified and modified.

You should be in the Home window.

Turning on the Bank Reconciliation Feature

Click on the **Accounts icon** and then **click on** the **Setup button** 🔧 to display the General Ledger Settings screen shown:

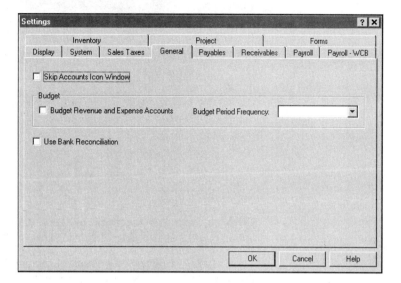

Click on Use Bank Reconciliation to turn on this option. A ✔ appears in the check box.

Click on OK to save the new setting and return to the Home window. As shown below, the Bank Reconciliation icon has been added below the General Journal icon:

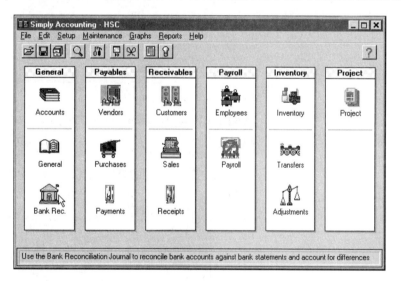

Double click on the **Accounts icon** in the General column to open the General Ledger Accounts window.

Select the account **1080 Cash in Bank**.

Click on the **Edit button** 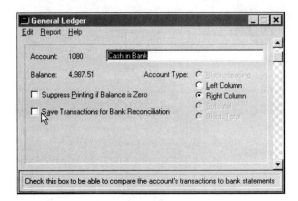 or choose Edit from the pull-down menu under Edit to open the account information screen below:

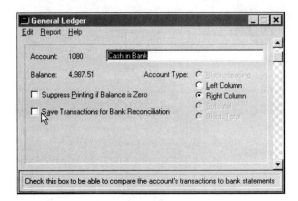

Notice that a check box has been added for bank reconciliation.

Click on **Save Transactions for Bank Reconciliation** to display the additional option buttons shown in the following screen:

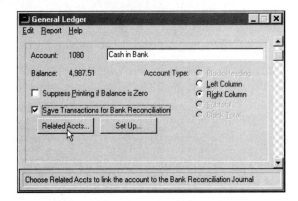

Naming and Integrating Reconciliation Accounts

Click on **Related Accts** to display the following screen:

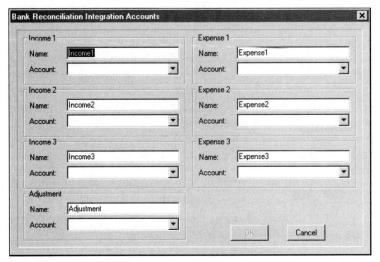

The fields on this Bank Reconciliation Integration Accounts form will be used to identify the appropriate General Ledger accounts for income (interest received) from bank deposits; for expenses associated with the bank account, such as bank charges or interest paid on bank loans; and for adjustments, or small discrepancies between the accounting entries and the bank statements, such as for amounts entered incorrectly in journal transactions. You can identify up to three sources of income, three types of expenses and one adjustment account for each bank account.

The first Income field is highlighted, ready for editing. The only source of income for this account that is not accounted for elsewhere is interest income. You can use up to ten characters for each name.

Type   Bank Int

Press   tab

Click on the arrow to the right of the Account field to list the revenue accounts that are available.

Click on 4160 Revenue from Interest, the account you created earlier as part of the reconciliation setup.

Press tab to advance to the next Income field. This field and the third Income field are not needed, so you will indicate that they are not applicable.

Type   n/a

Press tab twice to skip the Account field and advance to the third Income field. Indicate that it too is not applicable.

Leave the default name for adjustments unchanged.

Press tab repeatedly to advance the cursor to the Account field for adjustments.

Click on the Account field arrow to display the list of eligible accounts. Either an expense or a revenue account can be used for adjustments because they can increase or decrease the account balance. HSC School Store will use the expense account created for this purpose.

Click on 5170 Reconciliation Adjustments

Press tab to advance to and highlight the first Expense Name field. The School Store has one automatic bank account related expense, bank charges.

Type   Bk Charges

Press tab to advance to the Account field.

Click on the Account field arrow to display the list of expense accounts.

Select 5020 Bank Charges for this expense account.

Press tab to advance to and highlight the second Expense Name field.

Type   n/a

Press tab twice to skip the Account field and advance to the third Expense field. Indicate that it is not needed.

Check your work carefully. When you are certain that all the names and accounts are correct,

Click on OK to save the new information and return to the *Cash in Bank* account information window.

Close the account information window to return to the main Accounts window.

Notes

If there are other bank accounts, you must set up the integration accounts for them as well.

Setting up for Reconciliation

Print the General Ledger for the *Cash in Bank* Account from September 1 to September 30, the period covering all transactions after the last statement. The General Ledger and September bank statement for the HSC School Store follow:

General Ledger Report				Debits	Credits	Balance
File Help						
08-31-1999 to 09-30-1999				Debits	Credits	Balance
1080 Cash in Bank						203.60 Dr
09-09-1999	Cash, Cash sales summary	CSS-1	J7	2,536.28	·	2,739.88 Dr
09-10-1999	A.W. Publishers	100	J8	·	600.00	2,139.88 Dr
09-10-1999	Accounting Dept.	38	J9	299.00	·	2,438.88 Dr
09-12-1999	T.O. School Suppliers	101	J11	·	550.00	1,888.88 Dr
09-15-1999	Tudor Lock Co.	102	J13	·	450.00	1,438.88 Dr
09-16-1999	Phys. Ed. Dept.	31	J14	331.20	·	1,770.08 Dr
09-16-1999	Keyboarding Dept.	15	J15	10.35	·	1,780.43 Dr
09-16-1999	Cash, Cash sales summary	CSS-2	J16	969.45	·	2,749.88 Dr
09-18-1999	Data Processing Dept.	11	J17	69.00	·	2,818.88 Dr
09-20-1999	Data Processing Dept.	23	J19	69.00	·	2,887.88 Dr
09-21-1999	Keyboarding Dept.	62	J20	57.50	·	2,945.38 Dr
09-23-1999	Cash, Cash sales summary	CSS-3	J22	895.60	·	3,840.98 Dr
09-25-1999	Math Dept.	33	J23	46.00	·	3,886.98 Dr
09-26-1999	Accounting Dept.	103	J24	192.60	·	4,079.58 Dr
09-28-1999	Data Processing Dept.	29	J25	82.80	·	4,162.38 Dr
09-30-1999	Cash, Cash sales summary	CSS-4	J29	825.13	·	4,987.51 Dr
				6,383.91	1,600.00	

Double-click to display Journal Report for current entry.

Notes

In an ongoing business, print the Ledger report beginning on the date of the oldest outstanding item from your previous bank statement up to the date of the most recent statement.

Notes

The deposit on Sep. 16 includes the cash deposit for $969.45 and two cheques for $10.35 and $331.20. The Sep. 26 deposit includes two cheques for $46.00 and $192.60. Notice that the deposit dates are not always the same as the journal entry dates.

U Can Trust Co.
5621 Honesty Way
Toronto, Ontario
M2Y 3E4

Transit #61290
Account # 003 77238-2

September 30, 1999

HSC School Store
16 Phin Ave.
Toronto, Ontario M3B 9J2

Date	Transaction	Deposits	Withdrawals	Balance
08/31/99	Balance Fwd.			203.60
09/10/99	Deposit	2,536.28		2,739.88
09/10/99	Deposit	299.00		3,038.88
09/12/99	CHQ #100		600.00	2,438.88
09/15/99	CHQ #101		550.00	1,888.88
09/16/99	Deposit	1,311.00		3,199.88
09/19/99	CHQ #102		450.00	2,749.88
	Deposit	69.00		2,818.88
09/20/99	Deposit	69.00		2,887.88
09/21/99	Deposit	57.50		2,945.38
09/23/99	Deposit	895.60		3,840.98
09/26/99	Deposit	238.60		4,079.58
09/28/99	Deposit	82.80		4,162.38
09/30/99	Interest	4.35		4,166.73
	Service Fee		11.50	4,155.23
09/30/99	Closing Balance			4,155.23
	Total Deposits	5,563.12		
	Total Withdrawals		1,611.50	

When you compare this statement with the General Ledger Report, you will notice these differences:

- One deposit for $825.13 in the General Ledger Report at the end of the month is not listed on the bank statement.
- Interest of $4.35 received on the deposit account does not appear in the General Ledger Report.
- Monthly bank charges of $11.50 have not been recorded in the General Ledger Report.
- Two of the deposits, for $1 311.00 and $238.60 in the bank statement, do not match any journal entry in the General Ledger because they were multiple deposits (see Notes).

Sometimes items may appear on the General Ledger report that were part of the previous month's bank statement, as when bank charges are recorded late.

All of these items must be accounted for in order to have the bank statement match the bank balance on the Balance Sheet.

Open the *Cash in Bank* account ledger information form if it is not already on your screen.

Click on Set Up to display the following advisory screen:

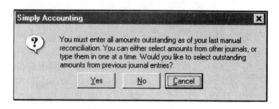

Click on Yes to display the following dialogue box:

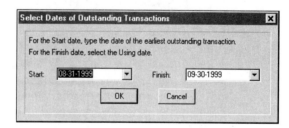

This screen asks you for the dates of the earliest and latest journal entries that have not yet been reconciled on your previous bank statement, usually for the previous month. For HSC School Store, this will include the journal entries made during the month of September that followed the August bank statement. The default start and finish dates are correct, so do not change them.

Click on OK to display these outstanding transactions, as shown here:

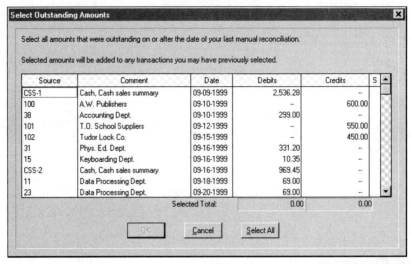

Click on Select All to select all of the journal entries because they are all outstanding.

If any items on the list of journal entries were in fact part of the previous bank statement, you should deselect them by clicking on the lines that contain these items. This action will leave all other items selected while the ones you click on are not selected. The unselected items are not outstanding according to the August bank statement.

Click on OK to advance to the next step and screen:

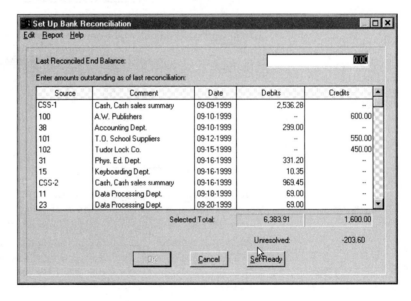

At this point you must enter the opening balance from the current bank statement as the Last Reconciled End Balance. For the School Store, this is the September opening *Cash in Bank* account balance from the bank statement (or from the General Ledger statement minus any not-outstanding items for the previous month, if there are any).

The Last Reconciled End Balance field is highlighted, ready to be changed.

Type   203.60

Press   `tab`

The unresolved amount is set to zero, and the bank reconciliation module can be set ready.

Click on Set Ready. A cautionary message appears on the screen

Simply Accounting is advising you that this step cannot be reversed. If you have not yet made a backup, do so before proceeding.

Click on OK to continue. You will return to the bank account information window. The Set Up button has disappeared because the setup is complete.

Close the *Cash in Bank* ledger account information window.

Close the Accounts window to return to the Home window.

To see what you have done so far, choose the Bank Reconciliation report from the pull-down menu under Reports. Choose the Summary option, enter the *Cash in Bank* account and click on OK. All the current month's journal transactions are still outstanding, but you have adjusted the report for the correct opening balance.

Close the displayed report when you are finished and return to the Home window. You are now ready to begin the reconciliation of the current bank statement.

Notes

The bank reconciliation detail report lists all individual journal entries and their status as outstanding.

Reconciliation of the Bank Statement

The bank reconciliation procedure consists of three steps to update the General Ledger. First, you record the bank statement account balance as the ending balance. Next, you identify all the deposits and withdrawals that have been processed by the bank. Finally, you must complete journal entries for any transactions for which the bank statement is the source document. All three steps are completed in the Bank Reconciliation Journal. The result should be a match between the bank balances in two statements.

Double click on the **Bank Rec. icon** (Bank Reconciliation Journal) in the Home window:

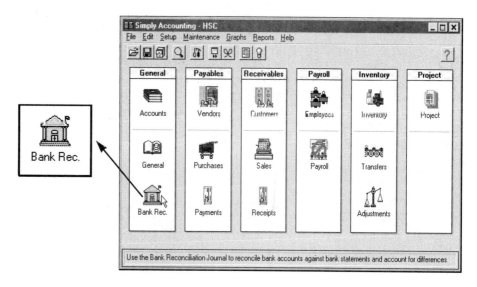

The Bank Reconciliation Journal entry form is shown:

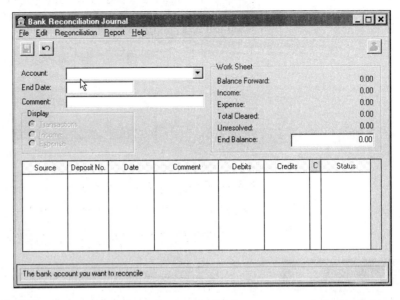

Click on the **arrow beside the Account entry box** to display the available accounts for reconciliation. The list displays the single bank account because it was the only one that was set up for bank reconciliation.

Select 1080 Cash in Bank to display the reconciliation information for this bank account:

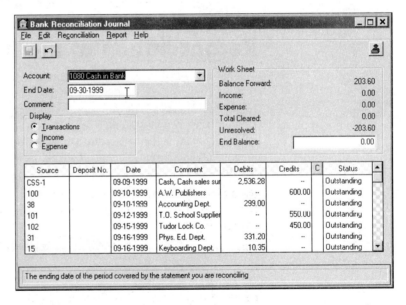

The account is entered in the Account field and the Using Date is entered automatically in the End Date field. The date is correct so do not change it.

Press (tab) twice to advance to the Comment field.

Type September Bank Reconciliation

Press (tab)

The cursor moves to the Transactions option in the Display box at the left side of the screen.

Press (tab) again to advance to and highlight the End Balance field in the Work Sheet area at the right side of the screen. This field will be used for the ending bank balance as it appears on the bank statement.

Type 4155.23

Press (tab)

Marking Journal Entries as Cleared

You are now ready to begin to process individual journal entries to indicate whether or not they have been cleared in this bank statement. That is, the bank has processed the items and the amounts have been withdrawn from or deposited to the account.

Your screen should now resemble the following:

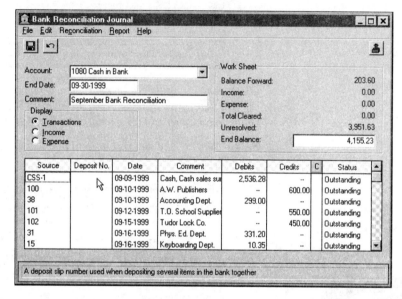

All outstanding items for the month are listed. These are the items that were left as outstanding during the setup stage. In addition, the unresolved amount has changed to reflect the new balance.

Sometimes several cheques are deposited as a group, as they were by the HSC School Store on September 16 and September 26. Each of these group deposits can also be cleared as a group.

Click on the **Deposit No. column beside the entry for Cheque #31.**

Type 1

Press ⬇ to advance to the next line in the Deposit No. column.

Type 1

Press ⬇ to advance to the next line in the Deposit No. column.

Mark the next transaction as belonging in group one as well so that all three items that were deposited at the same time have the same group number.

With one item in the group still selected, move to the C (cleared) column.

Click on the **C at the top of the column**. Your transactions list appears as follows:

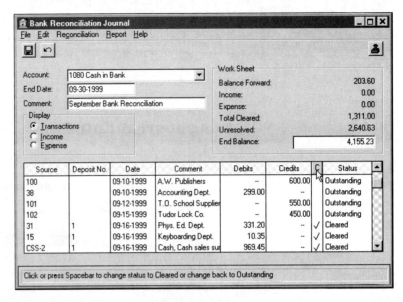

All items in the group will have their status changed to cleared at the same time. Deposit numbers can be entered in the Bank Reconciliation Journal at the time of the deposit and then saved until you are ready to reconcile the bank statement.

Beside the two cheques that were deposited together on September 26 — the ones for $46.00 and $192.60,

Type   2

Click on the **C at the top of the column**.

You are now ready to mark the remaining transactions that have been cleared.

Click on the **C column for the first entry on the list**.

A check mark appears in this column and the Status has been changed from Outstanding to Cleared. Continue to clear the remaining journal entries that appear on the bank statement and scroll as necessary to display additional items. You should leave only the last item as outstanding — the deposit that was not yet processed by the end of the month. As you clear each item, the unresolved amount is updated.

The next section describes the procedure for clearing transactions that are different in some way, like NSF cheques. By marking their status correctly, you will have a more accurate picture of your business transactions. Read the following section. You will use it to mark the NSF cheque for the October bank reconciliation.

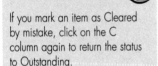

If you mark an item as Cleared by mistake, click on the C column again to return the status to Outstanding.

Marking NSF Cheques

For some items, you may want to add further information, in particular NSF cheques and their reversing entries. The available status alternatives are explained in the Status Options chart below.

STATUS OPTIONS

Cleared (C)	for deposits and cheques that have been processed correctly.
Deposit Error (D)	for the adjusting journal entry to account for the difference between the amount of a deposit that was recorded incorrectly and the bank statement amount for that deposit. Assign the Cleared status to the original entry for the deposit.
Payment Error (P)	for the adjusting entry to account for a difference between the amount of a cheque recorded incorrectly and the bank statement amount for that cheque. Assign the Cleared status to the original entry for the cheque.
NSF (N)	for customer cheques returned by the bank because there was not enough money in the customer's account. Assign the Adjustment status to the adjusting entry that reverses the NSF cheque.
Reversed (R)	for the entry for cheques that are cancelled by posting a reversing transaction entry to the bank account or the Sales or Purchases Journals. Assign the Adjustment status to the reversing entry that cancels the cheque.
Void (V)	for the entry for cheques that are cancelled because of damage during printing. Assign the Adjustment status to the reversing entry that voids the cheque.
Adjustment (A)	for the adjusting or reversing entries that are made to cancel NSF, void or reversed cheques. (See the explanations for NSF, Void and Reversed above.)

To mark a cheque as NSF,

Click on the word Cleared in the Status column for the NSF cheque.

Press (enter) to display the alternatives available for the Status of a journal entry as shown here:

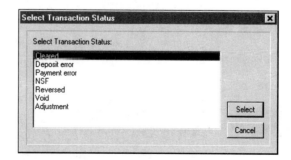

Click on NSF to highlight this alternative.

Click on Select to enter it. The word Cleared changes to NSF for this item.

The last step is to change the status of the customer payment that reverses the NSF cheque to Adjustment.

Adding Bank Statement Journal Entries

Click on Income in the list in the **Display** portion of the window to begin entering the journal information for income to this account. Bank Int, the income source we named earlier, is selected in the Income group list. The Bank Reconciliation Journal now includes a journal entry form for this income transaction as shown here:

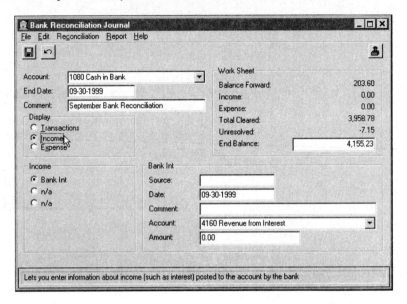

Click on the **Source field** to advance the cursor.

Type   Bk-Stmt

Press `tab`

The using date is highlighted and can be changed. Since it matches the bank statement entry date for interest paid on the account, it is correct.

Press `tab` to advance to the Comment field.

Type   Interest Earned on Bank Deposits

Press `tab` twice to skip over the correctly entered Account number and advance to the Amount field. The field is highlighted, ready for editing. Check the bank statement for the correct amount.

Type   4.35

Press `tab`

If there are other income categories, click on the income name in the Income group list to the left of the journal information. A new journal form will appear for this income.

Click on Expense in the list in the **Display** portion of the window. The expense, Bk Charges is selected on the left side of the screen and its journal form appears on the right-hand side.

Click on the **Source field**

Type   Bk-Stmt

Notes

You can edit these journal entries or transaction status entries at any time before posting. Choosing Save will save the work you have completed so far, and still permit you to make changes later.

Notes

Duplicate source document codes are allowed in this journal.

Press `tab` twice to advance to the Comment field, accepting the date as entered because it is correct.

Type Bank Charges and Service Fee

Press `tab` twice to skip over the correctly entered account number and advance to the Amount field. The bank statement contains the amounts for this expense.

Type 11.50

Press `tab`

If there are other expense categories, click on the expense name in the list to the left of the journal information. A new journal form will appear for this expense.

At this stage, the unresolved amount should be zero if everything is reconciled. If the unreconciled amount is not zero, check your journal entries to see whether or not you have made an error. Click on each option in the Display box to show your work for the corresponding part of the reconciliation procedure. Make corrections if necessary.

You should also review the reconciliation journal entry before proceeding.

Choose Display Bank Rec. Journal Entry from the pull-down menu under **Report**. Your journal entry should appear as follows:

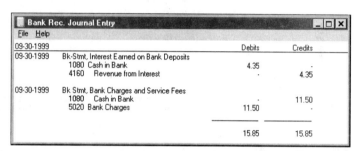

The income and expense journal entries are listed. In addition, an adjustment entry will be displayed if there is any unresolved amount.

Close the report window when you are finished.

Any discrepancy will be posted as an adjustment to the reconciliation adjustments expense account created earlier. This account should be used only for small amounts, not significant enough to warrant a separate journal entry.

Click on the **Save button** 💾.

Make a backup copy.

Click on the **Post button** 👤.

The program will warn you before posting an unresolved amount, giving you an opportunity to correct any mistakes you may have made before posting the journal entries.

The Bank Reconciliation Journal form is updated as shown:

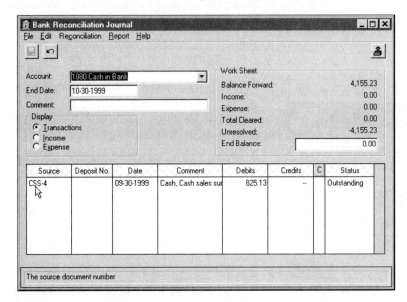

Only the outstanding journal entries remain on the list and the End Date advances to the next month.

Close the Bank Reconciliation Journal to return to the Home window to complete the transactions for October.

Displaying Bank Reconciliation Reports
Bank Reconciliation Journal

Notes

You can print the Bank Reconciliation Journal from the Reports menu. Click on the Bank Reconciliation Journal icon to select it. Then choose Display Bank Rec. Journal from the pull-down menu under Reports.

Click on the **Bank Rec icon** and then **click on** the **Report button** in the Home window. You will see the report options screen:

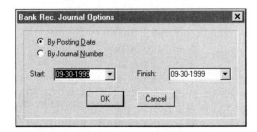

The journal can be prepared according to journal entry numbers or by date. By default, the report uses posting dates. Enter the starting and ending dates or journal numbers for the report you want.

Click on OK

Close the display when you are finished.

Notes

You can display the General Ledger Report, Invoice Lookup, Vendor/Customer Aged or Employee Reports (if applicable) from the Bank Reconciliation Journal.

Bank Reconciliation Report

Choose **Bank Reconciliation** from the pull-down menu under **Reports** to display the following report options:

Notes

You can display Journal Reports, Invoice Lookup, and Vendor or Customer Aged or Employee Reports (if applicable) from the Bank Reconciliation Detail Report.

Enter the bank account number in the Account field. Choose the Status categories to include in your reports. By default, all are included. Clicking on a category will remove the ✔ from the check box and omit this category from your report.

The **Detail** report lists all journal entries with their status.

Click on Summary

Enter the start and end dates. Usually these dates will coincide with the bank statement period. The Summary report provides totals for each type of Status, totals for income and expense categories and outstanding amounts that will reconcile the bank statement with the General Ledger account balance.

Close the displayed report when you are finished.

Printing Bank Reconciliation Reports

Display the report you want to print.

Choose **Print** from the pull-down menu under **File** to print the displayed report.

Close the report window when you are finished.

End of Month Procedures

Periodically a business will clear old information from its accounting files. In the manual system, it might store the details in archives or on microfiche in order to keep the current files manageable in size. Computerized systems should be similarly maintained by making backups of the data files and then clearing the information that is not required to keep the data files manageable. These periodic procedures include clearing journal entries for prior periods, removing paid invoices from customer and vendor records, and removing vendors and customers who no longer do business with the company.

Warning!

You must make a backup copy of your data files and print all reports before clearing any information. Once the journals and invoices are cleared, they cannot be recovered.

Before proceeding, back up the data files and print all the relevant reports: journals, vendor and customer detail reports, inventory tracking reports, etc.

Clearing Journal Entries

You should be in the Home window.

Choose Clear Journal Entries from the pull-down menu under **Maintenance** to display the following dialogue box:

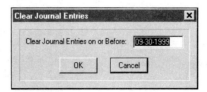

You must enter the date before the first journal entry that you want to keep. For HSC, September 30 is correct, so accept the date.

Click on OK

The following warning is shown:

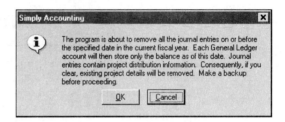

Click on Cancel to stop without deleting any information. If you have made a backup, you can continue.

Click on OK

The journal entries will be removed and you will return to the Home window.

Clearing Paid Vendor Invoices

Highlight the Vendors icon in the Home window.

Choose Clear Paid Vendor Invoices from the pull-down menu under **Maintenance** to display the following dialogue box:

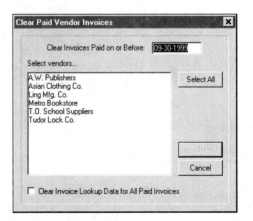

You can clear invoices for one or more vendors at the same time. Unpaid invoices will be retained.

Type the last date for which you want to remove invoices. September 30 is correct.

Sidebar notes:

Notes

Simply Accounting does not remove information without a warning. This gives you a chance to reconsider, make backups or just confirm that you have selected the option or entry you want. Always read the warning carefully.

Notes

If neither the Vendors nor Customers icon is highlighted, the menu option to clear invoices will be dimmed because the program does not know which invoices you want to clear.

Click on Select All (You can also select individual vendors by clicking on their names.) We also have stored lookup details, and do not need to keep that information.

Click on Clear Invoice Lookup Data for All Paid Invoices

Click on OK

Again, Simply Accounting presents the warning shown here:

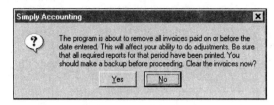

If you have selected correctly and are ready to proceed,

Click on Yes

When you choose to clear lookup data, you will see this additional warning:

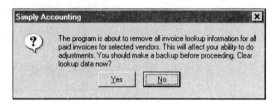

Again, if you are certain that you should continue,

Click on Yes

The information will be removed, and you will return to the Home window.

Clearing Paid Customer Invoices

Clearing customer invoices is very similar to clearing vendor invoices.

Highlight the Customers icon in the Home window.

Choose Clear Paid Customer Invoices from the pull-down menu under Maintenance to display the following dialogue box:

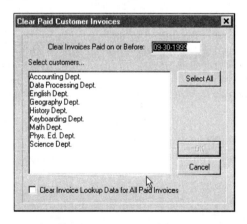

Notes

You can clear paid invoices for all customers by clicking on Select All.

Again, you should accept the date because we will begin entering new transactions in October. We will clear the invoices for a single customer, the Data Processing Dept.

Click on Data Processing Dept. We also have stored lookup details that we do not need to keep.

Click on Clear Invoice Lookup Data for All Paid Invoices

Click on OK

The next warning is the same as the one we saw for removing vendor invoices. If you are ready, you should proceed.

Click on Yes

Again, the additional warning for lookup data is shown. If you are certain that you want to continue,

Click on Yes

You will return to the Home window. The requested information has been removed.

Clearing Inventory Tracking Data

Choose Clear Inventory Tracking Data from the pull-down menu under **Maintenance** to display the following dialogue box:

You need to enter the date. Entries on and before the date you enter will be removed. You can accept September 30.

Click on OK

Again, you see the warning before any data is removed:

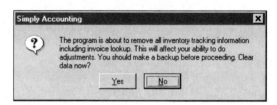

If you are certain that you want to proceed,

Click on Yes

The requested information is deleted and you will return to the Home window.

Clearing Invoice Lookup Data

Choose Clear Invoice Lookup Data from the pull-down menu under **Maintenance** to display the following dialogue box:

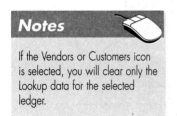

Notes

If the Vendors or Customers icon is selected, you will clear only the Lookup data for the selected ledger.

You need to enter the date. Entries on and before the date you enter will be removed. September 30 is correct, so you can accept it.

Click on OK

Once again, you see the warning before any data is removed. If you are certain that you want to proceed,

Click on Yes

The requested information is deleted and you will return to the Home window.

Removing Vendor and Customer Records

Sometimes you know that you will not be doing business with a customer or vendor again. Removing their records saves disk storage space, reduces the length of the displays to scroll through for journal entries and saves on mailing costs. Vendors are removed from the Vendors window. Customers are removed from the Customers window. We will remove the customer History Dept. because they will not be purchasing from the school store in the near future.

Double click on the **Customers icon** to open the Customers window.

Click on the **History Dept. icon** to highlight this customer.

Click on the **Remove button** or choose Remove from the pull-down menu under Edit to display the warning:

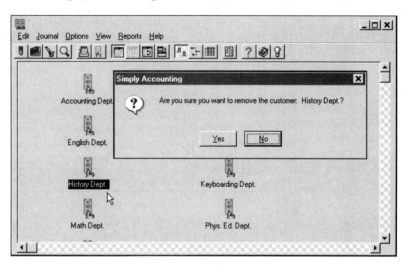

Again, you should check that you have selected the customer you want before continuing. If you have selected correctly,

Click on Yes

If you have selected a customer (or vendor) for whom the invoices have not been cleared, Simply Accounting will not permit you to remove the customer (or vendor). You will see the following warning:

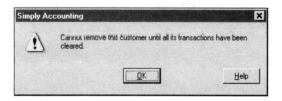

Click on OK to return to the Customers window. Clear the details, if appropriate, and then remove the customer's record.

SOURCE DOCUMENTS

USING DATE — October 7

 Sales Invoice #EC-11
Dated Oct. 2/99
To Accounting Dept.

10 Workbooks - Simply DOS Purbhoo	30.00	each
10 Workbooks - Simply Windows Purbhoo	30.00	each
GST	7 %	

Terms: Net 15 days

Notes

- Remember to delete the PST for all books that are sold — those items that have No PST as part of the item number.
- Accept the default selling price for all items in this application.

Cash Receipt #10
Dated Oct. 2/99
From Accounting Dept., cheque #52 for $642 in payment of account. Reference invoice #EC-10.

Notes

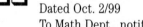 Sales Invoice #EC-12
Dated Oct. 2/99
To Math Dept., notification of NSF cheque #33 for $46 plus $20 handling charges. Mr. Farouk was notified of the outstanding balance still owing.

Cash Receipt #11
Dated Oct. 4/99
From Math Dept. (Mr. Farouk) money order #64321 for $66 in full payment of account. Reference invoices #EC-12, EC-8 and September bank statement. Mr. Farouk added a note of apology.

- Create new revenue account, 4200 Revenue from Handling Charges.
- Reverse the Receipts Journal entry and enter handling charges in the Sales Journal. If you have cleared the journal entries, use the Sales Journal to enter both parts. See Accounting Procedures.
- The bank charges expense will be recorded as part of the bank reconciliation at the end of the month.

Cash Sales Summary #5
Dated Oct. 4/99

No.	Item	Quantity Sold
010	ACCO 3 Ring Binder 1" spine	3
030	Accounting Paper - 25 sheets	4
050	Calculator - Basic Math	2
070	Clipboard - Acrylic Letter	1
110No PST	Dictionary - Pocket Eng	10
130No PST	Dictionary - Pocket Punj/Eng	1
140No PST	Dictionary - Pocket Viet/Eng	2
190	Eraser	3
220	Glue Stick	1
250	Gym Bag - HSC Logo	6
280	Lock - Combination	6
320	Paper - Lined 200 refill sheets	2
350	Pen - Blue/red	2
400	Pencil Crayons - 20 pack	2
510	Sweatshirt - HSC Logo	9
520	Template - Flowchart	1
560No PST	Workbook - Simply Windows Purbhoo	2

Notes

Remember to accept the default selling prices and to remove the PST for sales of books.

☐ Cash Sales Summary #6
Dated Oct. 7/99

No.	Item	Quantity Sold
020	ACCO 3 Ring Binder 2″ spine	2
040	Binder - Blue 3 Ring 2″ spine	2
060	Calculator - Scientific	1
100No PST	Dictionary - Pocket Cant/Eng	8
120No PST	Dictionary - Pocket Fr/Eng	3
150	Diskettes - DSHD 3.5″	12
270	Knapsack - HSC Logo	8
290	Markers - Self-stick 4 pack	1
330	Paper - Typing 50 full sheets	1
380	Pencil	2
500	Sweatpants - HSC Logo	7
550No PST	Workbook - Simply DOS Purbhoo	5

USING DATE — October 14

☐ Memo #1
Dated Oct. 9/99
From S. Gallo, Accounting Dept. Head: One scientific calculator in the store was damaged beyond repair. Write it off to the Damages and Losses expense account.

☐ Sales Invoice #EC-13
Dated Oct. 9/99
To Keyboarding Dept.,

50 Diskettes - DS-HD 3.5"		$1.00 each
GST		7%
PST		8%

Terms: Net 15 days

☐ Cash Receipt #12
Dated Oct. 11/99
From Accounting Dept., cheque #59 for $642 in payment of account. Reference invoice #EC-11.

☐ Cheque Copy #103
Dated Oct. 11/99
To A. W. Publishers, $1 680 in full payment of account. Reference invoice #AW-619.

Notes

Allow inventory to drop below re-order point.

☐ Cash Sales Summary #7
Dated Oct. 11/99

No.	Item	Quantity Sold
040	Binder - Blue 3 Ring 2" spine	4
060	Calculator - Scientific	2
110No PST	Dictionary - Pocket Eng	7
140No PST	Dictionary - Pocket Viet/Eng	1
240	Graph Paper - 50 sheets	3
260	Index Cards	1
280	Lock - Combination	8
340	Paper - Typing 50 half sheets	1
380	Pencil	2
410	Post-it Notes - 3x3	2
450	Ruler - 15 cm.	1
510	Sweatshirt - HSC Logo	3
550No PST	Workbook - Simply DOS Purbhoo	5

☐ Cash Sales Summary #8
Dated Oct. 14/99

No.	Item	Quantity Sold
050	Calculator - Basic Math	2
070	Clipboard - Acrylic Letter	2
100No PST	Dictionary - Pocket Cant/Eng	7
170	Duo Tang Folder	1
250	Gym Bag - HSC Logo	8
270	Knapsack - HSC Logo	4
310	Paper - Blank 50 refill sheets	2
350	Pen - Blue/red	4
390	Pencil Crayons - 8 pack	1
420	Post-it Notes - 3x5	1
500	Sweatpants - HSC Logo	6
530No PST	Workbook - Accounting D'Amico	1
560No PST	Workbook - Simply Windows Purbhoo	4

USING DATE — October 21

☐ Sales Invoice #EC-14
Dated Oct. 16/99
To Phys. Ed. Dept.

6 Sweatpants - HSC Logo	$25 each
6 Sweatshirts - HSC Logo	24 each
GST	7%
PST	8%

Terms: Net 15 days

☐ Cash Receipt #13
Dated Oct. 18/99
From Keyboarding Dept., cheque #68 for $57.50 in payment of account.
Reference invoice #EC-13.

□ Cheque Copy #104
Dated Oct. 18/99
To T.O. School Suppliers, $91 in full payment of account. Reference invoice #TSS-991.

□ Cheque Copy #105
Dated Oct. 18/99
To Tudor Lock Company, $150 in full payment of account. Reference invoice #TLC-632.

□ Purchase Invoice #TSS-1414
Dated Oct. 18/99
From T.O. School Suppliers
    50 Diskettes - DSHD 3.5" $25.00
    GST included in price
Terms: net 15 days

□ Purchase Invoice #LM-6123
Dated Oct. 18/99
From Ling Mfg. Co.
    20 Gym Bags - HSC Logo $240.00
    GST included
Terms: net 30 days.

□ Purchase Invoice #ACC-75110
Dated Oct. 18/99
From Asian Clothing Co.
    20 Sweatpants - HSC Logo $400.00
    20 Sweatshirts - HSC Logo   360.00
    Total (GST included) $760.00
Terms: net 15 days.

□ Purchase Invoice #MBS-4100
Dated Oct. 18/99
From Metro Bookstore
    15 Dictionaries - Pocket Cant/Eng $150.00
    GST included
Terms: net 30 days.

□ Cash Sales Summary #9
Dated Oct. 18/99

No.	Item	Quantity Sold
010	ACCO 3 Ring Binder 1" spine	2
080	Clipboard - Hardwood Letter	3
110No PST	Dictionary - Pocket Eng	0
150	Diskettes - DSHD 3.5"	6
210	Exercise Book - 4 pack	1
230	Glue Sticks - 3 pack	1
270	Knapsack - HSC Logo	1
290	Markers - Self-stick 4 pack	1
330	Paper - Typing 50 full sheets	1
380	Pencil	2
440	Reinforcements - Gummed	1
550No PST	Workbook - Simply DOS Purbhoo	2

Cash Sales Summary #10
Dated Oct. 21/99

No.	Item	Quantity Sold
050	Calculator - Basic Math	1
090	Clipboard - Hardwood Legal	1
100No PST	Dictionary - Pocket Cant/Eng	7
150	Diskettes - DSHD 3.5"	1
220	Glue Stick	2
250	Gym Bag - HSC Logo	7
280	Lock - Combination	3
320	Paper - Lined 200 refill sheets	2
370	Pen - Solo Cross	1
400	Pencil Crayons - 20 pack	2
470	Scissors - 5"	1
560No PST	Workbook - Simply Windows Purbhoo	5

USING DATE — October 28

Sales Invoice #EC-15
Dated Oct. 23/99
To Math Dept.

10 Math Sets	$5.00 each
GST	7%
PST	8%

Terms: Net 15 days

Cash Receipt #14
Dated Oct. 23/99
From L. Sialtsis in the Phys. Ed. Dept., cheque #39 for $338.10 in payment of account. Reference invoice #EC-14.

Cash Purchase #PR-223
Dated Oct. 25/99
To Patris Restaurant, cheque #106 for $150 to pay for school store staff and student luncheon.

Cash Sales Summary #11
Dated Oct. 25/99

No.	Item	Quantity Sold
020	ACCO 3 Ring Binder 2″ spine	1
080	Clipboard - Hardwood Letter	1
100No PST	Dictionary - Pocket Cant/Eng	5
180	Duo Tang Folders - 4 pack	1
210	Exercise Book - 4 pack	2
250	Gym Bag - HSC Logo	2
270	Knapsack - HSC Logo	5
290	Markers - Self-stick 4 pack	1
310	Paper - Blank 50 refill sheets	2
360	Pen - Blue/red 12 pack	1
390	Pencil Crayons - 8 pack	1
420	Post-it Notes - 3x5	1
480	Scissors - 7″	1
490	Shorthand Coil Notebook	4
510	Sweatshirt - HSC Logo	2
520	Template - Flowchart	1
550No PST	Workbook - Simply DOS Purbhoo	2

Cash Sales Summary #12
Dated Oct. 28/99

No.	Item	Quantity Sold
050	Calculator - Basic Math	1
110No PST	Dictionary - Pocket Eng	6
150	Diskettes - DSHD 3.5″	8
190	Eraser	2
240	Graph Paper - 50 sheets	1
260	Index Cards	1
280	Lock - Combination	5
300	Math Set	1
340	Paper - Typing 50 half sheets	1
380	Pencil	2
410	Post-it Notes - 3x3	1
460	Ruler - 30 cm.	1
500	Sweatpants - HSC Logo	2
530No PST	Workbook - Accounting D'Amico	1

USING DATE — October 31

Cheque Copy #107
Dated Oct. 30/99
To T.O. School Suppliers, $25 in full payment of account. Reference invoice #TSS-1414.

Cheque Copy #108
Dated Oct. 30/99
To Asian Clothing Co., $760 in full payment of account. Reference invoice #AC-75110.

Memo # 2
Dated Oct. 31/99
Reconcile the following Bank Statement for October.

U Can Trust Co.
5621 Honesty Way
Toronto, Ontario
M2Y 3E4

Transit #61290
Account # 003 77238-2

October 31, 1999

HSC School Store
16 Phin Ave.
Toronto, Ontario M3B 9J2

Date	Transaction	Deposits	Withdrawals	Balance
09/30/99	Balance Fwd.			4,155.23
10/01/99	Deposit	825.13		4,980.36
10/02/99	Deposit	642.00		5,622.36
10/02/99	NSF CHQ #33		46.00	5,576.36
	NSF Charges		20.00	5.556.36
10/05/99	Deposit	66.00		5,622.36
10/05/99	Deposit	669.85		6,292.21
10/07/99	Deposit	737.54		7,029.75
10/12/99	Deposit	1,085.65		8,115.40
10/14/99	CHQ #103		1,680.00	6,435.40
10/15/99	Deposit	693.57		7,128.97
10/19/99	Deposit	273.12		7,402.09
10/21/99	Deposit	437.37		7,839.46
10/21/99	CHQ #105		150.00	7,689.46
10/22/99	CHQ #104		91.00	7,598.46
10/24/99	Deposit	338.10		7,936.56
10/26/99	Deposit	376.23		8,312.79
10/28/99	CHQ #106		150.00	8,162.79
10/28/99	Deposit	208.77		8,371.56
10/31/99	Interest	13.10		8,384.66
	Service Fee		11.50	8,373.16
10/31/99	Closing Balance			8,373.16
Total Deposits		6,366.43		
Total Withdrawals			2,148.50	

CASE PROBLEM

The bank statement for the month of November listed a deposit for $188 but the journal entry shows that the amount deposited was $198.

a. How could you trace back to find the source of the error?

b. How can the bank help in finding the source of the error?

c. How would you complete the bank reconciliation journal for this entry?

CHAPTER FIFTEEN

Delhi Delights Inc.

OBJECTIVES

Upon completion of this chapter, you will be able to:

- *enter* corporation-related transactions in the General Journal
- *enter* transactions for two successive years
- *advance* the using date to a new fiscal year
- *display* and *print* reports from two years of data

COMPANY INFORMATION

Company Profile

Delhi Delights, a family restaurant in Sydney, Nova Scotia, serves East Asian and Oriental food in a buffet style. Ms Teegu Murchu, the owner, was advised to incorporate because of the restaurant's success and the corporation Delhi Delights, Inc. was formed. She will use the corporation to expand, with the immediate goal of opening one new restaurant each year. She will continue her marketing strategy of providing delicately spiced dishes to cater to the tastes of her North American clientele. Her menus also include a wide selection of authentic dishes for connoisseurs of Indian foods. Over time, even the North American customers are ordering more of these hot and spicy foods.

The corporation was authorized to issue 10 000 shares of cumulative preferred stock with a value of $100, and an unlimited number of no par value common stock. On January 1, 1999, Ms Murchu was issued 1 000 preferred stock valued at $100 000 and 20 000 common stock valued at $200 000 in exchange for the business assets. In addition, the new corporation secured a $300 000 loan at 8% for 10 years.

The following information is available for entering the business transactions:

- Chart of Accounts
- Share Register to record shares issued
- Trial Balance dated January 1, 1999

DELHI DELIGHTS, INC.
CHART OF ACCOUNTS

ASSETS
1080 Cash in Bank
1200 Visa
1220 Subscrip Rec: Common
1540 Building
1560 Equipment
1580 Furniture & Fixtures
1600 Land
1620 Vehicles
1680 Accum Deprec & Amort
1920 Organization Costs

LIABILITIES
2200 Accounts Payable
2220 Dividends Payable
2840 Term Loan Payable

EQUITY
3020 Common Stock
3040 Preferred Stock
3100 Common Stock: Subscribed
3180 Stock Div to be Distributed
3560 Retained Earnings
3580 Treasury Stock
3600 Current Earnings

REVENUE
4020 Revenue from Sales

EXPENSE
5020 Administration Expenses
5040 Deprec & Amort
5060 Food Costs
5100 Payroll Expenses
5140 Utilities & Maintenance
5340 Interest Expense
5450 Income Tax Expense

DELHI DELIGHTS, INC.
SHARE REGISTER

Date	Common Issued & Outstanding	Value	Preferred Issued & Outstanding	Value
Jan. 1	20 000	$200 000	1 000	$100 000

DELHI DELIGHTS, INC.
POST-CLOSING TRIAL BALANCE

January 1, 1999

1080 Cash in Bank	$300 000.00	
1540 Building	75 000.00	
1560 Equipment	50 000.00	
1580 Furniture & Fixtures	50 000.00	
1600 Land	100 000.00	
1620 Vehicles	25 000.00	
2840 Term Loan Payable		$300 000.00
3020 Common Stock		200 000.00
3040 Preferred Stock		100 000.00
	$600 000.00	$600 000.00

INSTRUCTIONS

1. Using the Chart of Accounts and Trial Balance, record the source transactions for the years 1999 and 2000 in the General Journal. Use appropriate codes for the source document numbers and use recurring entries wherever appropriate.

2. Print the following reports:

    a. General Journal for Jan. 1 to Dec. 31, 1999 (Click on the option Previous Year in the Journal Options window to access the data for 1999.)

    b. General Journal for Jan. 1 to Dec. 31, 2000 (The option Current Year should be selected.)

    c. Comparative Income Statement: Jan. 1 - Dec. 31, 1999 and Jan. 1 - Dec. 31, 2000.

    d. Comparative Trial Balance (Dollar Amounts) for Dec. 31, 1999 and Jan. 1, 2000. (Choose Comparative Trial Balance from the drop-down list beside Select a Report.)

SOURCE TRANSACTIONS

USING DATE — March 31, 1999 for First Quarter: January – March

Notes

When you post the January transactions with the March 31 using date, Simply Accounting will warn you that the journal date precedes the using date and will affect prior period reports. If you have entered the date correctly, you should proceed by clicking on Yes.

Jan. 3 Issued for cash 1 500 shares of preferred stock to investors for $150 000.

Jan. 3 Issued for cash 25 000 shares of common stock at $12 per share.

Jan. 6 Paid $30 000 to lawyer, Roche & Roche for services relating to forming the corporation.

Jan. 14 Building improvements costing $85 000 were completed and paid for.

Jan. 14 New equipment worth $200 000, and furniture and fixtures costing $15 000 were installed, set up and paid for.

Mar. 31 First quarter sales in 1999 for the period ending March 31 were $306 000. All sales are cash.

Mar. 31 Depreciation and amortization of assets for the first quarter was $11 275.

Mar. 31 A summary of other operating expenses paid for in the first quarter is as follows:

Administrative Expenses	$50 000
Food Cost	$99 725
Payroll Expenses	$36 000
Utilities & Maintenance	$3 000

Mar. 31 Interest expense on the Term Loan for the first quarter was $6 000 (paid out of cash).

Mar. 31 Income tax, at the rate of 40%, paid for the first quarter was $40 000.

USING DATE — June 30, 1999 for Second Quarter: April – June

Jun. 30 Sales for the second quarter in 1999 for the period ending June 30 were $321 600.

Jun. 30 Depreciation and amortization of assets for the second quarter was $11 275.

Jun. 30 A summary of other operating expenses paid for in the second quarter is as follows:

Administrative Expenses	$50 000
Food Cost	$102 725
Payroll Expenses	$38 000
Utilities & Maintenance	$3 600

Jun. 30 Interest expense on the Term Loan for the second quarter was $6 000.

Jun. 30 Income tax, at the rate of 40%, paid for the second quarter was $44 000.

USING DATE — September 30, 1999 for Third Quarter: July – September

Jul. 31 Issued an additional 20 000 shares of common stock in exchange for land for future expansion of the restaurant chain. The fair market value of the stock was $15 per share.

Sep. 30 Sales for the third quarter in 1999 for the period ending September 30 were $287 000.

Sep. 30 Depreciation and amortization of assets for the third quarter was $11 275.

Sep. 30 A summary of other operating expenses paid for in the third quarter is as follows:

Administrative Expenses	$50 000
Food Cost	$93 725
Payroll Expenses	$32 000
Utilities & Maintenance	$4 000

Sep. 30 Interest expense on the Term Loan for the third quarter was $6 000.

Sep. 30 Income tax, at the rate of 40%, paid for the third quarter was $36 000.

USING DATE — December 31, 1999 for Fourth Quarter: October – December

Nov. 15 Declared cash dividends to preferred shareholders of $10 per share on 2 500 outstanding preferred shares. Declared cash dividends to common shareholders of $2 per share on 65 000 outstanding common shares.

Dec. 15 Paid dividends declared on November 15.

Dec. 31 Sales for the fourth quarter in 1999 for the period ending December 31 were $330 500.

Dec. 31 Depreciation and amortization of assets for the fourth quarter was $11 275.

Dec. 31 A summary of other operating expenses paid for in the fourth quarter is as follows:

Administrative Expenses	$50 000
Food Cost	$105 725
Payroll Expenses	$38 000
Utilities & Maintenance	$4 500

Dec. 31 Interest expense on the Term Loan for the fourth quarter was $6 000.

Dec. 31 Income tax, at the rate of 40%, paid for the fourth quarter was $46 000.

USING DATE — March 31, 2000 for First Quarter: January – March

Jan. 2 Received subscriptions for 5 000 common shares at $15 per share.

Jan. 4 Sold 1 000 preferred stock to investors for cash at $100 per share.

Jan. 8 Issued 20 000 shares for construction of building for new restaurant on land purchased in 1999. The market value of each common share was $15.

Jan. 9 Purchased, installed and set up new equipment costing $125 000 and furniture and fixtures costing $75 000 in the new restaurant. Paid in cash.

Jan. 15 Received first installment of $37 500 from common stockholders.

Jan. 30 Received final installment of $37 500 owing for subscriptions from common stockholders and issued shares.

Mar. 31 First quarter sales in the year 2000 for the period ending March 31 were $454 000.

Mar. 31 Depreciation and amortization of assets for the first quarter was $18 150.

Mar. 31 A summary of other operating expenses paid for in the first quarter is as follows:

Administrative Expenses	$75 000
Food Cost	$145 850
Payroll Expenses	$54 000
Utilities & Maintenance	$5 000

Mar. 31 Interest expense on the Term Loan for the first quarter was $6 000.

Mar. 31 Income tax, at the rate of 40%, paid for the first quarter was $60 000.

USING DATE — June 30, 2000 for Second Quarter: April – June

Jun. 30 Sales for the second quarter in 2000 for the period ending June 30 were $498 000.

Jun. 30 Depreciation and amortization of assets for the second quarter was $18 150.

Jun. 30 A summary of other operating expenses paid for in the second quarter is as follows:

Administrative Expenses	$75 000
Food Cost	$162 850
Payroll Expenses	$60 000
Utilities & Maintenance	$6 000

Notes

To record transactions for the second fiscal year, first make a backup copy of your data files, then advance the using date to Jan. 1, 2000. Now you can advance the using date to any other date in the new fiscal year.

Jun. 30   Interest expense on the Term Loan for the second quarter was $6 000.

Jun. 30   Income tax, at the rate of 40%, paid for the second quarter was $68 000.

USING DATE — September 30, 2000 for Third Quarter: July – September

Aug. 8   Purchased land for future expansion for $250 000 cash.

Sep. 30   Sales for the third quarter in 2000 for the period ending September 30 were $448 400.

Sep. 30   Depreciation and amortization of assets for the third quarter was $18 150.

Sep. 30   A summary of other operating expenses paid for in the third quarter is as follows:

Administrative Expenses	$75 000
Food Cost	$151 850
Payroll Expenses	$52 000
Utilities & Maintenance	$5 400

Sep. 30   Interest expense on the Term Loan for the third quarter was $6 000.

Sep. 30   Income tax, at the rate of 40%, paid for the third quarter was $56 000.

USING DATE — December 31, 2000 for Fourth Quarter: October – December

Nov. 15   Declared cash dividends to preferred shareholders of $10 per share on 3 500 outstanding preferred shares.

Nov. 15   Declared a 15% stock dividend on the outstanding common shares consisting of 13 500 shares of common stock to be distributed on December 15, 2000 to common shareholders on record on November 30, 2000. Market price of shares is $15.

Dec. 1   Purchased for cash 5 000 shares of treasury stock at a price of $15 per share.

Dec. 15   Paid dividends on preferred shares declared on November 15.

Dec. 15   Issued 13 500 shares of common stock in respect of the stock dividend declared on November 15.

Dec. 31   Sales for the fourth quarter in 2000 for the period ending December 31 were $527 900.

Dec. 31   Depreciation and amortization of assets for the fourth quarter was $18 150.

Dec. 31   A summary of other operating expenses paid for in the fourth quarter is as follows:

Administrative Expenses	$75 000
Food Cost	$168 850
Payroll Expenses	$66 000
Utilities & Maintenance	$6 400

Dec. 31   Interest expense on the Term Loan for the fourth quarter was $6 000.

Dec. 31   Income tax, at the rate of 40%, paid for the fourth quarter was $75 000.

CASE PROBLEM

Teegu Murchu wants to analyze her financial statements more thoroughly, including calculating some ratio calculations. Export the year-end Balance Sheets and the quarterly Income Statements to spreadsheets and complete the following:

a. a horizontal analysis (trend percentages) for sales and food costs

b. a vertical analysis (component percentages) of expenses for each quarter

c. calculate the following ratios for the years 1999 and 2000

- Equity
- Debt
- Dividend yield
- EPS
- Return on Assets
- Book Value of Shares

Cheshire
Cheese & Butter Factory

OBJECTIVE

Upon completion of
this chapter, you
will be able to:

• *enter* transactions for depreciation on plant and equipment in the
General Journal

COMPANY INFORMATION

Company Profile

Cheshire Cheese & Butter Factory, located just outside of Saskatoon,
Saskatchewan, is owned and operated by Jack Farmer. After growing up on a
dairy farm, Farmer obtained an agricultural science degree and wrote his thesis on the
process of aging cheese. While working on his parents' farm over the next few years,
he completed further research and developed new methods that produced high quality
cheeses. He registered patents for these cheese processing methods, and in 1998,
started his own factory on a small piece of land that he purchased from his parents.
This ensured him a steady supply of fresh milk to use for the production of cheese and
butter.

Farmer has now completed his second year of operation and needs to calculate
depreciation expenses for his business. Since he uses the **straight-line** method for
his business financial statements, he keeps two sets of data files, because for income
tax purposes he must use the **capital cost allowance** method of calculating
depreciation. The following information allows you to calculate and record the
depreciation on Cheshire's plant and equipment using Simply Accounting:

• Chart of Accounts
• Trial Balance dated December 30, 1999 (using capital cost allowance — CCA)
• Trial Balance dated December 30, 1999 (using straight-line method)

CHESHIRE CHEESE & BUTTER FACTORY
CHART OF ACCOUNTS

ASSETS
1080 Cash in Bank
1200 Accounts Receivable
1240 Raw Materials Inventory
1300 Churning Equipment
1320 Accum Deprec: Churn Equip
1360 Computers & Peripherals
1380 Accum Deprec: Comp & Peri
1400 Conveyor Belt
1410 Accum Deprec: Conveyor Belt
1430 Escalator Belt
1440 Accum Deprec: Escalator Belt
1460 Factory
1470 Accum Deprec: Factory
1490 Factory Fixtures
1500 Accum Deprec: Fact Fix
1520 Land
1540 Machinery
1550 Accum Deprec: Machinery
1570 Refrigeration Equipment
1580 Accum Deprec: Refrig Equip
1600 Truck - 2TCX
1610 Accum Deprec: Truck
1630 Vats & Vessels
1640 Accum Deprec: Vats & Vessels
1660 Warehouse: Cold Storage
1670 Accum Deprec: Warehouse
1700 Organization Costs
1710 Accum Amort: Org Costs
1730 Patents

LIABILITIES
2100 Bank Loan
2200 Accounts Payable
2300 Accrued Liabilities
2940 Mortgage Payable

EQUITY
3500 Capital Stock
3560 Retained Earnings
3600 Current Earnings

REVENUE
4020 Revenue from Sales

EXPENSE
5020 Amortization: Org Costs
5040 Amortization: Patents
5100 Depreciation: Churn Equip
5110 Depreciation: Comp & Peri
5120 Depreciation: Conv Belt
5130 Depreciation: Esc Belt
5140 Depreciation: Factory
5150 Depreciation: Fact Fix
5160 Depreciation: Machinery
5170 Depreciation: Refrig Equip
5180 Depreciation: Truck
5190 Depreciation: Vats & Vess
5200 Depreciation: Warehouse
5400 Cost of Goods Sold
5500 Selling & Admin Expenses
5600 Utilities
5700 Wages & Salaries

CHESHIRE CHEESE & BUTTER FACTORY
TRIAL BALANCE

Using CCA Method of Depreciation
December 30, 1999

1080 Cash in Bank	$ 11 900.00	
1200 Accounts Receivable	25 000.00	
1240 Raw Materials Inventory	20 000.00	
1300 Churning Equipment	5 000.00	
1360 Computers & Peripherals	4 000.00	
1380 Accum Deprec: Comp & Peri		$ 1 200.00
1400 Conveyor Belt	8 000.00	
1410 Accum Deprec: Conveyor Belt		1 200.00
1430 Escalator Belt	12 000.00	
1440 Accum Deprec: Escalator Belt		2 400.00
1460 Factory	200 000.00	
1470 Accum Deprec: Factory		10 00000
1490 Factory Fixtures	6 000.00	
1500 Accum Deprec: Fact Fix		1 200.00
1520 Land	100 000.00	
1540 Machinery	36 000.00	
1570 Refrigeration Equipment	45 000.00	
1600 Truck - 2TCX	30 000.00	
1610 Accum Deprec: Truck		9 000.00
1630 Vats & Vessels	4 000.00	
1640 Accum Deprec: Vats & Vessels		800.00
1660 Warehouse: Cold Storage	100 000.00	
1700 Organization Costs	40 000.00	
1710 Accum Amort: Org Costs		2 100.00
1730 Patents	80 000.00	
2100 Bank Loan		30 000.00
2200 Accounts Payable		20 000.00
2300 Accrued Liabilities		10 000.00
2940 Mortgage Payable		300 000.00
3500 Capital Stock		150 000.00
3560 Retained Earnings		50 000.00
4020 Revenue from Sales		500 000.00
5400 Cost of Goods Sold	180 000.00	
5500 Selling & Admin Expenses	25 000.00	
5600 Utilities	6 000.00	
5700 Wages & Salaries	150 000.00	
	$1 087 900.00	$1 087 900.00

CHESHIRE CHEESE & BUTTER FACTORY
TRIAL BALANCE

Using Straight-Line Depreciation Method
December 30, 1999

1080 Cash in Bank	$ 11 900.00	
1200 Accounts Receivable	25 000.00	
1240 Raw Materials Inventory	20 000.00	
1300 Churning Equipment	5 000.00	
1360 Computers & Peripherals	4 000.00	
1380 Accum Deprec: Comp & Peri		$ 900.00
1400 Conveyor Belt	8 000.00	
1410 Accum Deprec: Conveyor Belt		562.50
1430 Escalator Belt	12 000.00	
1440 Accum Deprec: Escalator Belt		1 100.00
1460 Factory	200 000.00	
1470 Accum Deprec: Factory		6 000.00
1490 Factory Fixtures	6 000.00	
1500 Accum Deprec: Fact Fix		600.00
1520 Land	100 000.00	
1540 Machinery	36 000.00	
1570 Refrigeration Equipment	45 000.00	
1600 Truck - 2TCX	30 000.00	
1610 Accum Deprec: Truck		5 500.00
1630 Vats & Vessels	4 000.00	
1640 Accum Deprec: Vats & Vessels		400.00
1660 Warehouse: Cold Storage	100 000.00	
1700 Organization Costs	40 000.00	
1710 Accum Amort: Org Costs		2 100.00
1730 Patents	80 000.00	
2100 Bank Loan		30 000.00
2200 Accounts Payable		20 000.00
2300 Accrued Liabilities		10 000.00
2940 Mortgage Payable		300 000.00
3500 Capital Stock		150 000.00
3560 Retained Earnings		60 737.50
4020 Revenue from Sales		500 000.00
5400 Cost of Goods Sold	180 000.00	
5500 Selling & Admin Expenses	25 000.00	
5600 Utilities	6 000.00	
5700 Wages & Salaries	150 000.00	
	$1 087 900.00	$1 087 900.00

INSTRUCTIONS

1. Using the Chart of Accounts, Trial Balances and Source Transactions provided, calculate the accumulated depreciation and depreciation expense on the plant and equipment. Record the necessary General Journal entries for the using date December 31, 1999. Use two methods of depreciation:

   • the straight-line method (use the file named **CHES-SL.ASC**)
   • the capital cost allowance method for income tax purposes (use the file named **CHES-CCA.ASC**)

2. Print the following reports for each method used:

   a. Balance Sheet as at December 31

   b. Trial Balance as at December 31

   c. Income Statement for January 1 to December 31

   d. General Journal by posting date December 31

SOURCE TRANSACTIONS

USING DATE — December 31

☐ ☐ Cheshire purchased the churning equipment on January 1, 1999 in order to add the production of butter to their line of cheeses. The cost was $5 000. It was estimated that this equipment would have a useful life of ten years and a residual (scrap or disposal) value of $500. The capital cost allowance rate for this class of equipment for tax purposes is 20 percent.

☐ ☐ The computers and peripherals consisted of a 486 DX 100 mHz system with a laser printer, purchased and set up for use on January 1, 1998 at a cost of $4 000. The system was estimated to provide four years of useful service with a residual value of $400. The capital cost allowance rate for this class of asset for tax purposes is 30 percent. An updated pentium or 686 RISC system purchase was being considered for the new fiscal year.

☐ ☐ The conveyor belt was installed at a cost of $8 000 on April 1, 1998, a few months after the business started to accommodate the increasing workload. It was expected to last for ten years, after which time it would have a residual value of $500. The capital cost allowance rate for this class of asset for tax purposes is 20 percent.

☐ ☐ The escalator belt was installed at a cost of $12 000 when the business started on January 1, 1998. It too was expected to last for ten years and have a residual value of $1 000. The capital cost allowance rate for tax purposes is 20 percent for this class of equipment.

☐ ☐ The factory to process cheese was completed at a cost of $200 000 on January 1, 1998. It was estimated to have a 30-year useful life and a residual value of $20 000. The capital cost allowance rate for this class of plant for tax purposes is 5 percent.

☐ ☐ The factory fixtures were purchased at a cost of $6 000 when the factory was opened on January 1, 1998. The fixtures were expected to last for approximately ten years with a zero residual value. The capital cost allowance rate for this class of fixed asset for tax purposes is 20 percent.

☐ ☐ When production of butter began on January 1, 1999, the machinery was added at a cost of $36 000. The residual value after eight years of useful life was expected to be $4 000. For tax purposes, the capital cost allowance rate for this class of fixed asset is 20 percent.

☐ ☐ The refrigeration equipment replaced old refrigeration equipment on January 1, 1999 at a cost of $45 000. The useful life of this equipment was estimated to be eight years, with a residual value of $5 000. The capital cost allowance rate for this class of fixed asset for tax purposes is 20 percent.

☐ ☐ The two-tonne delivery truck model 2TCX was purchased on January 1, 1998 at a cost of $30 000. At the time, the truck was estimated to provide five years of service and then be worth $2 500. The capital cost allowance rate for this class of vehicle for tax purposes is 30 percent. It is anticipated that this truck will be traded in for a larger four-tonne model soon.

☐ ☐ The vats and vessels were purchased for $4 000 on January 1, 1998 when cheese production began. They were expected to have a useful life of ten years with a zero residual value. The capital cost allowance rate for this class of fixed asset for tax purposes is 20 percent.

☐ ☐ The cold storage warehouse was completed at a cost of $100 000 on January 1, 1999, a year after the startup of the factory. The warehouse was needed to keep up with the growth and expansion of the company's operations. The warehouse was expected to last for 30 years and have a residual value of $10 000. The capital cost allowance rate for this class of plant for tax purposes is 5 percent.

☐ ☐ The organization costs incurred to start the company will be amortized according to income tax rules. The tax rules permit three-quarters of the original organization costs to be written off at 7 percent annually, using the declining balance method. Therefore the amortization for 1999, the second year, will amount to $1 953. No other method of amortization is permitted.

☐ ☐ Cheshire registered its processing patents (rights) on January 1, 1998. The patents were valued at $100 000. Cheshire decided to amortize these patents over the shorter period of five years rather than the 20-year legal life permitted by tax rules. The amortization of the patents directly reduces the asset account so that an accumulated amortization account is not used.

Notes

Remember to reduce the accumulated depreciation account for the old computer system to zero.

☐ ☐ On December 31, 1999, the business decided to sell its old computer system to another local business for $1 200 in anticipation of buying a new system on January 1, 2000. Using both the straight-line and the capital cost allowance methods, calculate any gains or losses from this transaction. Create the new account that is required to complete this transaction for the loss or gain.

On December 31, 1999, it was decided to trade in the old truck model 2TCX for a new truck, model 4TCZ. The new four-tonne truck will reduce delivery expenses by allowing fewer delivery runs to be made. The company took out an additional bank loan for $20 300 to purchase the new truck. Under CICA rules, the trade-in should be treated as a sale with the respective loss or gain, and then a purchase of the new asset. The new truck was valued at $35 000 (for both depreciation methods) and there was no loss or gain on the trade-in under the CCA method of calculating depreciation. Create a new asset account for the new truck (1605 Truck - 4TCZ, Left Column) and if necessary, create a new account for the loss or gain under the straight-line method.

CASE PROBLEMS

1. Cheshire Cheese purchased batteries for both its delivery truck and its portable computer. The cost in each case was around $300. Will these purchases increase the values of the corresponding fixed assets? Explain your answer.

2. At the end of June 2000, Cheshire Cheese decided to install a new conveyor belt costing $10 000, estimated to last for six years with a scrap value of $1 000. If the company uses the straight-line method of depreciation, what accounting procedures would you follow:

   a. To dispose of the old conveyor belt at scrap value?
   b. To insert the new conveyor belt in the records?

3. Show the depreciation in chart form for the fixed assets at the end of 2000 and 2001, using the straight-line and capital cost allowance methods. Take into consideration case problem #2 above in your calculations. (You may wish to use a spreadsheet to assist you with this case.)

CHAPTER SEVENTEEN

OBJECTIVES

Upon completion of this chapter, you will be able to:

- *plan* and *design* an accounting system for a small business
- *prepare* a conversion procedure from manual records
- *understand* the objectives of a computerized accounting system
- *create* company files
- *set up* company accounts using setup input forms
- *make* the accounting system ready for operation
- *enter* accounting transactions from realistic source documents
- *display* and *print* reports
- *analyze* and *interpret* case studies
- *develop* further group interpersonal skills
- *develop* further oral and written skills

COMPANY INFORMATION

Company Profile

Notes

Serene Sailing and Boating is located at RR #5 Baysville Ontario P0B 1A0
Its Revenue Canada business number is: 12365 4987

Serene Sailing and Boating is located just outside Baysville, Ontario. Situated in the heart of the Lake of Bays cottage and tourist region, Serene earns its revenue from renting out its canoes, kayaks and small sailboats at daily or weekly rates. Individuals and small groups often use Serene's equipment for short term guided camping trips, booking on their own or through clubs at which they have memberships. Most of these clubs have opened accounts with Serene and are located in Toronto or other southern Ontario cities. Serene Sailing and Boating also has available for its patrons a comfortable lounge area that serves beverages, snacks and light meals. The nature of the business makes it seasonal, and Serene closes down each year at the end of September, re-opening in May the following spring.

Serene also has set up accounts for its regular vendors who supply food for the lounge area, and boats and other supplies and equipment for the marina.

The owner, Alicia Nemo, has chosen not to be involved in the day-to-day aspects of running her business. She leaves that to Sid Surfer, the manager, who supervises the other three employees, performs the full range of management duties and pilots the cruise yacht during the three-hour cruise around the Lake of Bays. Nemo handles the promotion and marketing aspects of the business, looking for new clients at the clubs in cities where she has connections, and negotiating prices and terms with vendors. The remaining three employees provide sailing, kayaking and canoeing lessons to clients. They also inspect and maintain all the boating equipment, performing minor repairs to ensure client safety, and they work in the lounge on a rotating schedule.

Although Nemo leaves the operating side of the business to her manager, she has chosen to do the accounting herself as a way of keeping track of the business. She has always enjoyed accounting work and excelled in her business studies, which included a course in Simply Accounting. She especially finds the reports that are so easy to prepare in Simply Accounting very informative and uses them as the basis for her weekly planning meetings with her manager. In preparing for the conversion of her manual records, Nemo and Surfer have gathered the following information:

- Chart of Accounts
- Post-Closing Trial Balance
- Vendor Information
- Customer Information
- Employee Information and Profiles

SERENE SAILING AND BOATING
CHART OF ACCOUNTS

ASSETS
Cash in Bank
Accounts Receivable
Food Inventory
Marine Hardware
Marine Supplies
Safety Gear
Boats and Canoes
Cruise Yacht
Kayaks
Dock & Marina
Dry Dock & Office
Computers & Peripherals
Fax/Scanner
Vehicles

LIABILITIES
Bank Loan
Accounts Payable
Vacation Payable
EI Payable
CPP Payable
Income Tax Payable
EHT Payable
WCB Payable
PST Payable
GST Charged on Services
GST Paid on Purchases
Mortgage Payable

EQUITY
Alicia Nemo, Capital
Alicia Nemo, Drawings
Current Earnings

REVENUE
Charter and Cruise Services
Instructional Services
Leisure & Hospitality Services
Rental Services

EXPENSES
Advertising & Promotion
Bank Charges
General Expenses
Hydro Expense
Maintenance & Repairs
Telephone Expense
Wages
EI Expense
CPP Expense
WCB Expense
EHT Expense

SERENE SAILING AND BOATING
POST-CLOSING TRIAL BALANCE

June 30, 1999

Cash in Bank	$ 55 591.25	
Accounts Receivable	1 150.00	
Food Inventory	2 000.00	
Marine Hardware	1 500.00	
Marine Supplies	**2 000.00**	
Safety Gear	1 000.00	
Boats and Canoes	14 000.00	
Cruise Yacht	75 000.00	
Kayaks	10 000.00	
Dock & Marina	150 000.00	
Dry Dock & Office	150 000.00	
Computers & Peripherals	3 500.00	
Fax/Scanner	500.00	
Vehicles	18 000.00	
Bank Loan		$ 24 000.00
Accounts Payable		1 380.00
Vacation Payable		0.00
EI Payable		806.18
CPP Payable		595.66
Income Tax Payable		2 660.17
EHT Payable		115.02
WCB Payable		364.22
PST Payable		3 200.00
GST Charged on Services		2 800.00
GST Paid on Purchases	1 680.00	
Mortgage Payable		200 000.00
Alicia Nemo, Capital		250 000.00
	$485 921.25	$485 921.25

SERENE SAILING AND BOATING
VENDOR INFORMATION

Vendor Name (Contact)	Address Phone & Fax	Invoice Terms	Invoice Date	Invoice Number	Outstanding Balance
Bell Canada (Gabby Feast)	2 Call Ave. Huntsville, ON P1H 2A4 Tel: (705) 412-7108 Fax: (705) 412-7777	Net 1			
Neptune Yacht Outfitters (Roy Poseidon)	142 Safety Ave. Bracebridge, ON P1L 1A4 Tel: (705) 699-0234 Fax: (705) 699-0220	Net 5	6/26/99	NY-347	$460
Ontario Hydro (S. Erge)	33 Power Ave. Huntsville, ON P1H 1A4 Tel: (705) 412-5323 Fax: (705) 412-6333	Net 1			
Pirate Marina (John Silver)	RR #5 Baysville, ON P0B 1A0 Tel: (705) 639-6503 Fax: (705) 639-7181	Net 10			
Pisces Nautical (Ryan Fish)	100 Lakeshore Rd. Dorset, ON P0A 1E0 Tel: (705) 834-7195 Fax: (705) 834-7100	Net 10	6/27/99	PN-411	$920
Pride Foods (Sherry Spicer)	33 Root Ave. Huntsville, ON P1H 1A3 Tel: (705) 523-8622 Fax: (705) 523-7155	Net 15			
Receiver General of Canada	Summerside Tax Centre Summerside, PE C1N 6L2 Tel: (902) 821-8186	Net 1			
Sharkey's Marine House (Len Sharkey)	43 Dwight Bay Rd. Dwight, ON P0A 1B0 Tel: (705) 721-6345 Fax: (705) 721-8246	Net 5			
Treasurer of Ontario	Box 620 33 King St. W. Oshawa, ON L1H 8H5 Tel: (905) 965-8470	Net 1			
				Grand Total	$1 380

SERENE SAILING AND BOATING
CUSTOMER INFORMATION

Customer Name (Contact)	Address Phone & Fax	Invoice Terms	Invoice Date	Invoice Number	Outstanding Balance
Burlington Sail Club (Sara Sayles)	650 Dundas St. Burlington, ON L7W 2J2 Tel: (905) 792-4710 Fax: (905) 792-5271	Net 10			
CEO Rowers (Keith Sorenson)	50 Bay Street Toronto, ON M4R 1K3 Tel: (416) 592-6252 Fax: (416) 592-0568	Net 10			
City College Rowing Club (Ellis Tranner)	255 King St. E. Hamilton, ON L9H 2E4 Tel: (905) 523-8883 Fax: (905) 523-6858	Net 10			
Guelph Seniors' Canoe Club (Jason Warren)	612 Woolrich Rd. Guelph, ON N1H 2G2 Tel: (519) 822-7109 Fax: (519) 822-6179	Net 10			
Scarborough Sailing School (Tracey Mullen)	55 Rift Rd. Scarborough, ON M7L 2N3 Tel: (416) 596-7265 Fax: (416) 596-8821	Net 10	6/23/99	SS-78	$1 150
Varsity Kayak Team (John Stamos)	33 St. George St. Toronto, ON M4R 2J2 Tel: (416) 923-8653 Fax: (416) 923-7192	Net 10			
				Grand Total	$1 150

SERENE SAILING AND BOATING
EMPLOYEE INFORMATION SHEET

Employee Name	Sid Surfer	Jennifer Charybdis	Joseph Mara	Scylla Siren
Position	General Manager	Assistant	Assistant	Assistant
Social Insurance Number	412 666 232	373 821 142	271 832 143	634 279 143
Address & Telephone	500 Fairy Lake Dr.	35 Whirlpool Circle	89 Seashore Blvd.	61 Alarm Rd.
	Huntsville, ON	Huntsville, ON	Huntsville, ON	Huntsville, ON
	P1H 1C3	P1H 1B1	P1H 1E3	P1H 1B5
	(705) 412-4589	(705) 632-4190	(705) 412-9023	(705) 632-7521
Date of Birth (dd-mm-yy)	04-07-62	08-08-74	21-05-73	02-03-75

Tax Exemption (TD-1)

Basic Personal	$6 456	$6 456	$6 456	$6 456
Spouse				
Children under 18				
Disability				
Education & Tuition		$2 900	$2 900	$2 900
Other				
Total Exemptions	$6 456	$9 356	$9 356	$9 356

Employee Earnings

Regular Wage Rate		$16.00	$16.00	$16.00
Overtime Wage Rate		$24.00	$24.00	$24.00
Regular Salary	$3 600			
Commission				
Vacation	2 weeks	4%	4%	4%

Employee Deductions
EI, CPP Income Tax   calculations built into Simply Accounting program
Additional Income Tax

SERENE SAILING AND BOATING
HISTORICAL PAYROLL INFORMATION

Pay Period Ending June 30, 1999

Employee Name	Sid Surfer	Jennifer Charybdis	Joseph Mara	Scylla Siren
Regular		$2 560.00	$2 560.00	$2 560.00
Overtime		48.00	48.00	48.00
Salary	$3 600.00			
Commission				
Benefit				
Vacation Paid		104.32	104.32	104.32
Gross	3 600.00	2 712.32	2 712.32	2 712.32
EI Ins Earnings	3 600.00	2 608.00	2 608.00	2 608.00
EI	95.88	80.01	80.01	80.01
CPP	92.63	68.40	68.40	68.40
Income Tax	955.81	568.12	568.12	568.12
Withheld	1 144.32	716.53	716.53	716.53
Net Pay	2 455.68	1 995.79	1 995.79	1 995.79

Advance Paid
Vacation Owed

Employee Profiles

Sid Surfer as manager oversees all aspects of the day-to-day business, including developing a balanced and fair rotating schedule of work for the three summer students. Surfer is married but does not claim his partner as a dependent for tax purposes. He has worked for Serene Sailing since May 1, 1993, and now receives a monthly salary of $3 600. At the end of each work season, he receives an additional two weeks of salary as vacation pay. There are no company benefits or other deductions.

Jennifer Charybdis, **Joseph Mara** and **Scylla Siren** are Physical Education students at the college in Huntsville. Since they were all hired on May 1, 1998, this is their second summer working at Serene. Together they perform the variety of tasks that Serene requires, dividing their time between instruction, guided cruise tours, serving and preparing food in the lounge, and maintenance work. All three have life guard, first aid and CPR training. They are all single and self-supporting but have their college tuition and education deduction as additional TD-1 claims. In addition to an hourly wage of $16 and $24 for each hour of overtime work after forty hours, they receive 4 percent vacation pay with their bi-weekly paycheque. That is, vacation pay is not retained. There are no company benefits or other deductions.

Additional Payroll Information

Employer contributions include:

- WCB rate at 3.103 based on maximum assessable earnings of $55 600
- EHT factor of 0.98
- CPP contributions equal to employee contributions
- EI contributions at 1.4 times the rate of employee contributions.

The salaried employee is paid monthly, hourly employees are paid every two weeks and vacation pay is included with each paycheque.

INSTRUCTIONS

Warning!

Save your work and make backups frequently.

1. Using the setup input forms provided in Appendix A and all of the information presented in this application, set up the company accounts for Serene Sailing and Boating in Simply Accounting using the following steps:

   a. **create** company files in a new data directory for storing the company records using the Integration Plus starter files
   b. **enter** the company information
   c. **enter** names and printer information
   d. **prepare** the settings by changing the default settings as necessary
   e. **organize** the Balance Sheet and Income Statement accounts
   f **turn off** the integration function for accounts not required
   g. **modify**, **create** and **remove** accounts to correspond to your Balance Sheet and Income Statement
   h. **enter** customer, vendor and employee information
   i. **enter** historical balances in all ledgers
   j. **back up** your files
   k. **set** ledgers to ready
   l. **finish** your session.

2. Using the information provided, record entries for the source documents using Simply Accounting.

3. After you have completed your entries, print the following reports:

    a. General Journal (all ledger entries) from July 1 to July 14, 1999
    b. the Vendor Aged Detail Report for all vendors on July 14, 1999
    c. the Customer Aged Detail Report for all customers on July 14, 1999
    d. the Employee Summary (all employees) for the pay period ending July 14, 1999
    e. the Income Statement for the period ending July 14, 1999

SOURCE DOCUMENTS

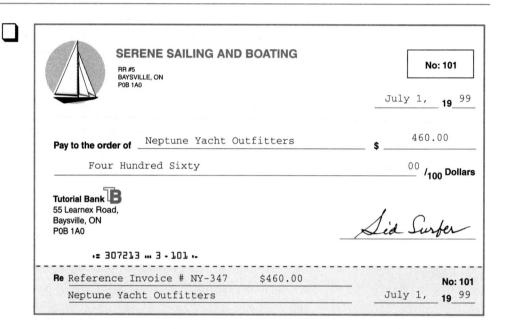

SERENE SAILING AND BOATING
RR #5
BAYSVILLE, ON
P0B 1A0

No: 101

July 1, 19 99

Pay to the order of Neptune Yacht Outfitters $ 460.00

Four Hundred Sixty   00 /100 **Dollars**

Tutorial Bank TB
55 Learnex Road,
Baysville, ON
P0B 1A0

Sid Surfer

·≡ 307213 ⑈ 3 - 101 ⑈

Re Reference Invoice # NY-347 $460.00   **No: 101**
Neptune Yacht Outfitters   July 1, 19 99

Lagoon Ad Agency
33 Muskoka Rd.
Huntsville, ON
P1H 1A2

LAA-691

NAME: Serene Sailing and Boating
ADDRESS: RR#5
Baysville, ON
P0B 1A0

phone: 705-412-8002
fax : 705-412-7909

Date	Description	Charges		Amount	
July 2/99	Advertising Flyers	100	00	100	00
		GST		7	00
Terms: Cash on Receipt		PST		8	00
GST # 345279128		**Total**		115	00

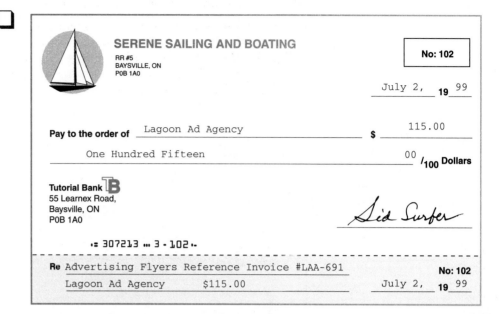

SERENE SAILING AND BOATING

RR #5
BAYSVILLE, ON
P0B 1A0

No: 102

July 2, 19 99

Pay to the order of ___Lagoon Ad Agency___ $ ___115.00___

___One Hundred Fifteen___ 00/100 **Dollars**

Tutorial Bank TB
55 Learnex Road,
Baysville, ON
P0B 1A0

Sid Surfer

·: 307213 ⫶⫶ 3 - 102 ·-

Re Advertising Flyers Reference Invoice #LAA-691
Lagoon Ad Agency $115.00

No: 102
July 2, 19 99

Metro Trust

33 Redway Rd.
Scarborough, ON
M7L 2N9

No: 139

July 3, 19 99

Pay to the order of ___Serene Sailing and Boating___ $ ___1,150.00___

___One Thousand One Hundred Fifty___ 00/100 **Dollars**

SCARBOROUGH SAILING SCHOOL
55 Rift Road,
Scarborough, ON
M7L 2N3

Tracey Mullen
Treasurer

·: 2022 ⫶⫶ 045 - 139 ·-

Re Reference Invoice #SS-78 $1,150.00
Serene Sailing and Boating

No: 139
July 3, 19 99

[JUST CRUISING ALONG]

SERENE SAILING AND BOATING

RR #5
Baysville, ON
P0B 1A0

Phone for reservations (705) 682-1021
Fax for reservations (705) 682-1000

SS-101

GST # 123654987

CUSTOMER STATEMENT

NAME: Guelph Seniors' Canoe Club
ADDRESS: 612 Woolrich Rd.
Guelph, Ontario
N1H 2G2

RENTALS:		RATE PER PERSON:
CRUISES	☐	$75 / Day
BOATS & CANOES	☑	$50 / Day
KAYAKS	☐	$40 / Day
INSTRUCTION	☐	$100 / Day

EQUIPMENT INCLUDED IN CHARGES.

Date	Transaction	Rate/Person		Amount	
July 4/99	Canoe & Equipment Rental for				
	party of 10 for 2 days	50	00	1000	00
	Terms: net 10 days				

Signature:	Jason Warren		Goods & Services Tax	70	00
Paid by:	Visa	M-C	**Provincial Sales Tax**	80	00
Cash	Cheque	Other	**Amount Owing**	1150	00

Serene Sailing and Boating
RR #5
Baysville, ON
P0B 1A0

WE TAKE PRIDE

Pride Foods

33 Root Ave.
Huntsville, ON
P1H 1A3
(705) 523-8622
(705) 523-7155 [Fax]

CUSTOMER COPY

PF-3312

Billing Date: July 5/99

Customer No: P4293

Date	Description	Charges		Payments		Amount	
July 5/99	Smoked Meats	200	00			200	00
	Prepared Foods (taxable)	500	00			500	00
	Fresh Fruits & Veg.	200	00			200	00
	Dry Goods	100	00			100	00
				SUBTOTAL		1000	00
Terms: net 15 days				**GST**	7%	35	00
GST # 267212432				**PST**	8%	40	00
Signature	Sid Surfer			**OWING**		1075	00

Overdue accounts are subject to 18% interest per year.

ONTARIO HYDRO

33 POWER AVENUE, HUNTSVILLE, ON P1H 1A4

Invoice Date: July 5, 1999

SERVICE NAME AND ADDRESS

No: 4017 09428 01

Serene Sailing and Boating
RR #5
Baysville, ON
P0B 1A0

Invoice No: 432174

CUSTOMER COPY

Months	Reading	Description	Net Amount	
1	63538	Commercial Consumption 5000kwh	200	00
1		Flat Rate Energy Charge-Water Heater	60	00
1		Water Heater Rental 3 (Tanks)	40	00

	Before	**GST**	**7%**	21 00
Average Daily kwh Consumption	July 15/99			

Same Period Last Year	**This Bill**	**Pay This Amount** 👉	**Total**	321 00
197	176			
GST # 367432432		**After** July 15/99	**Pay**	351 00

SERENE SAILING AND BOATING

RR #5
BAYSVILLE, ON
P0B 1A0

No: 103

July 5, 19 99

Pay to the order of Ontario Hydro $ 321.00

Three Hundred Twenty-One   00 /100 **Dollars**

Tutorial Bank 𝕋B
55 Learnex Road,
Baysville, ON
P0B 1A0

Sid Surfer

⑆ 307213 ⑈ 3 ⑉ 103 ⑈

- -

Re Reference Invoice #432174 $321.00   **No: 103**

Ontario Hydro   July 5, 19 99

[JUST CRUISING ALONG]

SERENE SAILING AND BOATING

RR #5
Baysville, ON
P0B 1A0

Phone for reservations (705) 682-1021
Fax for reservations (705) 682-1000

SS-102

GST # 123654987

CUSTOMER STATEMENT

NAME: CEO Rowers
ADDRESS: 50 Bay Street,
Toronto, ON
M4R 1K3

RENTALS: **RATE PER PERSON:**
CRUISES   ☐ $75 / Day
BOATS & CANOES   ☑ $50 / Day
KAYAKS   ☑ $40 / Day
INSTRUCTION   ☑ $100 / Day
EQUIPMENT INCLUDED IN CHARGES.

Date	Transaction	Rate/Person		Amount	
July 6/99	Canoes for 4 persons for 3 days	50	00	600	00
	Kayaks for 2 persons for 3 days	40	00	240	00
	Full Day Instruction for 2 persons	100	00	200	00
	Terms: net 10 days				

Signature: *Keith Sorenson*			**Goods & Services Tax**	72	80
Paid by:	Visa	M-C	**Provincial Sales Tax**	83	20
Cash	Cheque	Other	**Amount Owing**	1196	00

Neptune Yacht Outfitters

142 Safety Avenue, Bracebridge, ON P1L 1A4

To
Serene Sailing and Boating
RR #5
Baysville, ON
P0B 1A0

INVOICE NO   232

Date: July 7/99

Phone   699-0234
Fax   699-0220

Stock Code	Qty	Description	Price		Amount	
LJ-153	6	Life-jackets	40	00	240	00
WO-192	6	Pairs of wooden oars	60	00	360	00
			GROSS		600	00

CUSTOMER COPY	**Terms on Account:** net 5 days			**GST**	7%	42	00
Method of Payment	On account ✓	C.O.D.	Credit Cards	**PST**	8%	48	00
GST # 4 2 1 3 2 7 1 6 7				**TOTAL**		690	00

Sharkey's Marine House

FOR PASSIONATE SAILORS

43 Dwight Bay Road, Dwight, ON P0A 1B0

NO: 673

Date: July 7/1999

Phone 721-6345
Fax 721-8246

Sold To:

Serene Sailing and Boating
RR #5
Baysville, ON
P0B 1A0

Product Code	Qty and Description		Price		Amount	
CN-XZ250	2	Canoes	400	00	800	00
KY-AF100	2	Kayaks	300	00	600	00
			GST		98	00
Signature	Terms: net 5 days		PST		112	00
Sid Surfer	GST # 3 8 3 1 2 3 4 5 6		AMOUNT OWING		1610	00

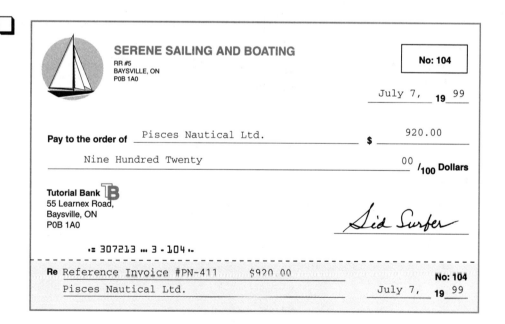

SERENE SAILING AND BOATING
RR #5
BAYSVILLE, ON
P0B 1A0

No: 104

July 7, 19 99

Pay to the order of Pisces Nautical Ltd. $ 920.00

Nine Hundred Twenty   00 /100 **Dollars**

Tutorial Bank
55 Learnex Road,
Baysville, ON
P0B 1A0

Sid Surfer

.: 307213 ... 3 - 104 ..

Re Reference Invoice #PN-411 $920.00   No: 104
Pisces Nautical Ltd.   July 7, 19 99

[JUST CRUISING ALONG]

SERENE SAILING AND BOATING
RR #5
Baysville, ON
P0B 1A0

SALES SUMMARY STATEMENT

NO: 5

CRUISES ☑
HOSPITALITY SERVICES ☑

Week	Transaction	Rate/Person		Amount	
July 1-7	30 Cruises # 121-150	75	00	2250	00
	Hospitality Services Receipts				
	#1093-1428			1250	00
	SUBTOTAL			3500	00

Approved: *Sid Surfer*	**GST**	245	00
	PST	280	00
GST # 123654987	**Amount Deposited in Bank**	4025	00

[JUST CRUISING ALONG]

SERENE SAILING AND BOATING
RR #5
Baysville, ON
P0B 1A0

Phone for reservations (705) 682-1021
Fax for reservations (705) 682-1000

SS-103

GST # 123654987

CUSTOMER STATEMENT

NAME: City College Rowing Club
ADDRESS: 255 King East
Hamilton, ON
L9H 2E4

RENTALS:		RATE PER PERSON:
CRUISES	☐	$75 / Day
BOATS & CANOES	☑	$50 / Day
KAYAKS	☐	$40 / Day
INSTRUCTION	☑	$100 / Day

☐ EQUIPMENT INCLUDED IN CHARGES.

Date	Transaction	Rate/Person		Amount	
July 8/99	Canoes for 6 persons for 1 day	50	00	300	00
	Full Day Instruction for 1 person	100	00	100	00
	Terms: net 10 days				

Signature: *Ellis Tranner*			Goods & Services Tax	28	00
Paid by:	**Visa**	**M-C**	**Provincial Sales Tax**	32	00
Cash	**Cheque**	**Other**	**Amount Owing**	460	00

BELL CANADA

2 CALL AVENUE
HUNTSVILLE ON
P1H 2A4

July 9, 1999

Call 412-7108 for enquiries about this bill.

Telephone : (705) 682-1021

Account: Serene Sailing and Boating
Address: RR #5
Baysville, ON
P0B 1A0

SUMMARY			
Service		120	00
Equipment Rental		80	00
Tax-Fed.	14.00	14	00
Tax-Prov.	16.00	16	00
Chargeable Calls			
Tax-Fed	0.00		
Tax-Prov.	0.00		
GST #412379129			
INVOICE NO: BC-1411 **PLEASE PAY THIS AMOUNT UPON RECEIPT**		$230	00

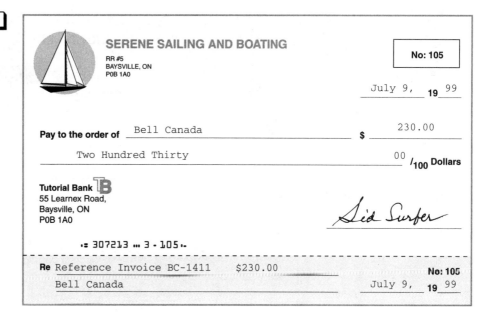

SERENE SAILING AND BOATING

RR #5
BAYSVILLE, ON
P0B 1A0

No: 105

July 9, **19** 99

Pay to the order of Bell Canada $ 230.00

Two Hundred Thirty   00 /**100 Dollars**

Tutorial Bank
55 Learnex Road,
Baysville, ON
P0B 1A0

Sid Surfer

·: 307213 ··· 3 - 105·-

Re Reference Invoice BC-1411 $230.00   **No: 105**

Bell Canada   July 9, **19** 99

WATERWORKS CLOTHING
64 Lake Road
Huntsville, ON P1H 2A1

IN MUSKOKA SINCE 1947

INVOICE NO: 5524
Phone: 705-699-2218

Date: July 10/1999

GST # 5 1 2 4 2 3 1 2 9

CUSTOMER

Serene Sailing and Boating
RR #5
Baysville, ON
P0B 1A0

CODE	Description	Qty	Price		Amount	
DS-1422	Deck shoes	3	40	00	120	00
			GST		8	40
Signature	**Terms:** net 30 days		PST		9	60
Sid Surfer	**Overdue accounts subject to 2% interest penalty per month**		TOTAL		138	00

[JUST CRUISING ALONG]

SERENE SAILING AND BOATING
RR #5
Baysville, ON
P0B 1A0

Phone for reservations (705) 682-1021
Fax for reservations (705) 682-1000

SS-104

GST # 123654987

CUSTOMER STATEMENT

NAME: Burlington Sail Club
ADDRESS: 650 Dundas Street
Burlington, ON
L7W 2J2

RENTALS:		RATE PER PERSON:
CRUISES	☐	$75 / Day
BOATS & CANOES	☐	$50 / Day
KAYAKS	☑	$40 / Day
INSTRUCTION	☑	$100 / Day

EQUIPMENT INCLUDED IN CHARGES.

Date	Transaction	Rate/Person		Amount	
July 10/99	Kayaks and Equipment Rental for				
	party of 8 for 3 days	40	00	960	00
	Full Day Instruction for 4 persons	100	00	400	00
	Visa# 4510 692 181 022				
	Terms:				

Signature:			**Goods & Services Tax**	95	20
Paid by:	**Visa** ✓	**M-C**	**Provincial Sales Tax**	108	80
Cash	**Cheque**	**Other**	**Amount Owing**	1564	00

GST # 2 7 9 1 2 4 3 2 7

QUALITY PARTS AND SERVICE

Invoice No: 451

Date: July 11/1999

Serene Sailing and Boating
RR #5
Baysville, ON
P0B 1A0

PIRATE MARINA
RR #5, Baysville, ON
P0B 1A0
Tel: 705-639-6503
Fax: 705-639-7181

CODE	Description	Price		Amount	
RPM-AWL	Repairs & maintenance and				
	overhaul of engines	800	00	800	00
		GST		56	00
APPROVAL:	**Terms:** net 10 days	PST		64	00

	CASH	ON ACCOUNT	CREDIT CARD	OWING		
Sid Surfer		✓			920	00

SERENE SAILING AND BOATING
RR #5
BAYSVILLE, ON
P0B 1A0

No: 106

July 12, 19 99

Pay to the order of Neptune Yacht Outfitters $ 690.00

Six Hundred Ninety   00 /100 **Dollars**

Tutorial Bank TB
55 Learnex Road,
Baysville, ON
P0B 1A0

Sid Surfer

⑈ 307213 ⑈ 3 - 106 ⑈

Re Reference Invoice #232 $690.00   **No: 106**

Neptune Yacht Outfitters   July 12, 19 99

SERENE SAILING AND BOATING

RR #5
BAYSVILLE, ON
P0B 1A0

No: 107

July 12, **19** 99

Pay to the order of Sharkey's Marine House $ 1610.00

Sixteen Hundred Ten   00 /₁₀₀ **Dollars**

Tutorial Bank TB
55 Learnex Road,
Baysville, ON
P0B 1A0

Sid Surfer

·⸬ 307213 ⸬ 3 - 107 ·⸬

Re Reference Invoice #673 $1610   **No: 107**

Sharkey's Marine House   July 12, **19** 99

Invoice: PN413

PISCES NAUTICAL

**100 Lakeshore Road
Dorset, ON P0A 1E0**

CUSTOMER

Serene Sailing and Boating
RR #5
Baysville, ON
P0B 1A0

GST # 167279142   Telephone: (705) 834-7195

Date	Transaction			Amount	
July 12/99	1 Sailboat	300	00	300	00
	1 Sail	100	00	100	00
			Federal Tax	28	00
Signature: *Sid Surfer*			**Provincial Tax**	32	00
Paid by:	on account		**Amount Due**	$460	00
Terms: net 10 days					

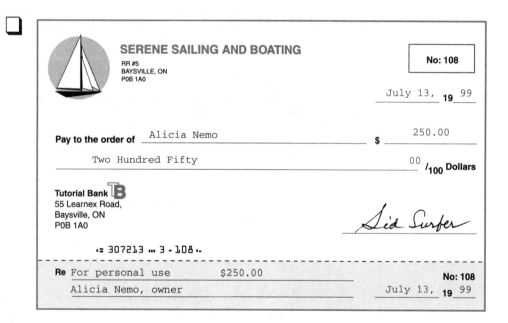

[JUST CRUISING ALONG]

SERENE SAILING AND BOATING

RR #5
Baysville, ON
P0B 1A0

Phone for reservations (705) 682-1021
Fax for reservations (705) 682-1000

SS-105

GST # 123654987

CUSTOMER STATEMENT

RENTALS:		RATE PER PERSON:	
CRUISES	☐	$75 / Day
BOATS & CANOES	☐	$50 / Day
KAYAKS	☑	$40 / Day
INSTRUCTION	☐	$100 / Day

EQUIPMENT INCLUDED IN CHARGES.

NAME: Varsity Kayak Team
ADDRESS: 33 St. George St.,
Toronto, ON
M4R 2J2

Date	Transaction	Rate/Person		Amount	
July 12/99	Kayaks and Equipment Rental for				
	party of 8 for 3 days	40	00	960	00
	Terms:				

PAID IN CASH

Signature:	John Stamos		Goods & Services Tax	67	20
Paid by:	**Visa**	**M-C**	Provincial Sales Tax	76	80
Cash ✓	**Cheque**	**Other**	Amount Owing	1104	00

SERENE SAILING AND BOATING

RR #5
BAYSVILLE, ON
P0B 1A0

No: 108

July 13, 19 99

Pay to the order of ___Alicia Nemo___ $ ___250.00___

___Two Hundred Fifty___ 00 /100 **Dollars**

Tutorial Bank ⊤B
55 Learnex Road,
Baysville, ON
P0B 1A0

Sid Surfer

•⊨ 307213 ⑾ 3 - 108 •⊨

Re For personal use $250.00
Alicia Nemo, owner

No: 108
July 13, 19 99

Guelph Seniors' Canoe Club

No: 43

July 13, 19 99

Pay to the order of   Serene Sailing and Boating $ 1,150.00

One Thousand One Hundred Fifty   00 /100 **Dollars**

NB **National Bank**
40 CLARK AVE.
GUELPH, ON
N1G 1X7

Klas VanderWaet
Manager

⑆ 3014 ⑈ 2 - 43 ⑈

Re Reference Invoice #SS-101   No: 43
    Serene Sailing Re: Rentals $1150   July 13, 19 99

CEO ROWERS

No: 124

July 13, 19 99

Pay to the order of   Serene Sailing and Boating $ 1,196.00

One Thousand One Hundred Ninety-Six   00 /100 **Dollars**

Toronto Trust TT
61 Bay Street
Toronto, Ont.
M4R 1K3

Rick Solway
ASSISTANT: FINANCE DEPT

⑆ 41414 ⑈ 4 - 124 ⑈

Re Reference Invoice #SS-102   No: 124
    Serene Sailing and Boating $1196.00   July 13, 19 99

SERENE SAILING AND BOATING
RR #5
Baysville, ON
P0B 1A0

Phone for reservations (705) 682-1021
Fax for reservations (705) 682-1000

SS-106

GST # 123654987

CUSTOMER STATEMENT

NAME: Scarborough Sailing School
ADDRESS: 55 Rift Road
Scarborough, ON
M7L 2N3

RENTALS:		RATE PER PERSON:
CRUISES	☐	$75 / Day
BOATS & CANOES	☐	$50 / Day
KAYAKS	☑	$40 / Day
INSTRUCTION	☐	$100 / Day

EQUIPMENT INCLUDED IN CHARGES.

Date	Transaction	Rate/Person		Amount	
July 14/99	Kayaks and Equipment Rental for				
	party of 25 for 1 day	40	00	1000	00
	Terms: net 10 days				

Signature:	*Tracey Mullen*		Goods & Services Tax	70	00
Paid by:	Visa	M-C	Provincial Sales Tax	80	00
Cash	Cheque	Other	**Amount Owing**	$1150	00

July 14, 1999

ACCOUNT NO.:	307213	**ADVICE TO**	DEBIT MEMO	
CODE:	12	**ACCOUNT HOLDER**	3246721	

PARTICULARS	AMOUNT
Bank Charges and Services	34.95

ISSUED BY:	LK	VERIFIED BY:	NTM	

M
A
I
L

T
O

Serene Sailing and Boating
RR #5
Baysville, ON
P0B 1A0

TB

TUTORIAL BANK
55 Learnex Road
Baysville, ON
P0B 1A0

July 14, 1999

ACCOUNT NO.:	307213	**ADVICE TO**	**CREDIT MEMO**
CODE:	14	**ACCOUNT HOLDER**	2143217

PARTICULARS	AMOUNT
Semi-Annual Interest on Bank Account	365.00

ISSUED BY:	LK	VERIFIED BY:	NTM	

M
A
I Serene Sailing and Boating
L RR #5
   Baysville, ON
T P0B 1A0
O

TB **TUTORIAL BANK**
55 Learnex Road
Baysville, ON
P0B 1A0

[JUST CRUISING ALONG]

SERENE SAILING AND BOATING
RR #5
Baysville, ON
P0B 1A0

SALES SUMMARY STATEMENT

NO: 6

CRUISES ☑
HOSPITALITY SERVICES ☑

Week	Transaction	Rate/Person		Amount	
July 8-14	35 Cruises # 151-185	75	00	2625	00
	Hospitality Services Receipts				
	#1429-1802			1400	00
	SUBTOTAL			4025	00

Approved: *Sid Surfer*

GST # 123654987

GST	281	75
PST	322	00
Amount Deposited in Bank	4628	75

**Employee
Time Sheet**

[JUST CRUISING ALONG]

SERENE SAILING AND BOATING
RR #5
Baysville, ON
P0B 1A0

NAME   J E N N I F E R   C H A R Y B D I S

EMPLOYEE NUMBER   1

SOCIAL INSURANCE NUMBER   3 7 3 8 2 1 1 4 2   PAY PERIOD ENDING   0 7 – 14 – 9 9

Day	Week 1 July 1 - July 7		Week 2 July 8 - July 14	
	Hours		Hours	
	Reg	Ovt	Reg	Ovt
Mon			8	
Tues	8		8	2
Wed	8			
Thurs	8	2	8	
Fri			8	
Sat	8		8	
Sun	8			
Total hours	40	2	40	2

**Employee
Time Sheet**

[JUST CRUISING ALONG]

SERENE SAILING AND BOATING
RR #5
Baysville, ON
P0B 1A0

NAME   J O S E P H   M A R A

EMPLOYEE NUMBER   2

SOCIAL INSURANCE NUMBER   2 7 1 8 3 2 1 4 3   PAY PERIOD ENDING   0 7 – 14 – 9 9

Day	Week 1 July 1 - July 7		Week 2 July 8 - July 14	
	Hours		Hours	
	Reg	Ovt	Reg	Ovt
Mon	8			
Tues	8	2		
Wed			8	
Thurs	8		8	
Fri	8		8	
Sat	8		8	
Sun			8	
Total hours	40	2	40	0

**Employee
Time Sheet**

SERENE SAILING AND BOATING
[JUST CRUISING ALONG]
RR #5
Baysville, ON
P0B 1A0

NAME S C Y L L A   S I R E N

EMPLOYEE NUMBER 3

SOCIAL INSURANCE NUMBER 6 3 4 2 7 9 1 4 3   **PAY PERIOD ENDING** 0 7 – 14 – 9 9

Day	Week 1 July 1 – July 7		Week 2 July 8 – July 14	
	Hours		Hours	
	Reg	Ovt	Reg	Ovt
Mon	8			
Tues	8		8	
Wed	8		8	
Thurs			8	
Fri	8	2	8	
Sat			8	
Sun	8			
Total hours	40	2	40	0

SERENE SAILING AND BOATING
[JUST CRUISING ALONG]

Memo   *From the desk of Sid Surfer*

July 14

For month ending June 30:
Remit to Receiver General of Canada

A) GST
B) EI
*   CPP*
*   Income Tax*

Remit to Treasurer of Ontario
C) PST less 5% Sales Tax Commission.

CASE PROBLEM

Many small businesses in your neighbourhood probably still maintain their accounting records manually, often relying on independent accountants to keep their records, prepare the required statements and file returns with Revenue Canada.

Take a survey of about ten to fifteen small businesses in your neighbourhood, including both service and retail types of business, to find out what accounting methods or systems they use. Prepare your questions ahead of time and keep them short and simple. Always maintain a professional, business-like and courteous manner with the businesses you are surveying.

Choose one of the businesses that is using manual accounting methods. Assume that you are their consultant and prepare a proposal for the conversion to Simply Accounting. Your report for them should include the following:

a. a description of the tasks involved in converting their accounting records and implementing the new system for the service centre
b. a time frame for completing each of these tasks
c. your rationale or decision-making criteria for each of the tasks and time estimates
d. an estimate of the training required to familiarize the owner/accountant with the new methods (assume they have no previous experience with computers)
e. a description of the problems they can expect to encounter in using the new system and any limitations of the new system.

To prepare your answer, you should visit the business to investigate its methods of operation. Use this information to guide your discussion of the conversion process. (Your instructor will tell you whether you should investigate an actual business as part of the case problem, or whether your proposal should be theoretical only.)

You may wish to work in groups. If so, suggest a plan by which members within your group could be given specific duties in helping to assess the needs of the business and to implement the computerized accounting system. Your group should decide the following questions in advance.

a. What information will you gather?
b. Who will gather information?
c. How much time will you allow for each stage?
d. How will you coordinate the work of the different team members?
e. How will you implement the conversion for the business?
f. How will the group members be accountable to one another?

Warning!

Establish a liaison first with the business you are investigating so that when gathering information, your credibility is established and company time is not wasted.

PART 3
APPENDICES

Input Forms

SYSTEM PREPARATION

Form SYS-1
Page 1 of 1

COMPANY INFORMATION

Name: _____

Street: _____

City: _____

Province: _____

Postal Code: _____

Business No.: _____

Fiscal Start: ____ - ____ - ____

Fiscal End: ____ - ____ - ____

Conversion: ____ - ____ - ____

PRINTERS

	Form/Paper Size	Margins TOP	LEFT
Reports/Graphs: _____	_____	_____	_____
Cheques: _____	_____	_____	_____
Invoices: _____	_____	_____	_____
Other: _____	_____		

	Number across page	Height	Width
Labels: _____	_____	_____	_____

NAMES

Tax: _____   Deduction C: _____

Income A: _____   Deduction D: _____

Income B: _____   Deduction E: _____

Deduction A: _____   Prov. Tax: _____

Deduction B: _____   Project Title: _____

SYSTEM PREPARATION

SETTINGS: Display

Display Font : _____   Size : _____

Hide Modules

Payables: Y ___ , N___

Receivables: Y ___ , N___

Payroll: Y ___ , N___

Inventory: Y ___ , N___

Project: Y ___ , N___

Display To Do Lists: At Startup Y ___ , N___   After Advancing Using Date Y ___ , N___

Home Window Backround: _____

Show Status Bar: Y ___ , N___

SETTINGS: System

Track Inventory Turnover: Y ___ , N___

Store Invoice Lookup Details: Y ___ , N___

Cash Basis Accounting: Y ___ , N___   Date _____

Use Cheque No. as Source Code: Y ___ , N___

Auto Advice: On ___ , Off ___

Backup Frequency: _____

SETTINGS: General

Skip Accounts Icon Window: Y ___ , N___

Budget: Y ___ , N___   Budget Period _____

Bank Reconciliation: Y ___ , N___

SYSTEM PREPARATION

SETTINGS: Payables

Skip Vendors Icon Window: Y ___ , N ___

Aging: _____ , _____ , _____

SETTINGS: Receivables

Skip Customers Icon Window: Y ___ , N ___

Aging: _____ , _____ , _____

Interest Charges: _____ %   Y ___ , N ___   Over _____ days

Include Invoices Paid in Last _____ Days

Terms: _____ % _____ Days, Net _____ Days

Apply these terms to all customers: Y ___ , N ___

SETTINGS: Sales Taxes

GST Rate 1:   _____ %

GST Rate 2:   _____ %

Use Quebec Tax: Y ___ , N ___

PST Rate: _____

Apply PST to Freight: Y ___ , N ___

Apply PST to GST: Y ___ , N ___

SETTINGS: Forms

Next Invoice Number: _____

Next PO Number: _____

Next Payables Cheque Number: _____

Next Payroll Cheque Number: _____

Confirm Printing   For Invoices: Y ___ , N ___

                     For POs: Y ___ , N ___

                     For Cheques: Y ___ , N ___

Print Address   On Invoices: Y ___ , N ___

                     On POs: Y ___ , N ___

                     On Statements: Y ___ , N ___

                     On Cheques: Y ___ , N ___

Default Invoice Comment: _____

_____

SYSTEM PREPARATION

SETTINGS: Payroll

Skip Employee Icon Window: Y __ , N __

Auto Payroll Deduction: Y __ , N __

Deduction A after Tax: Y __ , N __

Deduction B after Tax: Y __ , N __

Deduction C after Tax: Y __ , N __

Deduction D after Tax: Y __ , N __

Deduction E after Tax: Y __ , N __

EI Factor: _____

EHT Factor :   _____

Keep Employee Details for 1 year _____ or 2 years _____

SETTINGS: Payroll WCB

Province : _____

WCB Maximum Assessable Earnings: _____

SETTINGS: Inventory

Skip Inventory Icon Window: Y __ , N __

Profit Evaluation: Markup _____ Margin _____ (Choose one only)

Sort by: Number _____ Description _____ (Choose one only)

Allow inventory to go below zero: Y __ , N __

SETTINGS: Project

Skip Project Icon Window: Y __ , N __

Distribute Payroll Journal by: (Choose one only)	Distribute Other Journals by: (Choose one only)
Amount _____	Amount _____
Percent _____	Percent _____
Hours _____	

Warn if distribution is not complete: Y __ , N __

ORGANIZATION: BALANCE SHEET ACCOUNTS

ASSETS - [section heading]

T
Y
P
E

Account Description	Amount	Amount
	Left	Right

Account Description	Amount	Amount
	Left	Right

Account Description	Amount	Amount
	Left	Right

TOTAL ASSETS - [section total]

LIABILITIES - [section heading]

T
Y
P
E

Account Description	Amount	Amount
	Left	Right

Account Description	Amount	Amount
	Left	Right

TOTAL LIABILITIES - [section total]

EQUITY - [section heading]

Account Description	Amount	Amount
	Left	Right

TOTAL EQUITY - [section total]
LIABILITIES AND EQUITY

ORGANIZATION: INCOME STATEMENT ACCOUNTS

REVENUE - [section heading]

Account Description	Amount	Amount
	Left	Right

T
Y
P
E

TOTAL REVENUE - [section total]

EXPENSE - [section heading]

Account Description	Amount	Amount
	Left	Right

T
Y
P
E

Account Description	Amount	Amount
	Left	Right

Account Description	Amount	Amount
	Left	Right

TOTAL EXPENSE - [section total]
NET INCOME

SKELETON ACCOUNTS - MAINTENANCE

Account Title [Initial]	SECTION	TYPE	Initial Account Number	CODE	Account Title [New]	TYPE	New Account Number
CURRENT ASSETS	A	H	1 0 0 0				
Bank	A	R	1 0 2 0				
Accounts Receivable	A	R	1 2 0 0				
TOTAL CURRENT ASSETS	A	T	1 3 9 0				
CURRENT LIABILITIES	L	H	2 0 0 0				
Accounts Payable	L	R	2 2 0 0				
TOTAL CURRENT LIABILITIES	L	T	2 6 9 0				
EARNINGS	E	H	3 0 0 0				
Retained Earnings	E	R	3 5 6 0				
Current Earnings	E	X	3 6 0 0				
TOTAL EARNINGS	E	T	3 6 9 0				
REVENUE	R	H	4 0 0 0				
General Revenue	R	R	4 0 2 0				
TOTAL REVENUE	R	T	4 3 9 0				
EXPENSES	X	H	5 0 0 0				
General Expense	X	R	5 0 2 0				
TOTAL EXPENSES	X	T	5 3 9 0				

SECTION:
A = ASSETS
L = LIABILITIES
E = EQUITY
R = REVENUE
X = EXPENSE

TYPE:
H = Heading
R = Right
L = Left
S = Subtotal
X = Current Earnings
T = Total

CODE:
R = Remove
M = Modify
* = no change

CHART OF ACCOUNTS MAINTENANCE

Code: M = Modify   Type: H = Heading   S = Subtotal   Suppress: Y = Yes
       C = Create   R = Right   X = Current Earnings   N = No
       R = Remove   L = Left   T = Total

Code	Account Title	Account No.	Type	Sup-press

INTEGRATION PLUS ACCOUNTS - MAINTENANCE

SECTION:
A = ASSETS
L = LIABILITIES
E = EQUITY
R = REVENUE
X = EXPENSE

TYPE:
H = Heading
R = Right
L = Left
S = Subtotal
X = Current Earnings
T = Total

MODULE:
GL = GENERAL
AP = PAYABLES
AR = RECEIVABLES
PR = PAYROLL
IN = INVENTORY

CODE:
R = Remove
M = Modify
* = no change

Account Title [Initial]	SECTION	TYPE	Module [used by]	Initial Account Number	Account Title [New]	CODE	TYPE	New Account Number
CURRENT ASSETS	A	H	—	1000				
Bank A - Payable	A	L	AP	1060				
Bank B - Receivable	A	L	AR	1080				
Bank C - Payroll	A	L	PR	1100				
Cash - Total	A	S	—	1120				
Accounts Receivable	A	R	AR	1200				
Advances Receivable	A	R	PR	1240				
Inventory	A	R	—	1260				
TOTAL CURRENT ASSETS	A	T	—	1390				
CURRENT LIABILITIES	L	H	—	2000				
Accounts Payable	L	R	AP	2200				
Vacation Payable	L	R	PR	2300				
EI Payable	L	L	PR	2310				
CPP Payable	L	L	PR	2320				
Income Tax Payable	L	L	PR	2330				
Receiver General Payable	L	S	—	2340				
QPP Payable	L	L	PR	2350				
Que. Income Tax Payable	L	L	PR	2360				
QHIP Payable	L	L	PR	2370				
Que. Minister of Finance	L	S	—	2380				
EHT Payable	L	R	PR	2390				

INTEGRATION PLUS ACCOUNTS - MAINTENANCE

Account Title [Initial]	SECTION	TYPE	Module [used by]	Initial Account Number	Account Title [New]	CODE	TYPE	New Account Number
Deduction A Payable	L	R	PR	2 4 0 0				
Deduction B Payable	L	R	PR	2 4 1 0				
Deduction C Payable	L	R	PR	2 4 2 0				
Deduction D Payable	L	R	PR	2 4 3 0				
Deduction E Payable	L	R	PR	2 4 4 0				
WCB Payable	L	R	PR	2 4 6 0				
PST Payable	L	R	AR	2 6 4 0				
GST Charged or Sales	L	L	AR	2 6 5 0				
GST Paid on Purchases	L	L	AP	2 6 7 0				
GST Payroll Deductions	L	L	—	2 6 9 0				
GST Adjustments	L	L	—	2 7 1 0				
ITC Adjustments	L	L	—	2 7 3 0				
GST Owing (Refund)	L	S	—	2 7 5 0				
Refundable QST Paid	L	L	—	2 8 0 0				
QST Charged at Rate 1	L	L	—	2 8 1 0				
QST Charged at Rate 2	L	L	—	2 8 2 0				
QST Payroll Deductions	L	L	—	2 8 2 5				
QST Adjustments	L	L	—	2 8 3 0				
ITR Adjustments	L	L	—	2 8 4 0				
QST Owing (Refund)	L	S	—	2 8 5 0				
TOTAL CURRENT LIABILITIES	L	T	—	2 9 0 0				

SECTION:
A = ASSETS
L = LIABILITIES
E = EQUITY
R = REVENUE
X = EXPENSE

TYPE:
H = Heading
R = Right
L = Left
S = Subtotal
X = Current Earnings
T = Total

MODULE:
GL = GENERAL
AP = PAYABLES
AR = RECEIVABLES
PR = PAYROLL
IN = INVENTORY

CODE:
R = Remove
M = Modify
* = no change

INTEGRATION PLUS ACCOUNTS - MAINTENANCE

Account Title [Initial]	SECTION	TYPE	Module [used by]	Initial Account Number	Account Title [New]	CODE	TYPE	New Account Number
EARNINGS	E	H	—	3 0 0 0				
Retained Earnings	E	R	G L	3 5 6 0				
Current Earnings	E	X	G L	3 6 0 0				
TOTAL EARNINGS	E	T	—	3 6 9 0				
REVENUE	R	H	—	4 0 0 0				
General Revenue	R	R	—	4 0 2 0				
Sales Discounts	R	R	A R	4 1 0 0				
Freight Revenue	R	R	A R	4 2 0 0				
TOTAL REVENUE	R	T	—	4 3 9 0				
ADMINISTRATION	X	H	—	5 0 0 0				
General Expense	X	R	—	5 0 2 0				
Adjustment Write-off	X	R	I N	5 0 3 0				
Transfer Costs	X	R	I N	5 0 4 0				
Purchase Discounts	E	R	A P	5 1 0 0				
Freight Expense	X	R	A P	5 2 0 0				
Wages	X	R	P R	5 3 0 0				
EI Expense	X	R	P R	5 3 1 0				
CPP Expense	X	R	P R	5 3 2 0				
WCB Expense	X	R	P R	5 3 3 0				
QPP Expense	X	R	P R	5 3 4 0				
QHIP Expense	X	R	P R	5 3 5 0				
EHT Expense	X	R	P R	5 3 6 0				
TOTAL ADMINISTRATION	X	T	—	5 3 9 0				

SECTION:
A = ASSETS
L = LIABILITIES
E = EQUITY
R = REVENUE
X = EXPENSE

TYPE:
H = Heading
R = Right
L = Left
S = Subtotal
X = Current Earnings
T = Total

MODULE:
GL = GENERAL
AP = PAYABLES
AR = RECEIVABLES
PR = PAYROLL
IN = INVENTORY

CODE:
R = Remove
M = Modify
* = no change

VENDOR MAINTENANCE

Code	

____ **Code : M = Modify   C = Create   R = Remove**

Vendor Name	
Contact	
Street Address	
City	
Province	
Postal Code	
Phone Number	
Fax Number	
Terms	

Yes/No

Clear Invoices When Paid ☐

Include in GST Report ☐

Print Contact on Cheques ☐

____ % ____ Days, Net ____ Days

Code	

____ **Code : M = Modify   C = Create   R = Remove**

Vendor Name	
Contact	
Street Address	
City	
Province	
Postal Code	
Phone Number	
Fax Number	
Terms	

Yes/No

Clear Invoices When Paid ☐

Include in GST Report ☐

Print Contact on Cheques ☐

____ % ____ Days, Net ____ Days

VENDOR TRANSACTIONS (HISTORICAL)

Code: 1 = Purchase   2 = Payment

Code	Vendor	Invoice/ Chq. No.	Date (mm-dd-yy)	Amount	Cheque

CUSTOMER MAINTENANCE

Code	

Code : M = Modify   C = Create   R = Remove

Customer Name	
Contact	
Street Address	
City	
Province	
Postal Code	
Phone Number	
Fax Number	
Credit Limit	
Terms	

Yes/No

Clear Invoices When Paid ☐

Include in GST Report ☐

Print Statement for Customer ☐

_____ % _____ Days, Net _____ Days

Code	

Code : M = Modify   C = Create   R = Remove

Customer Name	
Contact	
Street Address	
City	
Province	
Postal Code	
Phone Number	
Fax Number	
Credit Limit	
Terms	

Yes/No

Clear Invoices When Paid ☐

Include in GST Report ☐

Print Statement for Customer ☐

_____ % _____ Days, Net _____ Days

CUSTOMER TRANSACTIONS (HISTORICAL)

Code: 1 = Sale   2 = Receipt

Code	Customer	Invoice/ Chq. No.	Date (mm-dd-yy)	Amount	Cheque

EMPLOYEE MAINTENANCE

Code

_____   **Code :   M = Modify   C = Create   R = Remove**

Employee Name

Street Address

City

Province

Postal Code

Phone Number

Soc. Ins. Number

Birth Date
_____ (mm-dd-yy)

Tax Table

Pay Periods per Year

Federal Claim
_____ dollar amount [TDI – TPD1]

WCB Rate
_____ (%) WCB = Workers' Compensation Board

EI Eligibility
_____   Y = Yes   N = No

EI Premium Factor
_____ (normally 1.4)

Vacation Pay Rate
_____ (%)

Retain Vacation Pay
_____   Y = Yes   N = No

Regular Wage Rate
_____ dollars / hour

Overtime Wage Rate
_____ dollars / hour

Salary per Period
_____ dollars

Salary Hours per Period

Hire Date
_____ (mm-dd-yy)

Deductions

Deduction A		Deduction D	
Deduction B		Deduction E	
Deduction C		Additional Fed Tax	

EMPLOYEE RECORDS (HISTORICAL)

PAYROLL LEDGER
Form EMP-2
Page ___ of ___

Employee Name			
Regular Wages			
Overtime Wages			
Salary			
Commissions			
Taxable Benefits			
Vacation Pay Paid Out			
CPP Contributions			
QPP Contributions			
EI Ins. Earnings			
EI Premiums			
Income Tax			
Quebec Income Tax			
Deduction A			
Deduction B			
Deduction C			
Deduction D			
Deduction E			
Net Earnings			
Advances Paid			
Vacation Pay Owed			

INVENTORY MAINTENANCE

Item No. Description	Asset Acct.	Rev. Acct.	Exp. Acct.	Var. Acct.	Unit of Sale	Price/ Unit (Sell)	Min. Stk. Lev.	Qty on hand	Total Value (Cost)

APPENDIX B | Setting System Security

ENTERING PASSWORDS

In Chapter 13, we provided an introduction to system security and passwords. Passwords may be needed when a company's computer is shared and files can be easily accessed by any of the users. It is very easy to remove and modify data in Simply Accounting, although it is not that easy to do it by accident because of all the built-in warnings. Nonetheless, security of confidential information is always important, and Simply Accounting's passwords offer an extra level of protection from unauthorized access or alteration.

Passwords are set from the Home window. To set passwords,

Choose Set Security from the pull-down menu under **Setup** to display the following control window:

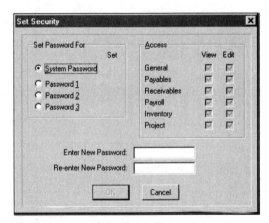

You can set up to four passwords for different users and for access to different parts of the program. The highest level of access comes with the System Password that allows the user to enter, use or modify any part of the data files, including the passwords. The System Password must be set before any other passwords can be set, so this password is selected initially. To enter the password,

Click on the **Enter New Password field** to move the cursor.

Type the word or code that you want as your password. You can use up to seven letters and/or numbers as the code.

Press `tab` to advance to the next field, Re-enter New Password. For security reasons, the password never shows on the screen — you will see an asterisk (*) for each letter or number you typed. As a additional precaution, Simply Accounting requires you to enter the code twice in exactly the same way.

Type the password or code again.

If the two entries do not match, Simply Accounting will warn you that they do not match and you can try re-entering the code again. It is possible that you mistyped the first entry, so if you still do not have a match, go back to the Enter New Password field and type in the code. Then re-enter the password in the Re-enter New Password field.

When you have entered the code twice, you can return to the Home window by clicking on OK, or you can set additional levels of security. To set a second password,

Click on Password 1 to activate this option and to make the Access part of the screen available as shown:

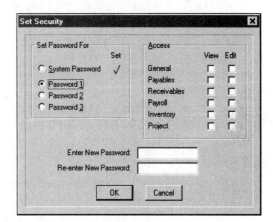

For each of the six ledgers, you can allow viewing only, editing or no access. Viewing access permits the users to see the reports and entries previously made but not to add to or change the information. Editing access allows the user to make journal entries and ledger changes but not to view reports.

To allow access, click on the check box beside the ledger in the appropriate column. For example, to allow viewing access only for the General Ledger, click on the box beside General in the View column. To allow no access, leave the check boxes empty.

After marking ledger access, you must enter the password. It must be different from the system password to serve its purpose of restricting access.

Click on the **Enter New Password field** to move the cursor.

Type the word or code that you want as your restricted usage password. You can use up to seven letters and/or numbers as the code.

Press [tab] to advance to the next field, Re-enter New Password.

Type the password or code again.

When the two entries match, you can continue to set the next two passwords in the same way as Password 1. After entering all the passwords,

Click on OK to return to the Home window. Nothing has changed yet.

However, the next time you open the file, the following dialogue box will appear and you will be required to enter the password before you can display the Home window:

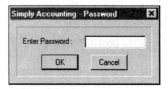

Type the password or code.

Click on OK

If you enter an incorrect code, nothing happens — the Password dialogue box remains open. If you enter the system password, you will have full access to all parts of the program, including the security settings. If you have set passwords, you must enter the program with the system password in order to change the security settings.

If you enter Password 1, or one of the other two ledger access passwords, you will be shown a restricted view of the Home window similar to the following one:

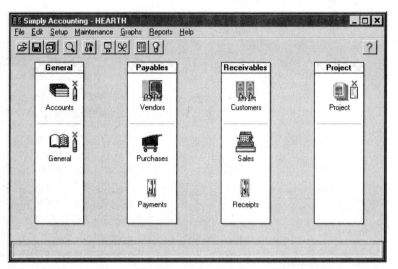

The window shown here allows no access to the Payroll or Inventory ledgers of journals — these icons do not appear. Full access to the Payables and Receivables ledgers and journals is available because these icons are shown in their normal manner. The Project ledger, with the X above the report icon, can be edited, but reports cannot be viewed. And finally, the General ledger and journal, with the X above the pencil icons, can be viewed but not edited. Several of the main menu options are also restricted, including the Set Security option.

Changing and Removing Passwords

To change or remove passwords, access the restricted files using the system password. To change a password, access the files with the System Password.

Choose Set Security from the pull-down menu under **Setup**.

Click on Password 1

Type a new code or password in the Enter New Password field. Re-enter the same code in the Re-enter New Password field. To change other passwords, select the password level you want to change and repeat the step of entering the new code in the two password fields.

To remove a password, you must click in the Enter New Password field and then press the Backspace key (pressing ⌈del⌋ does not work here). This leaves the field blank but the OK button will be highlighted.

Click on OK to return to the Home window.

Repeat these steps of adding blank passwords for each password that you have set and want to remove. The final step will be to remove the system password. You should now be able to access your data files without a password.

APPENDIX C | Correcting Errors After Posting

W e all make mistakes. This appendix outlines briefly the procedures you need to follow for those rare occasions when you have posted a journal entry incorrectly.

Obviously, you should try to detect errors before posting. Reviewing the journal entry should become routine practice. The software has built in a number of safeguards that help you not make mistakes. For example, outstanding invoices cannot be overpaid; employee wages and payroll deductions are calculated automatically, etc. Furthermore, names of accounts, customers, vendors, employees and inventory items appear in full, so that you may check your journal information easily.

Before making a reversing entry, consider the consequences of not correcting the error. For example, spelling mistakes in the customer name may not be desirable, but they will not influence the financial statements. After making the correction in the ledger, the newly printed statement will be correct (the journal will retain the original spelling). Sometimes, however, the mistake is more serious. Financial statements will be incorrect if amounts or accounts are wrong. Payroll tax deductions will be incorrect if the wage amount is incorrect. GST and PST remissions may be incorrect as a result of incorrect sales or purchase amounts. Discounts will be incorrectly calculated if an invoice or payment date is incorrect. Some errors also originate from outside sources. For example, purchase items may be incorrectly priced by the vendor.

For audit purposes, prepare a memo explaining the error and the correction procedure. A complete reversing entry is often the simplest way to make the corrections for a straightforward audit trail. With Simply Accounting's recall and lookup features, they are made easier because you can see an exact copy of the original entry that was incorrect. With invoice lookup turned on, you can automatically reverse and correct Sales and Purchases journal entries by adjusting the original entry. Choose Adjust Invoice from the pull-down menu under Sale or Purchase or click on the Adjust invoice button in the journal (page 220). Payroll entries can be reversed and corrected in the Payroll Journal by choosing Adjust Cheque from the pull-down menu under Cheque or clicking on the Adjust cheque button (page 183). Under all circumstances, Generally Accepted Accounting Principles should be followed.

Reversing entries in all journals have several common elements. In each case, you should use an appropriate source number that identifies the entry as reversing (e.g., add ADJ or REV to the original source number). You should use the original posting date and add a comment. Make the reversing entry as illustrated on the following pages. Display the journal entry, review it carefully and, when you are certain it is correct, post it. Next you must enter the correct version of the transaction as a new journal entry with an appropriate identifying source number, (e.g., add COR to the original source number).

Reversing entries are presented below for each journal. Only the transaction portion of each screen is shown because the remaining parts of the journal screen do not change. The original and the reversing entry screens and most of the corresponding journal displays are included. Explanatory notes appear beside each set of entries.

GENERAL JOURNAL: ORIGINAL ENTRY

Account	Debits	Credits	Dist
1200 A/R - Toller Properties	535.00	--	
2650 GST Charged on Services	--	35.00	
4100 Revenue from Roofing	--	500.00	
Total	535.00	535.00	

Reversing Entry

Account	Debits	Credits	Dist
1200 A/R - Toller Properties	--	535.00	
2650 GST Charged on Services	35.00	--	
4100 Revenue from Roofing	500.00	--	
Total	535.00	535.00	

PURCHASES JOURNAL (NON-INVENTORY): ORIGINAL ENTRY

Item	Rec'd	Order	B/O	Unit	Description	Price	G	G. Amt.	P	P. Amt.	Amount	Acct	Dist
					Repair work		3	7.00	8.00	8.00	100.00	5260	

☑ Invoice Received   Freight

GST		7.00
PST		8.00
Total		115.00

Terms: ___ % ___ Days, Net 1 Days

06-14-1999	Debits	Credits
2670 GST Paid on Purchases	7.00	-
5260 Telephone Expense	108.00	-
2200 Accounts Payable	-	115.00
	115.00	115.00

Reversing Entry

Item	Rec'd	Order	B/O	Unit	Description	Price	G	G. Amt.	P	P. Amt.	Amount	Acct	Dist
					Repair work		3	-7.00	8.00	-8.00	-100.00	5260	

☑ Invoice Received   Freight

GST		-7.00
PST		-8.00
Total		-115.00

Terms: ___ % ___ Days, Net 1 Days

06-14-1999	Debits	Credits
2200 Accounts Payable	115.00	-
2670 GST Paid on Purchases	-	7.00
5260 Telephone Expense	-	108.00
	115.00	115.00

Notes

PAYMENTS & RECEIPTS
- Click on Include Fully Paid Invoices.
- The only change you must make is that positive amounts in the original entry become negative amounts in the reversing entry.
- In the Payment Amt. field, click on the invoice line for the payment being reversed.
- Type a minus sign and the amount.
- This will restore the original balance owing for the invoice. Refer to Page 119.
- If you have already cleared the paid invoice, make a Sales Journal entry for the amount of the payment (non-taxable) to restore the balance owing.

Invoice	Original Amt.	Amt. Owing	Disc. Available	Disc. Taken	Payment Amt.
CE-714	575.00	575.00	0.00		575.00

☐ Include Fully Paid Invoices   Total   575.00

Reversing Entry

Invoice	Original Amt.	Amt. Owing	Disc. Available	Disc. Taken	Payment Amt.
CE-714	575.00	0.00	0.00		-575.00

☑ Include Fully Paid Invoices   Total   -575.00

INVENTORY PURCHASES

Notes

INVENTORY PURCHASE
- Change positive quantities in the original entry to negative in the reversing entry (place a minus sign before the quantity in the Rec'd field).
- Similarly, change negative quantities, such as for returns, to positive (remove the minus sign).
- Add a minus sign to the freight amount if Freight is charged.
- Use the same accounts and amounts in the reversing entry as in the original entry.
- If you have invoice lookup turned on, you can use the Adjust Invoice option instead (page 220).

Item	Rec'd	Order	B/O	Unit	Description	Price	G	G. Amt.	P	P. Amt.	Amount	Acct	Dist
MTB-A2	5			Each	Summit - 21sp S	1,000.00	3	350.00			5,000.00	1340	

☑ Invoice Received   Freight 3   3.50   50.00

GST   353.50

PST

Terms: ___ % ___ Days, Net 15 Days   Total   5,403.50

06-14-1999	Debits	Credits
1340 Mountain Bicycles	5,000.00	-
2670 GST Paid on Purchases	353.50	-
5200 Freight Expense	50.00	-
2200 Accounts Payable	-	5,403.50
	5,403.50	5,403.50

Reversing Entry

Item	Rec'd	Order	B/O	Unit	Description	Price	G	G. Amt.	P	P. Amt.	Amount	Acct	Dist
MTB-A2	-5			Each	Summit - 21sp S	1,000.00	3	-350.00			-5,000.00	1340	

☑ Invoice Received   Freight 3   -3.50   -50.00

GST   -353.50

PST

Terms: ___ % ___ Days, Net 15 Days   Total   -5,403.50

06-14-1999	Debits	Credits
2200 Accounts Payable	5,403.50	-
1340 Mountain Bicycles	-	5,000.00
2670 GST Paid on Purchases	-	353.50
5200 Freight Expense	-	50.00
	5,403.50	5,403.50

SALES JOURNAL (INVENTORY AND NON-INVENTORY

Notes

SALES

- For inventory sales, change positive quantities in the original entry to negative in the reversing entry (place a minus sign before the quantity in the Qty field). Similarly, change negative quantities, such as for returns to positive (remove the minus sign).
- For non-inventory sales, change positive amounts in the original entry to negative amounts in the reversing entry (place a minus sign before the amount in the Amount column).
- Add a minus sign to the freight amount if freight is charged.
- Use the same accounts and amounts in the reversing entry as in the original entry.
- If invoice lookup is turned on, you can use the Adjust Invoice option instead (page 220).

Item	Qty	Unit	Description	GST	PST	Price	Amount	Acct	Dist
BAG-N1	2	Each	Saddle Bags - ballistic nyl	3	8.00	35.00	70.00	4020 Revenue	
			Bicycle repair work	3	8.00		50.00	4040 Revenue	

Comments	Freight	3		10.00
	GST @ 7.0%			9.10
	GST @ 0.0%			
	PST			9.60
Terms: 2.00 % 10 Days, Net 15 Days	Total			148.70

06-14-1999	Debits	Credits
1200 Accounts Receivable	148.70	-
5060 Cost of Goods Sold	40.00	-
1310 Bags	-	40.00
2640 PST Payable	-	9.60
2650 GST Charged on Sales	-	9.10
4020 Revenue from Sales	-	70.00
4040 Revenue from Services	-	50.00
4200 Freight Revenue	-	10.00
	188.70	188.70

Reversing Entry

Item	Qty	Unit	Description	GST	PST	Price	Amount	Acct	Dist
BAG-N1	-2	Each	Saddle Bags - ballistic nyl	3	8.00	35.00	-70.00	4020 Revenue	
			Bicycle repair work	3	8.00		-50.00	4040 Revenue	

Comments	Freight	3		-10.00
	GST @ 7.0%			-9.10
	GST @ 0.0%			
	PST			-9.60
Terms: 2.00 % 10 Days, Net 15 Days	Total			-148.70

06-14-1999	Debits	Credits
1310 Bags	40.00	-
2640 PST Payable	9.60	-
2650 GST Charged on Sales	9.10	-
4020 Revenue from Sales	70.00	-
4040 Revenue from Services	50.00	-
4200 Freight Revenue	10.00	-
1200 Accounts Receivable	-	148.70
5060 Cost of Goods Sold	-	40.00
	188.70	188.70

PAYROLL JOURNAL

PAYROLL JOURNAL

- Redo the original incorrect entry but DO NOT POST IT!
- Click on the Enter taxes manually button to open all the deduction fields for editing.
- Type a minus sign in front of the number of hours (regular and overtime) or in front of the Salary and Commission amounts. Press `tab` to update the amounts, including vacation pay (i.e., change them to negative amounts).
- Edit each of the remaining deduction amounts by typing a minus sign in front of each amount. For the Advance field, change the sign for the amount. Advances should have a minus sign in the reversing entry and advances recovered should be positive amounts.
- Check the amounts for CPP and EI with the original journal entry because if the employee has reached the maximum contribution since the original entry, these amounts may be incorrect. Change them to match the original if necessary.
- Remember to click on the Calculate taxes automatically button before you make the correct payroll entry.
- You can use the Adjust Cheque option instead to reverse and correct the Payroll Journal entry (see page 183).

Period Ending	06-14-1999	EI		22.45	Gross Pay	774.00
Reg.	40.00	720.00	CPP/QPP	20.67	Withheld	-193.59
Ovt.	2.00	54.00	Tax	131.72	Benefits	0.00
Sal.					Advance	240.00
Commission			Medical	18.75		
Benefits			RRSP		Net Pay	820.41
Benefits (Que)						
Vacation		46.44				
Release						

06-14-1999		Debits	Credits
1240	Advances Receivable	240.00	-
5300	Wages	820.44	-
5310	EI Expense	31.43	-
5320	CPP Expense	20.67	-
5330	WCB Expense	8.44	-
1080	Cash	-	820.41
2300	Vacation Payable	-	46.44
2310	EI Payable	-	53.88
2320	CPP Payable	-	41.34
2330	Income Tax Payable	-	131.72
2400	Medical Payable	-	18.75
2460	WCB Payable	-	8.44
		1,120.98	1,120.98

Reversing Entry

Period Ending	06-14-1999	EI		-22.45	Gross Pay	-774.00
Reg.	-40.00	-720.00	CPP/QPP	-20.67	Withheld	193.59
Ovt.	-2.00	-54.00	Tax	-131.72	Benefits	0.00
Sal.					Advance	-240.00
Commission			Medical	-18.75		
Benefits			RRSP		Net Pay	-820.41
Benefits (Que)						
Vacation		-46.44				
Release						

06-14-1999		Debits	Credits
1080	Cash	820.41	-
2300	Vacation Payable	46.44	-
2310	EI Payable	53.88	-
2320	CPP Payable	41.34	-
2330	Income Tax Payable	131.72	-
2400	Medical Payable	18.75	-
2460	WCB Payable	8.44	-
1240	Advances Receivable	-	240.00
5300	Wages	-	820.44
5310	EI Expense	-	31.43
5320	CPP Expense	-	20.67
5330	WCB Expense	-	8.44
		1,120.98	1,120.98

METHOD ONE

- Re-enter the transfer as you did originally.
- Type a minus sign in front of each quantity in the Qty field.
- Also type a minus sign in front of the amount for Additional Costs.

METHOD TWO

- Switch the inventory items in the two parts of the Transfers Journal.
- All items from the Transfer Out (top) section should be entered in the Transfer In (bottom) section.
- All items that were in the Transfer In section should be entered in the top Transfer Out section.
- Type a minus sign in front of the amount for Additional Costs.

Items to Transfer out

Item	Qty	Unit	Description	Unit Cost	Amount
BM-2	10	ton	Base Material: Gravel 3/4 smo	20.00	200.00
CP-5	100	sqft	Cobblestone: Leeds texture re	0.70	70.00
PVS-1	200	each	Paver Slab: Natural expose 1	0.50	100.00

Additional Costs	
Total	370.00

Items to Transfer in

Item	Qty	Unit	Description	Unit Cost	Amount
EG-1	1	Each	Example for Reversing Entry	370.00	370.00

Total	370.00

04-14-1999	Debits	Credits
1500 Reserved Inventory for Projects	370.00	-
1360 Base Materials	-	200.00
1380 Cobble Pavestones	-	70.00
1440 Paver Slabs	-	100.00
	370.00	370.00

Reversing Entry (Method One)

Items to Transfer out

Item	Qty	Unit	Description	Unit Cost	Amount
BM-2	-10	ton	Base Material: Gravel 3/4 smo	20.00	-200.00
CP-5	-100	sqft	Cobblestone: Leeds texture re	0.70	-70.00
PVS-1	-200	each	Paver Slab: Natural expose 1	0.50	-100.00

Additional Costs	
Total	-370.00

Items to Transfer in

Item	Qty	Unit	Description	Unit Cost	Amount
EG-1	-1	Each	Example for Reversing Entry	370.00	-370.00

Total	-370.00

04-14-1999	Debits	Credits
1360 Base Materials	200.00	-
1380 Cobble Pavestones	70.00	-
1440 Paver Slabs	100.00	-
1500 Reserved Inventory for Projects	-	370.00
	370.00	370.00

Reversing Entry (Method Two)

			Items to Transfer out		
Item	Qty	Unit	Description	Unit Cost	Amount
EG-1	1	Each	Example for Reversing Entry	370.00	370.00

Additional Costs	
Total	370.00

			Items to Transfer in		
Item	Qty	Unit	Description	Unit Cost	Amount
BM-2	10	ton	Base Material: Gravel 3/4 smc	20.00	200.00
CP-5	100	sqft	Cobblestone: Leeds texture re	0.70	70.00
PVS-1	200	each	Paver Slab: Natural expose 1	0.50	100.00

Total	370.00

ADJUSTMENTS JOURNAL

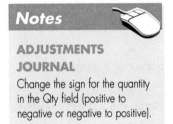

Notes

ADJUSTMENTS JOURNAL

Change the sign for the quantity in the Qty field (positive to negative or negative to positive).

Item	Qty	Unit	Description	Unit Cost	Amount	Acct	Dist
BAG-L1	-1	Each	Saddle Bags - leather	40.00	-40.00	5100 Damaged Inv	

Total	-40.00

06-14-1999	Debits	Credits
5100 Damaged Inventory	40.00	-
1310 Bags	-	40.00
	40.00	40.00

Reversing Entry

Item	Qty	Unit	Description	Unit Cost	Amount	Acct	Dist
BAG-L1	1	Each	Saddle Bags - leather	40.00	40.00	5100 Damaged Inv	

Total	40.00

06-14-1999	Debits	Credits
1310 Bags	40.00	-
5100 Damaged Inventory	-	40.00
	40.00	40.00

APPENDIX D | Supplementary Case Problems

CASE ONE

To be completed: after Reliable Roofing
Data used: Reliable Roofing

Complete the following purchase in the General Journal.

☐ Purchase Invoice #ID-67113
Dated July 31, 1999
From InfraRed Diagnostics, $200 for rental of diagnostic equipment, plus $14 GST. Invoice total $214. Terms: net 30 days. Charge to Consultation Expense.

After posting the above transaction, you realize that the expense should be charged to an equipment rental account.

Change the name of the Scaffolding Rentals account to Equipment Rentals and make the corrections necessary to reflect this expense accurately.

Why is it important to make the correction even though the income will not change on the income statement?

CASE TWO

To be completed: after Grandeur Graphics

Grandeur Graphics would like to keep track of credit card sales separately from other cash sales without sorting through all the sales invoices manually. Grandeur wants to determine whether or not to continue to pay the fees attached to the different kinds of cards. How can she set up the Receivables Ledger to track this information? How and why might she offer the credit card payment method even if it is relatively more costly than cash?

CASE THREE

To be completed: after Grandeur Graphics

Why might a business choose to set up customer records for all customers, including the cash or one-time customers? Do the same arguments apply to setting up vendor records?

CASE FOUR

To be completed: after Grandeur Graphics

The credit limit information in Simply Accounting can be very helpful. Discuss an optimum strategy for setting up customer credit limits so that the program warnings will be helpful.

CASE FIVE

To be completed: after Carnival Catering
Data used: Carnival Catering

Complete a payroll journal entry dated July 12 to pay Sylvia Mellon for 50 hours of work.

When you issue the cheque to Mellon, she points out that the number of hours for the two-week period should be 70 hours. Make the reversing entry to correct the initial payroll entry and then complete the correct payroll entry. What difference will it make whether you go through the reversing entry procedure or just complete an additional entry for the difference in hours?

CASE SIX

To be completed: after Meteor Mountain Bike Shop

At the end of the season, the Trycykels want to reduce their in-store inventory to a minimum for winter storage. Therefore, they are offering a 10 percent storewide discount, plus no taxes on the sale price.

Describe the accounting procedures for entering sales transactions for the reduced-price merchandise. Remember that although the customer pays no taxes, the store is still required to pay the sales taxes to the provincial and federal governments.

How would you record these sales in different provinces with their different tax policies? (Refer to Chapter 2 for information about provincial taxes.)

How would discounted sales like this be recorded using the quick method for GST administration?

CASE SEVEN

To be completed: after Meteor Mountain Bike Shop

Meteor Mountain Bike Shop is adding five styles of youth bicycles to its inventory line and wants to set up a separate inventory category for these new bikes. The other youth bikes that are already in the inventory ledger should be part of the new Youth Bike category. Advise the Trycykels on how to make these inventory changes.

Case Eight

To be completed: after Bonnie Brides

In the fall, when Brioche was purchasing new gowns for her upcoming busy months, she realized that several classic style gowns that she had been selling for two years had increased in price since she last purchased them. This meant that her own prices would have to increase in order to maintain her profit margins. She knew that Simply Accounting determines the cost of goods sold on an average cost basis so that the lower-cost gowns still in stock would be combined with the new higher-priced gowns in determining cost. She preferred to use the FIFO (first in first out) method to assess the cost of goods sold.

Describe how she can modify her accounts and inventory ledger so that she can use the FIFO cost calculation method.

Case Nine

To be completed: after Puretek Paving & Stoneworks

At the end of a project in May, 20 percent of the reserved inventory for the project was unused because of last minute changes in the design of a walkway. Since Simply Accounting allows fractional quantities, the customer was billed for only the inventory materials actually used. This was entered as .80 in the quantity field of the Sales Journal. The remaining 20 percent (quantity .20) should be transferred back to the regular inventory stock. Describe the procedures for making this transfer.

Case Ten

To be completed: after HSC School Store

The School Store wants to offer "Be Prepared Student Packs" for its next fall season. These packages would include an assortment of items needed on a day-to-day basis, such as a dictionary, math set, lock, paper, pens, etc.

Examine the inventory list and develop a strategy for bundling items in this way, including selling price. Describe the procedure for implementing the package offers.

Case Eleven

To be completed: after HSC School Store
Data used: HSC School Store

During the October sales transactions, the advisory message appeared that some inventory items had fallen below the re-order point. Export the appropriate inventory report (for the end of October) to a spreadsheet program so that you can prepare order information. Print a list of all items that have fallen below the minimum stock level. Print another list of all items that are very close to the minimum level that should be re-ordered soon.

CASE TWELVE

To be completed: after Hearth House
Data used: Java Jean's

Java Jean's currently uses only the Payables and General Ledgers because all sales are cash and payroll is looked after by the bank.

Set up the Receivables Ledger for Java Jean's. Can this be done without having any customer names? How? What will be the advantages for the Emporium in using the Receivables Ledger? (In other words, is it worth the time it would take to do this?)

Next, set up the Payroll Ledger for four part-time employees. Use yourself and three people you know as the employees to provide the information required, including deduction amounts.

CASE THIRTEEN

To be completed: after Hearth House

Hearth House has added passwords to its computer accounting records. Wanting to maintain the confidentiality of their payroll records, they have one system-level password and one password that allows access to all parts of the system except payroll. This second password therefore permits access to all the accounting information for entering the day-to-day business transactions.

One day, the employee in charge of payroll, the only person with the system-level password who could access the payroll journal and ledger, suddenly became seriously ill and was unable to complete the payroll or even to give the password to someone else.

Now that this situation already exists, is there any way to overcome the problem in order to complete the immediate payroll (pay the staff), to prepare year-end T4s and to submit the payroll deductions to the Receiver General? What precautions should be in place to prevent a situation like this from disrupting a business? — it could have just as easily been the Sales Journal that was inoperative. (Have you ever gone into a bank and been told that there was nothing they could do for you because the computer system was down?)

APPENDIX E | Integration with Other Software

INTEGRATION

Exporting Files

There may be times when you want to work with the financial data of your company in ways that cannot be accommodated by your accounting software. Simply Accounting allows both primary and secondary reports that are displayed to be exported to other kinds of software. Exporting is the ability to transfer information from one software application to another. These exported reports may then be used with a spreadsheet or wordprocessing application.

Simply Accounting allows files to be exported to a drive and path specified. File formats available for export purposes include Text files for wordprocessing applications, Lotus version workfiles, Lotus Symphony files, Microsoft Excel files, SuperCalc files and Comma separated files. Exporting report files to other software applications will allow the user to manipulate and interpret these reports for management decision making. Integration is an important step in making the accounting process meaningful.

Integrated files can be used by businesses in a number of different ways. They include preparing invoices, creating a mailing list of customers or vendors, preparing comparative statements, preparing budgets, sales forecasting and determining implications of new taxes and tax increases. Ratio analysis of financial statements is also possible as a decision support tool. Reports gathered from Simply Accounting and spreadsheet applications can be brought together in a wordprocessing or desktop publishing application to prepare comprehensive final documents.

Notes

Depending on the applications that you are using, there may be some loss of formatting when you transfer files from one application to another. You may need to reformat the document in the new application. Please refer to the manuals for the software you are using for complete information about transferring files.

Dynamic Data Exchange

A second method of linking Simply Accounting data with other software is through DDE — Dynamic Data Exchange. As the name suggests, the link is interactive. Each time you update information in your Simply Accounting file, the corresponding information in the other program is also updated.

You can set up links for any of the data fields from any of the Simply Accounting ledgers. A summary of the steps involved in setting up a DDE link would be:

Notes

This description provides a summary of the steps involved in using DDE. Refer to your Simply Accounting manuals for detailed instructions.

- Open your Simply Accounting company files.
- Choose (highlight) the ledger from which you want to use information.
- Choose DDE from the pull-down menu under Edit in the Home window.
- Select the fields and records for which you want to establish the link.
- Choose Send Data to copy the link to the Windows clipboard.
- Switch to the other software program and choose Paste Link or Paste Special so that you copy the link and not just the field contents to the other software.
- Repeat these steps for each link you want to establish.

Although a link may contain several fields and several records, each link will be treated as a single block of information. It is generally easier to manage the linked data if each link contains one piece of information. It may take longer to set up, but the end result is a more flexible file.

Clearly, using DDE takes more effort than exporting a report. However, you need to complete the setup only once and your end document will contain current information automatically whenever you need it. In addition, with DDE you can combine information from different ledgers or reports easily into a single document. For example, you can create form letters advising employees of their payroll deduction amounts. Another example might be a letter to all customers including an inventory list containing only item names and prices.

Customized Reports with CA-RET

CA-RET offers another way to link company data from Simply Accounting exported reports or from other company databases. Its main purpose is to prepare reports that are customized to suit the specific needs of your own business. The CA-RET program includes several predefined report styles or templates to get you started:

- Tabular reports for information presented in rows and columns like a spreadsheet. Simply Accounting Inventory reports would use a tabular report format.
- Form reports for data that looks like an input form (labels for each field beside the field contents). Simply Accounting's ledger input forms for new customers, accounts, etc. are like form reports.
- Labels for address labels, inventory product labels, name tags, etc.
- Form letters for a standard letter or report body for each person or record in a database. Information from each record is inserted into the letter where appropriate.
- Freestyle reports for building a report from scratch, with no predefined formats.
- Crosstab reports for combining data from two separate tables. For example, you might combine sales information for each inventory item on a month-by-month basis. (Column one has inventory items, row one has months and cells contain sales figures.)

A summary of the steps involved in producing a CA-RET report would be:

- Start the CA-RET program.
- Choose a report style.
- Identify the databases containing information needed in the report.
- Choose the data fields that are to be included in the reports.
- Add text, formatting or calculations to make the report look the way you want and then print.

Some Examples

The examples below were prepared using Microsoft Excel, WordPerfect 6.1 and CA-RET with reports exported from the Puretek Paving & Stoneworks and Hearth House files in Simply Accounting.

In Example 1, the ending balance sheet for Puretek has been exported to an Excel file. Using the calculating abilities of Excel, several key ratios were calculated.

EXAMPLE 1

PURETEK PAVING & STONEWORKS
COMPARATIVE BALANCE SHEET

ASSETS	As At 04-30-99	As At 03-31-99	Key Ratios	
			04-30-99	03-31-99
CURRENT ASSETS				
Cash in Bank	76,245.90	54,895.00		
Accounts Receivable	806.00	(9,500.00)	Current Ratio	
Construction Materials	1,600.00	2,800.00	Current Assets	
Office Supplies	108.00	0.00	Current Liabilities	
TOTAL CURRENT ASSETS	78,759.90	48,195.00	1.58	1.71
INVENTORY ASSETS				
Base Materials	4,875.00	6,500.00	Quick Ratio	
Cobble Pavestones	8,560.00	10,145.00	Current Assets-Inventory	
Edging Stone Blocks	1,500.00	1,950.00	Current Liabilities	
Patio Stone Blocks	5,860.00	6,600.00	1.00	0.82
Paver Slabs	3,860.00	4,380.00		
Stone Slabs	11,920.00	13,900.00		
Wall Building Blocks	8,900.00	9,000.00		
TOTAL INVENTORY ASSETS	45,475.00	52,475.00		
PLANT & EQUIPMENT				
Cash Register	1,200.00	1,200.00	Debt Ratio	
Computers & Peripherals	3,800.00	3,800.00	Total Liabilities	
Construction Equipment	45,000.00	45,000.00	Total Assets	
Delivery Truck	51,000.00	50,000.00	0.54	0.54
Furniture & Fixtures	3,000.00	3,000.00		
Loading Equipment	33,500.00	25,000.00		
Warehouse	150,000.00	150,000.00		
Yard	100,000.00	100,000.00		
TOTAL PLANT & EQUIPMENT	387,500.00	378,000.00		
TOTAL ASSETS	511,734.90	478,670.00		

LIABILITIES		
CURRENT LIABILITIES		
Bank Loan	39,840.00	40,000.00
Accounts Payable	21,445.40	20,330.00
Vacation Payable	673.24	0.00
Receiver General Payable	6,740.16	0.00
EHT Payable	197.35	0.00
CSB Plan Payable	700.00	0.00
WCB Payable	1,416.85	0.00
PST Payable	4,976.00	0.00
GST Owing (Refund)	2,779.00	(1,330.00)
TOTAL CURRENT LIABILITIES	78,768.00	59,000.00
LONG TERM LIABILITIES		
Mortgage Payable	199,900.00	200,000.00
TOTAL LONG TERM LIABILITIES	199,900.00	200,000.00
TOTAL LIABILITIES	278,668.00	259,000.00

EQUITY		
OWNER'S EQUITY		
R. Stoanfayce, Capital	219,670.00	219,670.00
R. Stoanfayce, Drawings	(2,000.00)	(0.00)
Current Earnings	15,396.90	0.00
TOTAL OWNER'S EQUITY	233,066.90	219,670.00
TOTAL EQUITY	233,066.90	219,670.00
LIABILITIES AND EQUITY	511,734.90	478,670.00

In Example 2, the Puretek project summary has been exported to a text file. Using WordPerfect 6.1, it has been reformatted as part of a memo to the owner.

EXAMPLE 2

MEMO TO: R. Stoanfayce   FROM: Mita Ashikaya   DATE: May 3, 1999

As requested here is the Project Summary Income Statement for April. Store costs are relatively higher than the project costs to the extent that the store project shows a net loss for the month. Perhaps we need to reconsider how we allocate such overhead expenses as hydro, telephone and interest. I have some suggestions that I would like to discuss with you.

PURETEK PAVING & STONEWORKS
PROJECT SUMMARY

Project	Store Operations		Briar Hill		Chaplin Estates		Forest Glen		Sherwood	
	Revenue	Expense	Revenue	Expense	Revenue	Expense	Revenue	Expense	Revenue	Expense
Rev. from Store Sales	15,800									
Rev. from Contracting			10,000		15,000		10,000		12,500	
Sales Returns & Allow.	(1,100)									
Returns Policy Rev.	253									
Other Revenue	15									
Advertising & Prom.		80		80		80		80		80
Bank Charges		32								
Construct'n Mat'ls				600		400		600		600
Cost of Goods Sold		8,715		1,395		3,000		1,690		2,270
Delivery Expense				0		0		216		0
Hydro Expense		200								
Int. Exp. - Loan		240								
Int. Exp. - Mortgage		1,900								
Legal Expenses				50		50		50		50
Repairs & Maint.		250		125		125		0		0
Telephone Expense		86								
Total Payroll Exp.		7,248		4,121		4,250		4,079		4,079
Revenue minus Expense	(3,783)		3,629		7,095		3,285		5,421	

In Example 3, we show the relative amounts of assets for the beginning and end of April. The graph was composed in Excel, using the comparative balance sheet.

EXAMPLE 3

Share of inventory assets for each asset group for Puretek Paving & Stoneworks

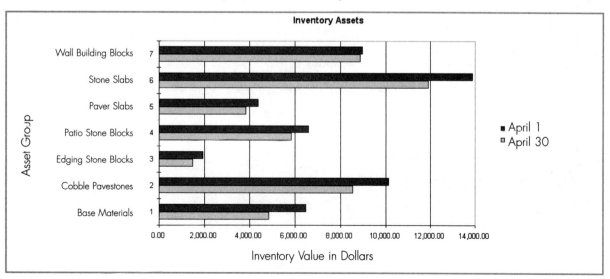

In Example 4-A, we show a form letter created in CA-RET to accompany the bonus paycheque for Hearth House employees. Example 4-B shows the resulting letter for the first employee.

EXAMPLE 4-A

Form letter in CA-RET

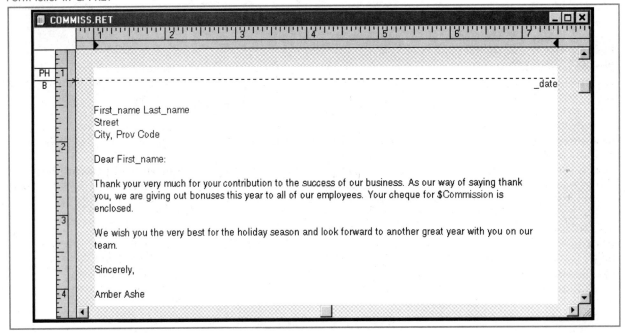

EXAMPLE 4-B

Preview of letter for first employee in CAR-ET

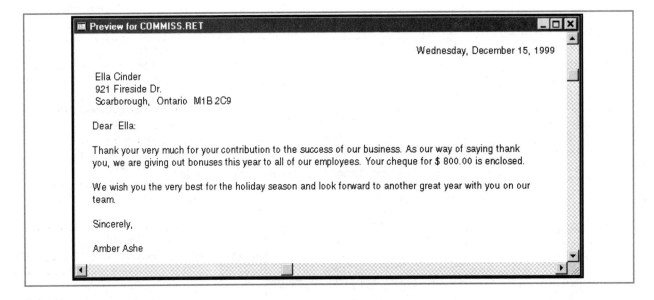

Index

GST *125, 352*
  inventory *226-31, 311*
  payroll *188-92*
  project *309-10*
  tool button *48*
  vendor *88-91*
Retained vacation pay *181, 385-86, 405*
Reversing entry *87, 183-85, 220-22, 517-23*

Sales
  cash *99, 118-19, 198, 243, 284*
  correcting *110, 209*
  discounts *198, 243, 222-23, 320, 352*
  freight *198, 208*
  inventory *206-10, 223-25*
  journal *106-10, 118-19, 206-10, 223-25*
  non-inventory *106-10*
  posting *110, 119, 210*
  returns and allowances *99, 284, 353*
  reviewing *109, 118, 209*
Sales tax *25-27, 170, 198, 285, 319, 352, 426*
Sample companies *9, 137*
Saving your work *18, 43-44, 428*
Section rules *151*
Security *365, 513-16*
Setting up
  bank reconciliation *428-35*
  budgeting feature *321-25*

company files *136-38, 245-46, 356-57*
company information *139-41, 247, 357-58*
Setup input forms *xx, 139, 247, 496-513*
Setup button *36, 145, 256*
Simply Accounting features, summary *338-39*
Size buttons *5*
Spreadsheets *392-94, 528-31*
Starter files *9, 136-37, 146-47, 356, 365-70*
Statements (see Reports)
Store entries *74-75, 87-88, 119, 223-25*
Subsidiary ledgers (see Accounting transactions keystrokes)
Summary (see Reports)
Suppressing zero balance *43, 151, 255, 377*

Tax
  exemption *167-68, 279-80, 317, 348-49, 474-75*
  GST *20-27*
  income *167-68, 279-80, 317, 348-49, 474-75*
  provincial sales tax *25-27, 170, 198, 285, 319, 352, 426*
  remittances *355*
  TD1 *167-68, 279-80, 317, 348-49, 385, 474-75*

To Do lists *185-89*
Tool buttons *15, 36, 37, 42, 71, 106*
Transfers journal entry *306-309*
Trial balance
  displaying *46*
  printing *49*

Unemployment Insurance (see Employment Insurance contributions)
Using date
  advancing *43-45, 105-106, 459*
  format *35*

Vacation pay *167-69, 181-83, 279-81, 317, 348-49, 385-86, 405, 475*
Variance account *218, 391, 400*
Vendor
  historical information *262-64, 379*
  new accounts *78-81, 260-62, 378-79*

WCB (Workers' Compensation Board) rate *169, 182, 183, 281, 317, 349, 385, 475*
Windows, working in
  with mouse *4-5*
  without mouse *5-6*